THE SEED OF YGGDRASILL

BY MARIA KVILHAUG

TLS

There dwells in the valleys a knowledge-hungry goddess; the Seed of Yggdrasill sinks down the Ash

Her name is Stream Returns to Source, of Elfin lineage, the oldest of the Inner Ruler's, and the youngest child.

Forspjallsljóð eða Hrafnagaldr Óðins, st. 6, Poetic Edda

*Ydun (1858)
By Herman Wilhelm Bissen*

*Herman Wilhelm Bissen (1786-1840)
Own work, Photography by Bloodofox,
2008-10-26*

TABLE OF CONTENTS

INTRODUCTION

Runes you must find and the Rune that is grasped the very Great Rune the very Powerful Rune, which is colored by the Great Sage and made by the Sacred Powers and carved by the Shattered One Among the Gods.

> *Runar munt þu finna*
> *oc raðna Stafi*
> *mioc Stóra Stafi,*
> *mioc Stinna Stafi,*
> *er fáþi Fimbulþulr*
> *oc gorðo GinnRegi*
> *oc reist Hroptr Ragna.*

Hávamál 142 (The Speech of the High One, Poetic Edda)

Back in the autumn of 1996, when I was 21 years old, I had left my world history and philosophy studies at the University of Oslo (UIO), Norway, and for various reasons begun studying art in England instead. It was there, in my "exile", that I first upon a copy of the Poetic Edda, translated into English. Of course I knew about the book, after all, the Poetic Edda is a collection of the mythical and legendary lore of my Scandinavian ancestors of the Viking Age, and as I mentioned in the Dedications, my grandfather had often referred to them. In school, we had read some extracts and summaries of certain myths of Snorri's Edda, as well as several sagas, and we had learned some rudimentary Old Norse grammars and read through some Old Norse texts, but no one could really accuse us of knowing the language and sacred lore of our ancestors very well, apart from some stereotyped notions about Þórr the Thunder god and his Hammer, Óðinn the King of the Gods, and Freyia, Goddess of love. My first encounter with the *"real"* Edda was a rather magical experience, described further at the end of this chapter. For now, let me just sat that when I first sat down and read a translated copy of the Poetic Edda, it immediately struck me that there was something that must have been lost in translation. Not because the translator was bad, or that I could determine the quality of a translation from the Old Norse language as I was not an 'expert' in that field, but because the names of characters, things and places were not translated. In modern languages, names are usually mere syllables that identify someone or somewhere, but I suspected that since names usually have an original meaning, perhaps people in the past placed more emphasis in these meanings.

To figure out the **real meaning** of the stories became quite an obsession to me, I felt a call, a vocation if you will, that I had to follow. The characters of the myths even began appearing as powerful characters in my dreams, seemingly urging me on! I had only had some rudimentary lessons in Old Norse at the high school level, but armed with a pile of dictionaries, some dating back as far as to 1886, and with copies of the Poetic and Prose Eddas in the original language, I sat down at the University library in Oslo for two months during my 1997 summer holiday, with the purpose of translating the mythical names.

Some of my translations at the time may have been questionable, or at least open for different interpretations, but they nevertheless provided me with a key to unlock the hidden messages of the myths. The simple stories about heroes battling giants suddenly became spiritual allegories, or parables on the importance of overcoming hatred, fear and greed, as the names of the hostile giants began to reveal their true meanings. In fact, the moment I started to apply my translated names to the old texts, a whole new world unraveled itself. A world of spiritual concerns, ageless wisdom, metaphysical and philosophical speculation, that is sometimes almost compatible with modern scientific theories. Ancient peoples were no less intelligent than modern people. They were just as capable of making rational observation and logical conclusions despite their lack of technical equipment to experiment with.

Rather than basing their thoughts strictly based on technology and science, they employed different aspects to understand reality. The would use more alternative forms of exploration, like meditation and altered states of consciousness. Inside these alternate states, a human being may intuitively grasp the unknown and thus gain the same understanding as one would have using a more scientific method. Due to the fact, that they lived in an animated universe where the sun, earth and moon are living beings, and where there was a spiritual purpose to existence. A more basic and fluid attitude that would seem unscientific to modern rationalists, but is not that far-fetched to those reclaiming the more animistic and natural methods employed by our ancestors. A spiritual and animistic approach to existence and learning is not necessarily a sign of ignorance or intellectual limitation, rather, their approach to reality was a matter of balancing the two parts of our brains, not censoring out the one in favor of the other like we are prone to do today. No real scientific breakthrough has ever come through using the rational mind alone, as Albert Einstein said himself, "the intuitive mind is a sacred gift and the rational mind is a faithful servant. We have created a society which honors the servant and has forgotten the gift." Einstein's theory of relativity would never have been discovered and carefully investigated without the initial, inspirational revelation. When I see what the Old Norse myth-makers have made out of their insights into the early universe, even before the Earth was created, I see a lore that is the result of such revelations, described with the language and the concepts that they had at hand.

Even if it is not always accurate from a modern point of view, there is no superstition in their view on the nature of the universe, it is metaphysical speculation, it is philosophy, it is the application of a symbolical language appearing like mythology which in reality is trying to reveal true insight. I could also begin to perceive likenesses between the underlying messages of Old Norse myths with several other world heritage spiritual traditions such as; **shamanism and with various Hindu, Buddhist and Classical philosophical/ spiritual traditions, particularly with Tantra, the Vedas, Neo- Platonism, mysticism and the ancient Mystery schools that most Greek philosophers actually were initiated into.** These schools taught mythology and symbols as allegories for the human soul on its quest towards wholeness, its return to true divinity and union with the universal soul. I quickly perceived that the same was the case with Norse myths; they are **allegories**, and they are designed to take the initiate on a journey towards spiritual wholeness.

I was hooked. Although, I was studying art at the time, studying the Old Norse myths became a time consuming hobby that eventually led me to return to university studies on the subjects of Old Norse Philology and the History of Religions. In the spring of 2004, I graduated with a Master degree in Cultural Studies, the History of Religions, at the University of Oslo (UIO), Norway, with the thesis, *"The Maiden with the Mead, A Goddess of Initiation Rituals in Old Norse Myths?"*

In my dissertation, I explored how the fundamental thematic structure of several Edda poems perfectly rendered the structure and themes of what could only be explained as a Pagan initiation ritual, and that the description of this ritual, albeit in the language of symbols, was a credible description of such ritual, accurate and detailed. Such a discovery challenges any notion held by some critics that the Old Norse myths simply reflect the time in which they were written down, well after Christianity was introduced. The discovery of the ritual structure of the myths and the detailed accounts of the various stages of the ritual experience strongly suggests that the myths as they have been left to us do in fact reflect, to a considerable degree, Pagan religion and its practices despite them having been written down by Christian monks. Since then, I have kept doing research on the essential meaning of Norse myths, taking seriously the fact that the myth-makers, the poets (skalds), were actually trying to convey meaning through metaphor. I took seriously the fact that the names of characters and places in the myths actually mean something, and that those meanings are essential if one is to understand the messages of these metaphors. By March 2010, after six years of doing research on the side, building upon my first thesis, I was almost brimming over with research material about the Old Norse myths and felt deeply compelled to share my insights. I created my first YouTube channel, the *Lady of the Labyrinth* and began making videos about ancient goddess symbolism and Norse mythology. By the end of the summer 2010, I sat down and presented my first lecture on how to decipher the myths.

I called my lecture series *Hidden Knowledge in Old Norse Myths*, which expanded within about a year and half into thirty lectures, ten slideshow, music videos retelling and analyzing Norse myths. I also wrote several articles on my blog(s) and was beginning to get noticed for my work. The feedback and interest I received after I began sharing, particularly my lecture series, have truly warmed my heart and propelled even new insight. The fun thing about myths is that they never cease to reveal something new. As I teach, I learn. In this book, there will be a mix of genres. Some sections, even a few whole Chapters, are edited and corrected transcripts of my lecture videos. These are more casual in style than the rest, lending an oral flair, lightness and a bit of humor to otherwise very heavy material. I have included personal stories about mystical experiences, although the conclusions I offer on these, are based on the same solid academic research fundamental as the more "serious" essays. Whenever a Chapter or a section within the Chapter is a transcript from an oral lecture, it will be referred to as such. In the oral lectures, I have sometimes included personal stories, when these serve to illustrate a point or explain the process of arriving at an understanding. The intense and very long-term study of the myths has often led to very interesting dreams and sometimes intensely mystical revelations. Being a natural skeptic (or at least rose to be one), I always question my own experiences.

But I have found that when I refrain from making judgments about the "reality" of such experiences, they provide me with deep insights and often revolutionary new ways of understanding not only the myths but also myself and the world. Human beings have always had such mystical experiences, it is part of our heritage and ourselves, and it was likely this kind of experiences that spurred the creation of mythology in the first place. If approached with a sincere wish to understand what our own subconscious or exterior messenger is trying to tell us, with an openness of mind combined with humble sobriety, these experiences may provide us with; increased life quality, increased understanding, increased depth with our studies, or perhaps, they like other aspects of life just turn out to be excellent stories we share around the camp fire. I hope you will enjoy this book.

Til árs ok fríðr! ["For a good year and peace!" (Old Norse prayer formula)]

TRANSLATIONS

The translations of Edda poems in this book are my own, as are any possible errors or misinterpretations. I am aware that I sometimes choose unusual interpretations and that my translations may thus differ somewhat from others. Translation of ancient texts are always a matter of interpretation, and even when a literal translation is possible to make, there might be other options on its meaning. The are instances in which a literal translation sounds so awkward in the modern language that a translator will often paraphrase or change the text in order to make it more accessible to the reader. Thus original meanings may easily be lost in translation. I have attempted to translate the texts as literally as possible, even when the literal rendering appears incomprehensible to moderns, and tried to show through further analysis why and how these interpretations still make sense. I also tend to include translations (i.e. interpretations) of the names of characters and place, which is actually unusual as most other translators treat names as if they were mere syllables. I am convinced that the meaning of the names is crucial to understanding the text. When there are several possible interpretations, I have chosen the one that fits best. For my primary source, I have used *Sophus Bugge's* compilation of Edda poetry; Sæmundar Edda (1867). This compilation of original Old Norse texts is available on-line at *http://etext.old.no/*. I have mainly looked to one English and two Norwegian translations of the Poetic Edda in order to verify or question my own translations. The source texts used as references were written by; Carolyne Larrington's, Ludvig Holm-Olsen, and Ivar Mortensen Egnund.

Note on spellings

I have employed the Old Norse spelling of mythical names rather than the anglicized kind. Thus, "Odin" is written as Óðinn, "Thor" as Þórr, and so on. In the genitive form of an Old Norse masculine name, the last letter of the noun form is often replaced with an "s", so that Þórr in the genitive form is written þórs, and Óðinn in the genitive form is written Óðins. I have made a compromise with English and write the genitive forms of these names with an apostrophe, still removing the last noun letter; Óðin's and þór's. The same rule will be applied to other male names. In the case of females, such as Freyia, I have, for the sake of easy reading, used the customary English genitive; "Freyia's", although the proper Old Norse genitive form of the name Freyia is Freyiu.

Pronunciations and norse letters

The letter ð is pronounced like a soft d, or more like a "dh", or like the "th" in the words "this" and "that". The letter þ is pronounced like the "th" in the name Thor and the word "thing". For those who want to pronounce the Old Norse words properly, it is important to note that the R's were rolled, unlike the English "r". An apostrophe above a vowel such as "ó" in Óðinn indicates pressure on that vowel, so that the name is pronounced with a long, emphasized "Ó-h-dhinn". The name Þórr, likewise, is pronounced with a long, emphasized "ó" followed by a short rolling "rr". Th-ó-rr. In modern English, the "o" tends to be accompanied by a "u" sound, so that it sounds like "ou" (making Óðinn sound like Oudin). This sound is not present in Old Norse "o". The letter ǫ is pronounced the same way as the German or Swedish letter ö or the Norwegian ø. In English, the equivalent would be the sound of the "u" in Thursday. An "i" is in Old Norse pronounced like the English "ee". An í (with the apostrophe) is pronounced like a long eeeh.

Important norse terms

Seiðr: Magic, sorcery, witchcraft, Divination, Oracle, Shamanism
Galdr: Spell-songs, charms
Blót: Sacrifice (ritual)
Són: Atonement (= sacrifice)
Vé: Shrine, sanctuary, sacred space
Hóf: Temple, sanctuary
Lundr: Grove (sacred grove), outdoor temple, sanctuary
Haugr: Mound, burial mound, cairn
Utiseta: "To sit outside" a pagan meditative "Vision Quest" practice
          performed during night at crossroads, mountain peaks, caves
          of burial mounds
Vǫl: Wand/staff (originally phallus of a stallion), carried by the vǫlur

SACRED PROFESSIONS

Vǫlva (sg.f.)/vǫlur (pl.f.): "Wed to the Wand"an oracle/priestess/witch who carries the sacred vǫl
Seiðmaðr (sg.m.): A man who performs seiðr
Seiðkona (sg.m.): A woman who performs seiðr (often a vǫlva)
Seiðberendr (sg.n.): "Seið-womb"-A male to female Transgender sorcerer
Skáld (sg.m.): Bard, poet (the rare female poet could be called "Skaldmey" [Bard-maiden]).
Skáldskap: Poetry, bardship
Þúl ("thool"): "Chanter", "Reciter" (from Þylja: to count up, to recite, to chant), Sage, Poet, Priest
Góði (sg. m.): Priest, lawman, god (pagan priest, the Christian priests were called "prestr")
Gyðja/Gyða (sg.f.): Priestess, goddess
Blótgóði: Sacrificial priest
Blótgyðja: Sacrificial priestess
Hófgóði: Temple priest
Hófgyðja: Temple priestess
Iarl: "Earl"-originally erilaR, the title of a court shaman, a counselor to the king, who knew the arts of sorcery, runes and divination

AN OVERVIEW OF THE OLD NORSE SUPERNATURAL POWERS

The Masculine Powers

Jotnar (m.plural, singular: Jǫtunn): Literally meaning «devourers», these are usually translated as "giants". The giants are primeval beings who often live in Utgarðr [Outer World] or the Jǫtunheimar [Worlds of the Giants], in the mountains, the rocks, the caves or in the ocean.

They are associated with the Mímisbrunnr [The Well of Memory] at one of the three roots of the world tree Yggdrasill, and are associated with magic, hidden knowledge and illusions. They are also known as Þursar [Thurses/trolls] and as Hrímþursar [Frost Thurses/Frost Giants], as Risi [Giants] and Bergrisi [Mountain Giants].

Tívar (m.plural): [Gods]. This is a term used to describe all the divine powers that together rule the universe. In singular, the word refers to male gods. They can also be referred to as Bǫnd [Bonds], as Hǫft [Fetters], Rǫgn [Powers/Rulers], Jólnar ["Yule-beings"?] and Díar [Deities], and could be used for the Aesir as well, often in the form of Sígtívar ["Victory gods"].

Aesir (m.plural, singular: Áss): [Ancestors/Gods]. The term is probably etymologically connected to the Vedic Asura and the Avestan Ahura, or else to Gothic Ansir: Ancestors. In post-pagan, Medieval times, people believed it meant "Asians", because of a legend that the Aesir were originally a migrating tribe from the eastern side of the Don river who came to Scandinavia, married the local women and influenced the language and the religions. In Norse myths, the Aesir are the tribe of gods who are responsible for intellectual and spiritual capacities, bestower of intelligence, speech, poetry, breath, inspiration and the urge to search for knowledge. They shaped the universe, protect humankind, and were the gods that people primarily worshiped.

Vanir (m.plural, sg. Vanr): The meaning of the term is uncertain, but could be related to the Old Norse word for "hope", vánr. The Vanir appear to be the powers behind the natural forces that are benevolent to human beings, associated with winds, waves, fertility, forests, crops, sexuality, death and magic.

Dvergar (m.plural, sg. Dvergr): [Mutilated Ones/Dwarfs]: Crafty, underground-dwellers who also appear to represent the form or shape through which spiritual powers may manifest in physical reality. They appear to also represent the archetypal craftsman or blacksmith.

Álfar (m.plural, sg. Álfr): [Elves]. These are strongly associated with the spirits of ancestors.

Ljósálfar [Light Elves]: Immortal souls who dwell in the three upper heavens of immortality. In the two highest heavens, only light elves exist. They have all been the lovers of Freyia.

Dǫkkálfar/Svartálfar [Dark/Black Elves]: Crafty spirits/souls whose identities are often blurred with the dwarfs, associated with craftsmanship and burial mounds. Received sacrifice like the gods.

Einherjar (m.plural, sg. Einheri): [Sole Rulers]. The souls of the chosen dead who are destined to fight for the gods at *Ragnarǫk*.

The Feminine Powers

Gýgjar (f.plural, singular: Gýgr): The original meaning of the word is unknown, but these are the feminine counterpart to the Jotnar and usually translate as "giantesses". They reside in the same realms as the Jotnar, and are even more often associated with the Underworld, symbolized as caves and rocks, and with rivers and lakes. They are credited with shaping the Earth from the inside, digging out valleys, hurling rocks into mountains, as well as to Fate, pulling the "Mill" of destiny and the Earth into motion. Giantesses are the origins of the Norns, goddesses of Fate, and several other Norse goddesses are of giant stock, but have become divine through their marriages or other interactions with the Aesir gods.

Also known as Mǫrnir (meaning unknown), who received sacrifice and worship, and as Iviði (f.sg: Iviðja) [Within Wood], which could also refer to a sorceress or a witch. They are associated with a place called Jarnviðr [Iron Forest].

Dísir (f.plural, sg.: Dis): [Goddesses]. This term is etymologically related to Old Indian Dhisana, a goddess of intelligence, wisdom, speech and prosperity, who could assume multiple forms/aspects/bodies, and who guarded the sacred Soma (the drink of immortality and illumination). In Norse myths, any female supernatural being could be referred to as a Dís, and the term is often used for the norns and the valkyrie in particular, but could also be used for giantesses and Ásyniur.

Even highly respected women could be so called. Many Norse female names end with *dís*. The Dísir received sacrifice in an annual ritual called the Dísablót. There are also references in the sources to a singular Dís, usually identified as Freyia, who could also be called Vanadís [Goddess of the Vanir].

Ásyniur (f. Plural, singular: Ásynia): [Ancestresses, Goddesses]. The Ásyniur are the wives and daughters of the Aesir, but often, even usually, come from other tribes of cosmic ruling powers, such as the giants, the Vanir, the norns or the valkyrie. It appears that they become Ásyniur through their marriages with the Aesir. They are said to be "no less powerful" than the Aesir, and keep their own collective hall.

Vanadís (f.sg.)[The Goddess of the Vanir]: The only female among the Vanir who is named and identified is the goddess Freyia, who by her adoption into the Aesir tribe is also an Ásynia. She is associated with Fate, death, magic, sex, wild nature, wild animals, cats, falcons, shape-shifting, witchcraft, sacrifice, love and spiritual mysteries.

Vættir (f.plural, sg. Vættir): Nature spirits, but may also be used to describe ghosts and all female powers. Landvættir are the spirits of the land/region.

Norns (f.plural, sg. Norn): Goddesses of Fate. Of giantess stock, these are the most powerful beings in the universe. The Aesir keep their Parliaments in their realm. The oldest norn, Urðr [Origin] is responsible for rejuvenating and revitalizing the world tree (the universe) every day. Every person also has a personal Norn or Fylgja to spin their fate.

Fylgjur (f.plural, sg. Fylgja): [Followers], these are a blend of the souls of ancestral mothers who «follow» their descendants in order to aid them, and Norns who are attached to particular lineages or to individual persons, and who spin their fates

Hamingjur/Hamingja: [Shape Walker]: Dísir who are a part of the human soul and may move outside the body or change shape.

Valkyrie (f.plural, sg. Valkyrie): [Choosers of the Chosen]. These are the Norns (fates) of warriors, specializing in choosing the Einherjar.

1: THE BOOKS OF OLD

-OUR SOURCES TO OLD NORSE PAGAN BELIEFS-

1.1: THE FORGOTTEN MANUSCRIPT (POETIC EDDA)

Óðinn spoke:
I advise you, Embracer of the Voluptuous Woman
Take this advice
Enjoy it, if you grasp it
It will do you good if you get it:
> *Óðinn kvað:*
> *Raðomc þer,*
> *Loddfafnir!*
> *en þv ráð nemir,*
> *nióta mvndo ef þv nemr,*
> *þer mvno góð ef þv getr:*

Never laugh at the ancient Sage
Often it is good what the old ones say
Often from the wizened old body
Wise speech issues
They that hang among leathers and hide between hides
> *At három þúl hleþu aldregi*
> *opt er gott þat er gamlir qveþa;*
> *opt or scarpom belg*
> *scilin orð coma,*
> *þeim er hangir meþ hám*
> *oc skollir meþ scrám*

-Hávamál, The Speech of the High One, St. 134, Poetic Edda

It is the year 1643 AD, and we find ourselves on an unknown Icelandic farm. The bishop of Iceland, Brynjolv Sveinsson, has just received into his hands an ancient leather manuscript. He is told that the farmer's family has kept the manuscript safe for quite some time now. In fact, the manuscript has been hidden away from the public throughout a period of four hundred years, almost since it was first written down during the late 12th century, copied from an even earlier manuscript long lost. As Brynjolv slowly turns the pages made out of hide, he realizes that an ancestral treasure has been recovered. Ancient legends and myths speak out from the leathery pages through the almost forgotten language of poetical metaphors. Most of the poems in the manuscript had been lost, only sometimes referred to and some stanzas quoted 400 years earlier by authors such as Snorri Sturluson, whose works had survived.

This was the first time in several centuries that Snorri's main source to his "Prose Edda", the source we know as "The Elder Edda" or the "Poetic Edda", had returned to the general public. Had the book been safeguarded against hostile Church authorities? Was it released now, that the guardians of the book realized that it would finally be safe, now that it would no longer be regarded as a threat to a new and fragile faith? Or was it just a coincidence, a family treasure forgotten for some four centuries until it occurred to some bright person that other people might like to know this book too? It is hard to say, but it is an interesting and true story. We know this hidden, now recovered manuscript as the Poetic Edda. What do we actually know about authentic, Old Norse Pagan mythology? Hardly anything at all, it could be argued.

All the sources on Norse mythology and cosmology are written sources, written in the Old Norse language, yet in the Latin alphabet by scholars and monks more than a century or more after the Conversion, and we just do not know to what degree "accurate" Pagan myths survived in the memory of Christian descendants across several generations. Another question is how "accurate" any myth could be in the first place, since the Pagan religion was not dogmatic [basing itself on the interpretation of holy books], but a religion based on magical activities and mystical experience. Instead of extensive and accepted dogma, the myths varied from culture to culture, person to person, storyteller to storyteller. It evolved and changed and adapted, creating a complex trail for any researcher to follow.

Since, poetry was a sacred art in Norse Paganism, and poets could take great liberty with they myths, applying endless variety in their use of allegory and metaphor in order to convey a message. What we are left with, when it comes to 'source texts' are the Poetic and Prose Edda. **The Prose Edda** [also known as the Elder Edda] is considered to be the most important source. It contains a collection of poems that are recognized as belonging to the Edda tradition. The Old Norse word Edda means "Great Grandmother". It refers to the lore of the ancestors (or more literally, the ancestral mothers. In Norse language stories and sagas were considered feminine concepts). Most of the Edda poems that we know of were collected in a manuscript known as the **Codex Regius**, which resurfaced in 1647 AD.

As mentioned above, an Icelandic family of farmers had been the keepers of the only comprehensive collection of Edda poems that survived what may have been the censorship of the Medieval Church. The leather manuscript was almost complete, with the exceptions of a few pages that had been torn out. Some of the poems in this manuscript were already known from other papers dating back to the 12th and 13th centuries, while other Edda poems have been preserved in other places, often through copying. The dates of various fragments and pieces are often very late date because the only source to it that we have was written down much later than their origin. Earlier transcriptions have been lost, and due to this fact, some scholars are very cautious about using poems that were written down later than the Codex Regius (which was written down during the early 12th century and probably copied from an older source still) because they may have been invented by Medieval scholars rather than by Pagan poets.

Thus many poems, such as the Gróagaldr, Fjǫlsvinnsmál, Hráfnagaldr Óðins, and the Sólarljóð ["The Spell of Growth", "The Speech of Much Knowing", "Óðin's Raven-Spell" and "The Song of the Sun"] are often left out of modern collections and translations. However, these poems are still called Edda poems because they do fit into the category of Edda lore, and in my opinion, an analysis of the structure and the symbolic details within the poems will show that these poems belong to an actual Pagan (and/or Pre-Christian) tradition in Scandinavia, because they resemble and fall into a thoroughly Pagan worldview and convey Pagan concerns (Except for, The Song of the Sun, which clearly reveals a conflict between the old religion and the new Christian one).

One of my major arguments concerning most of the Edda poems, whether they were collected in the Codex Regius or not, is that they follow a basic structure of initiation or refer to concepts and practices which could not have emerged in or been practiced legally during the Christian era. For the sake of simplicity, I will refer to the Edda poems as the "Poetic Edda" despite the fact that no such book really existed (since the Codex Regius manuscript did not contain all the Edda poems). Throughout this book, the assumption will be that the Poetic Edda represents lore that emerged in an Old Norse Pagan environment as a starting point. One important aspect of the Poetic Edda is that the poems, like all Old Norse poetry, are based on allusive metaphors and allegory. Due to the fact that the poetry is based on this premise of 'allusive metaphors and allegory, characters and themes are often never directly identified. Each line of poetry can be viewed as a riddle that is begging to be solved.

The poet expected *his* listeners to decipher the meaning themselves, based on their own knowledge of mythical cosmology and pseudo-history. To modern people, this task becomes very challenging since we no longer know the entirety of the Pagan worldview and must make do with the limited access we have, mainly through Snorri's Prose Edda and a few other sources. We do, for example, face a lot of challenges when we read Old Norse poems because the poems often are at odds with our preconceived ideas of the Old Norse pantheon and cosmology. Most of our preconceived ideas are derived from; secondary textbooks about Norse myths, what we learned through media and education, and from Snorri's Prose Edda. All these books, including Snorri's text, present a simplified overview of Norse mythology that often skip important details for the sake of making the myths appear more straightforward and simple than they really are. I am often faced with reactions from my audience when I refer to information that is not usually acknowledged in mainstream media, but which is known to those of us who actually study the primary sources.

Let me use a stanza from the poem Sólarljoð [the Song of the Sun, st. 79] to illustrate my point;

> *Here are runes that have been*   *Hér 'ru Rúnar,*
> *carved by Njǫrð's daughters, Nine:*   *er ristit hafa*
> *Counsel Drink the Oldest*   *Njarðar Dœtr Níu:*
> *Approaching Spring the youngest*   *Ráðveig hin elzta*
> *and their Seven Sisters*   *ok Kreppvǫr hin yngsta*
>   *ok þeirra Systr Sjau.*

If you already possess some general knowledge on Old Norse myths, you may react to these lines, like I once did myself, with the objection; "But, Njǫrðr did not have nine daughters, he only had, one daughter, Freyia, and one son, Freyr" You would not be the only one. Due to this kind of preconceptions, modern scholars have had the audacity to completely ignore information given in this Edda poem, that Njǫrðr had nine daughters, and moreover, that they are carving runes in the underworld quite exactly like the Norns, the goddesses of fate.

The information is dismissed as just another example on how this particular Edda poem must be read as a late Christian misrepresentation of Norse Pagan cosmology. By missing out on this crucial part of Old Norse cosmology; we completely overlook the fact that of the nine giantesses who birthed the universe[1]. Such an attitude is in fact extremely arrogant, since we, a thousand years later, cannot claim to know more about Norse Pagan cosmology than the people who clearly lived through the phase of transition between the old and new religion, which the poet obviously did.

The poet who created the Song of the Sun was clearly in some agony over the conflicting worldviews, and is repeatedly referring to Pagan concepts of the soul and the afterlife. Did he really know so little about the Pagan religion that he would make obvious mistakes? Or did he refer to concepts that were still common knowledge and that would be understood by his audience? When Snorri wrote his Prose Edda in 1220-1225, he did so because he perceived that young people were beginning to forget the myths of their ancestors, and were thus unable to understand their poetry. Young people were beginning to forget, more than two centuries after the Conversion. In other words, it is very likely that the concepts that surface in Old Norse poetry yet is otherwise unknown to us from textbooks or Snorri's work, is addressing and referring to actual Pagan concepts known by those who listened to the art of poetry.

---

1 This aspect of cosmology will be referenced throughout the book

List of edda poems
Original titles and author's title translations, with summary of content

Divine Poems

Vǫluspá: The Divination of the Witch.

Often known as The Seeress's Prophecy. This poem takes the form of a séance of oracular divination, i.e. the Old Norse art of seiðr. The diviner, a vǫlva [wand-carrying witch/priestess] divines the history of the universe from beginning to end and the new era to come, at the request of Óðinn before the children of Heimdallr [Great World]. This is the one poem that I deal with in its entirety throughout this book, as it provides a perfectly chronological framework explaining most of the basics of Old Norse cosmology. The first half of this poem, stanza 1-24, is chronologically dealt with in Chapter 2 on cosmology. Stanza 25 on the disappearance of Óð's maiden appears in Chapter 4, stanza 26-27 are dealt with in Chapter 5 on the Loss of the Golden Age, and the final part is analyzed in Chapter 6 on Ragnarǫk.

Hávamál: The Speech of the High One.

Hár [The High One], a name for Óðinn, offers guidance of wise and proper conduct for the traveler (of the world). The listener is later revealed to be one Loddfafnir [Embracer of Voluptuous Woman / Harvest/ Fate]. Towards the end of the poem, Óðinn recounts his initiation journey in three stages: **First**, he meets "Twin's Maiden" and is rejected by her. **Second**, he meets the maiden Gunnlǫð and is accepted, but after the marriage, he escapes with all the Mead of Poetry, rejecting her instead. Third, he sings charms until the three last charms allow him to yet attract "the maiden", keep "the maiden" and finally know the best of secrets in the arms of one who is also, perhaps, his own sister. The initiation journey involved being hanged in a tree for nine nights, receiving neither food nor drink. Then he receives the learning of runes and magical spells as well as the mead of poetry, a theme which forms the climax of the revelations of the High One.

Vafþrúðnismál: The Speech of the Powerful Head Veil.

After receiving the reluctant blessings and the advice of his wife Frigg, Óðinn enters the "halls" of the giant Vafþrúðnir [Powerful Head Veil, from váf = head veil, þrúðnir = powerful one] in order to see how these "halls" are created. The giant challenges the god to a duel of wisdom and knowledge, the one who is unable to answer a question must perish. Óðinn asks a series of questions about the order of cosmos, and as such the poem provides valuable information about cosmology same as the Vǫluspá. Óðinn wins the battle when he asks whether the giant knows what Óðinn whispered into the ears of his son Baldr on Baldr's funeral pyre.

Grímnismáll: The Speech of the Masked One.

Óðinn and Frigg argue about the worthiness of their respective wards, which they raised. Frigg's ward is Agnarr [Respect Warrior], who now lives in a cave with a giantess (a metaphor for the underworld and death). Óðin's ward is Geirrǫðr [Red Spear], who still lives and who has become a great king. Óðinn mocks Frigg for having a ward of no consequence, whereupon Frigg mocks Óðinn for having a ward infamous for his inhospitality, cruelty and general stinginess. Qualities much disfavored by the gods. Óðinn, enraged, goes to see if this is true, and is taken captive by his own ward, who does not recognize him. The god is placed on a log burning from both ends and must sit there for eight days. On the ninth day, Geirrǫð's son, named Agnarr after his uncle, thus representing a fusion between the ward of Frigg and the ward of Óðinn, offers a drink to the god and receives a revelation about the various dimensions of cosmos and the true pantheist nature of Óðinn as Spirit, the One Who is Many. Another valuable cosmology poem.

Skírnismál: The Speech of the Shining Bright One.

The god Freyr, ruler of order and the fertility of the land, sits in Óðin's high seat Hlíðskiǫlf [Seat of Openings] from where one can look into all the worlds. Freyr discovers a maiden whose arms shine so bright they illuminate the lands and the oceans. Her name is Gerðr [Enclosure], daughter of Gymir [The One that Hides Something], yet her true identity is subtly revealed through metaphor. It is likely the maiden is Freyia, Freyr's own sister, whom the gods and elves do not wish to see them together. There is also a reference to the *"Sun Goddess"*, who refuses to shine upon Freyr's desire, just as the shining giant maiden refuses to give herself to the god. Freyr sends his servant Skírnir [Shining Bright One] into the world of the dead, where he finds the bright golden halls of the maiden, and is allowed entry. There, he resorts to three kinds of arguments to win her hand for Freyr. The offering of sacred gifts, threats of violence, and finally, when nothing impresses the maiden, he resorts to witchcraft, painting out the terrible future if she refuses. The maiden finally accepts Freyr as a husband, but with one condition; **Freyr has to survive the nine nights of initiation and meet her in the Breezeless Grove of Barri [Pine Needle]** (which is a metaphor for immortality). Freyr laments, fearing how he shall survive even three of the nights.

Hymiskvíða: The Song of Hymir ["Slow One" or "Hymn"; uncertain meaning].

The Aesir are invited to the home of Aegir the Ocean giant, grandfather of the present cosmos. The giant's home is on Hlésey [Wind-Shield Island] and is thus a realm of immortality where Light Elves dwell and where the *Daughters of the Ocean*, who are also waves and rivers, provide the golden light of wisdom that illuminate the hall of Aegir. In order to gain entry to this realm, the Aesir, who are not actually immortal, need a cauldron that is big enough to contain all the mead of Aegir. The Thunder god, Þórr, is charged with finding the cauldron, and is accompanied by Týr (the god of battles, victory and strategy). They enter the hall of Hymir and find Amma [Grandmother], a terrible giantess with nine hundred heads. From this scary Grandmother comes the bright and friendly Móðir [Mother], who offers a power-drink to her son. Apparently, implying Þórr is the son of Mother is Earth, and that the terrible Grandmother is the giantess otherwise known as Nott [Night]. The Earth Mother offers counsel to her son as well as the powerful drink that enables Þórr to find the way to defeat the terrible frost-giant Hymir which he does, through strategy and deceit. The Thunder god challenges the frost giant to a fishing trip, on which the giant catches the Middle World Serpent on his hook. The giant Hymir cuts the string, and the serpent escapes, but despite Þórr's loss, he manages to steal the cauldron, heroically arriving at the Hall of Aegir to save the day.

Hárbarðsljóð: The Song of Long-Beard.

Þórr tries to cross the river that forms the border between Óðin's divine land and the Middle World. Þórr is the only god who is "too heavy" to enter the divine realms via the bridge called Bíflind [Gentle Shivering] or Bífrǫst [Shivering Voice], so he depends on a "ferryman" to row him across. The Ferryman is traditionally a being who ferries or takes people across the rivers to the land of the dead. However, this time, Óðinn, disguised as the Ferryman, wearing the name Hárbarðr [Long Beard], challenges Þórr. They Ferryman asks; *Why should the Thunderer gain entry into the divine realm?* Þórr begins to brag about his manly deeds, but is mocked by Long Beard, who points out that there are more important matters than being manly when it comes to entering the divine realm, such as the love of a certain Linen-White Maiden. Þórr fails to understand the message and, blinded by his own self-importance and rage, stomps off, while Long Beard offers his final advice; To seek his mother, the Earth, for she will be able to show him the way to the divine lands and to seek her soon, for she is dying, and also to rescue his wife from another man.

Lokasenna: Loki's Mocking.

In the Hymiskvíða, described above, the gods received an invitation to the Hall of Aegir, but in order to attend, they need a cauldron large enough to room all the mead of the Ocean lord in order to complete the banquet (of the immortals). Now they are waiting anxiously for Þórr to arrive with the cauldron, all depending on the Thunder god's success. While they are waiting, Loki kills the servant called Fímafengr [Clever Fingers] in a fit of jealousy. Loki is then thrown out of the hall, but is so blinded by rage that he demands new entry. The servant Eldi [Maturity] tries to stop him, advising him to stay away, but Loki threatens to kill him too. He walks into the hall and reminds Óðinn of their age-old pact of blood-brotherhood, and Óðinn relents. The god Víðarr [Expander] the Silent, son of Óðinn and the giantess Gríðr [Truce] offers a cup of mead to Loki, but Loki refuses to drink, and begins ranting on about the faults of the gods and goddesses.

The goddesses are generally accused of promiscuity and adultery, whereas the gods are accused of cowardice, unmanliness and self-humiliating activities. All the while, the gods and goddesses stand up for each other and attempt to explain for Loki that he has misunderstood the real meaning and value of these stories. Loki refuses to listen, always attacking the god or goddess who has stood up for another. Finally, Loki is so enraged that he reveals that he is the true murderer of Baldr, only to hear that Frigg knew it all along. Skaði, the goddess of injuries, finally expresses the rage of the gods against Loki, warning him, yet the mischief-maker continues his rant ever louder. Síf, Þór's wife, tries to calm him and soothe him by offering him a cup of mead, but even as Loki drinks the mead in his present state, he abuses the gift and brags that he has deceived even Síf, having her for his lover.

Then Þórr enters with the cauldron and finally manages to scare Loki into silence. Loki escapes, but is hunted down to answer for his crime of murdering Baldr. He is tied up in the underworld, and Skaði (who is also a goddess of death), places a poison-dripping serpent above his face. There he lies, protected only by his wife Sígyn [Victory Woman], who holds a jar above her husband's face so as to catch the poison before it hurts him. But sometimes the cup is filled to the brim, and the wife has to empty it and while she is away, the poison drips into the face of Loki, who trembles in agony, making the whole world shake. At Ragnarǫk, Loki is destined to break free just as his son Fenrir [Greed] is to do, attacking the world of the living.

Þrymskvíða: The Song of the Drummer.

In this comedy poem, Þórr wakes up one morning to discover that his hammer (a symbol of his masculine potency and power and thunderbolt. He seeks the aid of Loki, shaman among the gods, who in his turn seeks the aid of goddess Freyia. Freyia willingly lends out her falcon hide to Loki, who is then able to travel to Þrymheimr [The World of the Drum], the realm of giants such as Þrymr [Drumming One] Skaði and Þiazi [Slave-Binder]. There, he discovers that the giant Þrymr has stolen the hammer and keeps it well locked up.

He demands to marry Freyia in return for the hammer. Þórr approaches Freyia and asks her to dress up as a bride, a request that makes the goddess so angry that the whole Earth shakes, and the Necklace of Flames [Brísingamen] bursts, before she tells Þórr that he is mad to think that she would ever marry a giant. The Aesir gather at parliament, and Heimdallr [Great World], the wisest and brightest among them, declares that the only way Þórr will be able to retrieve his hammer [his manhood] is to become the bride himself. Þórr refuses at first, fearing that the Aesir will think him unmanly and perverted, but Loki urges the god to obey the will of the Parliament.

Thus Þórr dresses up in the dress and the veils of a bride, with rocks for breasts and keys in the belt, accompanied by an equally cross-dressed Loki who happily, even gleefully, plays the role as handmaiden. The wedding banquet proposes a few problems since Þórr, the manliest among gods, has trouble acting convincingly feminine, but Loki saves the day with his clever tongue until the wedding is sanctified. Traditionally, a replica of Þór's hammer was placed by the groom in the bride's lap, a symbol of intercourse, in order to sanctify the marriage. As Þórr now receives the hammer in his lap, a symbol of yielding femininity, he actually retrieves his manly power and kills all the giants who wanted his "red rings" (of life).

Allvismál: The Speech of All-Knowing.

Allvís [All-Knowing] is an unfortunate but very knowledgeable dwarf who seeks to marry the maiden þrúðr [Power], daughter of Þórr the Thunder god. The father challenges the dwarf in a contest of wisdom, where the dwarf provides valuable information about Pagan cosmology and how the various dimensions correspond and how one singular quality is perceived differently in all the different worlds. Even for all his knowledge, the dwarf is beguiled by Þórr who keeps the dwarf standing until the Sun goddess shines her rays upon him at dawn. Traditionally, this is understood as the dwarf being turned to stone in the light of the sun, being a dwarf and thus unworthy of marrying a god's daughter. Þórr tricked the dwarf, showing that for all his knowledge he would not be able to withstand the light of day. I think it may also be a way of symbolizing transformation, from the limited dwarf form and into an enlightened being. The dwarf has to transform this way in order to reach true Power.

Vegtamskvíða: The Song of Way-Wont.

Also known as Baldrs Draumar (The Dreams of Baldr). The god Baldr, son of Óðinn and Frigg, has terrible dreams about his own death. The Aesir and the Ásyniur gather at Parliament in order to discuss these omens, and Óðinn takes it upon himself to seek a dead vǫlva (witch) in Hel, in order to divine the future. He travels into the Underworld (which is described in detail), before he reaches the High Hall of Hel [Hǫll Hár Helju] and sings válgalðr [Death Charms or Choice Charms] for the "ancient wise woman".

As the witch reluctantly rises from her grave, she reveals, at Óðin's bequest, that the precious mead is kept beneath shields in Hel, awaiting the return of Baldr. She reveals the identity of the fated murderer, and also reveals who is going to avenge Baldr and who the mother of the avenger is (From other sources, we know that the revelations were kept secret by Óðinn, who allows the murder to happen and who then seeks the mother of the avenger in order to become the father). Óðinn proceeds to ask about some "maidens who wailing throw their veils towards heaven", but the witch refuses to answer, claiming that it is because she has understood who she is talking to; Óðinn. When the witch cannot answer his question about the maidens, Óðinn understands that the witch is not the actual wise woman that he had sought, but rather the "mother of three trolls", Loki the bound, who portends Ragnarǫk.

Rígsþula: The List of Ríg.

Describes how one Ríg ["Ruler"], walks through the world mating first with Edda [Great Grandmother] to make the class of thralls, then with Amma [Grandmother] in order to make the class of peasants, and finally with Móðir [Mother] in order to beget the noble warrior class. From Móðir is born Kon Ungr [Royal Descendant], who is destined to become a sage and a king.

Hyndlulióð: The Song of the She-Wolf.

A young man, Óttarr [Hope Warrior or Fear Warrior] sacrifices to the goddesses and prays until the altar, red with blood from the sacrificed animal (a boar, most likely), turns into crystal and the greatest of goddesses appears before him. Freyia, who transforms his soul into the body of the boar, which she rides into the Underworld, the "darkest of darkness". In a rock cave, they find an aspect of Hel in the form of a wolf-riding giantess vǫlva [witch], whom Freyia addresses respectfully as "sister" and "maiden foremost among maidens". She is called Hyndla ["Bitch"or "She-Wolf"}, and she owns a stable full of pitch-black male wolves that she rides. Freyia declares her purpose; To help Óttarr on his way to Valhǫll or Valland [The Hall or Land the Chosen Dead], where Óðin's warriors dwell after death. Obviously, the purpose of this quest, the sacrifice and the underworld descent, is to become an Einheri, a "One-Harrier" or, I suggest, a "Sole Ruler", one of Óðin's warriors to aid in the final battle against the destructive powers of Greed during Ragnarǫk.

In order to manage the journey, the young man is in need of good advice, for after "the third day" he will have to argue his case as an inheritor of the "gold of Valland" (gold is a metaphor for divine wisdom and light) against his opponent Angantýr [Pleasure Beast]. In a séance of seiðr, the She-Wolf divines the "ancestry" of Óttarr, revealing that he is related to the entire world, to all lineages and all kinds, all united in one single being born of nine mothers [the universe, or Heimdallr, the Great World].Then she divines the future and Ragnarǫk, prophesying the arrival of one being greater than all (the latter is often thought to be a reference to Christ).

Finally, Freyia declares that she will offer the precious Mead of Memory to Óttarr so that he may remember the teachings he has received. The She-Wolf then plays the Ogress of Death. Even as she reveals all wisdom, it is her nature to demand oblivion and death. Freyia plays the alternative fate, she is the one that leads to Valhǫll, granting glory rather than oblivion. She is compared to Heiðrún [Illuminating Symbol] who produced the mead of resurrection in Valhǫll by chewing the leaves (lives) of the World Tree. She declares that even in the face of massive challenges and Ragnarǫk, Óttarr, the Warrior of Hope (or, alternately, the Warrior who conquers Fear), will drink the mead of knowledge and remember the teachings, and that she will demand that all the Aesir help him.

Vǫlundarkvíða: The Song of the Sacred Grove.

Vǫlundr [Sacred Grove] is a smith, an elf and a son of the "Sami king". With his two brothers, he arrives in Wolf Valley by the Wolf Lake. The wolf, a symbol of; survival instincts desire, hunger, greed, and lust. These qualities are necessary for life's survival yet easily turned destructive in the wrong hands. On the Shore of the Soul [Sefarstrǫnd] at the Wolf Lake, the three brothers find three maidens who are both Norns and Valkyrie. Wearing *swan hides* and *spinning* the linen of fate. The maidens are presented as goddesses of abundance, provisions and wisdom. It is Vǫlundr [the smith/elf son of a king] who marries All-Wise, the youngest of the Valkyrie. The three couples live happily together for seven years.

Then the women begin to tire of life as house-wives and yearn for battles. On the eighth year, their yearning grows stronger. Until, finally, on the ninth year of marriage, the Valkyrie leave their husbands, flying into the Dark Forest in order to fulfill the fate of All-Wise the young. Without their wives, the brothers feel lost. Two of them begin to seek their wives in the direction of the east (world of giants) and of the south (world of gods and Norns), but Vǫlundr the elf-smith remains in Wolf Valley, forging hundreds of red gold rings, awaiting the return of his beloved. The story of Vǫlundr is discovered by King Niðuðr [Wave Beneath], who sends his warriors to capture Vǫlundr, and discover where the gold is to be found.

The King complains that he had not managed to find any gold on the "Path of Grani", which means the Path of Initiation (Grani is Sígurð's horse, used to carry the divine red gold of wisdom and to jump through the fires of death). Vǫlundr explains that the wealth the King is talking about was abundant when the three brothers lived in harmony with the three sisters.

The **red gold** in question is a symbol of divine power, knowledge and wisdom. The King is not satisfied with this answer and, following the counsel of his cunning wife, cuts Vǫlund's hamstrings [Hamstringing is a method of crippling a person or animal so that they cannot walk] and places him on an islet called The Place of the Soul [Sefarstaðir], where the elf is forced to forge riches for the King and his people.

The King takes Vǫlund's sword for himself and gives the Red Ring of All-Wise to his daughter Battle Intent [Bǫðvildr]. But Vǫlundr plots his revenge. Through cunning maneuverings and manipulations, he somehow succeeds in taking the lives of the King's two young and greedy sons, and rapes the King's daughter, who becomes pregnant, taking back and mending the Red Ring of All-Wise that the daughter had broken. Then he flies away in the shape of an eagle, letting the King know of the consequences of his actions. The pregnant and raped daughter is now placed under Vǫlund's protection, becoming the Woman of the Sacred Grove, birthing a new beginning.

Grottasǫngr: The Song of the Mill-Stone.

King Fróði [Wise One/Wisdom] receives a huge mill-stone from a "peasant" called Hangakiǫft [Hanging Gaping Mouth], a mill that will grind what the miller speaks, but no one has the strength to draw the mill except two giant maidens called Fenia [Heath-Dweller/Doer] and Menia [Necklace-Owner/Rememberer]. The maidens are taken as slaves and made to draw the mill while singing songs of abundance, peace, wisdom and prosperity.

But the king drives them too hard and refuses them rest, and finally, the giantesses grow weary and angry. Recalling their own strength and former glory, they begin to call upon the sleeping King Wisdom to wake up and listen to their tales. But as their songs fall on the deaf ears, as the household of Wisdom continues to sleep, the maiden begin to grind war, pestilence and poverty, ending the Peace of Wisdom that has long reigned.

Sólarlióð: The Song of the Sun.

This is usually thought to be a Christian poem, with remnants of Pagan concepts within. It was probably composed after the introduction of Christianity, in the year 1200, by a person who seems somewhat pulled between the new faith and old concepts and beliefs. A man has died, and is advising his son of the death journey he has walked. He tells of a chair in which the recently deceased must sit for nine days. The "Chair of the Norns" he says is the seat in which you await the Judgment of the Norns. He describes his vision of the Sun as a glorious goddess to whom he bowed one last time before he died, and many other visions.

The Sun-Song is composed in the style of the Edda poems, yet the poem is often not added to contemporary Edda translations because it is thought to be more of a Christian than a Pagan poem, despite the fact that it clearly explains Pagan concepts. The focus of the poem is in my opinion on Pagan issues, yet not the ones people today traditionally consider crucial to Paganism.

I believe the reason for this modern dismissal is the Sun-Song's focus on the female powers of the Old Norse cosmos, which does not correspond with stereotypical notions held in our day. It is my conviction that the poet who composed this poem in the year 1200 probably knew a lot more about Old Norse Pagan concepts than we do today and that his focus is, to a great degree, on Pagan issues, and that the poet is drawn between these ancient issues and the Christian faith. Various aspects of the Sun-Song will be discussed, particularly in Chapter 2 and in Chapter 6.

Hrafnagaldr Óðins eða Forspjallsljóð: Óðin's Raven Charm or Song of the First Speech.

Composed in the Edda style, this poem has often been dismissed by many scholars as a late poem, probably written down centuries after the Conversion by someone who was well acquainted with Edda lore. This 'author' has been dismissed as a hoax, due to the fact that they bragged about their knowledge of the use of metaphors and then made a completely unintelligible poem which makes the poem seem to be a fake. However, in my opinion, the most important reason for this dismissal seems to be the fact that the poem is almost impossible to understand from the traditional perspective on the myths as a kind of fairy tale. There is no story, no setting, but instead only a series of cryptic and subtle stanzas often referring to issues and concepts, mostly unknown to us.

Every attempted interpretation, ends up the same, with the poem being labeled as unintelligible and thus a fake, invented by some hoax perhaps during the 17th century AD. This is why the poem is hardly presented in any translation or collections. I found, when I tried a translation of my own, that this poem becomes deeply meaningful. When, I included the names of characters and places in my interpretations, it continuously alludes to the basic issues of the Mysteries that in this book are revealed to be at the heart and core of Edda lore. On this ground alone, I am firmly convinced that this poem deserves its space among the Edda poems, and I have, in some instances, used some stanzas from this poem as relevant sources.

Gróagalðr: The Spells of Growing.

A young boy stands before the "doors of death" at the mound of his long dead mother, a witch (vǫlva) called Gróa ["To Grow"]. The mother wakes up from the dead and speaks to her son, who tells her that his stepmother has forced him to seek the hand of the maiden Menglǫð [Invitation to Blend or Necklace Joy]. The boy is anxious, believing himself to be too young to undertake such a dangerous and difficult task, and asks his mother's advice. The dead woman declares that the path is terribly dangerous and difficult, but if he succeeds, fortune will be his. She sings nine spell-songs that will help him on the way. The spells she sings, deal with; letting go of the past, letting go of all things that holds the boy back, to follow his own way, and to not be distracted, especially by "Christian women". The dead witch says farewell with a final advice; That he shall always remember his mother's advice.

Fjǫlsvinnsmál: The Speech of Much Knowing.

The young boy of the Gróagalðr suddenly finds himself floating in the darkness of the Outer World [Utgarðr]. The place is dark, hostile and the home of giants. Yet the boy can see a beautiful, golden hall with a tree called the Mímameiðr [Tree of Memory] within, and at its root a mountain called Lyfjaberg [The Mountain of Medicine].

On top of this mountain by the root of the tree sits a dreaming, sleeping maiden, His beloved Menglǫð. She is accompanied by nine beautiful and friendly maidens. The boy knows that he has to enter this hall and wake up the maiden, but the hall is protected by fearsome walls and gates and blood-thirsty hounds, as well as by the guardian and servant of the maiden, Fjǫlsviðr [Much Knowing].

The guardian challenges the boy, saying that since he is neither dead nor dying, this is not a place for him (letting us know that this is a place for the dead and the dying). The boy, now calling himself Wind-Cold (a way of indicating that he is actually dead), begins to engage the

Bronze Age Rock Carving,
Scandinavia
Three males surrounding
the emblem of the Sun
goddess.

giant guardian in a word duel [similar to a battle of wits], asking questions to see if the guardian can answer. The questions lead to revelations of secrets about the properties and functions of the realm of the maiden, who is revealed to be The Great Maiden [Þióðmæra] and the ruling queen of the giant world. Finally, the boy asks the right question and realizes that he has been married to this maiden for an eternity, but that he has forgotten because of multiple deaths. When he remembers his true identity, the maiden wakes and calls for the guardian to let her beloved through, declaring herself as his fylgja ["follower", a guardian spirit/ancestral mother/soul].

HEROIC POEMS

Helgakvíða Hiǫrvarðssonar: The Song of Helgi Hiǫrvarð's son.

The poem begins with the story of King Hiǫrvarðr and his earl's son Atli [Intender]. Atli plays the role of a shaman, a priest and a guide through initiation. The title iarl [earl] is derived from the older erilaR and used to refer to a sage or a priest, one who knew runes. After seeking visions in a sacred grove where birds talk to him, Atli moves into the Land of Sleep [Svávaland] in order to woo a maiden there for King Hiǫrvarðr, Sígrlinn [Mild Victory]. The theme is similar to that of the Skírnismál (above) where the servant Skírnir enters the Underworld to woo a supernatural maiden for his lord Freyr. He does not succeed in bringing out the maiden, but must return with the King.

The two ascend a Sacred Mountain [Helga Fjǫll] in order to see the state of the Land of Sleep. Then they sleep by a river (a border between the worlds), and as they sleep, Atli moves into the realm and fetches the maiden for his King and her handmaiden for himself after killing the giant in eagle disguise (a symbol of death) who has guarded the maidens in a house surrounded by flames. Later, Hiǫrvarð's son by the supernatural maiden grows up unsociable and different from other men, and no name will stick to him. One day as he sits on a burial mound, nine Valkyrie ride past. Their leader is Sváva from Sefafjǫll [The Sleeper from Soul Mountain], who names the boy Helgi [Sacred One] and points out his sacred destiny. Helgi has to go through trials in order to win the hand of the Valkyrie in marriage. On the journey, he has to go into the Fjord of Hatred [Hatafiord] and battle the giants called Hatred [Hati] and Rage Ocean [Hróðmarr].

After a successful battle, Helgi and his men, who sleep aboard their ship, are attacked by the giantess Frosty Enclosure [Hrímgerðr], a daughter of Rán [Robbery, the death goddess of the ocean]. Frosty Enclosure, who is a deadly wave, tries to rock the boat into sinking, wanting the bodies of the drowned in her cold embrace, as her lovers (which means that she wants to kill them). Helgi's attendant Atli [Intender] manages to keep the giantess occupied in a verbal exchange until dawn breaks and the ogress is turned into stone. Before she dies, she reveals that only the light of the Valkyrie had prevented her from taking the men's' lives. Helgi and Sváva get married, and she protects, guides and loves him throughout his life like a Valkyrie, but Helgi must fight once more at the battle of the Rock of Greed [Frekasteinn], where he dies. Sváva, devastated, goes to sleep once more.

Helgakvíða Hundingsbani hinn fyrri: The First Song of Helgi Hunding's Bane.

Helgi, from the poem above, is reborn as Helgi, son of Sígmundr Vǫlsung, and later known as Hunding's Bane. In this first poem, Helgi's birth is described as if it was the birth of the present Universe itself. I believe this is a way of showing how Helgi's story is relevant to all men, it is the story of man's quest for and journey towards wisdom. In this life, Helgi begins his career as a Viking greedy for spoils. One day, as he dozes off after a battle during a near-death experience, the Valkyrie of his previous life appears before him, this time calling herself by the name Sígrún [Victory Symbol], reminding him of their previous life together, when he had her as his wife.

She urges him to change his life and go through the same trials of initiation that he did in his previous life. Helgi goes through more or less the same (at least very similar) battles as before, this time aided by his older half-brother Sinfiǫtli [Pale Fetters, i.e. "Death Gods"], who grew up as a refugee in the forest, learning to change his shape into animal form, to speak the language of birds and animals, and to know healing herbs. Sinfiǫtli helps the present Helgi much the same way as Atli helped the previous Helgi, and Helgi succeeds his battles. This time, he is also victorious in the crucial battle at the Rock of Greed. Helgi dies only when Óðinn chooses him for his own and leads the spear of the Valkyrie bride's own brother. The couple goes to stay together and drink precious mead in the burial mound, and Helgi is allowed entry in Valhǫll, moving between the two afterlife realms, the mound and the heaven. The Valkyrie Sígrún goes to sleep once more and is only woken up when Helgi's younger half-brother, Sígurðr, born after the death of Helgi, comes of age.

Helgakvíða Hundingsbani ǫnnur: The Second Song of Helgi Hunding's Bane.

This poem tells the same tale about Helgi Hundingsbani, some events are told in a different manner that the first part of the poem, and some events are added to. The comparison to the birth of the universe is not present in this poem.

Frá dauða Sinfiǫtla: About the Death of Sinfiǫtli [Pale Fetters].

This is not a poem but a prose interlude written by those who edited and wrote down the Edda poem collection of the manuscript that was hidden away until 1647, containing most of the Edda poems in a meaningful chronology (I have followed this chronology in this presentation, adding the Song of the Sun and the Raven Charm, which have been transmitted in torn-out pages). The editors explain that Sinfiǫtli, son of Sígmundr [Victory Origin] Vǫlsung [Descendant of the Witch's Wand] and brother to Helgi, was killed by his stepmother as a vengeance for his killing her brother. Sígmundr, in grief, takes the body of his son to the shores of death where the Ferryman awaits, and almost goes into the ferry with his son, but the Ferryman refuses him.

Sígmundr then leaves Denmark, where he had lived with his wife, and moved south to Frankland, where he marries Hjǫrdís [Herd Goddess], daughter of King Eylimi [Connects Islands] and sister to Grípir [Grasping One], which is a name for Óðinn. With Hjǫrdís, Sígmundr has a son, Sígurðr [Victory Beginning]. But the Hundings attack, killing all the men of the family. Hjǫrdís escapes with her young son and finds refuge with King Hialprèk [Communicator], where she marries the King's son Álfr [Elf, i.e. soul, ancestor]. There, her son Sígurðr grows up an orphan, raised to avenge his father and grandfather.

Grípisspá: The Divination of Grípir.

As a young man, Sígurðr seeks his maternal uncle, the sorcerer Grípir [Grasping One = Óðinn]. The sorcerer performs a séance of seiðr where he divines the young man's future and destiny. He tells Sígurðr that there is a; maiden, a Valkyrie, a golden goddess, who is the foster-daughter of "The Worlds" [Heimir]. She has been sleeping since the death of Helgi. If the young man can manage to wake her up, she will teach him knowledge about runes, healing and every language there is, everything that a human being would ever want to know. But there is a danger, namely that he may forget the Valkyrie bride and fall into the trap of cunning powers weaving for their own ends.

Reginsmál: The Speech of the Ruler.

Sígurðr is taught by the dwarf smith Reginn [Ruler] in his forge. They forge the blade called Rage [Grámr] as the Ruler tells Sígurðr a tale about how the Red Gold of Andvari [Alert Spirit] came into the possession of a giant in serpent's disguise, Fafnir [Embracer], Reginn's own brother. The serpent now "embraces" the Red Gold, keeping the inheritance of the gods hidden away from human kind, scaring them away while he snorts his poisons and wears the Aegishjalmr [Helmet of Fear, i.e. a fearful mind]. In this poem, Sígurðr and Reginn travel to fulfill the duty of the son towards his father and grandfather; to slay the Hundings. On the way across the ocean they enter a violent storm, yet in the middle of the storm they see a sorcerer standing calmly on a cliff. As they ask his identity, the sorcerer offers some clues, revealing that he is really Óðinn, the One Who is Many. Sígurðr invites the god aboard the ship, and the storm immediately calms down. The young man asks advice for his present quest, and is given counsel. He wins the battle against the Hundings, and Reginn sings his praise.

Fafnismál: The Speech of the Embracer.

Having fulfilled his cultural duty as a young nobleman, avenging his father, Sígurðr embarks on the quest for the Red Gold, urged on by Reginn, who pretends to be a beneficial spiritual guide, yet is spurred by greed and hatred only. Sígurðr goes up on a heath called Gníta [Lice Egg (?)], later described as a Sacred Mountain, where he digs a hole in the ground for himself. As the 'fear-helmeted' giant in serpent's shape moves over the hole, Sígurðr drives his sword through its body, and is surprised when the serpent begins to ask questions about his descent. Sígurðr identifies himself as the "Foremost Animal" whose courage had whetted[2] him and whose hands had assisted him, as well as the sharp sword [tool].

I suggest this is a way of saying that Sígurðr represents human kind in general. Sígurðr manages to turn the table and asks questions back, and the dying serpent reveals powerful and secret knowledge about himself, and about the true and secret intentions of his brother Reginn. He reveals that Sígurðr, man's representative, believes himself to be free, but that he is in fact a slave moving unknowingly towards his final destiny and towards the judgment of the Norns [fate-goddesses], and that he is in danger of drowning on the way. Sígurðr responds to this information by asking who the Norns are, who saves the mother from the children, and Fafnir reveals that there are three kinds of Norns.

An exchange about Ragnarǫk follows before the serpent dies, and Sígurðr returns to his mentor Reginn, now able to see through his mentor's base intentions. Reginn praises Sígurð's courage once more, but this time the young man rejects the praise, declaring that courage has nothing to do with killing others. Reginn, suspecting that he is losing his control over the boy, goes angry, but can do nothing. He demands the serpent's heart to eat in order to learn the whereabouts of the Red Gold, but falls asleep. Sígurðr tastes the blood of the serpent and immediately understands the speech of birds. The birds confirm that Reginn has bad intentions, advised Sígurðr to kill the smith, and to seek the Sacred Mountain once more. He will find the Red Gold of the gods, and then he will find the golden bright maiden who has slept, ever since his previous death. Sígurðr follows the advice of the birds and finds the Red Gold in the serpent's lair.

Sígrdrífumál: The Speech of Sígrdrífa ["Victory Snowfall", a Valkyrie].

Carrying the Red Gold, Sígurðr reaches a high hall on the mountain surrounded by flames made out of radiant river-light (the light of the Daughters of the Ocean). The flames reach high up into the heavens. Knowing no fear, Sígurðr rides through the flames, shining with the bright gold of "Alert Spirit", and finds a warrior sleeping within, hidden by shields. As he removes her helmet, he discovers that the warrior is a woman. Her armor has grown into her body.

---

2 Whetted: to sharpen the blade of (a tool or weapon)

He removes her armor, and the lady wakes up, revealing that she is a Valkyrie by the name Sígrdrífa, and that the god Óðinn has made her sleep because she chose a warrior she loved, Agnarr [Respect Warrior] rejecting Óðin's request, that she should choose a warrior that was called Hjalmgunnarr [Helmet-Fight Warrior, i.e. conflicting mind].

Óðinn had then put her to sleep, at the cost of the welfare of humankind, for as long as the Valkyrie sleeps, woe is in the world. The Valkyrie offers the Mead of Memory to the young man, and with it, she offers the knowledge about how to use the runes for all kinds of purposes; healing, midwifery, stilling storms, making enemies into friends, convincing others, ensure victory in all things, eloquence, protection. Finally, she reveals the existence of húgrunar ["Soul Runes"] which must be possessed in order to obtain true wisdom. She reveals how these runes were discovered, formed and distributed by Óðinn into all the worlds. Finally, the Valkyrie offers her guidance throughout the young man's life, if he chooses to listen to her, and the remainder of the poem consists of advice for proper conduct similar to those found in the Hávamál.

Helreið Brynhildar: Brynhild's Ride to Hel.

In the chronology of the Edda collection, this poem appears after two "poems about Sígurðr" and one "poem about Guðrún" that follow the Sígrdrífumál (above). In these, we hear about the circumstanced that led to the death of Sígurðr. In the present poem, Sígurðr is on his way to Hel, where all souls go after death. But his Valkyrie, now called Brynhildr (after she had married someone else), goes after him and saves him from the clutches of the "Rock Bride". She has to answer for her crimes in life before the death-ogress before she can justify her actions and retrieve the soul of her beloved out of Hel, forever to be together.

Guðrúnarkviður, Sígurðarkvíður and Atlakvíður

Poems about Guðrún (four poems), Sígurðr (two poems) and Atli (two poems) "Brynhild's Ride to Hel" is followed by two poems about Guðrún, explaining events that happened after the death of Sígurðr, when his widow Guðrún became a witch and then married King Atli of the Huns [based on the historical character Attila, who died in 452 A.D.]. The previous poems also contribute to the information about this ancient legend, partly based on and inspired by historical events. In the Edda, the Hunnish king is greedy for the Red Gold that he has heard that Sígurðr owned, a magnificent treasure, but a spiritual one. To Atli's great chagrin, none of this wealth arrives with his new bride, so Atli grows angry with his new in-laws. The in-laws are identified as Burgunds, a historical German tribe whose ruling class was massacred around the year 432 AD by the Huns under the leadership of a young Attila, who was in league with the Roman general Aetius. Aetis, who wanted to put an end to the many border squirmishes caused by rebellious Burgunds. These historical events of fifth century Europe have found their way into the legendary lore of the Scandinavian Viking Age, as shown in the Poetic Edda.

King Gunnarr [Warrior] of the Burgunds/Niflungs, whose character is based on the historical Gundahar, king of the historical Burgunds (who died during the 432 AD massacre of the Burgund court), appears in the Edda lore as the brother to Sígurð's wife Guðrún [Divine Symbol].

The Burgunds (of the Edda, at least) appear to have followed a matrilineal descent, since Sígurð's marriage to the Burgund princess automatically makes him the high king of the Burgunds, ruling together with his wife, her mother, and her two brothers Gunnarr and Họgnir [Thinker], implies that the marriage automatically grants him kingship. Gunnarr wants to seek the Valkyrie on the mountains just like Sígurðr (a way of alluding to the initiation into manhood and sagacity which was necessary in order to become a king) and to marry a princess. Sígurðr willingly accompanies his brother-in-law as his experienced mentor, yet Gunnarr is unable to complete the initiation, being too timid to dare to go through the fire.

Sígurðr wishes to save the face of his friend before his friends and family, and secretly, the two change shape so that it is Sígurðr, wearing the appearance of Gunnarr, is the one who actually goes through the fire and meets the Valkyrie once more. Later, Gunnarr is married to one Brynhildr [Armor Battle], a name which refers to her previous incarnation. It talks of a time when she was a sleeping Valkyrie whose armor had grown into her body. Brynhildr is two characters at the same time; on one side, she is a Hunnish princess, sister to King Atli, married to the Burgund prince after his initiation had made him worthy. Although this was in fact a hoax since he had not managed to complete the initiation himself.

On the other side, she is really the Valkyrie who has been appearing under different names in the previous poems, the Valkyrie who sleeps when her human is dead, and who reawakens when he, reborn, come to seek her and wake her up. As a Hunnish Princess, Brynhildr discovers that her marriage to the oldest prince among the Burgunds is not going to make her their first lady, since that honor goes to the oldest princess. This conflict is subtly revealed as the two sisters-in-law argue about which of them is the First Lady and ranks higher. For a Hunnish princess who was obviously used to patriarchy this was a shock. She felt tricked into marriage with a man that would never become king, and never be the foremost man among his people. Things do not improve as the argument makes Guðrún lose her temper and reveal a most humiliating fact; that she has received Brynhild's own wedding gift to her husband Gunnarr not from Gunnarr, but from her husband Sígurðr.

This is proof that her present husband is not even the man who entered her wedding bed, thus Guðrún's husband has not only bested her own husband when it comes to public status, but also though the entry into the marriage bed before the actual husband. This is a deeply humiliating fact for the princess, who feels gravely dishonored and tricked into marrying the lesser man and tricked into becoming the concubine of the king. As a Valkyrie, also described as the Goddess of Gold [Gullna Dís] and the Goddess of the Shield Kind [Skjoldunga Dís], Brynhildr is horrified to realize that she is married to a man whom she never actually knew, a man who was too timid to go through the fire, going against her sacred oath to marry a man who knew no fear.

Originally, she had not wanted to marry at all, but her brother, who turns out to be Óðinn thinly disguised behind the figure of Atli, was so greedy for the Red Gold of the gods that he demanded that she marry the one who could bring them the Red Gold.

After careful consideration, the Valkyrie, who is revealed to be Óðin's own sister, agrees on these terms. She will marry the one who is able to bring the Red Gold, a feat that will only be managed by a man who has no fear in his heart. Now she finds herself living like a human woman in a world of deceit where her husband is a timid man and where her true husband, the one who knows no fear, is married to another and appears to have forgotten her completely. The Valkyrie proceeds to have her husband and his brother kill the king in order to usurp the throne. The brothers, Gunnarr and Hǫgnir, make the arrangements and are later mocked by both their sister Guðrún and by Brynhildr for having broken their sacred wows for the sake of greed for power. The Burgund princes have usurped the power, stolen the High Seat from their own sister, and Guðrún, who in her shock and grief, leaves her people and disappears into the forest.

Where, she embarks on a journey of initiation, reaching the realm of the Norns, learning how to weave fate according to her liking. Brynhildr kills herself and travels into Hel in order to save Sígurðr. She weaves a terrible future for her own brothers in order to avenge herself and her dead husband, but her weaving is discovered by another weaver, Guðrún's own mother Queen Grímhildr [Mask Battle], who urges her sons to seek reconciliation with their sister in the place where she now dwells. The brothers ride to seek their sister's forgiveness, and after a great deal of begging, their mother offers a cup of mead to Guðrún that heals her from her anger and finally enables her to accept her brother's offer of peace. The trouble is that her previous weaving's have caused the Hunnish King Atli to turn his forces against the Burgunds, suspecting them of having driven his sister Brynhildr to suicide, or perhaps even killed her.

The only solution for peace is to offer Guðrún in marriage to the Hunnish king. Guðrún reluctantly agrees. During the wedding feast for Atli and Guðrún, Gunnarr falls in love with his dead wife Brynhild's "younger sister", Oddrún [Edge Symbol] probably yet another incarnation of the ever-reincarnating Valkyrie goddess. But Atli refuses the match. Later, he grows angry by the fact that Gunnarr has had relations with his sister despite the refusal to marriage, suspecting him of having caused the death of his other sister, and ultimately for not having brought the Red Gold that was Guðrún's heritage after her husband. He invites the Burgund princes to a banquet with the secret intention of destroying them. Guðrún sees through his intentions and tries to warn her brothers.

When she fails to prevent them from coming, she dresses up as a warrior and fights alongside her brothers during the battle that is to come. The Burgunds are defeated, and Guðrún forced to watch as Atli tortures and murders her brothers Gunnarr and Hǫgnir. Afterwards, Guðrún accepts Atli's peace offerings and expresses submission, stating that a woman must often bow to the dominance of men, and that he will rule on his own from now on, since she has no more power. But with her submission comes a warning of how a trunk (the masculine) will topple if the roots (the feminine) are cut from under it.

Atli, failing to understand the message, proposes that she arrange a funeral banquet to honor both their dead relatives. Guðrún agrees, and the banquet is a fact, a banquet where she serves the hearts of her own two young sons by Atli to their own father, their blood mixed into the mead and their flesh served as "calf-meat" to all the participants.

Although she reveals the gory contents of the food after they have eaten, the entire hall seems spell-bound, and everybody fall asleep beneath Guðrún's spell. Guðrún kills Atli with his own sword and reveals that she knew how he was the real mind behind the death of her husband Sígurðr, and that he had manipulated everybody to his own purpose, causing deaths and misery. Atli dies gracefully, acknowledging the formidable character of his wife, and asks for a king's funeral. Guðrún grants his wish by putting the entire hall of the Huns to the fire, with all the sleeping warriors within.

The Edda poet praises Guðrún as a warrior woman who fulfilled her duty, avenging her brothers with the utmost ferocity. The historical events behind this story are based on a rumor that spread soon after the death of the real Attila in 452 AD. The Hunnish lord had died during his wedding night to a German princess (he had many wives, however). His warriors claimed that he had died from heart attack, but rumor had it that it was the bride who had killed him, thus avenging her father and brothers who had died at his hands. The name of the bride was, according to Roman sources, Ildico, which probably is a Latinized version of Hildegunde.

We do not know what tribe she belonged to, but it is easy to see that her character has inspired the character of Guðrún in the Edda poems. The death of the historical Attila actually led to the rapid decline of the Hunnish empire, which had dominated and subdued the European tribes north of the Roman borders for a century already. The woman who reputedly and single-handedly brought down Attila indirectly also brought down the reign of seemingly invincible oppressors, ultimately causing the liberation of all the tribes. It should come as no surprise if that woman was remembered in legends afterwards. The Poetic Edda is the only proof that Hildegunde was thus remembered and praised in the lore of the tribes, even if the memory of her true identity was blurred and mixed up with the memory of the Burgunds' fall.

Oddrúnargrátr: The Lament of Oddrún.

The poem begins with a story about a girl who has concealed her pregnancy for a very long time. She calls the Valkyrie Oddrún [Edge Rune] to her aid. The Valkyrie arrives and sings powerful charms that finally bring about the birth of the children of New Fortress [Borgný] in Mornaland [Land of Tomorrow]. The Valkyrie then proceeds to tell her own tale of loss and sorrow. She had once loved Gunnarr the Burgund, and offered him her cup of mead. But, her relationship to the Burgund prince had been discovered by her brother Atli, who refused their match. After the battle between the Huns and the Burgunds, Gunnarr was thrown into a pit full of serpents, a symbol of the Well in Hel (the well of death) where serpents withdraw the life energy of the dead souls, grinding them into the water that runs back into the world.

Gunnarr is given a harp and begins playing with his toes, since his hand are bound. He plays so hauntingly beautiful that everybody begin to weep, even the most hardened warriors, and the serpents are held at bay. The tunes of Gunnarr's death song reaches the Valkyrie where she now stays in her father's house at Hlésey [Wind-Shield (i.e. Immortality) Island], identifying the Valkyrie and the eight sisters she mentions, as the daughters of Aegir the Ocean Lord. The Valkyrie rides as fast as she can muster to save her beloved, but the call came just too late. Upon arrival, she sees how Atli's mother, the ogress of death, has turned into a snake or reptile and entered the pit. The ogress of death is the only entity that remains unaffected by Gunnarr's tunes, and promptly bites through his liver, killing him.

Oddrún lives on, but in grief. The poem fills out several details of the story, especially regarding the motifs of King Atli, who once again is described in a manner that reveals his true identity. Óðinn in a greedy and destructive aspect, willing to do anything to get his hands on the Red Gold of divine wisdom, repeatedly attempting to succeed through dishonorable manipulation and failing miserably. It will take him quite a while to reach the state of perception where he can finally sing the last charm of the ultimate secret.

1.2: SNORRI STURLUSON'S PROSE EDDA AND YNGLINGA SAGA

Apart from the Poetic Edda, our most important source to Old Norse myths was written down by the Icelandic scholar Snorri Sturluson (1179-1241). It is usually known as the Prose Edda and is divided into separate books which should be called treatises about Old Norse poetry. In fact, the entire work is a treatise on Pagan poetry, the ancient art of bards known in Old Norse as skaldskáp (the "creation of the bard"). Snorri had a clear and outspoken agenda with his work. He realized that people were beginning to forget the myths of their ancestors. As a good Christian, he could not really defend his wish to preserve these Pagan myths, but as a poet and a scholar of poetry, he could claim the importance of the myths as the basis of the ancient art of poetry.

Since Old Norse poetry was based on metaphors, and the metaphors drew from mythology, it was necessary to remember Old Norse mythology in order to understand and continue the ancient and precious art of poetry. Snorri's Prose Edda was an attempt to preserve the very special Norse art of metaphorical poetry by writing down the most important myths that would explain the metaphors. Without knowledge of the myths, it would soon be impossible to understand the poetry of the ancestors. In fact, without the aid of Snorri's marvelous work, we would not today have been able to understand neither skaldic nor Edda poetry. The verses would have appeared unintelligible to us, created, as they are, in a language of riddles, allegories and metaphors.

THE VARIOUS PARTS OF THE PROSE EDDA ARE AS FOLLOWS:

The Prologue: In the Prologue, Snorri makes an effort to present the Pagan gods as ancestors who had been so marvelous and powerful that their descendants in their superstitious ignorance started to worship them as gods after their deaths. Snorri explained that the term Aesir ("gods") really meant "Asians", a name derived from the "fact" that the Aesir originated in Turkey, or to be more exact, in the famous Troy. Troy, and Turkey, belonged to the Asian continent as far as Snorri's contemporaries were concerned. This historical approach is usually dismissed as a fancy of Snorri, who was supposedly trying to establish an ancestral line to the Classical world which was quite fashionable in 13th century Europe.

However, there are aspects of the story which in my opinion curiously resemble very early movements from the Southeast to the Northwest towards the end of the Stone Age, aspects that I will be exploring in later Chapters. Also, the idea of ancestral worship is by no means unknown from other Viking Age sources, and it is not impossible that the term Aesir is related to the Old Gothic term Ansir, which means ancestors, who were indeed worshiped by the Goths. Whether there is any truth in Snorri's tales and if so, to what degree, is difficult to say, but we must not forget that Snorri's presentation of the Pagan gods as human ancestors was a very clever move; by letting the Christian authorities "understand" that these were really just tales of famous humans in the past, the myths no longer posed a threat to Christian doctrine. The Church could certainly accept ancestral history where it could not accept Pagan beliefs. It is almost certain that this Prologue saved the Prose Edda from the oblivion that was imposed on the Poetic Edda. Snorri simply made the myths acceptable to the Church, and it is not unlikely that this was a conscious move.

Gylfaginning: The first book of the Prose Edda treatise means "The Vision of the Sorcerer" and will be described more thoroughly in I.3.

Skáldskaparmál: The second book of the Prose Edda treatise means "The Speech of the Creation of Bards" and will be described more thoroughly in I.4

Háttatal: The third book of the Prose Edda treatise means "the List of Verses" is a systematized textbook on the rules of Old Norse poetry, using poetical examples usually created by Snorri himself.

Ynglinga Saga: Another important source to mythology written by Snorri Sturluson is the Ynglinga saga, the first part of the greater work Heimskringla [The World Circle], a collection of sagas of the Norwegian kings by Snorri. In the first part of his Ynglinga saga, Snorri elaborates the same story told in his Prose Edda Prologue, namely the origin of the Aesir as ancestors from the south. The saga is loosely based on several skaldic poems; in particular the skaldic poem Ynglingatál by the 9th century scald Thióðolf the Wise.

Other famous Viking Age scalds are also referred to and quoted, revealing a lore where various royal lines were indeed thought to be descendants of divine beings. In Norway, several noble and royal clans claimed descent from the mountain hunter and skiing goddess Skaði and her marriage to Óðinn, whereas Swedish lines such as the Ynglinga line claimed descent from Freyr and his marriage to Gerðr. Studies initiated by the Norwegian academic authority Gro Steinsland have shown that this kind of noble descent from a Sacred Marriage between a god and a giantess was extremely important in the lore and religious life of the Vikings. In the Ynglinga saga, Snorri emphasized the role of the Aesir gods and goddesses as powerful priests and priestesses who established the Norse religion in a distant past.

Óðinn in particular was a powerful sorcerer who performed marvelous feats, which was why he was worshiped after his death. Freyr was remembered and worshiped as a great king, and Freyia, who introduced the art of seiðr to the Aesir, was the last living and only surviving member of the ancestral pantheon. Snorri said that she still operates as a temple priestess even to this day (which would be the 13th century). Scholars have suggested that what Snorri was really referring to was the fact that the worship of and divinatory and private rituals associated with Freyia were the last to survive into the 13th century. Another interesting part of the Ynglinga saga is the Prologue, where Snorri refers to his sources. About his medieval sources to mythology, the great scholar wrote;

"In this book I let write down old rumors of the chiefs who had their reigns in the Northern lands and who have spoken Norse languages, such as I have heard wise men tell....some of this is found in the stories of the lineages which kings and other nobles count their descent after, some is also written after old songs ...that people use for entertainment, for even if we do not know if these are true, there is evidence that old wise men have thought them to be true... Thióðolf the Wise from Kvinir was a skald at the court of Harald Hárfagri, he made that poem known as the Ynglingatál...While Harald Hárfagri was the king of Norway, Iceland was settled [mostly by people who refused to bow to Harald's sole reign (author's comment)].

At Harald's court there were many scalds, and people still know their songs and the songs about all the kings who have been in Norway since. And we have gathered most of our knowledge from what has been told in the poems sung for the kings themselves, or for their sons....It is the way of scalds to praise most the man in front of whom they are performing, but no one would dare to tell a man about deeds he was supposed to have done, when everyone who listened knew them to be lies and bragging, and he himself as well. That would have been scorn, not praise. Ari priest the Wise...was the first man here in the land (Iceland) who wrote in the Norse language the knowledge of old and new times...Ari also learned a lot from Turid, daughter of Snorri the good, she was a wise woman and she remembered Snorri her father, and he was about 35 years old when Christianity came to Iceland...It was not so strange that Ari had good knowledge about ancient events both here and in other countries when he learned from such knowledgeable people, and he himself was knowledge-hungry and had a good memory. But the poems I think are the least misleading ones, if they are sung properly and interpreted with wisdom."

1.3: GYLFAGINNING THE REVELATION OF THE SORCERER

Gylfi was the name of a Swedish sorcerer king who went to seek Ásgarðr, the abode of the Aesir, usually translated as "gods" although the Aesir were but one tribe of so-called Powers in which the Old Norse Pagans believed in and related to. According to Snorri, the Aesir were "Asians" who had arrived in Scandinavia in the old days. In the Gylfaginning, the Aesir had reached Sweden and were in constant war with the native powerful sorcerer-king, Gylfi. When I first tried to look up the meaning of the name Gylfi, I found only one dictionary dating back to 1886 [Fritzner, Johan. Ordbog over det gamle norske sprog] which actually offered a translation, one which provided a very interesting clue. It literally said that Gylfi refers to a "werewolf", "shape-changer", or, most remarkably, a "sorcerer who changes into a woman every ninth night". Thus the true meaning of this name is lost in a worldview so different from our own that we would be hard put to explain it further. I can only point out the obvious; that the concept of changing sex was indeed associated with sorcery and that the number nine is a significant number in Norse mythology as a whole.

The precious ring Draupnir, for example, drips eight new rings every ninth night. This is the ring that burned with Baldr on the funeral pyre. Nine nights is the number of nights that Óðinn hung on the tree during his initiation, and is also the number of nights it takes to reach the heart of Hel according to the story of Hermóðr who attempted to save Baldr. Nine is also the number of nights that Freyr must wait before he can unite with his lover, and is the number of Freyia's heaven where she receives the chosen dead. It is also the number of worlds that existed before the present one, and the number of worlds in which Hel [death] rules. The Valkyrie of the Edda always appear in groups of nine, the famous hanging sacrifice at Uppsala lasted for nine days, and nine mothers birthed the great Heimdallr, whose name means the Great World. Some sources declare that a human being has nine Fylgjur (guardian spirits and ancestral mothers).

All these associations are significant, but we are still left dangling, knowing only that Gylfi is associated with magic, shape-changing, gender-bending and the very important number 9, which has to do with death, initiation and creation. The other word that composes the title Gylfaginning is ginning, which means "illusion", "hallucination", "optical trickery" or "vision" (as in "revelation"). In my opinion, the most correct interpretation of the title of Snorri's first book would translate something like "The Revelation of the Sorcerer". In "The Revelation of the Sorcerer", Gylfi, inspired by the powerful deeds of the goddess Gefion ["The Provider" and a name for Freyia], who knows all fate and who is the first among the Aesir who manages to trick the sorcerer king thoroughly. This makes Gylfi very curious, and spurs him to travel to the abode of the Aesir, that is, to Ásgarðr and Valhǫll. On his journey, he takes the name Gangleri, which means "Wandering Learner".

He seems conspicuously like the god Óðinn himself, a sorcerer and a shape-changer (who has certainly taken the shape of a woman several times), and who frequently move into the various dimensions of the universe in order to learn ever more, and who takes upon himself countless names. Indeed, Gangleri is listed among the important names of Óðinn. According to the rules of Norse poetry, a character will be hidden in words and identify itself through attributes such as these. How come Óðinn is in fact visiting his own abode, seeking himself, as if he was a stranger from a different land? Has it anything to do with the name he uses when he begins his quest, the "Wandering Learner"?

When the Wandering Learner arrives in Ásgarðr, he encounters another aspect of the god Óðinn, a threefold aspect disguised in three shapes; **The High One, Just-As-High, and Third** [Hár, Jafnhár and þríði], all names of Óðinn. These three take turn in answering Gylfi's questions about the universe, telling Gylfi all about the history of the world from beginning to end. Most of the revelations are based on the Edda poem Vǫluspá, but also makes reference to other cosmological Edda poems, especially Grímnismál and Vafþrúðnismál. When the three have finished their revelations, the entire Ásgarðr vanishes into thin air, and it turns out that the entire experience had been a ginning [an illusion, a hallucination, a trick, or indeed, a sorcerer's visionary revelation]. Gylfi finds himself on an empty field. An interesting feature that we will return to later is the fact that after this, Gylfi starts to walk through the world telling people everything he had heard, and one after the other people told the stories. Then, and only then, did the stories actually become real.

As Snorri mysteriously concludes; *"And they [the Aesir] recalled the things they had told the visitor. And to the people and places that were there, they gave the same names as in their stories, so that people, when great spans of time were gone, should not know that they were the same Aesir, those that they had just made up and who they now gave the same names. It was only then that Þórr got his name..."* That the world itself was considered a great story told by the gods and then retold by the living is a concept that is often hinted to in Old Norse sources. Such a concept of the world as a tale may very well have been part of the esoteric mysteries revealed through poetry. It is certainly not unknown from other cultures either. According to Joseph Campbell [The Mythic Image], a Kalahari bushman was known to have claimed that "there is a dream dreaming us", and according to the Indian Yogavashishta [2.3.11], "the world is like the impression left by the telling of a story". That the greatest creator god was the inventor of poetry is no coincidence, neither that his very name, Óðinn, indicates that he in fact is The Poetry. Neither is it a coincidence that one of the names of his wife, Frigg, is Saga, which means "Story".

1.4: Skáldskaparmál
Hidden meanings in poetical metaphors

"I wrote this book so that young students of poetry could learn to decipher that which has been composed in a subtle manner."-Snorri Sturluson, in his Introduction to the Prose Edda

Snorri's Skáldskaparmál [The Speech of the Creation of Poetry] is the second book of his Prose Edda. The book begins with the story of how a "man" named Aegir [The Sea, "The Terrifying One"] or Hlér ["Wind-Shielded" = Immortal] arrives in Ásgarðr. In the banquet that follows, the giant is entertained by the tales of Bragi, god of poetry (and husband to Iðunn). As god of poetry, Bragi is a specialized aspect of Óðinn. Snorri used this story as an entry to his own explanation of the traditional Norse art of poetry. Through the mythical tales we are introduced to the mythological background for the use of poetical metaphors, or what Snorri called heiti and kenningar. Snorri's mission was to make a study for *"young poets who want to learn the language of poetry and collect a treasure of old poetical words, and who want to understand that which is cleverly disguised in runes"*. Heiti are poetical words or synonyms that take the place of the nouns of everyday life.

They are often old-fashioned words no longer much used, that only survived as poetical words with the purpose of variation in the poetical vocabulary and to have an array of words to choose among in order to fit the rhymes. A kenning is also such substitute, but here, used in the form of metaphors. The word comes from the expression kenna við ["to know (something) by (something else)"]. It will always consist of at least two parts, where the basic word is "made known" by a second word that describes it. But each part may also be divided into a new two-part metaphor, so that one single kenning may consist of many parts. According to Margaret Clunies-Ross, Snorri's purpose must have been to show how *the language of early Icelandic poetry expressed basic principles in the Pagan Scandinavian religion*. Snorri, she claims, was of the opinion that Pagan poetry represented a serious attempt to understand the underlying principles of the cosmos.

She believes that this has to do with a particular medieval trend where scholars assumed that the authors and poets of the past had used metaphors and symbols called *integumenta* ["coverings"], in order to convey the inner meaning of their mythical narratives. I personally believe that Snorri and his medieval contemporaries were correct in their assumption and that Pagan poets really did apply a metaphorical language conveying hidden meanings. In the Skáldskaparmál, Snorri continues to relate Pagan myths, but this time with the more direct purpose of explaining metaphors. In my opinion, it would also seem that there is a hidden purpose, an esoteric revelation that must be deciphered, which basically has to do with the so-called "red gold". We are never told exactly what the red gold is, but we are given numerous examples of the metaphors for red gold, and the several examples of the mysterious mythology surrounding it.

As far as I have been able to understand it, the red gold seems to be a symbol in itself, a symbol for the hidden, divine knowledge that can only surface within a person through dire trials of initiation. A part of the Skáldskaparmál is the list of metaphors known as the þulur ("lists" or "recitals").

These are important listings of metaphors for things and characters which tell us quite a lot about the characters and the things. In the next essay on the skaldic poem Haustlǫng, I will go through some metaphors and how they serve to explain the function of poetical, mythical characters.

1.5: HIDDEN IN PLAIN SIGHT-WHAT SNORRI COULD NOT SAY

"That, I think, has been cleverly disguised in runes [symbols]."
Snorri Sturluson, Skáldskaparmál

The poems that constitute the lore of the fictional "Poetic Edda" belong to a Norse poetic tradition in which metaphor, allegory and parable was essential. Not only would the entire poem, like a riddle, be referring to mythical events that explain the poetical riddle. Basic mythical characters, even places, would in themselves be presented in riddles. A particular character would be "known by" countless names. Names that actually serve as metaphors which describe the character's essential nature, function and meaning. People would understand what character is really being referred to through these name-meanings and the attributes accompanying the character. Strangely enough, when the Edda is translated into other languages, the translator hardly ever attempts to translate the names of characters and places, and even less try to identify the "real" character behind the name-metaphor.

Names are perceived as mere sounds without meaning, left as they are or transcribed into a sound that fits better with the language that the poems are translated into. The original Norse listener or reader would have understood the meaning of names and known how to decipher the real identity of the characters, while we are left with hundreds of unintelligible, meaningless sound-names. Thus we are left with a translated poetry book where more than half of the meaning is missing. It is my mission to attempt to uncover the real meaning of the Edda myths, and thus I will attempt not only to translate names literally, but also attempt to identify the real character or meaning behind the name through the use of metaphor.

This is not as controversial as it may seem. Norse linguists are well aware of the metaphorical nature of myths and the fact that names have meaning and may be covers for other characters. It is no secret that Snorri Sturluson wrote his Prose Edda in an attempt to explain the real meaning behind the poetical metaphors, this was in fact his stated intent. Without his work we would have understood nothing at all of the Edda poems. The problem with using Snorri as a source to Norse myths is that his work, too, was biased. He was possibly a devout Christian who loved his ancestry and thus desperately tried to make it more acceptable to the Church.

Or he was a secret Pagan who desperately tried to preserve the myths in a fashion that would hide Pagan messages in plain sight. Snorri's way of making the Pagan ancestry acceptable was by explaining away the gods as actual ancestors that were misjudged by their descendants and turned into false gods.

The Church would not look kindly upon Pagan gods (demons, idols), but it would not mind ancestors. The Church would not accept Pagan doctrines of salvation and resurrection, but it would accept ancestral history. There is a reason why Snorri's work on the Pagan myths was known and accepted throughout the Middle Ages, while the Poetic Edda manuscript was hidden away. One aspect of Snorri's work is the repeated failure to describe or explain mythical events that directly describes initiation and resurrection, events that are described in the (once more clandestine) Poetic Edda. This failure is so thorough that one almost suspects his silence to be a pointer towards what we should look for in the Poetic Edda, and this suspicion should be considered in light of the factual knowledge that educated people in the Middle Ages really were big on codes, coded messages and riddles such as these. The difficulty with translating names (and, I hope, the reason why so few try to) comes when you try to actually do the translations and the interpretations. If one is to come close to the original meanings, this requires an understanding of the mythology as a complete system of beliefs. Since we are not actual insiders of this previous culture, such an understanding will be a matter of interpretation, a question of how we understand the myths and the culture in which they were nourished.

1.6: OTHER SOURCES TO OLD NORSE MYTHOLOGY

"But the old songs I believe are the least faulty [as historical sources], if they are correctly rendered and wisely grasped."
Snorri Sturluson, Prologus to Heimskringla

Skaldic Poems. One important type of sources existing is the skaldic poems. These were composed by named skalds [bards] during the Viking Age. Most of the surviving poems focus on praising kings and warriors or describing battles that have taken place, reflecting the poetry of a Viking chief's court. Some of them describe myths, such as the poem Haustlǫng [Prolonged Autumn] which we will be exploring in Chapter 4.

Whether the poems are dealing with almost journalistic reportage and propaganda, or with more subtle issues, they all base their poetic language on metaphors firmly based in a mythical worldview. Thus the metaphors applied even to the most mundane matters may offer insight into the mythology of the Viking Age. Saxo Grammaticus. Another written source to Old Norse mythology is found in the work of Saxo Grammaticus (1150-1220), a Danish scholar who in 1208 finished his work in Latin, Gesta Danorum, and "The History of the Danes". Like Snorri, Saxo described the Pagan gods as ancestors, particularly devious and immoral ancestors without much honor. Saxo obviously harbored a very hostile attitude to Paganism, and the Aesir were presented as human beings of particularly wicked and demonic persuasion. His book nevertheless provides some interesting additions to and versions of Norse myths.

Sagas. Sagas of kings and Icelandic families often provide invaluable insight into Norse folklore and Pagan practices. The only problem with the saga sources is that those who wrote them down would decide what and how to write things down on the basis of their own medieval (and Christian) conceptions. They were often very cryptic and sometimes directly hostile to the Pagan practices they were describing, especially towards witchcraft and sorcery, which held an important and age-old function in the Pagan era but which was, by the time of writing sagas, condemned as utterly evil.

They would also sometimes refer briefly to practices that they assumed their audience would recognize and understand without further explanation or description, showing that these practices were still known and applied or at least remembered. Our biggest problem today is that we have to figure out for ourselves what they took for granted that people knew. One very important saga for the student of mythology is the Flateyjarbók, which contains several sagas as well as short stories and myths and the Edda poem Hyndlulióð, which is not present in the main Edda manuscript (where several pages had been torn out, however).

Sagas of Old Times. Some sagas, the Fǫrnaldarsǫgur: The Sagas of Old Times, were not about famous families or royal courts, but claimed to be the heroic lore of Viking Age ancestors. They were written down late, no earlier than the 13th century, but they tell of Viking Age men and women who gained some reputation in their lifetimes, and often contain strong elements of myth and folklore. The heroes frequently move into other worlds and encounter supernatural beings. It is often possible to recognize Pagan mythical characters and Pagan activities such as initiation rituals and magic.

Source Criticism. Altogether, the sources provide an insight not into the entirety of Old Norse Paganism, but only into a few of the themes and stories that were remembered by Christian descendants. In the case of the sagas especially, attitudes towards magic and magical performers show clear signs of Christian influence, where Pagan practitioners are demonized. After the Conversion, legal texts show that new laws discriminating and oppressing Pagan practitioners, women, homosexuals and cross-dressers of both genders were quickly introduced. Legislation is a powerful changer of attitudes.

Thus the presentation of trolls, sorcerers, witches and magical arts are usually negative, which is probably a Christian rather than a Pagan attitude since Paganism embraced witchcraft and sorcery and included people who defied the usual gender roles. In my opinion, however, the themes, story lines, structures and symbolic elements of the sources point to a Pagan origin. The structures of initiation rituals that can only have emerged in a Pagan context are very dominant in much of this lore. Other themes are recognizable from comparative mythology that is certainly ancient, such as the Vedas dating back thousands of years. Finally, archaeological finds often provide illustrations of mythological events that we recognize.

1.7: MY METHODS OF INTERPRETATION

Do you know how to carve them?	*Veiztu hve rista scal?*
Do you know how to interpret them?	*veiztu hve raþa scal?*
Do you know how to color them?	*veiztu hve fá scal?*
Do you know how to test them?	*veiztu hve freista scal?*
Do you know how to ask them?	*veiztu hve bidia scal?*
Do you know how to offer them?	*veiztu hve blóta scal?*
Do you know how to send them?	*veiztuhve senda scal?*
Do you know how to stop them?	*veiztu hve soa scal?*

Hávamál 144 [The Speech of the High One], Poetic Edda

COMPARATIVE MYTHOLOGY

Like all mythologies, the Old Norse is the result of many cultural, religious and philosophical influences gathering over long time-spans. The shamanism and animism of the Ice Age ancestors run like powerful undercurrents through the entire Edda lore. The religions of the Neolithic and Megalithic cultures of Stone Age Europe would have provided another powerful current, as would the entry of warlike tribes from the Southeast of Europe towards the end of the Stone Age. There was a possible fusion between these three main groups of old cultures, happening during the Bronze Age, together with the influence of the Sacred Marriage ritual that began in Sumer and the Classical Mystery schools that began, possibly, in Minoan Crete. Shamanic Sami and Siberian cultures would continue to interact with the Norse throughout the entire era. Then there was the influence of Celtic, Roman and Eastern European Iron Age cultures, the entry of Mongolian Huns, and finally we know that the early Viking Age was powerfully influenced by Islam and Arab culture (and fashion) through trade and traveling, as well as by early medieval Christian attitudes. Like a language and a culture, a mythology is also the result of long-term, ever changing and ever-evolving development and the fusion of countless different influences. It is like a time-capsule, capturing a moment of fusion between historical streams, a fusion that is whole and complete in itself. Like a language or a culture, a mythology a complete and self-explanatory system on its own. We do not need to look to outside sources in order to find meaning in the myths as they actually exist within a mythological system. Looking at the various possible influences from other systems of belief may throw light upon the history and the original meanings of particular aspects of the myths, and also provide clues as to meaning when the meanings of a myth or a mythical character seems difficult to decipher.

However, I have found that in Old Norse mythology at least, even the most universal symbol takes a life of its own. The myths were composed and transmitted by professional story-tellers, most of them initiated into the arts of poetry through sacred ritual and sacred learning. The story-tellers had an agenda of their own, and would shape mythology according to their message, playing on the associations that were already there, and emphasizing what they thought would best serve the transmission of their message. Comparative mythology is very interesting and has been an important part of my research.

However, I find that the deciphering of the messages themselves, the messages that the poets attempted to convey through metaphor, is the most interesting and least researched aspect of Old Norse myths. This is why I rarely apply comparative mythology, except when I really believe it may help to deepen our understanding of the underlying messages.

THAT BY WHICH A THING IS KNOWN

I have three main methods that I apply together whenever I approach a prose story or a poem, stanza or a line of Old Norse mythology. **The first method** is to interpret the poetical metaphors. There is absolutely no doubt that the Norse poets used metaphors to disguise characters and phenomenon. They had two main types of metaphors; **The kenningar** ["that by which something or someone is known"], and **heiti** ["nicknames"]. The Icelandic scholar Snorri Sturluson (1179-1241) wrote his entire "Prose Edda" as a thesis on how to create and how to decipher the metaphors of kenningar and heiti, and how to understand the background to many famous metaphors used in the lore that Snorri knew about much of which we also know about.

Without his thesis, we would never have been able to understand the skaldic poetry which was based almost entirely on such metaphors, and the poems of the Poetic Edda would also have been indecipherable to us. Snorri stressed the importance of realizing that there were "subtle meanings" hidden in words, letters and songs. Hardly anything at all is ever said straightforward manner, something is always disguising something else, and one singular subject may be treated in countless ways, just as one singular character may appear in countless disguises.

THE MEANING OF NAMES

The second method I apply is the so-called "philological method" applied to names. It is of utmost importance, if we want to get a true understanding of the myths, to interpret all names, whether they are the names of characters, things or places. These names are always meaningful. For the most part, they are disguising an underlying character or rather an underlying universal quality, and the choice of nickname describes the function of this character or quality in the particular context it appears. To keep safe, I usually refer to interpretations that may be found in Rudolf Simek's Dictionary of Northern Mythology, which is a compilation of various interpretations of names offered by various esteemed linguists.

I choose the interpretation I believe, based on my own research, is the most accurate. Sometimes I choose interpretations found in other secondary sources, some of which may be slightly controversial, such as when I translate the name Menglǫð as "Invitation to (a) Blend" rather than the more common "Necklace Joy" or similar. This interpretation of the name was proposed and explained by the Icelandic author Svava Jacobsdottir in an essay about the sacred mead, and I agree wholeheartedly with her interpretation of the name, which has not been proven wrongful. There are also several instances where I myself have the audacity to make interpretations of my own based on the use of dictionaries.

An example of this is when I translate the name Gullveigr as "Gold Power Drink". This is a literal translation based on the assumption that the name is derived from the word gull ["gold"], and the word *veigr* ["power" or "drink" (or "power drink")]. The reason why this name is not usually interpreted on the basis of such a literal translation is because one famous scholar, Turville-Petre, back in the 1930s decided that the name meant "Greedy for Gold". His interpretation is not based on the actual meaning of any part of the words that make up the name, but is an imaginative paraphrasing based on his interpretation of the myth about Gullveigr and why she is "punished". It seems that no later scholars have dared to or even considered challenging this paraphrasing of the name.

Through my own studies, I found Turville-Petre's interpretation of the name Gullveigr is based on an erroneous interpretation of her myth, and that it makes more sense to stick to the literal translation of her name (as I proposed in my 2004 thesis, and as I will be explaining in parts of this book). Whenever I propose my own translations, I usually give an account of why I interpret the name the way I do. There are some interpretations that may be very uncertain (for example when I propose a new interpretation of the name Embla in Chapter 2.10) but which I have let stand with an explanation because it makes sense within the larger context of how I decipher the mythology at large. The responsibility for any error in this regard is of course my own.

READING MYTH AS A PARABLE

The third method is to approach all myths as parables that must be deciphered through discovering the basic structure or formulas that carries the story. This approach is inspired by two Norwegian authorities on the field. Professor Gro Steinsland, who is head of the Nordic Medieval Studies department at the UIO, interprets myths by revealing and defining "mythological models" in the sources, underlying models that may bring us closer to genuine Pagan beliefs. Eldar Heide, in his 1997 thesis on the Edda poem Fjǫlsvinnsmál, explains that the Norse myths must be read as parables where it is not the details of the story, but the underlying structure behind the details that actually provides the meaning and the ritual-religious background to the Edda poems. I myself applied a similar method in my own thesis, where I looked at the basic themes of a story and how the themes followed a chronological pattern that was identical to countless other seemingly different stories. This was how I discovered the same story of a Pagan initiation ritual behind several different myths.

THE FORMULA IS THE KEY

The realization that a myth is not just a fanciful story, but a parable made up by carrying structures, symbols and metaphors later also brought me to the realization that there are formulas within the myths that are repeatedly applied by the poets in order to convey a message. There are several basic formulas that are applied time and time again, and the variation between them is only due to what heiti or kenning is used to disguise the same elements of the same formulas. Such formulas will be explained throughout this work, but I will mention a few;

> A trinity of masculine entities is a formula that is repeated in endless variety in the myths, yet is always basically the same trinity; a formula that describes the three qualities of human consciousness.

> A trinity of female entities, and more often a group of nine female entities, which also constitute a formula that essentially has to do with the fate of the soul.

> Marriages, lovers, siblings, parents and offspring, even gender, also provide a formula with which to convey a message about how various qualities interact whether it is in the cosmos at large or within an individual person.

The discovery of the formulas made me realize that the characters of a myth really cannot be interpreted as superhuman persons who do weird and supernatural things, but must be interpreted as various qualities that reside within the macrocosm of the world and within the microcosm of human experience.

TRUTH OR FICTION? THE EYES THAT SEE

There are those who recreate the Norse Pagan religion today, adhering to it or rather, to a modern version of it, who may be provoked by the revelation of the formulas and the parables in myths. The idea that the gods and goddesses "merely" represent qualities within men and women or within the world at large (or both), means that the gods and goddesses of the stories are not ultimately "real". They are poetical inventions in a fiction made by human poets, yet this is fiction made by poets who wanted to reveal a profoundly spiritual message of a pan-human, universal character; a message of personal spiritual evolution and enlightenment. Some will find this appealing, while others will feel disturbed.

I want to convey one thing very clearly, one of the most beautiful thing about these myths is that they are composed in a manner that make them accessible to all people almost regardless of their basic beliefs and their level of insight and understanding. They can be read as sacred stories and as entertainment, as literal truth and as fiction. Even when read as fiction they can provide a valuable insight into the minds of the culture that created them, and they can become transmitters of ageless wisdom and to some, of spiritual truth. If one really wants to understand this ancient heritage, one ought to keep an open mind and try to avoid imposing stereotypical notions or personal beliefs upon the original sources, but let these speak for themselves. Even if this forces a more complex way of perceiving the Pagan gods, who are no longer just superhuman or deities but poetical characters used to convey a message, one should remember that the poets who created the myths were most probably devout Pagans.

It is possible to keep two things in one's mind at once. If you like to think of the gods as real super-persons that you can relate to on a personal and literal level, you can still recognize that the myths about them actually employ their personalities and their traditional stories in order to convey a message. It would be a bit like writing a very subjective biography with a secret external agenda about someone famous. If you are more like myself, thinking that the gods may be symbolic personalities, yet symbols that have been used to channel real powers of some kind on both a cosmic and personal level, you can also recognize that the powers and the symbols that describe them can still be used as poetical characters. And if you are of the opinion that the gods and their myths are mere fiction, why then you will still be able to appreciate the beauty and elegance of ancient literature employing the "superstitions" of their age in order to convey messages about the human condition and our quest for knowledge and experience.

DO THE MYTHS REPRESENT COMMON BELIEFS OR THE BELIEFS OF SPIRITUAL ELITES?

Within most ancient and contemporary religions, there have always been two or three levels to the religion. A *"lay religion"* where people can indulge in their attachment to the gods or "God", or "Goddess" as a more powerful being than themselves, to whom they can make ritual offerings and prayers, and relate to as a sort of divine parent, ruler or guide. On the level of the lay religion, most people will be satisfied to follow certain rules and participate in certain rituals, and otherwise just get on with their lives. Then there is usually the *level of professional priesthoods or self-proclaimed spiritual leaders*, who lead the rituals of the lay level, tend to the lay adherents and make an effort to maintain or promote the dogmas and rules of the religion.

The *third level is the level of mystical experience* and meditation on the true meaning of the divine characters. Those who seek this level within their chosen religion or within the religion they were born into will question the dogmatic and stereotyped rules and images of the divine, trying to reach a deeper communion. A very good example of this is the Sufi poet Rumi (1207-1273), a Turkish contemporary of Snorri; He was a Moslem, yet his mystical experiences and revelations completely transcended all Islamic dogmas, his poetry revealing a direct and personal relationship to the divine, which Rumi in his poetry described passionately as a lover, a lover present within all existence.

Today, we have Hinduism as a great example of a contemporary Polytheist religion that has given birth to several spiritual traditions that all seek spiritual illumination or "enlightenment". One of the deepest revelations of such spiritual traditions is that all the gods and goddesses are but aspects of the one great universal soul, and that all individual souls are, similarly, such aspects. This insight could be called Pantheism. In Tantra, the Great Goddess [a unification of all the goddesses] becomes the creative energy of Kundalini which resides as a potential, yet coiled up, sleeping energy in an area situated within the sexual organs of every human body, to be woken and raised through meditation and ascetic or yogic practices in order to unite with the Great God [a unification of all gods] that is universal consciousness, residing in the brain.

This idea thrives excellently side by side with lay people who worship a considerable number of deities, and even the Tantric will accept that there is a certain reality to these deities in their own right, just as there is a certain reality to the human body in its own right, although it is ultimately just one of a billion expressions of the divine whole. In the devotional Hindu cults known as Bhakti, the human soul seeks to unite with the great All-Soul, which is worshiped in the form of a chosen god or goddess, it could be any god or goddess since they are all one, but each cult usually chooses a particular deity to represent the great One.

Ancient myths become parables about this union, such as when the shepherd girls sleep with Krishna and the Krishnaites claim that this is a parable about the loving, intimately personal relationship between God and the human souls. It is impossible to say whether the myth originated as a spiritual parable of divine union or was turned into one by the mystics who paved the way for this layer within their religion. The same could be said about Old Norse myths. We know that most of the gods and goddesses of the myths originated as local or tribal deities, often patron deities of their land or tribe, or as deities protecting particular areas of life. In Norse myths, numerous gods from various historical backgrounds all come together as a colorful pantheon. We know that the importance of the respective deities varied according to location, tribe, clan and time, but that they were all accepted as "real".

But just as in other Polytheist religions, there would be people who were mystically inclined, people who would be seeing something deeper in the myths than just stories about supernatural personalities. They may have created secret societies, special sects, or sub-streams within their religion, spiritual traditions or Mystery cults such as those that existed in ancient Greece and ancient Egypt. Giving new meaning to ancient myths or claiming to know the original true meaning of these myths. The poets of the Edda were initiated into such deeper meanings, and treated the gods and goddesses as fictional characters describing qualities of consciousness, vitality and spirituality that they perceived to reside simultaneously on at least three levels; within men and women, within the society as an organism and within the cosmos at large. This does not mean that these qualities were not real, on the contrary, the qualities are real, eternal and cosmic, they appear to have a certain personality of their own yet they exist within everything at all times, their human shapes and names are but metaphors that describe them as qualities. The meaning of the myth is to describe how they work and how they may be worked with in order to reach a state of wisdom that may, eventually, lead to a state of immortality.

1.8: Gender as a mythical formula And some other observations about mythical formulas as a method to unlock the meaning of the Norse myths

The High One said: "There are twelve Aesir whose nature is divine.
Just-As-High said: "No less holy are the Ásyniur, nor is their power less"

Snorri Sturluson, Gylfaginning, Prose Edda

In the introduction to this book, I explained the methods I have applied when trying to interpret Norse myths. Most of my methods are known and acceptable methods;

➤ The interpretation of the kenningar and the heiti
➤ The philological method of interpreting of names
➤ The interpretation of the parable structure or mythical models

All good methods applied by other scholars work if applied thoroughly. Each scholar will perhaps use these methods in a particular fashion. Since interpretation, no matter what method is applied, will always be colored by the paradigm of understanding the scholar already has, or is trying to develop. A method of interpretation may be said to work well if it results in a wholeness of understanding. That is, if the method is applied to all the myths and all the stanzas, always rendering a result that makes sense in the greater context. A method does not work if it can only be applied to some myths, but does not yield satisfactory results in others. The method has to yield results that always fits into the greater paradigm of understanding. Sometimes, there will be other paradigms of understanding which are also supported by the same methods, and then there ought to be disputes and compromises.

Ideally, the understanding of a research subject will only be enriched by new input and new approaches, knowledge being a gradual patchwork of various contributions. Sadly, many esteemed scholars are so defensive about their established paradigm that they will rather ignore new input than add it to their understanding, as if there was really a case of one paradigm "winning" over the other. This is both a human weakness and the result of centuries of "thought-police" traditions where one way of thinking must violently suppress and exclude another, instead of working together towards ever expanding knowledge. One method applied in my research is a method I developed myself after more than a decade of studying the myths, related to the known use of mythical models, but which I will call the application of "mythical formulas". Such formulas may be represented in Norse myths as the appearance of a masculine trinity, a feminine trinity, or in a group of nine females. Other formulas are represented in couples; a married couple, a couple of lovers, or a couple of siblings. Then there is the formula of parents and offspring, and finally there is the issue of gender, which is also a formula. Rather than spending too much space describing these formulas, I have decided that I would rather let the interpretations unfold themselves throughout this book. Showing in practice how the formula is applied at every turn to reveal another a piece that fits into the greater puzzle.

Here, I will only give a brief introduction, leaving it to the rest of this book to prove my points. One of the first things I believe I understood about Norse myths was that a mythical character always represents something more complex and profound than just a troll, a giant, a dwarf or a deity. The Norse poets knew the art of hiding messages behind characters. That the characters, places and things always covered for something else; a state of being, an inner quality, or a cosmic natural force that exists both in the universe at large and within the human being.

As such, the stories about the many gods are often the stories about the many qualities within a human being; our breath and spirit, our soul and fate, our conscious intelligence, our passion and our fear, our greed and our desire, our various emotions, our attitude and our inner state of being, or the powers within that will work to develop us or to destroy us. This does not mean that the Old Norse people did not believe in their gods. It only means that the Norse myths are the result of a poetic and immensely esoteric and spiritual tradition where poets learned how to reveal the deeper mysteries of existence through the language of myth and through the application of sacred characters for this purpose only.

It also meant that they would use metaphors that were known to the people. A god or goddess would not be blindly applied in mythical poetry, but carefully chosen to reveal a particular message. This message could only be understood by the audience if the poet applied a god or a goddess who in one particular aspect represented something the audience already knew about that divine character in that particular aspect. The choice of nickname to the many-named deities was important, as was the identity of the deity behind the name. The audience would deduce the meaning of the metaphor by reflecting on what function the deity had, and what particular function the deity had when a particular nickname was applied. When the poets used the metaphor of human relations on the gods and giants, the audience would deduce something about the relationships based on their knowledge about such human relations. Thus a marriage would mean a lasting union between two qualities. A couple of lovers would mean a temporary or casual union between two qualities.

A couple or a group of friends or companions would mean the co-existence of two qualities or a greater number of qualities working together. Parents would always mean the causes of a quality. The parental couple, whether married (lasting) or lovers (temporary) would mean the union of qualities that created a result, the offspring. Siblings would mean that there was more than one result of the same union, perhaps more than one aspect to the result. When I began suspecting this, I began analyzing the various relationships, beginning with the famous divine sibling couple, Freyr and Freyia. The names of these old Vanir gods are titles, indicating a male and a female sovereign ("The Lord" and "The Lady"). I noticed that Freyr was associated with masculine sexuality, symbolized by the erect phallus. He was also associated with growth and fertility, rain and sunlight. He was associated with law and kingship, and with animals such as the horse and the boar. His major attribute is a sword. His sister, Freyia, was associated with female sexuality, symbolized by a ring, and childbirth. She was also associated with fate, witchcraft, death and the secrets of the underworld, with the mysterious "precious mead" and with animals such as the wild cat, the swan and the falcon.

While Freyr is a divine ruling king, his sister is a divine witch (vǫlva) and a sacrificial priestess (blótgyðja), roaming the world as a traveling teacher of witchcraft, initiating her female and male disciples into the esoteric secrets of the underworld.

The first thing that struck me as I contemplated these associations was that the masculine aspect of the sibling couple represented the growth of the fields, the fertility of cultivated nature, the law and order of the human world, and rulership. In short, his domain is the known and human sphere of existence. The feminine aspect of the sibling couple represents the wilderness, the unknown world, the other side, the spiritual quest, the mysterious aspects of existence, and fate, the secret powers that rule behind appearances. Suspecting that these two obviously "different but complimentary" masculine and feminine powers were examples of a repetitive formula, I began studying gender in myth and in Norse society more carefully.

VIKING AGE GENDER ROLES

"8. It stands on record that armies wavering on the point of collapse have been restored by the women. They have pleaded heroically with their men, thrusting their bosoms before them and forcing them to realize the imminent prospect of their enslavement—a fate which they fear more desperately for their women than for themselves. It is even found that you can secure a surer hold on a state if you demand among the hostages girls of noble family. More than this, they believe that there resides in women an element of holiness and prophecy, and so they do not scorn to ask their advice or lightly disregard their replies. In the reign of the deified Vespasian we saw Veleda [an oracular priestess] long honored by many Germans as a divinity, whilst even earlier they showed a similar reverence for Aurinia and others..."

Tacitus; Germania (98AD)

After many painstaking attempts, I realized that in order to truly grasp the meaning of the Norse myths, we have to leave aside all judgments and attitudes about what we think gender ought to mean and what we think it has meant before, and try to focus on the understanding that gender in Old Norse mythology actually symbolized some deeper spiritual message. In order to understand the message, we have to try to understand the metaphor that carries the message. A metaphor will only work if it builds on the associations and attitudes of its audience, and the audience would be the Viking Age clan society. Although gender is a metaphor for something else, the Old Norse gender metaphor would reflect Old Norse attitudes and associations towards gender. Thus we moderns can only understand the Old Norse gender metaphors if we attempt to understand Viking Age attitudes towards gender, an attitude which was neither modern nor "old-fashioned". The modern attitudes of Western society today are a blend of old die-hard gender role attitudes countered and sometimes even balanced by various branches of feminism and a general modern Western individualism. The idea that the sexes ought to be equal in all respects, the attitude that gender is but a social construction and that there is no real difference between the genders, or that an individual has a right to put him/herself before the needs of the community was non-existent in the Viking Age.

To them, the difference between the sexes was obvious and taken for granted, and individual pursuits had to compromise with the agenda or one's clan. By the time of the Viking Age, a patriarchal organization was dominant in the sense that men were the primary heads of the households in a legal sense, and children were named after the father (also if born outside of wedlock), and property passed primarily through the patrilineal. A woman moved to live with her husband's clan at marriage. There were clear gender roles, although there seems to have been some sacred or magical space reserved for "particular" people who transcended gender roles. The Viking Age was severely influenced by wars, battles and warrior ideologies, and men were usually the warriors.

This society was more of a clan society than a class society, and although there were noble clans that dominated due to wealth and tradition, even the poorest and lowest status peasant male would be a warrior if he was physically able. The ideal that a free man should always be a warrior had a tremendous impact on the psyches and the appearance of Viking Age society. Women could learn the martial arts and even be involved in battle if they were so inclined, but no woman was expected to do so or to carry arms. In a society where all people had to be able to participate in all kinds of productivity as a matter of survival, I suspect that it was this difference between the warrior male and the unarmed female that constituted the most considerable difference in the lives and roles of men and women.

Despite this severe gender role difference, and contrary to us moderns, the Viking Age Pagan did not carry a thousand year old history of obsessive misogyny, fear of sexuality and hostile underestimation of women and all things feminine which we moderns must still struggle to liberate ourselves from. The culmination of a millennium of development into the housewife ideal of the 1950s (which is, irrationally enough, thought to be "traditional" despite the fact that women have worked outside the home and provided for their families since before the Middle Ages) would have been totally unknown to the Vikings. The Church is not the first institution that systematized misogyny, but it did a very thorough job of enforcing it throughout the centuries.

After the Scandinavian conversions, which happened during the first decades of the 11th century AD, the Church introduced a series of laws which limited the rights of women and of people who did not fit into the male or female stereotypes. For the first time in Scandinavian history, women were given considerably less legal rights and value than men, and gay couples living together as an alternative to heterosexual marriage, was outlawed. No such laws existed before that, and Viking Age attitudes towards gender, even towards transgender behavior and homosexuality, were very fluid and different from those that followed the conversion. We are often presented with a very macho version of Viking Age society, and it is of course easy to be swayed by the intense warrior ideology that was obviously a crucial part of this Iron Age to Medieval culture.

It is easy to assume that women were just as invisible in that warrior culture as they were in warrior cultures dominated by one of the three monotheistic religions, with their exceedingly condescending and even hateful attitudes towards women. But to the Pagan, women were no less holy and important than men, just as goddesses were no less holy and powerful than gods.

*Detail from the Gosforth
Cross, 9th century.
A woman offers a drinking
horn to a man with a wand.*

They were different, but they were not lesser. When I first read the heroic poetry of the Edda, I was surprised at the central space taken up by women. Whenever I had earlier been presented with contemporary summarized versions of these heroic legends, such as the legend of Sígurðr the dragon-slayer, the focus was always on the actions of the men. The same is the case in medieval versions such as the Vǫlsunga saga and the Niebelungenlied.

However, in the oldest source to this story that we have access to, the Edda poetry, the central focus is actually on the emotional states of the female heroines. It would seem that the women's feelings and reactions to what was happening to them and to their beloved men and brothers was a favorite theme for the Viking Age Edda poets.

As to the myths, we are equally conditioned to not actually see the feminine entities and their fundamental importance, and when you read the next Chapter on cosmology, you may be surprised at the overwhelming evidence of a Norse cosmos where female entities are at least as important and powerful as the male ones. It is not a matter of what gender dominates, it is the complimentary balance between the feminine and masculine energies that best describes Norse cosmology, two universal and complimentary qualities that consistently interact and work together at every turn. To the Viking Age Pagan, there was no gender wars.

Both genders depended upon each other and worked together, brothers and sisters were equally important members of their clan unit and both genders remained a part of the clan into which they had been born even when marrying outside of it. We also see considerable evidence that brothers and other male relatives felt responsible for protecting their clan-sister against any abuse given by her in-laws or husband. A woman remained a member of the clan she was born into and could call upon her clan-members for support if needed. The clan she married into would remember that she was a representative of her clan, and treat her accordingly.

The Vikings and their Iron Age predecessors may have had gender roles that appear traditional, but after centuries of degrading all feminine experience we tend to automatically overlook the historical contribution to society that women provided and which was recognized by the non-misogynist Pagans. There were two leaders of a clan, two heads of the household, and the wife sat together with her husband in the High Seat. Where the male may have been a warrior, a craftsman, a sailor, a hunter, a fisherman and a builder, the woman was a housekeeper, not in the sense of being the little woman awaiting home with dinner at five, but in the sense of being a farmer.

The good woman would know every aspect of running a farm and how to produce the wealth of the clan from the land they owned. If she came to the position of "house-lady" [húsfrú], her reign, responsibility and authority would be similar to that of anyone who today leads and organizes a large work-force in some complex corporation. There is no coincidence that women were often referred to as the providers of this or that in Norse poetry, the women were seen as the providers, not the ones who were provided for. A man could return from a journey with precious gifts and other contributions, but it was the housewife who organized the daily business of gathering and processing provisions and products, deciding how the produce should be spent and shared.

She carried the keys to all buildings on the farm as a symbol of this authority. Men were often away, whether on trade or raiding or other pursuits. They may generally have had more adventurous lives than women, but they were also more dangerous lives; men often died young, women lived on. In no way did this lifestyle render women powerless, quite on the contrary; the women were the backbone of the clan's land, its heart and its center, and they knew their own worth and kept their own mysteries and rituals. Women often led rituals and performed magical duties. Women could be priestesses and chose spiritual careers before the domestic one if they so wished. No professional spiritual practitioner was more respected than the *vǫlur* [the oracular witches] who embodied the goddesses of fate on this earth.

Apart from being the provider of all basic needs, the average Viking Age woman would be a professional herbalist, surgeon and healer, a producer of textiles and clothing and dyes, a fashion designer, a professional brewer of alcoholic drinks, and a trader. Women's dominant role in the economy was fundamental to the heroic pursuits of their men, and their role as doctors and nurses to the sick and the wounded was a lifetime education, demanding the respect and appreciation of those they frequently had to heal. References to females who dress the wounds of males are numerous in the Norse sources and are a theme first mentioned by the Roman Tacitus in his Germania;

> *"The men take their wounds to their mothers and wives, and the latter are not afraid of counting and examining the blows, and bring food and encouragement to the fighting men."*

What about war and battle? Was it solely the domain of men, or did women ever partake in these? Mythical images of armed women abound. Saxo claimed that there were women back in the Pagan days who refused the soft lives of women and the loving embrace of men, choosing to live as warriors in all-female warrior communities. We have no way of knowing if this was actually true, and we may wonder how such women would have fared in a harsh Iron Age world unless they held some sacred function. Perhaps the concept of the shield maiden as a servant of Óðinn may be based on a priestess-community where women dedicated their lives to the war-god, looked like warriors and actually performed some ritual duties in connection to war, battle and sacrifice. Some classical sources refer to females, "angels of death", who performed human sacrifice after battle.

From the Viking Age, we do see a considerable difference in the grave finds, where men are often buried with an array of weapons that they probably also knew well how to wield, whereas only a third of women are buried with weapons. When women were buried with weapons, it was usually just one weapon, and it was usually a bow and arrows. We can only make some educated guesses about what this could signify. The guess that women hunted with bow and arrow is quite probable, and that these bow-women in question may have attended battles on a distance, as shooters. But when it comes to those women who were actually buried with a spear or a sword, we may wonder. It is my guess that most of the women who were armed in death learned to use their weapon in life. This is easily observed in modern athletics. We also know that women can be equally skilled in combat, however even with the similarity in skills, strength of the other warrior (regardless of gender) may create a serious matter of life and death.

The few sources that relate to this matter render little doubt that this general difference in strength was taken seriously and led to ideals of chivalry where it was a great shame for a man to fight or harm a woman or anyone else who could be considered blautr ["soft"] even if she attacked him with weapons. Adding to that, the few sources we have on the issue render little doubt that girls' physical training could not compare with the intense and diverse training into various kinds of weapons that a boy received. Women could learn martial arts if they so wished, but they were not expected to be warriors and there was no shame for a female who could not or dared not fight. For a man, there would be no greater shame, and only men could be called cowards. In the sources, we see traces of attitudes that can only be described as chivalry, where causing physical harm to a woman would dishonor a warrior for life. Despite the stereotypical formula of "raping and pillaging" that many Viking raiders certainly engaged in, the attitude of the Edda poem Vǫluspá is clear; rapists and woman abductors would end up wading forever in the harsh streams of Hel after death, together with oath-breakers and kin-murderers.

Even when a saga woman takes up the sword and fights, the warriors whom she fights always seem to avoid harming her back. In the Poetic Edda, brave Guðrún fights alongside her brothers and kills three men, yet is not harmed, just disarmed. In the warrior ideology of these people, the honorable man must only take on foes that can be expected to fight back on an equal standing, and in this world where boys learned to fight from the time they could walk, women were simply not to be counted as equal in this respect. It would seem that women's particular role in war was honored by friends and foes alike. If there had been a great danger to the women, they would not have been brought to watch the battles of their menfolk like the audience to a football game.

Yet there are indications that women were often present on the battlefields as spectators, watching, shouting words of encouragement, and ready to receive the fallen and the wounded. The image of the Valkyrie picking up the souls of the dead, choosing who shall die and who shall live, may very well have been inspired by the women who watched the battle and who afterwards walked across the battlefield looking for men they could restore to health, and to give the dead their final honors. Heroic sagas show that a man's heroic pursuit was nothing without female appraisal; just as Tacitus observed even back in the first century AD;

> "....Not chance or the accident of mustering makes the troop or wedge, but family and friendship, and this is a very powerful incitement to valor. A man's dearest possessions are at hand; he can hear close to him the laments of his women and the wailing of his children. These are the witnesses that a man reverences most; to them he looks for his highest praise.

As to sex and sexuality, rules and norms may have varied over time and differed from tribe to tribe, but generally there was a healthy and natural approach to sex as something both genders were allowed to enjoy. No importance was ever placed on virginity, and a "maiden" simply referred to a young unmarried woman. If a woman claimed that her son born out of wedlock was fathered by a king, the boy could demand a prince's status, and would be allowed to go through the trials that could show the parliament (who would elect kings) that he was worthy of kingship. According to the Spanish ambassador Al-Ghazal, who visited Denmark in the year 844 AD, Danish women could be with whomever they wished without fearing punishment or shame, as long as the male partner was not far beneath her in social status. The Arab envoys were surprised at how readily Danish women communicated with male strangers, and feared that their talking to the native women would lead to misunderstandings and thus violent retribution from their men.

When confronted with the anxiety of the visitor, who was worried about the rumors his friendship with the Danish queen could cause, she herself explained;

> "She laughed and told him, "We have no such thing in our religion and we have no jealousy. Our women stay with our husbands according to their choice. The woman stays with him as long as she wishes, and parts from him if she no longer desires him."

Burial chamber urn lid, Bronze Age Denmark, Gentofte

This statement should probably be treated with a bit of criticism, since Al-Ghazal came from a medieval Moslem culture and may have exaggerated the sexual freedom of Danish women, among other things, Al-Ghazal concluded that Danish women would not deny themselves to any man, obviously a very subjective interpretation of what it means to be able to choose one's sexual partners. But there is little doubt that relative to the medieval Moslem and Christian experience, Scandinavian Pagans were extremely liberal. What we are presented with in all the sources is a society that by no means was easy or perfect to live in, but nevertheless where the interaction and the relationships between the sexes is continuously balanced in every aspect of life, from the most harsh realities to the most joyful. This balance was considered sacred.

When the gods hold their sacred parliaments, where important legal decisions are made, they do so right in the sacred heart of the realm of the Norns [the goddesses of fate]. We learn that nothing is in fact decided without the actual decision of these goddesses, who rule the laws of the universe. I believe this mythical image is reflected in one of the major seats of political decisions in Sweden during the Viking Age, Uppsala. There, the parliament is called the *dísaþing* [The Parliament of the Goddesses] and this curiously named parliament of kings and noble men was accompanied by the dísablót [The Sacrifice to the Goddesses]. In order to sanctify the parliament, rituals were performed in honor of the Dísarsalinn, The Temple of the Goddess.

THE GENDER METAPHOR

> *Often are women subdued by the dominance of men*
> *But the trunk (male) collapses when his branches (female) are shorn*
> *The tree (male, female) topples if its roots (male) are cut from beneath...*
>> *Costom drepr qvenna*
>> *carla ofriki,*
>> *i kne gengr hnefi*
>> *ef qvistir þverra;*
>> *tre tecr at hniga,*
>> *ef heyggr tág vndan..."*

> *Atlamál hin Grænlenzku st.73, Poetic Edda*

When studying the Old Norse texts, we have to always bear in mind that they were written down well after the Conversion and by professed Christians. Even so, we may detect that the most basic attitude towards gender was one of mutual respect and appreciation. The texts were written down by men, and most of the oral transmissions that they were based on were transmitted by male poets, thus we notice that women and feminine entities are regarded as "The Other Sex". However, the attitude towards the feminine "Other" is basically and generally one of respect, high regard, admiration, and appreciation as the feminine is either a mysterious and scary quality that must be respected and treated with care, or else a beloved, attractive, much sought and needed quality that provides nourishment, pleasure and a sense of belonging.

Whether the feminine "Other" is of the scary underworld kind or the pleasant home kind, she is associated with wisdom and with the powers of fate. Snorri offered some interesting keys to gender associations in his Skáldskaparmál when he explains various metaphors that may be used to describe men and women. The metaphors would give associations to particularly masculine or feminine qualities in the Viking Age audience:

"How shall a man be referred to? He shall be referred to by his actions, what he gives or receives or does. He can also be referred to by his properties, what he owns and also if he gives it away; also by the family lines he is descended from, also those that have descended from him. How shall he be referred to by these things? By calling him achiever or performer of his expeditions of activities, of killings or voyages or huntings...and because he is a trier of the weapons and a doer of the killings, which is the same as achiever... all masculine tree-names... It is also normal to refer to a man using all the names of the Aesir.

A woman shall be referred to by all female adornment, gold and jewels, ale or wine or other drink that she serves or gives, also by ale-vessels and by all those things that it is proper for her to do or provide...woman is now referred to in terms of stone and all words for stone.

Woman is also referred to in terms of all Ásyniur, Norns and Valkyrie or Dísir. It is also normal to refer to a woman by any of her activities or by her possessions or descent. Woman is referred to in terms of gold, called dealer of gold... A woman is a dealer of the gold that she gives, and "dealer "[selia] is also the name of a tree [selia = willow], and as was noted above, woman is referred to by all kinds of feminine tree-names. She is also said to be the "consumer" [lóg] of what she gives, and lóg is also a word for a tree felled in a wood...woman is called "forest".... "rod"... "prop"... "pillar"... "birch"... "oak"... "linden"... Man is referred to as trees... "tree" and "beam"... "grove"... "fir"... "ash"... "maple"... "spruce"... "stave"... "thorn"...."

We need to apply a very open-minded attitude when we try to figure out the basic Viking Age concepts about the sexes, and the concepts that hide behind this text. Firstly, we see the reflection of a society where men were usually warriors, hunters, craftsmen and sailors, and could be the fathers of lineages. Women are less associated with action, even less with voyage, but clearly with provisions, trade and economy. We see the contours of a society where women ruled the household and thereby the entire economy symbolized by the keys to all the houses of the farm that the lady of the house would wear in her belt as a sign of her authority. While the men were out on more or less serious adventures, exploring the world and its oceans, battling their enemies and hunting game. How could this system be applied in poetry?

By thinking, first of all, of the male as the journeyman, the traveler, the one who is out on a quest, while the female is the companion who awaits his return at home, or else the unknown bride awaiting on another shore, representing the true home and destination of the journeyman on both the practical and the spiritual level. Then we can ask what the journeyman encounters out on his quests. Other people, of course. For the most part, other Scandinavian people or people with a similar societal structure as that he knew from home. He would, ideally, first encounter the males of the people he visits. The males would appear as the guards, the protectors, the obstacles that the visitor must pass before reaching the inner core, where the female rules. Perhaps this is his true home, but he has been away for so long that he is not immediately recognized.

The male guardians will be testing the visitor, checking out his true identity and purpose, deciding whether he is worthy of reaching the inner core. Once there, the female will represent the welcoming, providing energy that offers hospitality and nutrition. Women were also the doctors, the pharmacists who knew the medicinal properties of plants and who were taught from girlhood how to treat wounds and mend broken bones. After a battle, women would walk the battlefield in search of men who needed aid. Women would treat the wounded and sit with the dying, and carry out the rituals that guided the dead on their way to the other side, like midwives for the soul. As I reflected upon this, I realized that this physical and cultural reality is used to also describe the spiritual journey of any man or woman.

It does not matter whether the seeker is actually male or female. The masculine forces represent the seeking, voyaging, learning spirit that seeks a long lost, perhaps even almost forgotten home. The feminine forces represent the long lost home; the place of the soul and of renewal, where wholeness in union as well as the nourishment that provides new life is freely given, and where healing and mending is offered and a loving guidance through the underworld. Like the gender roles themselves, it is of course far more complex than that, and it includes the ages of the people, especially where females are concerned. A young woman symbolized something else other than an old woman. Let us say that the young feminine is always that bright, secret treasure which is guarded, protected and hidden from the outsider. She is the unseen and unknown element within. She is the subtle power, the one that cannot so readily be grasped, and the secret element that hides behind or even within the outer surface, represented by the male.

The older woman, sometimes a younger woman, but then she is always the fierce warrior type, is also hidden and secret, but not as protected; she represents secret knowledge and wisdom more than anything else. Often the dangerous, secret call of the wild, the spirit of the wilderness and the hush of the dark, cold rock caves. It is significant that a wall is considered masculine, while a gate is considered feminine; the gate opens and lets things through both ways, and must thus be guarded against intruders. The wall [the masculine] is massive and keeps things separate. As a guardian and a warrior, the masculine also represents the protecting and confrontational energy. The gate and the wall, the guardian and the protected treasure within, are metaphors revealing how Viking Age people perceived the basic qualities of the two genders, and was also applied as metaphors to disguise spiritual issues. Likewise, in a tree, a typical metaphor for a human being, the trunk is considered masculine, while the roots and the branches are considered feminine.

If you contemplate this image, you will realize that the feminine is associated with a free-flowing energy that will move in all directions on its search for nourishment, whether it is in the dark depths of the earth or in the bright high sky. Nourished by its roots and branches, the masculine trunk represents the holding power, the energy that gathers and maintains all this flowing energy into one solid, massive object, the physical channeling and a compact holding together of energy that begins as a fluid flow in the underworld (roots) and ends in a fluid flow in the heavens (branches). The tree is also a metaphor for the human body and for the universe itself. In the stanza quoted in the beginning of this section, the importance of power balance between these two energies is pointed out; the trunk collapses and topples without its branches and roots.

A similar concept is found in the metaphors given by Snorri where a woman may be symbolized by a forest and a man may be symbolized by a grove. The feminine forest is the free growing, wild and uncultivated energy, also a symbol of the underworld, the unknown power, the feminine source of the masculine grove, and also its animating power. The masculine grove is the enclosed and cultivated space, the known and the seen power, within which the unknown powers may be invoked and channeled and take a knowable form. When we understand that these associations represent basic attitudes and concepts about the feminine and the masculine qualities of cosmos, of society and within the human being regardless of its biological sex, we will better understand Norse mythology. Based on this realization, I discovered that it always makes sense to regard the male characters as representative of the known, the seen, the physical and the solid. It can also exist on the non-physical level, but it will always be that which is the most known to us, or at least knowable, the outer surface, the solidity and the massive holding together of a particular reality.

The male character will also represent, as mentioned above, the part of us that seeks learning and adventure "abroad", and another, older male character will often represent either a guide and teacher, or an obstacle and tester, often both. The female character will always represent the unknown, the unseen, the ethereal and the fluid. She represents either that which is sought, that which is hidden away, or the element within, that which is guarded and protected, the inner being or the soul. In this role, she will appear as a young bright maiden. As an older woman, she will represent the ultimate teacher, the secret knowledge within, the memory and wisdom that has been hidden away and which must be uncovered and enticed to reveal itself.

This key provides a better understanding of the meaning of relationships: A couple will represent the lasting or temporary union between a male seen, shaping and holding quality and a female hidden, animating and extending quality. A father will represent a known or knowable cause, a physical cause or a channeling cause. A mother will represent an unknown or unknowable cause, an unseen and secret cause, or a cause that is within/behind the father, being the animating, moving energy that is channeled. A daughter will, likewise, represent the unknown and unseen, hidden result, whereas a son will represent the known and seen result. Siblings will represent these two aspects; the known and the unknown, the shaper and the mover of a singular result.

1.9: THAT WHICH IS DISGUISED IN RUNES

In ever learned poetry by the water source. I never sang galðr and I never sat beneath hanged man.-The declaration of bishop Bjarni Kolbeinsson of the Orkney Islands at the beginning of the 13th century. What the bishop never did were Pagan rituals surrounding the sacred art of poetry.-

In this section, I have added three edited transcripts from my YouTube video lecture series *Hidden Knowledge* in Old Norse Myths, about my approaches when deciphering the myths. These lectures were adapted to a listening audience and thus take a more casual, oral form.

READING MYTH AS PARABLE
TRANSCRIPT FROM VIDEO 3: MYTH AND PARABLE

If you have seen any of my (two) previous lectures, you know that I stress the fact that Old Norse myths were told in a way that was poetical and metaphorical in style and that the myths should be read as allegories and metaphors and as parables. I am going to be a bit comparative; I am going to go all the way to India, to begin with, to see how the way Indian myths are supposed to be read. This may provide some insight into how Old Norse myths ought to be read. The connection between the two mythological systems is not so far-fetched actually and it has something to do with the term "Indo-European". There is an ancient connection between Old Norse myths and Old Indian myths. I am going to begin with the Indian epic legend known as the Maha Bharata.

The title means "The Great Story" and it certainly is a great story. There are six main characters in the epic, and they are Draupadi, a princess, and her five husbands. Now that is interesting in itself [a woman having five husbands] to a sociologist or an anthropologist or even a historian. Polyandry is not so common in the world today, but it does exist in some Indian cultures and it exists historically. That is probably why the metaphor works, because it relates to a phenomenon people in those days knew about but it is a metaphor, and that is the big point here.

Any learned Indian person, Brahmin, yogi, or just an educated person who knows about the Sanskrit texts knows that Draupadi, the princess, is not just a woman with five husbands, but that she is a metaphor for the human mind, and that her husbands represent the five senses. The whole story is about how these six aspects of human experience relate to each other, to the surrounding world and to God. It is perfectly possible to read the Maha Bharata just as a story, and it is a great story on its own, just as it is perfectly possible to read the Old Norse myths as stories without looking for metaphors or clues or hidden messages. When you know that the intention was to tell a hidden story about these aspects of human consciousness, the whole epic, the Maha Bharata, becomes a different story. It becomes philosophy, and it becomes a spiritual manifest. Then the whole experience of reading the story is transformed. This is also the point with Old Norse myths.

I am going to make another example, and I am going to go into Indian myths: I am going to talk about Krishna [a Hindu god identified with Rama]. To Krishna [Bhakti] devotees, he is, sort of, "God". We tend to think of the Indian religion, Hinduism, as polytheist, in the sense that they believed in lots and lots of different goddesses and gods, but the fact is that lots of Indians are not actually polytheist but rather Pantheist. Pantheism means that you perceive the multiple goddesses and gods as sort of real but essentially as aspects of a Supreme Being, the one, unifying entity at the source of everything. Krishna devotees believe that Krishna is that one, Supreme Being behind all the other goddesses and gods.

There is a myth about Krishna who plays the flute, and all these shepherd girls, the gopis, come flocking in order to listen to his music, now this is God playing, you know, so they listen to the divine music and they all fall violently in love. So how does Krishna, "God", react when all these girls fall in love with him? There are hundreds of them! Well, he splits up into several hundred images of himself and in this way he manages to make love to all the shepherd girls at the same time, and everybody are happy. Now that sounds a bit, odd, but every Krishna devotee and 'learned' Indian person knows that you are not supposed to read this story literally. This is not about how a guy named Krishna makes love to lots of girls. This is about how God is capable of giving his full attention and having a personal and deep relationship to every human being at the same time. The shepherd girls, the gopis, are not in fact "shepherd girls", they are metaphors for the human individual souls, whether male or female, and the story is about the union between the individual souls and the divine One.

The message is that every individual can have a strong, personal relationship with God. Now I am going to go a little bit closer to home but further back in time. The Greek-Roman empires created a widespread Hellenistic and later Roman culture which flourished from the time of Alexander the Great (356-323 B.C.E) and until the Goths sacked Rome towards the end of the fourth century after Christ. We are speaking of almost 800 years where the whole Mediterranean region and somewhat beyond was a big cultural melting pot, knowing lots and lots of different goddesses and gods. In this culture, there were several strong undercurrents of religiosity that was Pantheist and, just like in contemporary India, believed that behind all the goddesses and gods was a great Supreme Being. Pantheism was very much more common in this age than we tend to think. At the core of Pantheism were the Mystery cults.

The Mystery cults were certain sects, you could say, but actually more like religions, big religions [some of which were] gathering people who believed that the great Supreme Being was a sort of All-Soul. They believed that all human individual souls as well as the souls of goddesses and gods were all derived from the same source, that they were aspects of the unifying original All-Soul. They believed that the big meaning of life was to reunite with that source. These people read age-old myths in a way that was different from what most people (at least today) would. An example is the myth about Isis and Osiris, an old Egyptian myth which was imported into and adapted to the Greek-Roman empires, becoming very popular.

The main myth is about how the god Osiris dies and is scattered into tiny little pieces. His sister and wife, the goddess Isis, collects all the little pieces of Osiris and restores him to life. Every initiate into the Mystery cult of Isis knew that this was a parable, a parable where Osiris represents the individual human soul, regardless of gender, and Isis represents the All-Soul, who through her mercy and great love for humankind actually saves the souls [Apuleius described her as the Savior Goddess]. To the initiate of the Mysteries of Isis, the myth is a parable of the quest for salvation. I want to point out that the way that Indians and Classical Mystery initiates read the myths as parables is in fact the clue to how to read Old Norse myths; as parables, mainly as parables for the human soul's journey back to the divine All-Soul.

SKALDSKÁP, THE ART OF POETRY

TRANSCRIPT FROM VIDEO 4: SKALDSKÁP, THE ART OF POETRY

Those of you who have been watching my other videos know that I keep saying how Old Norse myths should be read as metaphorical allegories and parables. I have given a few examples on how the translations of names provide new insight into the metaphysical worldview of the Viking Age Pagan, and I have given some comparable examples to explain how a mythical parable may work. I still have not really gotten to the subject however, namely exactly how I claim that Old Norse myths should be understood.

If you have watched my "Old Norse myths of initiation" videos (the videos on Norse myths made with images, text and music) you may have a clue as to how I understand these myths, and you might as well, because like a vulture I keep circling my prey. Why go there directly when you can have your fun first. There are so many interesting subjects on the way. I am going to explain why I keep saying that Old Norse myths are metaphorical with such authority. You see, I do not say that just because I think so. I say that because it is obvious to anyone who has ever studied Old Norse poetry.

It has to do with the Old Norse rules of poetry, with the terms heiti and kenning, Old Norse terms that refer to metaphors. In 1225 AD the Icelandic scholar Snorri Sturluson wrote a whole book about the subject, parts of which has become known as the famous Prose Edda. I will provide more information about these terms and Snorri's work in the description, because now I want to go straight to today's subject, namely exactly how a typical Old Norse metaphor would work. For dramatic effect, let us imagine a credible, and I must say, an alarmingly commonplace Viking Age scenario: The aftermaths of a battle!

WE ARE BACK IN TIME, SAY, 1200 YEARS BACK. A Norwegian fjord, perhaps, just before the age of piracy, which is what the Viking Age actually means. [Víkingr was a Norse word referring to those who were "of the inlets" (from *vík* "inlet". The suffix "*ingr*" was (and still is, in Scandinavian languages) a way of attaching someone to a place such as the vík (in modern Norwegian, I could for example call myself a Nesodd-ing since I live in a place called Nesodden). That referred to pirates who would hide their ships in inlets while planning attacks. The Scandinavians of the time did not regard themselves as "Vikings" since that referred exclusively to those who were pirates]. Norway was not one country yet but a cluster of countless little kingdoms and chiefdoms. So we have a victorious tribe. Let's say they call their leader by the title of king.

The *king* wants to celebrate his victory and honor the dead, they are in fact going to hold a funeral feast! In Norway we still call that kind of feast gravøl, which means "grave-beer", which again basically means that up until quite recently my ancestors celebrated the departed by getting dead drunk. (Today we tend to drink coffee instead). Now despite the fact that the plan was for everybody to get absolutely plastered, the burial feast was still a sacred occasion, and the king turned to his most respected bard, the royal scald, and asked him to compose a suitable poem that was to be performed in the feast hall a bit before everybody had drunk too much. The *scald*, well aware of the sacredness of his profession, would go somewhere suitable, like a burial mound on which he would sit, or perhaps he would sit beneath the corpse of a hanged enemy, sacrificed to Óðinn, or maybe he would just sit at the battlefield where all these people died recently, this practice was called the **utiseta** which means to "sit out" and basically meant that anyone seeking inspiration or knowledge from the spirits or visions from the gods would go to a so called crossroads, where the borders between the spheres or between life and death were blurred.

The poet knew that his poem would have to graphically describe the battle, to honor those warriors who died courageously, whether enemy or friend, to ridicule those enemy warriors who might have behaved cowardly, and to praise the king and assure everybody how much the king was favored by the gods. The poet had probably himself partaken in the battle, as every free and able-bodied man was (supposedly) a warrior in those days, whether he normally worked as a farmer or as a bard or as a craftsman. Now he sits outside, on his chosen spot and is trying to mentally compose a poem. There is no pen, no paper, only his mind at work, the poem will be spoken and listened to, not read. The poet remembers, he remembers back to before the battle, standing next to his king, watching the first enemy ship slowly approaching into the fiord. Ah! "Ship".

There is the start. An enemy warship. A magnificent sight, both terrifying and glorious to his "barbarian" mind. How shall the poet make an appropriate metaphor for "ship"? There are rules of poetry, rules that demand that the poet may not just use the word "ship", plain and simple. He has to rewrite the whole concept of ship, or he is no poet. OK, so a ship is something you ride when you are at sea, and may thus be likened to a horse. So *the first layer* of the metaphor may be: "horse of the ocean". Established. This was a **common metaphor** for ship even in daily speech. In those days, even daily speech was strongly metaphorical.

But this is sacred poetry and the poet is not satisfied with an everyday figure of speech. "Horse" can be replaced by "steed", and "ocean" by "waves", so the *second layer* of the metaphor is "steed of the waves". It is **still too common** for our poet. What else than horse or ship may be a steed? Well, in his time, nothing...unless you looked to the steeds of the gods! The *third layer* of the metaphor takes us into the **mythical realm**. What about a "boar"? The god Freyr rides a boar, but that is not a suitable metaphor, because it is too positive.

The *boar is a metaphor* in itself, a symbol, that is, of fertility and abundance, and thus the allusion will be wrong. We are not talking about our ship, we are talking about their ship, and their ship is deadly and dangerous, and our poet wants to stress that fact. So what else? Oh yes! A wolf! A wolf is the steed of Hel, the goddess of death! Alright! That will give the proper feeling of dread and hostility and certain death that the poet wants to transmit. The poet settles for "wolf" [the third layer of the metaphor, from horse to steed to wolf]. Then he turns to the other part of the metaphor, waves. The word "wave" has to be taken into the third layer of the metaphor, to be taken into the same mythical realm. Now that is easy, because in the mythical realm, waves are identified as the nine daughters of the sea god Aegir and the sea goddess Rán. Let us say you choose the father, Aegir.

Then you have to move into the fourth layer of the metaphor, because you can't just go using the real and obvious name. You have got to make a little riddle about it. That is the rule. So, you look for things that are typical of Aegir and voila! He lives on an island. So instead of saying the nine daughters of Aegir, you say, the nine daughters of the Island Dweller! For example, there could be endless variations here. Maybe this metaphor does not work when our poet continues composing his poem. The metaphor has to fit into the context not only as far as meaning goes, but also with rhythm, rhyme and intonation.

So our poet keeps another alternative up his sleeve, rather than focusing on the nine daughters, he focuses on the fact that the same nine daughters are also considered the nine mothers of the god Heimdallr, whose name means the "Great World"! [From heimr = world, and dallr = great, awesome, dazzling, glorious] The nine waves are in fact the mothers of our present universe! So our poet may also describe our enemy ship as "the wolf of the nine mothers of Heimdallr". Although, to use the name Heimdallr is not enough. To make a riddle you will also know Heimdallr by something else, like his nickname "the White God" or by something that describes him, such as the "Horn Blower" (he is famous for blowing a horn). As a consequence, the word "ship" may become "the wolf of the horn-blower's nine mothers".

But why stop there! The rules of poetry allow our poet to skip the nine women and their relations, it is enough to use just the name of one of these wave-women, and our poet will pick the name that best describes the ship and its fate. Remember, this is after the battle. Our poet knows what happened to the ship. Let us say it was wrecked and the people on board drowned. Then to indicate its fate even before he has described it, our poet chooses the name Greipr, which means "the Grasping one" and indicate the kind of wave that grasps you and pulls you down below to certain death. Suddenly the poet sits with a metaphor that perfectly describes the ship in many different ways: it is a wolf, which indicates its deadliness and hostile intentions. It belongs to the wave that will drown it in the future.

This wave is also a giantess, and everybody knows that giantesses ride wolves, because all giantesses are really identical to Hel, the goddess of the underworld and the metaphor will now strengthen the impression of a dangerous and ill-fated ship, already wed to death. Actually there could be endless, countless variations of this metaphor that describes an enemy ship. Our poet may now turn to the word wolf and decide to use some metaphor for wolf instead, like "the sun-swallower" because a wolf is supposed to be eating the sun at the end of times, and so on.

He will draw on mythology and cosmology, the world of the supernatural. It does not stop here. He will have to go through the same kind of process for every noun in the whole poem. And it is not going to be a short poem. The listeners, before they get drunk, that is, will find the end-result, the poem, to be a refreshing riddle that has to be solved, and they need to have vast knowledge of the mythical world in order to understand the riddles and thus the poem itself.

To be able to solve the riddles quickly enough to follow the meaning of the poem was the entertaining challenge of the audience, to be able to make the riddles and let them all fit poetically with each other required an immense effort of creative mind, and a good poet was greatly honored. The poem is such a piece of art that the poet will probably find himself provided for another year because of it. These people, the so called Vikings, were barbarians, primitives, compared to the surrounding world of their time, but their minds were not primitive. Sophistication runs deep in the human brain and far precedes the sophistication of modern society.

THAT WHICH IS DISGUISED IN RUNES
TRANSCRIPT FROM VIDEO 7

I am going to talk a little about how I got into studying the Edda and how I "discovered" its metaphorical nature. Since I was about fifteen years old I was reading everything I could come across about Pagan mythology, from all over the world, especially goddess lore. However, for a long time I seemed to shun the Pagan mythology of my immediate ancestors, the Norse. Why? Well, I think it is because Norse mythology was a part of my cultural heritage, which meant that I was actually taught about it in school. The people who taught me either had a Christian or an Atheist worldview, and they would teach me about the Norse myths in a manner that was condescending and stereotypical.

I was taught that the myths of our ancestors were childish tales made by people for entertainment or for explaining natural phenomena that people at the time were too stupid to understand and thus feared. I was literally taught that the Norse myths were great and funny stories, but held no spiritual depth whatsoever, and that this was the reason why people easily let themselves convert to Christianity, because Christianity offered a hope of salvation and deeper spiritual truths. I remember wondering about that when I was a child, because, I read, a lot. I read in the sagas about the first Christian king in Norway, Olav the Holy, and the saga is actually very straightforward, this saint actually tortured people in the most gruesome ways, tearing out entrails, that kind of stuff, and killed them and persecuted them if they were not willing to convert, and a great war was fought before Norway actually accepted the Church.

I figured, if people easily let themselves be converted, then why did they have to be tortured first? Why did they fight a war for their old faith? Why, in fact, was Scandinavia not Christened until the 11th century AD, when the rest of Europe had long been Church-bound and Vikings had been visiting (in various manners) for many centuries? But even though I was an inquisitive child, what you are taught by adults when you are a child sort of sticks, it programs you in a way, it creates a filter through which you see everything, it is like a subliminal message, and this message was telling me that there was no interest in Norse mythology because it was primitive and silly and childish, not to say male dominated.

You had a god of this and a god of that and it all seemed very macho and rough, which frankly didn't interest me much at the time, and the only goddess worth mentioning was a goddess of love and beauty who seemed to be abducted and had to be rescued all the time. Not my style. So I read about other interesting mythologies, Egyptian, Greek, Mesopotamian, Native American, Siberian, you name it, wonderful mythologies of powerful goddesses, shamans and mind-altering states. The only thing I didn't pay much attention to what was that which was closer to my own roots.

When I was about twenty, I moved to England to study art, and I remember one day I was walking through a very beautiful park with my sketchbook and watching the trees. And I thought, the tree is like a perfect image of the universe, and I contemplated that for a while and had quite a galactic mind-trip while I was at it. And then I thought about Yggdrasill the world tree in Norse myths and thought, maybe the world tree is not a childish image that should be taken literally. Maybe it was meant to be a metaphor, and as a metaphor, it is perfect. That same day I walked into a bookstore and bumped into a stand on which was placed the Poetic Edda in English translation [by Carolyne Larrington]. I thought, wow, do they have that in English?

Do people really read it here? That was how much I knew, then I walked away and forgot about it! But, the same night, when I was going to sleep, the image of the book, the world tree, and that of three ladies spinning away at the roots of the world tree kept me awake for hours. When I finally slept, I dreamed a quite vivid dream about Hel, the goddess of the underworld, and that she told me to "seek", and I woke up suddenly with a clear memory from childhood. I remembered that I had been talking to my father about the Norse gods while we were on a mountain hike together. I had been nine years old. And my father had said that the gods died only when they were forgotten. He didn't mean so much with it I think, being a rational mind, but he said that and I remember feeling horrible about the old gods having to die because they were being forgotten!

I was out in the mountains that day, and I remember turning around and looking out across the plains and feeling that there were someone there. And I raised my arms and thought very intently. "Óðinn, Þórr and Freyia, I promise you that I will keep you alive! I promise you that I will remember you!"

I was absolutely certain that I was heard. Of course, I was nine and I instantly forgot about that promise and did not recall it until that night, eleven years later, when those images kept me awake and I had this strange sensation that someone was holding me to my promise. Well that's what it felt like. I realized that I better have a look at that book. The day after, I bought it. The Poetic Edda. The first time I read it, I was thrilled! To realize that my preconception about these myths being childish, were wrong. Also, to my surprise, I discovered that female characters were extremely important. And I realized that there was a spiritual treasure here, if only I could find it. And I read it over and over again, wondering why it still didn't make the sense I knew it was supposed to make.

I bought another translation, and found new insights there, but still, it was as if lots of the pieces of a puzzle were missing. So, quite obsessed, over the next year I bought and borrowed all the translations into English, Norwegian, Swedish and Danish that I could find, and with every new translation I realized that everybody were translating the same poems differently.

Although it helped to read various translations, there was still something important missing. One day I realized what was missing. It was the translation of names, the names of characters and the names of places and objects. They all had names that meant something, yet those names were hardly ever translated! And I figured, if the names had meaning in Old Norse, it meant that Old Norse people knew those meanings and understood them! It meant that we were not getting even close to hear what the Norse people had heard, unless we translated names! Following my realization, I spent months in the University Library in Oslo one summer, reading the Poetic Edda and the Prose Edda in the Old Norse language, accompanied by a tall pile of dictionaries, some of them hundreds of years old. Later, I went and studied Old Norse in the university so that I could modify some of my more interesting translations, yet, even back then, I finally came close to what I was looking for, and it was a revelation.

Suddenly, I no longer read a simple and primitive story about a hero called Helgi who conquered three trolls before he died by a famous rock. No, I was now reading about the Holy One who conquered the trolls of Hatred, Anger and Fear before he sadly died at the Rock of Greed. However, he managed to overcome the battle at the Rock of Greed in his next life and was thus finally allowed to enter Valhǫll, the hall of Death-Choice. It was an entirely different story. Another example, I was no longer reading about a giant called Ymir who floated in primeval space before its body was cut into pieces by Óðinn, Víli and Vé who shaped the world from the giant's limbs. No, I was reading about the great primeval Sound which was cut into pieces, little tunes, by the divine trinity of Spirit, Intent and Sacred Space. And on and on it went.

All the names in the Edda are meaningful and metaphorical. And it surprised me to realize that this understanding was non-existent. If I looked into a modern Norse dictionary, I could look up the name of a giant only to read that this was the name of a giant. As if I didn't already know that. To actually find out what the name of that giant meant, I often had to look at dictionaries dating back the nineteenth century. Later, when I got into serious academic studies and so forth, I learned from my betters that the book we know as Prose Edda by Snorri Sturluson was an attempt to explain how to understand the metaphors that are found in the older Poetic Edda, that which, according to Snorri, were hidden in runes.

Runes meaning words or secrets [rún (f.sg) = secret, whisper, letter, secret word, symbol]. Now, Snorri's Edda is a great introduction to Norse mythology, but you have to be aware that he was making a desperate attempt to preserve the mythical lore of his ancestors without offending the Church. There is a reason why the Poetic Edda was hidden away from the authorities throughout four centuries, this was an age when books and memories, even people, were burned if they could be accused of threatening the doctrines of the Church. Someone made an effort to hide the Poetic Edda and for four hundred years, that manuscript was considered lost. Snorri's work, however, was perfectly safe, mainly because Snorri made sure to present the lore in a way that was inoffensive. He made the tales of the gods into a tale of the ancestors and explained that people in olden days worshiped their ancestors until they believed that they were gods.

This has caused many people today to speculate in the historical origins of
Óðinn and the Aesir, which is interesting enough, although I think it is a lot
more interesting to look for the spiritual messages in the myths, because they are
certainly there. Snorri told us that the Aesir were ancestors from Asia and maybe
his story does reflect some Indo-European invasion that really happened, but I am
convinced that Snorri emphasized this aspect of the lore in order to make it appear
historical rather than spiritual. You see, the Church could accept pre-Christian
history, but it could not accept pre-Christian religion. Snorri also left out certain
very important aspects of several myths. To make an example: Snorri often cites
the poem Hávamál, the Speech of the High One (Óðinn).

But when you read the Hávamál in the Poetic Edda, you realize that the climax
of the story is the initiation by hanging that Óðinn goes through. Snorri must have
known about this climax, but he completely fails to mention it. Why? Now, he also
quotes heavily from the poem Vǫluspá, the Divination of the Witch, and uses that
poem as his main inspiration when he tells the story of creation and apocalypse.
Yet he completely fails to mention a most crucial aspect of that story, namely the
initiation by burning undergone by the goddess Freyia. He must have known about
it and how important it is in the poem, yet he simply ignores it. And this goes for
all the poems he mentions. He always fails to mention the aspects in those poems
that indicate a Thoroughly Pagan ritual of initiation. He always manages to make it
appear as a story about people, basically, disguising that which reeks of deep Pagan
beliefs, especially those that are concerned with resurrection and overcoming
death, into stories about people.

He lets Loki appear to be like Satan and dismisses almighty Hel as a poor girl
who was thrown into the underworld, lets Óðinn become the patriarch of the gods
although it might as well have been Freyr or Þórr, and leaves out almost completely
all the (numerous) goddesses that are not married. Mind you, Snorri truly made
a masterpiece and I am personally convinced that he really understood and
sympathized with the Pagan lore, yet, he also had to hide a lot of information.But
he didn't hide it away. Snorri hinted heavily towards his mission when he said that
he wrote this book so that students of "poetry" could understand that which has
been hidden in words. He cleverly disguised everything he wanted to say behind
stories that could be read as tales of entertainment but that held many deeper
layers. The whole prose Edda actually provides the key to understanding the myths
of the Poetic Edda if only the student looks behind the apparent.

2: Creation, cosmos and the ruling powers

2.1: Preconceptions and stereotypes
What the ancients knew about cosmos

*"The Ruler was my father an eloquent tongue my life-long love.
Wisdom was my only desire, so I studied the various customs of different
peoples as I traveled through many lands."*

Eirik the Eloquent, in Saxo: Gesta Danorum

When I was studying Old Norse linguistics at the University of Oslo, an important part of our studies obviously consisted in the reading and translating of various Old Norse texts. I remember very clearly an assignment where I was to translate a short passage from the Konungsbók ["The Book of the King"] written down in Norway around the year 1200. It was a textbook for princes consisting of all the necessary knowledge about the world that a medieval king was expected to possess. I read and translated as I went: "The Earth is round as a globe". I stopped, and looked at what I had written. Then I checked with the information about the text, clearly saying that it was written about 1200 AD.

I went back to the beginning of the sentence and began translating again, this time checking every word with my dictionary and my grammars. Again, I wrote: "The Earth is round as a globe". I was puzzled. I was absolutely certain that I had always heard, both in school and through other educational media, that people in the Middle Ages believed that the Earth was flat as a pancake. Here, on the other hand, in one of the most remote kingdoms of Middle Age Europe, someone had written that the Earth was round as a globe. I asked my teacher about it, and he said that my translation was correct, and that it was a great modern mis-comprehension that people in the Middle Age believed that the Earth was flat. They knew it was round like a globe.

At least, educated people knew that. When the sailors of Columbus several hundred years later feared they might reach the end of the world, it was a result of bad education, not because educated people believed it was so. The knowledge of the round Earth was known to the educated classes thousands of years ago. As little as we really know about our past, we are often a bit surprised whenever ancient evidence suggests that people in ancient cultures were in possession of scientific methods, technology and knowledge that we can only call advanced, and which is sometimes quite accurate from our modern perspective. The notion that the Earth revolves around the Sun had been proposed at least as early as the 3rd century BCE by Aristarchus of Samos. The concept of atoms, tiny, unseen particles that provide the basic building material for all physical bodies, date back to ancient Greece, Egypt and India. In India, the Ājīvika, Jain, and Cārvāka schools of atomism may date back to the 6th century BCE. The later Nyaya and Vaisheshika schools developed theories on how atoms combined into more complex objects. In the West, the references to atoms emerged as far as we know 2500 years ago with Leucippus, whose student, Democritus, systematized his views around the year 450 B.C.E.

Several Greek philosophers claimed that they had received a lot of their knowledge from Egypt and Ethiopia, and Democritus himself had traveled to both these countries as well as to Asia and India. Democritus held that the Earth was round, that originally the universe was composed of nothing but tiny atoms churning in chaos, until they collided together to form larger units, including the earth and everything on it. He surmised that there are many worlds, some growing, some decaying; some with no sun or moon, some with several.

He held that every world has a beginning and an end, and that a world could be destroyed by collision with another world. We may assume that Democritus built on the knowledge of many other traditions from around the ancient world. The point I want to make is that knowledge about our universe was developed and spread for thousands of years before our present time. The lack of general education for everybody meant that this knowledge was maintained, taught, spread and developed by certain elites, but it was spread and it was taught widely, shared across the continents for centuries if not millennia. The sharing and developing of knowledge about our cosmos and about nature was only suppressed by certain powerful religious institutions. In Europe that would mean the Church, where powerful influences stressed the basic Biblical tenet that the quest for knowledge is in fact the same as original sin.

The early Church was responsible not only for destroying Pagan temples and Mystery centers, but also for destroying the last libraries and universities of the Classical world. Philosophers, scientist and Pagans alike were persecuted, as symbolized by the cruel death of the last scientist to defend her vocation; Hypatia of Alexandria, Pagan philosopher, mathematician, astronomer and inventor of advanced instruments and technology. This famous female university professor was murdered by a Christian mob in the year 415 AD and burned as a witch, as John of Nikiu wrote about several hundred years later:

> "And in those days there appeared in Alexandria a female philosopher, a Pagan named Hypatia, and she was devoted at all times to magic, astrolabes and instruments of music, and she beguiled many people through Satanic wiles...A multitude of believers in God arose under the guidance of Peter the magistrate...and they proceeded to seek for the Pagan woman who had beguiled the people of the city and the prefect through her enchantments. And when they learnt the place where she was, they proceeded to her and found her...they dragged her along till they brought her to the great church, named Caesarion. Now this was in the days of the fast. And they tore off her clothing and dragged her...through the streets of the city till she died. And they carried her to a place named Cinaron, and they burned her body with fire."

If not the only culprit, the Medieval Church did a thorough job out of destroying the last remnants of the once famous Library of Alexandria, which had contained literature and knowledge from all over the ancient world for hundreds of years, if not more. Knowledge about ancient people and their ideas, their science and their philosophies was lost forever. Yet, we know that people had advanced knowledge about astronomy several thousands of years ago: Even Paleolithic cave paintings are now thought by some to be the depictions of astronomical configurations, even the entries to the sacred caves appear to be aligned with solstices or equinoxes.

We know that people thousands of years ago had technology enabling them to engineer and design enormous monuments. And from various strange archaeological finds and ancient texts, we know that our ancestors were capable of building machines and tools as well as presenting complex theories about the universe. This Chapter on cosmology will present the origin of the universe as perceived by Old Norse myth-makers in Pagan times and what happens when names of characters, things or places are translated in interpreted with an openness of mind and with respectfulness towards the intelligence of the myth-makers.

Many will be surprised at the almost scientific complexity, and sometimes surprising accuracy, with which these myth-makers actually described the earliest origins of our universe and our Earth. Blended with a magical and mystical-spiritual attitude and an animistic approach to all existence are observations of a gaseous, light-sound-vibrational universe where life is created through alchemical processes of various explosions and blends between different kinds of liquid matter and clouds of mist. As we shall see, Norse myths display, as did several ancient cultures, tremendous amounts of complex knowledge. Knowledge about nature, about cosmos, about astronomy and engineering and architecture that seems astonishing to us because we were raised to expect less from our ancestors than such advancement of mind. When the Norse myths present, as we shall see, if not always accurate then still profoundly philosophical and rational insights into the nature of cosmos and its early beginnings, powerful elements of nearly scientific theory, we should not really be that surprised or so ready to assign it to outside intervention.

People in the past were no less intelligent than we are today. They too had their geniuses, and were as capable of making rational observations and logical deductions as we are today. In our time, there is a tendency to ignore this fact and thus also miss out on the treasures that our ancestors revealed to us in their sacred lore. If we expect to see superstitious beliefs, funny trolls and "fertility idols," that is what we will see, at the expense of true understanding. Our species is an intelligent one and has been so for hundreds of thousands of years. We tend to severely underestimate "primitive" cultures. People who lived in so-called primitive cultures were not primitive in their minds. This advanced brain of ours was not developed for future purposes, it was developed out of the continuous necessity of each moment in our evolution, and out of our continuous curiosity about the world.

Our brain became big because we employed it for thinking and imagining possibilities, for millions of years before we became the species we are today. In many ways, I am certain that early humans (and their ancestors) employed more of the brains potential on a daily basis than most modern humans do today, being able to lean back on our technology and push a few buttons and draw a card in order to instantly get what we want. What modern person would be able to employ nature, say, the way our Ice Age hunter-gatherer predecessors did? We tend to picture them as simple-minded brutes, often thinking them less elegant and complex than apes actually are yet who among us could from nature alone make intricate clothing, buildings and tools that would enable us to live, and archaeology shows that they often lived very well, in a world full of dangerous predators and dramatic climatic changes?

Yet with their superior knowledge about all nature, they produced enough welfare to cultivate impressive botanical and pharmaceutical knowledge, medical operation skills, ways of making textiles, woven baskets, threads, fishing nets, fishing hooks and harpoons, dyes from all kinds of minerals and plants, as well as tools and baskets, clothing and lamp oil from the corpses of hunted animals. These people found ways of drilling tiny holes though shells and carved pearls only to decorate themselves, they developed advanced navigation and sea-faring vessels that brought our species all around the world. With such ability to observe and make use of all aspects of nature, with such imagination and practical skills, they were no doubt able to develop some serious knowledge based on long-term observations over the generations.

No doubt they knew songs and stories, and they certainly held knowledge about the equinoxes, the solstices and the astronomical movements thousands of years before they began to raise stone henge. The cultivation of a rational and practical mind came together with the cultivation of the intuitive. Dreams and visions induced by altered states of consciousness must have helped spur the imagination and the curiosity about the various dimensions of reality and about the cosmos. The use of entheogenic[3] substances has probably played an important role in the development of our species, or our philosophies and our religions. We also tend to greatly underestimate the advancement of the countless known and unknown ancient civilizations that preceded us.

Many if not most of these are actually known to us through archaeological digs and written accounts, but may surprise us yet. Just because advanced knowledge and technology was not mass-produced and profited upon as it inevitable is today does not mean that it did not exist. There are numerous examples of advanced technology and advanced knowledge from ancient cultures. Scandinavia of the Viking Age was not a very advanced civilization compared to other contemporary and earlier civilizations. It was a relatively poor peasant and seafaring society, clan-based and tribal, where magic and sorcery was as real as any other phenomenon, where shamanism, oracular divination, witchcraft and sacrificial cults dominated the worldviews of most people, which many today would dismiss as superstitious.

Yet it was also an ancient culture with roots far back into the Bronze Age and a time when Scandinavians interacted with the Mediterranean world on a regular basis. Trade in goods was not the only things that circulated across the seas, by the rivers and the continents for thousands of years well into the Viking Age. Despite their apparent barbarianism, the Pagan Scandinavians were lovers of knowledge and the exchange of knowledge. Nothing was respected more than knowledge, if not wisdom, and eloquence was a valued treasure, evidence for wisdom.

---

3 Psychoactive substances that cause altered states

In fact, knowledge was sacred, and they had their sacred knowledge keepers, the vǫlur [oracular witch-priestesses] and their seiðmennir [sorcerer-shamans], their þulur [reciting sages] and their skaldir [poets], their gyðjur [priestesses] and their goðar [priests]. Óðinn himself is called the Fimbulþúl ["The Great Reciting Sage"] and about his process of understanding the world it is eloquently spoken, in Hávamál st. 111, Poetic Edda:

It is time to speak	*Mál er at þylia*
From the Seat of the Sage	*þvlar stóli a*
Out by the Well of Origin	*Vrþar brvnni at*
I saw and was quiet	*sa ec oc þagþac,*
I saw and I contemplated	*sa ec oc hugþac,*
I listened to the speech of	*hlydda ec a manna mál;*
people	*of rvnar heyrda ec doma,*
Of symbols I heard	*ne vm rádom þagðo*
And counsel was given	*Hava hallo at*
By the Hall of the High	*Hava hallo i.*
In the Hall of the High	

2.2: VǪLUSPÁ, "THE DIVINATION OF THE VǪLVA"
THE WITCH WHO SPOKE THE WORLD'S STORY

All witches have descended from Wood Wolf (Tree of Desire)
All wizards from the Tree of Intent
All magical womb-men from Dark Mind
All giants are descended from Sound
> *Eru Vǫlur allar*
> *fra Vidolfui,*
> *vitkar allir fra Vilmeidi,*
> *seidberendr*
> *fra Suarthofda,*
> *jotnar allir fra Ymi komnir.*

Hyndluljóð [The Song of the She-Wolf] st. 33, Poetic Edda

In the year 1225 AD Snorri relates how Freyia is the only deity that is still alive and still performing rituals as a blótgyðja, a sacrificial priestess. Many scholars believe that the worship of Freyia was still secretly operating by the time Snorri wrote his book, although Iceland had been Christian for 225 years already, and that this was what he was referring to. I suspect that this may have to do with the clandestine continuation of a Mystery tradition which we will be exploring throughout this book, and/or with the continued existence of "wise women" performing Freyia's ancient art of seiðr hundreds of years after the conversion. Seiðr [an art which involved oracular divination and witchcraft]was an extremely important underlying practice of the Old Norse religion, a fact that is necessary to understand in order to understand the Old Norse myths. A recent study by Stephen Mitchell, Witchcraft and Magic in the Nordic Middle Ages, shows that the practice of witchcraft happened openly and without fear of prosecution until the end of the 15th century AD.

When Ragnhildr Tregagás in 1324 was persecuted for having (reason unknown) put a spell of impotence on a man by carving runes into the wood of his marriage bed, the only punishment was a forced pilgrimage. Before her court trial, Ragnhildr proudly boasted about her witchcraft, obviously not in any way afraid of being accused of it. Interestingly, the spell involved was recorded in the Old Norse language, which was still spoken until the mid-1400s, and referred to Gǫndul ["The Magician"] a known name for Freyia [The spell began with *ritt ek ifrá mer Gǫnduls ondu*; "I carve away from me the pleasures of Freyia" (i.e. the pleasures of love)].

Recordings from Arboga in Sweden during the 15th century give an excellent example of the survival and the sudden rapid decline of wise women in Scandinavia. During the 1460s, we hear of the existence of visa Kadhrin ["wise Catherine"]. Eleven years later, in 1471, the same woman is referred to, but this time as galna Kadhrin ["Crazy Catherine"]. A change of attitudes had obviously happened, and the first severe trials of witchcraft began after a few decades. Interestingly enough, such trials began for real only after the change to Lutheran Protestantism, when the recital of Catholic prayers could be enough to bring anyone to the stake for whispering spells! It is also interesting to note that Church illustrations in Scandinavia during the medieval era frequently show the Devil offering a horn of mead to a witch, a symbol of evil temptations.

The horn of mead offered by the Devil could appear to be an attempt to transform the ancient and extremely important (as we will see in Chapter 3) Pagan icon of the old goddess of witchcraft who also offers the mead of wisdom and poetry to the initiate. The Church paintings were obviously attempts at changing attitudes towards ancient Pagan practices that were either still practiced clandestinely, or towards the memories of these, turning the ancient symbol of the gift of wisdom into a matter of evil temptation, much as their predecessors had transformed the symbol of the serpent of wisdom into a symbol of the Devil. The existence of the wise women, Snorri's remark about the continued practice of Freyia as a priestess, and the paintings of the Devil and his drinking horn are all powerful hints that some aspects of the Pagan religion survived in Scandinavia until the witch trials began during the 16th century.

Wise women: *vǫlur*, who practiced the art of seiðr that was introduced by Freyia and practiced by Óðinn, performed what we today would call witchcraft, medium channeling, divination and shamanism. Which was held in high regard by Norse Pagans. The use of spells and the meddling with "dark forces" was as much a part of their religion as any other kind of ritual. The dark forces were not evil, they were as much a part of the powers that fuel this universe as the bright forces, their darkness representing not evil, but the unknown. There is no actual battle between good and evil in the Norse myths, try and look beyond that veil, and you will better understand the lore of the past. There are no clear-cut hierarchies in the divine pantheon of our ancestors, there are just complex entities that may or may not be beneficial in different situations.

The Viking Age man and woman lived in a world populated by an endless variety of aspects of a unified whole. Most mainstream presentations of the Old Norse Pagan cosmic genesis base themselves almost exclusively of Snorri's account in the Gylfaginning. I will try a different approach. Snorri himself based his own account of creation and the emergence of the primeval and divine powers of cosmos on the much older lore of the Poetic Edda, and in particular on the Edda poem Vǫluspá [The Divination of the Witch]. Snorri himself regarded his work as a helping tool to be used when trying to deciphering the meaning of mythical metaphors. Therefore, I will use The Divination of the Witch as a starting point and apply Snorri's Prose Edda mainly as a means to explain the older Edda sources.

Vǫluspá-The Divination of the Witch: is a poem supposedly spoken in a state of trance by a vǫlva (f.sg: "wand-witch", plural: vǫlur) during a séance of seiðr. Seiðr was the Old Norse art of divination and witchcraft, considered sacred and respectable within the Pagan worldview. It carries many resemblances to shamanism, but also to oracular traditions and what we today would simply consider sorcery.

Seated Oracle goddess Nehalennia from 2nd century Iron Age votive altar, holding the wand of the vǫlva, flanked by a dog (Hel-hound) and a vessel filled with apples (symbols of immortality).

Domburg, the Netherlands. [Domburgs Nehalennia altaar volgens Plaat 7 No. 15a van L.J.F. Janssen, De Romeinsche Beelden en Gedenksteenen van Zeeland, Leiden, 1845]

A séance of seiðr

Attention I demand from all the sacred families greater and lesser children of
Great World;
You want me, Choice Father to give a good account of the most ancient tales
that which I remember best

> *Hljóðs bið ek allar*
> *helgar kindir,*
> *meiri ok minni*
> *mǫgu Heimdallar;*
> *viltu, at ek, Valfǫðr!*
> *vel framtelja*
> *forn spjǫll fíra,*
> *þau er fremst um man*

Vǫluspá, st. 1 , Poetic Edda

The Divination of the Witch takes the form of a typical public séance of seiðr
where the practitioner (in this case the "Witch") would be seated outside in the
courtyard, either on a high platform surrounded by people, or inside the hall, where
she would be offered the High Seat that was usually reserved for the male and
female heads of the household, or for any visitor of higher rank than their hosts.

The Eiriks saga Rauða describes how the women of the farm visited by a vǫlva
(a female professional practitioner of seiðr), stood in a circle around the platform
and sang a song called the *varðlokur*["Invocation of the Spirits"] until the vǫlva,
in trance, could see that which had before been hidden. The divination involved
seeing the past, the present and the future, and the power of the divination was
the fact that the vǫlva by seeing the weave of fate so clearly could also alter it and
change the outcome. This was, according to Snorri in his Ynglinga saga, the most
powerful of all arts. We will see that the oldest known entity of the entire Norse
cosmos is thought to be an incredibly ancient vǫlva, remembering a time before
time itself, and keeping her séance before the gods and all the children of the world.
It gives us a powerful clue as to the underlying perception of existence:

AN EXISTENCE, A COSMOS, BROUGHT INTO BEING BY MAGICAL POWERS;
AS A GREAT BIG SÉANCE OF ORACULAR DIVINATION, OF EXPERIENCING
AND SEEING THE INTRICATE WEAVE OF FATE THAT IS THE HISTORY OF ALL
THAT LIVES, EVER LIVED, AND EVER WILL LIVE.

The Vǫluspá poem begins with the Witch addressing her audience. All the
children of Heimdallr. Heimdallr is usually known as a god of the divine Vanir
tribe who now remains with the Aesir gods, and we will be discussing him further
on several occasions. For the time being, we will bear in mind that his name
indicates what he is: Heimdallr is derived from the Norse words *heimr,* meaning
"world", and *dallr*, meaning "great" or "splendid", as in glorious, terrific, fantastic,
and awesome. In Old Norse mythical poetry, he is an embodiment of the universe
itself, the Great World. Thus the Witch is addressing all the beings of cosmos, the
children of the world. The Witch proceeds by referring to her *patron*, that is, the
one who has asked for her divination.

From the saga sources, we know that the vǫlur were traveling women who were approached by the head of a household (or his messenger, initially), who would invite her to their halls. There, she would be offered food and gifts and a place to stay the night. She was treated with the utmost reverence. It was a festive occasion were all the people attached to the farm gathered, and everybody, even slaves, were allowed to ask the Witch about things that concerned them. After she had received all the questions from all the people of the gathering, she would make her preparations in the night and usually begin her séance the day after, where she would enter trance and answer all the questions she had received as they were revealed to her.

The vǫlur were sacred women who were in league with the *Norns* [Norns or fate-goddesses] who, we later learn in the same poem, rule the lives of men and the laws of the universe. Only through seiðr could anybody hope to influence the Norna *dómr* ["the judgment of the Norns"]. In this case, we learn that the head of the "household" of cosmos, Óðinn, is the one who has invited her. The Witch tells the tale of creation, and later on in the divinatory poem, she arrives at the point of time in history where he invites her and where she begins her séance. That is when he wishes to learn about the future, the result of all that has happened in the world recently. As below, so above. What the clan leader would do when inviting a vǫlva to speak, so Óðinn did when he wanted this séance: He pays her gold and jewelry in order to learn her secret lore:

> 28. She sat outside alone when
> the aged one came the old-young
> of the Aesir and looked her in the
> eyes
>
> 29. For her, the Father
> of Armies chose rings and
> jewels for her wise speech
> and her magical divination
> she saw widely, and so
> widely into all the worlds

> 28. Ein sat hon úti,
> þá er inn aldni kom
> yggjungr ása
> ok í augu leit...
>
> 29. Valði henni
> Herfǫðr
> hringa ok men,
> féspjǫll spaklig
> ok spáganda;
> sá hon vítt ok um vítt
> of verǫld hverja.

Óðinn, whose name can be translated as "The Spirit", has many other names, and many of them are employed to describe him throughout the Vǫluspá poem. Which name is used when is actually significant because they indicate something about the function and role of the god at various turns in the fate, the history of the world. In the beginning, Óðinn is addressed by the *vǫlva* under the name or rather the title *Valfǫðr*. Val means "choice", which is why I translate the name as Choice Father. The word for choice is also used to describe The Chosen Dead. The souls that reside with Óðinn in Valhǫll. It is usually thought that Óðinn is the father of The Chosen Dead who reside in Valhǫll. I believe that the word val, "choice", refers to a choice that the soul must take in order to be worthy of Valhǫll or simply able to enter this realm. There are many stereotypical and superficial concepts of "Valhalla" in mainstream media, described as a kind of paradise for drunken brutes who happened to die in battle.

As we shall see throughout this book, the entry to and residence in Valhǫll is a far more profoundly intricate matter. One Edda poem, the Hyndlulióð, seems to be describing the path to Valhǫll as one going through a severe initiation trial where revelations about cosmos are offered during a state of symbolic or experienced death. Where the soul of the initiate has blended with the soul of a sacrificed animal. The goddess Freyia, who in another Edda poem [the Grímnismál], is said to be the deity who actually decides who shall go to Óðinn in Valhǫll. She offers to the initiate a "Mead of Memory" that will enable the initiate to remember the revelations he had during the state of death.

The heroic poems strongly suggest that the hero had to go through similar kind of mysterious initiation set of trials where the "golden goddess" in the shape of a Valkyrie had to be woken from slumber if he were to hope for such a glorious fate after death. The initiation involved sacred teachings about the nature of the universe, about fate, healing and magical arts.

As to the kind of choice that has to be taken by the soul, we get a powerful clue in the story of Váli, "The Chosen Dead", who was "born" to destroy Blind Strife in order to restore Baldr from Broad Vision. I have analyzed this myth in Chapter 5.6 (The Rape of the Rejecter). I will also analyze the meaning of Valhǫll in Chapter 7. For now, let me suggest that The Chosen Dead has to do with spiritual enlightenment and that Óðinn is the progenitor of that kind of illumination. It is from the position of being the first cosmic being to seek a state of illumination, as a "father" of the path of initiation, that Óðinn asks the mysterious Witch to reveal her knowledge.

Later, when he approaches her for the first time, she addresses Óðinn [The Spirit] as Herfǫðr [The Father of Armies]. In fact, Óðinn seeks her wisdom only after he has observed the state of war and misery and the loss of wisdom that has come to the world through the loss of deeply symbolical things: The Hearing of the Great World and the Eye of Spirit. Partly deaf and partly blind the original omniscience of the world and the whole Spirit that rides it, the Spirit has arrived at a point where he needs to know the background to, the outcome of and the solution to the present problems.

THE WITCH BEFORE TIME

When the vǫlva begins her divination, going back to the beginning, it is very interesting to note that she clearly reveals that she remembers, and that she was there, before it all began, as it is said in Vǫluspá stanza 2:

> I remember giants born before time
> those who in the olden days had me fostered...
>> Ec man iotna ár um borna
>> þa er fordom mic fodda hofdo ...

She was fostered among giants that existed before time. The identities of these giants are subsequently revealed, but for now, we should let this information sink in. It is a fact that is usually ignored. In fact, I have never ever read an account anywhere where this fact is pointed out: that there is a First Being in the Vǫluspá cosmo genesis, and that this First Being is the incredibly ancient Witch who reveals her knowledge to the Spirit and to all the children of the Great World. She remembers giants before time, and as we shall see, she also remembers the nine worlds that preceded the present one.

She is the one who knows all fate, for she was there from the very start, and has seen it to the very end. Who, then, is the vǫlva really? Are there any other female beings who could qualify as First Being, when using the vǫlva of the Vǫluspá story as the basic model? About her, we know only this:

1. Firstly, she knows all fate.
2. Secondly, being a vǫlva, she can influence and shape fate.
3. Thirdly, she was there in the beginning, raised among the earliest gigantic powers that came before the present universe was shaped.

Knowing all Fate: The fact that she knows all fate brings to mind at least two goddesses: Frigg and Gefion, both described as "knowing all fate" in the Edda poem Lokasenna. Frigg is the wife of Óðinn, and her name probably means Love or Beloved. She is also called Saga, which means "The Story". It is tempting to suggest that as Saga, she is the Story of the world, the History of the entire universe, which is why she can tell it from start to finish. Gefion's name means "Provider", a longer form of Gefn, which means the same and which is said to be a name for Freyia [Lady Sovereign]. We know that Frigg and Freyia originated as one goddess, Frija [To Love].

A Witch (vǫlva): We also know that Freyia in Norse myths is in fact the great traveling *vǫlva* [the wand-witch of the gods] the first teacher of the art of seiðr, as Snorri explained in Ynglinga saga 4. Another name for Freyia is Gǫndul ["The Magician"]. From this scant information it is certainly possible to suggest that Frigg and Freyia both are identifiable as the ancient Witch who tells the world's history in the Vǫluspá, and who is the First Being.

First Being: Another candidate to the First Being is the oldest of the Norns, Urðr, whose name means "Origin" or "Beginning". She is the ultimate goddess of fate, residing in the heart of the divine realm Ásgarðr, where she guards the Well of Origin [Urðarbrunnr] from where all fates emerge and ascend into the world. She provides the water and the soil that gives nourishment to the universe "tree", renewing its life every day, and the Aesir always hold their council by her sacred water source. She and her sister Verdandi, whose name refers to that which is happening right now, carve the runes of fate into the world tree's roots, as we shall see.

Identifications: The Fate-mother Urðr provides as certainly as does all-fate-knowing Gefion, lives in a water-hall as certainly as does all-fate-knowing Frigg (who lives in Fensalar, the "Moist Halls") and is certainly an entity related to the beginning of the universe itself. Moreover, she and is the writer of all fate from the very beginning. As such, the Norn called "Origin" also qualifies as the First Being.

Throughout this book, we will see that the myths reveal a very fluid concept of realities and entities where identities and functions frequently overlap. It can be hard to grasp for us moderns who are used to clear distinctions and separations, but our ancestors tended to be tremendously far more flexible in their outlook on spiritual realities than we are today. From the point of view of the Viking Age poet, one basic entity can hide behind countless names, its true identity only revealed through functions and attributes.

This outlook is at the heart and core of Old Norse poetry, and should be extended to mythology and sacred lore if we are to truly understand their spiritual reality. The First Being hides behind Frigg, Freyia and Urðr, and could well be behind several other female deities of the Poetic Edda. But for now, we should have a look at the Prose Edda, only to see that Snorri too described a First Being who was a female.

In Snorri's account, the female First Being comes together with or just after the male First Being, a being who turns out to be the body of the universe itself. The female First Being nourishes the male First Being with her liquid, causing him to expand, just as the fate goddess of Origin, Urðr, nourishes the World Tree with her water in the Vǫluspá.

AUÐHUMBLA , YMIR AND GINNUNGA GAP

Gangleri [Wandering Learning] asked: "Where did Ymir live? What did he live from?"

The High One replied: "The next was that, as the frost began to drip, there was a cow from this. She was called Auðhumbla, and from her teats ran four rivers of milk, and with these rivers she raised Ymir."

Wandering Learning: "What did the cow live from?"

The High One: "She licked the frost-covered rocks [of Niflhel [the World of the Dead] they were salty..."

Gylfaginning, The Prose Edda by Snorri Sturluson

The name Auðhumbla is derived from the Old Norse adjective *auðr*, which means "abundant" and the word humbla, which probably means what we today in Norway call humle [a very important brew ingredient in ale and beer]. For this reason, I translate the cow's name as Abundant Brew Ingredient. The interpretation is meaningful in light of the immense importance of ale, beer and mead as symbols of life-giving, life-restoring and wisdom-inspiring liquid power in Norse mythology. The Norn Urðr uses her sacred, life-restoring water to nourish the world tree, which is a symbol of the entire universe, while the cow Abundant Brew Ingredient nourishes the world giant, who is likewise a symbol of the universal body, with her rivers of liquid life-power.

The cosmic cow emerges from the frosty realm of death and feeds on the frost of death, a symbol of how death becomes life through a process within the cosmic cow: She transforms death into life within her body. This is exactly what the Norn Urðr also does with her water, which transforms the daily decay of the universe into restored life. Snorri explained that the Well of Origin has this property, that anyone who goes into it will emerge transformed, transparent and illuminated. The image of the cosmic cow is repeated in the image of a cosmic goat, Heiðrún [Bright Rune (i.e.: Symbol] who transforms the dead matter that she eats off the world tree into the life-giving mead that restores the souls of the chosen dead in Valhǫll.

The concept of the cosmic cow is recognizable from Old Indian lore, where the goddess Vac, whose name means both "Cow" and "Voice" emerged from the mouth of Brahman, the androgynous universal being that existed alone in the beginning. She represented the separation of the feminine active, dynamic and creative power, Shakti [Power] from the masculine passive, still and observing power within Brahman, whose voice or sound she is. From this first divine voice, the Vac, the world came into shape and the life stories began. The divine first voice that created the universe was symbolized as a cow.

Cows symbolize the mother goddess in many Indo-European traditions and seem to have been a very important symbol of goddesses in Europe and the Middle East ever since the Neolithic era. As a symbol, the cow is a perfect image of an abundant flow of nourishment. In the Norse tradition, it is the flowing streams of "milk" produced by the female First Being, symbolized as a cow, which gives life and growth to the universal body, the male First Being. The manifestation of feminine and masculine energies in the early cosmos is a basic mold for all feminine and masculine mythical beings ever after, where the male always ultimately represents the seen and known body of things, whereas the female always ultimately represents the hidden, unseen and unknown movement within the body that causes expansion and thus, fate.

The connection to Old Indian Vedic lore is powerful in this version of the creation story. When Vac came out as a voice from the mouth of Brahman, we are reminded that Auðhumbla also, according to Snorri, emerged from within a "mouth" [the Ginnunga Gap]. The word *gap* refers to an open mouth, indicating also that it is a swallowing, feeding mouth. The word *Ginnunga* is probably derived from the word **ginnr** [sacred] and **unga**, genitive plural of ungr [descendant]. As such, both the cow and the world giant she nourished came into being from streams of hot and cold that met within the Mouth of the Sacred Descendants. The element of sound and speech as crucial to original creation is hinted to, and as such, will need to be further explored. For now, we shall return to the Vǫluspá account and have a look at the giants who fostered the First Beings.

2.3: The nine within the wood

We will move on to the next lines in stanza 2 of the Vǫluspá in order to explore exactly what the cosmic vǫlva remembers happening before time itself:

> *Nine worlds I remember nine Witches Within-Wood before the precious Mead-Tree sprouted from the ground below*
>> *Nio man æc heima*
>> *nío iviþi*
>> *Miotuið moran*
>> *fyr mold nedan.*

The incredibly ancient vǫlva remembers nine worlds before the present, and clearly identifies these worlds as iviði, a plural form of the feminine noun iviðja which refers to either a sorceress or witch such as the vǫlva herself, or to a giantess. The vǫlva may very well also be a giantess as she was fostered among these primeval entities. There is a strong suggestion in these lines, pointing to a concept of crafty witch-giantesses actually embodying worlds.

The name for giantess or sorceress that is used, iviðja, literally translates as "Within Wood" [i = within, inside, in [viðja = wood, forest, tree]. The wood refers to the matter that makes up a tree, and the tree is here a symbol of the world, the universe, a connection that is clearly shown in the last line. Thus the giantesses or witches (or both) are beings that reside within the matter that makes up a "world" [a universe]. In the previous section, I mentioned that the physical universe, symbolized by the body of the giant Ymir represented the original masculine element in cosmos.

This was nourished by a mysterious power of abundant nourishment and creative movement, the original cosmic female element, the instigator of all fate. When we now hear of female "within woods", we must bear in mind that the wood is a symbol of the physical body, in this case the body of the universe, and that the lines reveal that the unseen female element resides within the seen male element, the invisible animating and nourishing power within the physical. The nine worlds that existed before the present "Mead Tree" would mean that we have nine male "trees" and nine female "within trees", the latter being imagined as crafty giantess witches who propel the expanding life and fate of the "tree" they inhabit.

These "Within Wood" giantesses have apparently, like immortal souls, survived the physical bodies of the previous universes and now come together to create our present universe, as we learn from two different Edda sources: In his *Gylfaginning*, Snorri Sturluson claimed that Heimdallr, whose name can be translated as "Great World" and who, therefore, is a representation of the universe and the world tree, was born by nine mothers. To support his claim, he quotes from an otherwise lost Edda poem titled Heimdalargaldr [The Charm of Great World].

In this charm, Great World himself reveals that he has been born by nine sisters:

> Of nine mothers am I child
> Of nine sisters am I son.
>> Niu em ek mœdra mögr,
>> niu em ek systra sonr.

The Edda poem Hyndluljóð [Song of the She-Wolf] also supports this concept. In stanza 35 we read:

> One was born in the days before time Immensely powerful, of the ruling lineages Nine women gave birth to the magnificent man Giants' maidens at the Earth's edge.

> Vard einn borin i ardaga rammaukin miok raugna kindar; niu baru þann naddgaufgann mann iotna meyiar vid iardar þraum.

These predecessors and mothers of the present universe are named in stanza 37:

> Howling One bore him
> Grasping One bore him
> The Achiever bore him and the Giver of Wealth
> Wolf-Rune (= Desire-Fate) bore him and Pleasure Island
> She-Wolf and Intender
> And Iron-Scissors.

> Hann Gialp vm bar,
> hann Greip vm bar,
> bar hann Eistla
> ok Eyrgiafa,
> hann bar Vlfrun
> ok Angeyia.
> Imdr ok Atla
> ok Iarnsaxa.

Some of the names of the universal mothers appear in other poetical sources, such as when the feeling of courage is called "Iarnsaxa's wind" in a skaldic poem, but as usual, the names of mythical entities in a particular poem serve only to describe some important aspects of these mythical entities in one particular context, and we must assume that they can show up with different names other places. In order to identify the giantesses, we must think of the nine maidens/mothers as a mythical and poetical formula and see where else we find such a formula.

THE DAUGHTERS OF THE OCEAN

The formula of the nine giantesses is repeated by Snorri in his description of the Ægisdætra [the "Daughters of the Ocean"]. Aegir may mean "Ocean" or "Terrifying One", and is usually thought of as the giant of the sea. According to Snorri, other names for Aegir are Hlér [Wind-Shielded] and Gymir [Hiding (something)]. He lives on Hlésey [The Wind-Shielded Island] and is married to Rán [Robbery], who is also described as his daughter. Rán is the mother of the nine giantesses. Rán is an ancient giantess of the ocean who owns a net with which she fishes the drowned people. People who drowned supposedly came to feast and make love in Rán's and her daughters' mead halls and beds at death. Rán is a giantess but is also listed among the goddesses [the Ásyniur of Ásgarðr].

Her daughters aid their mother in catching men at sea in order to bring them down to her realm. Snorri lists the names of the Daughters of the Ocean as Himinglæva [The Heaven-Shining One], Blóðughadda [Bloody-Hair], Hefring [The Rising One], Dúfa, Úðr, Hrǫnn, Bylgja, Bara [all these describe different kinds of ocean-waves], and Kolga [The Cold One]. According to Snorri (and often confirmed by other Norse sources) they are embodied in the waves of the ocean. However, as Snorri himself points out, and which is verified by Skaldic and Edda poetry, the ladies have many names. In Snorri's Skáldskaparmál, we hear how the nine Daughters of the Ocean are synonymous with the mysterious red gold that seems to represent divine knowledge in the Eddas:

"Why is gold called the Fire of the Ocean [Ægir]? The origin of it is this story: Aegir, as was told before, went as a guest to Ásgarðr, and when he was about to return home, he invited Óðinn and all the Aesir to visit him after an interval of three months. Undertaking this journey were first of all Óðinn and Njǫrðr, Freyr, Týr, Bragi, Víðarr, Loki and then the Ásyniur, Frigg, Freyia, Gefion, Skaði, Iðunn, Síf. Þórr was not there; he was away in eastern parts killing trolls. And when the gods had taken their places, Aegir had glowing gold brought into the middle of the hall which illuminated and lit up the hall like fire, and this was used as lights at his feast just as in Valhalla there had been glowing swords instead of fire...

Ran is the name of Aegir's wife, and the names of their nine daughters are as was written above. At this feast everything served itself, both food and ale and all the utensils that were needed for the feast. Then the Aesir discovered that Ran had a net in which she caught everyone that went to sea. So this is the story of the origin of gold being called fire or light or brightness of Aegir, Ran, or Aegir's daughters, and from such kennings the practice has now developed of calling gold fire of the sea and of all terms for it [the sea], since Aegir and Ran's names are also terms for sea, and hence gold is now called fire of lakes or rivers and of all river-names."

In Snorri's account, the Daughters of the Ocean are clearly not only symbols of the waves, but also of rivers, of light and of the divine red gold that appears to lead to wisdom and spiritual illumination. They provide the light of the gods in the Hall of the Ocean, a place of immortality. Aegir's hall is situated at the island called Hlésey, which means the Wind Shielded Island. The wind is, significantly, a symbol of death in Norse poetry, so that we understand that a place which is "breeze-less" (such as the Grove of Barri) or "wind-shielded" such as Aegir's island in the Ocean where his wife Death lurks, are places of immortality.

THE ONE AND THE MANY

The formula of nine supernatural females is often repeated in Old Norse sources. When the first warrior fates, the Valkyrie, appear in Vǫluspá stanza 30, they are nine in number, ready to ride the earth. In the heroic Edda poems, Valkyrie ride the "air and sea", always in groups of nine or three by nine. They are not only responsible for protecting and guiding their chosen hero, but also for bringing rays of light into the world, and causing the dew to fall in the valleys. They are always united in one head Valkyrie who speaks for them all, just like the Old English poem suggested when it said about the Valkyrie:
"Lo loud were they, lo loud, riding over the hills.
They were of one mind, riding over the land."
In the Edda poem Fjǫlsvinnsmál, we are presented with a description of a "court" with a "hall" within Utgarðr [The World Outside], which is the realm of the giants. The protective walls and guards of this court are described in very similar terms as those found within the realm of death in Níflhel [Hiding in Mist], but behind the hostile and dangerous walls is a bright realm with a hill called Lyfjaberg ["The Mountain of Medicine"] where the Mímameiðr ["The Tree of Memory"] grows. The Tree of Memory is obviously another name for the universe tree. Beneath this tree sits a maiden, dreaming, by the name of Menglǫð [Invitation to Blend].

She is called the Þióðmæra [The Great Maiden] and is said to rule the lands, the people and the halls of Utgarðr. Such a sole-ruling queen of the giant world is otherwise not mentioned in Edda poetry, but is mentioned in the Saga of Egill and Ásmundr, where she is called Queen Eagle Beak. She is dreaming beneath the tree, awaiting the return of her beloved, who has been gone for countless lifetimes. The image of a maiden "ruling lands and people" while weaving and dreaming in a secret chamber is repeated in the Edda poem Oddrúnargrátr, st.17, where it is the head Valkyrie of eight sisters, Brynhildr, who is the ruling power:

Brynhildr in the storage room	*Brynhildr i bvri*
made the embroidery (of fate) she	*borða racþi,*
had the people and the land in her	*hafþi hon lýði*
power,...	*oc lond vm sic,...*

By the knees of the giant queen, nine maidens are seated, all benevolent, as the Fjǫlsvinnsmál relates:

36. It is called the Mountain of Medicine and it has long been the joy of the sick and the wounded healed is any woman even from ages of sickness who climbs that mountain.

36. Lyfjaberg þat heitir en þat hefir lengi verit sjúkum ok sárum gaman; heil verðr hver þótt hafi árs sótt, ef þat klífr, kona

37...what are the maidens called who by the knees of Menglǫð sit together in unity?

37... vat þær meyjar heita, er fyr Mengladar knjám sitja sáttar saman?

38. Life is one called, another Life Tracker the third Guardian of People, Bright and Kind, Nice, Peace, Healing Goddess and Bids Abundance

38. Hlíf heitir, ǫnnur Hlifþrasa, þriðja Þjóðvarta, Bjǫrt ok Blíð, Blíðr, Fríð, Eir ok Ǫrboða

40. They offer salvation when men sacrifice to them in a high holy place; Never is the need so great that can come to the people that they cannot remove the need.

40. (Bjarga) svinnar, hvar er menn blóta þær á stallhelgum stað; eigi svá hátt forað kemr at hǫlða sonum, hvern þær ór nauðum nema

In the Sólarlióð stanza 79, we learn that the Vanir god of winds and waves, Njǫrðr, has nine rune-carving daughters. These are divided into one elder and one younger, followed by a formula of "Seven Sisters" which is repeated in another Edda poem, the Hárbarðsljóð, where the Seven Sisters are described as wild and independent yet very attractive women who were responsible for carving the ground out of the valleys and spin the threads of fate out of the ocean's sands. They are united in a mysterious "Linen White Woman" whose love is sought, found and then lost by Óðinn.

The daughters of Njǫrðr are obviously Norns, fate-goddesses, who like Norns carve the runes of fate, and they do it in the underworld where the soul arrives after death to receive the Norna dómr ["the judgment of the Norns"]. It seems obvious that the poet identified Njǫrðr with Aegir, and for good reasons; they are both lords of the "Ocean" and fathers of its "waves". Thus when we know that Freyia is the daughter of Njǫrðr and rules "the ninth world" of cosmos, where she also "chooses the chosen" like a head Valkyrie, we may suspect that she could also be the unifying face behind the nine sisters.

As above so below

Freyia is also the first *vǫlva*, the first Witch, the first teacher of the art of seiðr. The vǫlur operated as priestesses cunning in witchcraft and oracular divination in the Old Norse society, and were described as traveling around the land alone or in groups. Interestingly enough, we learn in Eiriks saga Rauda that the first Viking settlers on Greenland actually brought with them a coven of exactly nine vǫlur when they left Iceland, an obvious reference to the nine fate powers who together birthed creation and the fate of the world. The formula of a group of nine powerful priestesses who seem to be earthly incarnations of the nine cosmic mothers may have ancient European origins. In the year 44 AD, Pomponius Mela wrote a Description of the World where he mentioned Gallic oracular priestesses who held power over winds, waves and fate:

> *"In the Britannic Sea, opposite the coast of the Ossismi, the isle of Sena (Sein) belongs to a Gallic divinity and is famous for its oracle, whose priestesses, sanctified by their perpetual virginity, are reportedly nine in number. They call the priestesses Gallizenae and think that because they have been endowed with unique powers, they stir up the seas and the winds by their magic charms, that they turn into whatever animals they want, that they cure what is incurable among other peoples, that they know and predict the future, but that it is not revealed except to sea-voyagers and then only to those traveling to consult them."*

Apart from this reference to priestesses, there are also similar myths: From Greek mythology, we know about the nine muses, goddesses who inspire artistic and intellectual virtues in people. There are also the nine sisters divided into three trinities: *The Hesperides*, three nymphs who guard the apples of immortality.

The Charites, also known as the graces, who inspire virtues in people and who were associated with the Underworld and with the Eleusinian Mysteries, and then the *Moirai*, the three Fates. Apparently, the three by three ladies are interconnected and sometimes referred to as the nine daughters of Okeanus [the Ocean] and thus related to our nine daughters of Aegir the Ocean Lord.

The three Hesperides could also be known as three of the nine daughters of the ancient ocean deities Phorkys and Keto, the six others being the three Gorgons and the three Graiai. In Mircea Eliade's classic Shamanism, Archaic Techniques of Ecstasy, we hear that a Siberian people, the Buryat, believe that a shaman is initiated by several spirit entities from other cosmic dimensions, particularly the nine daughters of Solboni, god of dawn. The nine women are also the wives of Tekha, god of dance, fecundity and wealth, but nevertheless they will initiate the fledgling shaman through "amorous relations". Another Siberian tribe, the Teleut, believe that a shaman has a celestial wife in the seventh heaven, and that he also has relations to the nine daughters of Ülg n of the fourteenth heaven, who play a major role in the shaman's initiation, since they confer his magical powers. They also arrive when a person dies in order to take the soul and carry it to heaven. This is, as we shall see, a very similar function to that of the nine ladies of Edda lore, often described as Valkyrie.

Giantesses carry the ages and reside within the worlds

"...The Witch Within Wood carries the ages.
...elr Iviðia
aldir bera...

Hrafnagalðr Óðins st.1, Poetic Edda

The nine Daughters of the Ocean and Mothers of the Universe are associated with worlds. Worlds that preceded the present one. The iviðja, the Witch Within Wood, is said to "carry" or "bring forth the ages" in stanza 1 of the mysterious Edda poem Hrafnagalðr Óðins, as quoted above. The Witch Within Wood could well be identified as the ancient vǫlva who divines the story of the world in the Vǫluspá, a descendant or uniting power of the nine iviði who came before and birthed the present universe. They are the fate powers that carry each world, bringing forth time in space. In Old Norse myths, there is also concept of worlds that exist simultaneously, like different dimensions to the one cosmos. The poem Grímnismál lists twelve such worlds or dimensions. The ninth world is ruled by Freyia, who there both chooses and receives the chosen dead. It is also the realm where she "chooses the seating in the hall". The hall in question is called Folkvangr, which means "People Field".

I assume that the meaning of the goddess "choosing the seating" in the "People Field" is a way of saying that she rules the fate of human beings from the ninth cosmic realm. It is also a realm of death, where she chooses the destination for the souls after death, like in the judgment of the Norns. The three upper realms after Freyia's ninth dimension belong to Baldr and then to the immortal light elves who are higher even than the gods. When Snorri in the Gylfaginning claims that Hel, the goddess of the dead, rules supreme over "nine worlds", I take this to mean that the first nine dimensions of cosmos are mortal realms, ultimately ruled by death. The ninth of these mortal realms is the realm where some souls are "chosen" for immortality. The three higher realms are free from death. We ought to ask ourselves what kind of Ocean that really birthed the mothers of the Universe.

During the Viking Age, Aegir and Rán and their nine wave-stream daughters were undoubtedly perceived to be residing within all earthly oceans, but in Norse mythology, every earthly phenomenon has a cosmic mold: The body of the Ocean that is Aegir and the death-receiving wife Rán, who resides within him, birthing their daughters, is ultimately the cosmic Ocean from which the world tree sprouted. That heaven and the cosmos were associated with a primeval cosmic ocean is probably a very ancient concept. Rock carvings dating back to the Scandinavian Stone Age show images of a "world tree" and other universe symbols such as spirals, sailing aboard ships.

From the Bronze Age, similar carvings show the Sun goddess frequently traveling by ship through the heavens. The symbolic journey by ship across a mythical ocean is also associated with the journey between life and death well into the Viking Age. It seems very safe to say that the origin of the universe, long before the existence of Earth and its oceans, was imagined as an ocean since time immemorial. In the Vǫluspá, stanza 19, it is revealed that there is a sea beneath the ash, and it is identified as Urðarbrunnr, "The Well of Origin". It is from this water that the tree that is the universe sprouts, and this ocean that births the Norns, the goddesses of fate. The fate goddesses emerge, according to stanza 20 of the same poem, *ór þeim sal er und þolli stendr*, "from that hall which stands beneath the tree".

THE HIDDEN MEANINGS

To sum up my interpretation of all this information, we see that our world, the entire physical universal body, is symbolized in a threefold manner: By a world "giant" called Ymir [Sound] or Aurgelmir [Rock Matter Bellower], by a god called Heimdallr [Great World], and by a tree called Yggdrasill [The Old Steed], or Mjǫðviðr [The Mead Tree]. The universe is a living being and is "known" in the sense that it can be seen and touched, and is therefore presented as a male. It is also a seen result of other forces, which is why it is pictured as a "son". The origin of the visible, physical universe is a kind of water source filled with vitalizing liquid that is associated with waves and streaming rivers.

These are unknown, hidden and unseen, which is why they are represented as female. They are "mothers" of the present universe, a metaphor for unseen and hidden causes, associated with light, waves and streams, moving vibrating powers that bring the universe into growth and movement. When the mothers of the universe are described as "daughters" of the Cosmic Ocean, it means that they are the unseen and hidden results of the union between the physical (known and seen) body of the "father" Ocean with the unknown and unseen "mother" ocean [Rán, who receives the dead].

The Ocean is a metaphor for space, heaven and the source of the universe, his "wife", whose name means Robbery, is the suction power within this source, that which receives life back into itself. Ultimately, the goddess of death in her cosmic mold is also the grandmother of our world. While her husband is the seen body of the cosmic ocean, the physical Universe manifest, she is the unseen and unknown original moving power of the cosmos that draws all life back into herself, birthing the unseen "daughters" [the waves and streams that bring the present universe back into motion].

This very same metaphysical and philosophical concept is described in other terms by Snorri when he claims that the Well of Hel, Hvergelmir [Mill Bellower] is the source of all the "rivers" in cosmos. The same water source is also the place where all dead souls are ground (hence the "mill" part of the well's name) into oblivion and recycled into the Bellower and streaming rivers of cosmos.

THE SEED OF YGGDRASILL

There dwells in the valleys a knowledge seeking goddess
The Seed of Yggdrasill sinks down the Ash
She is of elf-lineage Her name is 'Stream Returns to Source' the oldest of the
Inner Ruler's the youngest child.

> *Dvelr í daulom*
> *dís forvitin,*
> *Yggdrasils frá*
> *aski hnigin;*
> *álfa ættar*
> *Iðunni héto,*
> *Ívallds ellri*
> *ýngsta barna*

Hrafnagaldr Óðins 6, Poetic Edda.

The existence of an unseen feminine moving power working within the masculine holding power (the holding together of a seen and physical aspect) is a concept repeated time and time again in Norse myths. On the human level, we will see that each human being, no matter the gender, has a female fate spinner within.

In the poem Hrafnagalðr Oðins, stanza 6, we hear that Yggdrasill the world tree, the universe, has a "seed" Frá Yggdrasills and that she is a "Knowledge-Seeking Goddess", Dís Forvitin. A seed is both a cause and a result of a tree, so that the goddess in question could be the "seed" of life and fate, the life potential that has produced and that is also produced by the universal body. This Seed "sinks down the ash", giving the impression that she is slowly making her way down through the universe and back to the source that birthed her (hence her name, as seen below). The Knowledge Seeking Seed of the Universe is subsequently identified as being alfa ættar "of elf lineage".

The elf in Norse mythology is a symbol of the soul of a person, so that the correct interpretation is to say that she is of "soul kind". She is then identified as Iðunn, the goddess of eternal resurrection. The name Iðunn is derived from the word iðr (f.sg) which means a stream that separates from the main stream and returns to the water source. Seeing the importance of water sources and streams as symbols of primeval creative powers, this makes a lot of sense. The realm of the immortals is significantly known as the Iðavellir ["The Fields of the Streams that Return to the Source"]. The unn ending in Iðunn's name is quite like the *inn* of Óðinn, indicating that she is The Stream that Returns to the Source. The stanza about the Seed of Yggdrasill culminates in the revelation that the Soul Goddess, the Knowledge Seeking Seed of the Universe, is both the youngest and the oldest child of Ivaldi ["The Inner Ruler"].

This reminds us of the nine daughters of Njǫrðr, lord of winds and waves, where the oldest and the youngest are named. The meaning of their names, "Ráðveigr [Council Drink] the oldest and Kreppvǫr [Returning Spring] the youngest", give obvious associations to the oldest Norn Urðr, whose Well of Origin is both the place where divine councils take place and the water with which she gives nourishment to the world tree, and to the youngest Norn Skuld, who represents the future and new beginnings. It should be clear now that the Norse myths subtly reveal the existence of a hidden, soul-like fate element, an animating and nourishing power existing within the physical universe. She is its source and its seed, the beginning and the end, mother and daughter of the world itself. She is the Witch Within the Wood, and each world before this one has had a similar Witch Within [the mothers of our world.] The concept of the "Within Wood" giantesses strongly suggest that the nine mothers have existed within nine previous worlds, which is possibly the reason why they are thought to be exactly nine in number. Curiously enough, the modern theory of vortex math offers a very interesting perspective.

According to this revolutionary mathematical theory a vortex of physical creative energy is produced through the interaction of exactly nine points working in unison. As far as I have understood, this is the basic cause of the universe itself, according to the theory. To suggest that the nine mothers of the universe have anything to do with an archaic version of vortex math is of course highly speculative, although we may assume that people back in the days had their geniuses just as we do today. I will not claim that it is so, but it is just too interesting not to mention in this context. Vortexes or not, we are starting to see a pattern where a male entity provides the physical and seen body while the female entity provides the unseen and non-physical spark of life and the movement of fate within the body.

This is the basic poetical mold for all mythical entities. Thus we can begin to look back at the First Beings of the previous section. If the vǫlva who tells the tale of the world from beginning to end is raised among the nine world-giantesses who preceded the present one, living within the matter of the previous physical universes, then she might also be the Witch Within the Wood of the present world tree, just as the "cow" Auðhumbla is the unseen cause of movement and expansion in the present physical universe called Ymir. It is time to have a look at what the name Ymir really means.

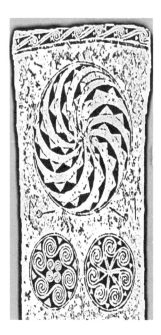

Painting on 6th century standing stone, Gotland, Sweden

2.4: IN THE BEGINNING WAS THE WAVE AND A BIG BANG!

THE FIRST COSMIC GIANTS

In the beginning was the Wave where Sound built was neither sand nor sea nor cool little waves,
Earth was not nor heaven above The Open Mouth of the Sacred Descendants was yet no growth.
Ár var alda
Þar er Ymir bygði
vara sandr né sær
né svalar unnir,
Jǫrð fannsk æva
né upphiminn,
Gap var Ginnunga,
en gras hvergi.

Vǫluspá st. 3, Poetic Edda

The Old Norse formula ár var alda is apparently very complicated, and usually refers to what was before, in the beginning. All the translations I have read offer slightly different variations. In Carolyne Larrington's English translation (1996) the interpretation is: "Young were the years". Ivar Mortensen Egnund's Norwegian translation (1905) goes "årle i old"["early in the old days"], whereas Ludvig Holm-Olsen's Norwegian translation (1975) is "i opphavs tider" ["in the times of origin"]. In his English translation of the Prose Edda, where the sentence is quoted, Anthony Faulkes (1987) suggested "it was in the beginning of time". Irmin Vinson, basing his English translation on Neckel and Kuhn's German edition, simply writes "years ago".

There are countless small variations, all emphasizing the basic meaning that this was something that happened a long time ago or even in the beginning of time. None of the translations, however, are the same simply because none of them are literal translation of the sentence: Rather than translating the sentence literally, one chooses a variety of the traditional understanding and opts for paraphrasing it into a more modern and entirely free rendering, "in the beginning", "in olden times" or "the years were young", or some of the other versions above. The reason for this, I believe, is that if translated literally, the sentence ár var alda, as it is, just does not really make that much sense grammatically. Some have tried to explain it to me. One anonymous YouTube commentator wrote: "Ár means year, and alda is the adjective form of alðr [age]. Years were old = a long time ago/in the beginning".

This describes well the common understanding of the sentence; the literal translation is thought to be "years were old", and is then paraphrased into something that sounds more accessible to moderns. However, if the plural years were old, I wonder why the verb form var is applied. If the "years were", we should have seen an Old Norse ár varu. The correct translation, if we are to understand the word ár as the neutral noun meaning "year", ought to be "the (singular) year was old". But, then we face the problem of the adjective form alda, which can only take that form if it is referring to (describing) a plural noun. Not content with just assuming that everybody before me have been correct, not content with assuming that just because it is traditionally understood in one particular way and that it has been understood that way for many years, I decided to try something else, and looked up my dictionary.

I quickly found that the word ár may mean "year" if it is a neutral noun, but that it could also mean an "oar" if it is a feminine noun and that as an adverb, it means "before" or "in the beginning". I remembered obsessing over this sentence already when I studied Old Norse in the university, and I remembered that one of my Old Norse professors pointed out that the sentence usually was translated with "in the beginning" because ár was an adverb. But then the word "year" is lost, and we have a really weird sentence going; "before was aged". I remember my professor just shaking his head as I pointed this out, strongly indicating that discussion was futile, this was what the sentence meant, and that was final.

I am too much of a rebel to accept that kind of argument, however, and I continued to fret over it until once more, a meaning appeared like a revelation, opening up fantastic possibilities. As an adverb, ár means "before", while var "was", indicates a singular thing that was before. Then it follows that the word alda is the noun that was before. Looking up the word alda as a noun, I found the feminine noun meaning "wave". I wrote my translation down for the first time, a direct, literal translation based on the idea that ár should be understood as the adverb. I got "In the beginning was the wave" (or "before was wave"). Maybe others have tried the same and dismissed the literal meaning of alda as impossible, but I immediately recognized that this was completely in tune with the general importance of waves and streams in the Old Norse mythical creation. I am aware that my interpretation is very controversial and at odds with what all other translators have decided before me.

I am aware that the expression ár var alda has been a fixed expression for a long time, meaning something like "back in the olden days", and that the noun ár could be understood as pluralis and that the verb might have been shaped relative to the intent or the context, although I have a hard time understanding the latter. I am aware that I could be wrong when I suggest that I have discovered the original meaning of the sentence, long forgotten due to the fact that people have not understood the essential importance of waves as symbols of cosmic energy movements essential to creation. But I can claim this; my interpretation is fundamentally correct if we look for a simple, direct, not paraphrased translation, if we look for one where the grammars actually make sense. No one can tell me that the sentence ár var alda cannot possibly be translated directly as ár [in the beginning] var [was] alda [wave].

The only real argument against my translation is the tradition of translating it otherwise. There have been countless traditional misinterpretations of many phenomena throughout the world's history. You do not have to agree with my interpretation of the sentence ár var alda in order to continue reading and appreciating my approach to Norse cosmology as a whole, but I believe that my unusual interpretation fits well with the whole and provides an even deeper insight into the minds of our ancestors. The following is an edited transcript of my first YouTube video of the series *Hidden Knowledge in Old Norse Myths* called: **Sound Waves and the Big Bang in the Poetic Edda**.

The fact that this is a transcript from an oral lecture accounts for the more casual language applied in this section. I am going to hold a lecture on the importance of translating names of characters and of place names in Old Norse myths in order to understand the coded messages that are in fact present in these myths; messages concerning philosophy, metaphysics and spirituality. Now, we know, at least scholars know, that the myths were told in a poetical style that was allusive and metaphorical. They were like parables, they were like riddles that had to be solved, deciphered so to speak. This was how the Old Norse people experienced them, as intellectual challenges that they had to solve. And yet, most mainstream publications about these myths leave us only with the impression that the myths were simple and straight forward A to B stories, like fairy tales.

I was actually taught in school that they were meant to entertain children and to explain natural phenomena that people at the time were too ignorant to understand. One of the reasons we are left with this impression is because the names of characters and the names of places in the myths are hardly ever translated. You see, today we tend to relate to names as just sounds used to identify someone or somewhere. But in Old Norse myths, as well as in, probably, other mythologies around the world, but I'll stick to my subject; the names of the Norse myths carry a meaning, and these meanings are the keys to understanding the underlying messages that are hidden within the parable that is the myth. These meanings were known to the Old Norse people, so if we want to get even close to what they perceived when they heard the myths being told, we have to try and understand these names. We have to try to make translations, and we have to keep in mind that the Old Norse peoples themselves perceived the myths as riddles that hid knowledge about the nature of the universe and our place in it.

So, I am going to give an example of how a translation may provide new insight into the minds of people who lived more than a thousand years ago. So let us talk about creation. Now, the creation of the universe is a topic in several Old Norse poems and myths, and I have chosen stanza 3 from the Edda poem Vǫluspá [The Divination of the Witch]. In the Vǫluspá this witch is telling the tale of how the universe was created, and the first line in this stanza is *ár var alda*. Now, ár [as an adverb] means "in the beginning" [or "before"], *var* [a verb] means "was" and *alda*, what does that mean? That is the noun. Now, I have never seen any translation of the Poetic Edda that actually translates alda as a noun. You will read "in the beginning of time" or "in the beginning of the ages" or "in the olden days", even, and this doesn't really make sense grammatically, for this is supposed to be the noun [and a singular noun, since the verb form var points to a singular noun]. So if you look up in an Old Norse dictionary, surely you have that lying around, you will find that alda as a singular (feminine) noun means "wave".

Maybe this is not being translated because it hasn't made sense to those who have tried to translate these poems, or maybe they just follow the [academic/linguistic] tradition, which is to say that this means "in the beginning of time". Whatever, alda as a noun actually means a big wave, and it makes sense because waves, rivers and streams were very important parts of the primeval forces in the cosmos. Vikings were a seafaring folk and they had many different words for waves. Alda is a big wave, like a tsunami [I may have been exaggerating there although that is how I envision it when I read the lines. Alda simply means wave, albeit not the small kind], then you have other kinds of waves, and one of these are the little waves, unnir (f.pl.).

Later on in the stanza, it is telling us first that "in the beginning was the (big) wave", and in the last lines of the stanza, it is telling us that there were no little waves, ne svalar unnir, "no cool little waves". So, there was a big wave, but not any small waves. Just a big singular one. OK, what are waves, and what are streams, and what are rivers? Well, if you read the myths as they should be read, as poetical metaphors, then waves, rivers and streams are movement, vibration so to speak. And that brings us on to the next line in the stanza: þar er Ymir bygði. Meaning, "that place where Ymir built". þar er means "that place where", and it is referring to the big wave of the previous line so that it is happening within the big wave: Ymir, inside the big wave, is building. Now, what is Ymir? Of course, we can look to what Snorri Sturluson [Prose Edda] says about Ymir.

He wrote this in the 13th century, and he said that Ymir was a giant, the first giant, and this giant was created by hot and cold streams (again) at the beginning of the universe, and he was nurtured by the four streams (again) coming out of the teats of the great cosmic "cow" Auðhumbla ["Abundant Brew Ingredient"], the Goddess, active force in the universe. He also tells us that this same cow, she brings forth Óðinn and his two brothers. So, these represent spirit, conscious intelligence and poetry, and these divine beings, entities, they killed Ymir and cut him into little pieces and from his limbs, they shaped the universe. What is Ymir? What does it mean? We do not have to look further than an Old Norse dictionary to find that Ymir must be derived from the masculine noun ýmr, which means a big (loud) "sound". So, inside the big wave, a big sound was building. This is getting interesting, it is becoming tempting to ask: "Did these people know about sound waves?" Maybe they did. It also makes sense out of the story of these three gods "killing" and cutting this giant into pieces, because if a sound, a big primeval, first, singular sound of the universe is "cut into pieces" it means that this big primeval first singular sound of the universe is cut into countless tunes, an orchestra of tunes that make up the universe. I have to stop here, but I just want to point out that this is not a fairytale. This is philosophy, this is metaphysics. I don't know much about physics but I think that they were onto something very close to the truth.

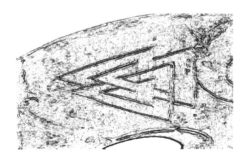

Contemporary Vortex glyph symbol with nine points and Valknutr symbol with nine points from Oseberg ship burial, Norway, 834 AD

WHEN FORTRESSES BURST IN THE GROVE OF BRIGHT SHINE

In the beginning was the Wave	*Ár var Alda*
when the eagles shrieked and	*þat er arar gvllo,*
sacred water poured down the	*hnigo heilog votn*
mountains of heaven;	*af himinfiollom;*
Then was the Sacred One of	*þa hafþi Helga*
powerful intent born to Fortress	*inn hvgom stora*
Battle	*Borghildr borit*
In the Grove of Bright Shine	*i Bralvndi.*

The first stanza in the Edda poem Helgakvíða Hundingsbani hin fyrri, quoted above, is an obvious reference to the creation stanza in the Vǫluspá, with some slight alterations. The great Sound giant, Ymir, is here replaced with the shrieks of eagles. The eagle is an important symbol of the original cosmic power.

According to Snorri, an eagle is seated in the top of the world tree, receiving "tidings" from the serpent that lies coiled at the roots of the tree through the squirrel-like messenger called Ratatǫskr ["The Wandering Container"]. The eagle is also mentioned as a power of death in the shape of the giant in eagle disguise, Hræsvelgr, whose name means "Corpse Swallower". He creates the mysterious "winds" of cosmos that may not be seen by human eyes, winds that ultimately bring the souls of the living back into his devouring beak.

The symbol of the death-eagle is very prominent in the myths and is a subject we will return to on several occasions, especially in Chapter 4, and then in a more in-depth study in Chapter 13. The poem of Helgi Hundingsbani elevates a human hero to the position of a First Being, probably a way of letting us know that his story and his actions are relevant on a cosmic level, a story that basically is about us all. Significantly, Helgi, "The Sacred One", undergoes a trial of initiation where he needs to overcome "giants" and other obstacles that symbolize hatred, anger, fear and greed.

Whirling sun disc symbol on brooch from Iron Age Denmark

The first lines of his first poem, however, also give an insight into alternative ways of describing cosmic creation. To sum it up, we have a wave, a shrilling sound, and streaming liquid pouring into the primeval cosmos. The physical universe, The Sacred One, is born from a symbolic mother, an unseen cause, whose name indicates a violent "battle" within an enclosed space (a "fortress"), all this happening in an enclosed place (the "grove") of intense bright shine. It is almost chilling to read such an account, written down in the Middle Ages and probably of a much older origin, nurtured by a relatively primitive Iron Age culture. An account which seems to almost accurately, though in poetical terms, seems to be describing the Big Bang that contemporary scientists believe is the origin of our universe.

The resemblance to modern scientific theory is blended with mythical concepts of fate and the weave of threads that make fate happen. The following will show that the fate goddesses and their threads are closely related to the unseen streams and waves that birthed the cosmos. After the birth of the cosmic Sacred One, the giantesses of fate that we discussed earlier (in Chapter 2.3) arrive on the cosmic scene, this time in the shape of Norns.

As such, they begin to weave the threads of fate from the very beginning, when all was still dark, as we see in stanza 2 to 4 of the first Helgi Hundingsbani poem:

2. There was Night in the settlement the fates arrived to the Descendant of Abundance did they shape time; (...)

2. Nott varþ i bo, Nornir qvomo, þer er auþlingi aldr vm scópo; (...)

3. They twisted with great power the threads of fate when fortresses burst in the Grove of Bright Shine; They prepared the golden thread (of divine fate) and beneath the Hall of the Moon [= Earth] they fastened it in the middle.

3. Snero þer af afli arlagþátto, þa er borgir braut i Brálvndi; þer vm greiddo gvllin simo oc vnd manasal miþian festo.

4. To the east and the west they secured its ends the High Descendant should own the land in between The Bright Shining kinswoman of Woman Beneath hurled towards the northern path one end, fastening it there, She bid it to hold forever.

4.Þer a/str oc vestr enda fálo, þar átti lofðvngr land a milli; brá nipt Nera a norþrvega einni festi, ey baþ hon halda.

The account given here clearly identifies Helgi with the First Cosmic Being and reveals to us the workings of the fates, who seem to be hurling, throwing, fastening and twisting the threads of fate throughout the universe. Knowing that the giantesses are also associated with cosmic waves, streams and glowing light, we may begin to grasp the true complexity of what fate, and what the "weaving and spinning" of fate, really meant to those who were initiated into deeper mysteries of Viking Age religion. In the middle of the great weave, born of the "Shining Grove" where "fortresses burst", the Descendant can rule his halls.

The "Descendant" is clearly a reference to the "son" of the giantesses. When he is called the Descendant of Abundance, it may be a reference to the "cow" Abundant Brew Ingredient, or simply to the fact that he is the descendant of previous worlds. He is the very embodiment of the present world, and also the cosmic mold for all living beings. Stanza 5 of the same poem reveals that neither the mother nor the son in the primeval cosmos knew of any grievances, it was a happy and powerful time. The son is called the dear one, and the maiden who birthed him has never known suffering. Then a cryptic remark follows, one about a raven sitting in a high tree hoping for food, saying to his raven companion that he "knows something".

The ravens are otherwise known as Óðin's two ravens, Huginn and Muninn, whose names indicate what they truly represent; The Thought and The Memory. These are the first sparks of consciousness in the new universe, and now they are "hoping for food", hoping for nourishment in this new world. Obviously, the nourishment in question is that which may promote the continued life of the conscious powers. The raven who says to the other that he knows something, continues by declaring that the newly born has eyes like a fighter and that he is a friend of wolves, concluding that the ravens of consciousness ought to be cheerful. The wolf is usually a symbol of desire, lust for life, and also the death that follows. Thus the newly born universe is a friend of desire and lust, the very nourishment for consciousness. The Helgi poem soon begins to concentrate on the human hero story, but the beginning is a valuable yet usually ignored source to Old Norse cosmo-genesis. The birth of consciousness will be dealt with more closely in the next Chapter, but for now, we shall continue to look at the primeval streams and sounds that made the young universe grow.

POISONOUS GASES, STREAMS OF HEAT AND COLD, MISTS, LIGHT AND SOUND VIBRATIONS

> *Powerful Head Veil said:*
> *"From the Stormy Waves dripped the poisonous drops they grew until they became a giant;*
> *From there have our lineages all come, together this is why they are so destructive."*
>
> > *Vafþrúðnir qvaþ:*
> > *«Or Elivagom*
> > *stvcco eítrdropar,*
> > *sva óx, vnnz or varð iotvnn;*
> > *þar ero órar ettir*
> > *komnar allar saman,*
> > *því er þat e allt til atalt.»*

> *Vafþrvðnismál St. 31, Poetic Edda*

Snorri Sturluson filled in the gaps of the Vǫluspá poem, drawing heavily on another Edda poem that deals with creation, the Vafþrúðnismál ["The Speech of the Powerful Head Veil"] [from váf (f.sg) = "head veil" and þrúðnir ["powerful one"]. Snorri's account is no less stunning in its description of a primeval pre-earth universe without order that was created by and consisted of hot and cold areas, poisonous gases and vibrational movement, as well as powerful sounds.

We can almost let his Gylfaginning account speak for itself (author's translation and interpretations of names):

"There were many ages before the earth was created that the Mist World [Níflheimr] was shaped. In its middle lies a well that is called Mill Bellower [Hvergelmir]. From it runs the rivers that are called thus: Cool, Battle-Desire, Life, Great Reciting Sage, Sheath and Shaker, Swallow and She-Wolf [Svál, Gunnþrá, Fjǫrm, Fimbulþul, Sliðr, Ríðr, Sylgr ok Ylgr], Bellowing [Gjǫll] is closest to the Hidden [Hel] Gates [i.e. the entry to death] (...)

But before that was that realm to the south of the world which is called End of the World [Muspell]; he is bright and hot, that heavenly lineage is flaming and burning, and it is impossible to travel there for strangers who do not have their homestead in that realm. Sooted/Sour [Surtr] is he called who sits there by the end of that realm, guarding his land; he has a flaming sword, and at the time when the world is about the end, he will come rushing and wreaking havoc, winning over the Aesir and burning up the entire world with fire. (...)

Some rivers are called the Stormy Waves/Age Waves [Élivágar]; when they had reached far away from their water sources, the poisonous cold streams within them hardened like the clinker that comes from a furnace, it turned to ice, and when the ice came to a halt and no longer flowed, the vapor that was rising from the poison froze on the top in the same direction and turned to rime, and this rime increased layer upon layer right across the Open Mouth of the Sacred Descendants [Ginnunga Gap]. The Open Mouth of the Sacred Descendants, the part that faces the northerly direction [i.e. the direction of Mist World (the underworld, world of the dead)], was filled with the weight and the heaviness of ice and frost, and there was a vapor and a blowing inwards from it. But as southerly part [the origin of heat and light] of the Open Mouth of the Sacred Descendants cleared up in the face of the sparks and molten particles that came flying out of the End of the World [Muspell].

Just as coldness and all grim things arose out of Mist World [Níflheimr], so everything that was close to the End of the World was hot and bright. But the Open Mouth of the Sacred Descendants was as gentle as the windless [i.e. deathless, without movement] sky. And when the frost and the blowing of the warmth met so that the cold particles thawed and began dripping, there was a quickening from these flowing drops due to the power of the source of the heat, and it took the shape of a man-being, and he was given the name Sound [Ymir]. The frost trolls call him Matter Bellower [Aurgelmir. Aurr = "sand", "gravel", i.e. basic matter], and from him are descended all the lineages of frost giants." If we look past the mythical language, the use of giants and mythical realms to disguise natural phenomena, we must realize that the account of the primeval universe in creation is based on the sincere, almost scientific observation of nature and natural powers. It may not be completely accurate seen from a modern scientific point of view, but is not that far from it.

The account of creation reveals a capacity for observation, rational thinking and a profoundly philosophical approach to reality. This thousand year old picture of a universe before our planet was born is one that poetically describe what we moderns have been brought up on. The concept of an early universe created by loud sounding bursts of hot bright matter into a cold and lifeless space, a place of acid, poisonous gases and mists, moved, perhaps, by vibrational energy and primeval physical matter that may take a liquid, gaseous ("misty") or burning form.

The first sparks of life are created through an alchemical process of cold particles that are heated up, a description that is not, I believe, very far from the truth. The capacity for an almost scientific approach to the natural world was always powerfully blended with the magical and spiritual outlook of the ancestors. Not long after we hear a detailed account of the various sorts of matter and vibration that create the primeval universe and the first sparks of life, we learn that the primeval Sound giant, who is also called Rock Matter Bellower [Aurgelmir], begins to generate new life in what appears to be a "funny troll" account. From the sweat produced inside his armpits, a male and a female being grow, and one foot mates with the other foot in order to produce a son; from these are the lineages of giants, or actually "hoar frost thurses" [hrímþursar] derived.

Of course, we do not know what armpits and feet may have symbolized, and the "sweat" could certainly refer to a kind of liquid energy produced by the primeval sound, so that it is more than likely that even this account has a rational observational base. What we are suddenly seeing is an early universe crammed with gigantic "hoar frost" entities, not a bad poetical description of early cosmic cold matter. The hoar frost giants are associated with rock matter through their progenitor, who they themselves know as "Rock Matter Bellower". The matter in question is *aurr*, meaning "sand" or "gravel", the particles that make up stones and rocks. The image of an early universe filled with hoar-frost covered rocks immediately springs to mind, at least in my case. This matter is clearly also produced from and shaped from a primeval sound vibration.

EVIL GIANTS, OR THE GUARDIANS OF WISDOM?

The first giant, which I by now will call the Sound of Matter, generate countless such hoar frost covered rocks, ancestors to the *iotnir* [the giants] of Old Norse myths. The word iotunn (m.sg), plural iotnir, does not originally mean "giant". It means "devourer", indicating their destructive and consuming nature. Snorri claimed that they were "evil". The "evil" of these ancient entities is probably partly due to Christian influence, where the world was divided into good versus evil powers, demonic versus angelic ones. Another reason is because the poem on which Snorri based his account, the Speech of the Powerful Head Veil, states that the giants were destructive in character because they originated from poisonous particles. However, if we look at the Old Norse description of the early cosmos, this entire universe came into being from poisonous particles and dangerous realms, which is in fact also scientifically the case; most of this universe is deadly, dangerous and poisonous to human beings, at least to our physical bodies. It does not really mean that the universe or the matter that makes it up is "evil". The reason why we should be careful about assigning the concept of evil to the giants is because the Edda poems clearly reveal that the giants actually appear to be ancient and knowledgeable guardians of sacred wisdom. The male giants continuously show up as guardians of esoteric secrets, the key to unlock illusion, and mostly as guardians of their own bright daughters, who in their turn are the providers of sacred wisdom.

The females of the species, the giantesses, known as the Gýgjur (f.pl.), Singular gýgr, are often referred to as beautiful, wise and benevolent, such as the nine maidens of the Mountain of Medicine who will help all men who pray to them and all women who climb their mountain by the Tree of Memory. The giantesses frequently overlap in function and identity with the Norns, goddesses of fate, and with the Valkyrie who lead the chosen souls to their immortal destination. In fact, the Edda poem Oddrúnargrátr reveals that the home of the Valkyrie sisters is at Hlésey, "The Wind-Shielded Island", which is the island of immortality and of Aegir, lord of the Cosmic Ocean and the father of the nine Witches Within Wood.

The giantesses are also the mothers and the wives of the gods, brought into the realm of Ásgarðr in their loving union with the Aesir, gods of consciousness, and given the assignation Ásyniur [the female Aesir]. We know for a fact that giantesses received prayer and sacrifice in the religious cults of Pagan Scandinavia. Giantesses were revered as the ancestral mothers of many clans and worshiped like goddesses. We do not know if the same was the case with the male giants, but it would seem that the giants represent obstacles rather than friends.

However, an obstacle is not necessarily an enemy. The giant usually represent an obstacle in the form of an inner quality that must be controlled, conquered and destroyed, such as greed, hatred, rage and fear. In that way, one could perhaps speak of "evil", although there are other stories where the giant seems to represent the master tester that confronts the initiate in order to see if he has reached the state of wisdom and eloquence that is necessary for him to gain entry into the lore of wisdom that the giant guards. As such, it would be entirely wrong to call the giants "evil". They are ambivalent, the creators of great illusions and potentially very dangerous, but mostly to the unworthy, to those who cannot decipher the riddles proposed by the illusions of the giants.

THE HIDDEN MEANINGS, A SUMMARY

To sum up my interpretations so far of, we see that our world, the entire physical universal body, is symbolized in a threefold manner:
1. By a world "giant" called Ymir [Sound] or Aurgelmir [Rock Matter Bellower]
2. By a god called Heimdallr [Great World]
3. By a tree called Yggdrasill [The Old Steed], or Mjǫðviðr [The Mead Tree].

The Universe is a living being and is "known" in the sense that it can be seen and touched and has a solid shape, an ordered form, and is therefore presented as male. It is also a visible and seen result of other forces, which is why it is pictured as a "son". The origin of the visible, physical Universe is a kind of water source filled with vitalizing liquid that is associated with waves and streaming rivers. These are unknown, hidden and unseen, which is why they are represented as female. They are "mothers" of the present Universe: a metaphor for unseen and hidden causes; associated with light; waves and streams; moving, vibrating powers; that bring the Universe into growth and movement.

When the mothers of the Universe are described as "daughters" of the Cosmic Ocean, it means that they are the unseen and hidden results of the union between the physical (known and seen) body of the "Father" Ocean, Aegir, with the unknown and unseen "Mother" Ocean: Rán. The Father Ocean is a metaphor for the origin of space, heaven and the solid matter source of the Universe, his "wife", whose name means Robbery, is the suction power within this source, that which receives life back into itself. Ultimately, the goddess of death in her cosmic mold is also the grandmother of our world. While her husband is the 'seen' body of the Cosmic Ocean, the physical Universe manifest, she is the 'unseen' original moving power of the Cosmos that draws all life back into herself, birthing the 'unseen' "daughters" [the waves and streams that bring the present Universe back into motion].

Some may compare this concept to the modern biological term osmosis, which is derived from the Greek words ἐνδον [endon: within], ἐξο [exo: outside], and ωσμος [osmos: push, impulsion] and which explains a particular movement of molecules. It has been pointed out to me that there might also be a similarity here to the more geometrical term torus. Being unable to adequately explain these scientific phenomena myself, I advise the interested reader to look up these terms on your own. This very same metaphysical and philosophical concept is described, in other terms, by Snorri when he claims that the Well of Hel, Hvergelmir [Bellowing Mill/Cauldron] is the source of all the "rivers" in the Cosmos. The same water source is also the place where all dead souls are ground into oblivion (hence the "mill" part of the well's name) and recycled back into the Bellower and the streaming rivers of the Cosmos.

THE LINEAGE OF THE GIANT SOUND

> *The Powerful Head Veil said:*
> *29. "Countless winters before the Earth was shaped*
> *The Fruit Bellower was born*
> *Power Bellower was his father, and he was fathered by Rock Matter Bellower."*

> *Vafþrúðnir qvaþ:*
> *29. «Orófi vetra,*
> *aþr veri Iorþ vm scopuþ,*
> *þa var Bergelmir borinn;*
> *Þrudgelmir var þess faðir,*
> *enn Aurgelmir afi.»*

As the first cosmic male trinity is introduced, as grandfather, father and son, we realize that it is all about sound, that is, primeval cosmic entities which produce sound on three subsequent levels. Of all the hoar frost rock giants that were produced by the first great cosmic Sound, only the youngest, Fruit Bellower [Bergelmir], survives into the present order of the universe. The official interpretation of his name is Mountain Bellower (from *bergr*: "mountain"), but I believe it could also be possible to translate it as Fruit Bellower (from *ber*, "fruit" and *gelmir* "bellower"). The symbol of the fruit would indicate the final and regenerating life- and growth- inducing product of the first Sound.

It would seem that creation happens in three roaring, resounding and bellowing stages: first, the Sound of Rock Matter, secondly, the Sound of Power, and thirdly, the Sound of Life Potential ("Fruit"). In the next Chapter, we shall analyze the myth of the first three Aesir, Óðinn, Víli and Vé, and how they shaped the universe. In the process, they destroyed all the hoar frost giants and parted the original Sound giant into pieces that gave shape to the ordered cosmos. In the cosmic massacre of the destructive rocks of the early universe, only one giant and his wife survived to become the progenitors of all later giants. The name of this giant is Fruit Bellower, representing the third stage of cosmic creation: the potential for life.

According to the Speech of the Powerful Head Veil, stanza 35, the couple hid within a luðr, which is sometimes translated as a "coffin" or as a "flour chest". The literal meaning of the word is a carved hole within a piece of wood which can be applied to a rocking bed, a sheath, a type of mill-house, the musical instrument we know as a lyre, a flour chest or a coffin for dead bodies. It is impossible to say which interpretation is the best, but what we know is that the object was a place within "wood", that is, within the physical body of the universe, where the giant and his wife could be stored until it was safe to emerge anew.

Within their storage chamber, the giant couple produced other giants in their image, and this is the first memory of the giant Vafþrúðnir [The Powerful Head Veil] whom we shall later discuss as an embodiment of cosmic illusion, one of the most tremendous opponents that the god of Spirit can possibly face. Another giant who is known to create great illusions (ginningar) that trick both men and gods, is the giant Utgarðsloki [Loki of the World Outside]. He is also known as Skrymir [The Bragging One / The Great/Loud Speaker]. Snorri tells the story of Loki of the World Outside, revealing that he is greater and more powerful than even the greatest Aesir god, and will easily trick them, although he will not let on how close they get to tear down the veils he create either.

It is likely that the Great Speaker and the Powerful Head Veil are one and the same giant. Another giant that appears and who may represent exactly the same as the ones above, namely the illusions of cosmos that makes it so difficult to navigate for the powers of conscious intelligence, is Þrymr [The Drummer] (who steals Þór's hammer). We also have Hymir [The Hymn], who owns the cauldron that is big enough to contain all the "mead of Aegir". The mead of Aegir is the liquid of the Cosmic Ocean, obviously, of which the giant Aegir is an embodiment. Aegir is the grandfather of the universe, not a descendant, yet the difference seems to be inconsequential.

The giants, it would seem, are all created from the same original cosmic mold. Aegir is also known as Gymir [The Hider (of something)]. What he hides is his daughter Gerðr [Enclosure] who guards the ancient and precious mead of memory, poetry and wisdom. She is the source of illumination on earth and may thus be compared to the Sun on a physical but also on a spiritual level, a secret, unseen (female) source of light and wisdom that is hidden away by the ancient giant of illusion. Another father of a mead-serving giantess is Suttungr [Heavy with Drink], father of Gunnlǫð [Invitation to Battle], who married Óðinn but was left weeping behind in the underworld. What we are seeing is actually countless ways of describing the same basic mold of the same basic power: The giant that produces the sound vibrations that become matter, and also the illusions that constitute the world.

THE DEATH-MOTHER GIANTESS

As to the giantesses, I have already described their role in creation and how they turn into fate goddesses and Valkyrie, and also into the wives of the gods. The collective giantess powers may be malevolent and benevolent at the same time, and appear in numerous guises, and are also known to come together in a unity. This unity may either appear as their leader, their oldest sister, or their mother. The ancient mother giantess is the unseen power that first created movement and thus life in the universe, and she is also the receiver of all that ever lived. In the myths, she appears in various guises. She may be Rán ["Robbery"] who "robs" people of their lives, receiving the dead in her woven "net" of ultimate fate. She may be Hel "The Hidden One", who receives the dead in the northern realm called Mist World [Níflheimr] that gave birth to life.

Like Rán, who gives birth to the life-giving streams of the cosmic ocean, Hel is also two-sided, described as black as a corpse on one side, bright as a young maiden on the other. This double-faced giantess frequently appears in the myths in two separate forms, a bright maiden and a terrible ogress. Another giantess who is molded in the same death-mother giantess is Skaði, who we shall hear more about in Chapter 4. The terrible ogress aspect of the death-mother giantess appears numerous times in the Edda, and in absolutely all the initiation stories, where she is the embodiment of the fate of death in oblivion, although she possesses the ultimate knowledge that the initiate needs in order to unite with the other aspect, the bright maiden who is the embodiment of the fate of resurrection and universal memory.

This giantess is often associated with wolves. In the Edda poem Hyndlulióð, "The Song of the She-Wolf", she appears as the wolf-riding ogress Hyndla [The Bitch/ She-Wolf]. She rides a pitch black wolf, keeps other male wolves in her "stable", and lives in the realm of darkness within the underground caves of Earth. She possesses the ultimate knowledge about the interconnectedness between all the beings in cosmos, a secret knowledge she reveals to young Óttarr, a disciple and lover of Freyia. In the poem, Freyia represents the benevolent maiden aspect who offers the mead of memory so that young Óttarr may remember all that the ogress taught him. The ogress herself declares that she will not offer anything but oblivion once the young man returns to life after his initiation. The wolf-riding giantess also appears in Snorri's account about the funeral of Baldr, where only the ogress Hyrrokkin [The Fire Spinner] riding a wolf and having serpents for reins, has the power to push the ship of Baldr towards the realm of death.

In the poem of Helgi Hiǫrvarðsson, an unnamed giantess riding a wolf, using serpents for reins, appears as a fylgja [a guardian spirit] who in this case is an omen of death. The she-wolf theme appears in the creation stories as well. In Snorri's account of the nine rivers that come out of the Mill Bellower, the well of death, one of them is called Ylgr, another word for she-wolf. In the poem Hyndlulióð, stanza 37, the giantess Imð, also meaning she-wolf, is mentioned as one of the nine mothers of the universe. The wolf gives associations to desire, lust, greed and hunger, seemingly negative qualities but also qualities that are at the basis of life itself, the instinct for survival at all costs. This is also what leads to death, another perfect image of the ambivalence of the power that birthed the universe and receives all life back into her ocean womb.

The ogress of death and oblivion appears in other guises as well, usually associated with rocks and caves, often called "bride of the rock cave", and is behind the figure of Sínmara [Pale Mare] who guards the key to the chest that contains the Thorn of Life, locked behind nine iron locks. The association to rock may belong to the realm of Earth, which came into being at a later stage. Giantesses are certainly associated with the shaping and the inner powers that move the Earth. However, I think that the rock is also a clear reference to the rock giants of the early cosmos, the descendants of Rock Bellower. If we keep in mind that the female element usually will represent the unseen animating power within the seen manifesting shape, the male element, we might begin to think of the Bride of the Rock as such an animating power existing within the "cave", the inner element of movement that hides within the still matter like a witch within the wood.

Image on Viking Age standing stone, Skåne, Sweden, a woman riding a wolf with serpents for reins.

2.5: AESIR, THE FIRST INTELLIGENCE

Before the sons of Storage Chamber lifted up the lands they who shaped the precious Middle World...

> *Áðr Burs synir*
> *bjǫðum um ypðu,*
> *þeir er Miðgarð*
> *mœran skópu;...*

Vǫluspá st.4, Poetic Edda

In the last Chapter, we saw how creation happened in three stages. Let us make a quick summary: First, there was Sound, built from hot and cold streams meeting within the Wave and also born from it and nourished by it. This giant Sound was also known as Rock Matter Bellower or we could say the Sound of Matter.

From the Sound of Matter came all the hoar-frost covered rocks of the early cosmos. The second stage was Power Bellower, the sound (or vibrational energy) of Power. This stage was the visible cause of the third stage, the Fruit Bellower, the vibrational energy of potential Life. The potential Life hid with his "wife", the fate spinning, animating and nourishing element within, inside an enclosed space within the "wood", the matter, of early cosmos and became the source of all matter, all illusion and all the things that giants and giantesses represent in the Norse cosmos. Yet at this early stage, life was nothing but a potential hiding within matter. In this early era, there was no sand, no sea, no cool waves, no earth, no heaven above, and no plant life of growth. Only the Sound that built within the Wave was. In one version of the Vǫluspá, stanza 3, the second line which describes Ymir the Sound is replaced with the words þat er ekki var [that which was nothing]. The fourth stanza in the creation poem introduces the first Aesir gods.

They are called the "sons of Búr". In the Gylfaginning, Snorri explained that Búr was another giant who lay dormant within the ice of Mist World [Níflheimr] even before the universe was created. Mist World is the realm of the dead in Norse mythology, but it was also the first realm in cosmos, the cold and misty sphere in the northern part of the still Open Mouth of the Divine Lineages. The melting frost from Mist World provided the matter that created Ymir, the first Sound. All this was described and analyzed in the previous sections of this Chapter on cosmology. When the world of the dead is also the world of primeval creation, from which the new universe sprung, and we know that nine worlds were thought to have existed before the present one, it is logical to assume that Mist World contains the remnants of earlier, dead worlds.

From Mist World all the streams of cosmos emerge, cold streams that when melted create new life-energy from the frozen remains of earlier worlds. Within these frozen remains there is a hibernating being, an entity which may have been hibernating since the death of a previous world, and that entity is called Búr or Búri. The name is often translated as "father" although it has also been suggested that it could be derived from the verb búa ["to inhabit"] so that the name means "inhabitant". However, we should not ignore the word búr, which means a special chamber or house where food was stored on the farms, or where maidens lived together.

I am quite certain that the original meaning of the name Búri must be the "Storage Chamber", a rather elegant way of suggesting an enclosed space where the potential for life is stored, much like the chamber within which the Fruit Bellower and his wife are said to have hidden. The concept of a space where life potential is stored within a dead cosmos is repeated in a vision about the future and the end of the present universe. Apparently, life will again be stored within a closed space, awaiting the birth of a new world, as is said in the Speech of the Powerful Head Veil [Váfþruðnismál] stanza 45:

The Powerful Head Veil said:
"Life and Heritage-Tracker shall both be hiding within Treasure Memory's Holt
The morning dew they shall have for their nourishment and from them new ages shall spring

> *Vafþrúðnir qvaþ:*
> *«Líf oc Leifþrasir,*
> *enn þa leynaz mvno*
> *i holti Hoddmimis;*
> *morgindaggvar*
> *ðav ser at mat hafa,*
> *enn þaðan af aldir alaz.»*

The Storage Chamber of a previous cosmos lays dormant beneath the ice of Mist World, but is brought forth and revived by the hot tongue of the cow Auðhumbla, the first animating and heating element in the cosmos. While nourishing the giant Sound with her streams of "milk", she also feeds herself from the frosty remains of the dead worlds. The image of an ultimate cosmic power that both brings forth life and consumes it, in fact consumes dead life remains in order to create new life, is repeated in the image of the "cow", the universal mother, as she licks forth the dormant Storage Chamber. This is another aspect of the first stage of cosmic creation, when Sound was building.

The second stage of cosmic creation involved the so-called "Power Bellower".

Much more is not said about that stage, but just like the appearance of the Storage Chamber [Búr] mirrors the appearance of Sound [Ymir], so the appearance of the Power Bellower [Þrúðgelmir] is mirrored in the appearance of a "son" and his "wife" within the Storage Chamber. Snorri informs us that the son of Búri the Storage Chamber is Bórr, usually translated as "son". The word borr in Old Norse, however, actually means "drill". Is this an energy that "drills" itself out of the Storage Chamber? The "wife" of this Drill, meaning its fate-creating, animating inner power, is called Besla, and her name is certainly derived from the word besla ["to beat"] or ["to hammer"]. The image of something drill-like that is being hammered or beaten through the walls of a cosmic storage chamber springs to mind, and yields results: the third stage of creation, when the potential for life is born into a long-dead world.

ÓÐINN, VÍLI AND VÉ

The third stage of creation, mirroring the birth of Fruit Bellower, is the birth of the three Aesir, born by the hammering, beating Besla of the Power Bellower's era.

1. One is called Óðinn, a name that is derived from the word óðr, meaning "spirit", "poetry" or "frenzy", and the suffix (h)inn, which signifies "the". Óðinn is The Spirit, The Poetry and The Frenzy.

2. The name of his brother Vé means "Sacred Space", as in a sacred grove, a temple, a shrine or a sanctuary. It could also mean "Awe".

3. The name of his brother Víli means "Will", as in intent and passion. The three names of Óðinn as well as the trinity of Óðinn and his brothers provide a mould for all other male Aesir, all of whom fit into the meaning of either Spirit, Poetry and Awe, or Frenzy and Will and Intent.

At the same stage of creation where "Fruit" is born [the potential for life] the first sparks of intelligence, awareness or consciousness is also born. It appears in the shape of a mysterious Spirit, a sacred space making Poetry and an intent, passion and will driven Frenzy. As soon as they come to Earth, we see that the Spirit is the source of breath and inspiration, the Poetry is the source of thinking, conscious intelligence, and the Frenzy is the source of vitality, color and heat. These first sparks of cosmic consciousness are the powers that "lift up the lands" in the poem Vǫluspá, giving shape to the sacred Middle World.

In the previous section we saw how the Sacred One, an image of the universe, received his place in cosmos from the Norns who let him stay "in the middle". We also saw that Ymir, representing Sound, was hacked into pieces by the three Aesir brothers, who shaped the world from his limbs. Obviously, this is not really a funny story about three guys who slaughtered a giant and made a world out of his body parts. It is a parable about how the original powers of cosmic consciousness, the spiritual, mental and emotional powers, arranged the universe and gave it order by dividing the one original sound into an orchestra of tunes. As the stars and planets begin to appear in cosmos, the three brothers attend the first þing, **the sacred Parliament, which is to be regularly held at the Well of Origin** [Urðarbrunnr] in the southern realm of the new cosmos ever after.

All the powers of cosmos attend this sacred Parliament, as it is said in the Vǫluspá stanza 6:

Then all the powers went to the fate-chairs the sacrosanct gods to discuss this; to Night and her kind did they give names there would be a Morning and a Midday, Afternoon and Evening to reckon the years.	*Þá gengu regin ǫll á rǫkstóla, ginnheilug goð, ok um þat gættusk; Nátt ok niðjum nǫfn um gáfu, Morgin hétu ok Miðjan Dag, Undorn ok Aptan, árum at telja.*

With the exception of the information about the "sons of Búr" who lifted the lands and shaped Middle World, no further introduction of the Ásyniur or other Aesir is actually given in the Vǫluspá, and we are not actually told exactly what powers attended the "fate-chairs" of the first Parliament. The audience was obviously expected to already know the myths behind. Snorri's account does not provide all the information we need, but in later accounts, we hear that both Aesir and Ásyniur (the female Aesir) attend sacred Parliament, as it is said in the Vegtamskvíða, stanza 1:

Then the Aesir [gods] went all of them, to Parliament and the Ásyniur [goddesses] all to have their say and about this did they speak, the powerful rulers...	*Senn vorv æsir allir a þingi ok asynivr alla a mali, ok vm þat ræðv rikir tifar...*

THE FIRST ÁSYNIUR

We do not know the origin of all the Ásyniur, but they seem to have come from different cosmic tribes, joining the rank of Ásyniur through relationships with the Aesir. Two of them, the Sun goddess and the Earth goddess, were introduced in stanza 4 and 5. Knowing that these cosmic bodies, a star and a planet, were counted among the Ásyniur by Snorri, it follows that we have been introduced to two Ásyniur appearing in connection to the actions of the first Aesir. The Sun and the Earth are followed by Night in stanza 6, introductions that we will discuss in the next sections of this Chapter.

Night is described as a giantess and not counted among the Ásyniur in Snorri's list, yet she is said to be the lover of Óðinn and the mother of the Ásynia Earth (as well as the mother of Day). As such, Night may be regarded as an Ásynia as well. If we are to follow the Vǫluspá chronology, the Sun, Night and Earth are the three first Ásyniur. Sun [Sól] and Night [Nǫtt] are easily recognized as a formula that repeats itself in Norse mythology all the time; the typical pairing of the goddesses into a bright and a dark aspect, a hot and a cold, a southern and a northern, a life-giving and a death-inducing aspect. We saw that in the beginning of creation, there was a southern realm of heat and brightness, and a northern realm of cold and darkness.

The cow-goddess from the south, her "licking tongue" and the streams associated with her melt the dead matter of darkness and creates new life. The realm of darkness, we know, is ruled by another female, called Hel, which means "Hidden", a power obscured by the darkness of the unknown. Sun and Night together repeat the image of the bright heat-giving goddess and the hidden power of darkness. The Sun goddess is said to have come from the southern realm of cosmos where also the Norns have emerged. Since the goddesses are usually paired, as described above we may assume that Night is the opposite of the bright Sun from the hot south, and belongs to the cold northern realm of misty darkness: Hel. Night probably represents the body of darkness that well describes most of the universe. Snorri reveals that the Earth goddess was born from this darkness; Night was her mother, and Óðinn was her father: the union between Spirit-consciousness and the dark unknown of the universe brought forth the Earth.

The birth of our planet repeats the ancient formula once more: Just as the body of the world giant Ymir, the Sound, is nurtured by the heat-cow and made to grow out of the darkness, just as the dead matter of the misty dark is revived by the heat from the south, just as the first conscious powers are born out of the cold darkness that is being lit up and heated, so the Earth is born out of Night, and nurtured by Sun. The ancient image of the maiden, mother and crone appears to be present in the first three Ásyniur. Beginning with the mysterious Night crone, the nourishing Sun mother and the young Earth daughter, although the mythical and cosmic roles could seem to switch eternally, the Earth being so clearly a mother, the Sun often appearing like the maiden, the Night being a mother as well as an ancient crone, and the lover of Aesir. In the next Chapter, The Steeds of Heaven, we will discuss the cosmic bodies in greater detail.

Bronze Age rock carving, Norway "She threw her right arm around the Door of the Steeds of Heaven"

THE GOLDEN AGE OF PRIMEVAL COSMOS

Apart from Óðinn and his brothers, we do not know the origin of the other Áss-gods either, unless they are described as his sons by Frigg. The only thing we do know is that the appearance of the first three brothers leads to a time-space reality within which all the various male and female powers of cosmos may come together to make order out of chaos. It is, apparently, a happy time, as the Vǫluspá continues its account of the early actions of the first conscious entities in cosmos (stanza 7-8):

*7. The Aesir met up at the Field of
Streams Returning to Source they
raised altars and high temples, they
set up their forges, they forged the
precious treasures, they shaped
tongs, and they made tools.*

*7. Hittusk æsir
á Iðavelli,
þeir er hǫrg
ok hof hátimbruðu,
afla lǫgðu,
auð smíðuðu
tangir skópu
ok tól gǫrðu.*

*8. They played checkers in the
meadow they were joyful then they
were content and knew no lack of
Gold [= Divine Wisdom]...*

*8. Tefldu í túni,
teitir váru,
var þeim vettugis
vant ór gulli;...*

This happy and carefree time, when the first spiritual and mental entities simply enjoy their shaping of the cosmos, is ended when three powerful giant maidens appear. The three giantesses are not identified directly, since the poet assumed that the audience would understand who the ladies were. They were powerful, and they were all-knowing, and there were three of them. We are reminded of the three first cosmic ladies, Night, Sun and Earth, and we are reminded of three equally "powerful and all-knowing" ladies who rule the laws of the universe and the destinies of lives. The three Norns, the goddesses of fate. The appearance of these ladies immediately leads to the Aesir creating the "dwarfs", a phenomenon that we shall discuss further in Chapter 2.9.

THE HISTORICAL ORIGIN OF ÓÐINN

Bronze Age, Spear God-rock carving

Of the entire cosmic family of early Aesir: Búri and his son Bórr, his wife Besla and their three sons, only Óðinn was actually worshiped as a god during the Viking Age. The first concrete evidence for his cult is from the Roman Iron Age, where he was obviously associated with the Roman god-planet Mercury and the Celtic hero-god Lugh (of the Tuatha de Danaan). He was strongly associated with his wife, a mead-serving, wand-wielding oracular goddess of Celtic origin, Rosmerta [The Great Provider]. His cult spread, and as Wodan, married to Frija, the god was important at least in the German tribe of the Langobardi before he became a most important deity in great parts of Scandinavia. Several Danish and Norwegian clans regarded him as their ancestor. When Snorri and the Edda poets elevate Óðinn to the position of All-Father and king of the gods, it is the result of a long development.

It was by no means always so. What deities were the most important to the various Germanic tribes varied over time and from tribe to tribe, even from clan to clan. The place-name material in Scandinavia certainly shows that there were many deities who are of little importance in the myths that were left to us, but who were very important in the local cults. The god Ullr, for example, had sanctuaries across all Scandinavia since time immemorial, but is hardly even mentioned in the myths. To many Scandinavians, both Freyr and Þórr were more important than Óðinn. Snorri offers a clue as to the development of the pantheon when he gives us a version of Aesir history where Þórr is the divine ancestral father, and Óðinn his descendant, instead of the other way around. Various kennings show that Freyr was certainly considered the King of the Gods and the King of Men by many. His name is also a title, meaning Lord or Sovereign.

Óðin's position as ancestral father to very powerful clans is an important reason why he was elevated to such a distinguished position during the Scandinavian Viking Age. Another reason was his importance as the god of poetry, we all know that the poets created mythical poems and thus were the transmitters of the sacred lore known to us. To them, Óðinn was certainly the most important male god. I also believe that Óðin's elevation to the position of ancestral father with very strong Pantheist elements originated from his importance in the spiritual path of initiation related to the mead of knowledge, memory and poetry that I will show was such a crucial part of Old Norse Paganism. The fact that Óðin's brothers and parents are of so little importance in the religious cult is an indication that they are poetical inventions, serving only one function: to make a point; to transmit a message about the cosmos.

The message is that Divine Consciousness was born from the revival of the memory of a previous universe, and that it took three basic forms; Spirit, Mind (Poetry/Awe) and Passion (Frenzy/Intent). These are the powers that give a time-space reality to cosmos, the powers that put an end to the chaos of primeval rock giants covered in hoar frost, and who provide shape, form and order out of the original Sound of cosmos. The Aesir are present in almost all subsequent myths, playing the role of divine consciousness in its various aspects, the power that gives shape, space and time to the world, as well as the power that plays itself out within each individual spark of awareness, within each individual life. When the Aesir pantheon is gradually introduced through myths, we see that all the Aesir belong to similar spheres. There is Bragi, the god of poetry, who obviously corresponds with the Poetry, Awe and the Sacred Space. There is Týr, the god of war, who obviously corresponds with Frenzy and Intent.

THE THREE QUALITIES OF BEING

Anyone who studies the Edda may at some point notice that a trinity of gods keeps appearing at crucial moments in Cosmic mythical history, and that the members of the trinity vary somewhat. Óðinn is almost always present in the trinity, while the two others tend to change names. Sometimes, they are familiar gods such as Þórr and Loki, at other times; they are characters that seem to have been created by the poet.

In the latter cases, it is obvious to me that they have a metaphorical significance which we can pinpoint if we look at the meanings of their names or at their function in the myth. More importantly, we should, I think, look at the trinity as a sort of poetical formula. One that always tells us more or less the same thing. I once sat down and compared all the trinities that appear in the myths, and made what I think is a discovery about the message of the male trinity formula in Norse myths.

Let us begin with the one character that always is a part of the trinity. Óðinn. His name is derived from the Norse word óðr, and the suffix, *hinn*. Hinn means "the" (masculine form), so Óðinn is the óðr. And óðr has, interestingly enough, three meanings:

1. The first meaning is "spirit". That meaning makes a lot of sense, seeing as Óðinn is the god of inspiration and otherworldly knowledge; also he is the giver of breath.

2. The second meaning is "poetry", which also makes sense, since Óðinn is the god of poetry.

3. The third meaning of the word óðr is ecstasy, or frenzy. This, again could refer to at least three things:

3a. The state of mind that a warrior enters during battle, the sort of concentrated rage or frenzy that is probably necessary to endure a battle situation. The Norse warriors apparently induced a state of ecstasy as a matter of ritual before a battle; rumors have it that they ate mushrooms. In any case, Specially initiated warriors of Óðinn would call this state of mind berserkargengu, which means to go berserk, and that word, ber-serk, means Bear-clad, that they sort of became like bears, like animals, fearless.

3b. The second meaning is sexual ecstasy and frenzy, the state of mind you need to. I think you get what I mean. It is about passion, life-force, and vitality.

3c. The third is spiritual ecstasy, the state of mind that a shaman, for example, enters in order to alter reality and move into other worlds.

Thus we have three basic meanings of the name Óðinn, with various associations. This is important when we want to look at the trinities in which Óðinn partakes. I will say now, in advance, what I realized after having studied and analyses each of the trinities. When Óðinn partakes in a trinity, Óðinn, wearing that name, always represents the first meaning in the trinity, namely spirit. The other two meanings, poetry and frenzy, is always adopted by two other gods. Let us look at the first trinity that appears: Óðinn and his two "brothers", Vé and Víli.

None of these were gods that actually were worshiped; they are purely poetical metaphors, so let us look at the meanings of their names:

➥ Vé means sanctuary, temple, a holy enclosure, and it could also mean awe, as in the awe we might feel when realizing the immensity of the Universe. I think this corresponds with poetry, because poetry was sacred, the mead of poetry was held in the vé, the sanctuary, of Earth, and poetry requires certain awe. This correspondence of Vé with Poetry is strengthened when we look at the brother, Víli.

➥ Víli literally means "will", as in "intent", and I think that concept corresponds fairly well with the aspect of Óðinn as ecstasy, the frenzy, the rage, the passion. You cannot really have intent or a will without passion.

Basically, these three "brothers", the qualities of spirit, poetry and passion, constitute the cosmic powers that make sure that the Universe falls into order. The next trinity that comes along consists of the three gods Óðinn, Hænir and Hlóðurr, as described in the Vǫluspá stanza 17 and 18:

17. Until Three (males) came
out of this crowd benevolent and
powerful
Aesir towards the Hall (Earth) they
found on the shore of miniscule
power
Askr and Embla (man and woman)
Without destiny

17. Unz þrír kvámu
ór því liði
öflgir ok ástkir
æsir at húsi,
fundu á landi
lítt megandi
Ask ok Emblu
örlöglausa.

18. They owned no breath/spirit
they had no mind/poetry vitality
nor heat nor beautiful colors;
Breath/Spirit gave Óðinn
Mind/Poetry gave Hænir
Vitality gave them Hlóðurr and
beautiful colors.

18. Önd þau ne áttu,
óð þau ne höfðu,
lá né læti
né litu góða;
önd gaf Óðinn,
óð gaf Hænir,
lá gaf Lóðurr
ok litu góða.

This is the first time that the Holy Trinity appears on Earth. We have already established that Óðinn in the trinity represents spirit. This corresponds very well with the fact that Óðinn is the one who offers breath and spirit to men and women. The second god, Hænir, offers thought. The meaning of the name Hænir is often thought incomprehensible. It actually means "chicken" (plural form). Norse linguists have really struggled with that one, and the only thing that I can think of is that the name is a humorous way of referring to the chattering, clucking sounds of thought within our heads. Hænir represents in my opinion exactly what he offers, thought. In the Ynglinga saga, it is said that Hænir was advised in all matters by the giant Mímir. Mímir means Memory, and that memory always advises thought is a very reasonable and descriptive poetical metaphor for how the mind works. Hænir is also referred to as the quick god, and the long-legged god, meaning that he can move far and quickly. Just like thought. The Ynglinga saga reveals that Hænir is not really that smart. He looks beautiful, appears to be the perfect chieftain, but he is completely dependent on Mímir, on his memory, to be able to rule at all.

This is one of many Norse myths that point out the limitations and illusions of the mind. Most of these myths feature Þórr. The third god in this trinity is Hlóðurr. He offers vitality, life force and beautiful colors to humanity. His name means Heat. I think we could safely say that Hlóðurr corresponds with the original trinity, taking the place of Víli, the intent, the passion. Hænir, the thought, the mind, corresponds with poetry, and with Vé, with awe. In another "Primeval Earth" myth, found in the Skaldic 9th century poem Haustlǫng, almost the same trinity that appears, with Óðinn and Hænir representing Spirit and Mind. But benevolent Hlóðurr, The Heat, has been replaced with the ambiguous god Loki.

Loki is a character that fits perfectly with the third meaning of Óðin's name; the frenzy. His is the blind rage, the intense passion, and the ability to alter consciousness and move into other worlds. His name might mean the fiery one, and he is often referred to as fiery. In the same poem, Loki is also referred to as Sagna Hrærir, the "Mover of the Stories". Indeed, what creates motion in the Universe and the necessary conflict of any drama is passion, intent. In this particular story, Loki, in a state of terror, offers the goddess of immortality, Iðunn, to the Eagle of Death in exchange for his own life at the present.

This short-sighted move (Passion is not famous for rational consequential thinking) leads to all the gods growing old very quickly, so Loki has to restore the goddess in order to save all their lives. The event leads to the entry of the giantess of death among the gods. It is perhaps illustrative that both Óðinn the spirit and Hænir the mind are completely passive in this story, because if Spirit and Mind had been engaged as much as Passion, all this drama may not have happened in the first place. Next time the trinity appears in the Edda, we see, again, Óðinn as Spirit and Loki as Passion. But the place of the mind, the thought, is now taken by Þórr, the Thunder god. He has two servants, a boy and a girl. The boy is called Þialfi, and is, just like thought itself, known to be able to move very fast.

His name means "Holding Together", a function of the mind which holds together mental reality. The girl is called Rǫskva. I have found two alternative meanings to that name, both making sense. The one is "to dig up", which is a quality of the mind; the other is to "mature" which is also a quality of the mind. In this story, the gods, all three of them together, Óðinn, Þórr and Loki, attempt to gather the divine red gold of a dwarf called Andvari [Alert Spirit]. Gold is a metaphor for divine light and wisdom. So this is about waking the spirit to a divine state. The trinity formula repeats itself in Norse cults. In the Viking Age temple of Uppsala, three male gods were worshiped next to the Dísir.

Again we have Óðinn, representing spirit, and then we have Þórr, representing mind, and thirdly, we have Freyr, a god whose huge phallic symbol was represented on standing stones all over Scandinavia, and who was the lord of growth, fertility, and, indeed, passion. At Uppsala, there are still three huge burial mounds in the vicinity of where the old Temple was situated. The mounds are traditionally thought to be the graves of these three gods. Looking to the myths again, we could look at the Aesir pantheon. We have seen how both Loki and Freyr could represent the passion of Óðinn. Þórr could represent thought, and thus poetry. Surely, there is always a lot of epic action around Þórr. We could look to other gods. Next to Óðinn, we have Bragi, the god of poetry, and Týr, the god of war. Obviously, the god of poetry is an incarnation of the poetry aspect in Óðinn, and the god of war corresponds with the frenzy, with passion.

We could also replace the Aesir trinity with the Vanir trinity: Heimdallr, whose name means Great World and who seems to represent the entire Universe, who hears all and sees all, would in my opinion represent the spirit. Then we have Njǫrðr, who controls the waves and the winds, if you look at it metaphorically, it is a good way of describing mind. And finally you have Freyr, who is clearly a candidate for passion, ecstasy and frenzy. There are also corresponding opponents to the divine trinity, such as the three monsters who will destroy the world at Ragnarǫk. Then, Spirit must face Greed in the shape of a great wolf, Fenrir. The Thunder god must face the raging Middle World Serpent, who coils itself around the known world (as a border against the unknown), a symbol of the mental structure.

Finally, Freyr, representing growth, fertility, passion and nature, must give way to the poisonous flames of Surtr [Sooted One]. When I first uncovered this trinity formula of spirit, mind and passion, I started to see it all throughout the Edda, even in the heroic poems, such as the characters of Sígurðr Vǫlsungr [Victory Origin of the Magic Wand Lineage], Gunnarr [Battle Warrior] and Hǫgnir [The Thinker] of the Niflungar [Mist Lineage]. I also find it very interesting that when going back to rock carvings from the Bronze Age in Scandinavia, three male gods dominate the picture, together with the central sun disc, the sun goddess with whom they all seem to seek, interact and unite. It is interesting that just as in the Edda thousands of years later, there were in the Bronze Age three gods, who all seem to interact with a goddess, the sun goddess, just as the three gods of the Norse pantheon all attempt to reach the golden, glowing maiden, whose arms illuminate the lands and the seas, and receive her drink of immortality.

A CHART SHOWING THE STAGES OF CREATION:
AS EXPLAINED IN THE EDDA

HLÉSEY [WIND-SHIELD ISLAND]
LORD: AEGIR/HLÉR/HYMIR/
GYMIR
[TERRIFYING/OCEAN/WIND-
SHIELD/HYMN/HIDING]
ASSOCIATIONS: GIANTS

•*Hræsvelgr [Corpse Swallow-
er]*
•*Þiazi [Slave Binder]*
•*Skrymir [Great Speaker]*
•*Utgarðsloki [Outer World
Loki]*
•*Fjǫlsviðr [Much Knowing]*
•*Vafþrúðnir [Powerful Head
Veil]*
•*Þrymr [Drummer]*
•*Surtr [Sooted One]*
Associations, Gods:
•*Þund [Thin Mist Óðin's oldest
name]*
•*Njǫrðr (steers winds and
waves)*
•*Búr [Storage Chamber, sleeps
in Hel before resurrection]*

*Functions: Steering Winds
and Waves, Creating Illusions,
Guarding/Hiding Knowledge,
Experiencing Fate*

*Masculine: Holding together,
steering, shape, form*

*Essence: Death/Immortality,
Ruling Fate, Beyond Illusion*

Element: Air, Fire

Animal symbol: Eagle

COSMIC OCEAN (URÐARBRUNNR/FENSALAR
[WELL OF ORIGIN/MOIST HALLS])
LADY: RÁN [ROBBERY]/THE FIRST WITCH
ASSOCIATIONS, GIANTESSES

•*Urðr [Origin (past, beginning)]*
•*Angrbóða [Bids Rage]*
•*Eldi [Old Age]*
•*Sínmara [Pale Mare]*
•*Nǫtt [Night]*
•*Amma [Grandmother]*
•*Gríðr [Truce]*
Associations, Goddesses:
•*Frigg/Saga/Hlín [Love, History, Tranquility]*
•*Nerthus (receives the dead in water)*
•*Mardǫllr [Great Ocean a name of Freyia's]*

*Functions: Birthing Winds and Waves,
Receiving the Dead, Weaving/Carving Fate,
Knowing Fate*

*Feminine: Free flow, movement, chaos,
vitality*

Essence: Death/Rebirth, Ruling Fate

Element: Water, Rock (matter, earth)

Animal Symbol: Serpents

Ægisdætra Aegir's Daughters(Plural)

•Nine Daughters of Aegir and Rán
•Nine Worlds
•Nine Witches Within Wood
•Nine Mothers of Heimdallr [Great World]
•Nine Valkyrie
•Three Giantesses, Three Fates, Three Lineages (Divine, Elfin and Dwarfish)

Associations: Dísir, Nornir, Fylgjur, Hamingjur, Valkyrie, Gygjur, Ásyniur

Functions: Creation, Creativity, Vitality, Birth, Life, Fate, Death, Flow, Energy, Life Force, Death Force, Knowledge (Guardians of Divine Knowledge, Challengers of those who know fear and guides for those who seek on the Path of Initiation, Resurrection, Enlightenment)

Cosmic Symbols: Streams, Waves, Light, Gold, Rivers

Animal Symbols: Swans, Ravens, Wolves, Serpents, Southern Heat and Northern Cold

Essence: Nine points of Creation: Nine Worlds, Nine Underworlds, Nine Nights of Death, Nine Nights of Initiation

The Giant's Daughter (Singular/Two-Faced)

North: Dark, Cold Death, Oblivion	South: Bright Warm Life, Memory
Hel [Hidden] Grim Face	Hel [Hidden] Bright Face/ Nanna
Hyndla [She-Wolf]	Freyia [Lady Sovereign]
Skaði [Injury]	Iðunn [Stream Returns to Source]
Gerðr [Enclosure] Bride of Giants in Hel	Gerðr [Enclosure] Bride of Gods at Barri
Gunnlǫð [Invitation to Battle]	Linen White Maiden, Wife/ Sister, Twin's Maid
Hrímgerðr [Frosty Enclosure]	Sváva [The Sleeper] from Sefafjǫll [Soul Mountain] Sígrún [Victory Symbol]
Guðrún, Grímhildr, The Bride of the Rocks	Sígrdrífa/Brynhild [Victory Snowfall/ Armor Battle]
Unnamed Ogress, mother of Atli [Intender]	Oddrún [Edge Symbol]
Sínmara [Pale Mare]	Menglǫð [Invitation to Blend]
Animal Symbols: Wolves, Serpents, Ravens	Animal Symbols: Cats, Swans, Small Birds, Hawk, Falcon

Functions: Death, Life, Fate, Guardians of Divine Knowledge

SECOND STAGE OF CREATION (POETIC EDDA)

1. Ymir/Aurgelmir [Sound/Rock Matter Bellower] Yggdrasill [Old Steed] -cosmic matter	1.Búr/Búri [Storage Chamber] Heimdallr [Great World] – cosmic awareness	1.Auðhumbla/Urðr [Abundant Brew Ingredient/Origin] The Witch in Vǫluspá Seed of Yggrasil [Iðunn] life-source
2.Þruðgelmir [Power Bellower]	2.....Bórr [Drill]	2.....Besla [Beater, Hammerer]
3.Bergelmir [Fruit Bellower] •Potential for Physical Life •Giants and Giantesses •Vibration/Sound •Androgynous, Known and Unknown	3.... Óðinn, Víli ok Vé [Spirit, ...Intent and Awe] •Conscious Intelligence •Spiritual, Mental and Emotional Awareness •Aesir •Masculine Known	3....Nǫtt, Sól ok Iórðr [Night, ...Sun and Earth] •Three Fates/Destiny •Past, Present, Future •Time/Death/Life •Feminine Unknown

THE THREE PRIMEVAL WORLDS (PROSE EDDA)

Muspellheimr – The World of Heat (South)	Níflheimr – The World of Cold Mist and Darkness (North)	Ginnunga Gap – The Open Mouth of the Sacred Descendants
Inhabitants: Surtr [Burnt], Sínmara [Pale Mare], Sól [Sun], Auðhumbla [Abundant Brew Ingredient – the Cow] Characteristics: Heat, Fire, Poison, Acid, Waves and Currents of Heat – nobody who is not a native inhabitant may survive Prophecy: Surtr is destined to destroy Freyr, the god of fertility and growth	Inhabitants: Búri [Storage Chamber, grandfather to the Aesir, revived by the heat of the Cow Auðhumbla] his son Bór [Drill] and daughter in law Besla [Hammerer] Characteristics: Cold, Darkness, Mist, Death.	Inhabitants: Ymir [Sound], created by the cold streams of the North and the hot streams of the South, origin of the iotnir ("giants"), nourished by the rivers of milk running from the Cow Auðhumbla. Characteristics: Stillness, Silence, Sudden Growth of Sound and Waves The Central Origin of the Universe and Miðgarðr - the Middle World

THE THREE ROOTS OF YGGDRASILL AND THEIR WELLS (PROSE EDDA)		
Ásgarðr – The Court of the Aesir (South)	Níflheimr – The World of Cold Mist and Darkness (North)	Utgarðr/ Iotunheimr – Outer Court/Giant World (East)
Inhabitants: Aesir, Ásyniur, Vanir, Nornir, Valkyriur, Einheri (dead warriors)	Inhabitants: Hel [Hidden, queen of the dead], Hræsvelgr [Corpse Swallower, the giant eagle who creates the winds of the world], Níðhǫggr [Waning Biter – the great serpent], dead souls, wolves, serpents, hounds, ravens, witches, Baldr, Nanna	Inhabitants: Giants and giantesses, thurses, Mímir, Aegir, Rán, Daughters of the Ocean, and many more
Cosmic Water source: Urðarbrunnr – The Well of Origin (the place of the norns)		Cosmic Water source: Mímisbrunnr – The Well of Memory
Places: Valhǫll and other abodes of the gods, the Bright Hall of the Maiden	Cosmic Water source: The Well of Hel called Hvergelmir [Bellowing Cauldron/ Mill],	Characteristics: Danger, Chaos, Illusion, Hidden Knowledge, Power, Sound, Vibration, Magic
	Characteristics: Cold, Darkness, Mist, Death, Rock, Caves, Nine Dimensions, Cold Streams and Rivers, Hidden Knowledge	Places: The Tree of Memory, The Mountain of Medicine, Wind Shield (Immortal) Island, the Bright Hall of the Maiden
	Places: Hel's High Hall as well as the Bright Hall of the Maiden	

CHART: THE HOLY TRINITY OF AWARENESS		
Spiritual: Breath, Inspiration, Spirit	Mental: Thought, Mind, Poetry, Awe/Wonder (Stupidity, Limitation)	Emotional: Intent, Will, Vitality, Passion, (Desire, Greed, Jealousy, Hatred)
Óðinn [The Spirit]	Óðinn [The Poetry]	Óðinn [The Frenzy]
Þríði [Third]	Hár [The High One]	Jafnhár [Just as High]
Óðinn [The Spirit]	Muninn [The Memory]	Huginn [The Intent/Passion]
Óðinn [The Spirit]	Vé [Awe/Sacred Space]	Víli [Intent/Will]
Óðinn [The Spirit]	Hænir ["Chicken"] Thought-giver	Hlóðurr [Heating One]
Óðinn [The Spirit]	Þórr [Thunder] protects the known	Loki (vs. Logi – Flame)
Óðinn [The Spirit]	Bragi [Great] - Poet	Týr [Beast/God] Warrior
Óðinn [The Spirit]	Geri [Doer]	Freki [Hungry One]
Baldr [Courageous]	Váli [The Choice]	Hǫðr Blindi [Strife the Blind]
Fenrir [Greedy One] Destruction, consumes Spirit (also corresponds with the Emotional)	Miðgarðsormr [Middle World Serpent] Forms border around the known	Surtr [Sooted One] The greater fire, burns out all life
Víðarr [Expansion] the Silent	Forseti [Front Seat] Justice	Ullr – Warrior, Hunter
Heimdallr [Great World] Sees, knows and hears everything (Kvasir)	Njǫrðr – rules winds and waves	Freyr [Lord Sovereign] rules growth, fertility, sexuality

2.6: THE STEEDS OF HEAVEN (SUN, MOON, STARS)

*41. I saw the Sun and it seemed to me that I
was seeing a glorious deity; to her I bowed
for one last time in this world of time*
41. Sól ek sá,
svá þótti mér,
sem ek sæja gǫfgan guð;
henni ek laut
hinzta sinni
aldaheimi í.

*Bronze Age rock carvings,
Bohuslän, Sweden*

*Sólarlióð, The Song of the Sun, stanza 41,
Poetic Edda*

As soon as the first cosmic intelligences attack the hoar frost rock giants and divide the original sound into many tunes, the ingredients of our present cosmos emerge on the scene: Stars, Sun, Moon and Earth. They begin swirling around without knowing neither their places, nor their powers or their possessions. But when the three Aesir begin their shaping of the precious Middle World, the heavenly bodies begin to act. These bodies seem to emerge out of Night, the darkness of the unknown. In this Chapter, I will go through what little is known about Old Norse astronomy from the Edda sources. There is very little that is known to us. I have heard that some people have methods of tracing a sort of astro-theology in ancient myths, but I have neither the knowledge nor the inclination to do so.

I think that myths may possible be interpreted differently on different levels of understanding, that they may be describing different things on different levels, so that one level of understanding does not exclude the other. When there is mention of "seven sisters", some will see a connection to the Pleiades, whereas I will focus on the function of these sisters as they appear in the myths; the shapers of reality within, the powers of fate within that each individual needs to woo. The mythical level that I have been drawn to explore is always the level that speaks to human beings on a spiritual level, what the myths may mean to our personal development and how they may have provided guidance to the initiates seeking wisdom. However, it is not impossible that the myth-makers and wisdom keepers regarded humanity as microcosmic replica of macro-cosmic powers, and that the movements and properties of cosmic bodies may be allegorical of movements and properties within the individual.

NIGHT AND ALL HER KIND

Hail Day,
Hail the sons of Day,
Hail Night and her sisters!
   Heill Dagr,
   heilir Dags synir,
   heil Nott oc nipt!

Sígrdrífumál, st. 3, Poetic Edda

There is hardly any information at all given about the stars or planets in the Edda lore, except the few lines above. As we saw in the previous section, there is mention of "Night and all her kind", [Nátt ok niðjum] to which the sacrosanct powers of the first cosmic Parliament "gave names" in order to count time, resulting in the settling of stars in their appropriate constellations. "Night and all her (female) kind" [Nott ok Nipt] is also mentioned in the Edda poem Sígrdrífumál, where the words are part of a prayer formula that invokes all the significant powers of the universe. Night is described as a dark giantess by Snorri, mother to the boy Dagr [Day], a way of saying that a dark and invisible quality is the unseen (female) cause of the bright and visible (male) quality.

Night is the daughter of a giant called Norr of Narfi [Narrow], a brother of Hel and the Fenris-wolf.

This is a powerful suggestion as to the identity of Night's father (i.e. knowable cause). The brother of Hel and Fenrir is the Miðgarðsormr, the Middle World Serpent, who personifies the border between the worlds, the border between the known and the unknown. This border, which serves to define the known against the unknown, is the knowable cause of the unknowable cosmic Night. Night marries one Naglfari [Nail Traveler] whose name is identical to the ship of death that will be steered towards Earth at the time of Ragnarok. This ship is built from the nails of the dead. Nails obviously symbolize something, but we cannot know what it symbolized to the Vikings. Despite this grim relationship, Night is not only the mother of Day, a symbol of brightness, but also the mother of Earth, our own ancestral mother. As such, Night was the lover of Óðinn, who supposedly fathered Earth. She is indirectly described in the Edda poem Hymiskvíða, st. 8, where Earth's mother (Þór's grandmother) is said to possess nine hundred heads:

The son (Þórr) found Grandmother to be a terrifying sight; she had heads nine hundred (heads)...
   Mogr fann Ammo
   mioc leiþa ser,
   hafði haufda
   hvndrvð nío...

The mysterious Night of the nine hundred heads may be an impersonation of the darkness of space that descends over our planet every night, her "kind" and her "heads" may be the inhabitants of this darkness, possibly the stars and other seen and unseen powers of cosmic darkness. Any absolute evidence for star-knowledge is not obvious from the lore. Yet we know that the planet Venus was called Friggjarstjarna ["The Star of Frigg"] a natural adaption of the Greek-Roman concept of the planet Venus and its connection to the goddess of love. We also know that the sun was called Dagstjarna ["The Star of Day"]. in the poem Sólarlióð [The Song of the Sun], suggesting that the medieval Norse poet knew that our sun is another star in cosmos. It is time to have a look at the shining Day Star.

THE SUN GODDESS

4...Sun shone from the south on the rocks of the hall then the Earth began to grow the green growth.	4....Sól skein sunnan á salar steina, þá var Grund gróin grænum lauki.
5. Sun hurled from the south together with Moon She threw her right hand around the Door of the Steeds of Heaven Sun knew not where she owned her halls Moon knew not what power he possessed the stars knew not where they owned their places.	5. Sól varp sunnan, sinni Mána, hendi inni hægri um Himinjódyr; Sól þat ne vissi hvar hon sali átti, Máni þat ne vissi hvat hann megins átti, stjǫrnur þat ne vissu hvar þær staði áttu.

Vǫluspá st. 4-5, Poetic Edda

The Vǫluspá stanzas above also give some interesting images of an early Sun hurling from the blazing heat realm of the southern cosmos [Muspell], shining upon the "rocks of the hall" so as to make the Earth begin to grow life. The Sun also throws her right hand around the Steeds of Heaven ["Door of the Steeds of Heaven"]. It is indeed very tempting to suggest that the "Steeds of Heaven" are the planets and satellites of our solar system, claimed by one of the "hands" of the Sun. When she shines upon the "rocks of the hall", it is equally tempting to suggest that the rocks, like the steeds, are the planets, and that the "hall" is space. Of course, the Rocks of the Hall may very well be the rocks of the young Earth as well.

This is how it is usually interpreted, since "hall" can be a metaphor for the Earth goddess, like when she is called the "Moon's Hall" in poetry. As such, we see a vision of the young Earth goddess as a barren hall of rocks that begins to breed when the Sun goddess shines her warming rays upon her, just like the primeval World of the Dead began to yield life when the hot tongue of the great cosmic cow began to feed on it. The Sun was a goddess to the Old Norse people, and as far as we know, if we are to follow the chronology of the Vǫluspá, she is the first Ásynia, a female Áss (the even older Night, who is related to the Aesir through her relationship with Óðinn is still considered a giantess.

She was a goddess that may have been far more prominent in older times than she is in the Edda lore. During the Bronze Age, she was probably the most important deity in all Scandinavia, as testified by countless rock carvings showing the symbol of the Sun goddess, often in illustrations where the Sun goddess is obviously worshiped with ritual dance and acrobatics. Her spiral and disc symbols frequently appear as driving a chariot across the heavens, or steering a ship. Her symbols continued to show up in jewelry and art, especially on burial monuments, well into the Viking Age. It is my impression that her symbol is almost as prominent on 5th-to 7th century Pagan burial stones in Sweden as the cross is on Christian burial stones later, relative to the amount of stones raised, of course.

The only other icon that seems to repeat itself on burial stones to an equal degree is the mead-serving maiden. The burial iconography of the Pagan era could be a very interesting study in this regard. The Vikings knew the burning goddess as Sól, and believed that there were two sides to her; she might be the bright red golden Sól of the gods, or she may be the dark Gygjar Sól [The Sun of the Giantess] who shines her darkness deep within Hel. This two-sidedness, obviously inspired by her journey into darkness every night, has provided a mold for Norse goddesses and female powers ever since, as we see reflected in Snorri's description of the death-goddess Hel in the Gylfaginning:

"She is pitch-black on one side and has bright flesh on the other, so that she is easy to recognize, terrible and scary she is..."

As the Sun of the gods, however, she is counted among the Ásyniur and married to a "man called Glen", her husband a poetical invention meaning "Opening Between Clouds", suggesting that the underlying message is that the great lady is married to the quality that lets her shine through the barriers. Another name for the Sun goddess is Alfrǫðull-"Elf Shine". Since elves are associated with souls, we may wonder if Sun is also associated with souls, and how. We do not know, but there is an interesting parallel in Sami mythology, where the Sun Maiden, Beaivi Nieida, is the mother of all souls. The souls come to the Earth mother in the shape of sun rays, where they are received by Mâtarâkka [The Ancestral Mother or Earth]. One of the Earth's three daughters is responsible for placing the souls within the wombs of females. Since the souls emerge from a female source, all souls begin as female as they enter the womb, but half of them are changed into males by another of the Earth's three daughters.

The Sami concept about the Sun Maiden and the souls of the living is part of a very ancient Finno-Ugric tradition reaching all across northern parts of the Eurasian continent. The Finno-Ugric cultural groups may have originated as a "Proto-Uralic" cultural group. By researching Finno-Ugric mythologies from the Sami in the West to Siberian in the East, one professor, V.V. Napolskikh (1992) found that it is possible to detect a common base to them all, a basic, Proto-Uralic cosmology that must be extremely ancient, reaching back at least five thousand years. Central in this basic cosmology stands the "Winter-Land of the South", a Southern realm ruled by a female being or a couple, who receive the migrating birds in winter.

While the Land of the Dead is situated in the North, a dark and frozen land, ruled by the "Death Mother", the realm of the South is placed in the warm land of the Sun. This Sun-Land or Winter-Land is always characterized by a lake or spring, a water source that gives new life and rejuvenation to the migrating birds. All new souls are born in this land; in fact, the water birds, especially swans and geese, symbolize the human souls. We may know this because these are still living mythologies employed as spiritual maps for contemporary shamans. The connection between swans, geese and human souls is indisputable. The same birds are strongly associated with the world of the dead.

This age-old Finno-Ugric cosmology is actually remarkably similar to the way Snorri describes the world of the Norns [fate goddesses] by the Well of Origin. This realm is placed in Heaven, and the Edda myths frequently refer to this place as the South. Its natives, the fate-goddesses and the Valkyrie, are repeatedly referred to as the "Southern Ladies" or the "Southern Goddesses" (alternately "southern-red" or "red-golden"). Opposed to this Southern Heaven is the North, where Níflhel is situated, ruled by the grim lady Hel, another striking similarity to Proto-Uralic Cosmology as described above. Like in Proto-Uralic cosmology, the water of the Southern land is ruled by a female, the Norn Urðr [Origin], and has the effect of rejuvenation and restoration of life on the whole world. It is also associated with swans, just like the fates and valkyrja of the Edda often wear swan hides when they travel.

I think that the widespread and ancient Proto-Uralic use of the swan or water-bird as a metaphor for souls that are reborn in the Southern water is extremely interesting as an analogue to the Norse fate-goddesses and valkyrja, well-known to possess swan hides, and associated with the rejuvenating Southern lake of Origin, from which they originate. Snorri relates how all human beings possess an individual fate-goddess who rules the fate of the individual. This idea is confirmed in the Poetic Edda. Could the Norse fate-goddesses of the individuals actually be analogue to human souls? We will look more closely at this issue in section II.11. In Proto-Uralic cosmology, the Southern land of rejuvenation is usually ruled by a female entity which is closely associated with the sun.

She is called "the Golden Woman of the South", "Sun Mother", "Sun Woman", "Geese Mother[i.e. mother of souls]", "the Old Woman of the South" or simply the "Mother Goddess". She appears as both an old woman and as a young maiden at the same time. By her life, and soul-renewing lake, where birds and souls submerge themselves before being reborn, due to the magical power of that water, there is also usually a tree, the Tree of Life. The birds and the souls are seated in the branches of this tree until the woman of the Southern Lands send them back into life. The Norse equivalent of this seems obvious. First of all, Sól, the Norse Sun goddess, just like the fate-goddesses, comes from the South, and lives in heaven.

This is basically the same place as where the fate-goddesses live, in that place in heaven which is called the Well of Origin [Urðarbrunnr], the water source by which Ásgarðr [The World of the Aesir] is actually situated according to Snorri. We must conclude that the Norse divine realm of the Aesir and that of the fates are identical, and that this realm is also closely associated to the Sun. The Sun, on her side, seems to be a strong influence on all other goddesses. The Norse Dísir [female spiritual entities of all kinds] are in fact always associated with gold, brightness, illumination, light and rays. Her association with souls is not clear, but it is interesting that one of her names is Alfrǫðull [Elf Shine], and that the Norse concept of elves may have an original connection with human souls. In the sagas, ghosts of ancestors are often referred to as "elves".

If this is so, Elf-Shine the Norse sun goddess translates to Soul-Shine, which corresponds to the Sami sun goddess Beaivi Nieida [The Sun Maiden] who produces the souls that are received by Mâtarâkka the Earth Mother. Souls transmitted to Earth in the form of sun rays. And if the Sun and the Well of Origin is basically the same place, it is interesting to note the parallel between the Sami concept of soul and the Norse concept of fate-goddesses that descend from that "well" to appear at the birth of each child. But we will hold that thought for later. Bronze Age Rock Carvings, Scandinavia, showing ships beneath a burning Sun and the Sun aboard ship, the realm of the fate-goddesses and the well of the oldest fate Origin are related to the Proto-Uralic myths of the Sun mother and the well of souls? I would cry a roaring yes!

Not only are the myths perfectly comparable, but there has been regular and intense contact between the Norse population and the Finno-Ugric populations for thousands of years. It is generally thought that some of the first people to populate Scandinavia after the last Ice Age were the ancestors of the surviving reindeer-hunting Sami populace that still forms a large ethnic minority in all the Scandinavian countries, as well as in parts of Russia bordering to these countries. The Sami language and ethnic culture and mythology belong to a Finno-Ugric family. The Sami and the Norse populations lived on the same peninsula for the last five thousand years at least.

*Bronze Age Rock Carvings, Scandinavia, showing ships beneath a
burning Sun and the Sun aboard ships
- Nationalmuseet i København*

Although the Sami were suppressed by the Norse populations since the late Viking Age, their religion almost totally crushed by the Church and the authorities during the 18th and 19th century AD, we know that the interaction between the culture groups before that was mostly a matter of peaceful trading, and that intermarriages happened quite frequently. When Norse Paganism was suppressed and the professionals persecuted, many Norse people began consulting Sami shamans instead. This respect for Sami shamans may have older origins as well, since there is a story of how Queen Gunnhild, wife of Eirik Blood-Axe, was an apprentice to Sami shamans in her youth. Apart from the obvious Sami connection, Norse people also had contact with people in Finland and Siberia for thousands of years. The people who lived in Scandinavia before the proto-Norse language became dominant may very well have been Finno-Ugric.

It seems safe to say that for thousands of years, a Proto-Uralic cosmos, with its Northern Underworld and its Southern Heaven, its Sun-Mother and its concept of souls originating in the Sun and coming to earth in the form of water-birds and sun-rays, dominated the Scandinavian Peninsula. I think this may very well be the Stone Age origin of an important part of Norse cosmology that became the cornerstone of Bronze Age religion, with the Sun goddess in the center of an important public cult attended to by kings and rulers. This Bronze Age religion was an important root foundation to the later Viking Age lore.

As to the survival of the ancient Sun goddess, the physical Sun goddess may have given way to other more abstract representations, or she may have provided a model for other goddesses. I have already mentioned the fate-goddess Urðr, "Origin", as an obvious power shaped in the ancient mold of the Sun mother. There is the mysterious sky goddess Síf, whose name only means "female relative", a good way of suggesting her importance as a sister, and whose hair is made of pure gold. Like the Sun, she is threatened by a destructive giant (Loki). Like the oldest fate, Urðr, she is associated with oracular divination: Snorri claims that she was a clairvoyant sibyl. Then there is Iðunn (see Chapter 2. 3, The Seed of Yggdrasill and Chapter 5), who is said to be of "elf-kind", just like the Sun goddess, and who is a "seed" of the universe, perhaps like a star.

There is the giantess called Gerðr [Enclosure], whose bright "arms" illuminate the lands and the seas even when she hides away in the underworld, a wife of Freyr the god of growth and fertility. There are the Valkyrie who shine with rays so bright that they "illuminate air and sea", who are called "golden goddesses" and "sun-bright ladies", and there is the lead Valkyrie, the goddess Freyia, who weeps tears of red gold and who owns the Brísingamen, "The Necklace of Flames", and who has the ability to be rebirth herself in fire.

THE MOON GOD (AND ÞÓRR, FREYR AND HELGI)

22. Óðinn said:
"Tell me the second if your
knowledge is sufficient and you,
Powerful Head Veil, knows:
where the Moon comes from he
who travels over people and Sun
the same?"

23. Powerful Head Veil said
"His name is Time-Traveler he
is Moon's father and for Sun the
same
Through heaven they must pass
every day to count the years of
the age

22. Óðinn qvaþ:
«Segðv þat annat,
ef þitt eþi dvgir
oc þv, Vafþrúðnir, vitir:
hvadan Máni kom,
sa er ferr menn yfir,
eþa Sol iþ sama?»

23. Vafþrúðnir qvaþ:
«Mvndilfori heitir,
hann er Mána faþir
oc sva Solar iþ sama;
himin hverfa
þa/scolo hverian dag
aldom at ártali.»

Vafþrúðnismál, st. 22-23, Poetic Edda

Máni [Moon] is hardly prominent in the Edda lore, although the Vǫluspá mentioned his "power": Before the Aesir provided places and names for all the steeds of heaven, Moon knew not yet "the power he owned". We must assume that just as Sun knew what halls she owned after the Aesir intervention, Moon also found his power. We do not, however, know what kind of power the lore refers to, and as far as I know there is little evidence for moon worship on any considerable scale. The lines that are left to us indicate Moon's importance as a way of reckoning time, however. The Sun is also important in this regard, but the Sun stands out as a goddess in her own right on many other levels than that.

Not so for the Moon, as far as we know based on the evidence that is left to us. The moon may be referred to in poetry as a relative of the Sun and the Earth, the Sun may be referred to as "Moon's Shining Sister", and the Earth may be referred to as "Moon's Hall". Two "children" follow Moon on his journey across the Heavens, according to Snorri, children from Earth: A girl called Bíl [Swift / Passing /Moment] and a boy called Hjuki [Returns to Health]. Bíl is also mentioned among the Ásyniur. These are the children of one Víðfinnr [Approximate Find] and may be seen in the shapes within the Moon disc. Here is one god of the Aesir pantheon who also has two human children as his companions: Þórr, the thunder god, who rules the weather, fertility and is the protector of marriages.

He is also a champion of his mother, the Earth goddess, protecting her from harmful onslaughts from the giant world. His hammer is a symbol of male potency. His child companions are the girl Rǫskva, whose name may be related to the word *rǫskvast,* "to mature", "grow", "come of age", and the boy Þialfi, whose name means "Holds Something Together". Þórr is married to a goddess called Síf, whose hair is of pure gold and whose name simply means "female relative", a sly suggestion as to the real identity of his wife, who could very well be his own sister. Like the Moon god, Þórr is known for his power. To suggest that Þórr the thunder god is identical to the Moon married to his golden-haired female relative, his sister Sun, is of course totally unusual, and many would probably say preposterous.

But if you look past all the preconceptions that centuries with oblivion about the original Pagan lore has created, and take seriously the suggestions offered by symbolic attributes and metaphors, it becomes impossible to ignore that the Moon and Þórr have some very essential features in common. If they were not once identical, then they may very well have emerged from the same conceptual mold. The same could actually be said for Freyr. As a Vanir god, he belongs to a different Pantheon than Þórr, and probably originated in a different tradition where he served many of the same functions. He too rules weather and growth, both symbolical and physical, he too is associated with fertility, sex, phallic symbols and marriages, and is believed to be very potent and powerful.

Like Moon, he has a sister who, as we saw earlier, is associated with bright golden shine, flames and rays of light. The Edda poem Lokasenna suggests that he had sexual relations with his sister, and in the Edda poem Skírnismál, he woos a maiden with arms so bright that they illuminate the land and seas. As we shall see in Chapter 6.4, there is evidence that this mysterious maiden is in fact his own sister, who fears that their marriage will be her brother's death. Snorri also lets us know that both Sun and Moon are driving chariots across the heavens on their eternal flight from two wolf-giants.

Moon's nemesis is called Hati Hróðvitnisson [Hatred Son of Rage Witness]. The names Hati, [Hatred], and that of the "father of Hatred", the "Rage Witness", also show up in the Edda poem of Helgi Hiǫrvarðsson, who has to conquer the giants called Hati and Hróðmarr [Hatred and Rage Ocean]. In that heroic poem, the battle against these giants is clearly a part of an initiation trial where Helgi has to overcome the qualities of hatred and rage within himself, before he can marry his sun-bright Valkyrie. Like the Sun, Helgi's sun-bright, southern-red Valkyrie bride is also threatened by an unwanted "marriage" to a destructive giant. Both Þórr and Freyr have to go through severe trials in order to win (or win back) their bright beloveds, who are threatened to be consumed by giant forces. On this ground, it is not impossible that the Moon could also symbolize the spirit of the initiate who seeks union with the bright goddess (a theme we will discuss thoroughly in Chapter 6), perhaps with his sun-bright sister, origin of souls. As we shall see, both Þórr and Freyr will follow the same path, staked out by Óðinn.

2.7: EARTH, THE ANCESTRAL MOTHER

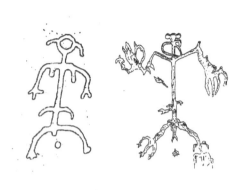

Hail the Aesir
Hail the Ásyniur
Hail the powerful, sacred Earth!
May eloquence and wisdom
be granted to us two
And healing hands in life!
   Heilir Esir,
   heilar Asynior,
   heil sia in fiolnyta Fold!
   mal oc manvit
   gefit ocr merom tveim
   oc lecnishendr, meþan
   lifom!
   -Sigrdrífumál, st. 4, Poetic Edda

Stone Age rock carvings; fertile women
Alta, Norway

In the previous Chapter, we saw that the powerful giantess Night of the nine hundred heads mated with Óðinn [The Spirit] and gave birth to Iorðr, the Norse word for "Earth". I have always thought that the name is conspicuously similar in sound to Urðr, the oldest fate. According to the Voluspá, Earth was then impregnated by her older relative, the Sun Goddess, whose life-giving rays made the green vegetation grow from the rocks of the Earth goddess. According to Snorri, who probably could not make sense out of this "female on female" procreation, Earth was impregnated by her own "father", Óðinn the Spirit. We must assume, however, that the older version, the Voluspá, is a valid version. It is the older version, and it is in sync with the Sami idea of the Sun Maiden's gift of souls to the Earth mother. As to the Sun's impregnation of the Earth, we must probably take a different approach than the idea of procreation by mating. After all, the Sun and the Earth are astronomical bodies on the physical level and goddesses on the spiritual level, not people who need to procreate by copulation.

If we rid ourselves of the concept that such mythical entities must copy our own biological functions, we will see the Sun as a source of soul-rays and the Earth as a place where the souls may grow (We could perhaps compare the Sun's rays with the nurturing milk of a mother which makes her daughter grow, although there is no direct evidence for this kind of concept). Snorri's version, that Óðinn impregnated Earth himself, although she was his daughter, is a version that is confirmed in skaldic poetry, so both versions probably existed and overlapped with each other. We know that the Sun is sometimes a dark Sun, the Sun of the Giantess, and that it might be this aspect of the old goddess that is behind Night, Earth's mother and Óðins lover. All this is of little consequence: Parents and children are metaphors for causes and results. Fathers are knowable causes, mothers unknowable. Earth is known by many names and kennings. Snorri listed a few, such as "Ymir's Flesh", which we now must see as the physical aspect of Sound.

She is also said to the Base of Wind's Hall, the physical foundation for the realm in which the wind. Also a symbol of death, can roam. She is of course also mentioned by all her relations, as the mother of Þórr, as the daughter of Night, as the daughter of Óðinn and as the "broad-faced wife of Óðinn". Another name for her is Fjǫrgyn [Life Struggle], a very perceptive description. I believe she may also be behind the name Laufey [Leaf Island], Loki's otherwise unknown parent. The mythical entities often appear in disguise throughout the myths. The Earth goddess is no exception: She is recognizable in several other characters appearing in the myths, and often appears as more than one character, that is, as a group. Earth usually appears in the shape of a vǫlva (a witch) and in the shape of a giantess, or even as a group or a pair of giantesses.

THE GIANTESSES AND THE MILL OF FATE

Earth is half giantess, a daughter of the nine-hundred headed Night. In the Hymiskvíða, Earth, known only as the Mother, lives with her terrifying grandmother in the halls of the frost giant Hymir [Hymn], where she guides her son Þórr on his quest to find a cauldron that may hold all the mead of the cosmic ocean. It is a beautiful way of describing a fact; that the Earth as a planet actually is a resident of the greater cosmos, represented by her mother, the darkness of space, and by her lover, the frosty halls of sound. The "Mother" appears in another poem (Gróagalðr), where she is the old dead vǫlva called Gróa ["To Grow"] who rises from her grave to teach her son the charms he will need on his quest for the sun-bright maiden. A similar dead witch is woken up from her grave, situated to the "East of Hel's gates", woken up by Óðinn to sing her secret songs of fate.

In the creation of the early cosmos, we saw that giantesses and Norns played an important role as the nourishing sources of streams, waves and light that laid the foundation for creation and for the weave of fate. We also saw that the threads of fate may be identical to such cosmic rivers and waves that are the giantesses. The same events now take place on Earth, as if earth is a microcosm where all the events and powers of the greater cosmos are repeated. In the poem Grottasǫngr ["The Song of the Mill-Stone"], we learn of giantesses who lived beneath the ground of Earth in the beginning, and who later moved into the world.

Their description of these early days on Earth is quite interesting. The mill known as Grotti is a mill that can grind fate if only drawn to revolve around itself by the power of the giantesses. This mill is described as a "revolving boulder" which makes the Earth shake, given into the hands of men by the giantesses themselves. The boulder of fate is said to come from the insides of the Earth, and it is tempting to suggest that it may be a symbol of the Earth itself or of a very vital part of Earth's total being. The giantesses, known as Fenia and Menia [Achiever and Rememberer], sing their ancient song, describing their own origin:

10. The Mill of Fate had not fallen from the grey mountains nor the hard stone block out of the Earth nor would we have ground so we rock giant maidens if we had not known how she (Mill/Earth) was made.

10. Komia Grotti or gria fialli ne sa hinn harþi hallr or iorþv, ne moli sva mær bergrisa, ef vissi vitt vetr til hennar

11. We grew nine winters as
playmates great maidens growing
nourished beneath the Earth
The maidens where the directors
of great deeds we ourselves moved
the flat mountain from its place.

11. Vær vetr niv
vorvm leikvr
avflgar alnar
firir iorð nepan;
stoþv meyiar
at meginverkvm,
færþvm sialfar
setberg or stað.

12. We rolled the boulder from
the world of the giants so that the
Earth began to shake we turned
then the fast-revolving stone to the
high hall so that people took it.

12. Velltvm grioti
of garð risa,
sva at fold firir
for skialfandi;
sva slongþvm vit
snvðga steini,
hofga halli,
at halir tocv.

The concept of giantesses shaping the Earth is known also from other sources. In the Hárbarðsljóð we hear that giantesses dug out valleys and spun the threads of fate. Long-Beard (Óðinn) said:

18. "The women would be like life-
sparks, if they were loyal to us
We would have owned these wise
women if they were benevolent,
minded towards us from the deep
valleys they dug the ground from
the sands they spun (fate-) threads
I was the one who managed to rule
them all, I rested with the Seven
Sisters and I had all their love and
pleasure

Hárbarðr qvaþ:
18. «Sparkar atto ver konor, ef oss at
spakom yrði; horscar atto ver konor,
ef oss hollar veri; þer or sandi síma
vndo oc or dali divpom grvnd vm
grofo; varþ ec þeim einn allom
efri at raþ hvilda ec hia þeim Systrom
Siav oc hafða ec geþ þeirra allt oc
gaman,

The Seven Sisters is a formula also mentioned in the Song of the Sun, as quoted earlier, where they are the seven sisters between the other two. The oldest, "Counsel Drink" and the youngest, "Approaching Spring", the nine giantess or Norn sisters who carve the runes of fate. The idea of giantesses shaping the earth's natural features is very prominent in the Edda lore. In the Helgi poems, the Valkyrie, who all have giant brothers, are described as causing the dew, the lightening, the rays of light and the hailstorms in the world.

Grimmer versions of the giantesses are causing the deadly waves and storms at sea. The greatness and importance of giantesses in Old Norse lore has often been overlooked by modern researchers, but is beginning to be appreciated by many. It is now known that giantesses were the objects of worship during the Viking Age, and that many giantesses were considered the ancestral mothers of tribes and clans. Kings and chiefs would symbolically marry the giantess ancestress in order to legitimize their rule, since the giantess represented the land and the fate of the tribe or clan.

To illustrate the awesomeness of giantesses, as well as an actual Viking Age explanation for how it is possible for a man to marry a giantess, let us quote from Saxo Grammaticus, where a giantess reveals her shape-changing powers to a prospective human lover (Gesta Danorum I.22):

"Young man, do not fear the dealings of my bed:
I change my corporeal shape in twofold manner
A double law I enjoin upon my sinews, molding myself in alternating fashion,
shifting my shape at will;
My neck touches the stars and soars high, near the Thunderer
Again rushes down and bends to human capacities pulled away to earth and
from the vortex of heaven
Lightly I transmute my body by variation fluctuating in aspect:
Now a tight cramping bunches my limbs
Now a freedom of height unfolds them and lets me touch the topmost clouds;
Now squeezed to dwarfish size
Now my pliant knees are stretched while my features change like wax
The Old Man of the Sea can do as much
Of indeterminate nature is my Twi-Formed Shape draws in vast expanse only
to thrust out its unlocked parts then roll them in a ball
Distend, contract, swell out, shrink, grow apace:
Immediate transformation gives me twin conditions, separate lives
I become huge to fight the fierce but small to lie with men."

Giantesses are also the rulers of death in its many shapes; Hel, the giantess of death in sickness and old age, Rán, the giantess of death in drowning, and Skaði, the giantess of death in the wilderness and of injuries. In the more glorious kinds of death, we have Freyia and the Valkyrie, but the giantesses, Norns, Valkyrie and goddesses all overlap, since death is death and fate is fate, merely taking different forms at different times. In the Song of the Mill Stone, the overlapping function of giantess, Norn and Valkyrie is particularly clear. As soon as the Earth, fast revolving boulder and mill of destiny, is brought into the realm of human beings, the giantesses, who had played such an important role in making these primeval movements happen, begin to walk the Earth in the shape of fate-goddesses, playing the role of Valkyrie, as they say.

13. But later we in the land of the Swedes we two who know fate moved among people (...)	*13. En vit siþan a Sviðioþv framvisar tvær i folk stigvm; (...)*
14. We overthrew some supported others (...)	*14. Steyptvm stilli, stvddvm annan, (...)*

It is becoming increasingly obvious, as we go along, that the separation between the various female powers of cosmos is severely blurred and that the female entities, whether they be Ásyniur, Gygjur, Valkyrie or Norns, all known under the common term Dísir ["goddesses"] overlap each other in function to such a degree that they may be identified with each other at every turn. They share basic attributes as powers of creative dynamic energy and as powers of fate and death, to such a degree that it becomes difficult to truly separate them. It is truly as Snorri declared in his Skáldskaparmál: *"All Ásyniur can be referred to by naming the name of another one and referring to them by their possessions or deeds or descent..."*

It may be less obviously the case with the male entities, but also here, Snorri reveals: *"It is also normal to refer to the Aesir by calling one by the name of another and referring to him by his deeds or possession or descent..."*

As you continue to read this book, you will begin to see that the fluidity between the female entities and between the male entities is so consistent and thorough that one must, finally, begin to realize that all the entities were created from the same original mold, ultimately divided only in the feminine moving power and the masculine holding power. The Earth and all the giantesses, Norns and Valkyrie who help shape her form and roll her fate-boulder are all different creatures, yet essentially the same, all created from the same original mold that began as the life-nourishing Auðhumbla who also feeds on the ice of death, and also as the Witch Within Wood.

SKAÐI, HEL AND THE WOLFRIDERS

> *"From this [observation of the Earth's properties over time] they [the ancestors] realized that the Earth was alive and possessed a kind of life experience. And they knew that she was extremely ancient of years and powerful of nature. She raised all that lived, and took all life back into herself when it died. For this reason they gave her a name and counted their lineages from her."*
>
> Snorri Sturlusson, Prologue to the Prose Edda

As Snorri suggested (see quote above), the Earth goddess was considered the ultimate ancestral mother of all lineages. She is our ancestral mother. In Viking Age society, it was very common for clans to honor their ancestral mother, often a mythical being, and very often a giantess, married to a god. The Norwegian professor Gro Steinsland has shown, from the 1990s onwards, that there is evidence of a cult of Sacred Marriage in Scandinavian prehistory that has greatly influenced Norse mythology. The Sacred Marriage happened in many different places, which is why it involved different characters. It was a ritual based on a myth of a divine ancestral father, a god such as Óðinn or Freyr, who married a giantess such as Skaði or Gerðr. There could also be evidence of a ritual where a human male married a goddess such as Freyia.

The giantess was the ancestral mother of the clan and seems to have represented the land and the fate of the people who lived in that land. The ritual meant that a king would legitimize his rule by ritually marrying this ancestral mother, and thus symbolically marry the land and the fate of the people, taking the place of the divine or legendary ancestral father. The Sacred Marriage may be a very old ritual introduced in Scandinavia already during the Bronze Age, inspired by the Sumerian ritual where the king also married the patron goddess of the people. The association between the ancestral mother and the land is very strong, suggesting that the ancestral mother may be one tribe's version of the Earth goddess. Skaði Ǫndurdís [Goddess of Skiing] is one quite famous giantess who became a bride of the gods and who was considered the ancestral mother of several Norwegian clans, who honored her as a goddess and as their ancestor.

Her son by Óðinn, Sæmingr, became the ancestor of Norwegian royal and noble lines. Skaði could have been an earth goddess in the ancient days, associated with wild nature, mountains, hunting, serpents, wolves and the underworld. She is the power that puts a poisonous serpent above Loki's face in the underworld. Skaði is also a goddess of death and injuries, as the assignment "rock bride" suggests, as well as her association with wolves. Her name means something like "fatal injury", and in poetry at least, she could simply be Death in that particular aspect, death by fatal injury. When she is depicted as a huntress skiing in the wolf-haunted mountains, it is the image of death hunting the living. This grim image of an earth goddess is actually quite fitting.

As Snorri pointed out, the mother Earth not only raised all life, but also took it back into herself when life died. As we will see in Chapter 4, Skaði began as a more ambiguous character than what she appears to be in Snorri's later account, as a goddess of two faces; one for death and another for renewed life. The same image of death is found in Hel, who has a face that is half dark as death, half bright as life. Hel, whose name means "Hidden" or "Hides (something) is also associated with wolves and serpents. She lives in the underworld, a kind of earthly version of the cosmic model Mist World. Her realm is Níflhel ["Hides in Mist"].

The wolf-riding giantess appears both in Old Norse art and in myths and poetry, often using serpents for reins with which she steers the wolf. She lives in the darkness and in the rock caves, and is all-powerful. She is an image of the dark aspect of the Earth goddess who receives and consumes all that dies. As such, the Earth goddess is created in the same mold as the other mothers of both origin and death, from grim Hel of the Misty World and life-robbing Rán of the cosmic ocean to Auðhumbla of the flowing life sustenance.

Skaði from Þrymheimr [The World of the Drumming] is also known as the Maiden from Iron Forest, which gives association to an old giantess who lives in that particular "forest", mentioned later on in the Vǫluspá, 40:

> To the East sat The Old One, in Iron Forest nurtures there birth to the kindred
> of Greed from all of these one of darkness comes
> Moon's abductor in the shape of a troll.
>
>> Austr sat in aldna í Járnviði
>> ok fœddi þar Fenris kindir
>> verðr af þeim ǫllum
>> einna nǫkkurr
>> Tungls tjúgari
>> í trolls hami.

The Old One of Iron Forest is probably Skaði or else an older, cosmic model for
Skaði, a giantess of the "East", the direction of the destructive giants of Utgarðr,
the World Outside. The children she gives birth to or nourishes are thought to be
"wolves", symbols of the instinct for survival and for the qualities of desire, intent
and greed, which can be very destructive. They are the "kindred of Fenrir", the
"wolf" of Greed. The one "wolf" that will be Moon's abductor is, as we already know,
Hatred. This destructive aspect of the old giantess who may be identical to Earth's
own grim aspect nourishes the qualities that are completely necessary for physical
life to happen, the survival mode, the hunger, the desire, the passion and the need
to devour other kinds of life. It is a two-edged sword, like the Earth herself, a planet
known by the name of Life Struggle.

ÓÐIN'S WIFE

> Óðin's wife rows the Ship of Earth eager for pleasures; her sails will late be
> reefed they are hung with the ropes of desire
> > Óðins kván
> > rœr á Jarðar skipi,
> > móðug á munað;
> > seglum hennar
> > verðr síð hlaðit,
> > þeim er á þráreipum þruma

> *Sólarlióð, st. 77, Poetic Edda*

Earth is counted as Óðin's wife and as one of the Ásyniur. As such, after Sun, she
is the second Ásynia to appear in the Vǫluspá. We know that one of the two most
splendid goddesses of Ásgarðr is Frigg, and that she is also regarded as a wife of
Óðinn. The other most prominent goddess is Freyia, whom I associate with the Sun
goddess. Could Frigg be an aspect of the ancient Earth mother? Frigg is associated
with Venus, called The Star of Frigg in Old Norse, and her name means Love or
Beloved. Her association to Venus does not necessarily exclude her association to
Earth. First of all, she could be related to both planets, or the association to Venus
could be derived from Greek and Roman lore.

Frigg lives in Fensalar [The Moist Halls] where only women (or men who can
change into women) may enter. She also knows all fate. Snorri relates how Loki
once entered Frigg's realm, and in order to do so, he took upon himself the shape
of a woman. We can only speculate what that truly means, but I have a suggestion.
The "Moist Halls" give certain associations not only to the bogs and lakes in
which the goddess probably resided, but also to the female sexual organs. Loki
frequently deals with magic and witchcraft, and we may assume that he was a male
practitioner of *seiðr*, the art of divination. It is in fact for the purpose of divining the
secret that may change the future that causes him to seek the realm of the goddess
who knows all fate. Male performers of seiðr where sometimes called seiðberendr,
a title which literally translates as "seiðr-vagina" or "seiðr-womb", as if the male
practitioner magically achieved a womb.

It is possible that the art of seiðr was considered a feminine art and that there was some kind of "womb-magic" involved. Perhaps a male practitioner had to acquire a magical womb in order to reach the realm of fate, which was a distinctly feminine realm. The history of shamanism is full of examples of transsexual shamans, and the existence of transsexual shamans in Scandinavia is very probably the reason why such a title existed. Not all male practitioners of seiðr would be particularly feminine. Warlike Óðinn himself was a famous divine practitioner. In a gender-divided society where a boy was expected to grow up to be a fierce warrior, less fierce boys, feminine boys and transgender male to female boys could find a respected path of their own by entering the rank of magical professionals. No doubt, boys who did not fit the masculine warrior bill flocked to this profession, where they would find acceptance and respect.

I am quite convinced that this is the reason why Snorri in the Ynglinga saga declared that there was so much unmanliness associated with the art of seiðr that men could not practice it without shame. An example of a famous seiðr-man was Ragnvald Rettilbeini, son of King Haraldr Hárfagri. His nickname, Rettilbeini, could be translated as "feminine spreading legs". Yet despite this comical nickname, the king's sorcerer son wielded great power until he came to be at odds with his father. The existence of multitudes of powerful and highly respected male practitioners in Pagan times suggests that Snorri's attitude was a Christian influence, not a Pagan one. Returning to Frigg and her Moist Halls, we may deduce that her moist realm is the realm of the womb, a powerful symbol of a place where creation and new life originates and from which it is birthed. This is also a powerful symbol of the planet Earth herself.

Adding to this, Frigg has power over all nature and can demand promises from fire and water, iron and all sorts of minerals, the rocks, the earth, the illnesses, the animals, the birds, the poisons, the serpents and the worms. She is called upon in childbirth and protects children, and she is the wife of the "All-Father", a suitable position for an ancestral mother, the "All-Mother". All these things may possibly identify Frigg as an aspect of the ancient, fertile and powerful ancestral mother Earth. She is called Fjǫrgvinsdottir [Daughter of Life Friend], and we should ask ourselves who this "Life Friend" is. In 2.10, we will see that Óðinn, Earth's father and husband, offers the gift of breath to human beings. I cannot think of a better Life Friend than the origin of breath. She is also sometimes called Fjǫrgyns Mey {"The Maiden of Life Struggle"}. I have found that someone's "maiden" usually refers to someone's fate. That the Earth is Life-Struggle's fate is a very comprehensible metaphor for our planet.

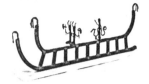

Bronze model of ship with acrobats at the prow, two male figures with ritual horned helmets and ritual labyris and a woman with a necklace accompanied by a serpent.

Bronze Age, Denmark.

Fjǫrgyn, Life Struggle, is also often used to describe the Earth goddess herself. Þórr, Earth's son, is often called Life Struggle's son. In the Sólarlióð [The Song of the Sun] Frigg is said to "row the Ship of Earth". As it were, Earth could itself be seen as a ship, a vehicle in which we are all being transported through life, moving through the ocean that is our cosmos. The rower of the "ship" is the ruler of its fate, and Frigg is the fate of Life Struggle.

There may be other potential candidates than Frigg and the giantesses for Earth goddess in the Edda lore, but it would be hard to say. Frigg's son, Baldr, is married to one Nanna Neprsdottir ["Nanna, Daughter of the Ring"]. The Ring is a symbol of spiritual wholeness. Her name could possibly be related to "understanding". In the Edda poem Hyndlulióð, stanza 20, Nanna is said to be the daughter of Nǫkkvé, which translates as Dark Sacred Space. It is not impossible that this is a way of saying Night, identifying Nanna as the daughter of Night and thus possibly as Earth herself.

2.8: THE EARTH'S PROTECTIVE FIELD AND ÞÓRR THE THUNDERGOD

Having discussed the Earth as both a planet, a Viking Age goddess and as the ultimate ancestral mother of human lineages, it is time to look at one very important property of planet Earth, its electromagnetic field of protection, without which we could never have lived. In mythical language, this is the realm of Þórr, the Thunder god, born of Earth as her firstborn son. Could ancient people have known about the atmosphere and its electromagnetic field? I can see no reason why they could not. Ancient people figured out the concept of atoms and of heliocentric concepts and many other complex insights based not on what they could perceive with their normal senses, but on observations of nature, logical deduction, and intuition.

It would seem that the Norse myth-makers had somehow managed to perceive the electromagnetic field intuitively and that they incorporated their ancient Thunder god mythology into their insights. As mentioned earlier, myths may be read on many levels. On one level, we have the stories of a deity with an actual cultural history behind it. "Thor", or actually Þórr, the Thunder god, is a deity associated with the sky, thunder and lightning, as well as with protection and marriages, and has very ancient origins. He was related to the Vedic god Indra and many other Indo-European thunder gods. In 98 AD, Tacitus mentions an earlier Germanic version, Tuisto, who had the son Mannus. Mannus had three sons who were the ancestors of all human lineages. In the Norse myths, Þórr had a son called Magni, as in Latin magnus, "The Great", and according to Snorri, he was the ancestor of the human Aesir. Like Norse Þórr, the German Tuisto was born of Earth, and his son was the progenitor of human beings, the first man.

We are thus seeing a very old mythology that has been incorporated into Norse myths and into Norse Pagan religion. The evidence for worship of Þórr during the Viking Age is very strong and widespread. His hammer was as common a symbol as the Christian cross. On another level, we can see the spiritual approach to the lore. This is where we have no way of knowing whether the poets of the Edda invented this or whether it was an ancient tradition of understanding behind it. That is, we do not know how ancient this spiritual approach is. It could be exceedingly old, or it could be that the Viking Age poets of the Edda used and manipulated the lore of this popular god with purposes of their own. We can only state that the lore of Þórr in the Poetic Edda, as it is left to us, provides spiritual and life-wisdom guidance. As the first man, the first "son of Earth", Þórr represents many of the challenges a man (and a woman) will have to go through in life.

We shall be exploring this spiritual lore at length in the Chapter about "The Son of Earth". On a third level, we have the metaphysical approach, the "scientific" approach of the Pagan philosopher who wants to explain the properties of Cosmos through the language of myth. We do not know how old that approach is either. We only know that as a power of the sky, Þórr is also used by the poets to describe electricity and the atmosphere from the perspective they perceived it. This is when Þórr must be understood by his nickname Hlórriði which could alternately translate as "Heat Swinging Back and Forth", "Heat Hurler" or "Heat Rider". Þórr the Thunder god appears as the great he-man of the Old Norse pantheon. In the myths about Þórr, he is often referred to as the "manly god" [þruðugr Áss] the adjective þruðugr meaning manly, powerful, vigorous, and virile.

In a pantheon of gods who appear to be able to take numerous shapes, including female and even birth-giving ones, Þórr actually stands out as the masculine god of Ásgarðr. We could ask ourselves what is all this masculinity about? I believe it is all about protection, the most important masculine function in Viking Age society. Þórr is the Son of Earth. He is often called Þórr Fjǫrgynsson, 'Þórr son of Life-Struggle', indicating his role as Earth's child. As such, Þórr is also more directly named sonr Iarðar [the Son of Earth]. Þór's main function as a god, his life mission, quite like the warrior who guards his family, is to protect his mother Earth from the perpetual attacks of gigantic destructive forces from Utgarðr [Outer World], which would be the world outside of Earth and which we today might call Outer Space, or just 'the unknown'. So what does Þórr actually represent on this level?

The name Þórr is derived from the Proto-Norse word þunraR, which means "thunder". Þórr is the thunder, and he, the thunder, is married to the goddess Síf. Síf means 'female relation' and should thus be understood as a female relative of, or counterpart to, thunder. Like all the other goddesses of solar origin, she is described as beautiful, golden, bright and shining. The solar goddesses, united in their shared solar origin, are conceived of as the source of all light, and the golden goddesses are often described as such; beaming with light, with sunlight, with rays of lightening, with flames and brightness, illuminating air, land and sea. The association to rays of lightening is particularly important in Síf's case. With her hair made out of pure gold, a powerful conductor of electricity, it seems safe to say that the goddess, in her aspect as þór's wife, the wife of thunder and its' "female relative", actually is the lightening. We have here, in the Thunder and the Lightening, a couple shaped in the ancient mold of the masculine Sound and the feminine Wave. Thunder's intimate connection with Lightening is described in many ways.

One is his marriage to Lightening. Another metaphor is the "hall" within which he lives. It is called Bílskírnir, which means a swift, momentary, passing shine [bíl: swift, passing, momentary, and skírnir, the "shining"]. This hall (a feminine word) would, like his wife Síf, also be a metaphor for Lightening. It actually makes sense that Thunder "lives inside" Lightening, quite like Sound grew within the Wave. Today, we know that thunder is in fact the sound that accompanies lightening. This "hall" of lightening is situated within a realm called Þrúðvangr, which literally translates as the 'Power Field'. This realm is situated in the sky, and today we know that the sky, the atmosphere, the ionosphere and the stratosphere, actually is a field of power, and that it is charged with electricity. In fact, atmospheric electricity in the atmospheric electromagnetic network (the power field) is what produces lightening.

We also know that this atmospheric electromagnetic field actually does protect the Earth from destructive influx from Outer Space. The fact, that this Thunder god lives inside the lightening, is married to the lightening and that this lightening is situated within something called the Power Field, which is in the sky, and that his main occupation is to protect the Earth from the negative influences of the so-called Outer World, may not prove that Old Norse people actually knew that the atmosphere really is a power field that does protect the Earth from influence from the world outside. But the myth is a fairly interesting indication that they may have known this. And there are, as we shall see, even more such indications.

Let us have a look at Þór's most famous attribute, his hammer. Þór's hammer is called Miǫllnir, a name derived from the Proto Norse melluniaR, which could be related to Old Slavic mlunuji or Old Russian molnija, which means "lightening". It could also be related to Gothic malwjan and Old Norse mala, which means "to grind". Thus the meaning could be either something like the Lightning Bolt, or the Grinder (or Millner). Both these meanings make sense and do not necessarily exclude each other. People in those days were big on double meanings. In the lore of Þórr, we see that lightening is described with three metaphors:

1. As the wife of thunder,
2. As the hall of thunder, and
3. As the hurling weapon of thunder.

It is the hammer that gives Þórr the power to protect; when Þórr hurls his hammer, it will destroy the giants that threaten the world by grinding them into tiny particles before the hammer returns to his hands. This is exactly what happens to the influx from Outer Space when it enters the electromagnetic field of Earth. This is actually exactly how the power field of Earth does protect the world; it turns things into little particles. Moreover, and here comes the best bit; we all know how electricity is conducted through metal, and that you need two ends that are polar opposites in order to make that power go around to conduct it. In order for Þórr to hurl his lightning bolt hammer and make it return to him in order to be hurled again, he needs to wear a belt, and this belt is made out of iron.

This belt has a name; it is called the Megingjǫrð, which means the 'Power Belt'. This iron power belt has to be fastened around Þórr, and he has to wear an iron glove on the right hand and an iron glove on the left hand. The gloves are called Járngreipr [Iron Grip] and Járnglófi [Iron Glove]. Only when wearing the iron Power Belt and the two iron gloves on his left and right hands may the Thunder god clasp his Lightening-hammer in order to hurl it and receive it.

It sounds conspicuously like the basic rules of how to actually make an electric circuit. Wearing the iron Power Belt and the iron gloves is the only way, the myths tell us, that he can control his lightning bolt hammer. Again, I would like to point out that people in the past were not more stupid than we are. They had the same capacity of observation, analysis and ability to make experiments. They were expert craftsmen capable of making very advanced metal equipment, and I think it is perfectly possible that people in the past have figured out how electricity works. If you had managed to conduct electricity a thousand years ago or more, you yourself and everybody around you would have considered this knowledge magical, sacred, divine. The only way to transmit this knowledge would be through a sacred language, and that was poetry. In the Old Norse world, poetry was based on metaphors, allegory and myth.

It would be easy to remember, it would be cleverly disguised as a story, but truly understandable only to those who had been initiated into the secret or to those intelligent enough to crack the code. This lore of Þórr may be a perfect example of how this kind of knowledge would have been transmitted during that time. I am not pretending to have proven that this lore of Þórr is actually about electricity and how to conduct it. It could, in fact be, completely coincidental. My notion is interesting enough, and if we are ever going to understand our past we have to stop limiting our minds into a paradigm of preconceptions of what these people may, or may not, have known.

2.9: DWARFS, THE BLUEPRINTS OF EXISTENCE

>*...until three females came there,*
>*the frost giant maidens;*
>*almighty and powerful,*
>*from the world of giants.*
>>*...unz þrjár kvámu*
>>*þursa meyjar*
>>*ámátkar mjǫk*
>>*ór jǫtunheimum.*

>*-Vǫluspá st. 8, Poetic Edda*

As the Earth is in her infancy and the Universe is newly shaped, the young Aesir are happily playing their games, building temples and enjoying their "gold", their divine knowledge. Then three giant maidens, "almighty and powerful" (and quite likely, related to the three fates), arrive, demanding that the young gods get down to business. The appearance of the giantesses is immediately followed by the creation of dwarfs. In her treatise, The Wise One of the Mountain: Form, Function and Significance of the Subterranean Smith; A Study in Folklore (1983), Lotte von Motz made a study of the legendary smiths of Northern European folklore and mythology. She concluded that the smiths generally seem to resemble an ancient priesthood, and strongly suggested that this priesthood originated with the Megalithic people of the Stone Age, a priesthood used and oppressed by the new ruling classes that appeared towards the end of that age. The dwarfs of Norse myths, who are also always craftsmen and smiths, fit this bill perfectly.

I agree with Motz on most of her analysis, but when it comes to the Edda poetry, I believe that the Edda poets have applied the dwarfs to serve their own ends; to reveal a message about the Cosmos and how the limitless spiritual entities could move into the sphere of physical forms and shapes. Usually, when we think about the dwarfs of folklore and myth, we tend to see them much as they appear in Disney's Snow-White, rude yet charming little forest creatures working in metals and mining.

Of course, the image of the dwarf is taken from ancient sources and draws heavily on very ancient mythical themes. The metal-working dwarf living underground is akin to the dark-elf [dǫkkalfr] who lives below ground, forging metals. They are associated with the souls of the dead, haunting the burial mounds. The dwarfs appearing in the Vǫluspá are quite different beings. Their importance is testified by the number of stanzas that they occupy. Nine stanzas, which is a lot, beginning with stanza 9. Most of these stanzas only render the many names of the dwarfs. The only way to possibly understand what the dwarfs represent in the poetical allegory of the Edda poem, is to interpret their names. This is easier said than done, since there are often many different possible translations, and few are absolutely certain. Even those translators who do attempt to make translations, make only a few, the ones that they can be most sure of.

This is understandable. However, I am completely convinced that the names are meaningful, as is every line and verse of the Poetic Edda and I have tried to offer a possible way of translating and understanding what the dwarfs mean. Some of my translations may be faulty or questionable, but as a whole, I believe that my interpretation of the dwarf lore in the Vǫluspá makes sense. Snorri explained that the dwarfs originated like germs in the flesh of Ymir the world giant, whom I have interpreted as primeval sound. According to Snorri's Gylfaginning, the dwarfs were given consciousness and shape from "the Power-Songs of gods": af atkvæðum goðanna urðu þeir vitandi mannvits ok höfðu manns líki ok búa þó í jörðu ok í steinum ["from the power-songs of the gods were they (the dwarfs) given the awareness of the human mind and had the likeness of men and lived in the earth and in the rocks"].

In the Poetic Edda, dwarfs appear on the cosmic scene after the ordering of cosmos and the establishment of the positions of the stars, the Sun, Moon and Earth. Then three giantesses, called "almighty" and "much knowing" arrive at the court of the Aesir. The three giantesses probably represent fate, being the same as the "much-knowing" Nornir that appear after human beings were created, after the dwarfs. So it is fate that demands that the gods must create the dwarfs. The entry of the giantesses leads to all the powers meeting in a first Cosmic Parliament:

9. Then all the powers went to the high chairs of fate the sacrosanct gods to discuss this: Who owed the King of Dwarfs to be shaped from the blood of Fire and the limbs of the Dead?	9. Þá gengu regin ǫll á rǫkstóla, ginnheilug goð, ok um þat gættusk: hverr skyldi Dverga Drótt um skepja ór Brimi blóðgu ok ór Bláins leggjum

The fifth and sixth line in the stanza form a question: Who owes The King of Dwarfs to be shaped? What is to be shaped is the King of Dwarfs, and the question is, who is to shape him? The riddle can only be answered if we understand who? Or what The King of Dwarfs is? The King of Dwarfs is a kenning for something else, something that we have yet to identify. The clues to understand who this dwarf is, comes when we hear the ingredients that make up the dwarf king: the blood of Fire [Brímir] and the limbs of the Dead [Bláinn, "The Blue", a poetical way of describing a rotting corpse, the dead]. It is interesting to note that the two names are typical dwarf names. Setting aside the charming forest creature concept and trying to see the underlying meaning here is necessary if the riddle is to be deciphered.

It is necessary here to look at Snorri's description of the creation of the world in Gylfaginning. Wandering Learner [Gangleri] asked: "What was the origin? How did it all start? What was before?" (...)

Equally High [Jafnhár] replied: "It was many ages before the Earth was created, that Misty World [Niflheimr] emerged. In the middle of that world lies a well (water-source) called Bellower Mill [Hvergelmir], from it runs the rivers (of the Universe)". In Snorri's account, the first "world" [cosmic realm] is actually Misty World, the world of the dead. This is the land of the "frost giants" [hrímþursar] with whom Snorri, a few lines before, had declared that the creator god lived before time itself. That was when he was known as Þundr [Thin Mist] as is also confirmed in the Edda poem Grímnismál st.54; "Óðinn I am now, Old One I was called before, Thin Mist before that". The world giant Ymir [Sound] was created as icy rivers from this realm of the dead entered the Ginnungagáp where they met with and were melted by, hot streams from a flaming realm in the south. As Snorri writes:

> Third [Þriði] said: "But first it was that world in the south of the world that is called Muspell, it is bright and hot, that sky is flaming and burning and impossible to traverse for those who are not natives. Sooted One [Surtr] he is called, who guards that land; he has a flaming sword (...)"

We know from the Vǫluspá st.2 that other worlds had existed before the present world, so that the existence of a realm of the dead even before this world was created makes sense: It is the frosty remnants of previous worlds, the dead worlds, which provide substance and matter in the shape of streams to the great point-zero of creation. Moreover, from the same realm emerges the frost giant Búri [Storage Chamber] who has been lying dormant beneath the ice of death, we must assume since the death of the previous world. As the hot tongue of the great cow Auðhumbla [Abundant Brew Ingredient] from the fiery south licks the ice of death in order to nurture herself, so that she in turn may nurture the world giant created by melting ice, he re-emerges from the death-ice and becomes the grandfather of the Aesir. The limbs of the frost giant make up the world. What we are seeing here is a mythical formula for creation. Ice and fire, which could be translated to cold still death and fiery moving life-force, come together at the very beginning. The fire of life, represented by the Cosmic Cow, melts the cold of death and nurtures new life, represented by Ymir and Búri, the Sound and the Storage Chamber from where awareness emerge in the form of Aesir. This formula of Creation [Fire and Death] is the same formula applied in the creation of the "King of Dwarfs".

One would almost assume that the King of Dwarfs either refers to Ymir or to Búri or both, as they could very well be ultimately identical to each other. Let us move to the next stanza about the dwarfs. It begins by declaring that:

> 10. Then was Móðsognir the greatest and the highest of all dwarfs,...

>> 10.Þar var Móðsognir
>> dverga allra,
>> mæztr um orðinn

Now we must try to identify Móðsognir. Since we are used to think of names as merely sounds, we will easily assume beforehand that this dwarf is a different one from that "King of the Dwarfs" we just heard about. However, it should be clear by now that a number of names may very well be referring to only one being, since names are merely metaphors describing the character, and to apply a new metaphor each time one character is referred to was a basic rule of Norse poetry. The name is difficult to interpret though. The first part of the word could either be móðr [a.: Exhausted, m.sg: mind/ intent, m.sg.: Courage, m.sg. Mental turmoil], or mót [n.sg: mark/ stamp/ image, shape/ form/ type or n.sg.: Assembling/ meeting/ counsel/ fusion or adv.: Against].

The second part of the name is sognir, which could be derived from the neutral noun *sog*; which means "sucking" and refers specifically to the suction force of a submerged wave, an inverted vortex. It could also just refer to the ocean, which was in itself perceived as a potential "sucker" for drowned people. It is also possible that the word is really sóknir, which could be derived from the feminine word sókn (f.pl.: sóknir), which means "application" or "seeking/ searching/ praying/ accusing". This is a good example explaining why translators of Old Norse texts are cautious about presenting a name in translation. It is hard to see what the most plausible interpretation is if none of the options make any sense from the point of our modern world-view, and without any certain knowledge about the ancient world-view. We need to look to the poem again and see if there are any clues as to which translation is the best. Further down in the same stanza, we read:

> ...and Sleeper was the second (in rank); images of humans they made many of from earth, these dwarfs as the Sleeper spoke it

> ...en Durinn annarr;

>> þeir mannlíkun
>> mǫrg um gǫrðu
>> dvergar í jǫrðu,
>> sem Durinn sagði.

The sentence building is a bit archaic, so I will render a more modern sentence. These dwarfs made many human images from earth, as the Sleeper (who was second to Móðsognir) spoke it. The Sleeper here appears to take the role of the power-singing Aesir. The human image theme is crucial, because we realize that one of the possible meanings of the name of the first king of dwarf refers to "images", "stamps", and "marks". The proper interpretation of his name should in my opinion be "image/ marker/ suction/vortexes" or "image/ mark- searchers". "Vortexes" or "searchers" are rendered in plural because of the word sógnir or sóknir being the plural form of the nouns. The plural within the one being is significant. This dwarf represents the greatest of all dwarfs, probably the King of Dwarfs himself, from which others seem to emerge, the archaic prototype for them all.

Another interesting thing is that it is almost impossible to distinguish the dwarfs from the "human images". As we shall see, the dwarfs are in fact connected to the creation of human beings. It is tempting to ask the question: "How would you have presented knowledge of genetic markers to a mythological minded audience?" Then, despite many interesting speculations about previous civilizations with a high level of technology, we must also consider the equally probable situation: **That no such knowledge existed**.

However, we should not underestimate the intellectual capacities of human beings no matter what time they lived in. It is perfectly possible that some people without any technology other than their brain capacity, simply figured out that the creatures of the world emerged from basic markers, basic images created by the gods, a basic image multiplying into countless variations. A third important aspect of this stanza is the dwarf Durinn [Sleeper] who is second to the first being. This reminds me of how Búri [grandfather to the gods], came second after Ymir, grandfather/mother to the giants, being, in fact, "sleeping" beneath the ice of death.

The two might be one, but the second is an aspect that serves a particular purpose: He "tells" the "images of humans" as they are created from the Earth. Earlier, we saw how the world seems to have been "told" or "sung" into being, as a huge "optical illusion" based on sound, speech or story-telling. We recall how Snorri claimed that the dwarfs were given form by the 'Power Words' of the gods. The "speech" of creation is followed by a long listing of dwarf's names, which I now assume represent the "images of humans". The forms, ideas or models for different basic potentials in human beings.

According to the Vǫluspá, these are:

11. Waxing, Waning, Northern, Southern *Eastern, Western, Ale-Thief, Hibernation* *Death and Dying, Close-Call and Dead One* *Shaking, Vibration, Bom-Tree, Ship* *Friend and Other One, Frightened One, Mead-Witness*	*11. Nýi, Niði, Norðri, Suðri,* *Austri, Vestri, Alþjófr, Dvalinn,* *Nár ok Náinn, Nípingr, Dáinn,* *Bifurr, Bafurr, Bǫmburr, Nori,* *Ánn ok Ánarr, Óinn.* *Mjǫðvitnir*
12. Power Drink, Wand-Elf, Wind-Elf *Daring One, Yearning and Desiring One* *Appreciated, Color, Wisdom Renewal and New Counsel,* *Now I have the dwarfs,* *Ruler and Counsel Wise, rightly counted.*	*12. Veigr ok Gandálfr, Vindálfr,* *Þorinn, Þrár ok Þráinn,* *Þekkr, Litr ok Vitr,* *Nýr ok Nýráðr,* *nú hefi ek dverga,* *Reginn ok Ráðsviðr,* *rétt um talða.*

13. Hiding, Wedge, Found One, Needle-Sized Shaft, Intent, Skillful One, Burner, Twin, Bushy-Browed, Blood-Knife, Chamber, Quick One, Horn-Blower, Famous, Lazy/Shining Gravel Field, Quarrelsome, Oaken(Crazy) Shields	13. Fili, Kili, Fundinn, Nali, Hepti, Vili, Hanarr, Svíurr, Billingr, Brúni, Bildr ok Búri, Frár, Hornbori, Frægr ok Lóni, Aurvangr, Jari, Eikinskjaldi.

After this impressive list of subtle, cryptic names, the vǫlva continues:

14. It is time to count the dwarfs of Hibernation to count the people of the Law They set out from the rocky halls from Gravel SpacesL to the Earth Fields.	14. Mál er dverga i Dvalins liði ljóna kindum i Lofars telja er sóttu frá salar steini Aurvanga sjǫt til Jǫruvalla.

A new list of names follows, meaning:

15. There was Dripper and Hidden Tracker High One, Burial Mound-Spurrer, Wind-Shielded (= Immortal) Field, Glowing One Fool, Snake, Sleepy, Alert Spirit Cut-Out-Part, Dyer, Part-Finder, Great Grandfather	15. Þar var Draupnir ok Dólgþrasir, Hár, Haugspori, Hlévangr, Glóinn, Dori, Ori, Dúfr, Andvari, Skirfir, Virfir, Skafiðr, Ai.
16. Elf (= Soul) and Sacred Youth, Crazy Shields Spyer and Frosty, Finder and Sacred Warrior As long as human kind exists the long list of the Laws shall be remembered.	16. Álfr ok Yngvi, Eikinskjaldi, Fjalarr ok Frosti, Finnr ok Ginnarr; þat man æ uppi, meðan ǫld lifir, langniðja tal Lofars hafat.

Something interesting has happened. Out of the great mass of almost incomprehensible dwarfs comes a special kind: The Dwarfs of Hibernation, who are also the people of "Laws", who "came from the Gravel SpacesL to the Earth Fields. We remember that the "images" were "spoken" by the "Sleeper", whom I identified as Búri, who slept or indeed hibernated beneath the ice of death, and who became the grandfather of the Aesir. It turns out that the Aesir indeed belong to these dwarfish "people of Laws" who came from the Gravel SpacesL to the Earth fields, as the next stanza reads:

17. Until Three came out of that flock, powerful and loving Aesir to the homes They found on the shore, of little power Ask and Embla, without destiny.	17. Unz þrír kvámu ór því liði ǫflgir ok ástkir æsir á húsi fundu á landi lítt megandi Ask ok Emblu, ǫrlǫgslausa.

It has become clear that the Aesir indeed emerged from the flock of dwarfs that, supposedly, the Aesir shaped. It is only through the flock of dwarfs that the Aesir could enter the human world and offer them the gift of spirit, thought and vitality, as they proceed to do in the next stanza. Before anyone inclined towards theories about ancient aliens automatically assumes that we are seeing evidence for alien intervention I would like to point out that my translation of Aurvangar to "Gravel Spaces" is derived from the assumption that the word is made out of *Aurr* ["gravel", "mud", "sand"], the same kind found in the Well of Origin, and the noun *vangr* ["open place", "court", "field" or just "cleared space"].

I have also considered the translation "Out-of-Illusion" from aur = "out of/from" and the adjective *vangr* ["false", "illusionary"]. If vangr refers to illusion, the aur- could still be from Aurr and mean "gravel", ultimately a symbol of matter. Then we would end with the translation: "Matter Illusion". There could be a double or triple meaning in this place-name where neither of these interpretations is "wrong", but rather complement each other and provides different layers of understanding.

Little Gray Aliens?

I have heard from those who consider these "dwarfs" to be little gray aliens. I do not automatically reject such theories, since I have no idea whether these really exist. What I often see when people present such interpretations of ancient myths is an almost consistent failure to regard all the details of these myths, in fact often carefully ignoring every aspect of the myth that does not serve to support their theory, and often adding a little "spice" that was not there in the first place in order to "support" their theory. In the case of the little gray aliens we are usually told that they are out to get us, clone us and perform genetic experiments on us. Thus the dwarfs who enter Earth from outer space and give their gifts to primeval human beings, helping to shape our destiny, could be seen as early alien intruders out to experiment genetically on the human species. As weird as this idea may seem to those who are not already into the alien stuff, the idea in itself is not entirely preposterous; as we shall see, the "dwarfs" do seem to be related to what we today call DNA or genetic markers.

Yet the theory mentioned above also fails. To counter the "alien gray" approach I would like to say that we are in fact not seeing a tale of how human beings already up and about are being messed with by alien powers. To think that would be to miss out on several important details in the myth, such as the crucial fact that the recipients, Askr and Embla, were not yet even alive; they were without destiny, without breath, without thoughts, without life. They were just drifting matter, a potential for life discovered by the Aesir gods of awareness, who are not from another planet but from the earliest emergence of cosmic consciousness. There is absolutely no evidence in the myths that the Aesir came from a particular planet or stellar system; they clearly emerged as non-physical consciousness in primeval space, and their gift to us is the gift of life itself. It was a gift of breath, free thought, poetry, color and heat, hardly the story of an alien conspiracy or of dubitable scientific and genetic manipulation. This is rather a tale of spiritual intervention, where spirit enters matter in order to create the very first life. It is only through the dwarfish dimension of limited form and shape that unshaped divine consciousness originating from the heart of the universe itself may take residence in physical bodies.

> This a tale of how spirit, awareness and vitality that was believed to have already existed without form in the early cosmos is made one with matter by going into and through the illusion of matter that they had prepared, so that conscious life may quicken and grow. Just as we are seeing a story where "gods" in the shape of "dwarfs" enter the young Earth from outer space (the rocky halls and gravel spaces), we might also be seeing a "deeper truth" of how unlimited, spiritual, cosmic awareness, by entering the "dwarfish" (limited, mutilated, made smaller) world of matter-illusion into Earth, breathe life and awareness into the potential for life-matter of Earth.

Returning to the creation of dwarfs and the gods who inhabit them: It all starts to make sense. Both "Hibernation" and "Sleeper" are good metaphors for the sleeping frost giant otherwise known as Búri, whose name means "Storage Chamber" and refers to something being "stored" in the ice of the world of the dead, the frozen remains of the previous worlds. His descendants are the Aesir, who rightly could be called the "people of laws", as they were the first to give order and laws to a chaotic Universe. Like every other force of the Cosmos, they all came from that one first universal being, the primeval Sound, born by the Wave (or the nine waves). But they were different from the first being because they emerged from the stored, slumbering dream-speech that contained the memory of a previous world.

> Finally, the question is, Why are giants and gods suddenly veiled and described as dwarfs? As long as we insist on reading the myths as literal renderings of childish fairy-tales, this poses a problem. We have gods there, giants here, and dwarfs are supposed to be different creatures entirely. When we integrate the fact that the ancient poets applied folklore to serve their own end; to use them as metaphors for deeper meaning, it is easier to see that these "racial" distinctions are of no importance or consequence, and serves only one purpose: to reveal what kind of force works, in what kind of way, and under what kind of condition.

According to Lotte von Motz, the Norse word for dwarf, dvergr (m.sg.), Actually means "mutilated", as in someone who has had a limb or part of himself chopped off, severed. Motz uses this to illustrate how the dwarfs in the myths seem to play the role of priests, as do their mythical relatives, the smith and the dark elf. There is some evidence that priests had a part of their body mutilated during initiation, something which may have been reflected in the myth of Óðinn sacrificing his eye for the mead of wisdom, or in the sorcerers who seem to have suffered castration as part of their profession. I wholeheartedly agree that dwarfs in other settings, together with smiths and dark elves, seem to represent typical Pagan priests in many myths, but this is not the only way that they appear. In the Vǫluspá, I believe they represent the original images of human beings emerging from the one to the many. Their craftiness is the craftiness of life itself. I believe that the term dvergr [dwarf] is used by the poets both because the concept dwarf brings to mind something that is "smaller", and because the word itself means "mutilated" and indicates something that is not whole. What we are probably seeing here is a version of an ancient and widespread philosophy, recognizable in the Indian poet Kamalakanta's Syama Sangit (Songs to Kali).

He describes the creator goddess in action, applying an age-old concept of creation: "limiting the Limitless." Here are the limitless powers of cosmic awareness, divided into a trinity of spiritual, mental and emotional qualities, entering the sphere of physical form, in which their original spiritual limitlessness is limited into "spoken" (mind-created) forms.

2.10: ASKR AND EMBLA-THE FIRST HUMANS AND THE AESIR GODS-

17. Until Three came out of that flock powerful and loving Aesir to the homes
They found on the shore, of little power
Askr and Embla, without destiny.

> *17.Unz þrír kvámu ór því liði*
> *ǫflgir ok ástkir æsir á húsi*
> *fundu á landi lítt megandi*
> *Ask ok Emblu, ørlǫgslausa.*

Stanza 17 of the Vǫluspá introduced the first human beings, the male Askr and the female Embla. They are found by the newly arrived Aesir, who have entered our dimension through or from the flock of dwarfs, and they are found "on the shore". Snorri explained that the first human man and women were two pieces of driftwood found on the beach by the sons of Bórr; Óðinn, Víli and Vé. The "driftwood" is obviously a metaphor. The tree is in itself a well-established metaphor for the physical body of the universe and of human beings in Old Norse poetry, and wood is thus metaphorically the matter that builds up the universe and the physical bodies. The "ocean" is both the Earthly waters and the great cosmic waters, a beach or a shore is then a place where the great "water" finds the frontier of an enclosed space, a land, a world. Thus the first people are drifting potentials discovered by the powers of cosmic intelligence as they roam the newly born Earth.

THE WOOD AND THE BREW: ASKR AND EMBLA

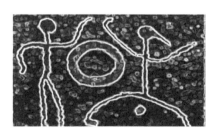

Bronze Age rock carving, Scandinavia a man and a woman flanking a Sun disc or other circular symbol, typically, the woman has a ponytail and an egg-like object dropping from between her legs.

The meaning of the name of the first human male, Askr, is beyond doubt: It means "Ash" and is a reference to the world tree, which is frequently referred to as an ash. When the first human male is referred to as an ash, the tree that ultimately symbolized the divine cosmic body, it is an indication that the first man is of the same original mold as the universe itself, created in God's image, so to speak. Could this be a Christian influence? I believe that it can safely be placed within the context of a Pagan worldview. First of all, the Christian approach leaves God outside of his creation, whereas the Pagan approach allows creation itself to be the original divine body.

According to Snorri, men in poetry can always be referred to as masculine trees such as the ash, the oak, the maple or the apple tree, as Snorri explains in the Skáldskaparmál: "...there is a tree called rowan. On the basis of these terms poets have called men ash or maple, grove or other masculine tree-names." On the basis of Snorri's information which is frequently confirmed in Old Norse poetry, it is probably also safe to assume that the image of the universe as a tree is in fact a metaphorical way of saying that the universal body is a kind of man. This is in its turn confirmed by the existence of a world giant which can also be depicted as a god, Heimdallr, the Great World. It would be natural to assume that the first human female, Embla, also is a tree. At least, this is what most interpretations assume. It is a logical assumption, seeing as Snorri claimed that women could be referred to as feminine trees such as the elm, the linden, the birch, the willow or the alder, as Snorri wrote: "It is proper to refer to her by calling her dealer (selia) or consumer (lóg) of whatever she hands out, but selia ["willow"] and lóg are trees. Hence a woman is called in metaphors by all feminine tree-names."

However, the name Embla proposes some serious problems, and no one has really figured out what tree she is supposed to be molded from. Sophus Bugge suggested that er name is a derivation from Elm-la, in its turn a derivation from the Germanic Almilon, related to the Old Norse *almr* {"elm"}. If this was really the case, I can personally not understand why the Old Norse poet did not just call her Almr or Alma. H. Sperber suggested that the name is related to Greek *ámpelos* ["vine" or "liana"], an interpretation which is just as vague and uncertain. Linguists desperate to come up with a solution to what Embla really means have proposed even more weird solutions: R. Much proposed the impossible idea that her name is derived from the Vandal king Ambri, who was a companion of the king Assi, supposedly the prototypical Askr.

Such an imaginative interpretation, the latter downright ridiculous approach on behalf of serious scholars gives me the courage to offer an interpretation of my own. What if Embla is not really a tree after all? What if she, just like her male counterpart, is shaped in the same mold as the first cosmic being, only that she is not molded in the male first being [the "tree"] but in the female first being, the mead-producing "cow"? Whereas the *mbla* ending in the name, with its emphasis on the *mb-sound* would not change easily, the *e* beginning would be easily changed. An h easily goes silent in spoken languages, and a vocal easily slips into a different vocal, so that the name Embla could originally have been Humbla; a meaning that indicates "Brew Ingredient" and is the same that makes up the name Auðhumbla ["Abundant Brew Ingredient"]. This interpretation would truly show that the first man and woman on Earth are created from the same mold as the first male and female element in Cosmos, the "wooden" shape of solid matter and the fluid, animating spark of life energy which nourishes and inspires the "brew" of life and movement within the matter.

THE THREEFOLD GIFT OF THE AESIR

They had no breath/spirit
They had no poetry/mind
They had no vitality, no beautiful colors;
The Spirit gave them breath/spirit
"Chicken" gave them poetry/mind
The Heat gave them vitality and beautiful colors

> *Ǫnd þau ne áttu,*
> *óð þau ne hǫfðu,*
> *lá né læti*
> *né litu góða;*
> *ǫnd gaf Óðinn,*
> *óð gaf Hænir,*
> *lá gaf Lóður*
> *ok litu góða*

Vǫluspá st. 18, Poetic Edda

In the Vǫluspá, stanza 18, the three sons of Borr offer to man and woman both the gifts of **breath, spirit, mind, poetry, vitality and colors**. In short, the Aesir trinity, having accessed the realm of physical life on Earth, share their essential qualities with human beings, or perhaps we should just say they share it with physical life itself, after all, Askr and Embla seem to represent microcosmic versions of the male and female aspects of the great universe (as discussed above).

The two, beginning as "driftwood", may very well just represent the drifting life potential that is found on the shores of the young Earth. Óðinn gives the gift of breath or spirit (ǫnd/and). One of the three meanings of Óðin's name is obviously emphasized here ["The Spirit"], which is also the same as breath. Óðin's brother Vé is disguised as the mysterious Hænir, who offers óðr to the life potential. Óðr is the very word from which the name Óðinn is made, here obviously signifying "poetry" and thus "mind" or "thought". Hænir shows up in another myth related by Snorri in the Ynglinga saga, where he is offered as a gift to the Vanir, who at first are impressed with his dazzling eloquence and nice appearance.

However, when they realize that he has to consult Mímir ["Memory"] whenever a decision has to be made, they are less impressed. Hænir corresponds with Vé ["Sacred Space"] and with the poetry/mind/thought meaning in Óðin's name. The name Hænir means "chicken" or "hens", in plural. This comical name has puzzled scholars for decades on end. Why would the mind-giver be called "chicken", as in a myriad of clucking birds? We tend to hold the rational mind in a very high regard, and it seems difficult to accept that the myth-makers are making fun of it. I believe, however, that the fact that the giver of thought is metaphorically refereed to as a "chicken" is a comical way of describing exactly how the thinking mind works. If you have ever observed a chicken, you can see how the behavior of clucking, plucking and babbling to either search out food or collaborate with other chickens is the perfect example of the constant movement, confusion and chaos the human mind exists in. The last brother, Víli, whose name means "Intent" or "Will", is replaced with Hlóðurr, meaning "Heat". He is the giver of vital life force and beautiful colors.

The underlying message is that in men and in women, perhaps in all physical life, these three basic **mental-spiritual-emotional** qualities exist and are divine in origin, microcosmic replicas of the greater universal consciousness.

2.11: Yggdrasill, the World Tree

19. I know an Ash stands
It is called the Old Steed
a tall tree, poured over with shining bright sand from there comes the dew
that falls in the valleys it stands ever green above
The Well of Origin.

> *19. Ask veit ek standa,*
> *heitir Yggdrasill*
> *hár baðmr, ausinn*
> *hvíta auri;*
> *þaðan koma dǫggvar*
> *þærs í dala falla;*
> *stendr æ yfir grœnn*
> *Urðar Brunni.*

Vǫluspá, st.19, Poetic Edda

Trees aboard a Ship of Life
Bronze Age Rock Carving
from Lökeberget, Sweden

Man and the world tree

In the Vǫluspá, the World Tree is only introduced after the birth of physical life on Earth (or the two first human beings). It is interesting that the first man is identified with the World Tree through his name Askr. This identification is very important to bear in mind when trying to understand the World Tree, and also the role that the various powers [Norns, gods and metaphorical animals] play in its existence. In a poetical manner, we may all understand how the tree is a metaphor for the universe at large. The metaphor for the human being, or for physical organisms as such, is even more obvious. If we consider the fact that the human nervous system actually looks a lot like a tree with countless branches, we moderns may better understand the likeness. The tree of the nervous system, with its roots, branches and trunk that in fact exists within the human body is subject to a number of influences that are both universal qualities shared by all physical organisms, some existing in the larger cosmos, as well as internal qualities operating differently within each individual. It is not impossible that our ancestors were able to perceive the nervous system through their knowledge of the insides of a physical body. We know that the Chinese developed knowledge about meridians within the physical body thousands of years ago, a system of energy movement through the body that is also mapped quite like a tree.

It is no coincidence that many meditative practices use the tree as a metaphor for the human body, and it is based as much on ancient sciences of the body as on imagination, poetry and religion. In this Chapter, I will explore the universal qualities of the World Tree, but remind the reader that the Universe Tree is also an image of the physical body, your body and the powers that rule it, eat from it and nourish it. When we see the eagle seated at the top of the world tree, with a hawk of immortality between its eyes, we may think of the eagle as the seat of the mind; the brain and the hawk as the third eye of divine vision. The "winds" that are sent down through the universe from the flapping wings of the eagle may be likened to the signals sent from the brain through the nervous system and other channels that move through the body like the branches and roots of a tree. The leaves that are being eaten by the forces of decay are like the cells that continuously die within our bodies.

The serpent that lies coiled at the base of the roots, feeding on the liquid that falls into the well of death, is as much a power within as a universal power of transformation and renewal. The squirrel that runs up and down the trunk of world tree carrying information between the powers that rule the tree corresponds to the communication that actually happens between the various compartments of the body, especially up and down the trunk of our spine where the central nervous system resides. The ladies of fate who carve runes symbols into the base of the trunk, weaving and spinning and shaping the life of the world tree, nourishing its universal body with the sacred liquid of ever renewing life-force, are also powers that run within the individual, the life-giving power of streaming movement, the sparks of life, carving, perhaps like the symbols of our DNA into the core of our bodies. The wells that nourish the world tree are wells of life-generating and consciousness-storing energy centers within the living body. This understanding just described is undoubtedly a modern version of what our ancestors may have perceived, but it is an understanding that is based on the archaic version, where many actual truths about the body and how it works were perceived and explained through the language then available. They may not have known about DNA, but they may well have intuited the existence of unseen symbols which seem to exist within, running the courses of our lives on a basic level.

THE WORLD TREE OF SHAMANS

The mythical world tree is so ancient and widespread that it would be impossible to determine exactly one function and one meaning, or exactly one origin to the concept. The closest comparative the Old Norse version of the world tree may perhaps be found in various Siberian mythologies. In his book Shamanism, Archaic Techniques of Ecstasy (ch. 8) Mircea Eliade suggests a basic meaning to this very old concept:

"Cosmologically, the World Tree rises at the center of the earth...and its branches touch the palace of [celestial divinities, heaven]...The Mongols imagine the Cosmic Mountain as a four-sided pyramid with a Tree in its center; the gods use it as a hitching post for their horses, as they do the Pillar of the World....It represents the universe in continual regeneration, the inexhaustible spring of cosmic life....on the other, it symbolizes the sky or the planetary heavens...expressing the sacrality of the world."

In the same Chapter, Eliade also offers various examples of world tree lore in connection to shamanism and initiation journeys:

> *"The Cosmic Tree is essential to the shaman. From its wood he makes his drum, climbing the ritual birch, he effectually reaches the summit of the Cosmic Tree..."*

From Eliade's great work, we also learn that the idea of the World Tree is closely connected to the concepts of soul and fate in various Siberian, shamanic traditions:

> *"The Tree connects the three cosmic regions...According to Siberian Tatars, a replica of the Celestial Tree stands in the underworld; a fir with nine roots... The Goldi reckon three Cosmic Trees, the first is in the sky (and the souls of men perch on its branches like birds, waiting to be carried down to earth to bring infants to birth), the second on earth, and the third in the underworld... The Goldi, the Dolgan and the Tungus say that, before birth, the souls of children perk like little birds on the branches of the Cosmic Tree, and the shamans go there to find them. This mythical motif...is not confined to Central and North Asia; it is attested, for example, in Africa and Indonesia. The cosmological schema Tree-Bird (= Eagle) or Tree with a Bird at its top and a Snake at its roots, although typical of the peoples of Central Asia and the ancient Germans, is presumably of Oriental origin, but the same symbolism is already formulated on prehistoric monuments."*

YGGDRASILL, THE STEED OF SPIRIT

In the Gylfaginning, Snorri described a world tree not unlike that which is described by Eliade after studying many different variations of the World Tree myth in Siberian cultures. According to Snorri, the World Tree, the "ash" Yggdrasill, was the High Seat or Sanctuary of the gods, where the gods keep their sacred parliament every day:

> *"The ash is the best and greatest among all trees; his branches reach out across the entire world and into the heaven. He has three roots that keep him upright, and which are spread unusually widely. One of them is among the Aesir [by the Well of Origin], another is among the frost giants [by the Well of Memory], where the Open Mouth of the Sacred Descendants was before.*
>
> *The third is above the Misty World, and beneath that root is the [death-well] Hvergelmir [Bellowing Mill], and Níðhǫggr [Biter Beneath, a serpent] eats of the root from beneath.*
>
> *Beneath the root that turns toward the frost giants, there is the Well of Memory [Mímisbrunnr]; in that water is hidden wisdom and knowledge. Memory [Mímir] is he called who owns the well. He is filled with wisdom, for he drinks out of the well with the horn called Bellowing Horn [Gjallarhorn, the same as Heimdallr uses]...*
>
> *The third root to the ash stands in the heavens, and beneath that root is there a well that is particularly sacred, and which is called the Well of Origin [Urðarbrunnr], this is where the gods keep their legal councils. Every day the Aesir ride up there on the Shivering Voice [Bifrǫst] which is also called the Bridge of the Aesir."*

The red horse of Tysoe.
Engraving in the ground

It is my guess that the world tree simply represents the physical universe, much like the world giant Ymir did. Where Ymir is the unshaped primeval universe, the sound vibration that makes creation possible, the tree is a universe of shape and form. The name Yggdrasill indicates that the physical universe is a steed, an ancient steed, but a steed for what? The word yggr means "old" or "terrible" but is also a name of Óðin's. It is not unlikely that the physical universe was considered the "steed" or traveling vehicle of what Óðinn ultimately represents; Spirit. The giant Mímir and the god Heimdallr also seem to represent the universe, but are more closely related to Óðin's role as the spirit that rides the physical world. While the tree obviously represents the physical matter universe, the three powers connected to it Óðinn, Mímir and Heimdallr seem to represent the three aspects of the consciousness of the universe. As Snorri explained (above), Mímir represents the universal memory and also drinks of it when he drinks of the Well of Memory, drinks of the hidden wisdom and knowledge that is stored in that well. Is it the Memory of the universe itself that the giant and his well represent? It is interesting to note here that the World Tree is sometimes called Mímameiðr [the Tree of Memory], as in belonging to the giant called Memory. Heimdallr uses the same Bellowing Horn as Memory does, but for the purpose of blowing out substance rather than drinking it. The god is by his very name, "Great World", identifiable as the world itself. He represents the universal consciousness that sees and hears absolutely everything that happens in the world that is his own body.

THE MEAD TREE

The first time the World Tree is mentioned in the Vǫluspá poem, it is called Mioðvíðr [The Mead Tree]. Interestingly, the sacred mead offered to initiates throughout the Norse myths, a mead that transmits wisdom and magical powers to the recipient, is often called the Mead of Memory, testifying once more to the conscious universe, a universe that stores experience like a memory, providing wisdom and power to those who may access this universal memory. When Óðinn the Spirit asks Mímir the Universal Memory for a drink of the Well of Memory, it is described as a cup of mead [The Mead of Memory]. He has to leave an eye in the Well as a payment for the drink, a symbol of the Spirit with one eye open in the ordinary world, another eye open in the eye of universal memory, which is the same as knowledge and power. The mead reference clearly associates the world tree with initiation, knowledge and also with the resurrecting powers of the source of all precious mead; the Well of Origin.

In stanza 19 (Vǫluspá), quoted in the beginning of this chapter, we learn that the world tree is poured over every day by white shining gravel. Snorri explains that this is the gravel of the Well of Origin, at one of the roots of the World Tree that lies in heaven and in the heart of Ásgarðr, the sphere of the gods who rule by parliament. The oldest of the Norns, Origin, is responsible for taking water and gravel from that well every day, and nourish the world tree with it. The rejuvenating power of the water prevents the tree from decay.

Snorri added that the Well of Origin had the quality that anyone who bathes in it will come out of it as a transparent being of white light, a sort of resurrection into spirit enlightened. The universe tree is continuously threatened by the serpent Biter Below and other animal symbols belonging to the world of the dead. The Biter Below gnaws eternally at the roots of the tree, its onslaughts healed only through the regenerating powers of the Mead of Origin. The serpent is a very ancient symbol of regeneration in itself, as it sheds it skin and thus transforms.

In Norse myths, it is strongly associated with death and what happens in death. The serpent in question is definitely residing in Hel or Misty Hel, the world of the dead. It is thus associated with a well that is described as being crowded with serpents. This well is called the Bellowing Mill, and is also the source of all the cosmic "rivers". The image of the souls being ground in this mill before they are recycled as flowing life force is powerful and ought to be scrutinized a bit more, which we will be doing in the Chapter 4 about Death and Creation.

THE SOUL TREE AND THE WELLS

As mentioned above, the souls of the living are symbolized in several Siberian mythologies as the leaves of the world tree. I think this concept is also found in Old Norse lore and is the only way to explain why, in the Norse lore, the leaves of the world tree are being continuously chewed by four stags that go by the names Dáin, Dvalin, Duneyrr and Duraþrór, meaning "Dead One", "Hibernation", "Brown Ears" and "Slumber-Boar". The names of the two first stags are identical to the names of dwarfs listed earlier, and the other two would be typical dwarf names as well, suggesting that the stags refer to limited, physical forms that feed on the green foliage of the universe tree. The association to death and hibernation obviously refers to the role of the stags as chewing the leaves that may well symbolize life. The boar is a symbol of sacrifice, an animal that would be slaughtered and then resurrected in the other world, and this one is "slumbering". It is difficult to determine exactly what the meaning of the four stags is, but we do get a very interesting clue in another stag that appears on the roof of Valhǫll, the stag called Eikþyrnir [Oak Antlers], who is accompanied by the she-goat called Heiðrún [Bright Symbol].

Both of these also chew continuously on the leaves of the world tree:

According to the Grímnismál poem, this nourishment causes an interesting alchemical reaction in these cosmic animals: The stag produces drops of liquid from his antlers, which fall down into the well of Hel, the well where souls are ground and recycled after death. The identical fate of the liquid product of the "leaves" of the world tree and the soul essence of the living points to the same thing:

The liquid substance of the leaf is a symbol of the life-force in the body, essentially what we would call soul poetically described as an eternal "liquid essence" of the physical matter (the leaf) which is being eternally recycled, emerging from the Well of Origin, returning to the Well of Hel. I suggest that the two wells are two aspects of the very same thing: the place of origin which is also the place of return after death. The Well of Memory is yet another aspect of the same phenomenon, the same place of origins and endings, the place where the memories of the life experience is gathered and stored before the liquid soul substance returns to the world as a new stream of life.

The she-goat Heiðrún also chews the leaves of the world tree, yet in her body, the liquid substance of the leaf, that is, the soul essence and life experience of the mortal body, is transformed into the Precious Mead that is served to the dead souls in Valhǫll and to the initiates into wisdom. The mead and the initiation it is associated with shall be thoroughly explored in Chapter 6.

THE SERPENT, THE SQUIRREL AND THE EAGLE

According to Snorri, there is an eagle seated in the branches of the ash (the world tree), "and he knows much". Between the eyes of the eagle is a hawk called Veðrfǫlnir [Wind Diminisher]. The eagle in the world tree appears several times in Norse myths and is a subject we will be discussing several times. For now, it is sufficient to say that the much-knowing eagle is the origin of winds, being described as silent, unseen movement that affects the entire universe yet is never seen by men. The same winds are metaphors for death, and in one account, the eagle is called Hræsvelgr ["The Corpse Swallower"}. We will discuss the death eagle a further in Chapter 4.8. For now, let me just suggest that the eagle's association to death lies, perhaps, in the fact that the eagle is a hunter, soaring above, observing majestically, then suddenly dropping down on its kill.

The eagle is usually associated with divine objectivity, the spirit that soars above and is able to grasp the great picture. According to Mircea Eliade, birds in the world tree are considered the manifestations of souls, and great vultures or eagles often represent the great spirit of the world tree that hatches new life, and that hatches new shamans during their initiation. In Native American traditions, the eagle is often a symbol of the Great Spirit. This is not entirely different from how the eagle appears in Norse myths, Óðinn, who represents Spirit, does take on an eagle hide, during his initiation. Apart from its role as a power of death, I believe the Norse eagle should also be seen as a power of Spirit, the much knowing observer that seats itself in the higher realms of cosmos, watching down on the living.

In between the eyes of the eagle, the hawk called Wind Diminisher seems to represent that which "diminishes" death, a kind of immortality. The hawk of immortality between the eagle's eyes does remind me of the concept of a third eye which is found in Indian Tantric chakra teachings. In fact, there are some elements that are similar to Tantra in the entire image of the world tree. First of all, we see that the world tree, representing the universe, also corresponds with the human body, as if the human being is a microscopic replica of the macrocosm.

Thus what happens in the world tree, the qualities and the descriptions of it, also happens within the human being, and we have the same qualities and "realms" within ourselves as those that we observe outside ourselves. In Tantra, the Great God (usually Shiva), who is the silent, passive observer of existence, resides not only in the mind of the universe, but also within an enclosure within the human mind, in the head, where we find the crown and the third eye chakras. The chakras are "wheels" of energy, centers in the body where life energy of the body is circulated and sent on its way through the physical and spiritual body. The third eye, when opened, represents seeing through illusion, which leads to immortality.

The hawk of the spirit eagle is possibly a Norse equivalent, since it is associated with the third eye of a spirit being that "knows much", and with immortality. The crown chakra is at the top of the head, where this wheel of energy may open up the individual's consciousness to become one with the great universal consciousness, the Shiva within becomes the Shiva without. It is possible that the Norse eagle represents this same universal consciousness.

If there ever was a tradition similar to Tantra in the Old Norse world, as I believe is certainly possible, the imagery offers a possible indication as to where deities would be situated within the body of a human being (since the body is a temple). The eagle is not only a symbol of the ultimate origin of movement (wind) and death (devouring beak), but also of Óðinn after he has conquered death. The hawk may, according to Snorri, replace the falcon in poetry, and the falcon is the bird of Freyia, Frigg and Freyr, who sometimes lend their falcon hide out to the shaman Loki when he needs to move into other realms.

Thus we see that the god Óðinn corresponds with the mind and what in Tantric traditions would be known as the Crown chakra, where the soul may achieve union with the greater universal consciousness, whereas Freyia/Frigg and her brother Freyr correspond with the Third Eye chakra, where the soul may travel into all dimensions and perceive beyond the apparent, beyond the veils of illusion. Going down to the base of the world tree, we see, in Norse myths, that a serpent lies coiled there, by the roots. In the Tantra tradition, there is also a serpent, lying coiled at the base of the spine of the human body, by the root chakra, the wheel of energy that opens up the connection to earth and the physical world.

The Tantric serpent is called Kundalini and represents the Great Goddess, the dynamic energy of Shakti, the universal goddess of creation in her raw energy form. Shakti simply means "Power". The aim of Tantric practice is to make the Kundalini serpent rise from the root chakra within the body and move up towards the crown chakra, where the Great Goddess and the Great God unite in an ecstatic union which leads to enlightenment. The relationship between the Goddess and the God is mirrored both in the universe at large and within the individual. Within the individual, the Kundalini serpent, the dynamic power energy (the Goddess), lies dormant, sleeping within, and must be awakened in order to move through the entire being and unite with the divine consciousness (the God).

Design from purse lid,
Sutton Hoo, 7th century:
An eagle behind a smaller
bird – a hawk/falcon?

There is no way of knowing for certain if something similar to Tantra was practiced in Scandinavia and mirrored in the image of the eagle in the top and the serpent at the base of the world tree, but I can see no better explanation for this imagery. In Norse myths, we do see how a goddess sleeping in the underworld must be woken up in order to reach the state of wisdom that is sought through initiation, and the goddess is sometimes associated with the serpent, yet not as directly linked as the Shakti is identified as the Kundalini serpent in the Indian tradition.

One such sleeping goddess is reached only after the hero has been able to retrieve the divine "gold" that has been guarded by a coiled up serpent, but the serpent and the goddess are not identical. Death as an entity often could appear in serpent shape, but mostly in a goddess/ogress shape, and the ogress of death steers her wolf steed with serpent reins. However, although wielded by a female, the serpent itself is usually referred to as a male, and Óðinn sometimes wears a serpent disguise. According to Snorri, he entered the realm of Gunnlǫð in the shape of a serpent and escaped in the shape of an eagle.

We also know that one of his many names is Svafnir [Sleep-Causer], counted among the serpents who dwell in the well of Hel. Not only is there a Biter Below in Norse myths, a great serpent coiled at the base of the world tree, but we also hear that this serpent is associated with the well of Hel, the Bellowing Mill where the souls of the dead are ground into oblivion before they are recycled into the cosmic rivers. This well is apparently crammed with serpents, carrying names associated with death and burial. In the poem Grímnismál, these serpents simply lie at the roots of the world tree. In Vǫluspá, they feed on the "life blood" of the doomed dead. Knowing the serpent's property of shedding its skin, and how its swinging movement may be symbolizing life energy, we see a grim image that may not, after the first sight, be quite as grim; the serpent imagery is one of regeneration and transformation in death. After Ragnarǫk, when the new world emerges in its enlightened splendor, the Biter Below will cease to lie coiled at the base of the world, but instead take the form of a feathered dragon, flying above, carrying the souls of the dead to their destination, as is said in the last stanza of the Vǫluspá:

66. *There comes the dark dragon flying*
That shining serpent from beneath from the Dark Moon Mountains he carries
in its feathers flying over the plain the corpses; Biter Below

    66. *Þar kemr inn dimmi*
    dreki fljúgandi,
    naðr fránn neðan
    frá Niðafjǫllum;
    berr sér í fjǫðrum
    — flýgr vǫll yfir —
    Níðhǫggr nái.

Unlike Tantra, there is no mention of the serpent moving up the spine of the body or the trunk of the world tree. There might have been such traditions, but we are left with no evidence for this, as far as I can tell. Instead of the serpent rising to unite with the eagle, Snorri describes a squirrel called Ratatǫskr who moves between the eagle and the serpent, carrying "hateful words" between the eagle and the serpent. What is meant by that image is uncertain, but the name of the squirrel is derived from the verb rata "to move", and tǫskr "container" as in a bag or a purse. The best translation would be "The Moving Container". This squirrel, running up and down the tree, "contains" communication between the serpent base and the eagle top, and this would be true both in the universe at large and within the individual. Why the communication is hateful is the biggest mystery, and no explanation is given. Additionally, we only have Snorri's word for it. If there is, as I have suggested, a similarity to Tantric concepts in the image of the serpent and the eagle, the squirrel may represent the negative thought-patterns that prevent the union between the lower and the higher "realms" of a being, which is so fundamental to spiritual awakening.

2.12: NORNS, FYLGJUR AND THE RUNES OF FATE

The Norns are introduced in Vǫluspá just after the creation of people and the first presentation of World Tree as a Universe of structure and form. Earlier, we saw how Norns arrive after the birth of Helgi [Sacred One] in the Grove of Bright Shine, Helgi here representing the birth of the Universe itself as the first "man" or conscious entity. When the gods found the lifeless driftwood that was to become life and humankind, it was noted that Askr and Embla were "without destiny". The moment the two are given breath, intelligence and vitality, they also obtain a destiny, symbolized by the arrival of the Norns in Vǫluspá, stanza 20:

20. From there (the Well of Origin) come maidens much knowing three, from that hall which stands beneath the (World-)Tree Origin, the first is called the second Is About To Happen they carved (runes) into the wood,
Debt was the third (maiden);
They made the laws
They shaped the lives
For the children of the ages they determined all fate.

20. Þaðan koma meyjar margs vitandi þrjár, ór þeim sal er und þolli stendr; Urð hétu eina, aðra Verðandi, skáru á skíði, Skuld ina þriðju; þær lǫg lǫgðu, þær líf kuru alda bǫrnum, ǫrlǫg seggja.

-Vǫluspá st.20, Poetic Edda

Let us have a short summary of Old Norse cosmological genesis based on the previous eleven Chapters:

    > To begin with, the universe comes into being in a way that seems to point to a resurrection from a slumbering state. This slumbering state is like death a state of stillness and oblivion between lives.

There were nine previous worlds, and the awareness that wakes up from slumber within ice and mist must be the reincarnating awareness of these previous worlds. Various universal qualities begin to play their parts; physical rock matter, streaming dynamic energies that bring matter to life and movement, and conscious energies that shape this matter.

> When Earth begins to grow fertile, the masculine, conscious and shaping powers; the "gods", are urged and pushed by the feminine, dynamic and moving powers; "the fates", to create limited (shaped, separated) forms through which the unseen and limitless may enter physical existence, the world of forms and shapes, symbolized as "dwarfs". Through these dwarfish molds, the limitless spiritual energies may become manifest in a physical world of shapes. Life is induced by these spiritual energies, matter is given spirit, mind and vitality, and are then subject to life and death and thus to fate.

> The World Tree is introduced as an allegory of the sacred universal body, as well as the sacred body of any individual. It is a symbol of life itself, and the human body is its perfect image. This is where the Norns, the goddesses of fate, begin to play their part in the world's history for real.

FATE AND THE WORLD TREE

Eliade also described how there were associations between the World Tree, the souls and the fates of men. In Shamanism etc., He describes this:

> *"Another theme, us that of the Tree [as a] Book of Fate. Among the Osmanli Turks, the Tree of Life has a million leaves, on each of which a human fate is written; each time a man dies, a leaf falls. The Ostyak believe that a goddess, seated on a seven-story celestial mountain, writes a man's fate, as soon as he is born, on a tree with seven branches."*

Detail from Oseberg tapestry, Vestfold, Norway, 834 AD. Three women in procession beneath a row of two-headed serpents. Each woman carries something; the first, a sword (valkyrie), the second, a loom (fate-spinning norn), the third, three serpents (giantess). Beneath them, we see a (magic) mushroom, the fly agaric. They are walking past a grove of serpentine trees in which nine men are hanging.

Just as the leaves could symbolize life, so fate was written into life like inscriptions within matter (the leaf). We have seen how the Norse lore clearly suggests that leaves symbolize life. The concepts of fate are also clearly associated with the world tree: The Tree is in fact nourished by the oldest power of fate, the equivalent of the Ostyak goddess above, the Norn called Origin [Urðr]. She and her sister Verdandi ["Happening Now", "About to Happen", "Present", "Being" or "Becoming"] also write fate into the substance of the world tree, only they write it into the roots of the tree. It is time to have a closer look at the concepts of fate and souls in the Edda tradition, concepts that are presented immediately after the creation of human beings who are molded in the shape of the universe tree itself and all its properties, ridden by the same Spirit, ruled by the same Fates.

THE WELL OF ORIGIN

The Norns, or Fates, originate in the Well of Origin [Urðarbrunnr], as is stated in the Vǫluspá stanza 20, quoted in the beginning of this chapter. To understand what they are, we must understand the place that birthed them. The Well of Origin stands beneath the World Tree, as a source of its life. Stanza 2 of the same poem suggests that the "Mead Tree" grew from the ground, which is where the Well of Origin is situated. The Tree is nourished daily by the water and the shining "soil" [aurr soil, gravel, sand, mud] that is taken from the Well of Origin, and this nourishment rejuvenates and resurrects the tree from the decay that it is also subject to on a daily basis. The "dew that falls in the valleys" (stanza 19) is derived from this sacred water, as it runs through the veins of the World Tree and seeps out through its the pores. This liquid dew is associated with honey and thus with the sacred mead.

According to Snorri in the Gylfaginning, the Well of Origin has several magical and life-giving, transformative properties:

> "It is further told that the Norns who live by the Well of Origin, every day take water out of the Well, and with it the soil that lies around it, and pours it over the ash, so that the branches will not dry out or rot. This water is so sacred that everything that falls into it becomes as bright and shining as the membrane within the inside of an eggshell... the dew that falls onto earth from there, people call honey dew, and it is what the bees live from. Two birds live in the Well of Origin, they are called swans, and from them are the birds that are called swans descended."

The transformative power of the Well of Origin is here emphasized to bathe in it is equal to emerge bright, shining and transparent much like a "light being". In fact, Snorri immediately after goes on to describe a place called "Alfheimr" the World of Elves" in fact the Light Elves, who reside in the upper heavens. In Chapter 3, we shall see that elves are described as the souls of the dead, and that Light Elves appear to be the immortal souls of the initiated and the enlightened.

NORNS AND SOULS

In Chapter 2.6, we saw that the mythology surrounding the Sun goddess as well as the Norns by the Well of Origin carries strong elements from Finno-Ugric or Uralic, shamanic traditions. The sacred realm of the Sun Mother contained elements that are similar to the realm of the Norns: It has a lake or a water-source which has a rejuvenating effect. In fact, it is the water from where all souls emerge and to where all souls return after death in order to be reborn. The souls are symbolized as waterbirds ducks, geese and swans. It is significant to note that Snorri mentions the existence of swans living within the Well of Origin.

Norns and Valkyrie are very much of the same stock in Old Norse myths the only difference being that Valkyrie seem to be the fates that are attached to warriors or men with divine or glorious fates. In one Edda poem, the Helreið Brynhildar [Brynhild's Ride to Hel], the Valkyrie Brynhildr states that she was one of eight sisters wearing swan hides. The Valkyrie are often described as wearing swan or bird hides, such as the "southern ladies" of the Edda poem Vǫlundarkvíða, where we hear that three brothers found three ladies on the shore. The ladies are first presented in the prose introduction:

> "One morning they found on the beach three women and they were spinning linen [= spinning fate], with them were their bird hides, they were Valkyrie."

The poem begins by further associating the Valkyrie both with fate, bird hides and the soul. The ladies have traveled through the Dark Forests and arrived at the shores of the Wolf Sea the wolf being a symbol of life-spark, desire, lust and the instinct for survival. In the poem, however, the shore where the ladies arrive is actually called "The Beach of Souls".

2 ...the beautiful maiden enclosed him in her bright embrace; Another was Swan White she wore the feathers of a swan on the Beach of Souls they sat down to rest the Southern Red Ladies spun the precious linen (of fate).	*2....fagr mer fira faþmi liosom; onnor var Svanhvít, svanfiaðrar dró, þer a Sevarstrond settvz at hvilaz, Drosir Suðronar dyrt lín spvnno.*

The fate-spinning Valkyrie are described as coming from the south, where all Norns and Valkyrie are derived, the same realm that birthed the Sun goddess, the same place of blazing heat waves from where the cosmic cow Auðhumbla emerged to revive the ice of a slumbering world. It is the southern read, bright golden realm of the Well of Origin, situated in the heart of Ásgarðr, where the gods gather to keep parliament. The association between Norns and swans is very clear, whereas the association between swans and the souls of people, and between Norns and the souls of people, must be scrutinized more closely. The association swan/waterbird and the souls of people can only be argued on the basis of comparative mythology. It is likely that the association is present in the Old Norse lore because it exists in comparative lores that seem to have inspired the Norse tradition.

The ancient Uralic concept of the Sun and Soul-Land with its Soul Source-Lake, where waterbirds symbolize the souls of the dead. The departure of such birds during winter is poetically used as an allegory of the departure of souls during death; the Southern Land of the Sun is the place where these souls are restored after diving into the Lake of the Sun. In Northern lands where winter often means months of darkness, where the sun is not seen at all, the bright and warm realm of the South easily comes to represent the place where life is restored after a period of dark cold and death.

The association between the Norns and the souls of people cannot be proven just by saying that the Norn equals the swan and the swan equals the soul, or by assuming that the Well of Origin in the southern bright realm of the Sun where life-restoring waters exist meant exactly the same to the Old Norse people as the very similar Uralic imagery meant to Uralic people and their descendants. It is likely, but we need more to go after. All we have are indications but there are many, and they are powerful. First of all, it is the mention of a Beach of Souls where the fate-spinning Valkyrie are discovered in the Vǫlundarkvíða. It is not the only time such an association is made. In the poem of Helgi Hundingsbani, we learn that the Valkyrie Sváva dwells on a mountain called Sefafjǫll The Mountain of Souls.

In the heroic poetry, the same Valkyrie follows the same man throughout his lifetimes sleeping between his lives, while he resides in the world of the dead. After he has successfully gone through his initiation trials in his third life of initiations, the Valkyrie saves him from oblivion in Hel and resurrects him into her own bright embrace like an enlightened self-merging with his own divine soul. In Edda the poem Fjǫlsvinnsmál, the young man, Svípdagr, discovers during his initiation that he has been married to the goddess who resides beneath the Tree of Memory, upon the Mountain of Medicine, since time immemorial: The only reason he has forgotten about this original marriage to the lady who "rules lands and people" is because he has died so many times or as the poem metaphorically describes this, he has been "taken on the wind-cold paths" so many times that he forgot who he really was.

The goddess to whom the young man is truly married to, and her company of nine sisters, are described much like Norns or Valkyrie, able to heal, teach and change a person's fate, and their realm is one of resurrection and renewal. Snorri Sturluson describes the Norns in his Gylfaginning as entities that follow a person throughout his or her life, spinning their fates:

> "There is a beautiful hall beneath the ash [the World Tree/the Body] by the Well [of Origin], and from this hall come the three maidens known as Origin, About to Happen, and Debt. These maidens set the fate for people; we call them Norns. There are other Norns too, and they come to every child that is born, and rule their lives' paths. Some Norns are of divine origin, others are elfin, and the third kind is of dwarf-kind, as it has been sung"

[In the Edda poem Fafnismál, stanza 13]:
Of much shattered birth
I believe the Norns are, they are not all the same kind:
Some are of Ás-kind [divine]
Some are of Elf-kind [immortal souls]
Some are the Daughters of Hibernation [dwarfish]

> *Svndrbornar mioc*
> *hygg ec at Norns se,*
> *eigoþ þer ett saman;*
> *svmar ero askvngar,*
> *svmar alfkvngar,*
> *svmar dotr Dvalins.*

Wandering Learning said:
> *"If the Norns rule the fates of people, then they shift it very unequally, since some live very well and in abundance, while others have little property and little glory, some have a long life and some a short one." The High One said: "The Norns that are good and of good lineage, they make a good fate. And when people have bad fortune, it is the cause of malevolent Norns."*

The essential message here is that our lives are ruled by our personal Norn, and that the fortune and misfortune in our lives depend on the kind of Norn that accompanies us throughout our lives. Our personal Norn, our personal Fate Goddess derives from the Well of Origin like all other Norns, yet there are different kinds, and they are "of shattered birth". The Norns that are divine, related to the Aesir, must represent fates that belong to the realm of the Aesir: a realm of mental powers and capacities. As Valkyrie, they bring fates of honor and glory the fate of the courageous warrior or successful king, for example. The Elfin Norns must be the fates of people who reach immortality in other ways, people whose souls are like the Light Elves, bright, silent and beautiful, elves who reside in the mysterious upper heavens of immortality, which we will be touching upon in the Chapter 6.

The "Daughters of Hibernation", the dwarfish Norns, are probably the ones who bring misfortune. It is easy to guess why. If they are the daughters of "Hibernation" or "Coma" [Dvalinn], they must be sleepwalking, and the fates they spin must be the lives of those who metaphorically sleepwalk, unconsciously, through life. In my opinion, the Daughter of Hibernation is the kind of fate that represents a slumbering soul, the soul of one who is not awake in his or her own life. When the heroes of Edda poetry seek to wake up their slumbering Norn or Valkyrie during initiation. I am pretty certain that this is an allegory of how the initiate through initiation wakes up his own slumbering soul. In the case of Sígurðr, the waking up of the sleeping Valkyrie leads to a glorious fate, and to the revelation of divine knowledge and magical powers. He was offered the guidance of the Valkyrie throughout his life, if he chose to listen to her. The Edda poem Sígrdrífumál, where the waking of the Valkyrie is described, clearly states that the only thing that could keep a man from listening to the guidance of his Valkyrie is fear, and the only thing that keeps us apart from the Valkyrie is fear.

Fear has kept the Valkyrie in a state of slumber ever since the previous life of the young man and fear has become an armor that has grown into her body: Once the armor is removed, cut away from her body, the Valkyrie wakes up and begins to reveal the sacred wisdom, transmitting her powers and divine fortune to her human.

THE FYLGJUR "FOLLOWERS"

Invitation to Blend sang:

48. Well it is that you have come now
I have had my will
The Follower shall give the kiss/say
the choice;
The best of happiness and fortune
come to those who hold each other
with love."

Mengløð kvað:

48. Vel þú nú kominn!
hefik minn vilja beðit,
Fylgja skal kveðju koss;
forkunnar sýn mun flestan glaða,
hvars hefir við annan ást.

Fjǫlsvinnsmál st. 48, Poetic Edda

Snorri's description of the personal Norns is very similar to the many references to Fylgjur in the saga sources. The word fylgja is a feminine noun usually translated as "follower", derived from the verb fylgja ["to follow", "accompany", "support", "align", "need", "keep inside", "have with oneself"]. It could thus be translated also as a "supporter", "companion", "alignment", "entity within" (or the more modern counterpart "inner being"). People had both animal Fylgjur and woman Fylgjur.

The animal fylgja of the sagas appear to be a symbol of the essential character of the person, and walks before her person on the path of life. When she is seen by her person, it is usually an omen of death the moment where the animal fylgja and her human being meet. The animal fylgja may also appear in dreams, symbolizing people and being omens of events that are to take place. The woman fylgja is something else entirely, although both the animal and the woman fylgja are related to the souls of people. The sources offer a variety of indications as to how Old Norse people perceived their Fylgjur. Sometimes, a fylgja appears as a female tutelary or guardian spirit to a clan or to the chief of a clan in particular.

In these cases, the fylgja is sometimes identified as the ancestral mother to the clan, and is thus the soul of a dead person who protects and guides her descendants. Thus the fylgja, like a Norn, is associated with the soul or a person, and as a clan's fylgja, she is associated with the soul of the ancestral mother. The importance and function of these ancestral mothers as well as the reverence paid to them clearly indicate ancestral worship. Ancient rituals of Sacred Marriage in Scandinavia may appear to have been the ritual "marriage" of a clan leader or tribal chief or king to the ancestral mother of the clan or the tribe, who guards the destiny and fortune of her descendants as a people.

One invaluable source to ancestral mother worship, sacred marriage and the clan fylgja function are the descriptions of Þórgerðr Holgabruðr, an ancestral mother to the Norwegian earls of Lade, who together with her sister Irpa was worshiped as a goddess by her descendants, with their own wooden idols and temple. Þórgerðr [Thunder Enclosure] was thought to be the fylgja of the Lade-clan, attached to all clan-patriarchs ever to follow, like she had once been married to the clan's male ancestor. Some, like Else Mundal in her dissertation Fylgjemotiva i norrøn litteratur [The Fylgja-Motifs in Norse Literature] (1974), suggest that this form of female ancestral worship may be a survival from a more matriarchal age.

Indeed, archaeology shows that the communal graves of early Scandinavian communities contain the remains of women who were all related, while the men were not. This is a strong indicator that men moved to their wives' clans and women represented the backbone of the clan, explaining why ancestral females were the ones who remained to protect their clans. Every human being regardless of clan was said to have a fylgja, and as often as not, the Fylgjur appear to be the souls of dead female relatives who after death begin their career as guardian spirits, sharing many properties with Norns and with female supernatural powers in general.

In fact, a fylgja often seems to be a soul that has become divine or supernaturally powerful after her death as a human woman. She is often also called a dís [goddess] or a Norn. The Fylgjur clearly have power over the fate of the individual they follow, suggesting a link to Snorri's description of the Norns who appear at birth and who follows a human being throughout her or his life. However, the ancestral mother fylgja is clearly associated with a human soul, but is not the soul of a living person, it is the soul of a dead ancestor operating as a guardian spirit to a descendant. How do these different descriptions of fate-spinning entities. The personal Norn who appears to be related to the soul of her person, and the personal guardian spirit who is also the soul of an ancestral mother or other female relative overlap and relate to one another?

The big question raised by those who discuss the subject is really whether the fylgja, also known as Hamingja, is really a goddess or Norn, an ancestral mother, or the soul of a person. I believe that scholars are confused by this issue because they insist that there must be a definite separation between these mythical species. I suggest otherwise. Let us begin with the fact that Snorri claimed that we all have personal Norns who spin the fortune or misfortune of our lives from birth to death. The degree of fortune depends on whether your Norn is divine, elfin or dwarfish. After analyzing the meaning of this statement further, we saw that the degree of fortune actually depends on whether your Norn is awake or in a state of slumber. This is in my opinion clearly an allegory of a person's soul. The Edda poetry strongly insinuates that it is possible to wake up one's Norn or Valkyrie [one's fate, through a ritual of initiation]. We will be discussing this on several occasions, particularly in Part II of this book.

This waking up of the fate has a considerable effect on the fate of the soul after death. The wakened fate offers guidance and wisdom, protection and spiritual illumination, and a kind of salvation in death. This is a very powerful indicator that the fate is related to the human soul and the fate of the soul in death. In the poem Fjǫlsvinnsmál, the young hero discovers that he has been married to the "great maiden" Menglǫð since time immemorial, and that he has only forgotten about their marriage because of multiple deaths and assume, multiple rebirths. There is a line in stanza 48, quoted earlier (in the section about Fylgjur), where the maiden identifies herself as a fylgja. From the rest of the poem, we know that the maiden is clearly much more than just a person's fylgjashe is also a goddess, ruling lands and people, seated beneath the Tree of Memory where she awaits the return of her true love, accompanied by her nine handmaidens, who are benevolent goddesses of healing, wisdom, kindness and abundance.

Their realm is situated like a bright golden oasis of resurrection within the icy darkness of the giant world, Utgarðr ["The World Outside"], which she, the maiden, is said to rule. Her rule happens while she dreams away beneath the Tree of Memory only to wake up when her true husband returns to her realm. The maiden is both the personal fylgja of the young man and a giantess queen of The World Outside, she possesses all the qualities of a goddess and of a Norn at the same time, and is the unifying head of a collective of Dísir [goddesses]. The theme of a personal soul overlapping or blending into the great universal soul is powerful in this story. Is the Valkyrie/Norn of the Edda poetry the one that must be wakened related to the fylgja? There are some indications that they indeed are exactly the same: as Else Mundal pointed out, the distinction between Fylgjur and Valkyrie in the skaldic poem Krákumál is non-existent the Viking Age poet clearly identified the two.

The Valkyrie are Óðin's Fylgjur, the Fylgjur of the warrior and the king. The Edda poem Fjǫlsvinnsmál is another powerful indication that this is so, since the queen of the giant world, who by the attributes and functions that describe her is clearly also a Norn, a goddess and a Valkyrie, identifies herself as the fylgja of her man. A person could have one fylgja, but he or she could also possess a whole group of them. Visible Fylgjur could appear in groups of three or nine a number that clearly associate them with the Norns and the Valkyrie. Apparently, there were also invisible Fylgjur, and a person could be surrounded by whole flocks of such Fylgjur. One important function of the fylgja in the saga sources is as an omen of death.

The death-omen fylgja has the habit of inviting a person to her home. Being the soul of a dead female relative, she has a function that overlaps with the goddesses of death who also invite people "home", which is the realm of the dead. In poetry, one can describe death or being about to die by saying that someone has been invited to the home of the Fylgjur, or to the home of the Dísir [goddesses]. Just like with the ancestral mother/female relative fylgja, the death-omen fylgja appears to be the soul of a dead person, not the soul of the living person to whom she is attached. How we understand this is still a matter of how we understand soul and death, and we should consider the possibility that our Pagan ancestors had a different and far more fluid way of perceiving these things. As a guardian spirit, the fylgja would counsel her person and help create good fortune.

She may advise a person and let the person know that if he advise is not followed, death will be the result. As long as the fylgja is benevolent to her person, fortune and luck will follow, but if she leaves her person, the person will suffer, and die early. The Fylgjur could leave their person if they no longer liked him or her possibly an indication that the woman fylgja is not necessarily attached to the human being in the manner of a soul or inner being, at least not the way we moderns would perceive it. There were many kinds of Fylgjur, often depending on what position you had in relation to a particular fylgja. A person could also be influenced by the Fylgjur of other people. The Fylgjur of your enemies, for example, could attack you, and then your life and fortune depended on how well your own Fylgjur could defend you.

The hostile Fylgjur of enemies are described in the sources as ófriðarfylgjur or óvinarfylgjur [Un-Peace Followers and Enemy-Followers] and could be perceived as such by their victims. The Fylgjur of the clan could be called ættarfylgjur [Clan-Followers], and the Fylgjur of friends and relatives could be called kynfylgjur [Kin-Followers]. Your own fylgja could be called by many different names: fylgjukona [Follower-Woman/Wife], draumkona [Dream Woman/Wife], the kind that would appear in and communicate through dreams, or she could be called a dís [Goddess] or spádís [Oracle Goddess] when she acted as a revealer of one's fate or purpose in life. She could also be called a Hamingja, which is most interesting, since the Hamingjur provide further light onto the concept of the Fylgjur.

2nd century Iron Age votive altar from Germany/Frisia with Latin letters, showing three Matronae- "mothers", also called Deae ["goddesses"]. Thousands of Germanic votive altars to the divine ancestral mothers have been found

THE HAMINGJA, A SOUL-WALKER

The Spirit spoke: *48. "Much did I travel* *Much did I try* *Much have I tested the Ruling Powers:* *Who are those maidens who move across* *the ocean, wise spirit maidens, as one* *troop?"*	*Oþinn qvaþ:* *48. Fiolþ ec for,* *fiolþ ec freistaþac,* *fiolþ ec vm reynda regin:* *Hveriar 'ro þer meyiar,* *er liþa mar yfir,* *frodgediaþar fara?*
The Powerful Head Veil spoke: *49. "Three great rivers run across* *the Earth [which belongs to] the Kin-* *Tracker's Maidens* *They are all soul-walkers when they are* *in the world although they were raised* *among giants."*	*Vafþrvðnir qvaþ:* *49. «Þriar þioðár* *falla þorp yfir* *meyia Magþrasiss;* *hamingior einar* *þer er i heimi ero,* *þo þer meþ iotnom alaz.»*

   -Vafþrúðnismál, st. 48-49, Poetic Edda

The word Hamingja is probably derived from the word hamr ["shape", "hide", "body"] and the word gengja ["to walk"]. Various interpretations have been proposed, most taking seriously the fact that the word means something like "shape-walker" or "to walk in a body/hide/shape". There is no doubt whatsoever that the Norse people believed in the ability of some people to move outside of their bodies, or to move within the shape of ah animal or take a different human shape. When a person could make his or her soul take a different shape outside of the original body, he or she could be called hamrammr ["shape of magical power"]. The Norwegian authority Anne Holtsmark has suggested that this referred to the ability to make the Hamingja within change her shape and move without, yet has been challenged by Else Mundal, who points out that it is the hamr [the shape], which is said to be changed, not the Hamingja.

The hamr, however, is not just a description of the outer hide of a person. It could be a way of describing a person's inner "shape", which is a way of referring to a person's soul, so that the Hamingja could well be called a "soul walker", indicating that she may be the power that makes the soul walk and take a shape/body at all. A person who was known to possess this ability of sending the soul out in a different shape or to be able to change shape, could also be called a or a hamhleypa, meaning a "shape-runner".

Essentially, the "shape-runner" and the "shape-walker" seem to belong to the same conceptual sphere. Hjalmar Falck, who in 1926 pointed out this similarity, claimed that the two words are identical in meaning. Thus the Hamingja would refer to an aspect of the human soul that may travel independently of the body. Knowing that the word fylgja actually could translate as "inner being", and that the fylgja is the same as a Hamingja, a "soul walker", there is a powerful indication that the fylgja and the Hamingja is related to the human soul as well as to the human fate, two concepts that seem to overlap. Yet again, we see the strong association between the fate-soul of the individual and the souls of dead ancestors:

The word hamr, which makes the word Hamingja, survived into Norwegian dialects as ham, meaning "ghost". From this perspective, the word Hamingja actually means "ghost walker". This would be related to the essential meaning of the contemporary word for a ghost in Norwegian: **gjenferd**, "to walk again". In the Vafþrúðnismál stanzas quoted above, we are introduced the concept of Hamingjur being Hamingjur "while they are in the world" that is, while they are in the world, they are soul-walkers. There is more to them: They were born among giants, and they run through the world like rivers, there are many of them, yet they move as one troop. They are wise spirits, they are the maidens of the "Kin-Tracker", which is a metaphor, perhaps for life itself. They also own and rule the Earth.

Obviously, the personal "soul-walker" or "shape-walker" of an individual is also more than this. Her role as a fylgja or personal fate-goddess or soul of an individual is one she wears "while in the world", outside this world, she is far more and far greater, an entity derived from the ruling powers of cosmos. So we see that the Norns, the Valkyrie and the Fylgjur and Hamingjur all belong to the same category: divine entities that descend into the world as the fate-spinning souls of people, to follow, protect, guard and advise human beings, and to rule their fates. They are all called Dísir on various occasions, which indicates that they are goddesses (or female supernatural powers). They rule lives, guide paths, offer warnings and bring the souls to their destinations after death.

They appear to be aspects of the souls of living people and the souls of dead people. Why it is so difficult to understand how they can be both and all these things at the same time beats me, but I guess it takes a bit of imagination and some insight into the many ways that "soul" has been understood in various traditions. So here we go, imagine that you have a soul. Your soul is your own, and you may have several aspects of your own soul, several qualities of yourself that all exist within you. Imagine that your soul is the invisible, inner, mysterious part of you that makes your life happen. The happening of your life, its past, its present and its future is what fate really is. Fate is the history and the destination of your soul, moving within the body-shape of your present life. Whereas you may have a fate-spinning soul or a collective of fate-spinning souls within, you may also be accompanied by the souls of dead relatives, the souls of tribal or clan ancestors and the souls of divine entities. They may all influence your fate, as may the souls of friends and the souls of enemies. Seen in this way, it becomes less hard to understand that the Fylgjur and the Norns of a person can be all these things.

There is the soul-fate of the person and the souls of the dead and the souls of supernatural beings, all operating together to create the complex weave of a life's destiny. The fluid overlapping between these fate-spinning powers, both the souls of the living person and the souls of dead persons, with divine powers such as Norns and death-goddesses indicate what we observed in the beginning: that they are all ultimately related to the same soul source from which they emerged [the Well of Origin]. Additionally, they all seem to be differentiated aspects of the same unifying core, which may be the soul-fate of the universal body itself; the Frá Yggdrasils, the "Seed of Yggdrasill", also known as Iðunn, that "elfin" giver of eternal resurrection, whose name translates as "Stream Which Separates from the Main Stream and Returns to Water Source Woman". They are all created in the mold of the first three Norns who carved the runes of fate into the root of the World Tree. To understand the Norse concept of fate, we must understand the meaning of the three maidens "who know much".

Past, present and future

The Three Fates arrive as the third female trinity after the "three giant maidens" and the goddesses Night, Sun and Earth, thus echoing the theme of nine feminine "waves" who birth the Universe and bring forth the ages. Let us have a summary of the appearance of female Fate-inducing entities in the Norse Genesis:

⟫ The Iviðja [Witch Within Wood] "brings forth the ages". This is the female side of the First Being, also identifiable as Rán, and perhaps as the vǫlva who speaks the Vǫluspá.

⟫ Nine Iviði [Witches Within Wood], associated with nine heimir ["worlds", i.e. World Trees, Universes] bring forth the present "Mead Tree", in other poems described as the birth of Heimdallr [Great World], birthed by nine sisters. The sisters are identifiable as the nine daughters of Aegir and Rán, giants of the Cosmic Ocean from which the World Tree and the Norns also emerged.

⟫ They represent the masculine and feminine mold of all Cosmos, the First Beings. The nine sisters are also said to be waves, rivers, streams and the source of light and red gold and thus associated with the streams of heat and cold that created another image of the physical Universe, Ymir [Sound]. Thus there is a masculine-feminine couple who precede the nine. They are birthed by their mother and assist her in bringing the dead back to her cosmic net, yet are steered and ruled by their father, the masculine power of giving shape and form.

⟫ One Cosmic Cow appears, also associated with streams and heat, her dynamic, active and nurturing energy makes the Sound grow and defrosts and revives a long dead consciousness which eventually give birth to the Aesir. The Cow may also be identifiable as the vǫlva who speaks the Vǫluspá, as she may be the Witch Within the Wood of the present World Tree its inner life-spark or soul, the Seed of Yggdrasill.

⟫ Grandmother Night emerges from the cold, northern Mist World, while the Sun goddess emerges from the southern realm of heat (Muspell).

⟫ Three giant maidens, all-knowing and very powerful, arrive in the golden court of the Aesir, demanding the creation of "dwarfs" and human life.

⟫ The Three Fates appear to give law, order and destiny to all living beings. The Earth goddess is born of the dark cold Night, who was impregnated by the Aesir (cosmic awareness), and given life and fertility as a result of the heating rays of the Sun. Her creation is quite like Ymir's the physical Universe, who was born from the encounter between (female) storm-waves from the Southern and the Northern realms, and nurtured to grow by the streams of milk from the southern Cow (i.e. an older, cosmic "Sun"). These are the prototypical Ásyniur, wives of the Aesir.

This is the stage we have arrived at, yet the number nine as a symbol of all the Fates that wield influence over existence will eventually be completed. These will be discussed further on, but I will offer a little sneak peak, revealing the three next fateful stages:

> The arrival of Freyia/Gullveigr/First Vǫlva on Earth
> Nine Valkyrie arrive to attend the Age of War
> The Golden Maiden of Resurrection/The Dark Bride of the Burial Mounds, Caves and Rocks two alternative Fates in Death.

The three Norns that formed the mold of all Fates to come first made their entry into the world's history when the Aesir [gods of intelligence, passion and spirit] had begun to play, to build and shape the primeval Cosmos. This was described in the Vǫluspá, st.8. The appearance of the three "powerful and much-knowing giant maidens" spurs the Aesir into creating the molds of limited shapes through which the non-physical spirit entities and powers could enter, and operate in the physical world. Obviously, we are here seeing a crucial turn of Fate.

However, because the ladies are said to be giantesses (or rather iotna meyiar ["maidens of the giants"]), many scholars refuse to accept that these are identical to the three original Norns. Trying to maintain a nicely ordered separation of the mythical species appears to be a concern of many modern scholars, completely in discordance with the Old Norse poets who would let the same basic characters appear in numerous shapes that often transcend species. It is not so hard to find evidence in poetry that the borders between the species of Gýgjur ["giantesses"] Norns, Valkyrie, Fylgjur and Hamingjur are completely blurred and overlapping, and that they are just different ways of describing the same essential type of entity the fate-spinning powers of both the universe and the inner self of human beings.

In the Chapter on Earth, we saw that giantesses turned the Mill of Fate, quite as if they were Norns which they are. They later took the role of Valkyrie and Norns, shaping the lives and choosing the deaths of human beings. In the Skaldic poem Darraðarlióð [The Spear Song], recorded in Njál's saga, it is a group of Valkyrie who weave the webs of fate, and this is just one of several examples which reveal that Norns and Valkyrie are very much of the same stock in Old Norse myths the only difference being that Valkyrie seem to be the Fates that are attached to warriors or men with divine or glorious fates- perhaps the divine Norns that follow men who achieve a glorious destiny. In the Edda poem Oddrúnargrátr, the Valkyrie Oddrún reveals that she and her eight maidens dwell on Hlésey [Wind-Shield Island], which we know to be the home of Aegir, the father of the original nine giantesses. In the Vafþrúðnismál, we hear of three great rivers of Hamingjur, who are fortune-shaping "shape-walkers" of the human world, yet were raised among giants.

The three original Norns thus began as maidens raised among giants, quite like the nine maidens "within wood" who preceded and birthed the present world. They seem to have ordered the beginning of physical reality in the shape of "dwarfs", as their presence immediately causes the gods to begin working. As soon as the Aesir enter the Earth the physical world through the "host of dwarfs", the human being, or perhaps life itself, begins its journey. As soon as physical life and death has become a reality, the three maidens appear once more, this time with names and the identity of Norns, goddesses of fate who ultimately rule all destiny and Cosmic laws. Fate and the goddesses of fate are presented as the most powerful ruling forces in the Cosmos; according to the Vǫluspá, stanza 19, they shaped the lives and decided the laws and decided the fate for all the children of the ages.

Matronis Aufaniabus, "The Mothers of Plenty". 2nd century shrine to the goddess collective/ancestral mother cult in the lower Rhineland.

That would mean every entity that was ever subject to time. No powers were greater, and this is acknowledged in the fact that the Aesir gods and the ruling powers keep their parliament by the Well of Origin, in proximity to the abode of the fates. **THE THREE ORIGINAL NORNS ARE CALLED URÐR, VERDANDI AND SKULD.**

→ The name Urðr means Beginning or Origin, and identifies the oldest Norn, the Norn of origins and beginnings, as the owner of the Well of Origin from where all fates and souls derive. She is usually understood to represent the past.

→ Then there is Verdandi, whose name means "Becoming", "About to Happen, or "Being», «Happening Now". She is thought to represent the present.

→ The third is Skuld, whose name directly translates as "Debt" or "Blame", representing the future.

In the poem Vǫluspá, fate is not just a blind power of destiny that overrules everything it is the result of the joint actions of the past and the present the combination of what has happened before and what is happening right now. This becomes clear if we look closely at the lines in stanza 20:

Origin, the first is called the second Is About To Happen they carved (runes/ symbols) into the wood

> *Urð hétu eina,*
> *aðra Verðandi,*
> *skáru á skíði,*

The lines clearly state that it is the past and the present together that carve runes into the World Tree. The third Norn, Skuld, is mentioned only afterwards, as a "Debt" to follow the fate-carvings of the first two Norns:

> *Debt was the third (maiden);*
>
> *Skuld ina þriðju;*

The future is represented by the mysterious Skuld, whose name literally translates as "Debt". Simek suggests "blame", but the word skuld may mean both debt and blame. Realizing that this Norn represents the future, and that she represents the result of the actions of past and present together, it is in my opinion most likely that the meaning is "debt", what the future owes. The future is clearly the result of the "carvings" of past and present together, the debt accumulated by past and present actions. The deeper message of this stanza is that fate and the future by no means is a set plan. It is the result. The "debt" that is created through the actions of the past combined with the actions of the present. The present "is about to happen", the present is the moment of choice, the one place where a person can influence his or her fate. This is in my opinion the great secret of seiðr, which is the art of not only divining the past, present and future, but also the art of changing fate, including the ultimate fate for all mortals, which is death.

This is a subject we will return to when the art of seiðr is first introduced by the divine, wandering Witch. This fluidity in the concept of destiny may not seem so revolutionary to us today, but to the ancients, who believed that fate overruled everything else, a concept frequently referred to in poetry, the Vǫluspá stanza 20, as quoted above, must have provided a revelation of divine mysteries. The three original Norns represent the mold from which all fate is created, the mold from which all souls are born: How to shape your personal destiny in life and in death may well have been linked to the mysteries of reaching into the carvings "that are about to happen". What are these "carvings" anyway these runes that were first carved into the roots of the World Tree by the Norns?

THE RUNES OF FATE

The very first mention of the runes in Edda poetry is in the Vǫluspá, the stanza 20, when the Norns carve into the wood (of the World Tree). Here they are the symbols of fate carved into "the wood", the matter of the universe and the matter of the physical bodies, carved there by the Norns of past and present. We generally know the runes to be the letters of the Old Norse system of writing. The runes were developed over time and evidence suggests that they were used at least some two thousand years ago. Their origins in other letter-systems such as the Latin or Greek alphabets have been much disputed, since the runes possess a likeness to several ancient letter systems.

The runes were used by both men and women and often held a quite sacred function, although they could also be practical. Most rune stones that we know of are memorial stones in honor of somebody dead, usually accompanied with a proud signature of the name of the carver, who emphasizes that he carved these runes. The image of the rune-carving female Norns is consistent with the fact that high-born women obviously learned the runes as well as any man.

In the heroic Edda poetry, runes are used by the lady Guðrún, carved into a wooden rune stave, to send a secret message of warning to her brothers. Interestingly, it is the wife of the brother who interprets the runic message and explains the interpretation to her warrior husband, who seems to regard knowledge about the runes as one of the many mysterious matters of women, alongside the interpretation and use of dreams, omens and magic.

There are some indications that the ancient Germans and Scandinavians used runes for divination and magic. In 98 AD, Cornelius Tacitus wrote in his *Germania* (ch.10) that the runes were used for the casting of lots:

> *"For auspices and the casting of lots they have the highest possible regard. Their procedure in casting lots is uniform. They break off a branch of a fruit-tree and slice it into strips; they distinguish these by certain runes and throw them, as random chance will have it, on to a white cloth. Then the priest of the State if the consultation is a public one, the father of the family if it is private, after a prayer to the gods and an intent gaze heavenward, picks up three, one at a time, and reads their meaning from the runes scored on them. If the lots forbid an enterprise, there can be no further consultation that day; if they allow it, further confirmation by auspices is required."*

There are many rune manuals, rune cards and rune interpretation divinatory systems that have been invented in our day and are much used by Neopagans and others who have interest in the runes. I have often been asked about the interpretation of runes for the purpose of divination and magic, but as an historian, I can only state that apart from what little we learn from Tacitus' account, there simply is no detailed record as to how the runes were understood and used for divination and magic. The runes that appear in the Edda represent not the letters used for writing, but the esoteric, allegorical meaning of the word rún in a wider sense. The Old Norse word rún (f.sg.) Refers to a letter, a symbol, a secret or a whisper, something that is conveyed subtly and secretly.

As such, the concept of the rune takes on a more allegorical meaning in the sacred poetry than the actual letter, they are the secret symbols created by the soul-powers of fate, imprinted into the matter of the cosmic body, and as such, into the matter of the bodies of all that lives. As a modern person, I have often thought of DNA in this context, although I would not claim that the Vikings or any of the myth-makers before them actually knew about this secret, invisible encoding that actually does play a major role in shaping the fate of a physical body, seemingly carved into the root cores of our cells. People in ancient times were able to deduce the existence of atoms, invisible compartments that provides the building material for all shapes and all beings. They could very well have been able to imagine that there were secret writings of fate carved deep into the core of all existence. The symbols of fate, the carvings of destiny, perhaps we could say the decisions of the soul in the past and in the present are made in the hidden realms, the secret realm of the divine fates by the Well of Origin. These are realms of existence that belong to the subconscious and the unknown, realms that can only be reached through special states of consciousness.

As long as the runes remain hidden in the secret realms, there is no way of truly knowing them, or of controlling fate. In order to access the power to influence and conquer one's own fate, one must bring knowledge of the secret workings of fate to the surface. This is exactly what Óðinn [the Spirit] did during the course of his initiation.

Detail from Oseberg tapestry (834 AD, Vestfold, Norway): Men hanging from trees in a grove of serpentine trees. [Illustration by Peter Robinson]

ÓÐINN UPROOTING THE RUNES

> *139...I peered downwards*
> *I took up the runes*
> *Screaming I took them*
> *I fell then back there (from*
> *where I peered)*
> *139...nysta ec niþr,*
> *nam ec vp rvnar,*
> *opandi nam,*
> *fell ec aptr þaðan.*

Those are the words of Óðinn in the Edda poem Hávamál. It is the second time the runes are mentioned in the chronology of the Edda poems. In a trial of initiation not unlike those practiced by shamans, yogis, ascetics and mystics, Óðinn has let himself hang onto the World Tree like a sacrifice, stabbed with spears he hung there without food or drink for nine nights the magical number of initiation and of death and of creation. He states that he sacrifices or actually gives himself to Óðinn himself to himself, The Spirit given to The Spirit. Thus The Spirit hangs, given self to its universal self on the universal body that is the World Tree.

In a fashion, it is the tale of the knowledge-seeking Spirit that is sacrificed and given over to physical life as a gift to itself in each and every one of us, life itself the initiation, and his discovery thus relevant to us all. It is while he hangs there that he suddenly sees the runes and take them back up to the place where he hangs. We must conclude that Óðinn found the runes that had been carved into the root of the World Tree by the Norns, that this is what he sees as he looks down, and that it is from this realm that he screamingly falls back to the place where he hangs. As such, the place in which the runes are found is the Well of Origin, which offers resurrection and transformation.

Óðin's trial is accompanied by the offering of the precious mead of poetry and by the transmission of sacred spell-songs [galðr], so that the "precious mead", the spell-songs and the runes are all interconnected. The same is true about the three worlds with their respective "wells", since each of the gifts given to the initiated Spirit derive from each of these worlds. The Mead of Poetry is given in the Underworld, where we find the Well of Hel, better known as Hvergelmir Mill Bellower. It is the place where souls are ground into oblivion, and from where the rivers of life stream back into the world.

The spell-songs are given to Óðinn by his own maternal uncle, a giant in the giant world, and the well found there is the Mímisbrunnr, the Well of Memory, where all universal memories are stored. Snorri let us know that Óðinn asked the giant Mímir for a drink from this well, to be drunk through the Gjallarhorn ["The Bellowing Horn"]. He had to leave one of his eyes in the well as a sacrifice for the wisdom of the Well. It is a good way of saying that Spirit has one eye in the place of Universal Memory, and one eye in the ordinary world.

Finally, the runes are found in the realm of the Norns, by the Well of Origin, where the secrets of life and fate may be revealed, and from where a soul may re-emerge transformed, bright and shining like the immortal Light Elf of the upper heavens. In the Hávamál, we hear more about the runes after the description of the initiation ritual that Óðinn endured. In stanza 142, we hear that in order to achieve the wisdom and spiritual progress that Óðinn achieved, we must find the runes too, and that there is one particular rune, one very important rune that has been colored (influenced) by the "Great Sage", Óðinn himself ["The Shattered One Among the Gods"]:

142. Runes you must find and	*142. Runar munt þu finna*
the Rune that is grasped the very	*oc raðna Stafi,*
Great Rune the very Powerful	*mioc Stóra Stafi,*
Rune, which is colored by the	*mioc Stinna Stafi,*
Great Sage and made by the	*er fáþi Fimbulþulr*
Sacred Powers and carved by the	*oc gorðo GinnRegin*
Shattered One among the Gods	*oc reist Hroptr Ragna*

The Shattered One is also Óðinn, who is the universal Spirit shattered into countless individual forms. It would remind us of how the Norns are of "much shattered birth" and how they represent both individual souls/fates as well as the unifying soul and fate of the entire cosmos, all emerging from the same Well of Origin. In the next Hávamál stanza, we learn that Óðinn, just like the Norns, has different functions among the Aesir, the elves and the dwarfs (and the giants):

143. Spirit with the Aesir and for	*143. Óðinn meþ asom*
Elves the Dead One Hibernation	*enn fyr alfom Dáinn,*
for the dwarfs	*Dvalinn oc dvergom fyr,*
Divine Tree (World Tree) for the	*Asvidr iotnom fyr,*
giants, I carved some (runes)	*ec reist sialfr svmar.*
myself	

I suggest that this correspondence is due to the fact that Óðinn represents the masculine aspect of exactly the same that the Norns represent. The Norns are the feminine aspect of the soul, associated with fate, representing the inner, hidden, all-.knowing, animating and subtly moving forces of the soul. As a masculine aspect, Óðinn the Spirit represents the outer surface of the soul, the knowledge-seeking, consciously thinking and thus shaping aspect that gives a perceivable form and orderly system to existence. To the Aesir, representing the mental, emotional and spiritual qualities of consciousness, he is Óðinn [The Spirit], the origin of the life-breath. To the elves which as we shall see are symbols for the souls of the dead he is Dáinn [The Dead One].

To the dwarfs, the limiting, molding forms that provide physical shape and physical existence, he is Dvalinn the Hibernation father to the slumbering fate-souls of most people. To the giants, representing matter, he is the Tree of Life itself, the body of the universe. The Hávamál stanzas about the runes culminate in mysterious and suggestive lines urging the initiate to learn how to use the runes properly:

143. Do you know how to carve them?	*143. Veiztu hve rista scal?*
Do you know how to interpret them?	*veiztu hve raþa scal?*
	veiztu hve fá scal?
Do you know how to color them?	*veiztu hve freista scal?*
Do you know how to test them?	*veiztu hve bidia scal?*
Do you know how to ask them?	*veiztu hve blóta scal?*
Do you know how to offer them?	*veiztuhve senda scal?*
Do you know how to send them?	*veiztu hve soa scal?*
Do you know how to stop them?	

The Hávamál rune lore concludes that it is necessary to have the proper wisdom and control over the runes:

145. It is better not to pray than to sacrifice too much the one who gives wants something back;	*145. Betra er obeþit enn se ofblotiþ, ey ser til gildis giof;*
It is better not to send than to send too much	*betra er osennt enn se ofsóit.'*
Thus Thin Mist (Óðinn) carved it before time began, when he ascended up there and when he returned back	*Sva Þvndr vm reist fyr þioþa rauc, þar hann vp vm reis er hann aptr of kom*

That Óðinn is called Þundr in this stanza is interesting. The name means "Thin Mist", and in another Edda poem, the Grímnismál, Óðinn reveals that this was his name when he lived among the frost giants. Snorri explains that Óðinn lived among the Frost Giants before the world was created. The Thin Mist, thus, refers to the mists of Níflheimr, the world of the dead that existed before the birth of the present universe. The Spirit was clearly present in the mists of death and slumber, to be woken up and resurrected by the heat of the Cow from the South in due time. The fact that Óðinn is said to have made his journey of initiation already at this early stage of the life of the universe links the initiation with creation itself.

My guess is that the sacrifice of Óðinn must be understood in light of the fact that he represents The Spirit of the universe. The "Tree" on which he hangs is the universal body, the mold of physical life. Each and every one of us is such a world tree, the masculine seen and shaped aspect of life, fueled by the unseen feminine streams of life-giving liquid brew. The Tree is called Yggdrasill, meaning that it is a "steed" of The Spirit. Today, we would probably replace the word "steed" with a "vehicle". It is not a new or rare concept to regard the body as a vehicle for The Spirit. As The Shattered One, it is the universal original Spirit that has shattered into countless pieces as it rides each vehicle of life that is a physical body.

As The Spirit rides the steeds of physical shapes, it experiences the challenges of suffering and death, which is its sacrifice to itself in order to gain knowledge and understanding. The secret quest, as we shall be seeing throughout this book, is The Spirit seeking reunion with the wholeness of his feminine counterpart, the all-knowing Fate-Soul within. The poem Hávamál then proceeds to a description of the nine spell-songs received by Óðinn during his initiation, and Óðinn then proceeds to create nine more, ending with the interesting stanza of the secret spell, akin to the "meaningful rune", in which he seems to achieve his union with the female aspect:

163. I know the eighteenth (spell-song) that is known to no one neither maiden nor a man's wife, — all that is best is known only to the One, and that is the end of this song only (known) to the One who hides me in her arms and who may be my sister.	*163. Þat kann ec iþ átiánda, er ec æva kennig mey ne mannz kono, — alt er betra er einn vm kann, þat fylgir lioða locom, nema þeirri einni, er mic armi verr eþa min systir se.*

Óðin's initiation may be of a universal character the initiation of The Spirit when it experiences the limitations and sufferings of physical life, where the purpose is to attain knowledge about fate and reunion with wholeness, with the true self. Yet, his journey also reflects a very typical ritual of initiation that may have been practiced in Pagan times by those who wished to seek the wisdom revealed by The Spirit in bygone days. There is another Edda poem where Óðin's initiation and the rune lore is further explored, the Sígrdrífumál.

In this poem, the human hero Sígurðr is one of the many heroes who walks in the footsteps of Óðinn, seeking the initiation and the mysterious lady who knows the secret spell and the meaningful rune. Sígurðr does find a Valkyrie sleeping on the sacred mountain of the soul, a Valkyrie who has been sleeping since his brother Helgi died. The same Valkyrie had followed Helgi through several lives as he was reborn. The subject of reincarnation will be dealt with in Chapter 3. For now, suffice that the Old Norse Pagans believed in reincarnation and that the Valkyrie/ fylgja/Norn/ Hamingja was thought to be sleeping between the lives of a person, sleeping while her person moved through the realms of death.

Since Helgi died before Sígurðr was born, we may assume that the Valkyrie, who has slept since Helgi died and who is now woken up by Sígurðr, represents his undying soul, to be woken up again through initiation trials in the present life. As Sígurðr wakes his Valkyrie from her long slumber, the fate-spinning lady within offers the Mead of Memory to the young man and reveals knowledge of the runes and how to use them. She also completes the story of Óðin's initiation, revealing how the Spirit released the runes, or the knowledge of the runes, into the world. There are elements of a creation story in these lines that are otherwise unknown, elements of the concept of a "first speech", or else the secret truths of life that is revealed by universal memory.

13. The Runes of the Soul/Intent
you must know if you want to be,
among common people, a wiser
person in spirit:
They were interpreted
They were carved
They ran through the soul of the
Shattered One from that drink
(the Mead of Poetry/Memory)
that had leaked from the skull of
Bright Drops and from the horn of
Treasure Release.

13. Hvgrvnar scaltv kvnna,
ef þv vilt hveriom vera
geðsvinnari gvma
þer of réð,
þer of reist,
þer vm hvgði Hroptr
af þeim legi,
er leciþ hafdi
or hausi Heiddraupniss
oc or horni Hoddrofnis.

14. He (Óðinn) stood on the
mountain with the blades of the
Flaming One
On his head there was a helmet;
Then the Head of Memory spoke
wisely the first word and stated
the true rune (symbol, secret)

14. A biargi stoþ
meþ Brimis eggiar,
hafdi ser a hofði hialm;
þa melti Mims haufvþ
froþlict iþ fyrsta orð
oc sagdi sanna stafi.

...18. (The Runes) were all cut
off that had been carved on and
poured over with the Sacred Mead
and sent on their wide ways:
They are with the Aesir
They are with the Elves
Some are with the wise Vanir
Some are with human beings.

...18. Allar váro af scafnar,
þer er váro a ristnar,
oc hverfðar viþ inn Helga Mioþ
oc sendar a viþa vega;
þer 'ro meþ asom,
þer 'ro meþ alfom,
svmar meþ visom vanom,
svmar hafa mennzkir menn.

19. Those are book-runes
Those are the runes of salvation
and all are ale-runes and great
power runes one who can possess
them without confusing them
without destroying them but have
them whole and complete:
Use them, if you get them, until the
rulers are torn apart!

19. Þat ero bocrvnar,
þat ero biargrvnar
oc allar aulrvnar
oc metar meginrvnar
hveim er þer kná oviltar
oc ospilltar
ser at heillom hafa;
niottv, ef þv namt,
vnz rivfaz regin.

The stanzas reveal that the runes are the secret carvings of Fate that are uncovered by The Spirit, made holy and potent by the sacred mead of life, and sent out into all the dimensions of cosmos. Some of them are with the Aesir, some with the Elves, some with the Vanir, and some with human beings. They are all different, all belonging to different kinds of worlds, and there have been counted many types of runes used for different purposes, yet they are all united in the one meaningful rune, the sanna stafi ["true rune"] spoken by Universal Memory when The Spirit wears its "helmet".

2.13: VANIR, SEIÐR AND THE SACRED MEAD

The Vǫluspá account of the world's history only relates the most important cosmic peak events, and even then, it uses an allusive language, leaving it to the audience to fill in the gaps with knowledge that the poet expected the audience to already possess. Sadly for us moderns, some of the allusions remain unexplained to a considerable degree. There were parts of the Pagan lore that Snorri probably judged "too Pagan" to explain or elaborate upon, too Pagan to be acceptable in his time. The hanging of Óðinn, an event which actually constitutes the climax of the Edda poem Hávamál, was not mentioned by Snorri at all! He moves around it with a seriously censored tale about Óðin's quest for the mead of poetry, a story that is good for entertainment but which lacks the depth and secret revelations of the older, and ultimately more Pagan Hávamál version, where the mead of poetry is clearly linked to the runes and the spell-songs, and where the tale of the ritual hanging sacrifice provides the background scenery. Likewise, the burning of the witch Gullveigr is not mentioned by Snorri despite the fact that this event takes up two whole stanzas of the Vǫluspá and provides a turning point in the composition of the poem. It is doubtlessly a very important cosmic event that follows the introduction of the Norns and which introduces the age of war and ignorance that eventually leads to Ragnarǫk, the apocalyptic transformation where old gods must give way to new ones, and where the Earth is renewed through severe natural disasters. Again, I assume that Snorri's complete censorship of this story has to do with the profoundly Pagan initiation ritual that forms its backdrop.

The stanzas of Vǫluspá stanzas 21-22 go:

21. She remembers the first war in the world
When Gold Power Drink was hoist on the spears and in the High One's hall they burned her
Three Times they Burned the Three Times Born often, not seldom (did they burn her) yet she still lives!

22. She was called Bright One/Illuminated One when she came to the settlements (of people)
The well-divining witch she could cast spells she did seiðr wherever she could she did seiðr with a playful intent
She was always loved by wicked women.

21. Þat man hon fólkvíg fyrst í heimi,
er Gullveigr geirum studdu
ok í hǫll Hárs hana brendu;
þrysvar brendu þrysvar borna,
opt, ósjaldan,
þó hon enn lifir!

22. Heiði hana hétu,
hvars til húsa kom,
vǫlu velspá,
vitti hon ganda,
seið hon hvars hon kunni,
seið hon hugleikin,
æ var hon angan illrar brúðar.

These two stanzas tell the story of how a vǫlva called Gullveigr was first stabbed and burned in Hǫll Hárs [the Hall of the High One], the High One [Hár] being a name for the god Óðinn. She is burned three times and is reborn each time, and then she was often burned yet still lives. In the next stanza, she has taken another name, Heiðr, and is working like a typical Old Norse vǫlva, traveling among the people performing her magical art of seiðr, an art originated among the Vanir, apparently teaching it to the women.

RESTORING GULLVEIGR TO CULTURAL MEMORY
HOW AND WHY THE BURNED WITCH OF THE EDDA HAS BEEN MISINTERPRETED

There have been many interesting interpretations of the myth and character of this first vǫlva to enter the world history of the Vǫluspá. The only part of these interpretations which I agree with is the one where most scholars identify the vǫlva as the goddess Freyia. The reason for this is that the vǫlva is obviously associated with the subsequent war between Aesir and Vanir, when the Vanir, and particularly Freyia, are the ones to introduce the art of seiðr to the Aesir. In fact, in Ynglinga saga 4, Snorri states that Freyia taught this art to the Aesir:

> Dóttir Njarðar var Freyja, hon var blótgyðja, ok hon ken
> di fyrst með Ásum seið, sem Vönum var títt
> ["Njǫrð'daughter was Freyia, she was a sacrificial priestess, and she was the first to
> acquaint the Aesir with seiðr, which had been common among the Vanir"].

Thus when the Vǫluspá introduces the first Witch to practice and teach the art of seiðr, and links her to the first encounter with Aesir and Vanir, we are very likely seeing an aspect of the goddess Freyia as a divine priestess and witch, entering the scene of world history right after the Fates have decreed the universal laws of destiny. However, the divine Witch does not teach it to the Aesir first, she teaches it first to the women of the human settlements. It is when the rest of the myth is analyzed that my own analysis differ radically with those of other scholars.

The Swedish professor Britt Mari N sström, in her book Freyia, Great Goddess of the North (1998), N sström assumes that Freyia's function as a witch among the hostile Vanir is to infiltrate the stronghold of the Aesir with witchcraft, and even as they try to kill her, she returns, continuing her "destructive plan", first and foremost through demoralizing the women. Already while operating secretly within the fortress of the Aesir, the Vanir gods break down the fences of the Aesir, entering with their spell-songs of victory.

The name Gullveigr, N sström concludes, must be "Gold Thirst", showing her insatiable greed for gold and jewelry, while the name Heiðr is dismissed as a common name for a sorceress.

The problem with this interpretation is that it is not actually based on the only source we have to the myth, the Vǫluspá stanzas 20-21, nor is it an accurate description of the way neither Snorri nor the subsequent Vǫluspá stanzas describe the war between the Aesir and Vanir. Neither is the "translation" of Gullveig's name accurate. With all due respect to this by me otherwise much esteemed scholar, the interpretation just referred to can only be based on N sström's own imagination combined with the interpretations made by earlier modern writers, equally imaginative and equally without any fundamental link in the actual Norse texts.

Before I proceed to more detailed criticism, I will add a few other typical examples of how this myth is traditionally misrepresented. Margaret Clunies-Ross (1994) also identifies Gullveigr with Freyia through her role as a vǫlva practicing seiðr and being associated with the Vanir-Aesir war. Thus Freyia and Gullveigr perform the same mythological functions. Furthermore, that Gullveigr appears to be sacrificed links her to Freyia's function as a sacrificial priestess. So far, so good. Clunies-Ross proceeds by analyzing the myth in light of her understanding that the Norse cosmos is divided into polarities where male and female is one of them.

She claims that the Aesir are fundamentally male, representing order and the reasoned world. Gullveigr is female and a master of sorcery, which in itself makes her appear threatening to the Aesir. According to Clunies-Ross, Freyia/Gullveigr offers herself sexually as well as her magical arts to the Aesir, but they will have none of it. Their stabbing her with spears is a symbolical penetration, leading to death rather than to the kind of penetration desired by Gullveigr and the Vanir.

This horrible treatment of Gullveigr leads to the war because the Vanir were angry on behalf of their kinswoman. Thus the war is the result of a sort of symbolic war between the masculine world of "reason and order" and the feminine world of sex and magic, where the masculine violates the feminine because the feminine threatens the "male order". Both Clunies-Ross and N sström fail in their analysis by moving far beyond what the texts actually say, and by understanding the myth within particular paradigms that in my opinion do not provide accuracy. The fact is that nobody ask such questions because it has long since been recognized that the trials on the World Tree follows the basic structure of initiation into sacred mysteries and professions, a structure which is summarized here in simplified form:

→ Symbolic Death
→ The Transmission of Sacred Knowledge During "Death"
→ Resurrection
→ A New Profession/Identity/Name to go with the New Powers

Seen in this light, the previous interpretations of Gullveigr become absurd. It is a fact that the burning of Gullveigr is described in much the same way as the hanging of Óðinn, and follows exactly the same structure of initiation. The same terminology we find in the Vǫluspá stanzas is right there in the Hávamál stanzas about Óðinn. In both accounts we have someone invisible and unnamed called "they" who appear to attend (or torture) the suffering deities. "They" whoever they are gave him no food or drink, and "they" stabbed him with spears as he hung.

Likewise, we have the mysterious "they" who burned and stabbed Gullveigr. In both cases, we are seeing a form of sacrifice which is transformed from sacrifice into a ritual of initiation, where conquering death is the final, ultimate test. In both stories which can only initiation stories the successful initiates, after conquering death begin their new lives as practicing professionals and wise people.

Óðinn describes how he barely survived his trials and how he now experiences increased wisdom and eloquence with every day, and how he is now a sage living among the gods, and how he brought the mead of poetry to the "Shrine of Earth". Gullveigr, who performed the feat before him and was his teacher, begins her career as a vǫlva who does what all vǫlur did travels and offers her services to people, and teaches the women who are unconventional enough to want to learn.

Her new name after the initiation is Heiðr, which means "illuminated", "bright", "open space" and is the same word that is used in the name Heiðrún, the she-goat who produces the precious mead at the roof of Valhǫll which brings eternal resurrection to its inhabitants. Interestingly, it is also the word that makes up the Old Norse word for "Paganism", Heiðindómr [Judgment of the Open Space/ Illumination/Brightness].

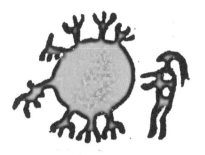

Bronze Age rock carving of woman with a ponytail approaching a burning Sun disc

SEIÐR THE SECRETS OF FATE

The chronology of Freyia-Gullveig's path is an exact replica of the typical career of any shaman or similar spiritual professional in Pagan cultures; She goes through her mortally dangerous trials, survives, and begins to work within her profession, eventually teaching on her knowledge. The fact that this leads to a war between the Aesir and the Vanir will be understood better if we realize that the war that Óðinn started and then almost lost eventually led to Óðinn learning about seiðr from Freyia. Seiðr, ultimately, has to do with altering fate, and the ultimate fate of all mortals is death. The Ynglinga saga first relates how Freyia taught the art of seiðr to the Aesir, and then describes Óðinn as a practitioner, explaining the essentials of this art, clearly associating it with the arts of poetry, shape-changing soul journeys, runes and spell-songs [galðr]:

> "He said everything by rhyme, just like one now speaks that which is called the Art of Poetry, he and his temple-priests were called verse-smiths...Óðinn could make it so in a battle that his enemies were blinded or deaf or filled with terror...but his own men went without armor and were crazed like hounds or wolves, biting their shields, being strong as bears or oxen...it is called to run berserk ["bear-clad"].
>
> Óðinn often changed his shape, then his body lay like dead or sleeping, while he himself was a bird or a four-footed animal, fish or serpent, and could travel in a moment to distant countries, in service of himself or others. He could also do other things, only with words could he quench a fire, silence the ocean and turn the wind in the direction he wanted...
>
> Óðinn had with him the head of Memory, which told him the tidings of other worlds beyond; sometimes he woke up the dead from the ground of sat beneath a hanged man, that is why he is called the Lord of Ghosts [Draugardrottin]. He had two ravens, which he had taught to speak, they flew widely across the lands and told him many tidings. From all this he became very wise. All these arts he taught in runes and in a kind of songs known as galðr [spell-songs, charms], that is why the Aesir are called galðr-smiths. Óðinn knew that art which carries with it the strongest power, and he practiced it himself, it is seiðr, and through it he could know the destiny of people, and of things that are yet to happen, he could give people death or misfortune or bad health, he could steal the wit and the power from people and give it to others. But this sorcery brings with it so much perversion/unmanliness for those who practice it that men cannot practice it without shame, and therefore they taught this art to the priestesses."

Within the Old Norse context, seiðr was particularly concerned with fate with knowing and controlling fate, even that most ultimate fate which is death. There are some saga descriptions where practitioners change shape and travel in the form of an animal, practice forms of witchcraft, and in Snorri's Gylfaginning, one vǫlva chants galðr in order to heal a wound, her chants drawing a splinter out of Þór's body. One account claims that a vǫlva could chant to call the fish into the bay during times of hunger. Many Medieval accounts, including Snorri's, emphasize the use of seiðr for harmful purposes. However, even the Medieval sagas seem to harbor enormous respect for the vǫlur, who primarily were the performers of seiðr. The art and societal position of the vǫlva in Norse Paganism resembles shamanism in most respects. In most shamanic cultures, the mythology clearly mirrors the world of the shaman who travels between dimensions and contacts spirit beings.

The world of the dead is a particularly important place as it is the place where knowledge about fate is hidden. This is also the case with Norse mythology. Most of the accounts describe a séance that can best be identified as a divination. This divination had to do with seeing the past, the present, and the future, something which could happen through the help of spirits invoked through song. It was not just passive prophecy. The real power of seiðr was that the divination was operative, that is, the master of this art could not only see destiny, but also alter it.

The ultimate fate of all mortals is death, and even that could be conquered through this most powerful of all arts. I believe that the clue to changing fate is to capture it as it is caught in the present moment. We recall from the previous section that fate is a matter of fusion between the past and the present. This fusion happens within the realm of the Norns. The person who could enter this realm and alter the carvings that are taking place in the present moment would actually be able to alter fate itself. This is the true secret of fate, and of the art of seiðr, and why Óðinn sought the knowledge of this art. It is exactly the uncovering of the carvings of fate that is the main purpose of his initiation. As the goddess Freyia showed him that it is possible to conquer even the ultimate fate, death, the god of Spirit began his quest for knowledge.

THE PRACTITIONERS

All witches have descended from the Wood-Wolf [Wood of Desire]
All wizards from the Tree of Intent
All seiðr-wombs [transsexuals] from Black Head [= Dark (unknown) Mind]
All giants have descended from Sound
      Eru vaulur allar
      fra Vidolfui,
      vitkar allir
      fra Vilmeidi,
      seidberendr
      fra Suarthofda,
      jotnar allir
      fra Ymi komnir.

Hyndlulióð st.33, Poetic Edda

The professional seiðr-practitioner had honored titles. A male practitioner was either called a seiðmaðr a seiðr-man, or a seiðberendr "seiðr-vagina", a title that brings to mind the very common phenomenon of transsexual shamans in countless shamanic cultures. This title may indicate why Snorri in the Ynglinga saga claimed that "men could not practice it without shame". It is also possible that seiðr involved some kind of womb magic. Snorri let us know that Frigg, who knows all fate, resides in the "Moist Halls" where only women can enter. Loki, in order to learn the secrets of the goddess, enters her hall after taking the shape of a woman. Indeed, there are several indications that the art was considered feminine, belonging to the spheres of women, and that men who performed it were bending the gender roles and considered somewhat unmanly.

After all, as the Vǫluspá reveals, the art was introduced by a female, the witch Gullveigr, who is also the goddess Freyia, the Viking Age prototype of divine femininity. In several saga accounts, the vǫlva is described as a traveling woman, who could travel alone, or with apprentices, or in groups of nine vǫlur. She would be invited to settlements and treated with the utmost respect.

The texts also indicate that she was outside of or above the usual societal hierarchies and could speak to people exactly as she liked no matter what kind of status they had. She would be placed in the High Seat which was normally reserved for the head couple of the household or for guests of higher standing.

She could employ local women for ritual purposes, such as in the Saga of Eirik the Red, where the women of the household hold hands and make a circle around the vǫlva and sing to "call the spirits" [varðlokur]. The vǫlva not only follows in the shoes of the most powerful among goddesses, but is also in league with the Norns and considered a supernatural species. In fact, although born as a human woman, she is spiritually descended from a giant called Viðolfr.

The olfr in the name of the Vǫlva's ancestor suggests a wolf, a symbol of various qualities related to the survival instinct, everything from hunger and desire to greed. The wolf may link the vǫlva to the wolf-riding giantesses in the underworld. One such wolf-rider, Hyndla, certainly performs a séance of seiðr as she divines the secret knowledge of the underworld to an initiate in the Edda poem Hyndlulióð. The word við may be related to viðr, meaning "tree", "wood" or "forest". It is the same word used to create the word iviðja ["within wood"] the title of the sorceresses who birthed the world. An interpretation of the name of the witches' ancestor may be the Tree of Desire, referring to the world tree and the body, as well as to the quality that keeps it alive, keeps it moving along the paths of fate.

There are other possible interpretations of the word við- , such as "proximity", or viðr, such as "weather", "wind" [i.e. «death"] or "wide", "expanding", "prolonged", but none of these makes as much sense as the association to the world tree, not the least because the vǫlva carries and wields a wand that is ultimately related to the same tree. Despite this, we know for certain that there were many powerful and influential male practitioners in Pagan times. Óðinn himself practiced it, and the vitgar ["wizards"], had their own parallel mythical ancestor in Vílmeiðr The Tree of Intent.

So did the so-called "seiðr-wombs", the (probably) male to female transsexual sorcerers, they are descended from Svarthofði Black Head. The meaning of this is uncertain, but the blackness refers to darkness, and darkness is the way of describing the mysterious, the hidden, the unknown and the beyond. It was not an evil association in Pagan times. The distinction between good and evil, light and darkness was simply not the same to the Pagans. One had wanted things and unwanted things and whether a thing was wanted or not wanted depended on one's perspective at any given moment. No powers were actually evil they could be destructive, but that would simply be their nature. Darkness denotes the mystery of the unknown, of the underworld, of death, exactly the things that the seiðr-practitioner sought, to see that which has been hidden.

It is more than likely that attitudes towards transsexual sorcerers and towards male sorcerers who meddled with women's mysteries changed towards the end of the Viking Age as a result of Christian and continental influence. The sagas of the kings actually show this change in attitude in some stories. We have, for example, the story of the seiðr-man Ragnvaldr "Spreading Legs" Rettilbeini, son of King Haraldr Hárfagri, who held much power in Norway until the time when Haraldr suddenly began to hate his own son and persecuted him "for sorcery". The title vǫlva is derived from the word vǫl (m.sg.).

Which refers to a sacred wand or staff and also to a stallion's penis and thus indirectly to the god Freyr, lord of growth, sexuality, vitality and fertility.

One single source has preserved information about the importance of this symbol in Old Norse cults, the Vǫlsa þáttr [The Story of the Wand], where a stallion is sacrificed and the penis preserved for a ritual in which it is offered to the giantesses who apparently enjoy such a gift. The horse is generally associated with Freyr, but also with Óðinn, one of whose names is Ialkr, which refers to a gelding, a castrated horse. This could be a reference to his sacrifice, something is given in a sacrifice, and the penis could be a metaphor for the creative and reproductive potency or power of the god, in this case of The Spirit itself. The phallus was a very important symbol in Pagan times, huge standing stones were erected all over Scandinavia to promote abundance and fertility in the land. There are castrated gods throughout history, such as Osiris, who like Óðinn was shattered into pieces and had to be restored through the love of his sister-wife.

There is also Attis, who offered his penis to the ancient Anatolian mother goddess Cybele, known to the Romans as Magna Mater The Great Mother. Her male priests were known to cut off their genitals and dress like women. Both Osiris and Attis represent the individual souls of human beings separated from the universal soul-core, the mother goddess. The Norse concepts of castration and other gender-bending themes related to sorcery and to the great mysteries of initiation may belong to a similar conceptual universe and share some age-old unknown history. We do not know enough to make certain conclusions about these similarities however. What we do know is that the horses of Freyr and Óðinn as well as other horses in the Poetic Edda are, without exception, associated with travel into other worlds, the Underworld in particular. The world itself is seen as a steed, as is shown in the name of the world tree Yggdrasill, which means "The Old Steed". In the case of the vǫlur (f.pl.), Their title, vǫlva, meant either "Carrier of the Wand" or "Wed to the Wand", or simply "Sacred Wand".

The wand was a symbol of her profession's authority and possibly of the World Tree itself. Seeing as it represents the (phallic) potency of a horse which is also associated with inter-dimensional shamanic travel, the staff may have been perceived as a channel of magical power. A similar tradition is found in Siberia where female shamans commonly (and to this day) carry a wand that represents the World Tree as well as a "steed" with which to travel into other worlds [Dioszegi, Vilmos (1968): Tracing Shamans in Siberia The story of an ethnographical research expedition]. That the vǫlur carried wands is testified both in written sources and from archaeology, where female graves containing cult like objects and wands have been found all over Northern Europe from the early Iron Ages to the Viking Age.

The much revered priestesses who were buried at Oseberg, Norway, in 834 AD had, among large amounts of ritual equipment, a wand between them. Shamanic mythologies also tend to revere a "First Shaman" a semi-divine but also once human character who was the inventor of shamanism and who still exists at the crossroads in order to help fledgling shamans. Often, the First Shaman is closely associated to the divine creator realms. Sometimes there is more than one First Shaman. The concept of a First Shaman or Shamans also appears to be the case with Norse seiðr, especially if we are to believe what is said in the poem Vǫluspá about Creation, where Gullveigr-Freyia of the Vanir is the first master of this art.

THE WAR OF THE TRIBES WHO ARE THE VANIR?

23. Then all the rulers went to the Chairs of Fate/Origin (= parliament) the sacred holy deities to discuss this: Ought the Aesir alone owe to suffer the loss, or ought all the deities together owe to pay the debt?	*23.Þá gengu regin ǫll á Rǫkstóla, ginnheilug goð, ok um þat gættusk: Hvárt skyldu æsir afráð gjalda, eða skyldu goðin ǫll gildi eiga.*
24. Óðinn hurled (his spear) and shot against the people there was a war, the first (war) in the world; broken were the wooden walls of the Aesir fortress the Vanir, victorious, openly swarmed the fields	*24.Fleygði Óðinn ok í fólk um skaut, þat var enn fólkvíg fyrst í heimi; brotinn var borðveggr borgar ása, knáttu vanir vígská vǫllu sporna.*

-Vǫluspá st. 23-24, Poetic Edda

In the Vǫluspá, the divine tribe of Vanir suddenly enters world history seemingly out of nowhere. The word Vanir (sg; Vanr) has an uncertain etymology. If the word is Norse in origin, it may be related to various words:

→ Ván (f.sg.) ["Hope"]. I.e. Vánarstjarna, The Star of Hope (= Sun)
→ Vanr (a) "Accustomed", "used to"/ "normal", "common", "ordinary"
→ Vanr (a) "Lacking", "missing"

The latter meaning would make sense insofar as the Vanir were once "lacking", their arrival among the Aesir was a great gift to them. In that sense, the Aesir got their "missing links", the ones that were needed to complete the divine pantheon. The only thing that seems certain is that the Vanir are the people and family of Gullveigr, who is the Goddess of the Vanir [Vanadís], otherwise known as the great goddess Freyia [Lady Sovereign]. A "great goddess" is a term much misunderstood, so we shall have to provide a definition before we move on. Within a polytheist religion, it is quite common that there are certain gods and goddesses who are more universal and less specialized than others.

These deities will have functions that range widely across many different areas of life, fate and death. They will be worshiped by both genders and all social classes, and they will receive particular attention in the public, government sponsored cult. This is the basic definition of both a Great Goddess and a Great God, and we know that Freyia, Óðinn and Freyr were such Great Deities within the Norse Pagan religions of the Viking Age.

Sometimes, there are mystical trends of Pantheism ("the one behind the many") within the larger polytheist religion where such "great deities" are considered Supreme Beings, the original source and origin of all other gods, who in some respect are merely specialized hypostasis of the Supreme Being. It is very common to acknowledge both a male and female aspect of the Supreme Being. Such mystical, Pantheist trends are known from Indian religion as well as from Classical religions, and may in my opinion have been a sub-trend also in the Old Norse religion.

→ In the Vǫluspá, the divine tribe of Vanir suddenly enters the cosmic scene seemingly out of nowhere. The only thing that seems certain is that they are the people and family of Gullveigr, who is the Goddess of the Vanir [Vanadís], otherwise known as the great goddess Freyia ["Lady Sovereign"]. The sources are very vague as to the origin of the Vanir, who until then appear to have played no role in the creation of the world. However, that is only how it appears.

→ In the Ynglinga saga (Chapter 4) Snorri claimed that the Vanir were a tribe of people who in prehistory were invaded by the Aesir, also described as a tribe of people. They warred for a long time, but no one was victorious, and both sides used magic against the other. Eventually, they came to terms and made a truce, and exchanged hostages according to the customs of the day.

→ The Aesir sent their wisest man, Mímir [Memory], together with the most handsome man they had among them, Hǫnir, who in the Vǫluspá plays the role of Óðin's brother Vé and offers the gift of intelligence and thought to men and women.

→ The Aesir received the best men among the Vanir; Njǫrðr and his two children, the twins Freyr and Freyia, as well as the wisest man they had, Kvasir. Snorri adds that Njǫrðr had a sister-wife who was left behind: "When Njǫrðr was among the Vanir, he had been married to his own sister, for it was legal among them; their children were Freyr and Freyia. Among the Aesir it was forbidden to marry such close kin."

The Vanir are offered positions as sacrificial priests and priestesses among the Aesir, and the priestess Freyia teaches the art of seiðr to the Aesir, and art that according to Ynglinga saga originated among the Vanir. In his Prose Edda account, the Skáldskaparmál, Snorri offers a slightly different version, where Kvasir is not one of the Vanir hostages but rather the product of a brew that was made from the spit [brewing essence] of all the Aesir and Vanir gods together. After a journey through the world of human beings and other entities, Kvasir was murdered and his blood was turned into the Mead of Poetry that plays such a major role in Old Norse myths, as we shall be exploring in the next Chapter (Chapter 3). In the Poetic Edda, Kvasir is replaced by Heimdallr as the third Vanir god, as the Þrymskvíða poem reveals:

> 15. Then spoke Heimdallr,
> the brightest among Aesir,
> -he knew well the future
> like all Vanir do...

> 15. Þa qvaþ þat Heimdallr,
> hvitastr ása,
> —vissi hann vel fram
> sem vanir aþrir...

 That Heimdallr is also an Ás is true but so are Njǫrðr, Freyr and Freyia from the moment they join the Aesir tribe; they now belong to both tribes. That Heimdallr, like all Vanir, knows the future is a reference to their Vanir inheritance the art of seiðr, which was the art of divination more than anything else. As I suggested earlier, I believe that the war against the Vanir was instigated by Óðinn because he wanted the Vanir among his own people he wanted their art of seiðr, which Freyia had shown was more than just divination. She had shown before the Aesir court that the art of seiðr ultimately had to do with taking control over fate even over that ultimate fate which is death.

The Aesir, although gods, were not immortal. Freyia of the Vanir tempted the Aesir when she displayed her powers, showing them the path towards immortality. The Vǫluspá poem reveals that the Vanir were victorious in the battle, yet somehow the Aesir managed to turn events in their favor, and Óðinn got exactly what he wanted the most powerful Vanir deities among his own tribe. The big question here remains the same as before. Who were the Vanir really, where did they come from? In Chapter 5, I touch upon the possibility that the Vanir represent some historical/ prehistorical people just as Snorri suggested, and that the war reflects events that may have taken place towards the end of the Stone Age, when "battle-ax people", Indo-European tribes, invaded or migrated into Northern Europe, encountering resistance from the Megalith-builders who already lived there.

The Megalith builders, who also left their significant marks in southern Scandinavia, may very well, much like the Vanir, have been regarded as particularly wise and crafty with their impressive knowledge about architecture, engineering, astronomy and mathematics. In my 2004 thesis, as referred to before, I suggested the possibility that they actually represented a myth of human beings who displayed divine powers and thus frightened the gods. However, none of these possible origins of the Vanir myth remove the fact that within the Edda context, the Vanir have become symbols of something far more cosmic. In order to understand who the Vanir really are, or rather what they are, we shall have a closer look at the Vanir who came to be priests among the Aesir.

Njǫrðr, father of the nine

According to Snorri's Gylfaginning, Njǫrðr was regarded as the third man among the Aesir after Þórr and Baldr. He lives in Noatún, which means the "Ships' Court" (noa is a genitive plural of nór ["ship"]), ultimately meaning the "Ships'Harbor". Ships are ancient Scandinavian symbols of the vessel of life that journeys through the ocean of existence, and which ultimately takes the travelers to their destination: death. Let us see what Snorri has to say about this god who stands at the very cosmic destination of all ships:

> "He lives in heaven, where it is called the Ships'Harbor. He rules the paths of the winds, and can silence both ocean and fire; to him one should pray for a fortunate journey across the oceans and for a good fishing harvest. He is so abundantly rich and blessed with property that he can offer land and precious gifts to anyone he wants, therefore he shall be prayed to in order to have your wishes fulfilled."

In the Poetic Edda, Njǫrðr is mentioned with further elaboration. In the poem Grímnismál, Njǫrðr lives in the eleventh dimension of cosmos and is the Ruler of Men:

> 16. Ships' Harbor is the eleventh (world) and there Njǫrðr keeps his halls standing high;
> The Ruler of Men who is without fault rules the High Timbered Fortress
>
> > 16. Noatún ero en ellipto,
> > enn þar Njǫrðr hefir
> > ser vm gorva sali;
> > Manna þengill
> > enn meinsvani
> > hatimbroþom hargi reðr.

In the poem (Grímnismál), there are twelve worlds or dimensions in "heaven" (cosmos), and we know from what Snorri has earlier stated, that only nine of them are subject to death ("Hel rules in nine worlds"). Thus the place where Njǫrðr receives the "ships" of the living is a place of immortality. The world that precedes his realm is the tenth dimension, Glitnir [The Glittering], a place of justice, which corresponds with Snorri's description of the world called Gimlé [The Glimmering], where good and just people will be living for all eternity.

Snorri also describes the eleventh world, but calls it Andlangr ["Expanded Breath"], clearly a name that refers to immortality. The next world, according to Snorri, is Viðbláinn ["The Wide Death"] [or "The Wood (= matter) Death"] which corresponds to the twelfth world of the Grímnismál, which is Valhǫll. According to Snorri, only Light Elves may live in the three upper heavens. We will be discussing what Light Elves are soon. For now, we shall state that the sources offer clues as to the real identity of Njǫrðr as a cosmic power when they place him at the shore of the cosmic oceans, the ruler of the "winds" of death that moves the world, the source of abundance and the fulfillment of wishes.

The ships are the vessels of life that manage to reach his shores of immortality without drowning on the way. According to the Gylfaginning, Njǫrðr replaced Hǫnir, the giver of conscious thought, when he came to live with the Aesir, suggesting that the god is associated with the mind and its thoughts:

> "Njǫrðr is not of Ás-kind, he was raised in the World of the Vanir. But the Vanir offered him as a hostage to the gods, and received in return a hostage called Hǫnir, and thus there was peace between the gods and the Vanir."

In the Edda poem Vafþrúðnismál, the hostage theme is further elaborated:

38. "Tell me the tenth one, since all the fate of the high gods is known by you, Powerful Head Veil: From where did Njǫrðr come To dwell among the sons of the Aesir? - Temples and sanctuaries he rules in plenty yet he was not raised among Aesir."	38. Segðv þat iþ tíunda, allz þu tiva rac a/ll, Vafþrúðnir, vitir: hvaðan Njǫrðr vm kom meþ asa sonom? — hofom oc hargom hann reðr hvnnmorgom oc varþaþ hann asom alinn.»
39. "In the World of the Vanir wise rulers created him, and sent him as a hostage to the gods; When fate is completed by the ages he will return back again to dwell in the world of the wise Vanir."	39. «I vanaheimi scopo hann vis regin, oc seldo at gislingo goðvm; i aldar rac hann mvn aptr coma heim meþ visom vanom.»

The lines leave us with the same mystery. Who were the Vanir, and what is this mysterious "World of the Vanir"? Who are the wise rulers of that realm? Interestingly, the Vafþrúðnismál poem mentions Njǫrðr and his realm just after the mention of the giant in eagle's hide called Hræsvelgr [Corpse Swallower], who is the cause of all winds, and who obviously receives the dead. Just like Njǫrðr, who receives the "ships" and who steers the winds.

I mentioned above that there is some connection between Njǫrðr and the mind, and in the same way, there is a connection between the eagle and the mind. In Chapter 2.11, I mentioned the eagle who sits in the top of the world tree with a hawk between his eyes, a hawk called "Wind-Diminisher", and suggested that he eagle corresponds with the mind of the universe tree and with the mind of human beings.

Further clues are given in the Edda poem Lokasenna:

Loki said: 35. "Shut up, Njǫrðr! You were sent to the East a hostage of the gods: The Maidens of Hymir had you for their chamber pot and made your mouth moist."	Loci qvaþ: 35. «Þegi þv, Njǫrðr! þv vart austr heþan gisl vm sendr at goðom; Hymis meyiar hafð þic at hlandtrogi oc þer i mvnn migo.»

Njǫrðr said:
36. "I had compensation for this
that I was sent far away a hostage
given to the gods;
For I begot a son who is hated
by no one, and he seems a Lord
among the Aesir."

Niorþr qvaþ:
36. «Sv eromc licn,
er ec varc langt heþan
gisl vm sendr at goþom:
þa ec mag gat,
þann er mangi fiár,
oc þiccir sa asa iadarr.»

The stanzas are as puzzling as they are informative. First of all, the Lord of Winds is obviously sent to the East, which is the world of the giants, not that of the gods! Yet he is still called the hostage of the gods. The line seems to rather describe the god as a Vanir hostage among the Aesir. In the East, the giant world, he is "had" by the "Maidens of Hymir". Loki mocks the god for having his mouth used as their pissing pot, yet Njǫrðr reveals that there was no dishonor and that this was how he begot his glorious son Freyr [Lord Sovereign]. Who are these maidens/daughters of Hymir? We must first ask who Hymir is. Hymir ["Hymn" or "Slow One"] is a frost giant who plays a significant role in the Edda poem Hymiskvíða.

In this poem, he is the husband of the bright browed, ale, and advice, serving but unnamed "mother", whom I have taken to be Þór's mother, the Earth goddess. In Hymir's halls we also encounter the "Grandmother", Night, who has nine hundred terrifying heads. Hymir owns the cauldron that is big enough to contain all the mead of Aegir, that is, the entire cosmic ocean. In the poem, Þórr and Hymir rows the boat of the giant out to sea and gets an unusual catch, **The Middle World Serpent**. A serpent whose function is to create a border between the known and the unknown worlds. Acquiring the cauldron of Hymir is necessary if the gods are ever going to hope to join the banquet of the immortals in Aegir's halls.

The cauldron that can hold the entire cosmic ocean is said to cover Þór's body entirely when he achieves it, and may be a way of describing fulfilled and complete knowledge integrated within the entire being. The connection to Hymir and his mysterious daughters is also a connection to Aegir and his nine daughters, the daughters who birthed the present world. Interestingly, Njǫrðr shares some important features with both giants. First of all, Njǫrðr is the lord of winds and waves, associated with a safe harbor in the great cosmic ocean. The winds are the unseen movements of life that lead to death. The waves are also unseen movements of life, identified as the daughters of Aegir, who is thus also a ruler of waves. Like Njǫrðr, Aegir lives in a safe harbor, Hlésey ["The Wind-Shield Island"], which is a reference to immortality. Like Njǫrðr, he quenches fire [a symbol of passion] and offers instead his daughters to provide the rivers of golden light in the hall of the immortals.

The light of his wave/river daughters is identical to the "red gold" of divine wisdom and enlightenment, and the formula of the nine sisters represents the power of creation that birthed this world. The realm of Aegir and his daughters is in the east, the place of sunrise. What about Hymir, is there cause to say that he can be identified with Aegir, and thus with the nine daughters of the Ocean? Snorri offers a clue in his lists of metaphors, pointing out that Hymir was called the "Breeze-Sender" by the skald Bragi. Thus Hymir too is the lord and origin of the winds, just like Njǫrðr the Vanir god, Hræsvelgr the Eagle and Aegir the Giant. It is more than likely that the four entities described here represent different guises for the same cosmic power, a power that is related to the mind of the universe and the source of movement, as well as to the final destination of the soul.

We find a further clue in the Edda poem Sólarlióð, which is usually dismissed as a Christian poem, but which nevertheless provides important perspectives, the poet would never have alluded to concepts that were not already known and taken for granted by his audience, who would still remember much of the ancient lore:

79. Here are Runes that have been carved by Njǫrð's Daughters Nine (...)	79. Hér 'ru Rúnar, er ristit hafa Njarðar Dœtr Níu (...)

This stanza leaves no doubt whatsoever that the poet and his audience, living around the year 1200 AD, identified Njǫrðr with Aegir. He is the father of nine daughters. Daughters who are here also obviously identified as Norns, the goddesses who carve the fates of all beings. To complete the picture, we should have a look at Njǫrð's unnamed sister and wife and mother to his children. Scholars generally agree that the name Nerthus is a Latin form of the name Njǫrðr, or rather of his feminine counterpart, who may have been known as either Njerðr or Njórunn.

According to Tacitus, Nerthus was the mother goddess jointly worshiped by a confederation of German tribes known as the Suebi, who back in the days (the account was written between 80 and 98 AD) lived in Central Europe and Denmark. She was a goddess associated with the ocean or a lake, and she received the drowned:

"They are distinguished by a common worship of Nerthus, or Mother Earth. They believe that she interests herself in human affairs and rides through their peoples. In an island of Ocean stands a sacred grove, and in the grove stands a car draped with a cloth which none but the priest may touch.
The priest can feel the presence of the goddess in this holy of holies, and attends her, in deepest reverence, as her car is drawn by kine. Then follow days of rejoicing and merry-making in every place that she honors with her advent and stay. No one goes to war, no one takes up arms; every object of iron is locked away; then, and then only, are peace and quiet known and prized, until the goddess is again restored to her temple by the priest, when she has had her fill of the society of men. After that, the car, the cloth and, believe it if you will, the goddess herself are washed clean in a secluded lake. This service is performed by slaves who are immediately afterwards drowned in the lake. Thus mystery begets terror and a pious reluctance to ask what that sight can be which is allowed only to dying eyes." [Germania, 40]

That Pagan goddesses received human sacrifice in lakes and bogs is beyond doubt, archaeological evidence suggest that this was common during the Bronze and Iron Ages. The essential features ought to be noted, the mother goddess is concerned with the "affairs of men", associated with fate and law, like the Norns. She is also a unifying figure which creates peace between people. She receives the dead [by drowning]. These essential features of the prototypical wife/sister of Njǫrðr are actually shared by Aegir's wife and the mother to their nine daughters, Rán [Robbery], who in Norse mythology is pictured as standing at the bottom of the ocean with a net, ready to catch the drowned.

She and her daughters want the drowned for their lovers. This destructive aspect is balanced by the other side of her, as the grandmother to the present universe, birthing the streams and waves that jointly create the world. Njǫrðr, a god of immortality, is indeed married to the goddess of death, mother of life. Even as he leaves his wife among the Vanir, he next marriage is similar, he marries a giantess who is another aspect of the death goddess, Skaði [Injury], who seems to represent death in the mountains, the wilderness or from injuries, but a point is made out of how the two are incompatible.

This analysis of Njǫrðr throws a revealing light upon the identity of the Vanir. We are back at the beginning, with the very powers that created the universe, with the giant and the giantess who are the grandparents of all existence. Just like the Hamingjur were cosmic river giantesses who became the "soul-walkers" of people when they entered the world of human beings, so the Vanir are giants powers of cosmic creation who become something else. A new aspect of themselves, when they enter the world of the Aesir gods, the world of conscious intelligence, order to the universe, and physical life.

FREYR THE LORD OF ELVES

As we saw in the previous section, the birth of Freyr was associated with Njǫrðr being held hostage among the nine maidens, his own daughters and we cannot exclude the possibility of a myth where the father is also the lover, and where the daughters give birth together as one being to their own brother. In Chapter 1.7 I described how formulas must be used to unlock the meanings of the myths, and how a parent metaphorically describes a cause, a child describing a result. The male parent is the seen and known cause, or else the cause that has a shaping, holding-together quality. The female parent is the unseen and unknown cause, or else the cause that fuels movement and fate.

Antlered Man with Ring and Serpent, surrounded by Stags and Boars and other Animals, a detail of the Gundestrup Cauldron which was sacrificed in the Gundestrup Bog, Denmark, around 300 AD. The symbols are associated with Freyr

The birth of Freyr is not certain, but on one level, we could say that Freyr represents man on a divine, ideal level, just as the universal tree, the World Tree, also represents man on the human level. Thus the birth of Freyr seems to echo the birth of Heimdallr and the sprouting of the World Tree. As we saw in the previous section, the Lokasenna poem mockingly describes the conception of Freyr as Njǫrð's humiliation when the maidens of the ocean giant used his mouth as a pissing pot. Yet the essential meaning is hidden behind the mockery. The creation of Freyr, the mold of man, involved the mouth of his cosmic father, a mouth moistened by liquid streams produced by the nine maidens.

This image will make more sense if we recall that Ymir, the World Giant, came out of the Mouth of the Sacred Descendants [Ginnunga gap], when hot streams of liquid moistened this Mouth, and that Helgi, who represents both the universe and the fate of man, was born to the shrieks from the mouths of heavenly eagles when sacred liquid ran down the mountains of heaven. Thus, in Freyr, we see yet another image of the divine world-being and original mold of man. According to Snorri's Gylfaginning, Freyr is foremost among the Aesir:

"Njǫrðr of the Ships' Harbor later had two children, the son Freyr and the daughter Freyia; they were beautiful in appearance and very powerful. Freyr is the foremost among the Aesir. He rules rain and sunshine, and by this he rules the harvests of Earth. He is good to invoke for the purpose of a good harvest and peace. He also rules the welfare among people."

In his Ynglinga saga, (ch.10) Snorri describes Freyr as a powerful Swedish king and priest, the founder of the temple of Uppsala which became a famous center of parliament and worship, thriving until the last days of Paganism:

"Freyr took the kingdom after Njǫrðr, and he got the nickname "Lord of the Swedes", and received gifts and taxes from them [the Swedes]. He was friendly and aged well, just like his father. Freyr built a huge temple complex by Uppsala and kept his main seat there, and to the temple he invested everything he owned, land and properties. Thus the Uppsala-Wealth was established, and it has kept ever after.

In his days, there was a Peace of Wisdom [Fróðafríðr], it was then good harvests in all countries and the Swedes gave credit to Freyr for this, therefore he was worshiped more than other gods, and still more as long as the people of the country were richer during his realm than before, because there was peace and good harvests. Gerðr Gymis-Daughter was his wife, and their son was called Fiǫlnir [The One Who is Many]. Freyr had another name, Yngvi [Sacred Lineage], and the name Yngvi was since used as a name of honor in his lineage, and his descendants were called the Ynglings.

Freyr became ill, and as his illness worsened, his men pondered the solution, and let people come and watch him, and then they built a huge mound with a door and three windows. And when Freyr was dead, they carried him to the mound in secret, and told the Swedes that he still lived, and they hid him there for three years, and all the treasure they poured into the mound, the gold through one window, the silver through the second, and the copper through the third. Then the harvest and the peace were maintained."

Freyr's association to worship in the burial mound after his death may be one reason why he is also associated with the elves. In the Grímnismál, st.5, we learn that Freyr is the lord of Alfheimr the World of Elves, the second dimension of "heaven", after Þór's realm Þrúðheimr [Power World]. We also learn that Freyr is associated with a very ancient Scandinavian god, Ullr, whose mythology is mostly unknown to us, except that he is associated with hunting, especially hunting with the bow and arrow, like Skaði also was.

We only know that Ullr was widely worshiped because of his importance in the place-name material, countless areas were named after his sanctuaries and fields dedicated to him:

5. Yew Valleys it is called where Ullr has built his halls; Freyr received the World of Elves in the days of origin from all the powers, as a tooth-gift.	*5. Ydalir heita þar er Vllr hefir ser vm gorva sali; Alfheim Freý gáfo i ardaga tivar at tannfe.*

The yew [ýr, m.sg.] Is a masculine tree and is thus a metaphor for man, in whose "valleys" (interiors) the god of hunting and archery has taken up his residence. The yew is also a reference to the bow that he uses to shoot with, since it was the wood matter most commonly used for bows. The association to masculinity, male potency and fertility is more than hinted at, an impression that is strengthened by the fact that of all gods, Freyr was the one most associated with sexuality and phallic symbols. We could say that Freyr on one level represents the essence of manhood and masculine power. That he is the ideal man model is strengthened by the image of the just king who provides peace, prosperity and fertility to his land and his people.

He rides a horse or a boar, and carries a sword. However, there is more to Freyr than the potency of life and procreation, he is also the Lord of Elves. The elves were objects of worship in the Pagan religion. During the annual alfablót ["The Sacrifice to the Elves"] the elves were honored as the spirits of dead ancestors. These were thought to reside underground and within the burial mounds or within mountains. The festival took place around the same time as the Halloween and the Day of the Dead is celebrated in other places and is clearly related, a very ancient ritual in honor of the souls of the ancestors.

Some elves were particularly honored: When King Olaf Guðrøðsson of Vestfold, brother to Halfdan the Black (810-860 AD) died, his burial mound at Geirstað became associated with great fortune for those who went there to pray. It was thought that the soul of Olaf heard their prayers. The dead king was referred to as the Geirstaðalfr-"The Elf of Geirstað". Thus we see that in Old Norse lore, the elves are strongly associated with souls. There were Light Elves and Dark Elves. In the Gylfaginning, Snorri describes the Dark Elves as darker than tar and offers a very somber vision of them, in contrast to the Light Elves:

"There lives the people called Light Elves [liósalfar]; but the Dark Elves [dǫkkalfar] live beneath the ground. These two elfin kinds are very different to look at, and even more unlike within. The Light Elves are brighter than the sun to look at, whereas the Dark Elves are blacker than tar."

Yet, the sources to our knowledge about the Sacrifice to the Elves and other references to elves as the souls of dead people give a more complex picture; the Dark Elves are not evil, they are simply the souls of the dead that reside in the underworld, perhaps ready to be reborn at some point. In Chapter 7, I will discuss the subject of reincarnation for now, let us say that the elves represent souls and that there is considerable evidence that the Pagans believed in reincarnation. The Dark Elves represent the souls of the dead that still reside in the world, albeit in the underworld, still able to communicate with the living. They may have been kept in the world by their descendants, who prayed to them and sacrificed to them for their wisdom, their guidance and their protection exactly as it was said that people could pray to Freyr in his mound after his death.

Pagans would sit on burial mounds or on the sacred hills and mountains where the dead were thought to reside, meditating until communication with the dead could be obtained. Their darkness is the darkness of the unknown, that which is not seen by the living, of the hidden reality that is death. The Light Elves, on the other hand, may very well refer to the souls of the dead that have achieved immortality. Perhaps they have become shining bright and transparent through a descent (or ascent) in the Well of Origin, a feat achieved through spiritual training and initiation, leading to the transformation and the immortality of the soul? Whatever the key to their position, the silent Light Elves dine with the gods and the immortals in the Hall of Aegir at Hlésey, The Wind-Shielded Island, where the history of the world is recounted and the nine Daughters of the Ocean provide the golden light of illumination for this mysterious banquet.

The Light Elves belong to the three upper heavens, where not even the gods may dwell; shining, bright heavens to the south. The first of these heavens is called Gimlé ["The Glittering"] brighter even than the Sun, where "deceit-free" lineages live for all eternity. The second is called Andlangr ["Long Breath"], and the third is called Viðbláinn ["The Wide Death"], where only Light Elves may dwell. As the Lord of Elves, Freyr is ultimately the Lord of Souls. What kind of soul or what aspect of the soul is an open question, the sources indicate that the elves are the souls of the dead, although there are instances where apparently living entities, such as Vǫlundr the smith (to be described in Chapter 5), is referred to as an elf, even as the Lord of Elves. Earlier, we saw how the Norns and Fylgjur were also associated with souls, both with the souls of dead female ancestors and with the fate-spinning souls of all people.

The word for elf in Old Norse, alfr, is a masculine word, and when elves are mentioned in Old Norse sources, they are mostly masculine, the souls of dead men. Like the fylgja, they may represent a dead ancestor, but unlike the fylgja, who then is an ancestress, the elf is a male ancestor. Unlike the fylgja, the elf soul does not seem to follow his descendants or play the guardian spirit, nor does he seem to appear or play a significant role within the soul of the living. The elfin ancestor resides in the burial mound and may be helpful to those who seek him there. To all appearances, the elf is the embodiment of the soul of a dead male. If he resides in the mound or in other aspects of the Underworld, he is a Dark Elf. If he resides in the upper heavens, he is the immortal soul of the enlightened, and is a Light Elf. There are some elves that are feminine, however.

The Sun goddess is the Shine of the Elves [Alfrǫdull], and the goddess of eternal rejuvenation (i.e. immortality), is said to be of "elf-kind" [alfa kindar] in the Edda poem Hrafnagalðr Óðins. None of these are said to actually be elves they are said to be associated with elves, with their bright shine and their "kind", I suggest the female kindred of the male elves, that is, the feminine aspects of the soul of both sexes, and/or the souls of females. We are starting to see the shape of a complex picture, the Old Norse concepts about the soul.

Apparently, all human beings regardless of gender possess a female soul, a fate-spinning goddess who follows us, is within us, aligned with us, yet also one who may take on a shape of her own and call on the company and aid of other fate-spinning souls. She may be awake or sleeping. A dead woman could act in the world as a fylgja without a body attached, mostly in order to help her descendants or loved ones. Apparently, a man could not, but he could live on in the elf, a concept that at least seems to refer to the souls of dead men only. When Freyr is the Lord of Elves, he is also the Lord of dead men, the lord of the realm where the souls of dead men linger. In a fashion, he represents or rules the soul of males. In the living, he is the source of masculine energy, potency and fertility. As a deity of these things, he not only begets fertility in the land, but also resides within all men and is a mold for men: What Freyr does is relevant to all men.

The only important myth about Freyr that we are aware of, is the Skírnismál story about how he wooed his wife, Gerðr, a story that will be discussed in the next Chapter. During the quest, Freyr offers up his "horse which can carry its rider high through the dark and flickering flames" and his "sword that can fight giants on its own, as long as it is carried by the fearless". He gives these gifts to his symbolical "servant", Skírnir [The Shining One], who then is able to enter the world of the dead, where the bride is hidden. As we shall see, the marriage proposal constitutes and instigates a trial of initiation where the object is the union with the mysterious giantess of the illuminating arms within the sacred and, most importantly, breeze-less Grove of the Pine.

The breeze-less grove is the same as the Wind-Shielded Island a place of immortality, in union with the maiden within the soul elf united with the soul fate. This difficult quest is the most important story about Freyr and thus the most important story about all men who embark on the quest of the soul to become a Light Elf in the upper heavens. It is interesting to note that these three upper heavens of immortality, brightness and Light Elves are counted as the three last among the twelve cosmic dimensions in the Edda poem Grímnismál. The remaining nine worlds belong to various gods, and we should bear in mind that Snorri stated that Hel the personified Death "rules in nine worlds". In the Grímnismál, the ninth world is the place where Freyia rules the fate of people in life and in death. This is where the goddess receives the souls of the dead, deciding which path they will take from that point. In the Edda poem Lokasenna, it is said that the goddess has held all the gods and Light Elves of the Hall of Aegir the Hall of Immortality in her embrace. It is time to have another look at Freyr's sister.

FREYIA, THE THREE TIMES BORN

> *13. Your father had a mother abundantly necklace-adorned*
> *I believe that she was called*
> *Wind-Shield-Goddess, the Priestess*
> *Wisdom was her father and Love her mother all that lineage is full of the best*
> *people.*
>
> > *13. Modur atti fadir þinn*
> > *menium gaufga,*
> > > *hygg ek at hon heti*
> > > *Hledis Gydia;*
> > > *Frodi var fadir þeirrar,*
> > > *enn Friaut modir;*
> > > *aull þotti ætt su*
> > > *med yfirmonnum.*

Hyndlulióð, st.13, Poetic Edda

Freyia already made her entry in the beginning of this Chapter, playing the role of Gullveigr-Heiðr, the "three times born", the first vǫlva, the first initiate, and the first to conquer death. Since the Middle Ages, Freyia has been reduced to a "Goddess of Love", although this aspect plays a minor role compared to her role as a goddess of witchcraft, seiðr, initiation, fate, death, wisdom and shape-changing.

In his Gylfaginning, Snorri first says of Freyia:

> *"Her hall, Room for Seats [Sessrumnir said to be a ship] is large and fair. When she is out traveling, she drives with her cats and sits in a chariot. She is the one who is most likely to respond when people invoke her. And from her is that honored title derived, that high-born or great women are called freyias [ladies, dames]. She well likes love-poems, and it is useful to call upon her if one wants to win love."*

This is the only source where there is indication that Freyia actually was concerned with love as such and it is only one sentence among several others that mentions this role, so her aspect as "goddess of love" is hardly as important as we have been led to believe through popular traditions. In his Ynglinga saga, Snorri emphasized Freyia's role as a priestess:

> *"Njǫrð's daughter was Freyia, and she was a sacrificial priestess [blótgyðja], she was the first to teach the Aesir how to perform seiðr, which had been an art among the Vanir (...) Freyia then maintained the rituals of sacrifice, for she was the only one who survived after all the gods, and she was then so honored that after her name one should call all high-born women, they who are now called ladies; likewise all women are the "Freyia" of her property, and "house-Freyia, the one who owns a farm."*

More than anything else, Freyia is the ideal prototype of a Pagan high-born woman who owns and runs her property and who takes responsibility for religious ceremonies and she is also the prototype of a wand-carrying witch and a priestess, a keeper of holy secrets. Where Freyr is the ideal King, foremost among men, his sister is the ideal Priestess, foremost among women.

Where Freyr was the great Elf of the autumn alfablót [Sacrifice to the Elves], Freyia was the great Dís of the spring dísablót [Sacrifice to the Goddesses] where all female powers were worshiped together as Dísir [goddesses], whether they were giantesses, Ásyniur, Norns, Valkyrie, Fylgjur and Hamingjur. At this annual nine day celebration, which took place together with the annual parliament of the clans, a temple was raised to the first Dís, called the Dísarsalinn [The Hall of the Goddess].

There is no doubt among scholars that the one Dís who owned this hall was Freyia, whose name is a title: "Lady Sovereign". Freyia will be discussed on several occasions in this book, so at this point, we shall only add a little to what has already been conveyed about the Lady Sovereign. To the Vanir, she was obviously the Goddess she is called the Vanadís, "Goddess of the Vanir". In Snorri's Edda, she is said to be the "foremost among the Ásyniur", a position she shares with Frigg, Óðin's wife. As I mentioned in the beginning of this chapter, Frigg and Freyia originated as one goddess, and Snorri solves the problem by letting Freyia be married to Óðr, which is the short, unspecified form of Óðinn and means exactly the same; Spirit, Poetry, Frenzy.

According to Snorri, Freyia's husband vanished, and the goddess went to search for him throughout the world, and everywhere she came among people, she took upon herself a new shape and a new name, and left behind her tears of Red Gold a metaphor for divine wisdom. In the Poetic Edda, Freyia appears first in the guise of Gullveigr, and it is in this story we see her primary function, as a vǫlva who practices and teaches the art of seiðr, and who knows how to conquer death through resurrection. Her trial of initiation is the first, staking out the path for gods and heroes to follow. Her name Gullveigr [Gold Power Drink] also connects her with the precious mead of wisdom, poetry and resurrection that is served to initiates in the underworld. Gold is a metaphor for divine knowledge.

Freyia may very well be behind the figure of the first vǫlva, who remembers the nine worlds before the present and who were raised among giants. As we have seen, her father Njǫrðr is the father of nine sisters, the rune-carving fate spinners who are also the rivers and waves of the world, and the mothers of Heimdallr the Great World another Vanir god. My educated guess is that Freyia is the unifying, singular aspect of the collective of nine or three by nine Dísir who form the mold of all female supernatural powers. The image of Freyia as a divine witch-priestess is strengthened throughout the Poetic Edda. In the Þrymskvíða, she lends out her falcon hide to Loki, who can then travel into other worlds in order to find lost power, like the classical shaman.

In the Hyndlulióð, she plays a major role as the teacher of a young man who has prayed to the goddesses for help. The goddess appears and takes the young man, changing him into the shape of a sacrificial boar, and rides him into the underworld, where secret, esoteric teachings are conveyed to him by the she-wolf below. Only when the goddess offers the Mead of Memory to the young man will he be able to remember these teachings when he is resurrected into the world of the living. The goal of this initiation journey is clearly stated to be Valhǫll, so that we learn that this poem may be conveying what actually had to happen when a young man wanted to reach this upper heaven.

In the Grímnismál, it is said that Freyia decides the fate of chosen men after death, and that she sends half of them to Óðinn and to Valhǫll. Apparently, the journey went through the underworld, guided by the goddess as if she was a fylgja and in a fashion, she is. If Freyr is the Elf among elves, then Freyia is the Fylgja among Fylgjur, the Dís among Dísir. In the Poetic Edda, there is very little information that even indicates the famous (yet almost undeserved) love-and-sex aspect of Freyia.

The Lokasenna accuses her of having all the Light Elves and gods of the hall of Aegir as her lovers, a piece of information which can only be truly understood if we realize the fact that the Light Elves are souls and the gods are divine souls who have reached the realm of immortality, through the embrace of the goddess. It is when she receives a soul into her loving embrace during initiation, like we see described in the Hyndlulióð, that the gates of Valhǫll and the realms of the immortals are opened.

The Lokasenna also accuses her of having been the lover of her own brother, Freyr, a fact which is not denied. However, as we shall see, it is Freyia herself who hides behind the figure of Freyr's wife Gerðr, whom Freyr reached through a trial of initiation, and who will only be his when he has reached the breeze-less grove of immortality after the nine nights of his initiation. Freyia's aspect as a "goddess of love" can only be fully appreciated when we understand her aspect as soul, and as the seat of the soul's enlightenment and immortality. In Grímnismál, stanza 14, Freyia is said to "rule the seating of the hall" in her realm Folkvangr, which literally translates as "People Field", suggesting that she rules the cosmic "field" of human destiny:

14. People Field is the ninth (world) and there Freyia rules the seatings of the hall Half the chosen (slain) she chooses every day and (the other) half belongs to Óðinn.	14. Folkvangr er inn nivndi enn þar Freyia reþr sessa costom i sal; halfan val hon kyss hverian dag, enn halfan Oðinn á

I suggest that the ruling of the seats of People Field actually refers to how the goddess arranges the fates of people in the world, a "hall" is often used to describe a realm or a world. The Earth is often called a hall, for example the "Hall of the Moon". Our human dimension, Miðgarðr, actually means "farm" or "settlement" of the "middle". The impression of Freyia as the ultimate fate-goddess is strengthened by the next lines of the same stanza, when she is said to be the chooser of the dead, the one who chooses who shall die, particularly in battle.

It is said that she "chooses the chosen", and the words used [val hon kyss] refers to the action of kiosa val, "to choose the chosen (dead)", the exact words that make up the word Valkyrie, "Chooser of the Chosen". In the Vǫluspá, stanza 33, counts nine Valkyrie heralding the age of war that precedes Ragnarǫk among them are Skuld, the Norn of the future, and Gǫndul, which is a name for Freyia. There is mention of Freyia being invoked after a childbirth in order to bless the midwife, and the later Flateyjarbók calls Freyia a concubine of Óðinn who frequently committed adultery, in order to obtain her "Necklace of Flames" [Brísinga Mén], she slept with the dwarfs of the four directions. I believe this originally had more to do with the necklace being a symbol of the Sun which shines in all directions.

The necklace was later stolen by Loki, but retrieved by Heimdallr, who plays the role of Freyia's hero. The Necklace of Flames is an important attribute of Freyia, inherited from a Bronze Age goddess of necklace and golden eyes that appears frequently in archaeological finds, and may be used in poetry to describe the goddess, such as when an otherwise unknown ancestral mother, Hlédís Gyðia [Wind-Shield-Goddess Priestess], is said to be "abundantly necklace-adorned" in the Hyndlulióð stanza quoted in the beginning of this section. When this necklace-attribute is combined with the information given through the meaning of the name, it is even easier to understand that Freyia is behind the figure.

She is a divine priestess, a gyðia, and she is associated with immortality and the wind-shielded island of immortality where her father Njǫrðr/Aegir lives. Hlésey, the island that is shielded from the winds of death and life. In this stanza, she is also described as both a singular person and also a-sexual [meaning dual persons or using the more fluid term "they"] ("their father was Wisdom"), one of several indications that the nine daughters are also one, Freyia, the Lady Sovereign. The stanza also reveals that the parents of Freyia (and thus also of Freyr) can be described as Wisdom and Love. In the Flateyjarbók story, Freyia takes the shape of a giantess called Gǫndul [Magician], identifying the giantess-goddess as a Valkyrie, who affects the fates of men in the direction that Óðinn craves, towards war.

She does this unwillingly because Óðinn has taken her necklace as a hostage. The story clearly carries elements of the goddess's power to change fate (through the art of seiðr) and resurrect the dead so that they may return to the same battle over and over, in my opinion a metaphor for the reincarnation of the soul. Apart from "Magician", Freyia has many other names, and some of them are listed with Snorri. Among these name is Mardǫllr, which means "The Great Ocean". It links the goddess to the ocean, just like Rán and the Nine Sisters, with whom we have seen that Freyia is certainly closely related. Being the Great Ocean, we are reminded of the cosmic ocean from which the World Tree sprung. Another name is Hǫrn, which means "Flax", and is a reference to the linen threads that is spun by the fates.

Freyia is here identified as the very substance of fate and thus life. Then there is the name Gefn, also known as Gefion "who knows all fate", and whose name means "The Provider". The meaning of the name is an ancient epithet of the goddess of the land all over Europe and beyond she is the source of all abundance and nourishment. There is also the name Sýr, which means "Sow", corresponding with the boar shape that Freyia's lover takes and the boar of her brother Freyr. The sow is also a very ancient symbol of the mother goddess in Europe.

It was a symbol of Demeter, the mother of grain and growth, who was also the Great Goddess of the Mysteries in Eleusis and who introduced the initiation mysteries at that ancient learning center. The sow was also a symbol of the Celtic goddess Cerridwen, who owned the cauldron of the "three inspirations" that was sought by bards. Scholars usually identify the maiden Menglǫð of the Fjǫlsvinnsmál poem with Freyia, based on the many similar attributes, among them her gate that will only open if she so wishes. In this Edda poem, Menglǫð sits beneath the Tree of Memory, awaiting her true love on the Mountain of Medicine with her nine handmaidens, who are goddesses of benevolent fate.

She is called Þióðmæra ["The Great Maiden"] or ["The People's Maiden"], and she is said to be the true ruler of Utgarðr, the world of giants. The image corresponds with the fact that Njǫrðr, her father, is identifiable as the most powerful giant, Aegir who rules the winds and waves. In the Vǫluspá, st.21, Freyia-Gullveigr is called þrysvar borna ["The Three Times Born"]. This may allude to the three powerful and much-knowing giantesses who came out of the giant world in order to spur the Aesir into creating the dwarf shapes of the physical world.

It could also allude to the three Norns of past, present and future, who wrote the laws of fate and carved the runes of fate into the World Tree. It could allude to the three kinds of Norns that may follow a man or a woman like a fylgja or Hamingja in their lives, one of Ás-kind, one of Elf-kind and one of Dwarf-kind. It could allude to the three "great rivers" of Hamingjur that own the Earth. It could allude to the three nights of initiation that sometimes alternate with nine, just as the three Norns sometimes appear as nine. Freyia as the Three Times Born may in fact be an allusion to all these things at once.

God from the Gundestrup cauldron, Bronze Age Denmark. Flanked by a male to the right and a female to the left, his two children? On his left, there is also a warrior riding towards the woman, a suitor?

SOCIETY AND RELIGION

As I have strongly suggested, there is evidence that the Vanir are identical with the most ancient creative powers of cosmos. They become "Vanir" as they enter the world of gods and human beings, echoing their original cosmic power to create and change fate on a physical, human and mental level. If we look back towards the beginning, we may realize that the account of creation has come full circle by now.

The Vǫluspá poem begins with a time before the present world existed, follows history from the emergence of matter in the early cosmos, the reawakening of conscious spiritual qualities, the fertilization of the Earth, the creation of a physical molds (dwarfs), and the entry of divine consciousness into life matter.

Then we saw the impact of fate from the moment that living beings attained breath, spirit, thought, intelligence, vitality and life's colors. Here is when the vǫlva enters the picture as the first spiritual leader and teacher, teaching the art of immortality and the arts of magic and healing. That the vǫlva, with her initiation ritual and her witchcraft, represents the entry of religion on this scene of cosmic history speaks volumes about the importance of seiðr and of the vǫlur in Old Norse Paganism. The arrival of Freyr and Freyia also heralds a time of rulership and societal order, i.e. civilization. Freyr is the ultimate King archetype, the sacred King whose sacred function is to ensure the peace, the justice, the morals and the education, the prosperity and the happiness of the people and the land.

The emphasis on peace is natural even for a warrior society; without peace there can be little prosperity, little wisdom and little happiness for the common man and woman. Ensuring the internal peace sometimes meant the ability to keep external enemies at bay, so that the King of peace was also a military leader who made sure to protect the land. The ideal King maintained the peace and performed the religious ceremonies and sacrifices that were thought to ensure fertility and abundance in the land. The marriage myth of the Skírnismál poem is usually thought to be related to the ritual of Sacred Marriage where the King entered a sacred union with the soul of the land and the tribe the Goddess. His ability to please the Goddess of the land, who is often also the ancestral mother of the tribe, was symbolized by phallic stones and figurines thought to inspire fertility.

The sister, Freyia, represents the feminine counterpart to masculine power. She was the priestess and the house-keeper, the one who practically ran the economy that her brother protected, and the keeper and teacher of sacred knowledge. This complimentary power balance between the male and the female ruler (both siblings are called "sovereign") was once an ancient, sacred and "natural" order of things, introduced by the gods themselves. It is reflected on many levels of society and seeps through in many ancient sources. The deeply patriarchal Romans were continuously surprised at how German and Celtic tribes would keep women as counselors, even on military campaigns, women who were revered as matronae [mothers] or else referred to as priestesses and oracles.

The complimentary powers may also be seen in the image of the Aesir holding their sacred parliament within the confines of the Norns' realm and in their presence, likewise, the great Parliament of all Swedes in Uppsala during the Viking Age was held in conjunction with the Dísablót [Sacrifice to the Goddesses] and was even named after the goddesses: Dísaþing [Parliament of the Goddesses]. The sibling-lovers Freyr and Freyia not only represent the ultimate, sacred power balance between the Priestess and the King, between the Witch and the Warrior. The two gods also represent the ultimate man and the ultimate woman according to ancient, sacred ideals; two different but equally powerful complimentary powers united in order to create the legendary Peace of Wisdom [Fróðafríðr] where prosperity, peace, high morals, happiness and the pursuit of wisdom and knowledge was the ruling quality of human society.

In Old Norse myths, the divine reality is the mold of all other realities. On every level of society, each man is his own Freyr, his own ruler, and each woman is her own Freyia, her own ruler. A man may not be a king, but he may ensure the safety and the happiness of his kind by using his power to protect and his abilities to create wealth and contribute to the prosperity of his "realm", and he may relate to the sacred powers in whatever way appropriate to his means and status. A woman may not be a high priestess, but she may organize and run her "realm", producing and providing wealth from it, she may learn to cure illnesses, she may cultivate knowledge and wisdom and perform the magic and the divinations that all women were expected to have a certain talent for, being shaped in the Norn's mold.

Heimdallr, Kvasir and the Precious Mead

In the section 2.3, I mentioned Heimdallr as a metaphor for the universe itself, just like the World Tree and the world giant Ymir. It is the name that gives the god's true identity away. It simply means Great World from heimr, "world", and dallr, "great", "awesome", "glorious". That, and his descent, being born from nine mothers. Heimdallr is one of many examples that there is an underlying concept of a "Universal Being" in Old Norse Paganism. There are many ways of describing the Universal Being, perhaps according to the dimension within which the Universal Being is perceived at any given time. As we saw in 2.12, Óðinn was Spirit to the Aesir (consciousness), yet Dead One to the elves (dead souls) and Hibernation to the dwarfs (physical molds) a different aspect of himself in every dimension of the universe.

Likewise, the Universal Being is represented by different aspects on different levels. It is the giant Ymir, primeval Sound and Bellowing Rock Matter. It is the World Tree Yggdrasill, providing the basics of a physical shape, a steed for the spirit. It is Heimdallr who hears all and sees all, and who guards the ethereal bridge between the worlds. He is disguised behind the figure of the giant Mímir [Memory], who drinks Memories from the same Bellowing Horn [Gjallarhorn] as Heimdallr uses to blow his breath into. As a god, Heimdallr represents the consciousness of the Universal Being, its eyes, ears and memories. I will be discussing Heimdallr as the Universal Being at length in Chapter 8.

As the third male Vanir god, Heimdallr is replaced by Kvasir in some sources, and the two are really indistinguishable, Heimdallr sees, hears and remembers every detail of every event in cosmos. Kvasir is knowledge and wisdom personified he can be asked anything, and there is nothing he cannot answer. One myth has it that Kvasir was created by the spit, i.e. the essence, of all the Aesir and Vanir deities together, emerged as a cauldron of mead yet shaped into a wandering sage who walked freely through the world during the era of the Peace of Wisdom [Fróðafríðr] when Freyr ruled as King Wisdom [Fróði Konungr]. In Chapter 5 about the Golden Age, we will look more closely at the myth of how Kvasir was killed and how his blood was hidden in three cauldrons, constituting the Precious Mead that was sought by seekers of divine wisdom ever since.

The Precious Mead is ultimately the collected consciousness of the Universal Being, the experience it stores, the knowledge it provides, the power of creation and eternal resurrection that is its essence. As I said earlier, the arrival of the Vanir gods heralded the era of civilization, and with it, the dawn of religion or perhaps we should rather say the dawn of a spiritual path, for "religion" is often associated more with mental and moralistic dogmas than with the pursuit of knowledge and divine insight through experience. In Old Norse myths, the Precious Mead is the center point of the spiritual path of initiation that was introduced by the vǫlva called Gold Power-Drink and sought by the god whose name means Spirit. This mead will be the subject of the next Chapter.

3: THE MAIDEN WITH THE MEAD

**INITIATION AND CONSECRATION THROUGH RITUAL DRINKING
AND SACRED MARRIAGE**

INTRODUCTION: A PATH OF INITIATION

*I have tasted the sweet drink of life...all the gods and mortals seek it together,
calling it Honey-Mead (madhu).The glorious drops that I have drunk have set
me free in wide space....The drop that we have drunk has entered our hearts;
an immortal inside mortals...*
-(Rig Veda 8.48)

A recurrent motif of the Edda poems is the woman who serves mead to a god or
to a hero. An in-depth study of every different setting in which this motif plays a
role shows that there are striking structural similarities between them. In my 2004
thesis, I explored some of these stories, uncovering the fact that their structure
follows a perfectly detailed and credible path of initiation where the initiate,
whether god or hero, has to seek a vision of the mead-woman through "techniques
of ecstasy" before entering the Underworld, where he would encounter obstacles
in the form of dangerous entities, usually representing fear, hatred, greed and
oblivion, or a guardian who challenges him so that he must prove his knowledge,
eloquence and wisdom.

When he succeeds, he would reach a golden bright realm of resurrection where
he would be restored and transformed through the consecration of the mead and
the embrace of the woman who serves it. The focus in my thesis was on the ritual
structure that ran as a basic underlying structure throughout several different
Edda poems. I found that we could speak of five stages of ritual, beginning with the
Vision Quest, followed by a Vision. This would lead to the third stage, the Descent
(into the Underworld), followed by Trials leading, eventually, to the Consecration.
The Consecration happens at the moment of mead-serving and sacred marriage,
or simply the loving embrace of the Mead-Woman. Adding to these five stages, the
hero or god, representing the role of the initiate or neophyte, would return to the
world worthy of a new role in society; a sage, a sorcerer, a god or a king.

» Vision Quest
» Vision
» Descent
» Trial
» Consecration

To sum up the stages of initiation as they appear in the Edda poems I dealt with.
We have, first, the Vision Quest stage. This is where the initiate applies so-called
techniques of ecstasy. In the poem Hávamál, Óðinn lets himself be hanged for nine
nights. He also fasts, abstaining from food and drink, and is pierced by spears. All
this seems to reflect a typical Norse human sacrifice, which we know happened in
Pagan times, and which the sagas strongly suggest was the fate of kings who failed
to inspire fertility in the land.

However, the ritual can also reflect a so-called "mock sacrifice" where the intention is not to actually kill the victim, but to induce a state of altered perception. Such severe trials are not unknown to shamanic initiation rituals, to yogis or ascetics, as a means of reaching communication with the other world or to have a near-death experience. The number of nights corresponds with the number of nights it takes to reach Hel (according to the Snorri in his story of Hermoð's journey to save Baldr). It also corresponds with the number of cosmic worlds (dimensions of reality) in which Hel, Death, is said to rule. The nine nights probably included the journey through all these nine worlds, as is suggested in the Edda poem Vafþrúðnismál, st.43:

About the runes of the giants and of all the gods
I can truly speak for I have been within every world:
To nine worlds I came beneath Misty Hel where the dead come from Hel's
halls.

> *Fra iotna rvnom*
> *oc allra goða*
> *ec kann segia satt,*
> *þviat hvern hefi ec*
> *heim vm komit:*
> *nio kom ec heima,*
> *fyr Níflhel neðan,*
> *hinig deyia or helio halir*

The number nine also corresponds with the number of worlds that existed before the present universe, and the nine sorceresses who birthed it. It is also the usual number in which giantesses and Valkyrie appear, and is repeated like a formula on several occasions. In the case of the Hávamál and Óðin's trials, the result of the hanging for nine days is that he "peers down" and sees the runes that the Norns have carved into the roots of the world tree the runes of fate. This is his Vision. Through his Descent, he is able to reach them and drink them like mead and bring the knowledge of them into all the worlds, before he himself "comes among" the "binding powers", i.e. the gods.

On the way, he has to face terrible giant forces, the Trial theme, and needs the embrace, the mead and the guidance of the Mead Woman [the Consecration Theme] in order to resurrect from the underworld. The Vision Quest theme is particularly elaborated in the story of Óðin's hanging, but is recognizable also in other stories. In the poem Skírnismál, Freyr induces his visions by sitting in the seat of Óðinn ["The seat of Spirit"]. The seat is called Hliðskjálf, which means the Seat of Openings, and enables the seated one to gain vision into "all the worlds". Again, we see the theme of conscious presence in several worlds.

The Vision Quest seems to be a little less dramatic in this one, involving something like meditation in a power spot, also well-known from shamanic, ascetic and yogic traditions. Freyr then has his Vision, the maiden with arms that illuminate the world. The Descent is undertaken by Freyr's servant Skírnir, who, like Óðinn, has to contend with a giant guardian and with the maiden herself, appearing like a rather hostile giantess, the Trial theme, where eloquence and a quick mind is his way out of trouble. The Consecration theme is promised, although not culminated, since Freyr has to survive the "nine nights" before he can earn the soft embrace of the Mead-woman with the shining arms.

This can only happen in the mysterious, breezeless "Grove of Barri", barri referring to a pine needle. The fact that this grove is "breezeless" is highly significant since wind is a metaphor for death. As such, the theme of immortality is introduced. In the poem Hyndlulióð, the initiate, Óttarr, resorts to blót (blood sacrifice), for his Vision Quest. The sacrifice of an animal, which appears to be a boar, is what leads to the Vision of the altar turning into crystal while the goddess Freyia reveals herself and transforms Óttarr into the very sacrifice. The Descent follows as Freyia rides Óttarr in the shape of a boar down to the "darkness of darkness itself". The Trial theme is the encounter with the scary, wolf-riding giantess of the rock caves and how to extract her knowledge without getting killed in the process. Whereas Óðin's purpose with his trials seems to be knowledge about the runes of fate, and Freyr's purpose is to reach union with the shining maiden, the express intent of this initiation journey is to reach Valhǫll, an alternative afterlife realm.

All of these journeys involve as their culminating point the ritual drinking of a precious mead served by a giantess within the underworld, the Consecration. In the stories of Hiǫrvarðr and the two Helgis, we see the same pattern repeat itself: the initiates or their accomplices perform a number of acts designed to induce visions of bright, golden maidens from other dimensions, mainly from dimensions that appear to belong to death and the afterlife. Sleeping by a river or on the top of a sacred mountain, dozing off within sacred groves or sitting in silence upon a burial mound are all practices that are described in the Edda as Vision Quests, allowing us to conclude that deep, all-night meditation in power spots, that is, in a sacred space thought to be particularly powerful in a magical, mysterious and religious way, was a known practice during the Viking Age.

These practices all lead to the vision of a land sometimes known as Sváaland, the "Land of Sleep", in which the glorious maiden is to be found. This time, the maiden appears to be a Valkyrie, and she reincarnates between the lives of various heroes. One of the last reincarnations of the Valkyrie happens in the story of Sígurðr the Serpent-Slayer, which takes place across several Edda poems. This story is one of the most detailed in its descriptions of an initiation journey. My 2004 thesis provides a quite thorough discussion of all the five stages throughout various poems. In this Chapter, however, I will focus on the Mead woman herself, her realm, and the meaning of the mead that she serves.

3.1: THE MEAD OF POETRY -HÁVAMÁL, THE HIGH ONE'S SPEECH-

The mead-woman motif occurs twice in the Hávamál in connection with what may very well describe some kind of initiation ritual in connection to the god Óðinn. In the Hávamál we find the oldest version of the story of Óðin's quest for the mead of poetry. Snorri Sturluson explained that the mead of poetry had been created by the spit (essence) of all the Aesir and Vanir gods together after their truce, and that it contained all the divine knowledge of the universe. The mead took the shape of a sage that moved through the world so that everybody who so wished could get answers to their questions about the nature of existence. The sage, who went by the name Kvasir, was killed by two dwarfs who wished to monopolize all this knowledge for themselves.

They did not succeed, and as they died, the giant Suttungr [Heavy with Mead] took the three cauldrons of mead, the biggest of which is the Óðrerir [Spirit/ Poetry/Ecstasy Blend]. The meaning of Suttung's name suggest a link to the giant Mímir ["Memory" or "Murmurer"], who drinks from the sacred mead of universal memory and wisdom through his horn called Gjallarhorn [The Bellower Horn], and who, through the name of his horn, is identifiable with the god Heimdallr ["Great World"], a universe-deity who sees all and hears all. The name of the cauldron Óðrerir is made from the word óðr (m.sg) which simultaneously means "spirit", "poetry" and "ecstasy" and the word rerir which means a "stir", a "blend" or a "brew", as in a liquid substance of ingredients cooked together or blended.

The word Óðr is also the name of the goddess Freyia's lost husband, and is the word that makes up the name Óðinn [Óðr + hinn (= "the")], a meaning that identifies Frigg's husband Óðinn and Freyia's husband Óðr as one and the same. The separation between the two gods must have been created after the goddesses Frigg and Freyia separated into two goddesses from the original one, the older Germanic goddess Frija, the meaning of whose name has to do with love, peace, wisdom and sovereignty. The name of the cauldron also suggests some mystical identification between the mead and Óðinn himself.

Suttung's daughter Gunnlǫð ["Invitation to Battle" or "Battle Hospitality"] then guards the mead within the Hnítbergr ["Clashing Rock"]. As was suggested by the Icelandic writer Svava Jacobsdottir, the name of Gunnlǫð's abode suggests a comparative link to the mythical complex known in Greek mythology as the Symplegades the perilous entrance to the world of the dead. These were described as rocky cliffs clashing together. There is indeed a myth about how two doves were sent to fetch the sacred Ambrosia, the nectar of immortality, in the Other World and who had to go through the clashing rocks to reach it, where one of them died. There is a similar entrance to the world of the dead in Indian mythology, described as two golden rocks clashing together, where the Soma-thief in the shape of an eagle tries to get the sacred drink known as Soma, which, exactly like the Old Norse mead, was a honey based liquid said to provide eloquence, wisdom and immortality.

In Old Indian mythology, the sacred Soma is guarded by the dhisanas, the numerous hypostasis of the great goddess Dhisana. The word is in fact etymologically linked to the Old Norse word Dísir, referring to the female powers, who also guard the precious mead in the Edda lore. The common etymology added to their common function makes it natural to assume that the Old Norse Dísir and their sacred mjǫðr share the same ancient origin as the Old Indian dhisanas and their sacred madhu ("honey"), another name for Soma. The time of separation between the eastern and the western traditions is probably thousands of years old. The name of Gunnlǫð herself, which means Battle Hospitality/Invitation, is thought by many to indicate that she is in fact a Valkyrie, a thought that is strengthened by the fact that she serves the precious mead.

*6th Century AD Gotland Picture Stone
Detail: Eagle with Human Legs is
met by a Woman carrying a Drinking
Horn, apparently urged on by a Man,
her Father? Probably inspired by the
myth of Óðinn, Gunnlǫð and her father
Suttungr.*

The Valkyrie are indeed said to be born among giants, and whenever they are presented with a family (usually a hostile father or brother), they are all giants. I will show, however, that the mead-serving woman comes from all the various worlds of the Old Norse cosmos and suggests that the borders between the worlds may not have been as geographically strict as we may think at first sight. In Snorri's account, the god Óðinn then sneaks into the mountain (a symbol of the world of the dead or the giants) in the shape of a serpent (a symbol of death and transformation) where he seduces Gunnlǫð, sleeps with her for three nights before he drinks all the mead within the three cauldrons. Then he changes shape into an eagle (symbol of the ruler of death) and flies off to Ásgarðr where he leaves most of the mead.

A few drops of mead landed in other worlds though, including the human world, which is why some people have the gift of poetry and eloquence to a certain degree. The older version of this myth is found in the Edda poem Hávamál and tells a different story, where Óðinn openly enters the halls of Suttungr and displays his wisdom and eloquence before the giant's court, like a man wooing for a wife in her father's hall. He swears a sacred ring-oath, which is a symbol of marriage, and is offered the precious mead by Gunnlǫð while she sits on a throne another symbol of marriage, kingship and initiation. In stanza 105 of this poem, we are told (supposedly by the god himself):

Gunnlǫð gave me on the golden throne the precious drink of mead...

> *Gunnlǫð mer vm gaf*
> *gvllnom stóli á*
> *drycc ins dyra miaþar*

Further on, stanza 140 of the Hávamál poem repeats the theme of the precious drink (drycc ins dyra miaðar), this time in connection with Óðin's trials as he hangs on the World Tree for nine days and nights. After having peered down and picked up the runes, Óðinn receives nine powerful spell-songs and then has a drink of mead:

...and I had a drink of the precious mead ladled from Óðrerir

> *...oc ec dryc of gat*
> *ens dyra miaðar*
> *ausinn Oðreri...*

It is generally known that Óðrerir was the mythical cauldron that contained the mead of inspiration, knowledge and poetry, guarded by the giantess Gunnlǫð. Stanza 140 makes it quite clear that the experiences of Óðinn in the halls of the giants, of Suttungr and of Gunnlǫð, are mysteriously connected to Óðin's trials by hanging on the World Tree. It appears that the god hung on the World Tree, stabbed with spears, fasting, in order to descend ("peer down") to a place where he simultaneously obtains the knowledge of the runes, learns the magical songs, and experiences the famous encounter with Suttungr and Gunnlǫð as told in stanzas 104-110 as well as by Snorri. Only then does the god learn to "be wise, learned, to grow and to live well". Essentially, we see that Óðinn enters three worlds simultaneously three worlds associated with the three roots of the world tree:

1. The realm of the Norns in Ásgarðr, where he receives knowledge of the runes of fate.
2. The realm of the giants in Utgarðr, where he receives the nine spells of memory.
3. The realm of death in Hel, where he receives the embrace of the mead woman. His new wife then helps Óðinn escape and become a god, but he leaves her behind, weeping in the underworld. Thus she must be sought there again by everyone who wants to taste her sacred mead.

All the three worlds are associated with a "well", or to be exact, a water-source:

1. The Well of Origin belongs to the oldest Norn, Urðr, and has the property of transforming those who enter it so that they emerge transparent and bright. It also has the property of nourishing the world tree, preventing its decay and death every day. It is the source of life itself, and of its regeneration.
2. The Well of Memory belongs to the old giant Mímir, and has the property that those who drink from it will know all the memories of the entire universe.
3. The Well of Hel, called "The Bellowing Mill", has the property of recycling the souls of the dead, and is the source of all "rivers" (movements) in the world.

Since Óðinn seems to simultaneously visit all three worlds, we may suspect that the mead he drinks carries the quality of all these worlds, and that the mead woman who guards the drink may be a divine Norn, a giant's daughter and the lady of the underworld all three at once. The three wells, roots and worlds are also reflected in Snorri's account, where the mead of poetry is guarded in three different cauldrons.

The most famous is the Óðrerir [Poetry/Inspiration Blend], the two others are called Boðn [Vessel] and Són [Reconciliation/Atonement/Sacrifice]. Like the three cosmic wells, the three cauldrons are different, yet all contain the same mead the same essence. The unity of the three worlds may be illustrated in the famous Old Norse design known to us as the valknutr ("choice knot") three interconnected triangles above which the Eagle soars in a standing stone depiction from the 6th century, a design I have used for the front page of my book. (Today, modern people tend to render the valknutr as a kind of three-fold pyramid pointing upwards, for some obscure reason or other. In ancient depictions, the valknutr always points down and to the left, indicating a more "feminine" symbolism).

3.2: ORIGIN'S WELL -HRAFNAGALDR ÓÐIN'S EÐA FORSPJALLSLJÓÐ
ÓÐIN'S RAVEN CHARM OR THE SONG OF THE FIRST SPEECH-

This often unknown poem is of obscure origin and has thus been much debated by scholars, the question being whether it is a "real" Edda poem, that is, dating back to Pagan times or just "made up" later by someone who was learned in Old Norse poetry and mythology but who was not an insider to Pagan religion. However it is, the poet certainly knew more about Pagan mythology and poetry than we do, and made a curious connection between Gunnlǫð and the oldest among Norns , Urðr, whose name means "Origin":

> *2. The Intentions of the Aesir are difficult riddles*
> *You want to throw weight to the runes*
> *Urðr is oath-bound to hide the Óðrerir*
> *I managed to use the greatest part*

> > *2. Ætlun æsir illa gátu,*
> > *verpir villtu vættar rúnom;*
> > *Óðrerir skyldi Urðr geyma,*
> > *máttk at veriamestum þorra*

These stanzas are spoken by the god Óðinn who is referring to how he managed to drink almost all the mead of the cauldron Óðrerir which was guarded by Urðr, making us realize that he is talking about exactly the same incident that happened between him and Gunnlǫð. It is clear that the poet who created the Hrafnagaldr, at least, identified Gunnlǫð with the oldest Norn Urðr. The association with runes only strengthens this impression, as does the reference to riddles and secret divine intentions. There is some controversy as to whether the poet of the Hrafnagaldr was "authentic", that is, if he (or she) was really a Pagan insider or just a later medieval wannabe Norse poet.

The major reason why this poem is hardly ever translated or allowed into collections of the "Poetic Edda" is because modern translators since the 1860s have dismissed the poem as unintelligible. The stanzas are written like riddles so obscure that it is almost impossible to understand by modern people so modern people have decided that the ancient poet was a fake. In my opinion, the poem becomes perfectly understandable the moment one decides to translate all the names and take seriously the fact that the names actually signify something. In the light of my own analysis of the Edda lore as representative of a kind of Mystery tradition, I find that the Hrafnagaldr fits perfectly. The poet obviously knew the art of Old Norse poetry and had grasped the great riddles of metaphorical poetry, and when the poet decided to identify Urðr with Gunnlǫð, I assume that the poet knew more about this than we do today.

The identification between the giantess Gunnlǫð and the Norn Urðr offers us more insight into the mead-woman's ultimate function, as well as into the nature and origin of the mead itself. The first among the Norns is the one who made all the cosmic laws and carved all the fates of everyone who ever lived, live and will live, as is described in the Edda poem Vǫluspá. She is responsible for nourishing the World Tree Yggdrasill from her sacred Urðarbrunnr, the Well of Origin. She wrote the first runes the runes that Óðinn later discovered while he hung. This water, according to Snorri Sturlusson's Prose Edda, has the quality that everyone who walks into it will come out transformed, shining, bright and "transparent like the inner membrane of an eggshell."

The water also nourishes the universe itself, revives it every day against the constant destruction that feeds on it. The same water is in fact the very origin of the universe. The World Tree, which is also called the Mjǫðviðr [The Mead Tree], actually springs from this cosmic water source, the Well of Origin. Other beings that constantly emerge from this Well of Origin are the individual Norns who follow each human being through his or her life, as we saw in Chapter 2.12. Adding to this source is the account of Snorri's in the Prose Edda, to which I have referred above. The sources indicate a powerful connection between fate, the mead, the original cosmic waters and the runes. I earlier mentioned that it has been suggested that Gunnlǫð was a Valkyrie. A Valkyrie is a specialized kind of Norn, spinning the life and choosing the death of warriors, so that the identification between the Valkyrie and the Norn makes sense. If Gunnlǫð was a giantess, the identification with the Norn still makes sense. In the Edda poem Grottasǫngr, giantesses are clearly identified not only as Norns , but as Valkyrie, moving among the hosts of warriors and choosing their fate.

Image from the Medieval Church at Yttergran, Blåkulla, Sweden: The Devil serves Drink from a Horn to Three Broomstick-Riding Witches carrying Drinking Horns. Images such as these abound in early Scandinavian Churches, suggesting a serious Christian attempt of Demonizing the Ancient Icon of the Woman who Serves the Sacred Mead from a Horn. Thanks to Stephen Mitchell for providing photos I could draw from.

3.3: HEL'S PRISONER -VEGTAMSKVÍÐA EÐA BALDRS DRAUMARTHE SONG OF WAY-WONT OR THE DREAMS OF BALDR-

In this poem, the god Baldr is plagued by evil omen dreams, and all the Aesir and Ásyniur [gods and goddesses] go to the sacred parliament by the Well of Origin in order to discuss what the dreams may portend. In order to find out, Óðinn, as the great shaman of the Aesir, travels to Níflheimr, the world of the dead. He arrives at the "high hall of Hel" where he makes sure to move to the east, direction of sunrise and new beginnings/light, of the dangerous hall. With spell-songs he wakes up a long dead vǫlva and asks why the death-hall of Hel is decorated as if to welcome an honor guest. This is where it is revealed that the precious mead is in fact guarded by Hel in the world of the dead, as is said in stanza 7:

Here stands for Baldr the brewed Mead the Bright Power-Drink is covered with shields

> *Her stændr Baldri*
> *of brvgginn Mioðr,*
> *Skírar Væigar,*
> *liggr skiolldr yfir*

Thus we are seeing that the precious mead is guarded by a supernatural female both in the world of the giants (Suttung's hall), the world of the fates (Urð's Well of Origin), and in Hel simultaneously. The question arises as to whether there really is a difference between the three worlds at all. Later, when Baldr is in fact dead and living like an honored guest in Hel's hall, the hero Hermóðr makes the journey into Níflheimr in order to beg the queen of the dead to let Baldr return to the living. Precious mead is certainly associated with the realm of the dead.

In Valhǫll, Valkyrie serve mead to the einherjar milked from the eternal she-goat Heiðrún [Bright Rune/Symbol]. Snorri provides a very detailed account of the journey to Hel: Hermóðr has to borrow Óðin's eight-legged steed Sleipnir, a horse that has the power to move in all worlds. The path is dangerous, slippery and dark, so dark that nothing can be seen, and only illuminated by a golden bridge called the Gjallarbrú [The Bellower Bridge], guarded by a giantess. When he crosses the bridge over the river Gjǫll [Bellower], the bridge resounds powerfully, and the giantess comments that "you do not have the color of dead men" and wonders what he is doing in Hel if he is not dead.

3.4: THE FROSTY CUP -SKÍRNISMÁL THE SPEECH OF THE BRIGHT SHINING ONE-

> ....for Elf Splendor (the Sun goddess) she shines all days but not upon my desire.
>> ....þviat Alfraþvll
>> lysir um alla daga
>> oc þeygi at minom mvnom

> Skírnismál, st.4 (Freyr laments his impossible love for the mead woman)

The poem Skírnismál also contains two references to the precious mead. This time, the mead is offered by another giantess, Gerðr [Enclosure]. The background story is that the god Freyr sits in Óðin's seat Hlíðskiǫlf [The Shelf of Openings], from which he can gaze into all the cosmic worlds and see everything, even that which is hidden. Hidden deep within the realm of her father Gymir ["Hides (something)"], the maiden lives in a hall surrounded by flames and she is so shining bright that her arms illuminate the lands and the seas (as if she was the sun goddess Sól herself). Frey's servant Skírnir [Bright Shining One] offers to undertake the dangerous journey to her realm in order to ask if she will accept Frey's hand in marriage.

Skírni's journey to her realm is described almost exactly like Snorri describes the journey of Hermóðr: The journey is dangerous, slippery and dark, so dark that nothing can be seen. He is riding a magical horse borrowed by a god (in this case Freyr), a horse that is able to move "through the flames". Just like Hel's halls, Gerð's hall is described as high and dangerous. Adding to that, they are flaming. Just like the giantess asked Hermóðr his business in the world of the dead when he is so clearly alive, a "shepherd" asks Skírnir whether he is dead or dying, and realizing that he is neither, says that Skírnir cannot expect to see the maiden and live. We are clearly in the world of the dead, and it is easy to see that Gerðr might be a disguise for Hel.

When Gerðr realizes that an unusual guest (neither dead nor dying) has arrived, she orders her servant guardian (the shepherd) to allow entry to the visitor:

16. Let him walk into our hall and drink the adored mead
Though I think it seems that out here I see my brothers bane

     16. Inn biþþv hann ganga i occarn sal
     oc drecca inn mera mioþ!
     þo ec hitt óvmc,
     at her vti se
     minn broðvrbani

Apart from our interest in her "adored mead", Gerð's last comment, that Skírnir is her brother's bane, provides an ingenious riddle. The answer to the riddle is found both in the Lokasenna poem and with Snorri, who explained that Skírnir is indeed the bane of a brother. The brother in this passage, refers to Freyr himself, on whose behalf Skírnir is acting.

Skírnir, the Shining Bright One, is the ultimate bane of the passion god because he demands the magical horse and the magical sword that Freyr will need in his last battle at Ragnarǫk. The god of passions is doomed to die because Skírnir took his most precious weapons. The ultimate conclusion thus seems to be that Gerðr actually may be identified with the goddess Freyia.

In the poem Lokasenna (st. 32), it is indeed revealed that the siblings, Freyr and Freyia, made clandestine love. Like Gerðr, Freyia is said to live in a high and impenetrable hall that no one may enter unless she herself wills it so, a point that is also made in the Skírnismál, where only Gerðr decides if Skírnir may enter. Like Gerðr, Freyia is associated with flames, as she owns the Brísingamen, the Flame's Jewel. Like Gerðr, Freyia is a recipient of the dead (Grímnismál st. 14), a function they both share with Hel.

It is interesting to note here that even Gunnlǫð is living in a realm that is described as slippery and dark, from which it is almost impossible to escape alive. Suttungr takes the shape of an eagle in pursuit of Óðinn, and a giant in eagle hide is indeed the very image of death itself in Old Norse myths. All of these maidens are mead-women guarding and offering the mead in an underworld realm. Later on in the poem, Gerðr repeats the action of welcoming the hero, offering him the "frosty cup full of ancient mead":

37. Be rather whole, lad!
And take the Frosty Cup full of ancient mead

     37. Heill verþv nv heldr, sveinn!
     oc tac viþ hrímcálki
     fvllom forns miaðar

The "frosty cup" is a reference to death, which is a realm of ice cold, frost and mists. The "ancient" mead is a reference to its origin at the well of the beginning of the universe itself. According to Snorri Sturluson, Gerð's mother was called Aurboða, and she was of giantess origins. The name Aurboða is interesting, since it seems to be referring to the precious aurr the sand from the Well of Origin that the oldest Norn Urðr uses to nourish the universe every day.

In fact, the name Aurboða seems to be referring to the one who creates these sands, since boða means "she who bids". Gerð's mother is the one who "bids", or "orders" the sand.

To see a link to the Norn Urðr, who pours the sand over the roots of the world tree, and thus provides the nourishment or our universe is not far-fetched in my opinion. In the poem Hyndlulióð, st.30, Gymir, Aurboða and Gerðr are said to be the "kinspeople" of Þjazi and Skaði. The most interesting genealogy, however, is offered by Snorri Sturluson in his þulur (Skáldskaparmál), where he clearly identifies Gymir with the sea giant Aegir and Gymir's wife with Rán, building his argument on how ancient skalds obviously identified them:

"How shall the sea be referred to? By calling it Ymir's blood, visitor to the gods, husband of Rán, father to Aegir's daughters, whose names are Himinglæva, Dufa, Bloðughadda, Hefring, Unn, Hronn, Bylgia, Bara, Kolga [most of these are names for different kinds of waves](....)and as Ref said; Gymir's spray-cold oracle-wife [Rán] often brings the twisted-rope-bear [ship] into Aegir's jaws [under the waves] where the wave breaks."

Snorri continues: *"Here it is implied that they are all the same, Aegir and Hlér and Gymir..."*

This implies to us that Gerð's father is in fact Aegir, the sea giant, and that her mother is Rán, the goddess of death at the ocean. She is one of the nine daughters who often appear wearing various names. How, then, can she also be Hel and Freyia at the same time? And how can Rán be the same as Aurboða, who is the same as Urðr? If we are to understand this, we have to learn to be as flexible in our minds as the Old Norse poets and their Old Norse audience actually were.

We have to stop thinking in terms of clear separations and rather apply a very fluid worldview where one being is known by many names and shapes. To ease the journey towards understanding such an alien worldview, let us look again at the Sólarlióð poem referred to earlier (Chapter 1.1:)

Here (in Hel) are Runes that have been carved by Njǫrð's Daughters Nine;
Counsel Drink the oldest
Approaching Spring the youngest and their Seven Sisters.

> *Hér 'ru Rúnar,*
> *er ristit hafa*
> *Njarðar Dœtr Níu;*
> *Ráðveig hin elzta*
> *ok Kreppvǫr hin yngsta*
> *ok þeirra Systr Sjau.*

A 7th century memorial stone from Lärbro in Gotland, Sweden shows the image of a giantess waiting by a bridge that is about to be crossed by a man riding an eight-legged steed. Significantly, she is offering a drinking horn to the visitor.

In this poem, there is no doubt that the poet and his audience "knows" that the god Njǫrðr has nine daughters! One of them, the oldest, is also clearly associated with a drink that provides wisdom (counsel). Another, the youngest, is associated with renewal, new life after death ("approaching spring"). Now, from other sources and mainstream education, we moderns "know" that Njǫrð's children are Freyr and Freyia, and we hear of no other daughters. However, the poet probably knew more about this than we do today, and he was addressing an audience that would also understand what he meant.

It is more likely than not that the Old Norse audience of the time of transition between Paganism and Christianity "knew" that Njǫrðr had nine daughters, and that they were clearly related to the Norns and to the world of the dead. So what does that make us think about Njǫrðr himself? We know that Njǫrðr "steered the winds and the waves", and that he lives in the ship's harbor, because that is what Snorri let us know.

As we saw in Chapter 2. 13, it is entirely possible to identify Aegir with another father of nine daughters, the sea giant Aegir, who also, significantly, steers the waves (his daughters).

Like Aegir, Njǫrðr was also married to a woman who was associated with drowning. We only have one description of Njǫrð's ancient wife, and that is the 2000 year old account by Tacitus, who made clear that the goddess Nerthus received sacrifice in a lake, by the drowning of the victims. Nerthus is a Latin form of Njerðr or Njórunn, Njǫrð's wife and sister, according to Snorri. When Njǫrðr comes among the Aesir, he may not be married to his own sister, but he marries a woman who greatly resembles her instead, Skaði, who is also a goddess of death, albeit of death in the mountains and death by fatal wounds.

The ladies of death actually seem to represent different kinds of deaths. Death at the ocean was the catch of Rán and her daughters, death by injury or in the wilderness was the catch of Skaði, death of sickness and old age the catch of Hel, and death in battle or by courageous acts the catch of Freyia and the Valkyrie. Overlapping all of these cosmic entities is the powerful concept of the ancestral mother or soul Fylgjur, who gather the spirits of their dead descendants, taking different shapes according to the individual death of the person. If we want to understand the ultimate interconnectedness between these apparently different entities, we need only realize that they are all, ultimately, just death. Death in its countless forms, death an individual experience for every entity, yet ultimately just the same. Thus we are seeing something interesting; Gerðr, the mead-woman, is through attributes and family relations in many ways identifiable both as one of the nine daughters of the sea giants, associated with waves, but also with light and "gold".

She is also perfectly identifiable with the sisters of Freyr, and thus with Freyia. There are associations to the death goddesses Rán and Hel, relations to Skaði, and to Urðr as well. As we shall see, the nine daughters of Aegir/ Njǫrðr are even identified as the Valkyrie. We can also see them in connection with the nine mothers of Heimdallr, the Great World, and with the nine sorceresses who existed within the previous world-trees, and who came before our present "mead-tree". If we are to truly grasp this strange and complicated series of associations and identifications and jumbling family relations, we have to understand that they reflect an ancient and very different worldview where the one is the many, and the many are the one, and that this fluidity was a natural part of the Viking Age mind.

3.5: THE MEAD OF MEMORY -HYNDLULIÓÐ THE SONG OF THE SHE-WOLF-

Wake, maiden of all maidens!
Wake, my friend!
She-Wolf, sister!
Who lives in the rock cave;
Now is the darkness of darkness itself
And we should ride together to Valhalla and to the sacred temple.

    Vaki mær meyia,
    vaki min vina,
    Hyndla systir!
    er i helli byr;
    nu er rauckr rauckra,
    rida vit skulum
    til Valhǫllr
    ok til vess heilags

Hyndlulióð st. 1, Poetic Edda: Freyia's invocation

The poem Hyndlulióð also refers to a precious drink. This time the mead-woman function is held by the goddess Freyia. Her lover Óttarr has "wagered for the gold of Valland" and the path is said to go to Valhǫll, Óðin's afterlife realm of warriors and Valkyrie. Valland and Valhǫll is the same. The realm of the Val usually understood to be the chosen slain. Vál means "choice" but also refers to the dead or the chosen dead. Freyia has appeared before the young man in the moment of his sacrifice to the goddesses and transforms the young man into the sacrificial animal itself, a boar on the path to death. She rides him as a boar into the underworld, which is described as the "darkest of darkness", and in which they find Freyia's "sister", "first among maidens", an old, terrifying giantess living within a rock cave.

She is called Hyndla, "the Bitch", and we are likely talking about a wolf-bitch since the old lady keeps a stable of pitch-black male wolves on which she rides. The antiquity of the wolf-riding giantess is revealed in art such as Viking Age carvings of a giantess riding a wolf using serpents for reins (see illustration to Chapter 7).

The character of the wolf-rider shows up once in Snorri's Prose Edda as well, where she is called Hyrrokkin [The Fire Spinner]. Hyrrokkin is invoked when the gods realize that for all their might, none of them, not even Þórr the manly god, has the strength to push Baldr's funeral ship on its way to Hel. Only the old giantess possesses this power, an indication that associates Hyrrokkin and Hyndla with Hel [Death] herself. An unnamed wolf-riding giantess is also mentioned in the Edda poem Helgakvíða Hundingsbani, where she is said to be a fylgja, a "follower", the kind of personal Norn that "follows" people through their lives. When she appears in the shape of a wolf-riding giantess, she is an omen of death, ready to take her human into her realm of souls.

Freyia, riding her "boar", convinces the old giantess to sit down and reveal esoteric knowledge about the interconnectedness between all beings in the universe, which is, apparently, the "heritage" that Óttarr needs in order to reach Valhǫll. In aiding her devotee to Valhǫll, Freyia acts in the manner of a Valkyrie. The Edda poem Grímnismál is indeed identifying Freyia as a sort of queen Valkyrie, since she "chooses the slain" the Old Norse words used are kiosa vál, which are exactly the words that make up the word Valkyrie ["chooser of the slain"]. At the end of the underworld revelations, Freyia asks Hyndla if she will also offer to Óttarr the "ale of memory" so that he will be able to remember the revelations when he returns to the world of the living on the "third day". Three days are exactly the time that Óðinn is said to have spent with Gunnlǫð.:

Carry the Ale of Memory to my guest, so that he can remember all these your words that you have spoken on the third morning.	*45. Ber þu minnis aul minum gesti, sua hann aull mune ord at tina þersar rædu a þridia morni*

The theme of the danger of memory-loss after having resided in the underworld is evidently a common issue, as we shall see. It is also mentioned in the Hávamál, stanza 13, where Óðinn reveals:

13. The Heron of Forgetfulness sits above the ale-room He steals the power of many; In his feathers I was fettered in the halls of Gunnlǫð.	*13. Ominnis hegri heitir sa er yfir a/lþrom þrvmir, hann stelr geði gvma; þess fvgls fia/drom ec fiotraþr varc i garði Gvnnlaþar*

The reference to Gunnlǫð's halls and the "ale-room" clearly reveals that the theme of forgetfulness has something to do with Óðin's dealings with Gunnlǫð, perhaps explaining why he left her behind in the underworld. He forgot her, exactly like Sígurðr forgot his beloved Valkyrie once he had returned to the world of men with tragic consequences. More importantly, the theme of memory and memory-loss is just another of the numerous evidence that links the mead-women to each other to the point of identification. Clearly, forgetfulness about the sacred teachings of the Underworld is a danger to both Óttarr and Óðinn.

Hyndla refuses to offer the drink of memory to Óttarr, offering a number of reasons that may mirror Óttar's own fears, but Freyia then declares that she will give the drink to him:

50....he shall drink the precious power-brew and I bid all gods to help Óttarr.	*50....hann skal drecka dyrar veigar, bid ek Ottari aull god duga*

The ending of the poem appears to consist of "bickering" between the giantess She-Wolf and the goddess. If we look past the "bickering", we may understand that this is a trick, a way for the poet to impart information in a manner that is hidden behind poetical comedy and only then may we start to get what is actually being revealed. It is repeatedly stated that Hyndla offers only oblivion, that is, forgetfulness. She will mingle the mead of knowledge with curses and poison. She wishes to sleep. In stanza 46, for example, the She-Wolf states:

Turn away from here! I wish to sleep! Little will you get from me no pleasant choices You run, noble girlfriend! Outside at night just like with the rams Bright Rune/ Bright Open Space Symbol fares	*Snudu braut hedan! sofua lystir mik, fær þu fatt af mer fridra kosta; hleypr þu, edlvina! vti a nattum, sem med haufrum Heiðrun fari.*

The "obvious" meaning here is the insult; Freyia is accused of running outside at night, compared with a she-goat (in heat) that runs with the rams or bucks. However, the she-goat in question is actually Heiðrún. This particular she-goat, whose name implies bright knowledge or bright secret or symbol (rún means "secret", "knowledge", of "symbol"), is actually the producer and provider of the sacred mead of resurrection that gives new life to the one-harriers in Valhǫll after death. This is a hint towards the true purpose of this journey; to reach Valhǫll. Freyia is the Valkyrie who takes her chosen hero there, and in order to do so, she has to take him through the realm of death, where he can receive the knowledge that is needed.

Scene of sacrifice.
7th century Gotland.

It is also Freyia who, according to Grímnismál 14, receives the chosen dead and "arranges the seating in the hall", a hall that is called the People Field (Folkvangr). We are talking about the ruler of fate and the receiver of the dead in her aspect of bright goddess of bright choices. When she is compared to the she-goat in this poem, she is compared to the very power that produces and provides the Mead of Memory. The other aspect, however, is the grim ogress. We will see this same duality in the next Chapter on Iðunn and Skaði (Chapter 3.10-12). Like Skaði, who is also associated with wolves, Hyndla represents the darkness of death, sleep and oblivion, whereas Freyia, like Iðunn, represents resurrection, the brightness of life and knowledge, or memory.

The same "bickering" is applied in another poem, Helreið Brynhildar [Brynhild's Ride to Hel], where the Valkyrie Brynhildr goes into Hel in order to save her beloved Sígurðr. In Hel, she meets an ogress who demands to know what she, the "goddess of gold" [Gullna dís] from the Land of Choice [Valland] is doing here in her rocky realm. Like Hyndla, the ogress is associated with rocks and caves, and is called the Bride from the Rock [bruþr or steini]. The Valkyrie, who is repeatedly said to be "from the south", which is the direction of the Aesir and the Norns , has nothing to do here in this northern realm, she should be at home tending to her "weaving", which is to say that she should be concerned with fate-spinning rather than move about in dark, rocky and misty Hel.

Brynhildr, the Valkyrie, explains the dramatic events that have led her to be "a Viking" that is, a pirate, causing death and destruction where she ought to have caused resurrection and wisdom, and then she declares that she will have Sígurðr for herself, and bids the ogress to "sink". The sinking of the ogress is a way of conquering death, now the resurrecting Valkyrie remains to receive the dead, rather than the ogress who only "wants to sleep". I believe that what we are seeing here is the choice between two fates in death, as shown through the ritual of initiation; death in oblivion and darkness, or a death that leads to resurrection and memory of the self.

The latter is closely related to the waking up of one's own fate-goddess, her guidance and her love. The goddess Freyia and the ogress Hyndla represent these two sides of fate and death. Interestingly, it is in fact the hostile ogress of darkness who provides the secret knowledge and the friendly lover-goddess of light who allows the memory of this knowledge to surface. As ultimately soul, fate and death-choice (or all these things together), the ogress and the maiden represent the two sides to the same coin, as Snorri suggested when he described Hel as half dark as death, half bright as life.

3.6: EARTH'S GUIDANCE -HYMISKVÍÐA, THE SONG OF HYMIR-

Little time it takes to show the way, a very long time it takes to walk it(...)
keep to the left-hand path until you reach the Human Realm.
There may Life Woman (= Earth) find Þórr her son and she may let him
know the path of his kinsmen to the lands of Spirit."

> "Litiþ er at synia,
> langt er at fara (...)
> haltv sva til vinstra vegsins
> vnz þv hittir Verland.
> Þar mvn Fjǫrgyn
> hitta Þór son sinn,
> oc mvn hon kenna
> hanom attvnga brautir
> til Oðins landa.»

Hárbarðsljóð, st. 56, Poetic Edda

The theme of the two-faced mead-woman seems to be present also in the poem
Hymiskvíða, in which Þórr and Týr travel to the realm of the frost giants in order to
find a cauldron big enough to contain all the sacred mead of the world giant Aegir.
The realm of the frost giant Hymir is cold, dark and terrifying, but Þórr receives
unexpected help from a bright lady, who in the poem is identified as his mother.
However, the bright and benevolent mother has a mother of her own, a terrible
creature with nine hundred heads. The two are presented together to create the
usual contrast between the hag and the beauty:

8. The boy thought Grandmother a terrible sight; Nine hundred heads she had; but another walked forth, All Golden Bright-Browed she carried ale power drink to her son.	*8. Maugr fann Ammo mioc leiþa ser; hafði hafda hvndrvð nío; enn annvr gecc Algvllin fram brvnhvít bera biorveig syni*

The fact that the all-golden, bright browed mead woman here is called þór's
mother, identifies her as the goddess Iǫrðr, the Earth goddess herself. According to
Snorri, in his Prose Edda Prologue, the Vikings and their ancestors reasoned that
the Earth was a living, sentient entity and counter her as their ancestral mother the
ancestral mother of all people:

> *"From this they realized that Iǫrðr was sentient and possessed a kind of life. And*
> *they also knew that she was extremely ancient of years and powerful of nature. She*
> *produced all life, and took to herself all that died. For this reason they gave her a name*
> *(Iǫrðr "Earth") and counted their lineages from her."*

Looking closely at Snorri's account, we realize that the description of the Earth
goddess fits perfectly with the description of the goddess of death and renewed life.
In the image of the Earth goddess we see both the ancient ancestral mother of all
fates, Origin, who nourishes the world tree.

The receiver of the dead in all her aspects; Rán, Hel, Skaði and Freyia. Like all the other mead-serving ladies, whether they appear as Norns, Valkyrie, goddesses or giantesses, the Earth goddess appears as a bright woman in the underworld, offering guidance and power. Iǫrðr is counted among the Ásyniur the wives of the Aesir, and like Frigg, Freyia and Skaði, she is mentioned as a wife of Óðinn. Earth is also known as Fjǫrgyn, which means Life Struggle, and many other names. According to Snorri's Gylfaginning, our planet, the Earth goddess is the daughter of Óðinn and Nǫtt a giantess who embodies exactly what her name means; the Night.

Night here should be seen as primeval darkness, the kind from which Iǫrðr, Sól (the Sun goddess), the Moon and the stars emerged within, or indeed, was birthed from. This is the Old Hag of nine hundred heads which so frightened young Þórr before his mother provided light within the darkness. In the Sígrdrífumál, "Night and all her kind" are invoked together with the powers of daylight, the powerful and sacred Earth herself, and the deities. The terrible Night is shown in contrast to the light-offering Earth, reminding us, perhaps, of the description of Hel as half dark as a corpse, half bright as life.Most importantly, Iǫrðr is extremely powerful. Her power should be invoked while drinking, as we see in the Hávamál stanza 137:

Where you drink ale choose the Power of Earth for Earth takes up the ale
> *hvars þv aul dreckir,*
> *kios þv þer Iarðar Megin,*
> *þviat Iorð tecr við aulþri*

Her power is also a very important ingredient both in the sacred mead and in the creation of this world, as the following to stanzas show. The first is taken from the Hyndlulióð (st. 38) where the growth of the present universe, or Heimdallr, is described:

He (Heimdallr) was made to grow by the Power of Earth, by the Cool Cold Sea 7 and by the Blood of the Atonement (Sacrifice)
> *Sa var aukinn*
> *Iardar Megni,*
> *sualkaulldum sæ*
> *ok sonardreyra*

The second stanza is taken from Guðrunarkvíða ǫnnur (st. 23) or "The Second Poem of Guðrún", where the heroine receives the precious mead from her mother and reveals its ingredients:

It (the drink) was made to grow by the Power of Earth by the Cool Cold Sea and by the Blood of the Sacrifice
> *þat var vm aukit*
> *Iarþar Magni,*
> *svalcaldom se*
> *oc sonar dreyra*

I earlier drew a link between the Well of Origin, which nourishes and rejuvenates the World Tree every day, and the precious mead, which rejuvenates the initiate who gains access to it. The formula stanzas from two completely different poems show that this linking is well founded the ingredients that make the healing drink are identical with the ingredients that make the universe grow. It is not a coincidence that the World Tree itself is referred to as the Mead Tree, nor that Heimdall's horn, Gjallarhorn, is identical to the horn used by the giant Mímir (Memory) to drink mead from the Well of Memory.

3.7: THE DRINK OF THE BURIAL MOUND
HELGAKVÍÐA HUNDINGSBANI QNNUR THE SECOND POEM OF HELGI HUNDINGSBANI

You rather desire her, Helgi, she who found your harbor when you traveled here last night
The Ocean-Golden Maiden she took my power away
Here it was that she disembarked and fastened safely your fleet and she is the only one with the power to keep me from becoming the bane of all the ruler's men

> *Hína vildo heldr, Helgi!*
> *er reþ hafnir scoda*
> *fyrri nott meþ firom;*
> *MarGvllin Mer*
> *mer þotti afli bera;*
> *her ste hon land af legi*
> *oc festi sva yþarn flota;*
> *hon ein þvi veldr,*
> *er ec eigi mac*
> *bvþlvngs monnom bana*

Helgakvíða Hiǫrvarðssonar st. 26, Poetic Edda: the Lament of Hrímgerðr

HELGI'S PREVIOUS LIFE

In the second poem of Helgi Hundingsbani, the hero, prince Helgi, receives the help and guidance of a Valkyrie, Sígrún, who lets him know that he is a reincarnation of one Helgi Hiǫrvarðsson, and that she was his Valkyrie Sváva [The Sleeper] in that life. As we learn from the poem of the previous Helgi, this young man, under the guidance of Sváva and her three by nine Valkyrie, had battled the giant Hati [Hatred] and the giant Hróðmarr [Furious Ocean], but died at the Frekasteinn [Rock of Greed].

The rock of Greed and the giant called Hatred probably indicate that Helgi has to battle the qualities of hatred and greed within himself. Seen from this perspective, it seems plausible that the giant called Furious Ocean represents emotional rage, since water could easily be seen as a metaphor for emotions. A very important part of the previous life initiation experience was Helgi's encounter with the terrible giantess called Hrímgerðr [Frosty Enclosure], who takes the shape of an ocean wave and tries to drown Helgi and his men as they travel to their fated destination. Obviously, the giantess is a daughter of Rán, assuming a hostile attitude.

Helgi's sorcerer mentor, Atli [The Intender] engages the grim ogress in a duel of eloquence where he manages to wrest considerable information out of her. As usual in Norse myths, the destructive giant adversaries are also the possessors of esoteric knowledge and those who are courageous enough to not be overcome by fear at the sight of their terrible apparitions may seek this knowledge by voicing the right questions. With his display of eloquence, the young hero initiate's mentor manages to keep the attention of the personified wave until daybreak, when the sunlight transforms her into rock.

Image from 7th century Gotland memorial stone showing Rán or one of her nine daughters about to fetch a drowning man.

As she transforms, the giantess reveals that the real reason that she has not been able to drown the men that night is the protection they have from Sígrún and her host of eight other Valkyrie. These, the ogress declares, have kept his ships safe, found the harbor for them, and protected them against her violent onslaughts.

Then dawn breaks, and Frosty Enclosure looks to the east, to the rising rays of the Sun goddess, and turns into rock. The fate of cold death and oblivion has given way to the fate of brightness and resurrection. The Valkyrie are repeatedly described as golden-bright and emanating rays of light as they move through the air and sea.

The formula of light across the air and sea is identical to the effect of Gerð's shining arms in the Skírnismál. Thus, the bright rays of the Valkyrie and the rays of the Sun goddess simultaneously have the effect of removing the destructive power of the ogress of cold death. Protected by this divine golden light, Helgi and his men can continue their mission at the Rock of Greed. The comparison of the Valkyrie to the Sun goddess is often repeated in descriptive terms such as "sun-bright", "southern red" or "golden" goddess. The verbal duel with the giantess represents the culmination of the trials; after having battled Hatred and Raging Emotions, Helgi overcomes his fears and the frosty enclosure of death at the ocean.

Rather than succumbing to the terrible onslaughts of the death-wave, he seeks her knowledge and transforms her. Below, we will soon see how the life-saving Valkyrie may also be identified as the daughters of the ocean rulers. Ultimately, the grim ogresses and the bright maidens are two sides of the same coin the bright version usually appears when the grim version is overcome, representing two different fates in death and in initiation. The result, at least, is that Helgi now can marry his gold-bright Valkyrie and live with her guidance throughout his life.

Although they are married, the text clearly states that Sváva continued to live as a Valkyrie as before. However, Helgi continues to live as a war-leader and ends his days in battle in fact, he dies at the famed Frekasteinn "The Rock of Greed". The warrior may have overcome his hatred, his fear and his rage, but it would be greed that keeps him on the war path, greed for riches and the spoils of war. Thus as he dies, he is no longer a candidate for Valhǫll, but must be reincarnated once again. The poem of Helgi Hiǫrvarðsson clearly states that Helgi will return in order to "avenge himself", and the prose ending states: "It is told that Helgi and Sváva were born anew".

THE SECOND HELGI

As Helgi is born again, he is exalted. His birth is likened to the birth of the universe itself, as the First poem of Helgi Hundingsbani begins (stanza 1):

1. In the beginning was the wave
when eagles hawked holy water
ran from the mountains of heaven
then was Helgi he the great of
intent born by Fortress Battle in
the Grove of Bright Shine

Ár var alda
þat er arar gvllo,
hnigo heilog votn
af himinfiollom;
þa hafþi Helga
inn hvgom stora
Borghildr borit
i Bralvndi

Battle Scene from Viking Age Memorial Stone. A Woman with a dog and drinking Horn overlooks the Battle like a Valkyrie deciding who shall have her Drink. The Dog is a common symbol of the Underworld, Guardian of the Goddess of the Dead

This likening to the birth of the cosmos is otherwise unexplained, but continues with the arrival of the Norns who set down the destiny of the princeling. His childhood is very different from that of his previous incarnation, where he was a silent young man who kept to himself until he had his vision of the Valkyrie while meditating on a burial mound, a vision that led him to become a warrior and a king. In this life, he is obviously destined to be a king and a war-leader from the start, a fact which makes the young Helgi become fierce a little too fierce, since he and his men managed to break the Peace of Wisdom, succumbing once more to Greed. It is while he is dozing off after battle that the Valkyrie of his previous lifetime reappears in the present.

Significantly, Helgi is sleeping by the Rock of the Eagle [Arasteinn] which suggests that he is very close to death, when he obviously has a vision (st. 15):

15. Then a bright shining broke out
from the Mountains of Fire (the
starlit sky) and rays of lightening
flickered from the light-shine they
(the Valkyrie) were under helmets
across the Fields of Heaven their
armors were splattered in blood
their spears emanated rays of light

15. Þa brá lioma
af Logafiollom,
enn af þeim liomom
leiptrir qvomo;
þa var vnd hialmom
a Himinvanga,
brynior váro þeirra blopi stocnar
enn af geirom geislar stoþo

The Valkyrie, who in the present life is called Sígrún [Victory Symbol], reminds Helgi of their ancient union and urges him to stop his folly his life as a purposeless pirate who lives primitively and sheds blood needlessly, and spurs him onto more worthy challenges. She lets him know that he is in danger of losing her altogether to a grim ogre unless he gets his act together.

Helgi wakes up and immediately begins to pursue the path she has shown him. The Valkyrie aids the reincarnated Helgi in a new battle where he again overcomes two giants, Hoðbrodr [Treasure Thorn] and Guðmundr [God Origin]. Helgi also has the help and guidance of his sorcerer brother Sinfiǫtli [Pale Fetters] who plays the same role as Atli in his previous life, and as Skírnir in the Skírnismál poem. The paleness in his name indicates death or dying, the fetter is an Old Norse metaphor for a ruling power. The new Helgi now sets out to win the battle he lost in his last life the Battle of the Rock of Greed. After having won the battle of the Rock of Greed in this life, Helgi lives in joy and glory with his Valkyrie bride, who continues to "ride the air and sea".

One day, the god Óðinn decides that he wishes Helgi's presence in Valhǫll among the einherjar, and lets a spear be thrown against the king a symbol of the god wanting someone for himself. Sígrún returns to her hibernating state, as the Valkyrie all seem to do when their beloveds die, symbolized by her return to her home at Sefafell [The Mountain of Souls] where she claims that she will rather sleep than remain in the world without Helgi. The theme of the sleeping Valkyrie is repeated time and time again, and we understand that she sleeps while she awaits the reincarnation of her beloved man. Before Helgi leaves the Miðgarðr permanently, she wakes and goes into Helgi's burial mound and sleeps with him in his grave, uttering the following words (stanza 43 and 46 of the Second Poem of Helgi Hundingsbani):

43. *Now I am as happy to see you again as the hungry hawks of Óðinn when they see the slain corpses, their hot blood or when they, moist with dew, see the dawn*

46. *Well shall we drink the Precious Power Drink, even if we have lost our lives and lands; no man shall sing any angry songs of lament even if he sees me wounded in my chest: Now has the Bride arrived in the Burial Mound the High Goddesses are with us dead ones.*

Nv em ec sva fegin fvndi ocrom, sem átfrekir Oðins haucar, er val vito, varmar braðir, eþa dagglitir dagsbrvn siá.

Vel scolom drecca Dyrar Veigar, þott mist hafim mvnar oc landa; scal engi maþr angrlióþ qveþa, þott mer a briosti beniar líti: nv ero brvþir byrgþar i haugi, lofda disir hiá oss liþnom

The stanzas clearly reveal a theme of drinking the precious mead within the burial mound and link it, like the other mead-woman stories, with a marriage bond. The Bride of the Burial Mound is a common theme, echoed in the Provider of the Mound [Bjarggefn, i.e. Skaði] and the Bride of the Rocks (Hyndla).The Valkyrie compares her love with the blood-thirsty ravens of Óðinn, and it has often been thought that the ravens that arrived at the battle-fields were indeed the visible shape of Valkyrie. That they are called hawks is a poetical metaphor hawks are used to replace ravens when the rules of rhyming demanded a different word.

From Snorri we know that the Valkyrie were thought to choose life and death, victory and loss bring the warriors, bring them to Valhǫll and offer them the mead of the goat Heiðrún (bright rune). The Edda poems give a more complex image of Valkyrie attached to human beings throughout lifetimes, like the Norns said to follow each person through their lives. The entry to Valhǫll obviously requires a lot more than just to die in battle, it requires the guidance of the awoken fate goddess through difficult trials of personal evolution, and the union between the person and his Valkyrie in life and in death.

3.8: THE SLEEPING VALKYRIE

Sigrdrifumál The Speech of Sígrdrífa

15. Sleeps on the mountain, a ruler's daughter bright in her armor after the death of Helgi...
>   *Sefr a fialli fylcis dottir*
>   *biort i brynio eptir bana Helga...*

17. She will teach the courageous about runes all that people wish for the most to be able to speak all the languages of men and to heal lives;
Live you whole, king!
>   *Hon mvn rikiom þer rvnar kenna*
>   *allar þer er aldir eignaz vildo,*
>   *oc a mannz tvngo mela hveria,*
>   *lyf meþ lecning;*
>   *lifþv heill, konvngr!*

Grípisspá st. 15 and 17

The poem Sígrdrífumál constitutes the climax in the story of young Sígurð's initiation quest. After liberating himself from a lifelong apprenticeship to the dwarf smith sorcerer Reginn [The Ruler], who also seems to represent negative qualities such as anger, hatred and greed, Sígurðr learns from a dying serpent and from talking birds about a mysterious maiden who sleeps on the mountain called Hindarfell, which means either Mountain of Obstacles or Mountain of the Doe.

The maiden is a Valkyrie called Sígrdrífa, and is said to be a reincarnation of earlier Valkyrie such as Sváva and Sígrún from the poems of Helgi Hiǫrvarðsson and his later reincarnation Helgi Hundingsbani. Unlike her human hero, she has not actually died in between her incarnations, only slept, as the stanzas above suggest. The chronology suggests that the editors of the Poetic Edda manuscript believed that Sígurðr was the third reincarnation, and that they believed that the same Valkyrie slept between the lives of the warriors, and that she assumed a new name every time her human was reborn. Sígrdrífa sleeps high on the Hindarfjǫll, caught in an armor that has grown into her body. Like the mead in Hel itself (see Chapter 3.3), she is covered with shields, and like the mead-woman Gerðr, she is surrounded by a dangerous fire which illuminates the heavens. In the poem Hyndlulióð, we also learned that the ogress of death was surrounded by fire a fire placed there by her own alter ego, Freyia. She is only woken by the hero Sígurðr, who knows no fear and who rides his very special horse called Grani through the terrible bright fire. Within the hall, he uncovers the Valkyrie beneath the shields and wakes her up by cutting off her armor.

The Valkyrie wakes, and, interestingly, laments the fate of human beings when the Valkyrie is asleep (st. 2):

2. Long did I sleep	*2. Lengi ec svaf,*
Long was my slumber	*lengi ec sofnoþ var,*
Long is the woe of people	*long ero lyða le;*
Óðinn caused this that I could	*Óðinn þvi veldr,*
not empower myself to break the	*er ec eigi mattac*
runes of slumber	*bregða blvnnstafom*

She then offers prayers to the forces of light and darkness, to the gods and goddesses and to the holy Earth. She prays for wisdom, eloquence and healing hands in life, before she offers to Sígurðr the "ale of memory", giving to the precious mead the same name as Freyia did in the Hyndlulióð. Then she reveals the powerful properties of the drink, as stanza 5 of the Sígrdrífumál goes:

5. Beer I take to you, apple-tree of	*5. Biór fori ec þer, brynþings*
armor-parliament!	*apaldr!*
It is blended with strength and	*magni blandinn oc megintíri;*
powerful glory;	*fvllr er hann lioþa oc licnstafa,*
It is filled with spell-songs and for-	*godra galdra oc gamanrvna*
tunate runes, benevolent charms	
and runes of pleasure	

Apple Tree of Armor Parliament refers to Sígurðr himself; an apple-tree is a metaphor for an outstanding and attractive young man, the "armor parliament" refers to battle or warfare. It is a way of addressing and complimenting a young warrior that the woman finds attractive. The Valkyrie then proceeds by instructing Sígurðr in the sacred lore and secrets of the runes, counting up different kinds of runes and explaining how to use them, making it clear what is only subtly revealed in the Hávamál that there is certainly a connection between the precious drink and the knowledge of runes. In fact, as we shall see in the stanzas below, the runes were imparted through the drink itself, and before the runes were released into the world, they were poured over with the sacred mead. It is obvious from the stanzas that the runes are not mere letters or symbols, but poetical metaphors for something else something that has to do with the realm of fate in which they were first carved by the Norns. Sígrdrífa makes this rune-drink connection more than clear in the stanza 13 and 18, where she refers to how Óðinn, here called Hroptr [Shattered One], first discovered the runes. According to Sígrdrífa:

13. They (the runes) were cut	*13.þer of réð,*
They were carved	*þer of reist,*
They ran through the Shattered	*þer vm hvgði Hroptr*
One's soul from the drink that had	*af þeim legi,*
dripped from the head of Bright	*er leciþ hafdi*
Drops and the horns of Treasure	*or ha/si Heiddraupniss*
Release	*oc or horni Hoddrofnis*
18. All (the runes) were cut off that	*18. Allar váro af scafnar,*
had been carved in and poured	*þer er váro a ristnar,*
over with The Sacred Mead and	*oc hverfðar viþ inn Helga Mioþ*
sent out on the wide ways...	*oc sendar a viþa vega;...*

We are back to the beginning, when Óðinn sought the knowledge of runes, charms and precious mead as he hung in the world tree and lay in the embrace of Gunnlǫð. The lines not only elaborate more that which was hinted to in the Hávamál what Óðinn was up to when he undertook his trials but they also show that Sígurðr, the human hero, is walking in the footsteps of the great god, and that his reunion with his Valkyrie, his waking her up, resembles Óðin's own sacred marriage to Gunnlǫð, the maiden who guards the mead resembles it to the point of identification.

Like Óðinn, Sígurðr is destined to walk out on his goddess, not because he wants to but because the fetters of oblivion make it so. Óðinn forgot the goddess in the underworld, earning the name Harm-Causer [Bólverkr], and so he also caused the Valkyrie of men to sleep, to the great woe of all people. Later, we learn that the reason for this is that she chose different men than he wanted, revealing a conflict of interest between the two beings who together receive the chosen dead. This theme repeats itself many times in Old Norse myths. The concept of the forgotten goddess who is made to sleep while humanity suffers because of it, can only be understood, in my opinion, if we understand the goddess of the mead, in all her shapes, as a metaphor for the fate-spinning soul, the soul that is either sleeping, causing havoc, or awake, causing bliss.

3.9: THE MAIDENS OF THE WIND SHIELDED ISLAND- ODDRÚNARGRÁTR, THE LAMENT OF ODDRÚN-

...richly, Oddrún sang powerfully, Oddrún sang bitter spell-songs for New Fortress
> *...rict gól Oddrún,*
> *rammt gól Oddrún*
> *bitra galdra*
> *at Borgnyio*

- Oddrúnargrátr st. 7, Poetic Edda

In the Oddrúnargrátr, we hear a version of a story told over various poems in the Edda, this time from the perspective of the Valkyrie Oddrún [Edge Symbol], a younger sister of Sígrdrífa/Brynhildr who unexpectedly turns up after the death of her older sister. In this way, she follows in the footsteps of the reincarnating/ reawakening Valkyrie cycle which began back with the first Helgi each time one Valkyrie sleeps, another takes her place. A young man, Gunnarr, wishes to seek the Valkyrie who sleeps on a mountain, this time under the name Brynhildr [Armor War]. It is a name that may be referring to the armor worn by Sígrdrífa before she was freed from it and woken up by Sígurðr. In Brynhildr, the metaphorical "armor" is never removed. Gunnarr receives the help and guidance of his brother in-law, Sígurðr, who has undertaken the journey before when he woke his Golden Goddess on the mountain. Gunnarr is too timid to ride through the fire, and the two men conspire. They exchange their physical shapes. After his journey to the mountain of the Valkyrie, Sígurðr has magical powers and is able to create an illusion of shape.

Wearing the shape of Gunnarr, Sígurðr goes through the fire and sleeps with the Valkyrie for three nights the same number of nights that Óðinn slept with Gunnlǫð. Later, the Valkyrie Brynhildr arrives as Gunnar's wife, only to find out about the treason. How her husband never had the courage to enter her realm, so that she is now living with an unworthy man. She realizes that Sígurðr is to blame, and has him killed. However, in the manner of a Valkyrie, and because Sígurðr had in fact reached her golden halls, she decides to save him from Hel. In the poem Helreið Brynhildar, we hear how the Valkyrie moves into Hel in order to save her lover. Later on, Gunnarr obviously grow into more courage and maturity, for he receives the love of Brynhild's sister Oddrún, and her love for him is symbolized by a drink:

> 12. I remember what you said that eveningwhen I made for Gunnarr the drink...

>> 12. Man ec, hvat þv meltir enn vm aptan,
>> þa er ec Gvnnari gerþag drecco;...

Later, when Gunnarr faces death, we hear how Oddrún hears his song all the way to her realm and then tries to save him from Hel. She arrives too late, just in time to see how Gunnarr is taken by the ogress of death in the shape of a serpent. The serpent pit is in itself an image of death in Hel. Another poem, the Vǫluspá, reveals that in the Bellowing Mill the well of Hel, there are numerous serpents, among them the serpent Svafnir [Sleep-Maker], which suck at the life-blood of the dead souls.

Detail from the Oseberg ritual chariot, woodcarving, Norway 834 AD: Gunnarr in the serpent pit being bit in the liver by the ogress of Death, while his valkyrie attempts to save him.

Obviously, in the Valkyrie stories we see how the Valkyrie has a function in death: salvation from Hel, from the frosty enclosure of the ogress who, as Hyndla said, offers only oblivion and loss of consciousness. The love of the golden, bright mead-woman clearly has to do with resurrection from the misty realm of ice and darkness, where the dead gradually disintegrate into the great cauldron of Hel from which all rivers stem.

What is most interesting about the Oddrúnargrátr is that we are offered a more detailed description of the realm of the reincarnating Valkyrie. One would have assumed that the Valkyrie lived in Valhǫll, but in the Edda poems, the only place said to be the home of the Valkyrie is Hlésey [Wind-Shielded Island]. This island happens to be the very home of the ocean giant Aegir, who is also known as Gymir and Hlér [The Wind-Shielded]. This giant, who is identical to the father of Gerðr, also happens to have nine daughters. The Valkyrie tend to show up in groups of nine, so this is highly significant.

We realize that the difference between the nine daughters of Aegir and Rán may be identified not only as giantesses, not only as the personified waves of the ocean, the gold light of the gods, or the mothers of the present universe; they are also identifiable as the Valkyrie, and said to be the sisters of Óðinn. The reference to a wind-shielded place is likewise significant, since wind is a metaphor for death in Old Norse poetry. This is a realm of immortality, shielded from the "winds" the power of death, and Gunnar's tunes are trying to reach this realm at the moment of death. Sadly, his death-song arrives too late. It might seem a bit confusing to accommodate the idea of the Valkyrie as much more than the rather uncomplicated barmaids of popular imagery. A Valkyrie may appear to be intimately connected with one person throughout his or her life, like a personal Norn, but she might also be associated with more general and cosmic purposes, like this stanza, describing the arrival of benevolent Valkyrie from Helgakvíða Hiǫrvarðssonar demonstrates:

28. *Three times nine maidens*	28. *Þrennar niundir meyia,*
though before them one, bright	*þo reiþ ein fyr*
beneath the helmet the mares	*hvit vnd hialmi mer;*
shook themselves and from their	*marir hristvz,*
manes dew fell into the valleys and	*stoþ af manom þeirra*
hail into the wide oceans; from	*da/gg i diupa dali,*
them come all growth of time	*hagl i hava viþo;*
	þaðan komr meþ aldom ár,

As an endnote, a helmet could be a metaphor for the mind, or a mind structure. That the maidens exist brightly beneath the helmet, shaking themselves in order to produce movement in the world, could perhaps also refer to qualities residing within the mind of sentient beings. The three by nine, before them one, and the reference to the growth of time could also have to do with the 28 (3×9+1) day biological and lunar cycle of time.

3.10: THE MOUNTAIN OF MEDICINE- THE TREE OF MEMORYBEHIND THE DOORS OF DEATH FJǪLSVINNSMÁTHE SPEECH OF MUCH KNOWING

This poem is a continuation of the poem Gróagalðr, where a young man invokes a dead vǫlva exactly like Óðinn did in the Vegtamskvíða (Chapter 3.3). The vǫlva is the young man's long dead mother, and when she asks why he has woken her from "the doors of death" [daudra dǫra], he explains that his stepmother has urged him to seek the maiden Menglǫð, but that he fears that he is too young and inexperienced to undertake the difficult trials involved.

The vǫlva Gróa [To Grow], otherwise known as the vǫlva who healed Þórr by singing galðr over his wounds after his battle with the giant Hrungnir, now sings nine spell-songs of advice that empower the young man to move into Utgarðr the Outer World of the giants, where he arrives at a bright, golden hall surrounded by poisonous flames and a wall that will kill anyone who touches it. The description of this realm is identical to the descriptions of the halls of Gerðr and similar to the descriptions of Freyia's hall in the Flateyjarbók and with the flaming walls surrounding the Valkyrie Sígrdrífa. The death theme is strengthened by the young man now calling himself Vindkaldr [Wind-Cold], which is a symbol for being dead.

Image from Urn Lid in a Bronze Age Burial Chamber, Gentofte, Denmark. A Man reaches out to a Woman who stands by a Conifer or Pine Tree, surrounded by Pine Needles. A reference that appears to be present also in much later Edda myths such as that of Menglǫð by the Tree of Memory and Gerðr in the Grove of Barri, The Pine Needle.

As usual, the obstacle to the realm is a powerful giant, a guardian servant who plays the same role as the shepherd did in Skírnismál, although the conversation is long and detailed. The giant's name is Fjǫlsviðr [Much Knowing] and like Óðinn in the halls of Suttungr, the young man has to display his eloquence and knowledge to the giant before he is allowed entry to the bright hall.

The word-duel between the young man and the ancient giant centers itself around the theme of the realm of the maiden Menglǫð and how to gain entry. The task seems impossible, but when the young man suddenly remembers that his name is Svípdagr [Swift Day], that he has in fact returned home after numerous deaths, and that the maiden in the hall is his true wife, the maiden within wakes up from her dreams and orders the doors to open, receiving him with a loving embrace.

The stanzas go like this:

Wind-Cold (= Svípdagr in disguise) sang:
41. "What kind of man has the honor of sleeping in the soft embrace of Invitation to Blend?

Much Knowing sang:
42. "No one is the man who has the honor of sleeping in the soft embrace of Invitation to Blend but Swift Day only;
He was once to the Sun Bright wedded to him she was sung to be wife.

Swift Day sang:
47. "I am called Swift Day
Sun Bright was my father
The Winds blew me onto cold ways (= I died)
The decrees of Origin (Urðr = Fate) no man can speak (change) although fate seems made heavy.

Vindkaldr kvað:
41. hvárt sé manna nǫkkut,
þat er knegi á Menglaðar
svásum armi sofa?»

Fjǫlsviðr kvað:
42. «Vætr er þat manna,
er knegi á Menglaðar
svásum armi sofa:
nema Svipdagr einn,
hánum var sú in Sólbjarta
brúðr at kván of kveðin.»

Svipdagr kvað:
47. «Svipdagr ek heiti,
Sólbjart hét minn faðir,
þaðan ráumk vindar kalda vegu;
Urðar orði
kveðr engi maðr,
þótt þat sé við lǫst lagit.»

Invitation to Blend sang:
48. "Well it is that you have come now
I have had my will
The Follower shall give the kiss/speak
the choice;
The best of happiness and fortune to
those who hold each other with love.

49. Long did I sit on the Mountain of
Medicine
I waited night and day for you
Now it has turned out as I wanted:
You have returned, man, to my halls.

50. I had such yearning desire for the
joyful pleasure of your company And
you have yearned sorely for me;
Now it is the truth that we two shall
fight together, through eternal ages."

Menglǫð kvað :
48. «Vel þú nú kominn!
hefik minn vilja beðit,
Fylgja skal kveðju koss;
forkunnar sýn mun flestan glaða,
hvars hefir við annan ást.

49. Lengi ek sat Lyfjabergi á,
beið ek þín dœgr ok daga;
nú þat varð, er ek vætt hefi,
at þú ert kominn, mǫgr! til minna
sala.

50. Þrár hafðar
er ek hefi til þíns gamans,
en þú til míns munar;
nú er þat satt, er vit slíta skulum
ævi ok aldr saman.»

In this poem, the mead-offering is not actually mentioned, but the structure and themes of the poems follow the exact same basic patterns as the others. The name of the maiden, Menglǫð, could, according to the argument of Svava Jacobsdottir, means "Blend Invitation/ Hospitality", from menga to blend (a mixture, a drink) and lǫð "invitation" or "hospitality". The name indicates an invitation to a drink, or even an invitation to blend together. The descriptions of Menglǫð and her realm thus offers even more insight into the concept of the Mead Woman and who she is behind all the various shapes and names she wears whenever meeting personally with a man who has dared to go through fire for her sake.

Like the giantesses Gunnlǫð and Gerðr, she lives in the realm of giants. In fact, as we shall see in the stanzas quoted below, the poem reveals that she is the very ruler of Utgarðr, the Outer World of giants. As usual, the realm is guarded by a very wise and powerful giant, sometimes posing as the father of the giantess, or else as her guardian, protector and servant. Both in the case of Gerðr and Menglǫð, the poems reveal that the giant guard is subservient to the maiden, as she orders him to open the doors. The hero has to test his intelligence and eloquence with the guardian first, though.

Like the reincarnating Valkyrie, Sváva, Sígrún, Sígrdrífa, Brynhildr and Oddrún, she is sleeping on a mountain, awaiting the arrival of her beloved, and like the Valkyrie, she is associated with sleep and dreams. Like the Valkyrie, too, is she described as sun-bright and in the company of nine maidens. Thus Menglǫð would seem to be a Valkyrie. In their cases, the guardians seem to vary between fathers, brothers and in one case, a giant serpent. These always have to be overcome in battle, although the battle seems to be about words. However, her hall is called "elfin", which associates Menglǫð to the immortal light elves in the three upper heavens, a feature she shares with the goddess Iðunn, whose name indicates a female stream that separates from the main stream and returns to the water source and one may wonder if the water-source is not in fact the Well of Origin.

Elfin Iðunn actually serves the same function as the mead-women through the fact that she offers the apples of immortality, just as the mead offers immortality. Iðunn is also associated with a tree, with memory, healing and rejuvenation, even resurrection, just like Menglǫð is, and just as the old Norn Urðr is. The tree by which root this maiden is dreaming is described as the tree "which few knows from where the roots have run" and whose branches grow into all lands the exact description of Yggdrasill the World Tree. To the greatness and importance of this maiden, who is indeed called the Þióðmæra the Great Maiden, stanza 8 testifies, for here she is identified as the actual ruler of the giant world, which also resembles the world of the dead, as well as the divine world. I let the following lines speak for themselves:

8. Her name is Invitation to Blend but her mother had her by the son of Sleep Thorn she rules here (in Utgarðr) and owns the lands the properties and the great halls.

8. Menglǫð of heitir, en hana móðir of gat við Svafrþorins syni; hon hér ræðr ok ríki hefir eign ok auðsǫlum

19. What is the tree called whose branches grow into all lands?

19.... hvat þat barr heitir, ... er breiask um lǫnd ǫll limar?»

20. It is called the Tree of Memory and few know from where its roots have run...

20. Mímameiðr hann heitir, en þat mangi veit, af hverjum rótum renn;

35. What is that mountain called where I see the bride seated, the Great Maiden, dreaming

35. ...hvat þat bjarg heitir, ... ver ek sé brúði á Þióðmæra þruma

36. It is called the Mountain of Medicine and it has long been the joy of the sick and the wounded healed is every woman even from ages of sickness who climbs that mountain.

36. Lyfjaberg þat heitir, en þat hefir lengi verit sjúkum ok sárum gaman; heil verðr hver, þótt hafi árs sótt, ef þat klífr, kona

37...what are the maidens called who by the knees of Menglǫð sit together in unity?

37... vat þær meyjar heita, er fyr Menglaðar knjám sitja sáttar saman?

38. 'Life' is one called, another 'Life Tracker' the third, 'Guardian of People', 'Bright', 'Kind, 'Nice' 'Peace' 'Healing Goddess' and 'Bids Abundance'

38. Hlíf heitir, ǫnnur Hlífþrasa, þriðja Þióðvarta, Bjǫrt ok Blið, Blíðr, Fríð, Eir ok Ǫrboða

40. They offer salvation when men sacrifice to them in a high holy place; Never is the need so great that comes to the people, that they cannot remove the need.

40. (Bjarga) svinnar, hvar er menn blóta þær á stallhelgum stað; eigi svá hátt foráð kemr at hǫlða sonum, hvern þær ór nauðum nema

The theme of the dreaming maiden who rules people and lands is echoed in another poem, the Oddrúnargrátr, where it is said that the Valkyrie Brynhildr/ Sígrdrífa awaits her true love in the same manner:

17. With Brynhild in the Storage Chamber the threads (of fate) she worked she held the people and the land in her power...	*17. Brynhildr i bvri borða racþi, hafþi hon lyði oc lond vm sic;...*

A similar impression is given in the Grímnismál, st. 14, where we learn that Freyia rules the fate of people in the world (the "seating" of her realm, the "People Field"):

14.People Field is the ninth (dimension) and there, Freyia rules the seating of the hall...	*14. Folcvangr er inn niundi, enn þar Freyia reþr sessa costom i sal ...*

Not incidentally, this is also where the goddess receives her chosen dead. Once more, the realm of the fates and the realm of the dead overlap with each other. We remember that both Freyia, in the Song of the She-Wolf, and Sígrdrífa/ Brynhildr serve the Mead of Memory to their lovers. We also know that these two are hidden behind deadly walls that will only open up to the worthy, those who have conquered their fears. Now we see that a very similar maiden, also the ruler of people and lands fate from a hidden realm, is seated by the Tree of Memory.

The theme of memory in fact of remembering oneself is strongly present in this poem, as is the theme of healing. We also get the image of a realm where the world tree itself is growing from, associated with nine ladies. We are very likely back to the beginning of the cosmos, when nine witches came before the "mead tree", as is said in Vǫluspá st. 2. In the Hyndlulióð, st. 35-37, we hear of how the "one" probably Heimdallr, who is a personification of the universe was born by nine giantesses:

35. One was born in the days of origin Very powerful, of the ruler's kind Nine women bore the famous man Giant maidens by the Earth's edge.	*35. Vard einn borin i ardaga rammaukin miok raugna kindar; niu baru þann naddgaufgann mann iotna meyiar vid iardar þraum*

The next lines list up and name the nine mothers of the universe, all given different and more formidable names than the nice names of Menglǫð's maidens. As anyone who ever studied Norse poetry knows, characters will appear with ever new names that describe them. The nine maidens are mentioned in connection with the nine worlds that came before the present, and are also mentioned in Heimdalargalðr, quoted by Snorri in the Prose Edda, where the god Heimdallr reveals that nine maidens bore him ("Of nine mothers I am the child, nine sisters bore me").

We also hear that there are nine daughters of the world giant Aegir who play a significant role as the waves and rivers of the world, as well as being the "lights of the gods". In the poem Sólarlióð, the Song of the Sun, we hear of the nine daughters of Njǫrðr who have, like Norns, carved runes in the underworld where the dying person awaits the Norna dómr the judgment of the Norns , and are indeed associated with a "counsel drink". Is the Fjǫlsvinnsmál, by taking us to the Tree of Memory and its nine maidens taking us back to a place of cosmic beginnings?

In Chapter 3.6, I mentioned the fact that the ingredients of the sacred mead were associated with the ingredients of the very creation of the world. There is little doubt that the Great Maiden is ruling a realm which is at the very core of creation, death and universal memory. What must also be taken into consideration is the highly personal relationship between the young man and this Great Maiden of the sun-bright realm within the darkness of death. He is said to be very young, yet married to the lady in bygone days, and separated from her by fate and by the "winds" a metaphor for death. The winds are named in plural, indicating numerous deaths, and they have sent him onto "cold paths", also metaphors for deaths. The reincarnation theme in other initiation stories is so crucial that it is almost obvious that we are talking about the numerous deaths of one reincarnating soul, and that he has suffered the oblivion that is the great challenge of all mortals, gods and men alike.

It is when he remembers who he truly is and names his true name, going from the pretended Wind-Cold which insinuates death to the true name Swift Day which insinuates sudden illumination and knowledge, that the doors to the lady open up and she wakes from her slumber. Despite the fact that the woman appears to be a goddess, a goddess associated with cosmic sovereignty, there is also a hint as to her being a fylgja the young man's own follower guardian spirit or personal fate goddess. The possible interpretation that she is an individual Norn or fylgja, would at first sight appear to be in conflict with the other equally possible interpretation; that she is indeed a universal Great Goddess. This conflict is only there, however, if one insists on a world of strict separation between various entities. There is absolutely no reason to believe that the Vikings and their predecessors lived in that kind of world, and numerous reasons to believe that the separation between mythical entities was fluid and of no real consequence.

Their very language testifies to this fact, and not the least their poetical language, which was also the language of religion and mythology. This poetry derives from a world where the many can also be the one, the one can be the many, and one entity may appear in numerous shapes that transcend the apparent separation of cosmic species. A giant, a god, an elf and a dwarf both male and female entities appear to freely inhabit all species or races whenever it suits their purpose. I think that we are seeing, again, the theme of waking up one's sleeping soul, in order to unite with the great All-Soul. The subtle message is that the individual fate soul is an aspect of the great cosmic soul, and that it is when she is woken or rather remembered, that the person remembers his or her true self, and that this individual self is ultimately in a lasting union (a "marriage") with the great cosmic self.

As such, the Norse myths range among the mystical traditions of countless world religions through the ages where the union of the individual soul with the great divine soul is at the heart and core of their spiritual paths. This "male seeker female treasure" is the usual formula of Norse myths, as I discussed in Chapter 1.8. The female is the ruler of the inner world, the male represents the journeyman. This may reflect the Viking Age gender roles, but is ultimately a metaphor. It does not matter what gender the seeker is, or what gender the divine is, because gender is only used to describe the journey of the individual soul towards the great cosmic soul.

This is a journey to the human being's inner world, where the divine power is awakened. The gender polarity, whichever way it goes, only serves to illustrate the passion and desire involved in the quest and in the union. The spiritual union is a passionate affair, and an issue of balancing and complimenting apparent opposites. This kind of spiritual parable is well known from other spiritual traditions, such as those of certain classical Mystery cults or Bhakti and Tantra traditions in contemporary India. In the next section, we shall see the Norse poets could turn the tables in order to illustrate the initiation journey of a female, uniting, ultimately, with the great divine in a male form.

3.11: A WOMAN'S PATH OF INITIATION-GUÐRUNARKVÍÐA QNNUR THE SECOND POEM OF GUÐRÚN-

> *23....That drink was imbued*
> *With the Power of Earth*
> *With the Cold Sea*
> *And the Blood of the Atonement/Sacrifice*
>> *23...þat var vm aukit*
>> *Iarþar magni,*
>> *svalcaldom se*
>> *oc sonar dreyra*

Guðrunarkvíða qnnur, st.23, Poetic Edda

This is the poem where the mead is described with the same formula as the magical, symbolical powers that caused creation itself, as we saw in section 3.6. The poems of Guðrún [Divine Symbol] are the only ones in the Edda lore known to us which describe a woman as the recipient of the mead and not just as the one who offers the mead. Since women were actually the ones who brewed alcoholic drinks in Viking Age society, it is somewhat witty that she is the only recipient who is able to recognize and name the ingredients of the drink. Guðrún's path to the mead follows the same structure of initiation through the underworld journey as the men's path. In my thesis, I explored at length the details of this initiation that was undertaken by gods and male heroes.

It always involved several steps: The initiate had to seek a vision of the mead-woman through various techniques of ecstasy. This could mean hanging and fasting, sitting on a burial mound, going into a sacred grove, sleeping in a sacred place, making sacrifice and prayer or making invocations. He would then have a vision of the mead-woman and her realm, and she would sometimes speak to him and offer guidance on the way. Then he would move into the underworld, which could alternately be the world of giants, the world of the dead, or the world of the gods/Norns or all three at once. The three realms would seem to overlap. Here, he would encounter obstacles, usually in the form of giants and giantesses representing things like Hatred, Greed and Fear, or he has to display his eloquence and intelligence before a guardian. Eventually, the flaming, dangerous walls surrounding the maiden would open up before him, and he would reach her golden, bright realm of knowledge and love, and he would resurrect.

He returns to the world a sage or a king, or as a person with the right to enter Valhǫll or be called divine. Guðrún, after suffering a terrible shock and disillusionment about everything she believed in and cared for, symbolically leaves everything she owns, walks into the wilderness and suffers a symbolic death. She compares her emotional suffering with death, more terrible than having ones bones burned like birch twigs and blood sucked by wolves. Her "death" is thus akin to the terrible sufferings of Óðinn when he hung for nine days, stabbed with spear and bereft of food and drink.

After spending a good while in the wilderness, which is a symbol of the realm of death, she walks down from the mountains and reaches a "high hall" where she is healed from her great grief and where women teach her how to weave fate. The hall is owned by one þóra, daughter of "Half". Guðrún seems to have arrived in the realm of the Norns , the rulers of all destinies, and employs her new powers with the intention of wreaking vengeance on her own brothers for the grief they have caused her.

This is when Guðrún's mother arrives in order to heal her daughter from her anger, a healing that is accompanied by the serving of a drink in a horn carved with secret runes that even the powerful and wise Guðrún cannot decipher. As the daughter drinks the mead of the mother, she is healed from her anger against her brothers and declares the ingredients of the mead, as quoted above. That women also sought the realm of the mead-women is suggested in this story as well as in the Fjǫlsvinnsmál (st. 36) where it is said that women may climb the Mountain of Medicine where the maidens are seated beneath the Tree of Memory, and be healed of life-long grievances, illnesses and sorrow.

Eventually, Guðrún accepts marriage with "Atli", a character that is in fact based on the historical figure Attila the Hun. However, in the Edda poems Atli is clearly a disguise for Óðinn in one of his more apparently destructive aspects, and is also said to be the brother of the Valkyrie, Brynhildr and Oddrún. When Guðrún travels to her husband her journey takes her through three realms, each lasting for seven days, and finally she reaches another "high hall", where the guardsman is always alert and where shield maidens roam.

The realm of the Huns is clearly described in a way that allows the audience to deduce that we are really talking about Valhǫll. Later in this book, we will explore how the god Óðinn in his own way also represents the Great Divine, the spirit in everything. As such, we are probably seeing a structural basis for female initiation within a Mystery tradition which resembles that of the men. After a symbolic death and magical instructions, as well as the drinking of sacred mead, the woman enters sacred marriage with the deity that represents the Great All.

3.12: Bright rune, the mead-producer above, Valhǫll, and valkyrie ready to ride the earth-

GRÍMNISMÁL THE SONG OF THE MASKED ONE

Bright Open Space Rune that she-goat is called who stands above Ruler-Father's hall eating from the limbs of Immortality Counsel
A huge cauldron she shall fill to the brim of the Bright Mead that power-drink that shall never fade

> *Heiðrún heitir geit,*
> *er stendr hallo a Heriafadrs*
> *oc bitr af Leraþs limom;*
> *scapker fylla hon scal*
> *ins scíra miaðar,*
> *knaat sv veig vanaz*

Grímnismál 25, Poetic Edda

In Snorri's Gylfaginning, Snorri lets Gangleri [Wandering Learning] ask whether it is so that the one-harriers of Valhǫll drank water. Snorri then lets the High One reply that obviously, the great men of Valhǫll would be served the finest mead in Óðin's halls:

> "There is a she-goat called Heiðrún [Bright Rune/Bright Open Space Symbol], she stands at the roof of Valhǫll, and eat the foliage of that tree which is very famous there, and is called Læráðr [Wind-Shield Counsel = Immortality Counsel].
> And from her teats mead is running so that she fells a great cauldron every day, which is so grand that all the one-harriers can drink there fill thereof."
> Gangleri replies, much impressed: "That is one useful she-goat! And it must be an awesome tree, that she eats from!"

In fact, the tree that provides the nourishment that the Bright Rune employs in order to produce the sacred mead of immortality is the world tree itself, a fact that is conveyed through a riddle. We learn that there is also a hart, Eikþyrnir [Oak Antlers], right there with the she-goat, who also eats from the same tree.

Rather than producing the mead of immortality and wisdom, his nourishment turns into drops dripping from his antlers, which are a symbol of the branches of the world tree itself, right down into the water-source beneath the tree, here identified as the well of death, Hvergelmir [Bellowing Mill], where all dead souls are recycled. From this well, the "rivers" of all the worlds spring. We are returning to the cosmic well beneath the world tree, in its threefold nature; the Well of Memory, the Well of Origin, and the Well of Death.

It is from this water-source that the world tree is nourished, given its life-force through the power of fate, and it is from the life-force of the tree that the mead is produced. What Snorri presents us with, through riddles, is the contrast between two kinds of deaths; the mead of Bright Rune, which provides the chosen dead with eternal resurrection, and the mead of the hart Oak-Antlers, whose mead returns to the source, where all life is recycled. If one starts to think of the mead as life-force, perhaps soul itself, this will be more easily grasped.

The she-goat Heiðrún is compared to the goddess Freyia in the poem Hyndlulióð. This goddess also appears as a vǫlva wearing the name Heiðr [Bright One], teaching her arts while traversing the world in her countless shapes. That runes and mead are connected to each other should not come as a surprise, neither the concept of a particular rune that spells a concept of immortality achieved. The association to Valhǫll and the mead served there makes us draw a line to the Valkyrie again.

In sections above, we showed how individual Valkyrie may be the particular guides and confidantes, even the wives, of certain warriors throughout their lives, guide them through their initiations, consecrate them in a ritual of mead-serving, the imparting of esoteric secrets, and sacred marriage. The same Valkyrie will save that is, resurrect from Hel their beloved heroes. From Snorri and other saga, Edda and skaldic sources we know that the concept of the Valkyrie was intimately associated with Valhǫll, where the Valkyrie serve the mead from the cauldron of Illuminated One. In the poem Grímnismál, stanza 36, Óðinn names the nine Valkyrie who serve the mead of resurrection to the one-harriers/ self-rulers/ sole rulers:

36. 'Vibration' and 'Mist (or Cloud)'	*36. Hrist oc Mist*
I wish shall carry to me the horn	*vil ec at mer horn beri,*
'Ancient Battle-Axe' and 'Battle'	*Sceggiald oc Scagvl,*
'Fighting' and 'Powerful'	*Hildr oc Þrvðr,*
Battle Noise' and 'Army-Fetters'	*Hlaucc oc Herfiotur,*
'Bellower' and 'Spear Charger'	*Gall oc Geiranvl,*
'Shield Truce' and 'Counsel Truce'	*Randgriþ oc Raþgriþ*
and 'Ruler Heritage'	*oc Reginleif;*
They carry ale to the Sole Rulers	*þer bera einheriom aul.*

The names of the Valkyrie indicate what they represent, as well as their functions.

» The vibrations and the Bellower themes are related to universal creation, which in Old Norse myths is imbued with symbols of shaking movements, vibrations and the sounds these make.

» The name Þruðr [Power] is identical to the name of the Thunder god Þór's daughter, whose hand is sought in marriage by the dwarf All-Wise in the Edda poem Allvísmál. To get the girl, the dwarf must display his extensive wisdom and eloquence to her father, Þórr himself, who in this poem plays the role of the giant guardian that is such a common theme in the myths of initiation.

» Mist is a reference to the world of the dead, such as Níflhel [Misty Hidden or Misty Frost].

» The name Ruler Heritage is very interesting, because it seems to refer to that which is referred to as the true heritage of the initiates in both the myth of Óttarr, (Hyndlulióð) and Svípdagr (Fjǫlsvinnsmál), and strongly indicated in the other heroic poems: That the revelations and powers imparted through initiation by the mead-serving woman is the divine heritage, the birthright, the spiritual heritage of human beings.

Almost all the other names refer to battle, fighting and matters of war (such as truce), which indicates that as specialized Norns, the Valkyrie embody the fates of war and battle, as we see in the Vǫluspá poem, stanza 30, here listed by the vǫlva:

30. She saw Valkyrie widely arriving *Ready to ride to the divine peoples* *'Debt' held a shield, and 'Battle' another* *'War', 'Fighting' and 'Magician' and 'Spear Battle';* *Now are they counted, the women of the Ruler* *Valkyrie ready to ride the Earth*	*30. Sá hon Valkyrie vítt um komnar* *gǫrvar at ríða til Goðþjóðar:* *Skuld hélt skildi, en Skǫgul ǫnnur,* *Gunnr, Hildr, Gǫndul* *ok Geirskǫgul;* *nú eru taldar nǫnnur Herjans,* *gǫrvar at ríða grund Valkyrie*

We should certainly pay attention to the fact that again, we see a number of nine Valkyrie listed up, although most of them have switched names. We should bear in mind that the names of characters are fluid and changing, and that the important matter here is the formula of nine maidens. In this case, we see that the youngest Norn Skuld [Debt], who represents the future, is present, as is the lady Gǫndul [Magician], who in Flateyjarbók is identified as Freyia.

The rest are, again, clearly representatives of the state of war and battle, and their arrival signifies the era of war and unrest that begun after the death of Baldr and which is going to lead to Ragnarǫk. The formula of the nine maidens associated with the fate of the world, however, is repeated time and time again. It is present in the number of mothers to the present world, and in the number of cosmic "waves", also said to be the "lights of the gods".

The Valkyrie of the Edda heroic lore usually ride in groups of nine, or three by nine, as they supervise battle and guide their heroes, the maidens at the Mountain of Medicine, whose names are altogether about peace and healing, are simply representing fate when the human being arrives "home" that is, reaches the blissful union with his original fate, perhaps his soul.

Usually, the group of nine are led by one, either the ninth in the group, or a tenth outside of the group. In the case of the mead-serving Valkyrie in Valhǫll, it would seem that the unifying point of origin to the mead that the ladies are serving, is the "she-goat", Bright Rune, who stands above the hall of resurrection after death, probably the very same being who chooses the chosen dead in the first place; Freyia, who receives the slain.

3.13: Freyia, gullveigr, the goddess is the drink-

In Chapter 2.13, we were presented with the Goddess of the Vanir, Freyia, who first arrived on the cosmic scene as a vǫlva who conquered death before the eyes of all the gods. Later, she moved through the world as a wandering witch, helping and teaching the people through the art of seiðr. The Aesir, wanting to gain control over this most powerful of all arts, started a war with her people, the Vanir, and ended up with a truce involving the arrival of Freyia and her three kinsmen into the realm of the gods. Then Óðinn and his Aesir could learn the art of seiðr also. Freyia thus stands out as the great spiritual mentor of the Aesir, and takes up her position as a priestess among them.

The fact that the goddess is called Gullveigr Gold Power Drink is a way of identifying the goddess with the sacred drink itself. This is in accordance with the name of Njǫrð's eldest daughter Ráðveig Counsel Drink. It is also in accordance with the way both the mead is said to be covered by shields in Hel, and the way the sleeping Valkyrie is, likewise, covered by shields in the realm of death. If we also realize that the mead offers rejuvenation and resurrection, we can see the mead in connection to the apples of Iðunn, who is also called the Ǫlgefn the Ale Provider, and who is obviously identified with her apples.

No one can eat the apples unless she is present, and her nickname Seed of Yggdrasill is not coincidental. The drink and the drink-serving and drink-guarding goddess are ultimately connected and seem to be the same. The mead is also served by the goddess Síf in the Lokasenna, where she tries to ease the anger of Loki. After Loki has drunk her mead, he declares that he has tricked her and "had" her, as if drinking her mead is the same as sleeping with her. Curiously enough, the drink is also served by a male god, Víðarr [Expanding/Wood Warrior] the Silent.

There is one other poem where a male serves the mead to another male, and that is the Grímnismál, where the young boy Agnarr [Respect Warrior] serves the mead to Óðinn and receives great cosmic revelations in return. I will write more about these cases later. A male entity also provides the blood that becomes the mead: Kvasir, who may be a disguise for Heimdallr and who consists of the essence of all gods and goddesses of all tribes put together. If the goddess represents something like the core soul of all gods regardless of gender, the ultimate Fate-spinner, much like all humans regardless of gender possess a personal Fate-spinner attached to their souls, we may better understand how the goddess can be the mead or the origin of the mead that she offers, yet how the mead and its provider may sometimes be disguised within masculine entities as well.

It seems to me that the two cases of male drink-providers metaphorically describe the offering of nourishment to a quality within the man. In the case of Víðarr the Silent, this god probably represents the expanding wisdom that comes out of inner silence, attempting to quiet the incessant raging rant of blind Loki, the inner wisdom reaching out to the foolish mind. In the case of Agnarr, the offering of drink to the bound god is a young man's choice to nourish his own Spirit. The fact that the essentially same realm, the same mead, and the same woman is described within all the various worlds, the worlds of giants, gods, elves, Norns and Valkyrie, is only obscure and confusing as long as one insists that were are speaking of geographical borders and physical species.

We could compare this with how the same mead is contained in (three) different vessels. The underlying message is unifying, suggesting that there is a deeper reality behind the metaphors of poetry where a golden bright maiden serves a mead of wisdom, light, healing, universal memory and a path of salvation along with her own self. The maiden seems to be associated with creation, death and fate, and indeed also with the fates that follow each person through their lives, spinning their fates. It is said that the fate must be woken lest she spins in a state of slumber, causing unfortunate lives. Perhaps we are seeing a path towards waking one's own fate.

3.14: SOMA AND HAOMA, AMBROSIA AND KYKEON-AND CERRIDWEN'S CAULDRON, THE INDO-EUROPEAN CONNECTION-

And the Holy Spirit...Took Zoroaster's hand and filled it with liquid all-encompassing knowledge and said "drink it". And Zoroaster drank it, and all-encompassing wisdom was blended within Zoroaster...and he was in the Holy Spirit's Wisdom for seven nights.
(Zand Wahmand Yasht III 6-12)

"Oh, you Golden One, I invoke your intoxication...All other intoxications bring the violence...but Haoma's intoxication bring blessed justice...To you, Haoma, the just, you who provokes forth the Truth!"
[Yasna, Avesta, 9.17, 10.18, 11.10]

SOMA AND HAOMA

The precious mead of the Edda lore is in my opinion certainly related to the sacred Soma of the Old Indian Vedic religion, predecessor of Hinduism, and the Haoma of the Iranian Avesta religion. There is also a connection to the Greek Ambrosia and to various references to a sacred drink in Celtic, particularly Irish, traditions. Soma was at once a god, a plant and a drink, inspiring ecstatic hymns, many of which were gathered in the Indian collection of religious hymns, the Rig Veda, three thousand years ago. The plant once known as Soma is today unknown to us, but Gordon Wasson (1971) argued that the Soma was the fly agarics, whereas David Flattery and Martin Scwartz believe that Soma and Haoma was made from harmaline, found in wild rye.

Soma was the deity that descended and manifested itself in the rituals, a mediator between human beings and the gods. Soma is described as bright, compared to the sun and its rays and shine, as well as to fire. The deity is a sage, a poet and a seer who stimulates thoughts and inspires hymns. As a drink, Soma gives power to the gods and immortality to human beings it is in fact the Drink of Immortality. It produced an ecstatic trance that could enable the soul to travel into the divine realms, see everything and travel everywhere, even between dimensions.

In Kundalini Yoga, Soma is seated in the highest chakra, the crown, and is described as the Nectar of Immortality. In the quote at the beginning of this Chapter about the Mead Woman.

Soma is described as the expander of the mind, the drink that is sought by both gods and men, and that it will take you to the "place where they stretch out our lifespan", that is, to the realm of fate, and that it will make you immortal. This is exactly the function of the Norse mead, which is also strongly associated with fate and immortality, and which is also sought by gods and men alike.

Likewise, Iranian texts describe the drink Haoma in similar terms.

"Ahura Mazda the Holy Spirit, creator of just bodily existence, took Zoroaster's hand and poured into it liquid all-encompassing wisdom, and said: "Drink it"...and Zoroaster drank it, and all-encompassing wisdom was blended into Zoroaster. Zoroaster was within the wisdom of the Holy Spirit for seven nights...on the seventh day, all-encompassing wisdom was removed from him..."
[Zand Wahmand Yasht, III 6-12]

The link between Soma, Haoma and the Old Norse miǫðr [mead] is powerful and cannot be doubted. Etymologically they are connected, as Soma is often called madhu [honey, mead], whereas the Avesta calls the intoxication of Haoma itself by the related word mada, from the same root as the Norse and Iranian words, originally meaning honey, an important ingredient in mead. Furthermore, all three cultures describe their sacred drinks as golden and bright, bringing illumination, wisdom, eloquence, poetry, and having to do with immortality. Reading the Indian Vedas and the Iranian Avesta, there can be no doubt that the drink was strongly associated with intense, personal mystical experiences, a state of trance and a passionate union with the divine.

Runic inscription and image of riding warrior being met by a woman with a drinking horn, 7th century Gotland memorial stone.

THE NORSE DÍSIR AND THE INDIAN DHISANAS

The references to death and the underworld are overwhelming in connection to the serving of the precious mead in Old Norse myths, so are esoteric teachings and the theme of resurrection. We are seeing a mythology that has to with initiation into the mysteries of death, resurrection, runes, spell-songs, fate and the afterlife. What is more, an in-depth study of the mead-women shows that we are speaking of the same concept as that found in the Old Indian concept of the dhisanas. The dhisanas were individual goddesses of intelligence, growth and well-being, worshiped in plural, but who were known to be mere aspects different shapes of one original and unifying Dhisana.

Several Vedic hymns honor the Dhisanas, and associate them also with the Goddess of Infinity or Eternity Aditi ["Infinite/ Eternal"], a cosmic deity (from the Yayur Veda, 1.4, 4.1):

> *May Aditi [the goddess of infinity], connected with the All-gods dig thee on the abode of Earth...*
>
> *May the wives of the gods, the goddesses connected with the All-gods place thee on the abode of Earth*
>
> *May the Dhisanas, the goddesses connected with the All-gods cook thee on the abode of Earth...*
>
> *Do ye, O goddesses, place this sacrifice among the gods*
>
> *Do ye, invoked, drink the Soma...*
>
> *Ye Dhisanas, that are strong, be strengthened, gather strength, and give me strength...*
>
> *O Mother, come forth, thy unerring, watchful name*
>
> *O Soma, to that of thee, O Soma, to Soma, hail!*

The Dhisanas [wives of the gods] are interesting to us because they are also etymologically connected to an Old Norse concept. The Dísir, which can be translated as "goddesses" or "female powers". The term could be used to describe any kind of female power in the mythological cosmos, whether she be an Ásynia, a Valkyrie, a Norn, or a gýgr (giantess). Just like the Indian Dhisanas, who were one and many at the same time, the Norse Dísir were praised and worshiped as a collective, but there was also a concept of a singular, unifying dís, as is seen in the concept of the Dísarsalinn [The Temple of The Goddess] in connection with the annual dísablót [The Sacrifice to the Goddesses].

In this important Pagan celebration, the Dísir, a term covering all kinds of female entities, were worshiped as a collective yet a temple was also raised in honor of the one, great Dís, usually thought to be Freyia, since she was the most important goddess and her name is a title, meaning the Lady Sovereign.

In the Old Norse myths, we see that women from all realms giantesses, Norns, death-goddesses, Valkyrie and Ásyniur such as Earth, Síf and Freyia, all are described within the same kind of realm, performing the same essential function. This ultimate unity at the core of the numerous aspects is probably as old as the concept of the Vedic Dhisanas, reaching back, it is thought, at least five thousand years. The mead-offering woman in Old Norse lore has her functional and etymological counterpart in Indian texts that are of extreme antiquity. The connection point between the Old Norse and the Old Indian is most probably equally old the creators of the Vedas and the forerunners of Edda lore must have parted company at a time that was still prehistoric, very possibly towards the end of the last Stone Age.

Seeing that the Vedic Soma was undoubtedly of this nature, there is no doubt in my mind that the original purpose of the ritual mead was to transmit a spiritual mystery which was experienced in a state of trance. What links all the different species of mead-serving females together despite their apparent differences where mythical species are concerned, are their shared functions, attributes and essential meaning, as well as the word Dísir, which is applied to them all no matter what world they belong to on the surface. The Old Norse word Dísir is certainly etymologically connected to the Old Indian dhisana.

It is thus not so hard to imagine that if the words are connected, related to a common origin reaching back several thousand years, so the mythical complex of goddess of many shapes and the golden drink she guards, called mjǫdr in Old Norse and madhu in Old Indian (referring to honey and the golden color of the mead), are also linked. Freyia, the Vanadís [Goddess of the Vanir] was worshiped in the Dísarsalinn the Hall of the (one) Goddess during the annual celebration known as dísablót the Sacrifice to the (many) Goddesses.

There certainly seems to be a Pantheist concept of "many-one" at the heart of Norse mythology, which may be detected in the lore of the female powers. Although not discussed in this essay, I am convinced that we find the same concept as well as in the lore of the male powers, especially regarding Óðinn and Heimdallr. I will be exploring this issue in depth in Chapter 13.

AMBROSIA AND KYKEON

"I have fasted, I have drunk Kykeon"
Password for the initiate at Eleusis (D'Alviella, 1981)

In Greek mythology, the sacred drink of the gods is called Ambrosia [ἀμβροσία], is related to Sanskrit amrita and means "immortality". It is identifiable also as Néctar [νέκταρ], which means "Overcoming Death" (from nék, "death" and tar "overcoming"). In Greek mythology, goddesses usually transmit this drink to gods and mortals, such as when Heracles receives the drink from Athena and it can be used to restore youth and cleanse the body of all defilements. Like the Norse gods, the Greek gods drank this liquid in order to achieve immortality through repeated rejuvenation.

The probable origin of a ritual use of Ambrosia or Nectar is lost in myth, and later Greek texts usually refer to the drink as a metaphor for any delightful and cleansing liquid used in cooking, botanics or medicine. A drink was, however, served during the Mystery initiations of Eleusis. Kykeon ["Mix", "Stir"]. Apparently, this drink was made from water and barley and other natural substances. It was used to break a nine day fast and provided the climax of the initiation experience, when the initiate followed in the footsteps of the divine grounder of the Mysteries. The goddess Demeter, who broke her fast after nine days of searching for her daughter, with this drink. The Kykeon was said to be used by the sorceress Circe, who blended into it honey and a magical potion.

It has been proposed that the Kykeon used during the Mysteries was imbued with psychoactive substances so as to provide a climax to the initiation experience. Since the drink was based on barley, it has been speculated that the drink received its particular powers from the ergot a fungus which grows on barley, the sacred corn of Demeter. By mixing this fungus with water we will produce a mild hallucinogen not unlike LSD. The temple of Eleusis was carved and painted with images of mushrooms and poppy, the plant used to produce opium. The Minoan religion that preceded the Eleusinian mysteries. The temple of Eleusis was said to have been established by Minoan refugees after the destruction of the Minoan culture around 1400 BC. Minoans also have a poppy goddess, and there are good reasons to believe that the Minoans used an opium-blended drink to reach communion with the goddesses and the gods.

TALIESIN'S BOOK

> *Remarkable when they come from the Cauldron;*
> *The Three Inspirations of Cerridwen*
>   *-Taliesin's Book*

Taliesin Pen Beirdd was a Welsh bard and druid who is said to have lived during the late 6th century AD. He was a popular and recognized bard who composed a great number of songs and poems that have been transmitted through later sources such as Taliesin's Book from the 14th century and in Hanes from the 16th century, as well as through references in the epic Mabinogion and Historia Brittonum from the 9th centuries. In his poems, Taliesin often refers to a mythical reality and to his own experiences within this reality as an initiate.

He declares himself to be all-knowing, he is the first bard, the first druid, the one who can answer all questions and who has been into all the elements and all the worlds he can take upon himself all kinds of shapes and he knows the truth behind all things. His inspiration and his knowledge and his powers have been acquired while he resided with the goddess Cerridwen in her Underworld abode. The goddess Cerridwen showed up in the shape of a hen who swallowed the young Taliesin and kept him within her womb for nine months. Then he was born anew, and escaped Cerridwen by taking upon himself the shapes of all animals and all elements. Even if he fears the old goddess, there is no doubt that she was the one who taught him everything.

The first bard has learned in her halls and drunk from her magical cauldron:

> *"Firstly I was formed in the shape of a handsome man in the halls of*
> *Cerridwen in order to be refined. Although small and modest in my behavior I*
> *was great in her lofty sanctuary.*
> *While she kept me prisoner, sweetness of inspiration educated me*
> *Laws were imparted me in a speech without words But I had to flee from the*
> *angry, terrible hag whose outcry was terrifying."*

There are several interesting similarities between the basic world of the bard Taliesin and that of Viking Age skalds. Like them, Taliesin belonged to a tradition of bards who kept and transmitted age-old traditions where poetry was considered the result of divine inspiration and journeys through the many spheres of the universe. Taliesin's poetry makes it clear that an experience of death was an important part of the initiation, and that this experience was associated with a stay in the realm of the goddess Cerridwen, sometimes a painful experience, where a magical cauldron was brewed with the purpose of transmitting wisdom to those who have been born in darkness.

The learning of wisdom, magical powers and poetical inspiration was closely associated with the drink brewed in Cerridwen's underworld cauldron, and her realm is obviously one of death. Like in Norse mythology, the number nine and three are repeated. Nine months the initiate must stay in the Underworld, and three is the number of inspirations emerging from the cauldron. The goddess is terrifying and must be escaped from, often in the shape of animals, quite like when Óðinn had to flee Gunnlǫð in the shape of an eagle or a serpent.

At the same time, Taliesin, like Óðinn, praises the goddess who has shaped him and given him her wisdom. Like the mead-woman of Norse myths, she has been initiated herself, and she stands foremost among gods, as Taliesin lets the old lady boast:

"When all the thrones are compared mine is preeminent
My throne, my cauldron, my laws
My searching speech give them consistency
I am an initiate of the halls of Don [Cassiopeia]"

The reference to the cauldron of the goddess is also a reference to the mead of poetry, immortality, wisdom, eloquence and inspiration, and the magical drink shows up in other parts of Taliesin's poetry. In these lines, the dark rock cavern and the serpent that is so important in some of the Norse initiation myths are also present:

"A deep cavern opens up before me shadowed by great rocks
The dragon comes out and crawls towards the Cup of songs
Of the song
Of the cups of gold
The golden cups are in his hand"

Engraving on Minoan signet ring showing woman/goddess on top of a peak in front of a temple, flanked by big cats, reaching out a staff (of office?) to a man standing to attention. Bronze Age Crete.

In my mind, there is very little doubt that there are clear similarities between Taliesin's experiences and the world-view that is expressed in the Norse myth of the mead-woman. In other Celtic mythologies, particularly from Irish sources, we repeatedly hear about a goddess who, through the transmission of a golden or a red drink, consecrates young men to the status of king or chief. The goddesses in question usually have names that either indicates "intoxication" or "sovereignty" just like Freyia has a name that indicates sovereignty, and another name, Gullveigr, which indicates the power of the golden drink. In the Irish sources, the young hero can only become worthy of ruling his people after having accepted the drink of the goddess as well as her sacred embrace (as in marriage or sexual relations with her). The drink is poured from a cauldron by a golden serving spoon, and served from a golden cup. The hero must swear an oath to the goddess much like Óðinn swore a sacred ring-oath. Often, the goddess appears first as a terrifying old hag, but when the hero swears his oath of marriage and kisses the hag, she turns into a beautiful young woman. Likewise, in Norse myths, the beautiful maiden and the old hag keep appearing in the same stories, representing two sides of the same coin.

3.15: Beowulf and archaeology: the real mead-women

"Hrotgard's queen, of noble countenance gold-adorned she greeted the men of the hall and the noble woman offered the cup first to the king of the East-Danes, the guardian of the land."

Beowulf, line 613-616. Translation by Michael Enright

Priestess-graves were found all over the North-Western European world from about 500 B.C.E and into the Viking Age. Priestesses or witches were buried with full ritual gear, the most important items being their cult staff, their pouch of herbs (often containing cannabis), magical amulets, and the equipment needed for serving mead in a ritual setting. The last known priestess burial is also the grandest, namely the Oseberg ship burial of 9th century Norway (now to be seen in the Viking Ship House of Oslo), where two elderly priestesses were laid to rest in the most splendid Viking Age ship burial ever found, surpassing even Sutton Hoo, and with full ritual gear, including the pouches and the staff and equipment for brewing. The ship was designed for moving in shallow waters, probably to take the priestesses along the coast. Most priestesses just traveled by foot it would appear, these had wealthy patronage and were honored with more splendor even than royalty. There is still a common misconception that they were a queen and her handmaiden although this theory has been disproved several times and the findings clearly show their cult like religious status and the equality between the two women. Archaeologists and historians such as Ingstad, Solli and Røthe (see bibliography) have provided extensive and overwhelming arguments for this view. No one would seriously deny the importance of drinking rituals in Iron Age and Viking Age Northern Europe. The concept of a mead-offering woman appearing in a ritual context is well-known both from written sources and from archaeology.

The lady of the hall

In his book "Lady with a Mead-Cup", historian Michael Enright emphasizes the importance of the drink-serving woman in Germanic societies, and focuses especially on her role within the warrior band. Like many other historians, he believes there is evidence that such bands of warriors bound together in sworn foster- or blood- brotherhoods and that such bands were important in the formation of early states in Northern Europe among both Celts and Germans. Enright discusses the role of the wife of the chieftain within the band, where she plays a role that may have been inherited from earlier religious professions.

The priestess ritually consecrating a warrior or chieftain through an offering of drink while offering a prophecy and/or a challenge. The mead-offering ritual at banquets would be performed by the queen or chief's wife, such as described in the Old English poem Beowulf (see above). In this context, the queen publicly acknowledged and honored the king by serving him first, offering a formal welcome, a prophecy and a blessing. She proceeded by moving about to the other warriors in the band, offering them drink one by one, according to their rank within the band. She gives prophecies and blessings as she moves around, and finally challenges the newcomer (Beowulf), spurring him on to heroic deeds.

According to Enright, the mead-serving queen of Beowulf is playing an age-old role of noble women, inherited from priestesses and oracles, serving to emphasize hierarchy within the warrior band as well as gluing the band together as one, all drinking from the same cup served by the same woman.

Iron Age (ca. 200 AD) Celtic votive altar to the goddess Rosmerta and her companion; Lugh-Mercury-Wotan.

THE GODDESS, ORACLE AND PRIESTESS COUNTERPARTS OF THE IRON AGE

Enright, being concerned mostly with the social function of the ritual (establishing hierarchy and community at once), nevertheless sees the ritual in connection with older religious cults, drawing a quite specific line to a popular cult rooted in the Celtic Iron Age around the goddess Rosmerta, a mead-offering, staff-carrying oracle goddess married to Wodan the German predecessor of Norse Óðinn. Rosmerta was an important goddess in the Rhineland and Eastern Gaul and central to a cult of Sacred Marriage. Tribal chiefs and kings would undergo marriage to this goddess in order to legitimize their power. Enright claims that this early cult of Wodan and the prophetic goddess originally was based on a Gallo-Roman myth about Mercurius-Lugh as the original king and his marriage with Rosmerta. Older evidence for the cult associate the goddess either with Mercurius, the Roman messenger of the gods, or with Lugh, and an ancient hero-king deity associated with the legendary tribe of Tuatha De Danaan, as well as with the pan-Celtic god Lugus.

When the cult of the prophetic goddess and her sacred king husband reached German territories, the male god was replaced by Wodan, who resembled his Roman and Celtic counterparts and may have been influenced by them or shared their origins. Furthermore, Enright sees the queen's role in the drinking ritual in connection with the existence of powerful female oracular priestesses in the Iron Age of Germanic societies. Such women accompanied the rulers and kings of the tribes as political counselors, pushers and oracles. They contributed divinations and were probably considered mediums for higher powers. They supervised ritual oaths and could urge the people to war with promises of victory. There was a strong connection between these women and a prophetic cult of the goddess, and especially to the cult of the goddess Rosmerta [The Great Provider] who again was connected to Wodan [i.e. Óðinn] through a myth of Sacred Marriage. Enright envisions a development where the symbolic and ritual role of the powerful priestesses was slowly taken over by the wives of the warlords.

ARCHAEOLOGICAL EVIDENCE

Enright also refers to archaeology, finding evidence, as mentioned in the beginning of this section, reaching back to at least 500 BCE of powerful Northern European women being buried with all the necessary gear for serving mead, and even buried with their serving spoon in hand. The same women's graves would display a number of cult like objects such as a staff, amulets, and divination tools. Their graves also show that they had a very high status in society, and they also carried the symbolic set of keys that indicated ladies of the house rather than serving maidens.

Other works have also emphasized the social and symbolic function of drinking rituals in Germanic and Viking Age Pagan societies, such as the historian Bjørn Qviller in his "Bottles and Battles", who also relate the importance of the ritual use of cannabis and opium in early societies but few have emphasized and appreciated the symbolic and ritual role of the drink-serving woman such as Michael Enright, who concludes:

"Neither the antiquity, continuity, intensity nor popularity of the woman/ liquor/prophecy complex can now be seriously doubted."

The fact that real mead-women certainly did exist, and that they were, originally, priestesses, provides, in my opinion, evidence that the emphasis and importance of the "maiden with the mead" in Edda poetry is derived from actual, ritual paths. That the maiden usually appears in the context of a journey to the underworld in order to learn esoteric secrets only strengthens this impression. We are seeing the evidence of a long forgotten path of initiation where men and women sought the golden lady within the underworld, and doted on her for their resurrection.

3.16: THE MEAD AND THE SUN GODDESS

41. I saw the Sun and it seemed to me that I was seeing a glorious deity; to her I bowed for one last time in this world of time
> 41. Sól ek sá,
> svá þótti mér,
> sem ek sæja gǫfgan guð;
> henni ek laut
> hinzta sinni
> aldaheimi í.

-Sólarlióð st. 41

The Sólarlióð, the Song of the Sun, has, compared to other Edda poems, often been "dismissed" as a Christian visionary poem. It is thought to be a poem created, perhaps, by a poet who felt pulled between the new and the old traditions, but who is mainly Christian. His references to Pagan lore are numerous, but modern scholars often describe these references as "confused", as if the poet did not really know the Pagan lore properly. The reason for this is that whenever the poet of the Sun Song refers to Pagan lore, it is done in a fashion that does not fit into the image we moderns generally have on the myths.

At the website Voluspa.org, otherwise a very recommendable page, we can read an example, sadly, of a very typical attitude:

> *"The composition exhibits a strange mixture of Christianity and Heathenism, which it would seem that the poet's own religion was in a transition state. Of the allusions to Heathenism it is, however, to be observed that they are chiefly to persons and actions of which there is no trace in the Odinic mythology, as known to us, and are possibly the fruits of the poet's own imagination."*

We do not know exactly when the poem was created, although it seems safe to suggest that it was created after the Conversion, that is, sometime after the year 1000 AD, perhaps as late as the 13th century, when it was written down. Although Christianity was introduced and most had converted, at least officially, the poets of this time most certainly knew a lot more about Pagan lore than we do today. To sit back here in our own century and claim that the poet was "imagining things" or confused because he was making references and placing emphasis on aspects of the lore that we are not accustomed to pay attention to, and which do not fit into our stereotypical, preconceived ideas about the myths, is downright arrogance.

All poets used language that could be understood by the audience. Metaphorical riddles, certainly, but these would have no effect or purpose unless based on the worldview that was still at the heart and core of the average Scandinavian until several centuries after the Conversion. The quotation above shows what underlies this attitude, as the term "Odinic mythology" is applied. The reason neither scholars or modern heathens have been able to really appreciate the intensely Pagan worldview that underlies a rather more superficial Christian approach throughout the whole poem, is because they automatically assume that Old Norse Paganism was all about "Odinic mythology".

I am going to recite several stanzas from this poem where I offer my own translations and make comments on each stanza in order to let us see exactly how well these fit into central, Old Norse concepts. The "problem" many face when they try to understand Norse myths is that they are unable to see what is right in front of them, right there in the text: the Goddess. In the website referred to and quoted from above, this refusal to recognize the Goddess is very well illustrated in the way the translator of the Song of the Sun even refuses to literally translate the word hon, meaning "she", which is used to describe the goddess Sól.

The sun is, by the modern translator, reduced to an "it", a thing, although the ancient poet clearly regarded her as a goddess, and describes her as such. This is completely in accordance with the Old Norse concept of the goddess Sól, known on the continent as Sunna, the Sun goddess. Before I begin going through the Pagan parts of the poem, let us have another look at the old lady Sun. Snorri described her as such:

> *"A man was called Time-Tracker. He had two children; they were so fair and so beautiful that he called his son Máni [Moon] and his daughter Sól [Sun], she was married to a man called Glen [Gap Between Clouds]. But the gods were angered at this arrogance and placed the siblings up on the heaven. They let Sól steer the horses that pulled the sun disc which the gods had created from the fires that flew out of the world of Muspell (the heat world) in order to illuminate the world...there is no wonder that she travels fast, as if she was afraid, for he is closing in on her, who is after her life. And she has no other option than to run..."*

*Bronze Age model of the chariot of
the Sun goddess, Denmark*

Whereas Snorri described the Sun goddess, whom he lists among the Ásyniur (the wives of the Aesir), as a girl who was driving the chariot of the sun, always haunted by the great wolf that is destined to swallow the sun eventually, no distinction is made between the sun disc and the goddess in the Poetic Edda.

As we saw in Chapter 2.6, at the time of creation, we learn that the Sun emerged from the South, the direction of Muspellheimr, her rays creating the life on Earth, but did not know her place in heaven. It is actually interesting to notice the emphasis placed on the direction from which Sun originated, the south. This is in fact a clue. At the time of settling the primeval cosmos, the goddess Sun arrived "from the south", as a power of heat and life-giving rays, with the power to control "the horses of heaven", which are also her "halls", and which I guess refer to the planets. She nurtures the Earth goddess with her rays, creating the first organic life.

The south from which the Sun arrives is Muspellheimr, the place of primeval cosmic heat, from where hot streams reached into the ice of primeval Níflhel, beginning to melt the ice of death in order to create a new universe. From this place, Snorri tells us, a great "cow" came also, a giant, cosmic cow by the name of Auðhumbla, which means "Abundant Brew Ingredient". The cow is an ancient and widespread symbol of the great mother goddess, nurturer of all life. In Old Indian mythologies, the goddess Vac represents the first cosmic speech, and takes the shape of a cow. In Old Norse myths, likewise, the first cosmic being, the goddess in the shape of a cow, nurtures the first sound.

This "cow", the first named being in the entire universe, nurtured the giant Ymir [Sound], with her life-giving streams of milk. At the same time, she fed on the ice of death, the heat of her moving tongue bringing forth and waking (restoring to life) the giant Búri [The Storage Shed], who sired the first Aesir. The theme of heat that creates first life, and the fact that the "cow" arrives from the southern realm of cosmic heat, makes it fairly reasonable to see a correspondence between the cow and the Sun goddess. The cow is also related to the life-giving and life-restoring mead, through her name and her streams of milk. Another she-beast who made such potent streams was the she-goat, Bright Open Space Symbol/ Illuminated Fate, who produced the mead of Valhǫll.

The Sun goddess is referred to in the poem Vafþrúðnismál, where Óðinn asks what will happen after the Sun goddess is extinguished by the wolf Fenrir [Greed]. The giant replies, referring to Sun as Alfrǫðull, "Elf Splendor";

17. One daughter is born by
Elf-Splendor after her, Greed runs
she shall ride when the rulers die
the path staked out by her mother

17. Eina dottvr
berr Alfraðvll,
aþr hana Fenrir fari;
sv scal riða,
þa er regin deyia,
modvr brautir mer

Bronze Age rock carvings from
Scandinavia showing worship
of the Sun goddess.

During the Bronze Age, the Sun was in fact the most important, central deity of Scandinavia, represented by discs and various energy wheel symbols. From countless rock carvings, we see testimonies of her central importance, in fact her dominance, in the public cult, and that she was worshiped through ritual dances and acrobatics, often from ships, and carried as an emblem on the shields of warriors, or depicted as the emblems or inner power of priests. Moving into the Viking Age, however, it would seem that the Sun goddess has withdrawn from the cult and from the mythical lore but it would also seem that her withdrawal is only skin deep.

If we look at countless standing stones, often memorial stones, dating back to the Viking Age and some centuries before, we see that the symbols of the Sun the swirling discs were extremely common, as they were in art and jewelry. If we look to the written lore, that which has been left to us, we might find that the ancient Sun goddess, once undoubtedly the Great Goddess of Scandinavia, shows up with different shapes and names. In Chapter 3.4 on the poem Skírnismál, we were introduced to the giantess Gerðr, daughter of Gymir, who was said to be identical to Aegir. Thus Gerðr is identical to one of the nine daughters of Aegir and Rán, and also, as we later saw, to one of the nine daughters of Njǫrðr and Njórunn/Njerðr/Nerthus. She is also a mead-woman, and her realm is described in such a way as to identify her to a number of other Dísirwhether they be Valkyrie, Norns, giantesses or Ásyniur. As already argued, we see that the separation between the various entities is very fluid in the Old Norse perception. Thus to identify an entity with another never really excludes the identification with another entity, and another, and yet another.

What is special about Gerðr here is that she is described quite exactly like anyone would describe a Sun goddess, in fact, the Sun is directly referred to:

4. How can I tell you this you be-ing so young! This great grievous need?	*4.Hvi vm segiac þer,*
	seggr enn vngi!
	mikinn móðtrega?
It is so that Elf-Splendor (the Sun) shines all day but refuses to shine upon my desire.	*þviat alfraþvll*
	lysir um alla daga
	oc þeygi at minom mvnom

These lines are hardly ever taken seriously it is generally ignored, the interpreter assuming that Freyr is talking metaphorically in the sense that his desire is not met. However, Freyr clearly identifies the reason for his misery; it is the Sun goddess who refuses to "shine upon his desire", and for this reason, he cannot have Gerðr. What does the Sun have to do with Gerðr? Why is her refusal so devastating? I would say it is because she is Gerðr, and the whole point of the entire story is her initiatory refusal to accommodate Freyr's desire. The identification between Gerðr and the Sun goddess is further elaborated:

6. In the halls of Hiding I saw her walk a maiden, most dear to me her arms shone like flickering flames through the air and the ocean	*6. I Gymis ga/rþom*
	ec sa ganga
	mer tiþa mey;
	armar lysto,
	en af þaþan
	alt lopt oc la/gr

Snorri described Gerðr as the fairest among maidens, who stayed in the North (the realm of death and darkness) with her father Gymir [Hiding something], where she lived in a grand hall. When she lifted her "arms", the light transmitted from them illuminated the air and the sky. The power to illuminate the world is in itself another good indication that Gerðr actually is a disguise for the Sun goddess, hidden in the world of darkness, as the Sun does at night and during Northern Scandinavian winters, which could also be metaphorically describing the bright soul that hides within the unknown (i.e. dark) parts of the self.

Moreover, her "hall" is described as golden, fair, shining, indeed flaming. In order to reach her, the hero needs a horse that can jump through the "flickering flames". She might be hiding in the Northern realm of death, as the sun does during winter, but she has taken her abode of heat and illumination with her. The description of the golden, fair, shining and flaming hall hidden in the realm of death and darkness is repeated in the Mead Woman stories, and particularly elaborated in the Song of Much Knowing (Chapter 3. 10), where the "Great Maiden" Menglǫð, "Invitation to Blend" is seated at the Mountain of Medicine.

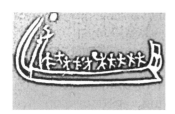

Bronze Age rock carving from Hvitlycke, Bohuslän, Sweden: A man, aroused, approached a black Sun disk while a whirling Sun disk is nearby, the dark and the bright Sun of Norse myths?

Her hall described exactly the same way as that of Gerðr. Likewise, the abode of Sígrdrífa, the Valkyrie, is surrounded by a "powerful light, burning like fire, reaching up from the realm of death to the heavens. Sígrdrífa's other alter egos, the reincarnating Valkyrie, are also described exactly like Gerðr, emitting rays of light.

In Helgakvíða Hiǫrvarðssonar, the first Valkyrie, Sígrlinn, is taken out of the realm of Sleep by the hero, who marries her. The realm of Sleep (Svávaland) happens to be a land of flickering flame, afire. Later, in Helgakvíða Hundingsbani I, we learn that the third reincarnation of the Valkyrie and her following of eight other Valkyrie come from the Mountain of Flames:

15. Then light radiated from the Mountain of Flames and from that radiance came the bolts of lightning they wore their helmets in the Fields of Heaven	*15. Þa brá lioma af Logafiollom, enn af þeim liomom leiptrir qvomo; þa var vnd hialmom a Himinvanga*

If the references to heavenly illuminating powers such as the sun was not clear enough, the Valkyrie are continuously called Southern Goddesses throughout all the heroic poems, just as the southern direction was clearly associated with the Sun and her origins. They are also called "gold-adorned" and "sun bright". Is the Sun goddess the "real" face behind all the ladies who serve mead in a ritual context? Is she behind all the other Dísir? I would not go that far, seeing as there are some who seem to be more descriptive of the Earth goddess, such as Hel, Urðr, Gunnlǫð and Þór's bright mother.

Maybe we do not need to look for any "real face", but just accept what seemed to be taken for granted by the myth-makers that the separation between entities is fluid and superficial. We really do seem to be talking of some inherent unifying core, an inner soul, perhaps a "central sun" to all the aspects of feminine divinity. This does not make one entity more real and true than any other. They coexist, sharing an inner unity, the function of illumination, whether cosmic and natural or spiritual and metaphorical. It would seem that the ancient Sun goddess has been the model for most of the mythical maidens associated with spiritual illumination, although the Earth goddess comes a good second.

Sámi symbol of the Sun on a rune drum

As to the Sun, the identification would certainly include the goddess Freyia, who owns the precious Brisingamén the Jewel of Flames and whose eyes weep golden tears. I have touched upon the subject of the goddess representing something akin to the soul, perhaps a universal soul, as well as the inner soul-fate-goddess of each individual. The fact that one of the Sun goddess's most important nicknames is Elf Splendor is significant here. The elves in Norse traditions seem clearly enough to be representing the souls of the dead. Dead souls who haunted the burial mounds were called elves, and the spirits of the ancestors were worshiped during the autumn celebration known as Alfablót the Sacrifice to the Elves.

The dǫkkalfar "dark elves" were associated with the underworld and the burial mounds, but there were also the Ljósálfar "light elves" who lived in the three upper heavens that are higher than the gods and where Hel does not rule, insinuating that they are the immortal souls of people and gods who have achieved spiritual illumination. These are silently present at the banquets of the gods, and all of them have, according to Lokasenna, been Freyia's lovers. Seeing that the elves represent the souls, we realize that the name of the Sun goddess could in fact be paraphrased as "Soul Splendor".

The splendor in question, Rǫðull, has to do with light and illumination, so that we could perhaps be speaking of an Illuminated Soul. Before we dismiss this possibility as pure speculation, we ought to have a look at the closes neighbor to Old Norse mythical lore; the mythology of the Sami people. Here, the sun goddess Beaivi Nieida [Sun Maiden] was believed to be the sole origin of all souls, mother to all life. The souls were perceived to be rays of light emerging from the mother source, reaching the Earth where the Ancestral Mother received them and distributed the souls into the wombs of female earthlings. The concept echoes the idea of the Sun goddess shining upon the Earth goddess, who then brings forth life. No comparison to actual organic male-female procreation is made here but this does not mean that those who originally created the myths were ignorant of the role of fathers in conception.

It just means that they saw the Sun and the Earth as goddesses, and were able to observe how the two cosmic entities interacted in order to create life. The idea of the Sun mother as the origin of all souls is actually widely known all over the Siberian and Finno-Ugric traditions, reaching back into prehistory. In countless myths from these regions and language groups, the Sun is the mother of souls, and the receiver of the dead souls, usually existing in the South, where there is a great lake of resurrection, and where the souls are compared to waterbirds. Likewise, in Old Norse myths, the South is not only the place from which the Sun emerges in various disguises, but is also the realm of the Norns , who nourish the World tree, who own a water of resurrection, and where the Norns and Valkyrie take the shape of swans. I think there are plenty of indications that the goddesses, particularly the Norns and Valkyrie, are associated with souls. This also takes us back to the great Norn Urðr, who is the Origin of them all.

3.17: NOT QUITE THE CHRISTIAN POEM AFTER ALL-SÓLARLIÓÐTHE SONG OF THE SUN-

I think that when we begin to appreciate the importance of the Dísir and their great, unifying Dís in Old Norse Myths, it also becomes possible to understand lots of myths and poems that have been dismissed as unintelligible and confused. The basic myth of the Mead Woman shows a structure of initiation undertaken by important men and women, where the Bright Maiden is an icon and a symbol of the illuminated state. This icon was important in the Old Norse religion, and continuously referred to by poets, who assumed that their audience knew what they were talking about.

When the poet of the Song of the Sun switched between a Christian and a Pagan worldview, he was comparing the two different concepts of death and resurrection, in fact salvation. It is the goddesses who offer salvation in Old Norse Paganism, representing the resurrected soul and the power over fate, even after death. This is why the poet always refers to female powers in his vision of death and resurrection. He also refers to known themes from the lore of initiation. I am now going to go through several of the Pagan stanzas of the Sun Song:

11. United they were, Sleep Wave and Abundance Heath Dweller The one could not be without the other until they were driven to frenzy over a woman: She was created for their downfall	11. Sáttir þeir váru Sváfuðr ok Skartheðinn, hvárgi mátti annars án vera, fyrr enn þeir œddusk fyr einni konu: hon var þeim til lýta lagin
12. They cared no longer on account of the Bright Maiden for games nor happy days no other thing could they pay attention to than Her illuminated shape.	12. Hvárskis þeir gáðu fyr þá Hvítu Mey, leiks né ljósra daga; ǫngvan hlut máttu þeir annan muna en þat ljósa lík.
15. No man should entertain arrogance I have in truth seen that those who follow Her, for the most part turn from God	*15. Ofmetnað drýgja skyldi engi maðr, þat hefik sannliga sét; því at þeir hverfa, en hánum Fylgja, flestir guði frá*

Without any understanding of the Bright Maiden as a central icon of the Pagan path towards spiritual illumination, crucial to our true understanding of Norse myths, we cannot understand these lines as anything but a "confused" reference to men who fight over women, a kind of moralistic nagging, a Christian disapproval of the female lures, otherwise irrelevant to the context of the poem. However, if we realize that the woman in question is the icon of the illuminating and resurrecting goddess soul, we begin to see an entirely different transmission one of esoteric, spiritual wisdom. Who are the two men who fight over the girl? Their names indicate something, Sleep Wave and Abundance Heath Dweller, but I cannot make a certain statement.

However, I am reminded of the concept of the battle between two kinds of attitudes that are seen in the poem Hyndlulióð. In this poem, the young man, Óttarr, must seek esoteric knowledge in the underworld, in order to reach Valhǫll. He will have to use this wisdom against his opponent Angantýr. This latter name actually means "Pleasure Beast". To overcome the desire for pleasure is not unusually a quite important element in the quest for enlightenment in many traditions. Óttar's name has an uncertain meaning, but could possibly mean Fear Warrior (from otti, m.sg: "fear" and arr (m.sg.) "Warrior"). The importance of overcoming fear is emphasized time and time again in the initiation lore. These two have to fight if Óttarr is to claim his "heritage" and come to Valhǫll.

The combat between the hero initiate and an ogre opponent who also seeks to own the bright maiden is very common. In the case of Helgi Hiǫrvarðssonar, one of the opponents is called Hatred. That the giants want to own "the Maiden of the gods" is a known theme, as we see in the abduction of Iðunn and the threats against Freyia. Another important theme is to wake up one's sleeping powers, and to overcome the oblivion of "sleep". This seems to be referred to in the name Sleep Wave. The Heath Dweller is a reference to someone who lives in a holy place.

As I see it, this is a matter of whether one is to own and marry one's own soul, or let it disappear to darkness, oblivion and destructive powers. That to seek the Bright Maiden is compared with arrogance is consistent with the Christian idea that the seeking of knowledge is sinful, in fact the very reason why we were expelled from paradise. God did not want us to eat of the Fruit of Knowledge, lest we might also eat from the Fruit of Immortality and become like gods ourselves.

Whereas this is considered a terrible, mortal, arrogant sin in most Christian dogmatic traditions, mysteriously associated with sex, mainly because the first to eat from the Fruit of Knowledge was a woman. The Pagans and their path were all about Knowledge and Immortality a quest worthy of gods and accessible to people. When the poet states that those who "follow Her" turn from God, he is possibly referring to people who rather follow the Pagan path and thus turn away from the Christian god. A little good advice is given, about the power of the goddesses to grant your desires:

25. Ask you the goddesses to your aid they who are of the speech of the Ruler to be benevolent to you in intent for a week after all shall pass according to your will all shall pass as you wish

25. Dísir bið þú þér
dróttins mála
vera hollar í hugum;
viku eptir
mun þér vilja þíns
alt at óskum ganga

LLater, the poet moves into the realm of death, letting the main character describe his experience in the Pagan realm of Hel. First, his experience of being close to death:

37. The ropes of Hel came tightly bound around my sides I wanted to tear them but they were very hard It is easy to go free

37. Heljar reip
kómu harðliga
sveigð at síðum mér;
slíta ek vilda,
en þau seig váru;
létt er lauss at fara

38. I alone knew how on all sides
my pains increased The Maidens
of Hel to my horror, invited me to
their home, each evening

38. Einn ek vissa,
hversu alla vega
sullu sútir mér;
Heljar Meyar
er mér hrolla buðu
heim á hverju kveldi

The Maidens of Hel refers to the forces of death. That they seek the (sexual) company of men is a typical Pagan Norse way of describing death. Death is frequently described as a sexual encounter between a man and one of the countless faces of Hel, and their invitation "home" is an indication that death is close by. Our hero proceeds to have a last vision before his death, and the vision is clearly about the Sun goddess, the ultimate Pagan symbol of the resurrecting goddess:

39. I saw the Sun true Star of Day
sink into her roaring home and by
the Gate of Hel I heard, from the
other side A heavy creaking.

39. Sól ek sá
sanna Dagstjǫrnu
drúpa dynheimum í;
en Heljar grind
heyrða ek á annan veg
þjóta þungliga.

40. I saw the Sun beset with blood
beams I was fast declining from he
halls of the world she seemed more
powerful in many ways than she
had been before.

40. Sól ek sá
setta dreyrstǫfum,
mjǫk var ek þá ór heimi hallr;
máttug hon leizk
á marga vegu
frá því er fyrri var.

41. I saw the Sun and it seemed
to me that I was seeing a glorious
deity; to Her I bowed for one last
time in this world of ages

41. Sól ek sá,
svá þótti mér,
sem ek sæja gǫfgan guð;
henni ek laut
hinzta sinni
aldaheimi í.

42. I saw the Sun she beamed so
splendidly that I thought myself
to know nothing and the streams
of the river of Hel roared from
the other side blended much with
blood

42. Sól ek sá,
svá hon geislaði,
at ek þóttumk vætki vita;
en Gylfar straumar
grenjuðu á annan veg,
blandnir mjǫk við blóð

43. I saw the Sun with quivering
eyes appalled and shrinking
because my heart was to a great
degree torn apart in languor

43. Sól ek sá
á sjónum skjálfandi,
hræzlufullr ok hnip inn;
þvíat hjarta mitt
var heldr mjǫk
runnit sundr í sega

44. I saw the Sun and was seldom
sadder I was now far from the alls
of the world my tongue had turned
into wood and all around me was
cold.

44. Sól ek sá
sjaldan hryggvari,
mjǫk var ek þá ór heimi hallr;
tunga mín
var til trés metin,
ok kólnat alt fyr utan.

45. I saw the Sun and then never
again after that gloomy day for
the waters of the mountain closed
around me and I was called from
my pains.

45. Sól ek sá
síðan aldregi
eptir þann dapra dag,
þvíat fjallavǫtn luk tusk
fyr mér saman,
en ek hvarf kallaðr frá kvǫl

When I began to take these lines seriously, it finally dawned on me that our "Christian" poet actually described a vision of the Pagan goddess of illumination before death. This is actually in accordance with your typical initiation structure in Old Norse myths, where the hero or god has a vision of the Bright Maiden before he enters the realm of death. The poet also seems, in my opinion, to lament his ancient goddess, bowing before her one final time.

When we realize that all Old Norse Paganism was not "Odinic" but included an extremely important path of illumination where Óðinn was a first seeker, but where the Bright Maiden was that which was sought, the true depth of Pagan thought in this "Christian" poem reveals itself. That there is a link between the Goddess and the personal soul is made clear by the poet in the next stanza, where the Sun the Star of Hope is compared to the heart, and where the poet feels as if she has been cut out of him perhaps because of the new religion:

46. The Star of Hope flew when I
was born cut out from my chest
she soared high never settled so
that she might have found peace

46. Vánarstjarna flaug,
þá var ek fœddr,
brot frá brjósti mér;
hátt at hon fló,
hvergi settisk,
svá at hon mætti hvíld hafa

The poet proceeds to describe his experiences in the realm of death, where he finds himself in the "Seat of the Norns", reminding us of the "judgment of the Norns" which according to the Fafnismál poem is due for all humans after death.

51.In the Seat of the Norns I sat
for nine days then I was placed
on a horse The Sun of the Giantess
shone in disguise through the
dripping clouds of the sky

51. Á Norna stóli
sat ek níu daga,
þaðan var ek á hest hafinn;
Gýgjar Sól
er skein grimmliga
ór skýdrúpnis skýjum

The nine days are typical of the death journey in Norse myths, as it is of the initiation journey. Hel rules nine spheres, the number of days it takes to reach her High Hall is nine, and Óðinn hung for nine nights before he reached his illumination. The horse is a symbol of the journey between worlds, and the sun, the Soul, shines "in disguise". After the journey and some Christian interferences, more Pagan references are made:

55. The Hart of the Sun I saw arrive from the South he was led by two together his feet stood planted on Earth his horns spread into Heaven.

55. Sólar hjǫrt leit ek sunnan fara, hann teymðu tveir saman; fœtr hans stóðu foldu á, en tóku horn til himins

56. From the North I saw riding the sons of Below and they were seven together from brimming full horns they drank the pure mead from the Well of the Lord of the Ring is horns spread into Heaven

56. Norðan sá ek ríða Niðja sonu, ok váru sjau saman; hornum fullum drukku þeir hinn hreina mjǫð ór brunni Baugregins

After a long list of more Christian interruptions, we are back in Hel, learning about the two female guardians of the gates of Hel (the Army Goddess):

76. Bow Spring and Wisdom Spring guard the doors of Army Goddess from the Bellower Seat (death) blood of iron fall from their nostrils this kindles hatred among men

76. Bjúgvǫr ok Listvǫr sitja í Herðis dyrum organs stóli á; járna dreyri fellr ór nǫsum þeim, sá vekr fjón með fyrðum

77. Óðin's woman rows the ship of Earth she is bound towards pleasure her sails are reefed late they are hung with the ropes of desire

77. Óðins kván rœr á Jarðar skipi, móðug á munað seglum hennar verðr síð hlaðit; þeim er á þráreipum þruma

It would seem, here, that Óðin's woman, Frigg or Freyia, is here presented as the ruler of the journey of life its fate but that she may be despised as bound to pleasure and desire, a Christian attitude to what was once regarded as divine, the lust for life and the sacredness of enjoyment. Still, the poet proceeds to refer to the ancient path of initiation, as if trying to say that he has revealed what he can of the ancient path disguised behind Christian interference:

78. Son! As your father
I have counseled you, as have the
sons of Sun Cauldron Woman,
towards the Horn of the Heart that
he brought from the death-mound
that wise Hibernation of War

79.Here are runes that have been
carved by the nine daughters of
Njǫrðr :
Counsel Power Drink the oldest
Approaching Spring the youngest
and their seven sisters.

78. Arfi! faðir
einn þér ráðit hefi,
ok þeir Sólkǫtlu synir,
hjartar horn,
þat er ór haugi bar
hinn vitri Vígdvalinn

79. Hér 'ru rúnar,
er ristit hafa
Njarðar dœtr níu:
Ráðveig hin elzta
ok Kreppvǫr hin yngsta
ok þeirra systr sjau

4: Retrieving the Soul of the Gods

Haustlǫnga Skaldic Poem: What poetical metaphors convey about mythical characters

4.1: A shield poem of the Viking Age

Then all the powers went to the chairs of fate (parliament) the high holy gods to discuss this matter: Who had blended the air all with harm? Or to the giant kind given Poetry's Maiden?

Þá gengu regin ǫll
    á rǫkstóla,
    ginnheilug goð,
    ok um þat gættusk:
    hverr hefði lopt allt
    lævi blandit
    eða ætt jǫtuns
    Óðs mey gefna

Vǫluspá st. 25, Poetic Edda

In this Chapter, I will use the famous myth of the abduction of the goddess Iðunn by the giant Þjazi in order to discuss some very basic yet often overlooked features of the Old Norse worldview. The myth is one of the few Old Norse myths that we can say, with certainty, was known during the Pagan era, as we know it was retold in a poem at the court of King Harald Hárfagri in Norway around the year 900 AD, and thus during the Viking Age. The Viking Age source to the myth is the skaldic poem Haustlǫng, a title that refers to the long autumn. The poem was composed around the year towards the end of the 9th century by the Norwegian poet Þióðolfr ór Hvíni [Thiodolf of Kvinir], who was a scald [bard, poet] at Harald's court, and who was also known as Þióðolfr Fróði Thióðolf the Wise.

As such, Thióðolf's poetry ranked among Snorri Sturluson's most important sources to mythology, and as a poet was his greatest inspiration. Haustlǫng is what is called a "shield-poem" or an "image-describing poem", that is, a poem describing the painted images on a shield. Thióðolf, the poet, received a precious, painted shield by a certain Þorleif as a gift. The Vikings believed that a gift demanded a gift in return, and whereas Þorleif could make painted shields, Thióðolf could compose poetry, so his return gift for the precious shield was this poem, describing the mythical scenes painted on the shield.

On one side of the shield was an illustration describing the myth of how the goddess Iðunn was stolen by the giant Þjazi, on the other side an illustration to the myth of Þórr and Hrungnir. This poem is thus a source which serves as evidence that these myths were authentic Pagan myths already well known at the beginning of the 10th century. These myths were explained and retold by Snorri in his Prose Edda 320 years later.

4.2: SHAMANIC SOUL-RETRIEVAL

I decided to focus on the first part of the poem describing the myth of Iðunnn's abduction with the emphasis on how the poetical metaphors applied in the poem may serve as an insight into how the mythical characters were perceived in the Pagan era, since the metaphors describe these characters and because we know that these description were referring to actual Viking Age perceptions and cosmology. I will also look at how the myth may be analyzed as a description of a shamanic journey with the purpose of retrieving a lost soul. A shaman is someone who travels into other worlds, often in a different shape than the usual human body, and who brings revelations from the other side and from the gods. The shaman is an intermediary between different existential planes in the cosmos.

Loki's journey in this myth, wearing the shape of a falcon in order to fly into another world is a typical shamanic journey. Shamanism was certainly known in the Old Norse world, through interaction with the Sami and with Siberian cultures, as well as through strong native shamanic elements within the Old Norse arts of seiðr and galðr. Shamanic elements are without doubt strongly present within Old Norse myths, which are rich in their countless descriptions of changing shape and traveling into other worlds in order to retrieve lost souls or acquire hidden knowledge.

Shamanic journeys are often about healing. A common explanation for sickness and death in shamanic cultures is the loss of one's soul. It is either the soul (or one of the souls) of a person that has lost its way during its many journeys in other worlds, or it has been abducted by powerful forces and kept in the underworld. Loss of soul will lead to sickness and eventually to death. The healing in a shamanic culture is thus the journey to that other world where the soul is held captive or finds itself lost, so that it may be found and restored to its person.

4.3: THE MYTH OF IÐUNN AND ÞJAZI SNORRI'S VERSION (1225 AD)

In Snorri's work, the poet Bragi tells the story of Iðunn and Þjazi with an explanation of a kenning as a starting point. He wants to explain why Iðunn, his wife, is called "Þjazi's booty". This is the entry to the entire Prose Edda treatise known as the Skáldskaparmál. It all begins with three Aesir, Óðinn, Loki and Hænir, going for a journey through "un-built mountains and forests", that is, through the wilderness. The wilderness is in itself often a symbol for the underworld or the land of giants. The three gods have trouble finding food, and when they finally manage to kill a bull, it turns out impossible to cook.

The reason for this is the sorcery wielded by a huge eagle which turns out to be seated in the tree above the Aesir. This eagle is in reality the giant Þjazi [Slave-Binder], who demands a share of the game if they want to succeed in cooking it. The Aesir agree, but are tricked. The eagle takes the whole bull. This provokes Loki, who hits the eagle with a staff, but the staff glues itself between the shoulders of the eagle, and Loki's hands are glued to the staff, and thus Þjazi flies a way with Loki as a captive.

Loki begs for mercy but is told that if he wants to be freed he has to swear to bring the goddess Iðunn with her apples to the giant. Loki promises to do this and as he returns home, he tricks the goddess out of Ásgarðr and lets the giant eagle abduct her. The gods immediately start to age, because only Iðunn can restore their youth and thus keep them immortal. The aging, desperate Aesir accuse Loki of treason and demand that he shall get the goddess back. Loki then borrows the falcon hide of Freyr and flies north to the giant worlds. He finds Iðunn, changes her into a nut and flies away with her.

Þjazi follows in his eagle hide "so that it blew from his wings", but is killed by a fire that the Aesir have put up as he enters the divine realms. The consequences of the murder of Þjazi is that the giant's daughter, Skaði ["Harm" or "Injury"] threatens to destroy Ásgarðr. The Aesir promise to appease the powerful giantess by giving her a husband among the Aesir and by making her laugh. Skaði accepts this and marries Njǫrðr (because his feet are the most beautiful), but laughs only when Loki falls into her lap after having had a goat pulling his genitals.

The joke can be understood if we take seriously the fact that Skaði's name means "harm", "injury", and that the joke is on Loki falling right into harm's lap. Skaði later divorces Njǫrðr and returns to her abode, Þrymheimr where she hunts in the mountains and enjoys the howling of wolves. She later has children by Óðinn who become the ancestors of several Norwegian royal clans, as Snorri describes in his Ynglinga saga 8:

> "Njǫrðr had a wife called Skaði, she would not have intercourse with
> him and later she married Óðinn; they had many sons, one of them called
> Sæmingr, about him Eyvind Skaldaspiller [920-990 A.D] sang this;
> > With the Maiden of Iron Forest [= Skaði]
> > The Ancestral Father of the Aesir [= Óðinn]
> > Made a Treasure Earl [= Sæmingr]
> > When these two, the Friend of Warriors [= Óðinn] and Skaði settled in
> > the world of men; and many other sons bore the Goddess of Skiing from
> > the mountains [= Skaði] to Óðinn.
> > Hákon Earl the powerful counted his line back to Sæmingr."

Skaði's and Þjazi's abode Þrymheimr means "The World of Þrymr" and is named after the giant who stole Þórr's hammer in Þrymskviða. The name seems to refer to drumming, if Þrymr is derived from Þruma, which means to drum, to beat, or just to "make sound". Thus Þjazi may very well be identified with the giant Þrymr, and the essential function of his stealing the hammer may be compared with the stealing of the goddess. Like Iðunn, the hammer of Þórr is associated with resurrection from death and the restoration to life, as shown when Þórr wields it over the bones of his rams, bringing them back to life.

Likewise, Iðunn, symbolized by her apples or by the seed she possesses in the myth, is the power that restores the youth of the gods and thus gives them a kind of immortality. The story ends with a short dialogue between Aegir and Bragi. Aegir wants to hear about the lineage of this Þjazi, and learns that he is one of Ǫlvaldi [Ale-Ruler]'s three sons. This giant was very rich and his sons had to share the gold after him by each taking a mouthful of it, which is why the gold is called "the mouth-speech of the giants" or the "tongue" or "words" or "speech" of the giants. Aegir has the last words, concluding that "this is cunningly disguised in runes."

4.4: The myth of Iðunn and Þjazi Thióðolf's version (900 ad)

I am going to render a translation/ interpretation of the part of the poem Haustlǫng describing the theft of Iðunn, following the suggestions of Finnúr Jónsson when it comes to the sentence building. The sentence building of the poem is almost incomprehensible to modern eyes, so Finnúr Jónsson rearranged the words in his 1912 rendition in order to make more sense. It is this rearrangement which is rendered here. I have also used Jónsson's translation as my most important source to translating these lines. The actual sentence building of the poem may be read at Heimskringla[4] In the first stanza, the bard Thióðolf declares that he wishes to thank Thorleif for a shield that he has given him.

The shield is painted with mythical images, and Thióðolf introduces us to the myth: He can see (on the shield) three gods and Þjazi. We are thus placed in the beginning of the myth, which Thióðolf's audience knew was the story of how the three Aesir traveled and met Þjazi in the "un-built mountains".

Haustlǫng ["prolonged autumn"] by Þióðolfr ór Hvínir, rearranged by Finnúr Jónsson. Translation by Maria Kvilhaug (based on Finnúr Jónsson 1912 edition).

Norse text (Rearranged sentences by F. Jónsson)	Literal Translation	Meaning
2. Snótar Ulfr fló glammi fyr ó-skǫmmu at móti Segjǫndum Sagna í gǫmlum Gemlis ham; ǫrn settisk ár, þars Æsir bǫru mat á seyði; Byrgi-Týr Bjarga Gefnar vasa bleyði vændr.	2.The Eloquent Woman's (= Iðunn's) Wolf (= abductor) flew with loud sounding wing-flapping for a non-short time ago to The Tellers of the Stories wearing the ancient shape of the Year-Old (= young bird =) Eagle The Eagle settled in the beginning (of time) where the Aesir carried food to the earth-oven The Fortress-Animal (= giant) of the Mountains of the (female) Provider (= giantess) (= burial mound) was no lowly coward.	2. = Þjazi (Slave-Binder = Death/ Mortality) flew with the power of Death a very long time ago to the Aesir/gods wearing the ancient shape of Death Death settled in the beginning (of time) where the spirit entities brought nourishment to matter Þjazi = Death was bold/fierce.

---

4 (http://www.heimskringla.no/wiki/Haustlǫng_(B1))

3.

Meðal-tálhreinn
vas tormiðluðr beina
tívum;
hjalmfaldinn
hapta snytrir
kvað hvat valda því;
margspakr valkastar
bǫru mór of nam
mæla af fornum þolli;
Hœnis vinr vasat hollr
hǫnum

3. Partly Unblended Treason as late to begin the cooking for the godsL The helmet clad Giver of Eloquence to the Chains (= gods) claimed that someone was behind this

The Very Wise Corpse-Thrower of Wave Guts-Seagull (= Eagle) spoke from the Age-Old Tree (Yggdrasill) Hænir's (Mind's) Friend was not fond of him.

3. = Þjazi (Death) failed to nourish the gods

The physical manifestation .of = Óðinn (Spirit) claimed that someone was behind this

The Very Wise = Þjazi (Death) spoke from the physical universe Loki (Passion, friend of Mind) hated/feared it

4.

Fjallgylðir
bað fet-Meila
deila sér fyllar
af helgum skutli;
hrafnásar vinr
hlaut blása;
Vígfrekr
Vingvagna-Rǫgnir
lét sígask ofan,
þars vélsparir varnendr goða
vǫru farnir

4. The Mountain Howler (= Wolf) asked Armor Step = Hænir to share with him a part of the sacred meal The Friend of the Raven God(= Óðinn) had to blow the fire The Battle-Hungry Ruler of the Wagon of Friendship let himself descend from above to where the Loyal Protectors of Gods had arrived.

4. = Þjazi (Death) asked Mind to share with him a part of the sacred life = Loki (Passion) had to ensure life = Þjazi (Death let himself descend from above to where Spirit,Mind and Passion had arrived.

5.

Þekkiligr dróttinn foldar
bað fljótt Fárbauta mǫg deila
hval Várar Þrýmrseilar

með þegnum,
en bragðvíss ósvífrandi ása
lagði at þat fjóra þjórhluti
upp af breiðu bjóði

5. The Decent King of the Earth quickly told the Son of Farbauti to share the Whale of the Goddess of the Drumming Belt with the Serving Man And the Cunning-Clever Defier of Gods now parted the bull in four up from the broad table

5. = Óðinn (Spirit) quickly told Loki to share

= The bull (matter/ sacrifice) with Þjazi (Death)

= Loki (Passion) now parted the matter in four, up from the altar

6.

Ok svangr
faðir Marnar
át síðan slíðrliga okbjǫrn
af eikirótum
- þat vas fyr lǫngu,
áðr djúphugaðr hirði-Týr
herfangs dræpi stǫngu
ballastan dolg vallar
ofan meðal herða

6. And the Hungry Father of the Giantess(= Skaði) then ate greedily the Yoke-Bear = bull of the oak-roots (= oak = ash) - This was a long time ago before the Deep-of-Soul Hiding Beast battered the War-Trophy with a staff: (he hit) the Powerful Enemy of Earth from above between the shoulders

6. And the hungry = Þjazi (Death) then ate greedily of life of the roots of Yggdrasill This was a long time ago before Loki (Passion) battered Death with a staff: (he hit) Þjazi (Death) from above between the shoulders

7. Þá varð farmr arma
Sigvinjar,

sás ǫll regin eygja í
bǫndum,
fastr við fóstra ǫndurgoðs;

.

rǫ́ loddi við ramman
reimuð Jǫtunheima,
en hendr holls vinar
Hœnis
við stangar enda

7. Then was The Burden of Sigyn's Arms whom all gods perceive in chains, tied to The Educator of the Ski-Deity(= Skaði)(= Þjazi)		7. Then was Loki (Passion) whom all gods perceive in chains, tied to Death The staff was glued to
The staff was glued to the Ghost of the Giant World and the hands of Hænis (= Mind's)Faithful Friend were glued to the staff.		= Þjazi (Death) and the hands of Passion were glued to the staff.

**Norse text
(Rearranged sentences
by F. Jónsson)**

Literal Translation

Meaning

8. Sveita Nagr
fló fangsæll of langan veg
með Fróðgum Tívi,
svát Ulfs Faðir
mundi slitna sundr;
þá varð Ofrúni Þórs
biðja mǫlunaut miðjungs
friðar,
hvat's mátti;
þungr Loptr vas of
sprunginn

8. The Vulture of the Flock happy with the catch, flew a long way with the Clever God so that the Wolf's Father was about to be torn apart.

Then Thor's Friend had to beg for mercy from Giant-Child despite all his power the Heavy Air was about to break

8. Þjazi (Death) happy with the catch, flew a long way with Loki so that Loki was about to be torn apart
Then Loki (Passion) had to beg for mercy from Death(Þjazi) despite all his power = Loki (Breath/Life) was about to break

9. Áttrunnr Hymis
bað sagna hrœri,
sorgœran,
fœra sér Mey,
þás Kunni Ellilyf Ása;
Brísings goða girðiþjófr
of kom síðan
Brunnakrs Bekkjar Dísi
í garða grjót-Níðaðar

9. The Lineage-Tree of Hymir asked the Stirrer of Stories, mad with pain, to bring to him The Maiden Who Knows the Age-Cure of the Aesir
The Belt-Thief of the Fiery Gods then brought
The Goddess of the Well-Field-Benches
to the world of the Rock-Ruler Beneath

9. Þjazi (Death) asked Loki (Passion), mad with pain, to bring to him Iðunn (Immortality) Loki then brought Iðunn (= Immortality) to the world of Þjazi (Death)

10. Byggvendr Brattra
Barða
urðut hryggvir at þat;
þá vas Iðunnr nýkomin
sunnan með jǫtnum;
allar áttir Ingvifreys,
gamlar ok hárar,
gættusk at þingi
regin vǫ́ru heldr hamljót

10. The Residents of the Steep Mountains were then not sad that Iðunn had come from the South to the giants
All the clans of Yngvi-Freyr aging and grey-haired went to the Parliament
The Rulers were rather ugly to watch

10. The Giants were then very happy that Iðunn (Immortality) had come from Ásgarðr to the giants All the gods aging and grey-haired went to the Parliament The gods looked terrible

Norse text (Rearranged sentences by F. Jónsson)	Literal Translation	Meaning
11. Unz (Text and translation: uncertain, reconstructed by Finnur Jónsson) Qlgefn þú skalt vélum véltr, Loki, Vreiðr mælti svá, nema leiðir aptr Mæra Mey, Stærandi Mun Hapta.	11. Until they found the Blood-Hound of the Flowing Corpse Sea (= wolf = thief)of the Ale-Provider and bound the thief, the Tree of Treason who had led the Ale-Provider astray "You shall suffer terribly, Loki," thus spoke the Angry One "until you return with The Wonderful Maiden Who Increases the Joy of the Chains (= gods)	11. Until they found the abductor of the Source of the Drink of Immortality (Iðunn) (= Loki) and bound the thief, Loki (Passion), who had led Iðunn (Immortality/ Wisdom) astray "You shall suffer terribly, Loki," thus spoke Thor; "until you return with The Goddess Who Bestows Immortality on the Gods (Iðunn)."
12. Heyrðak svá, þat Hugreynandi Hœnis síðan sveik opt Ösu Leikum Fló aukinn hauks bjalfa, ok lómhugaðr faðir Marnar, ern fjaðrar blaðs Leikreginn lagði Arnsúg at Öglis Barni	12. I have heard this that Hænir's (= Mind's) Intent-Tester later tricked back the Lover of the Aesir He flew away in the shape of a hawk and the Father of the Giantess = Þjazi that swift wing-flapping King-Tricker followed with Eagle-Wind the Child of the Hawk	12. I have heard this that Loki (Passion) later tricked back Immortality (Iðunn) he flew away in the shape of a hawk and Þjazi (Death) that swiftly fatal Þjazi (Death) followed with Mortality after Loki
13. Skǫpt hófu skjótt brinna, en Ginnregin skófu, en sonr Biðils Greipar sviðnar - sveipr varð í fǫr.	13. The wood began to burn that the Sacred Pow-ers had made into fuel and the son of the Wooer of the Grasping One (= giantess) burnt. In suddenness his journey ended.	13. The matter began to burn that the gods had made into fuel and Þjazi (Death) burnt. In suddenness his journey ended.

As we can see, Thiodolf's skaldic poem only refers to the first part of the myth about Iðunn and Þjazi the part which is about Skaði is only indirectly referred to through kennings for Þjazi as the "father of the giantess" or the "father of the skiing deity" (Skaði is the goddess of skiing). We are going to go through particular themes and characters in the story and see how the metaphors may provide clues to understanding the myth itself and Pagan cosmology in general.

4.5: The meaning of the journey of the three gods

In the first stanza, we are introduced to a familiar scenario. Three gods are traveling abroad. The second stanza makes it clear that this happened a "non-short time ago". That is typical Old Norse understatement signifying that this happened an extremely long time ago, in fact at the dawn of time itself. The impression of archaic origins is strengthened by expressions such as "the old" eagle hide and the "age-old" tree. The scenario itself is known from other genesis myths. In Skáldskaparmál, Snorri tells a story about how the gold is known as the Otter-Ransom, and it begins in the same way, with Óðinn, Loki and Hænir out to explore the newly created world. What happens on that journey also has consequences for all descendants. In the Vǫluspá of the Poetic Edda, we also hear about three gods who travel "out" in the beginning times.

In the stanzas 17 and 18 the vǫlva explains that Óðinn, Hænir and Hlóðurr ["Heat" a probable heiti for Loki] "came out from the flock" (of dwarfs, actually) and gave to human beings spirit, breath, thought, mind, vitality and "beautiful colors". According to Mircea Eliade, all myths are tales of origin, beginnings and creations. They function to give humans existential orientations by explaining the sacred origins of their own practices. The myths are archetypal, they explain why the world became what it is. These genesis myths continue and compliment the first cosmic creation myth. All the myths beginning with the three gods are in my opinion such genesis myths telling about the start of an important event. According to Gro Steinsland, the number three is not coincidental. Important cosmic events that create great change in the world always happen after the appearance of three gods, three Norns or three giantesses. The number is dynamic and symbolizes change. Thus our first conclusion is that what happens in the myth of Iðunn and Þjazi is a myth of origin, but origin to what?

4.6: The origin of a sacred path

From stanza 4 we learn something that Snorri does not tell us. The meal of the gods is sacred, and the giant wants to partake in a sacred meal a sacred act. The food is prepared in an "earth oven" (seyð) and laid out on a "broad table", i.e. an altar. A point is made out of how Loki has to work that is, to "blow" to make the cooking fire, and I think that this is not coincidental. The stanza is about how this terrifying, enormous cosmic power the eagle-giant "descends" into the sacred act, and how the "friend of the gods" is ordered to establish a particular and sacred course of action. Since the sacred act is a meal shared between cosmic powers, and involving the killing of a sacrificial animal (the bull), I lean towards to the sacred course of action known as sacrifice, performed by "the friend of the gods", which not only refers to Loki but probably to a sacrificial priest.

The sacrifice also leads to a journey into the other world, implying a death. This journey is shamanic in itself. The goddess Iðunn is left in the world of the dead, with the result that all the gods begin to age and die. The restoration of the goddess brings resurrection and rejuvenation to the gods, and happens only after a shape-changing journey undertaken by Loki, the prototypical shaman, who finds and rescues the goddess from the underworld.

This is akin to a shamanic soul-retrieval journey with the purpose of healing, and in this specific case, is about the relative immortality of the gods. That the otherworld journey follows a sacrifice is not unknown from Old Norse myths. In the Edda poem Hyndlulióð, such a journey is undertaken by Óttarr in the shape of a boar, under the guidance of the goddess Freyia. Óttarr is changed into a boar and travels to the underworld only after having "colored the altars red with blood from the sacrifice" in order to honor the goddesses. We can almost certainly assume that the sacrifice was a boar and that Óttar's soul through the magic of the goddess actually merged with the soul of the sacrifice a boar.

It is the sacrificed boar's journey to death that empowers Óttar's own journey. It is very likely that the sacrificed bodies of beasts or of men were thought to be "steeds" for the souls of the living when they wanted to enter the underworld, a concept that may explain the practice of "sitting beneath hanged man" or the sitting on burial mounds in order to travel into other worlds. The eight legs of Óðin's horse Sleipnir may be a reference to the "eight legs" of the funeral bier carried by four men; it is this steed that Óðinn and his followers employ when they want to move into the underworld and other cosmic realms.

Like Óttarr, Loki rides with the sacrificed animal into the world of the dead in this story this is symbolized by how Loki is attached, almost glued, to the sacrificed bull as it is taken by the eagle (death). The second time, however, Loki borrows the hide of a deity (Freyr) in order to travel. It is likely that we are being offered two possible ways of traveling into the unknown. It could happen through the grace of a deity, such as when Freyia changed Óttarr into a boar or when she lent her falcon hide to Loki in the Þrymskvíða, or when Frigg lent her falcon hide to Loki in the, or here, where it is in fact Freyr who lends his falcon hide out to Loki. Or it could happen by taking a ride with a dead or dying entity such as a sacrificed boar, bull, horse or man.

In all the cases we know of, the purpose of the journey is either immortality and resurrection, initiation, or the access to hidden knowledge leading to initiation and resurrection from death. The sacrifice is a means to empower the journey and to beseech the grace and guidance of the gods or goddesses. That the origin of such a practice was remembered in a famous myth indicates that the practice of undertaking the journey to the underworld with the hope of restoring one's immortal soul was a crucial concern in Old Norse Paganism. This origin myth is paralleled only by the story of how humans received their gifts of thought, intelligence, vitality and fate, and the story of how the gods discovered the mysterious "red gold of Alert Spirit" (Andvari), which also seems to be associated with divine wisdom, initiation and resurrection.

4.7: THE VERSE-SMITHS: HOW THE GODS ARE KNOWN

The gods are also called "the tellers of the stories" (Segjandi Sagna). This could refer to the gods being the tellers of this particular tale, but I find it tempting to draw a line to Snorri's presentation of the gods in Gylfaginning and in Heimskringla.

The three gods are referred to as "rulers" or "kings" (regin) and "sacred kings" (ginnregin). This could either just be understood as "rulers", which is obvious since they are gods, or it could be taken more literally as referring to the Aesir as the fathers of royal lines. It could possibly be seen in connection with the kingship cult. That kings were seen as bodily incarnations of gods in some way or other is common in many ancient societies, and many scholars, the most famous being Folke Ström and Gro Steinsland, have emphasized the role of the kings as playing the role of the ancestral god in marriage with the giantess ancestral mother of the land/clan/tribe (Steinsland) or with the great goddess (Ström).

The god may have been perceived as intimately connected with the ruling king, in a way embodying him, whereas the goddess or giantess ancestral mother may have been represented by a priestess during rituals of sacred marriage. Thus "kings" may be referring to ancestors, divine ancestors, and be associated with the ritual of sacred marriage. Gylfaginning is framed by a story of how King Gylfi travels to Ásgarðr. We learn that the Aesir divine his approach and that they prepare great "optical illusions" for him, within which they tell his all about the gods, and the beginning, fate and end of the world. After the entire history of the world is told from beginning to end, Gylfi discovers that he is standing on an empty plain and that all the halls, walls and gods he had just seen and spoken to, are non-existent. He then goes home and tells everybody on the way what he has seen and head, and "one after the other people told these stories".

Not just that, but the Aesir then sat down together and held parliament and remembered what they had told Gylfi, and they gave people and places names according to their own tales. It is in fact only after everything was told that the stories became real. I understand this as meaning that reality was in fact created by their stories. The same theme is actually present in the Skáldskaparmál where it is Aegir who comes and listens to stories. There too we learn that: "a lot of what the Aesir did there were just optical illusions". In Snorri's Heimskringla [The World Circle, his introduction to the sagas of the Norwegian kings] we learn that Óðinn "said everything with rhyme, just like one today performs that which is called skaldskáp (poetry), and he and his temple priests were called verse-smiths." The "temple priests" (hófgoðar) had already been identified as the other gods. A few lines down, the gods are called "charm-smiths" and "verse-smiths".

It has been claimed that Snorri's texts cannot be taken as a source to actual Pagan mythology because he may have invented the stories himself, but the skaldic poem Haustlǫng, dating back to the climax of the Viking Age, shows that the idea of the gods as storytellers is ancient and Pagan in origin.

The Edda poem Vǫluspá is a poem that also tells the entire history of the universe from beginning to end. It is spoken by a vǫlva (a priestess-witch) as a divination that takes the form of seiðr. This art was a form of operative divination which means that what is seen is also made to happen the diviner does not just passively observe but actively makes things happen, as is testified by many descriptions of this practice in the sagas. In this case, the being who tells the story of the universe (and thus creates at the same time) is a witch who lived before time itself started (Vǫluspá st.2) and thus may be counted among the first beings, the creator entities. She, too, "tells" the world into being.

That the gods are verse- charm- and story-makers could on the simple level refer to the gods being powerful bards, but these are in fact gods, and what gods do has to do with the creation and maintenance of the world. One could get the impression that the gods were seen as a sort of magical divine bards who actually "told" the world into being. That the world is a story, dream or illusion is not an unusual idea in the history of the world. We have the saying of a Kalahari bushman rendered by Joseph Campbell in The Mythic Image, and which testifies to the possible antiquity of the idea: "There is a dream dreaming us". We can also go closer to home, in the Old Indian Yogavasistha text (2.3.11) we learn that "the world is like the impression left by the telling of a story". I understand the concept of the gods as storytellers as a way of saying that what they did created a pattern of behavior and course of action for future generations to follow, a sort of matrix for the dramas of life, possibly ritual but also perhaps existential.

4.8: ÞJAZI, THE EAGLE OF DEATH

Óðinn said:
"Tell me the ninth, since you
are said to be wise and you,
Tremendous Veil, know:
From where comes the wind that
moves across the waves?
It may not be seen by men."

Tremendous Veil said:
"Corpse-Swallower he is called
who sits at the end of Heaven
devourer/giant in the shape of
an eagle from his wings, that
said wind comes that is above all
men."

Óðinn qvaþ:
Segðv þat iþ níunda,
allz þic svinnan qveþa,
oc þv, Vafþrúðnir, vitir:
hvadan vindr vm komr,
sva at ferr vág yfir?
e menn hann sialfan vm siá.»

Vafþrúðnir qvaþ:
«Hresvelgr heitir,
er sitr a himins enda,
iotvnn i arnar ham;
af hans vengiom
qveþa vind koma
alla menn yfir.»

Vafþrúðnismál [The Song of the Tremendous Veil], stanza 36 and 37

The unwanted element in the sacrifice is the giant eagle Þjazi, who wants the entire sacrifice for himself. In order to understand this conflict, we need to understand who, or rather what, Þjazi is. The most obvious attribute is his eagle-hide, and his status as a giant. He is of enormous size, which is what Snorri meant when he described the giant as "not small". These little descriptions are significant because this is how we know a character through its particular attributes and functions. In Snorri's Gylfaginning, we hear about two eagles both described as giants in eagle disguise. One of them is called Hræsvelgr and sits by the "end of heaven", and from his wings come "the wind across all people".

Both Snorri and the Edda poem Grímnismál emphasize the wing-flapping and the mysterious cosmic wind that it creates. What kind of "wind" is this? In order to understand what the wind symbolizes, we must look at its origin, the giant in eagle's hide:

→   *Corpse Swallower and Corpse Thrower: It is significant that the name of the giant eagle means "Corpse Swallower" and that he is situated in the northern end of the universe, which is synonymous with Hel, the realm of death. The wind of the wings of the giant eagle is the force of death, the beginning of invisible cosmic movement yet also the devourer of all life. If we compare this with the way Þjazi is described, we see that both Snorri and Thiodolf emphasized the blowing whistling sounds of wind when the eagle flaps his wings. We are probably speaking of exactly the same concept: Death in the shape of an eagle. That impression is utterly strengthened by the metaphors Thiodolf uses to describe Þjazi: He is the "very wise corpse-thrower", [Margspakr válkastar] and he is very svangr "hungry". He also hunts Loki with arnsúg "eagle wind".*

→   *Death-Feeding Vulture: Moreover, he is the "seagull of entrails". Snorri explained how masculine birds (such as seagulls) could be used as metaphors for the eagle, whereas entrails give certain associations to corpses and death. Another bird metaphor for Þjazi is "the vulture of the flock", again giving associations of death, or more specifically, the devouring, demolishing, destructive aspect of death that eats away at the remains of the dead. Again, Snorri mentioned vultures among the masculine birds that could in poetry replace the real meaning, "eagle", and thus embody the very image of devouring death.*

→   *Ghost and Slave Binder: Other associations to death is when Þjazi is called the "ghost of the giant world" and he is the giant of "the mountain of the giantess", which refers to the burial mound. His name Þjazi means the "Slave-Binder", and there is probably no more powerful abductor of "slaves" than Death itself. Like the eagle Hræsvelgr, he lives in the wilderness, which was a common symbol of the underworld and death, and is associated with a giantess (Skaði) who probably also symbolizes death, just like the corpse swallower Hræsvelgr is associated with Hel, the lady of the underworld.*

→   *Top of the Tree: The other giant in eagle hide of the Gylfaginning is not named, but said to be living in the top of the world tree, having constant communication with the roots of the tree and the serpents coiling them through the mediator squirrel Ratatoskr [The Moving Container]. It also has similarities with Þjazi to the point of identification. Apart from the obvious "giant in eagle hide" formula, both sit in an age-old, huge tree, and both are very knowledgeable.*

Interestingly, and probably not incidentally, the question of the eagle of death in the poem Vafþrúðnismál (as quoted above) is the ninth question. The number nine being an important number in Norse poetry. The number nine is among other things associated with death. Not only is the eagle of death mentioned as the ninth question in the Edda poem, Snorri also lets us know that Hel the goddess of death, rules over nine worlds.

In the Edda poem Grímnismál [The Speech of the Hidden One], stanza 14, we learn that the goddess Freyia [Lady Sovereign] receives the chosen dead in the ninth heaven from where she also chooses the slain and decides who shall remain with her and who shall be sent to Óðinn's Valhǫl:

14. People Field is the Ninth (world) and there, Lady Sovereign rules over the seating in the hall (fate) Half the choice (fallen dead) she chooses every day Half she sends to Óðinn	*14. Folcvangr er inn niundi enn þar Freyia reþr sessa costom i sal; halfan val hon kyss hverian dag, enn halfan Óðinn á.*

The giant in eagle disguise is a mythical formula for Death. His creation of "winds" in the universe may be a way of saying that Death is the origin of movement, as well as being the force that ceases all movement as he "swallows" the corpses. His position in the top of the world tree or at the end of the world hints strongly to his immense power over all creation. Þjazi's main function in the poem is exactly to make the Aesir aware of their own mortality.

The eagle is all powerful and even called the leikreginn "the one who plays (tricks) the gods", or else, "the Ruler of Trickery", probably referring to him being the creator of illusion. This in turn identifies the Eagle of Death with other giant masters of illusion, such as Utgarðsloki and Vafþrúðnir. Realizing that the eagle represents the death that devours everything offers a new understanding of the myth. The gods/ancestors who are establishing a ritual of sacrifice or a sacred meal, are confronted with their own mortality in the end, only death receives nourishment.

METAPHORS FOR ÞJAZI IN HAUSTLǪNG

[Þjazi by Elmer Boyd Smith Page 62 of Brown, Abbie Farwell (1902). "In the Days of Giants: A Book of Norse Tales" Illustrations by E. Boyd Smith. Houghton, Mifflin & Co.]

- Þjazi = The Slave Binder.
- Snótar Ulfr = The Eloquent Woman's (= Iðunn's) Wolf (= abductor).
- í gǫmlum Gemlis ham = wearing the ancient shape of the Year-Old (= young bird =)Eagle.
- Byrgi-Týr bjarga Gefnar = The Fortress-Animal of the Mountains of the Provider woman (= giantess) = The Giant of the Burial Mound.
- Meðal-tálhreinn = Partly Unblended Treason .
- margspakr Valkastar bǫru mǫr of nam = The Very Wise Corpse-Thrower of Wave GutsSeagull (= Eagle).
- Fjallgylðir = Mountain Howler (= Wolf).
- Vígfrekr Vingvagna-Rǫgnir = The Battle-Hungry Ruler of the Wagon of Friendship.
- Þegn = Man Servant.
- Herfang = War Trophy (= Death).
- Ballastr dolgr vallar = The Powerful Enemy of Earth.
- Fóstra ǫndurgoðs = Educator of the Ski-Deity (Skaði) .
- Reimuð Jǫtunheima = Ghost of the Giant Worlds
- Miðjungs friðar = Child of Peace/Giant.
- Áttrunnr Hymis = Hymir's Lineage Tree (Ancestor/relative of the giant Hymir from the Hymiskviða).
- Grjót-Níðaðar = Undercurrent's Rock / Rock-Ruler.
- Lómhugaðr faðir Marnar, ern fjaðrar blaðs leikreginn = Hardwilled Father of the Giantess (= death), that swift wing-flapping King Tricker.
- Sonr biðils Greipar = Son of the lover of the Grasping One (= one of the giantesses who gave birth to Heimdallr/the universe).

4.9: THE WOLF AND THE GIANTESS OF THE BURIAL MOUND

The second animal with which the giant is associated with is the "mountain-howler", which means a wolf and is a symbol of death and the underworld. He is also called the "wolf of the eloquent woman". This refers to him as a thief and abductor of the goddess Iðunn [the eloquent woman] but it also connects him to wolves again. We also know that he lives in Þrymheimr [The World of the Drum] and that he is thus probably identifiable with the giant Þrymr who stole Þórr's hammer, and who had a giant sister representing death and old age. In this story, the sister is replaced by a daughter, Skaði, who, because of the meaning of her name, poetically represents harmful and fatal injury and thus death. In the story of Skaði's marriage to Njǫrðr, we learn that wolves always howl in Þrymheimr, wolves howls being an omen of death.

Giantesses and wolves are closely connected in Norse myths, always related to the underworld, death, and to initiation rituals. The greatest wolf of all is the brother of Hel, Fenrir, whose name strongly indicates "greed". Another wolf has offspring by a giantess in the Iron forest in the east, and among their descendants are the wolves that will devour Sun and Moon. The giantess Hyrrokkin [Fire-Spinner], who is the only being in cosmos strong enough to push Baldr's funeral ship into the ocean on his way to Hel, rides a wolf and has serpents for reins. The same steed is used by an unnamed giantess that meets Heðinn, Helgi's brother in the Song of Helgi Hundingsbani, where her appearance is an omen of Helgi's death and also a call for Heðinn to accept initiation, which he refuses. The ogress on the wolf asks Heðinn to ride with her, something he refuses to do, and then the ogress prophecies his doom. When Helgi dies, he asks his Valkyrie to marry Heðinn, which she refuses.

From other poems we know that the Valkyrie will only marry someone who is not afraid of death, which the ogress represents, and from the Hyndlulióð we know that the ogress of wolves is the teacher of the initiate. In the Edda poem Hyndlulióð, the giantess Hyndla [She-Wolf] has (male) wolves in her stables in the dark underworld, which she can ride to Valhǫll if she can be convinced to do so. She is also the power that reveals important knowledge in the underworld which will enable the hero to enter Valhǫll. It seems that we are always speaking of the same cosmic being, and that her most descriptive name is Hel [from helja "to disguise"].

Her realm, moreover, is guarded by "Hel-hounds", and wolves (and serpents) are said to devour the corpses of the dead. The connection between male wolf and female giantess is very clear and always points to death and the underworld, which makes me think that they are all identifiable with the siblings Hel and Fenrir. Seeing as Þjazi is twice referred to as a wolf, and the importance placed in metaphors on his kinship with giantesses in this poem, I think that the wolf strengthens the idea that Þjazi represents death, as does his daughter Skaði. Þjazi is repeatedly associated with "the giantess", such as when he is called "The Father of the Giantess", the "Educator of the Ski-Deity (i.e. Skaði) or "The Giant of the Provider of the Mountains". The Provider of the Mountains [Bjargar gefn] is in the female form and thus refers to a goddess or giantess of the mountains, which again refers to the burial mound or the realm of death.

Votive altar to the Matronae (divine ancestral mothers), Iron Age Germany: An unmarried maiden, hair loose, is seated in the center, in her lap she holds a basket of fruit. She is flanked by older women wearing the headdress of married women.

4.10: THE BRIDE OF THE GODS

The goddess Iðunn is described by the poet as Ása Leika "the Lover of the Aesir" and as Mey Þas Kunni Ellilyf Ása- "The Maiden who knows the Cure Against the Ageing of the Aesir". Without her, the mortal Aesir grow old and must die, but the lover of all the gods is restored by Loki, and thus the gods are again rejuvenated. However, the abduction happened because Loki was afraid of death in the first place, and a new being is introduced and integrated in Ásgarðr. Skaði whose name means "(Fatal) Injury".

The powerful giantess now puts on her armor and threatens to destroy Ásgarðr in order to avenge the Slave-Binder, her foster-father. In order to appease the powerful giantess, the gods let her choose a husband among them, and promise to make her laugh, something she believes will be impossible for them.

The dangerous lady, also known as the Ǫndurdís [Goddess of Skiing], who runs with wolves and hunts with bow and arrow in the mountain, marries Njǫrðr for a while and is made to laugh but only at the cost of Loki, who must humiliate himself and fall into the lap of Injury before she starts to smile. She later become one of Óðin's wives, as told by Snorri in the Heimskringla and remembered by those royal clans who regarded and worshiped her as their ancestral mother [See 2.3]. According to the Lokasenna poem, she also had Loki as a lover, and in the Grímnismál poem, as we shall see, she is called the Bride of the Gods, indicating, just like in Iðunn's case, that she is a singular lover/bride of the plural gods.

2nd century votive altar to the goddess Nehalennia at her temple in Domburg, the Netherlands. She is flanked by a basket of apples (immortality, regeneration) and a hound (death, the underworld journey).

THE ORIGINAL UNITY BETWEEN SKAÐI AND IÐUNN

It is curious how Skaði suddenly takes over as the lead female in the story after Iðunn has been sent to the underworld it is almost as if the goddess returns from the underworld in a new and grimmer guise. Interestingly enough, Skaði is known by similar terms as Iðunn. In the Edda poem Grímnismál (st. 11) she is referred to as scír bruðr goða, The Shining Bride of the Gods. In fact, the two females, who at first sight would appear to be polar opposites, bright, gentle innocence versus grim, ruthless fury, and seem to have a common origin in the Iron Age goddess Nehalennia, who was depicted with the Hel-hound on one side and the basket of life-giving apples on the other.

There are several examples of how Norse goddesses known from the Viking Age have split up from a common origin. The goddesses Frigg and Freyia, for example, are both derived from the Iron Age Frija, wife of Wodan. Their common origin is echoed in the fact that in the Viking Age/medieval sources they are still both married to Óðinn, although Snorri disguises this fact for the sake of Christian decency and claims that Freyia's husband was Óðr which is only the short form of Óðinn (the inn ending in "Óðinn" simply means "the"). We also hear of the goddess Gefion (Gefn in the short form) as a separate entity, yet her name, among several other goddess-names, is listed among the countless names of Freyia, who according to Snorri "took upon herself new shapes and new names wherever she came among people".

Gefion means Provider, which corresponds with the earliest Iron Age wife of Óðinn/Wodan that we know of, namely the witch-oracle goddess Rosmerta, whose name means The Great Provider. The name Gefn also turns up as a name of Iðunn, in the form Qlgefn the Ale-Provider. In the next Chapter, "The Maiden with the Mead", we will see that the ale-providing aspect is a feature common to almost all the female powers, and always has to do with death, initiation, the accumulation of esoteric knowledge and, significantly, resurrection from death, which is exactly what Iðunn and her apples are all about. According to several academic studies made in Scandinavia, as summed up by the Swedish authority Britt Mari N sström in the year 2000, it is possible to see all the Norse goddesses as overlapping in function and attributes to such a degree that we may be talking of a Great Goddess of many shapes, a very common notion in ancient times. That there were strong Pantheist elements, the belief in many gods that are united in a common source or core, such as this in the Old Norse lore is in my opinion beyond doubt.

Although I think that Pantheism may have been a philosophy harbored by intellectual and spiritual elites. I will be exploring this subject on many occasions throughout this book. In any case, it is a matter of fact that Old Norse poetry the language of the myths would use countless metaphors and nicknames to describe just one kind of being. The powers appear with so many different names. Names that seem to describe their function in particular stories rather than being their one and only name.

We have to recognize a character through analysis of his or her attributes and function, as I have been trying to show throughout the previous pages. The major attribute of Skaði is the wolf, which identifies her with other giantesses of the underworld, and ultimately with Hel. The major attribute of Iðunn is the basket of apples representing rejuvenation, immortality and renewal.

These two crucial attributes are united in the older, oracular goddess Nehalennia. She was named in numerous votive altars of central Europe, especially during the third century AD, where she appears seated on a throne within a shrine, like an oracle or sibyl. To one side of her there is a wolf or a dog, to the other a basket of fruits. Sometimes she has a smaller basket of apples in her lap, or she wields the well-known cult-staff of the vǫlur (witch-priestesses). Her name is possibly related to the word necare "to kill", and thus indicates her association with death, as does the dog or wolf.

There are other possible interpretations of her name as well, such as "the goddess of seafaring" (sometimes she also steers a ship, a well-known symbol of the journey to the other side after death), or as Simek has suggested; "the helpful goddess coming close" Nehalennia is probably identifiable with another Germanic goddess known to us as Nerthus, a Latin form of a German or Norse name, probably derived from Njerðr or Njórunn, thought to be identifiable as Njǫrð's sister-wife and mother to Freyr and Freyia. The connection to Freyia reminds us again of the concept of the lover or bride of the gods. According to the poem Lokasenna, Freyia has known all the gods and elves in the hall of Aegir, the hall of immortality, as her lovers.

This goddess was worshiped all over central Germany, and her cult described as such by the Roman scribe Tacitus around 80 A.D.:

"There is nothing particularly noteworthy about these people in detail, but they are distinguished by a common worship of Nerthus, or Mother Earth. They believe that she interests herself in human affairs and rides through their peoples. In an island of the Ocean stands a sacred grove, and in the grove stands a car draped with a cloth which none but the priest may touch. The priest can feel the presence of the goddess in this holy of holies, and attends her, in deepest reverence, as her car is drawn by kine.

Then follow days of rejoicing and merry-making in every place that she honors with her advent and stay. No one goes to war, no one takes up arms; every object of iron is locked away; then, and then only, are peace and quiet known and prized, until the goddess is again restored to her temple by the priest, when she has had her fill of the society of men.

After that, the car, the cloth and, believe it if you will, the goddess herself are washed clean in a secluded lake. This service is performed by slaves who are immediately afterwards drowned in the lake. Thus mystery begets terror and a pious reluctance to ask what that sight can be which is allowed only to dying eyes." Nerthus-Nehalennia is also clearly associated with other archaeological finds of votive altars showing goddesses as seated oracles, such as the numerous finds of three seated ladies, often just called matronae "The Mothers", and who were supposedly associated with fate and the naming of children. They, too, would be depicted with baskets of fruits and in company of dogs. It is significant to note that the important attributes of the female characters in this myth, Iðunn and Skaði, appeared in combination with each other at an earlier stage the symbol of death on one side, the symbol of renewal on the other. This brings to mind Snorri's description of the lady Hel: "Hel is black like a corpse on one side, and pink like a maiden on the other..."

In fact, the combination ogress-maiden is extremely powerful in Old Norse mythology and legend. The grim ogress and the bright maiden are rarely outright identified with each other as bluntly as by Snorri in his description of Hel, but they often appear together in the same stories, one representing death in oblivion and darkness (ogress), the other representing the possibility of conquering death and achieving immortality (bright, golden maiden).

Despite her dark countenance, the ogress is also a provider of the most profound wisdom the problem is to wrest that wisdom from her without dying in the attempt. It is interesting to note that grim Hel of the two sides herself is a guardian of the sacred mead, as stated in the poem Vegtamskvíða. The sacred mead has the same function as the apples. It provides renewal, immortality and divine wisdom.

The point is that the combination Iðunn and Skaði in the poem takes its place among a series of similar scenarios and must be known as a metaphorical formula for two possible fates or deaths. Both are the "lovers of the gods", and the one appears when the other is gone. Ultimately, and originally, they were the same. They represent the two faces of fate or death; the grim, harsh fate of oblivion, or the bright, gentle fate of resurrection.

4.11: THE KNOWN AND THE UNKNOWN: GENDER AS METAPHOR IN OLD NORSE POETRY

Iðunn is the first female character to appear in the poem, and plays a subtle role. Although the most crucial figure in the myth, she appears more like an abstract concept around whom everything revolves, than as an acting character. The only impression we get of her as a personal character rather than something abstract is the little joke on her behalf offered by Snorri. She is eager to follow Loki when he says that he knows an "apple tree" she might take pleasure in. As Snorri otherwise explains, trees are metaphors for people, male trees for men and female trees for women. An apple-tree is a poetical metaphor for a particularly attractive young man.

The male-female polarity of the Norse cosmos should be taken into consideration when trying to understand what Iðunn and what Skaði represent. This polarity reflects the warrior society where men would represent the outward face of the tribe, the protectors and the mediators, whereas women would represent the core of the tribe, the providers and the counselors. To outsiders, the men of a tribe would ideally show themselves before allowing any close encounters with the inner circle of women and children. This societal structure is reflected in the use of metaphors in poetry. The poetry thus traditionally employs male characters to describe the obvious, known, seen side of reality, and in the case of other people (giants, for example), the male representative would appear as the first obstacle, the guardian. The female characters are "behind the scenes", subtle, mysterious powers, the unseen, and often represent that which is sought once the male obstacle is gone. This polarity is reflected whenever there is a male-female couple:

➤➤ To begin with, we have the siblings Freyr and Freyia, who even by their names (actually titles being "Lord and Lady Sovereign") indicate "two sides to the same coin". Freyr, the brother, represents fertility, crops, cultivated nature, mostly domestic animals (horse and pig), as well as law and order and kingship. His sister, on the other hand, represents magic, witchcraft, fate, death and hidden wisdom, the mysteries of initiation. She is primarily associated with wild animals (big cats and falcons).

➤➤ Then there is the couple Óðinn and Frigg, where Óðinn represents that in human beings and the cosmos at large, which seeks to uncover hidden knowledge the known seeking the unknown. Frigg is said to "know all fate but speaks not", thus being, in fact the unknown, the hidden knowledge. Whereas there are three meanings to the name Óðinn: Spirit, Poetry and Frenzy, Frigg comes with three corresponding, complementary names to those of her husband's: Love, History (Saga) and Tranquility (Hlín).

Realizing that gender has a metaphorical role in itself in Old Norse poetry is important and gives us an indication that whereas the gods and Þjazi represent conscious, known powers, the goddess and the giantess in the story represent the unknown, hidden and subtle powers. It is significant that Loki easily gives Iðunn away only to realize the terrible consequences afterwards, when he learns how important her power actually is. It was difficult to see before it was lost. If we then think that Óðinn is the giver of breath/spirit, Hænir the giver of thought/intelligence, and Loki/Hlóðurr the giver of passion, vitality and color, we realize that the gods may be representing what composes the known side of the human perception or point of view.

Iðunn as a goddess will be representing some complementary, invisible, unknown, hidden aspect of the human and divine point of view. Þjazi, likewise, represents the direct, visible "first sight" aspect of death, which appears destructive and all-consuming. He is a iotunn a concept usually translated as "giant" but which literally means "devourer". Skaði as a giantess will be representing the invisible, mysterious, hidden aspects of death which reveals itself to be different from what appeared to be the case before Þjazi, the first sight image of destruction in death, was "murdered". Likewise, family relations will be significant. If the couple is husband and wife, the meaning seems to be that they are two different forces coming together to create a complimentary union, often with an outcome (offspring).

Male offspring will represent the obvious, known result of their union, female offspring will represent the unknown, hidden result. A sister and brother, as in the case of Freyr and Freyia, represent the hidden and known sides to the same thing.

Iron Age votive altar to the mothers, Bonn, Germany

Then there are the cases of fathers and daughters without other known relations, which is typical of the giant world, in this case a formula represented by the father-daughter couple Þjazi and Skaði, where the daughter represents the hidden results of the father's known actions, or in this particular case the hidden or unknown result of his known death (Skaði only appears after her father's death). Skaði could have demolished the world of the gods, a way of saying that the gods' actions in this story may very well have destroyed them forever, gambling out their most prized possession, the goddess who gave them eternal life.

Instead of destroying them, Skaði is offered truce and persuaded to become, once again, the bride of the gods, and a nut a symbol of new life and the new shape of Iðunn is allowed to grow in Ásgarðr. Interestingly, there is another giantess known by the name Gríðr "Truce". She is a benevolent giantess and vǫlva who lives in the rocky mountains just like Skaði. And just like Skaði, the truce-giantess eventually becomes the lover of Óðinn, giving birth to Víðarr the Silent. Víðarr means "to expand", as in "Silent Expander", and is one of the young gods who will survive Ragnarǫk. Gríðr is also a priestess who helps and guides Þórr on his path of initiation, lending him her own sacred staff, iron gloves and belt which will allow him to wield the power of thunder. It is time to explore what Iðunn actually represents in humanity and among gods in order to truly understand this myth.

4.12: THE KNOWLEDGE-HUNGRY GODDESS-THE SOUL OF THE GODS?

There dwells in the valleys a knowledge-hungry goddess:
The Seed of Yggdrasill gliding down the ash:
She is of elf-kin
Her name is Iðunn [Stream Returns to Source]
The Oldest of the Inner Ruler's
The youngest of children.

> *Dvelr í daulom*
> *dís forvitin,*
> *Yggdrasils frá*
> *aski hnigin;*
> *álfa ættar*
> *Iþunni héto,*
> *Ívallds ellri*
> *ýngsta barna.*

Hrafnagalðr Óðins eða Forspjallsljóð [Odin's Raven Charm or the Song of the First Speech] st. 6

The theft of a goddess is a recurring theme in Norse myths. Freyia is threatened with abduction by or unwanted marriage to giants in three different Norse myths, and Síf together with her in one of them. Adding to that, we have stories about the theft of important attributes owned by the goddesses (Síf's hair, Freya's necklace and Iðunn's apples). These attributes may be seen as symbols of the power of the goddesses, eternal youth, fertility and secret knowledge. Most scholars today assume that Iðunn (and Síf) are hypostasis of Freyia. Iðunn is the maiden aspect of the goddess with her gift of resurrection, rejuvenation and transformation.

The apples of immortality (eternal rejuvenation, actually) may be seen as another image of the "precious mead" offered by the female characters in the myths to male initiates so that they may be resurrected from the underworld. As mentioned earlier, the apples or fruits with which the goddess is so strongly associated that the gods may not have the apples without the goddess offering it and are known from numerous early Iron Age images in Germany and areas where Germanic tribes dwell during the Iron Age. Where she is the seated, mother goddess Nehalennia who keeps a basket of apples on one side and a dog on the other.

The image is extremely interesting because it includes the dog or wolf, which is an attribute of Hel and the giantesses who represent Hel, such as Skaði. It would appear that the characters represented in Norse mythology by Hel/ Skaði and Iðunn /Freyia once were unified in this older goddess, a remnant of which is seen in Snorri's description of Hel as half black as a rotting corpse (death) and half rosy-cheeked maiden (life). This original union is interesting in light of the story featuring exactly these two female opposites. The death vs. life theme is obviously extremely important in this story.

The first metaphor for Iðunn in the poem is Snót, according to Snorri a replacement word or "true description" for women who are "clever in speech" [Snótir heitir þær, er kyrrlátar eru "Snótir are they called (feminine), who are eloquent (women)"]. Thus Iðunn is associated with eloquence. This is important because learning to be eloquent was an important part of the mystery initiation and an important result of drinking the precious mead of the underworld. It had to do with learning the art of poetry and perhaps to do with mastering poetry the way the gods did as a way of creating reality. Later, the goddess is called "the maiden who knows the age-cure of the Aesir" which refers directly to her power to restore the youth of the gods. Without her, they would quickly grow old and die. As I argued in my thesis, resurrection from death and a sort of immortality was at stake when the initiate entered the golden halls of the underworld mead-serving maiden.

The connection with the mead is strengthened when Iðunn in stanza 11 is called "Ale-Provider" (Qlgefn) twice. The metaphor for Iðunn as "the goddess of the well-field-benches" is very complicated but if we take the words apart they start to make sense. The well is the water beneath the world tree from which the original Norn Urðr ["Origin"] nourished the world tree. That water, like the mead which was produced from it after it had flowed through the world tree and into the belly of the goddess in the shape of Heiðrún [bright secret/rune/fate], had the quality that anyone bathing in it or drinking it will be restored and transformed into a transparent light being (Snorri's Gylfaginning). The field is harder to interpret but a field is always a part of the realm in the underworld in which the goddess with the mead is hiding.

Benches and seating are metaphors for fate such as when Freyia chooses the arrangement of seating in Folkvangr the "People-Field" (= the world, Freyia's abode. This indicates that Freyia rules fate in the world of people). Finally, Iðunn is called ása leika the lover/girlfriend/playmate of the Aesir. It is significant that Iðunn is the one singular lover of all the plural gods. This may be understood further in light of Loki's true statement in the Edda poem Lokasenna when he tells Freyia that in the hall of Aegir, all the elves and gods have been her lovers. Loki ignores the fact that the hall of Aegir is a realm of immortality (Hlésey, the Wind-Shielded Island, shielded from the wind that is death) and exists outside of the world.

He also ignores the fact that the loving embrace of the goddess is a part of the initiation through death and resurrection. Iðunn is not very present in any of the Edda sources, which may be because she is just an aspect of Freyia. In another poem, Óðins Hrafnagalðr or Forspjallsljóð, stanza 6, which was quoted in the beginning of this Chapter, Iðunn reappears. Here she is known as dís forvitin the "Knowledge-Hungry Goddess" who "dwells in the valleys", a poetical formula otherwise used in the Vǫluspá to describe the "dew that falls in the valleys" from the well of Origin, from which Norns and Valkyrja [Archaic form of Valkyrie] ascend into the world. She is also called Frá Yggdrasils, the "Seed of the World Tree" and described as sinking down (descending) the ash (the world tree). The seed may be seen in connection with the apples of the goddess with which she may also be identified, and with nuts. Loki carries her home in the shape of a nut a symbol of the potential for new life.

Iðunn is also called "the oldest of the In-Ruler's, the youngest child", a very cryptic statement that indicates that she is both old and young and that she is a daughter (result) of the forces that rules within. The name of the goddess used in these poems, Iðunn, is derived from the word iðr and unn, the latter just a suffix indicating a female. The word iðr refers to a small stream going out of a river that takes the opposite course of the main stream, returning to the source. The proper translations should thus be "Woman Who Returns to the Source of the Flow". I think that meaning is very significant if we realize that the goddess has something to do with enlightenment. In any case, the reference to a source of water and to streams is important, seeing as watery streams were what brought the entire cosmos into being in Old Norse mythology.

From all this, we may still be a bit puzzled as to what Iðunn, and consequentially, the great goddess in this aspect, really means. As pointed out, as a female she represents the unknown and the mysterious forces that are of great consequence but which are hard to perceive. As a restorer of life, provider of knowledge, eloquence, rejuvenation, potential for enlightenment, and her character as the essence of life or potential life (seed, fruit, nut), and as a unifying aspect that is the "lover" of all the initiated gods and immortal light-elves (= souls) that may access the realm of immortality. It is not entirely preposterous to suggest, as I do, that she represents the immortal soul, and the unifying all-soul at that, shared by all individuals. Understanding Iðunn as the immortal soul of the gods makes it a lot easier to understand the origin of this myth as a shamanic journey of soul-retrieval. The effect of the loss of Iðunn on the gods is immediate aging and approaching death.

Her role as the seed of life itself, and that her loss immediately brings about the action of changing shape so as to travel into the realm in which she is held captive, and the instant rejuvenation and healing experienced by the gods at her return, is a perfect description of a soul-retrieval. Significantly, this interpretation opens up a new dimension in our understanding of the many theft-stories and of the significance and symbolic meaning of the goddess in her many shapes. I am quite convinced that the goddess that must be discovered or rediscovered in the underworld, a theme that is in fact central to Old Norse myths, has to do with the discovery or rediscovery of the soul, which is also strongly associated to fate, and in particular the ultimate fate of all mortals, gods and men alike: death.

Snorri let us know that all human beings were followed through life by Norns goddesses of fate that were attached to their individuals from birth to death. These Norns all have their origin in the Well of Origin the Urðarbrunnr which lies in the heart of Ásgarðr, the divine world. They would thus all seem to be aspects of the three first Norns that represent past, present and future. According to Snorri, some of these fates are divine, and will spin lives of fame and glory to their humans. Others are elfin, and these are immortal and mysterious, belonging to the upper heavens of pure golden light. Most fates, however, are dwarfs, lesser fates, the daughters of Dvalinn. Significantly, Dvalinn means "the Hibernation", indicating sleep.

It is most interesting that when the hero Sígurðr is on his way to find the mysterious goddess on the sacred mountains, he asks about these Norns, and receives the same information that Snorri offers, as said in the Edda poem Fafnismál, st. 13:

> *Of much shattered birth I think the Norns are, they are not all the same;*
> *Some are of the Aesir*
> *Some are of the Elves*
> *Some are the daughters of Hibernation*
>
> > *Svndrbornar mioc*
> > *hygg ec at Norns se,*
> > *eigoþ þer ett saman;*
> > *svmar ero askvngar*
> > *svmar alfkvngar,*
> > *svmar dotr Dvalins*

Sígurðr then proceeds to the sacred mountain, which is described as a realm of death, within which he finds a sleeping, in fact hibernating Valkyrie. Valkyrie are specialized Norns, spinning the fate of men who are destined for glory. When the hero after tremendous and dangerous trials manages to wake up his fate goddess, he immediately receives esoteric knowledge and magical abilities. As us shown in the poem Helreið Brynhildar, the love of the Valkyrie awaken also saves him from the oblivion of Hel after death; in short, she saves him from the cold embrace of the ogress fate and brings him to Valhǫll. We also learn that the same Valkyrie is reborn time and time again in order to reunite time and time again with the re-birthing hero (yes, the Vikings believed in reincarnation). In all these lives, the Valkyrie guides and protects her hero throughout his lives, like a good following Norn, or, indeed, a so-called fylgja (a "follower", otherwise understood to be guardian spirits).

The theme of the sleeping goddess who must be found in the underworld and woken up in order to provide knowledge and resurrection from death, as well as providing active guidance in life, is actually extremely important in Old Norse mythology, as we shall see in the next essay. I think it is almost completely safe to claim that she is a representation not only of the fate, but also an important aspect of the immortal soul of human beings. It would seem that the gods who are not immortal also has one. Finally, it would also seem that, at the heart and core of the theology of the soul-fate-follower goddess that must be woken from her slumbers through initiation, is a Pantheist concept of a unifying soul source; the multifaceted goddess.

4.13: LOKI, THE MOVER OF THE STORIES

Metaphors for Loki in Haustlöng:

➤ Hænis vínr = Friend of Hænir (the giver of thought).
➤ Hrafnásar vínr-The Friend of the Raven God (Óðinn).
➤ Farbauta mǫg The Son of Farbauti.
➤ Bragðvíss ósvífrandi ása The Cunning-Clever Defier of Gods.
➤ Djúphugaðr hirði-Týr Deep-of-Soul Hiding Beast.
➤ Farmr arma Sigvinjar Burden of Sigyns arms
➤ Fróðr tív The Wise/Clever God.
➤ Ulfs faðir- Father of the Wolf.
➤ Ofrúni Þórs- Thor's friend/counselor.
➤ þungr Loptr Heavy Air.
➤ Sagna hrærir The Mover of Stories.
➤ Brísings goða girðiþjófr The Belt thief of the Flame's gods.
➤ Hugreynandi Hœnis Hænir's (= Thought's) Intent-Tester
➤ ǫglis barni Child of the Hawk.

A few other typical metaphors for Loki:

➤ Bölvasmiðr: Mischief-Smith
➤ Sleipnis frænda: Kinsman to Sleipnir
➤ Inn slægi áss: The Sly God
➤ Frænda ok föðurbróður, vársinna ok sessa Óðins ok ása: Kinsman and Uncle and Comrade and Seat Companion to Óðinn and the Aesir
➤ Inn bundni Áss: The Bound God

Finally, we must have a look at Loki, who plays an active role in this poem. Obviously, he assumes the role of the shaman, as he often does, and thus represents the shamanic pattern to follow by human descendants. Let us now look at the metaphors describing Loki metaphors by which Loki "was known" to the Norse audience. He is called the "friend of the Raven-God" and "Hænir's faithful friend. The Raven-God is Óðinn, and his ravens represent The Intent [Húginn] and The Memory [Muninn]. Loki is a "friend" of (associated/allied with) intent and memory.

He is also a friend of Hænir, who gave thought and intelligence to humans and thus represents conscious intelligence. Thus Loki is associated and allied with intent, thought and memory, corresponding with the original trinity representing intent/will, thought/intelligence and memory/spirit. He unifies these cosmic divine forces within himself, representing the three gods together. As such, he is described as the cunning and clever god, the Tester of Hænir's Intent, that is, that fiery passionate part of ourselves which experiments with the intentions made by thought. He is also the Mover of the Stories [sagna hrærir], showing that the poet was conscious about Loki's role as a poetical character applied in the stories in order to create movement, drama and conflict, which is essential to all poetry and to the drama of life. Importantly, Loki is the "child of the hawk".

We know of only one hawk in the Gylfaginning, and that is Verfǫlnir, which actually means "the One Who Diminishes Wind". We know that wind is a metaphor for death, so to diminish it is significant, especially as we know that the myth is centered around the themes of death, resurrection and immortality. The hawk Verfǫlnir is seated "between the eyes" of the giant eagle that sits in the top of the world tree (the northern end of the world) and which indeed represents death. There seems to be a theme here of the hawk coming out of the eagle, and is interesting as the hawk and the falcon means the same thing according to Snorri, and because Loki flies in this shape in front of the eagle of death.

In this myth, Loki and the hawk that diminishes death, represent the same thing: the conquering of death. Loki is a complex character of extreme importance in the myths left to us. But as a deity, there is no evidence in any kind of record that he was ever worshiped by anyone. Like some other characters such as Baldr, Loki seems to be a literary character applied by poets in order to create conflict [being the driving force of all dramas]. That he is called "the Mover of the Stories" only shows that poets were well aware of this fact.

If Loki represents anything more than this, it must be the passion of human beings, reflected in the sound-play of his name. Loki rhymes with logi, which means "flame". Passion in itself is not a bad thing from the rather laid-back Old Norse point of view, but it is complicated and may be destructive, since it can be moved by all sorts of emotions, including jealousy, greed and anger. We will see more of Loki in the *Golden Age Essay*, where he plays an important role in the death of Baldr.

Summary

The name of the goddess used in these poems, Iðunn, is derived from the word iðr and unn, the latter just a suffix indicating a female. The word iðr refers to a small stream going out of a river that takes the opposite course of the main stream, returning to the source. The proper translations should thus be "Woman Stream Who Returns to the Source of the Flow". I have shortened it to "Stream Returns to Source". I think that meaning is very significant if we realize that the goddess has something to do with enlightenment. In any case, the reference to a source of water and two streams is important, seeing as watery streams were what brought the entire Cosmos into being, in Old Norse mythology. From all this, we may still be a bit puzzled as to what Iðunn, and consequentially, the goddess in this aspect, really means. As pointed out, as a female she represents the unknown and the mysterious forces that are of great consequence but which are hard to perceive.

As a restorer of life, provider of knowledge, of eloquence, and of rejuvenation, of the potential for enlightenment, her character is the essence of or potential for life, as symbolized in the seed, fruit or nut. As a unifying aspect, she is the "lover" of all the initiated gods and immortal light-elves (= souls) that may access the realm of immortality. It is not entirely preposterous to suggest, as I do, that she represents the immortal soul, and the unifying all-soul at that, shared by all individuals. Understanding Iðunn as the immortal soul of the gods and the path back towards the source of Origin makes it a lot easier to understand the origin of this myth as a shamanic journey of soul-retrieval.

The effect of the loss of Iðunn on the gods is immediate aging, sickness and approaching death. The character who from the beginning of the story was the performer of sacred rituals, Loki, changes shape and travels to the Underworld in order to retrieve this seed of life. The instant rejuvenation and healing experienced by the gods as she returns to them is a very good and typical description of what is otherwise known as shamanic soul-retrieval, as defined in the beginning of this chapter. Significantly, this interpretation opens up a new dimension of understanding in the many Norse goddess abduction and theft of power object stories. I am quite convinced that the lost goddess or lost treasure which must be discovered in the underworld has to do with the discovery or rediscovery of the soul, which is also strongly associated with fate. Particularly the ultimate fate of all mortals, gods and men alike: death. This is a theme that is central to Old Norse myths.

METAPHORS FOR IÐUNN:

➤➤ Snót: Eloquent, intelligent woman
➤➤ Mey, þás kunni ellilyf Ása: the Maiden who knows the age-cure of the Aesir
➤➤ Ása Leika: The Lover of the Aesir
➤➤ Brunnakrs bekkjar dísi: The Goddess of the Well-Field-Benches
➤➤ Qlgefn: Ale-Provider
➤➤ Mæra Mey, Stærandi Mun Hapta: The Precious Maiden who increases the Joy of the Gods
➤➤ Frá Yggdrasils: The Seed of Yggdrasill
➤➤ Dís Forvítin: The Knowledge-Hungry Goddess
➤➤ Ivalds Ellri: The Oldest of the In-Ruler's
➤➤ Yngsta Barna: The Youngest Child

5: The loss of the golden age in old norse myths

[Note for the present edition of this book: I wrote this chapter back in 2011-12. Since then, new discoveries have led to a reconsidering of the Indo-European migration thesis: it does appear that a people we now refer to as the Yamna, and which Gimbutas referred to as the Kurgans, indeed did migrate on a large scale from the area to the north of the Caucasus and the Black Sea around 5.000 Years ago. They spread and blended into the European as well as some Asian areas, bringing shared traditions and religious elements with them. Today, an estimate of 50 % of Scandinavian males are directly descended from these people through the father lines (Y-DNA), that is, from men who entered Scandinavia ca 4.500 Years ago and obviously mated with the native women. They also spread into the rest of Europe.]

5.1: Golden ages in human prehistory?

"The use of the word civilization needs and explanation...The civilization that flourished in Old Europe between 6500 and 3500 BCE and in Crete until 1450 BCE enjoyed a long period of uninterrupted peaceful living which produced artistic expressions of graceful beauty and refinement, demonstrating a higher quality of life than many androcratic, classed societies."

(Marija Gimbutas The Civilization of the Goddess)

Many cultures have myths about a Golden Age, a prehistoric time of peace, prosperity and happiness, a time of innocence and of wisdom, a time without poverty, cruelty and suffering. Whenever a myth of the Golden Age occurs, it serves not only to offer the comfort of the knowledge (real or not) of a bygone time of harmony and happiness, but also to explain, and sometimes legitimize, the suffering and inequality that we experience today and know that people have experienced for several millennia. Some traditions seem to think in terms of a natural cosmic cycle you simply have bright ages and dark ages, changing place over the course of history on both cosmic and mundane levels.

According to some Hindu traditions, we are presently living through the Kali Yuga the Age of Kali an era of spiritual decline and darkness. Whereas the Kali Yuga, depressingly enough, is supposed to go on for several hundred thousand years, other traditions, such as that of the Maya, offered the intriguing idea of a new cosmic cycle that would be instigated from the time of winter Solstice 2012. Popular interpretations of this change in the Mayan estimates of the cosmic cycle today often involves a deep fascination with catastrophic events and an expectation of a great apocalypse, inspired, perhaps, more by Biblical Doomsday prophecies as those seen in the Book of Revelations, than in the Mayan records.

If we look to contemporary Mayan elders and wisdom keepers, there is little need for panicking. According to the Maya calendar, a new astrological cycle begins every 5125 years and we would be hard put if each cycle involved a total destruction of the world. A new cycle is thought to have an astrological impact on the world, but as far as the contemporary Mayan elders go, this one might bring about a restoration of ancient knowledge and the return of ancestral wisdom keepers perhaps even the dawn of a new Golden Age.

I personally find the concept of cycles lasting approximately 5000 years quite curious, not because I am uncritically ready to believe in preordained cycles but mainly because if we look back, a great change really did occur in Europe and Asia at least around 5000 years ago, give and take, when an era of peace gradually made way to an era of war and conquests. The previous era in Europe, a fact often neglected by historians, stands out with its many quite advanced and civilized cultures, hundreds of towns all over Europe, interconnected through trade, marriages and shared artistic and religious symbols that some have suggested were an early form of writing.

Historians tend to ignore this era and focus on Bronze Age civilizations in Egypt and Sumer, or the very late Greek civilizations, although lately, archaeologists seem to recognize that Europe as a whole seems to have formed a number of interconnected cultures where traveling and exchange of cultural values and ideas as well as knowledge and objects was the order of the day, probably explaining how Minoan labyrinth symbols appear in North Scandinavian rock art from this era. It seems increasingly possible that Bronze Age Europe actually formed a culture in its own right, with powerful connections to North Africa and the Middle East, even some parts of West Asia all the way to India. As archaeologists are slowly opening up for the idea of a Bronze Age civilization where the various parts of Europe held more in common than not, the era preceding the Bronze Age, the Neolithic, was equally universal.

This is a fact often ignored, apparently, as I see it, because the first archaeologist to propose significant evidence for the idea proposed it together with mention of goddesses and women in power. If certain scholars could disregard the personal discomfort they may feel because of Gimbutas' focus on the feminine imagery that actually dominated the era, they might realize that Gimbutas made a very good case. She showed that Neolithic Europe actually saw a considerable number of quite advanced and interconnected Stone Age town cultures which displayed all the signs of civilization. Approximately between 7500 BCE and 2500 BCE we see the rise of flourishing European town cultures that were interconnected.

Specialized work, trade routes, fashions, advanced architecture, town planning and organized religion, as well as an astonishing creativity and advancement in art. They painted and carved sacred symbols that seem to have been the same all over Europe and lived, generally, in peace and prosperity, enjoying cultural continuity over several thousands of years. Their art and their use of symbols show along with other features that these cultures were connected to each other all over Europe and had strong ties to Anatolia and the East, as well as North Africa. These are the cultures that also saw the rise of famous megaliths, especially in the western and northern parts of Europe, where megalithic monuments, stone henge and abstract art take precedence.

In the southeast, figurative art was more prominent, displaying an overwhelming fascination with the female body, especially the mysteries of childbirth and, pregnancy, yet often in connection with death and burials, which points to deeper meanings than just the biological function of birth giving. There is also a fascination with shape changing transformation. Women who were part animals are extremely common in this art. The abstract symbols applied to the figurines and monuments alike; however, were shared all over Europe, many symbols recognizable from earlier Paleolithic art.

In Malta, which flourished as a Megalithic temple culture towards the end of the era, between 3600 B.C.E and 2500 B.C.E, we see the blend of figurative art with Megalithic architecture, in which the naturalistic female figurines of the continent grew into huge, stylized and three meter tall stone statues, placed in the temple complexes. The European town cultures of the Neolithic and Megalithic age seem to have been preceded in Anatolia and the Middle East, beginning with the 12 000 year old megalithic monuments of Göbekli Tepe in Turkey, followed by the Stone Age cities of Catal Höyük in Turkey and Jericho in the Middle East some 10 000 years ago 5000 years before the warlike era that followed. In the beginning of this era of Stone Age civilized cultures, there is no evidence whatsoever of warfare, nor of violence on any significant scale, not until a different culture began to appear, first in the eastern parts of Europe from about 3500 BC and then slowly, gradually, spreading out over the following millennium.

It means that we can speak of at least four thousand years of an actual Stone Age civilization (7500-3500 BC) that knew general societal peace and cultural continuity. Add another thousand years before the culture declined completely, leaving its symbolic and thus possibly its religious heritage in one Bronze Age civilization only, The Minoan. Before this era ended, significant signs of violence or hierarchy were hardly present at all, and equality between the sexes seems to have been the order of the day. If a gender takes prominence at all, it is in art, where female figurines and female symbolism completely dominate the picture, probably an indication that the figurines portray goddesses or a great goddess that was worshiped by both sexes, especially since many of the figurines are found in shrines or carry iconography that is recognized in later Classical goddesses.

The well-known Classical concept of the Great Goddess of many shapes, mother to all the other gods, as we see in the Mystery religions such as that of Isis, Cybele or Demeter, may very well have originated in this era. After two millennia of exclusively male god worship, this fact seems hard to swallow for many moderns, who, despite all the overwhelming material and written evidence, have a difficult time imagining that a female god could be anything but a "fertility idol". I speak of an era, because whatever terms people want to put on this time period, there was clearly a quite intense cultural interaction between the various cultures all over the European continent, with significant contacts to the Middle East.

THE NEW CULTURE TYPE

"And thou shalt consume all the people which the Lord thy God shall deliver to thee; thine eye shall have no pity on them; neither shalt thou serve their gods... And he shall deliver their kings into thine hand, and thou shalt destroy their name from under heaven... the graven images of their gods shall ye burn with fire..."

The Old Testament: Deuteronomy 7.16, 24, 25

"And they warred against the Midianites...and they slew all the males... And they took all the spoil of all their cattle, and all their flocks, and all their goods. And they burnt all their cities wherein they dwelt, and all their goodly castles, with fire...Moses said unto them, Have ye saved all the women alive?... Now therefore kill every male among the little ones, and kill every woman that hath known man by lying with him. But all the women children, that have not known a man by lying with him, keep alive for yourselves."

The Old Testament: Numbers 31.7, 9,10, 15, 17, 18

From about 3500 BCE, a new kind of culture, perhaps not one culture but rather a culture type, began appearing in East and Central Europe. Gradually, over more than a millennium, this culture type spread into the rest of Europe and the Middle East. When they finally acquired horses and metal weapons, their success in conquest was a given. This new culture type was more warlike, more hierarchic, more barbaric and more male-dominated than the previous Megalithic and Neolithic cultures of Europe.

Its art and building style was simpler, testifying to less civilized origins, perhaps more of a pastoral and nomadic culture, and as it took over Europe, the ancient art of megalithic architecture gradually vanished, as did much of the figurative art style and impressive pottery styles and fashions of the southeast. Only in the Minoan culture did much of the previous, old European culture survive in art, fashion and religious expression, well into the Bronze Ages. Towards the very end of the peaceful era, around 2500 B.C.E, this new culture began appearing in Scandinavia, mingling with the old Megalithic culture that already existed here. The previous, megalithic culture in Scandinavia had been connected to the continental cultures. It had apparently been a clan-based culture.

The whole clan lived together in huge communal buildings, also being buried in communal clan graves. The material shows little evidence of hierarchy within the clan, and may have been ruled by elders or in a democratic fashion we know that later Scandinavians ruled society through parliament where, even into the Viking Age, kings had to be elected by the people. We do not know if the Megalith people had kings or even chiefs, however. The women of the graves were usually related to each other whereas the men came from outside, suggesting matrilineal succession where men moved to their wives' clans. This matrilineal pattern seems to have been the norm also in the rest of Europe at the time.

The cultural change, although happening gradually over a period of a millennium, must have been revolutionary on the local scales, taken many different forms from invasion to gradual interaction, truce and compromises and left its mark in European culture and mythology. Many have suggested that the new culture were the "Indo-Europeans", a people that may have originated in Caucasus and spread in all directions, explaining why most European languages are related, and also related to the Sanskrit and Persian languages. In India, there are legends of a white-skinned people, the Aryans, who overran the ancient and peaceful Indus valley civilizations and introduced class hierarchy, warrior castes and male domination.

These were the Sanskrit speakers who also created the Vedas, a body of sacred lore, hymns and myths which are clearly related to many European traditions, including the Old Norse Eddas. The Indo-European hypothesis, however, is challenged by many, and the evidence for such a culture is very uncertain. It has been suggested that the linguistic and mythical connections across the Eurasian continent may be far older, we know that trade, traveling and interaction was common for thousands of years during the previous era, the Neolithic, as well as before: Nomadic and less nomadic Ice Age hunters across the Eurasian continent also shared many cultural traits and symbols, from the westernmost parts of Europe to the easternmost parts of Siberia.

Thus the "Indo-Europeans" may never have existed as a people, the cultural and linguistic interconnections being rather based on countless millennia of cultural interaction. If we begin to look closely, we will see many different mythologies, such as the Finno-Ugric, the Middle Eastern, the Mongolian and the North African, also share many significant features and basic themes. We are a species that has been migrating and emigrating, returning and sharing for ages uncountable. The connection between cultures is as old as human kind. The very long-term and gradual cultural change may thus be a sign that the "revolution" may have been more internal and less based on invasion.

Of course, there might have been both. There is no reason to believe that invasions and the destructions of cultures never happened either. The Bronze Age civilizations, at least, certainly reveal many stories of invasion, where the men were killed and women and children of an entire culture were made slaves or forced to marry their invaders. The oldest evidence of warfare and possible cultural destruction in Europe, however, dates back to the same era as the first appearances of the new culture type, some 5000 years ago. Wherever we have written sources, we seem to hear similar stories of invasion.

MYTHS AND LEGENDS OF CONQUEST

> *"I came not warring here for any ill the Trojans had done me. I
> have no quarrel with them. They have not raided my cattle nor my
> horses, nor cut down my harvests...We have followed you, Sir...for
> your pleasure, not ours- ....You forget this, and threaten to rob me
> of the prize for which I have toiled...Never when the Achaeans sack
> any rich city...do I receive so good a prize as you do, though it is
> my hands that do the better part of the fighting. When the sharing
> comes, your share is far the largest, and I, forsooth, must go back
> to my ships, take what I can get and be thankful, when my labor of
> fighting is done."*

> *Homer The Iliad (800 BCE).*
> *(Achilles complains about the privileges of his lord after a raid)*

In Snorri's introduction to the Prose Edda, as well as in the beginning of his
Ynglinga Saga, we hear a story of conquest in ancient times a conquest made by
a people who came from the southeast. To be exact, Snorri gives the exact origins
of the Aesir as a people coming from Troy, in present day Turkey. In the Prologue
version, the migration seems to have happened back in the day when Troy was still
a great city Troy being destroyed sometime during the Bronze Ages whereas the
Ynglinga Saga version mentions a time when Romans were conquering the world,
bringing the origin myth closer to us in time. In the first version, Snorri lets the
Aesir meet native resistance in Sweden only, whereas the latter version indicates
that the Vanir also had to be dealt with before the migration, a people somewhere
to the northwest of Turkey. That the Aesir were supposed to be a people from Troy
is usually considered a preposterous idea invented by Snorri in order to keep up
with medieval fashions it was simply very fashionable to claim Classical ancestry:
The Romans claimed to be descended from Aeneas, a Trojan refugee after the
Trojan war, and, according to my Norse teachers, most other people who wanted to
appear civilized and special claimed similar ancestry without there being any reality
behind it. When Snorri claimed that the word Aesir meant "Asians", referring to
their Asian origins (Turkey was considered a part of Asia), this is also a claim that is
very doubtful.

When he claims that the Aesir were so powerful and gifted that others began to
think they were gods, he is trying to legitimize his own interest in Pagan lore. By
allowing the audience to think that the Aesir were simply people, ancestors, that
the Pagans had mistaken for gods, Snorri's works became palatable to the 13th
century Church. Rather than fretting about the many historically incorrect details
and inconsistencies of Snorri's story and there are many I think it could be useful to
look at the basic structure of his story. If there is any truth behind his story, it must
be referring to events so breathtakingly long ago that there is no wonder if the story
has been mixed up with more recent events or confused by mythical imagination.
Beneath the surface, what he is telling might very well be a legend of immense
antiquity about a people who came from the southeast and settled all over Northern
Europe in some bygone time.

In the Prologue, Snorri wrote:

> "Óðinn had the gift of clairvoyance and so did his wife. And so they discovered
> that his name would be honored in the Northern parts of the world, and that
> he would be honored before other kings. For this reason he wanted to migrate
> from Turk-land. He had with him a huge crowd of people, young and old,
> men and women, and many precious things. And wherever they traveled a
> country, much great things were told about them, until they seemed more like
> gods than people (...)
>
> The Aesir took wives in these countries to themselves and some to their
> sons. And their lineages flourished, and in the entire Saxland and the North-
> countries did the language of these Asia-men spread so that it was the same
> language in all these countries."

If we look beyond details and names, and into the basic structure of the story,
which Snorri cared enough about to relate in two different versions, we can deduce
that there might have been a legend behind, an ancestral legend of people who
came from the southeast, from Asia Minor, a people of powerful warriors who
spread out in the whole known world, and whose language became the norm in the
areas they conquered. They married the women and created new theocratic social
systems, also described in detail by Snorri. What he is describing is in my opinion
suspiciously close to the real, prehistoric migrations that actually did take place
towards the end of the Stone Age some 4500 years ago in Scandinavia.

Of course, Snorri could simply be basing his story on the many migrations of
tribes that happened during the Roman Iron Age, but one would almost expect him
to be more accurate about tribal history that was so much closer to him in time.
The 3rd-5th century AD tribal migrations happened from north to south and from
east to west, the latter due to Hunnish interference during the fourth century AD.
The moving tribes were already related and spoke similar languages, and there is
no evidence of significantly new social systems or of one particularly powerful tribe
that settled in one place to spread a new culture.

Additionally, the memory of the Huns and of the Scandinavian emigration to
the continent around two thousand years ago was all recorded in the tribal lore,
as when the Goths claimed Scandinavian ancestry in the Getica. In the Poetic
Edda, the memory of the Huns is a memory of an Asian warrior tribe that actually
differed very little culturally from the Germans, and the Huns certainly did not
contribute the Norse language. What Snorri is describing is something quite
different, a new kind of people, a new kind of language, a new kind of social order,
a whole new culture settling in both peacefully through marriages and truces, and
violently through conquest. This kind of migration has not really happened in
historical times, but it did happen in prehistory, and it would not be that surprising
if memories of such a revolutionary event survived, however blurred, in legend.
In the Prologue, Snorri claimed that the "Asians" from Troy worshiped a heroic
thunder god as their ancestral father; " þro the one we know as Þórr". The new
culture type that spread out in Europe towards the end of the Stone Age was also
prone to worship a thunder god.

The monster-bashing thunder god has been worshiped by most Indo-European people, from Indra to Zeus, and was once the most important male god. In the 12th century Norse records, Þórr was born by the Earth goddess and had a son called Magni. According to 1st century Tacitus, the Iron Age German tribes thought that they were the descendants of a thunder god born by the Earth mother, who had a son called Mannus a Latinized form of a German word for "man":

> "In their ancient songs, their only form of recorded history, the Germans celebrate the earth-born god, Tuisto. They assign to him a son, Mannus, the ancestor of their people" (Germania, 2)

Tacitus wrote these lines down almost exactly 1127 years before Snorri wrote his work. It is a testimony to the possibility of how very ancient memories may have survived in oral legend as is the fact that many of the Viking Age Þórr-myths have obvious counterparts in the Vedic myths of Indra written down thousands of years earlier in a completely different part of the world, myths that are considered as old as 5000 years. One of the oldest written works of Europe is the Iliad, dating back to approximately 800 BCE and showing how Greek town-cultures grouped together in order to invade Troy in present day Turkey a legend which has turned out to be based on true events, as Troy was excavated during the 19th century. We also have the Roman legends of how the early Roman settlers, all men, abducted the Sabine women and forced them to become their wives probably a reason why Rome became so obsessively patriarchal according to legend the first Roman women were all unwilling abductees.

There are other and similar stories of whole towns of warriors marrying captive women, having to introduce severe laws that limited the freedom of their less than loving wives. Wives who had seen their brothers and fathers massacred by their husbands. Some misogynist laws seem to be nothing but safety measures against the hatred nurtured by these women, who were by law mere property. I believe this degradation of women is a result of such abductions and massacres, creating unequal relationships between the sexes from the very start of a new town settlement. In Bronze Age Egypt, there are stories of the terrible, invading Hyksos, red-haired and white-skinned people who used new and impressive techniques, such as driving horses into battle. The Hyksos really did come from the Caucasian mountains. In 1780 BCE, they managed to invade Egypt and ruled there for 200 years, before Pharaoh Ahmose managed to learn the art of chariot-driving and chased the Hyksos out of the homeland and into Canaan (Palestine). Apparently, he also drove out some other foreigners at the same time, Semitic people who were accused of collaborating with the Hyksos during the occupation, possibly the real background story of the Biblical exodus, when Moses left Egypt with a considerable number of people.

The Old Testament gleefully describes countless aggressive invasions by primitive and poor pastoral tribes where ancient Canaanite city-states, among them Jericho, the oldest known city in the world, were completely destroyed, burned to the ground and its people massacred. Except for a few young virgins who were raped and then forced to marry their rapists, who had also killed their parents and siblings.

In this biblical case, such terrible and cruel invasions were all "pleasing to the Lord", who even demanded that livestock was destroyed, every trace of the previous culture trampled and burned to ashes. There might very well be some truth in these old Bible stories, although there is more archaeological evidence that Semitic tribes at a very early stage invaded the Sumerian city states, than the Canaanite ones. In Sumer (present day Iraq), there are countless stories of aggressive pastoral tribes attacking the early, very advanced and civilized city states some 5000 years ago, leaving many in ruins.

For the most part, the city-states managed to maintain their culture, the invading forces rather becoming a significant influence, yet adapting quickly to the more advanced cultures of Sumer. Some of these invading tribes; however, were described as excessively primitive and barbaric, bringing nothing but destruction. We are not speaking of one invading culture, but rather a series of raids instigated by many different tribes, some related to the Caucasian Hyksos, others Semitic, the ancestors of Arabs and Jews. It is no coincidence that Abraham was born in the Sumerian city-state of Ur. Soon, the city states, inspired by or infiltrated by the new warlike cultures, were fighting regularly among themselves. Legislation texts show that the earlier equality between people and between the sexes gradually gave way to increasing hierarchy. Around 2400 B.C.E, the reformer Urukagina of Ur outlawed polyandry, forbidding women in the city-state of Ur from having more than one husband.

Several centuries later, the same punishment that was once passed against polyandry was now passed against women who disobeyed their husband, testifying to the gradual decline of women's rights, which had once been considerable in Sumer. The old Sumerian cultures had been ruled partly by a caste of priests and priestesses, partly by democratic election, but the many invasions led to a need for a "big man". Someone who could lead the city-state in war. This was the origin of kingship in Sumer. The compromise between the old democratic and theocratic system and the new king-general rule may have found one outlet in the ritual of Sacred Marriage, where the newly elected king had to ritually submit to, worship and then marry the goddess of the city-state. The oldest religious texts of Sumer are hymns used during this ritual, where the goddess was incarnated in a priestess who performed the Sacred Marriage with the king on a stage for all to see. The king would legitimize his rule and show his worthiness by displaying how the goddess loved him. This ritual became extremely important in the Middle East and its myth, its basic mythical theme and its function soon spread into Europe to form the basis of public religion, where sacred kingship and the king's marriage to the patron goddess of the land or the people was central.

In the German and Celtic areas, this ritual was extremely important even into the late Iron Ages. No man could become king unless he was elected by the people, went through severe rituals of initiation to show himself worthy, and entered marriage with the goddess of the people. The Norwegian professor Gro Steinsland has shown how crucial this myth of sacred marriage actually is in the Edda lore, testifying to the importance of the ritual well into the Viking Age. Others have shown how this ritual was central to public religion in Scandinavia during the Bronze Ages. I believe that the myth of Sacred Marriage has inspired more than just public kingship inauguration rituals.

It has spurred the lore of mystical union with the goddess in death, as testified by the overwhelming presence of sacred marriage symbolism in graves and grave monuments during the Scandinavian Bronze Age and Iron Ages, as well as in the Edda lore, as I showed in my thesis and in the previous essay. The cultural revolution, which happened towards the very end of the Stone Age, significantly shaped the Bronze Age cultures of Europe and the Middle East. It was not just a time of war and invasion. It was also a time when modern civilization was shaped, when trading and cultural interaction across the continent intensified or continued as intensely as ever. Whether the Norse myths about a Golden Age are based on real historical events or on pure fantasy, they are highly relevant even today. They offer clues as to why the Golden Age was crushed what qualities were nourished to make it so and clues as to how to restore that era of wisdom and peace both on a societal and a personal, spiritual level. The Golden Age as such is not just an era, but a state of being, an inner state of peace.

5.2: THE PEACE OF WISDOM AND THE SONG OF THE MILLSTONE

> *Grottasǫngr*
> *Wake you, Wisdom!*
> *Wake you, Wisdom!*
> *If you wish to hear our songs and our ancient tales*
> > *vaki þv Froþi!*
> > *vaki þv Froþi!*
> > *ef þv hlyþa vill*
> > *songvm ockrvm*
> > *oc sagvm fornvm.*

> *Grottasǫngr st. 18, Poetic Edda*

> *"Shield had a son called Peace Heritage [Fríðleifr], and he ruled the kingdom [Gotland-Denmark] after him. The Son of Peace Heritage was called Wisdom [Fróði]. He took the kingdom after his father at the time when Augustus held the peace over all the world, the age when Christ was born. But since Wisdom was the mightiest of all kings in the Northern lands, the peace was called after him as far as the Danish [Old Norse] language reached, and people called it the Peace of Wisdom [Fróðafríðr]. In that era, no man hurt another, even if he were to stumble upon, lose or bound the one who had killed his father or brother. And there was no thief or burglar in those days, so that a gold ring lay a long time on the Jalangr-heath."*

This is Snorri's account of the Peace of Wisdom, the Golden Age in Norse mythology. Snorri lets the Golden Age be a peaceful era in the North, corresponding with the Pax Romana of the emperor Augustus and the era around the birth of Christ. He gives to King Wisdom a designated geographical rule, namely Gotland and Denmark.

I do not know how the society worked in Scandinavia in those times, although we do know that it was relatively peaceful compared to the times that were to follow. We should not lose ourselves further into historical speculation, however, since that will easily blind us to the messages conveyed by the poets. The inner message of the myth is much more important than its historical truth value. A message of wisdom and of peace, and a description of the forces that may destroy such a state of being, whether it is on a personal or a societal level. The real, underlying message is to be understood by taking seriously the meaning of the names. King Wisdom represents wisdom ruling an individual, and the dominance of wisdom in the world. It is the result of peace, the Heritage of Peace, and it brings peace, as in the Peace of Wisdom. It is a state of being, or an era real or imagined, when no one would think of exerting violence, not even in vengeance.

To the general Norseman, even by the time of Snorri (13th century AD), to resist avenging oneself on the killer of a father or brother was a highly impressive feat which really served to illustrate how incredibly peaceful those times were. The gold ring is a symbol of the divine wisdom, the illumination offered by the Pagan path of initiation. The end of the Peace of Wisdom is also explained, and Snorri based his account on an older Edda poem, the Grottasǫngr: "The Song of the Millstone". To understand this poem, we need to look at Snorri's account, which serves as an introduction. After his descriptions of the Peace of Wisdom and King Wisdom, Snorri continues.

> *"King Wisdom when to Sweden to attend a banquet at a King's called The One Who Is Many [Fiǫlnir (= Óðinn)]. There he bought two slave girls who were called Fenia and Menia; they were awfully huge and powerful."*

The names Fenia and Menia reveal that we are not talking about ordinary slave girls. This is merely a disguise. According to Rudolf Simek's Dictionary of Northern Mythology, the name Fenia means "Heath-Dweller" or "of the Heath" (from fén: heath, clearing, a bright open place). This name is not coincidental. The heath was a sacred place in Pagan times, a place where the darkness of the underworld wilderness opened into brightness, a natural temple. When the Pagans wanted a name for their faith so as to counter the new faith, they chose the word Heiðindómr, the Rule of the Heath as opposed to Kristinndómr, The Rule of Christ. A Pagan was called a heiðningr a heathen. The name Heiðr was used by Freyia when she traveled the world as a witch and is part of the name Heiðrún, the she-goat who produces the sacred mead of the afterlife.

It means both "illuminated space" and "heath". Likewise, Simek explains that the name Menia means "Necklace-Owner" or "Of the Necklace", from the word mén necklace or jewel. This is a reference to Freyia's necklace, and she, the owner of the Brísingamen the Flames' Jewel is the famous necklace owner of Norse mythology. Thus we are seeing that the two "huge and powerful" slave girls are related to the two sides of the goddess. The witch-hag and the beauty-maiden. However, there are two other possible translations of the names Fenia and Menia. Fenia could be translated as the Achiever, whereas Menia could be translated as the Rememberer. As such, the two "slave girls" could in fact represent the goddesses of fate, Urðr and Verðandi. Urðr (Origin) represents the past, and corresponds with Menia the Rememberer, whereas Verðandi (Becoming) represents the present and corresponds with Fenia the Achiever.

In the creation poem Vǫluspá, these two carve the runes of fate into the roots of the world tree. In the poem Grottasǫngr, the Rememberer and the Achiever draw the millstone of destiny. Their role as Norns fates is strengthened throughout the story since their main purpose is to shape fate whether it is as the constructors of the Earth landscapes, as the grinders of destiny in general or as the Valkyrie who choose the dead. I will stick to these two latter translations although the former are not thereby excluded. It is my conviction that the Norse poets often used double or triple meanings on purpose.

Snorri continues:

> *"At the time there were two millstones that were so huge that no one were strong enough to draw them. And this mill had the property that the one who could pull her, could get ground that which was spoken. This mill was called Grotti, and the one who gave it to Wisdom was called Open Hanging Mouth [Hengikioptr]. King Wisdom led the two slave girls to the mill and ordered them to grind gold. This they did, at first they ground gold, peace and happiness for Wisdom. But he did not let the girls rest or have their sleep longer than the cuckoo was silent or the time one needs to utter a verse. It is said that they then sang the song known as the Grottasǫngr, which goes like this:…"*

The mill, made out of two millstones, can grind whatever the one who grinds speak. It is the millstone of destiny, where fate is "ground". The Open Hanging Mouth that owned the mill at first seems to be yet another reference to the speech and sound that is the basis of creation in Norse cosmology. However, no one in the world is strong enough to draw the mill, except the two women, Fenia and Menia, the Achiever and the Rememberer. The concept of the very powerful giantesses is a repeated theme in Norse mythology. In Snorri's story about Baldr's funeral, none of the Aesir, not even mighty Þórr, is able to push the great Ring Horn ship onto the ocean. They need the help of the old giantess Hyrrokkin, the Fire Spinner, who pushes the ship towards is death journey without effort. In another story, when Þórr visits Utgarðsloki, the mighty Þórr is beaten in a wrestling match against an old giantess called Eldi (Old Age). In the poem, the Achiever and the Rememberer reveal their true and immensely powerful nature as shapers and movers of the Earth itself, as I described in Chapter 2.7. To be able to rule the giantesses of fate is the equivalent of ruling the fate of the world and the natural forces, since this is what the sisters represent.

The concept is very similar to the Indian tantric concept of Shakti the cosmic dynamic creative power that is the Goddess, which must be channeled through the containing, and preserving holding power of the male principle, the God, lest it becomes destructive. But the God must love and cherish the Goddess in order to contain her. The enlightened state is achieved when the two powers melt together in a loving, equal union. In the Norse lore, the ruling, likewise, goes both ways. The sisters have to be benevolent in mind towards their ruler. He must please them and love them, respect and cherish them, lest they become destructive. Only through loving them can he contain and rule their creative power. This is where the sleeping Wisdom fails. As we learn, King Wisdom enslaves the goddesses of fate so that they will create destiny according to his liking. He wants peace, prosperity and happiness, and so the ladies grind. The slavery in question is interesting, and it would not be so far-fetched to wonder if we are seeing yet another myth of how male-dominated ruling elites enslaved and suppressed ancient goddess-oriented and more matriarchal and egalitarian cultures.

If we are to choose this interpretation, we will be missing out on some important points. I think that we have to take seriously the fact that the king in question is an incarnation of Wisdom, and that the kingship indicates that Wisdom dominates this society, which allegedly produced peace, happiness and prosperity. This does not fit well into the image painted above. It is as such not really a story of how an aggressive and warlike royal and noble class began to subjugate women and workers at least it is not the only layer of the myth. We have to look beyond the possible historical background and into the message about wisdom that the poet was trying to convey.

The slavery is a metaphor, meaning only that Wisdom has taken control over Fate, the fate of the world itself. In fact, as the poem shows, these ladies embody the natural forces in general, not just "fate". They are the forces that shaped the earth and moved it. As such, the "slavery" is a good thing. It is the "enslavement" of the natural forces and the world's destiny to the rule of peace, wisdom and prosperity. Despite their "slavery", the women seem very happy and content to grind peace and prosperity for Wisdom, creating, in fact, the Golden Age, the Peace of Wisdom.

However, Wisdom begins, as the poem reveals, to "fall asleep", while refusing his slave-girls their rest. He forgets to care for them, becomes greedy for their produce, and abuses his power over them. We must keep in mind that the giantesses represent the natural forces and the fate of the world, which was as real to the Vikings as any natural force. As soon as "Wisdom falls asleep", the ruler fails to appreciate the true power of the giantesses, acknowledge them and meet their needs. His household, the household of Wisdom, falls asleep. This is what leads to the end of the Peace of Wisdom, as the poem goes:

8. Beware, Wisdom you are not fully wise you friend of human eloquence when you bought your people and chose us for our strength and for our appearance But of our lineage you asked not	8. «Varattv, Froþi! fvllspakr of þic, malvinr manna! er þv man keyptir; ka/ssþv at afli oc at alitvm, en at ætterni ecki spvrþir.

The ladies then begin to count up their lineage, revealing that they are of the kind of Þiazi the Slave-Binder, the eagle of Death, and Hrungnir the Roarer, among others, before they go on to reveal their own significance and their connection to the Mill and the Earth herself. Then they move onto their role in the fates, the lives and deaths of men, and the outcome of all battles. The giantesses reveal how they have shaped great wars in bygone times, but that they finally became enslaved to Wisdom, and when they came to the house of Wisdom they ground peace, happiness and prosperity. They did not mind until they were treated without respect and taken for granted, and forced to never rest. Again, in order to understand this, we must bear in mind their function as natural powers, the dynamic and creative principle. This is what has been abused. Wisdom has become a prey to his own greed. As Wisdom and his household metaphorically fall asleep, the giantesses call for them to wake up Wisdom if they want to hear their ancient songs. No one wakes up.

The giantesses, listening to the silence their calls are met with, complain that the king shows no mercy to slave girls, that they are forced to work too hard, that his greed causes him to abuse them, that they are not respected, and that the king is underestimating the power of the slave women's anger. As no one wakes up, the giantesses begin to grind war, famine and pestilence. In fact, they begin to grind Ragnarǫkthe Shattering of the Rulers. The death of multitudes is prophesied, as well as the death of Wisdom. However, the ladies continue with a very subtle revelation:

22. "Let us grind more! The son of the She-Bear on the Half-Lord will avenge Wisdom so that he is famed both as her son and as her brother as we two both know."	22. Molvm enn framarr, mon Yrsv sonr, niðr Halfdanar, hefna Froþa; sa mvn hennar heitinn verþa bvrr oc broþir, vitvm baþar þat.»

This curious stanza raises some interesting, yet usually ignored questions:

➼ Who is the She-Bear, and who is Wisdom, and the Half Lord? The question will be answered later, but cannot be understood before we have had a look at another Golden Age myth; the myth of Baldr.

➼ Very few, if anyone, have previously actually asked the question "Who killed Baldr"? The answer would seem obvious, since the killer is clearly said to be Hǫðr Blindi, whose arm was directed by the mischievous Loki.

➼ We shall take a new look and find that we may very well be dealing with a veritable murder mystery. But first, we will look at another related theme; the story of how Týr lost his arm.

5.3: WHEN THE GOD OF WAR LOST HIS ARM TO GREED

The war-leaders travel to the clash of arm which was to take place at the Mountain of Flames
The Peace of Wisdom was torn
Between enemies, runs the wolf of the Expander blood-thirsty around the island.
> *Fara hildingar*
> *hiorstefno til*
> *þeirrar er lagdo*
> *at Logafiollom;*
> *sleit Froþa friþ*
> *fianda a milli,*
> *fara Viþriss grey*
> *valgiorn vm ey.*

Helgakviða Hundingsbani hin fyrri, st. 13, Poetic Edda

LOKI AND HIS THREE CHILDREN

The story of how Týr, the god of war, lost his arm to the Fenrisulfr The Wolf of Greed is told by Snorri in his Gylfaginning. It begins with his account of Loki, who is described as the origin of all deceit and betrayal, a shame to Aesir and to human beings, a god of false rumors, speaking behind other's back, and of treason. Loki is beautiful to look at, Snorri continues, but very ugly in his intentions, and very ambivalent in his actions. More than anyone else does he possess the quality of cunning. It is possible that Snorri's description of Loki is influenced by Christian concepts of Lucifer and the Devil. In poetry, Loki is certainly very ambivalent and often mischievous, but he helps the Aesir as often as he brings them into trouble. The name Loki has a very uncertain meaning.

The likeness to the word logi "flame" has led some to believe he was a god of fire. He was not, but the likeness is played upon in the Eddas as well as in folklore, and I think that the association to the metaphorical flame of passion is certainly there. In one story, Loki's appetite/hunger is compared to that of Logi of Utgarðr "Flame of the World Outside", and he may well be the real figure behind Hlóðurr "Heat" who gave vitality, passion and colors to men and women in the creation story. The Norse words that may have given Loki his name, apart from the rhyming logi, is the verb loka "to close" or the noun loka (f.sg), which could mean "closed door" or generally something that closes/hides something else. There is also the word lok (n.sg) which also indicates something that closes something, such as a lid, but also an ending, something that is completed or finished.

Til loks means "to the very end", at lokum means "thoroughly" or "fulfilled" or "reached", loksins means "finally", or "at last". I suspect that the concept of closing or hiding something is behind the meaning of the name Loki, and that the associations with logi ["flame"] is based on the rhyming sound together with the passionate, "flaming" nature of the god, although it is originally not related. But I have found no linguistic support elsewhere for this suspicion. Loki is, Like Óðinn, one of three brothers. His other brothers are called Byleistr or Byleiptr ["Wind Lightening"] and Helblindi ["Death Blinder" (or "Blind to Death")]. The latter is recognizable as one of Óðin's names. It is my conviction that Loki, thus, is a name for one of Óðin's brothers, Vili or Vé, who are ultimately all aspects of the same three-fold god Óðinn: Spirit, Poetry and Frenzy, or Spirit, Mind and Passion.

In a trinity, all will play one of these three parts. Helblindi is the Spirit that blinds death itself, or is blind to death it is the part of consciousness that could be immortal. Wind Lightening is a good way of describing the quality of mind, thoughts being like swift stormy charges of lightening. Seeing Loki's role in stories, I suggest that he is a character based on the quality that Víli represents. The Will or Intent, the passion to move forward and make things happen. Loki is called Sagna Hrærir in the poem Haustlǫng, meaning "The Mover of the Stories". Passion or intent is always the mover of all stories, the creator of conflict. I will refer to Loki as Passion on many occasions, indicating vitality, intent, desire, life-force and will, qualities of Passion that can be both destructive and creative, indeed ambivalent and deceitful of nature, although often bringing great products and stories.

To the three original qualities of Spirit-Mind-Passion, there are always three negative counterparts, just as the bright golden maiden of glorious fate is always seen in contrast with the terrifying hag of oblivion and sleep. Loki has three sons, two by a giantess called Angrbóða ["She who bids Aggression"]. In Norse mythology, children mean results, the results of a quality or of the union between two qualities. Sons mean seen and known results, daughters mean unseen and hidden results. The seen and known results of the qualities of Passion coupled with Aggression is the quality of Greed and the quality of a closed mind, a mind that closes itself around the known, keeping all that is unknown outside of its perception. The two seen results are represented by Fenrir and the Miðgarðr serpent.

→   Fenrir [Greed], is also known as Fenrisulfr ["The Wolf of Greed"]. The name indicates his function; the wolf is a metaphor for the quality of greed, gluttony, hunger, destructive desire. The wolf is the major enemy of Óðinn as Spirit, and is destined to kill the Spirit, only to be killed himself by Spirit's son Víðarr the Silent, a name that indicates silent expansion of Spirit. The wolf is a negative mirror, the destructive counterpart, of the quality of Passion.

→   The other son of Loki is Iormungandr ["Powerful Spell/Magic"] also known as Miðgarðsormr the Middle World Serpent. This serpent-shaped giant coils himself around Miðgarðr the Middle World and represents the border between the known and the unknown. He is the main enemy and nemesis of Þórr, the god whose main purpose it is to protect Earth, Middle World and the known against the threats of the World Outside and the unknown. This serpent is a negative mirror or destructive counterpart of the quality of Mind, closing the doors of perception against all that is not known.

→   A third son of Loki is Sleipnir ["The Glider"] an eight-legged steed who has the ability to move swiftly between all the dimensions of cosmos. The steed is given to Óðinn as a means of moving between worlds and into the unknown, and is used by heroes who seek the precious mead in Hel. It was borrowed by Hermóðr when he went to seek Baldr. The steed is, unlike the two other sons, not born through the union of Loki with "She who Bids Aggression". It is born by Loki himself in the shape of a mare. In that female shape, Loki coupled with the stallion Svadilfari [Harm Traveler] a stallion that was used to build a wall of protection around the world of the Aesir against the giants.

→   The theme of a boundary between the safe and ordered world of the known (gods and men) against the dangerous and unpredictable world of the unknown (giants) is strongly present in association with Loki, whose name could possibly mean "the Closer" (of doors between the worlds). Although the wall that closes the doors between worlds is built through the effort of the Harm Traveler, a foal is born that can jump across any high wall of the cosmos, including the high walls of Hel. When Sleipnir is ridden by Óðinn or those who walk in his footsteps on the path of initiation, it is ultimately the power to move between the worlds that is employed by Spirit. It is a counterpart to Spirit, born of a very weird union between two destructive-creative ambivalent powers Loki as a female means Passion in an unknown, hidden form, coupling with Harm Traveler, a negative but useful force that builds a wall around the known world against the unknown.

→ There is also a daughter which may replace Sleipnir within the trinity, a daughter of She who Bids Aggression. Hel, the goddess of the dead, the third child of Passion coupled with Aggression. That she is a daughter means that she [Death] is the hidden result of this union.

→ Hel as Death rules the nine mortal worlds and represents according to Snorri particularly the death of everyone who dies from old age and disease. However, many of the myths and stories show that this is only partially true. Baldr died from a wound, but became Hel's property at once. When Hermóðr travels to Hel, he learns of whole armies of men who died in battle, traveling the Hel-Path. Sígurðr, who avenged himself on his own murderer and thus died in battle, was sent right to Hel and only saved from the dark realm through the efforts of his Valkyrie lover. It would seem that Hel is ultimately just death, although she has many aspects and names.

→ As Hel, she is the death of old age and disease, but she has "sisters" who represent different kinds of death. They are, ultimately, all the same. Death in all its forms. Like Sleipnir and his parents, Hel has two faces, she is half rotten and dark like a corpse, half rosy-cheeked and fresh like a young maiden. The metaphor for life and death is obvious in this image death is both these things at once destruction and decay, but also the origin of new life and resurrection. In the Viking Age, Hel has become the daughter of Loki, although if she originated as anyone's daughter it would probably rather be the daughter of Utgarðsloki "Loki of the World Outside". This tremendous giant is the cause of illusions that may blind both gods and men, and the brother of the giantess called Eldi "Old Age".

→ Like the little Loki, the great Loki is associated with the Middle World Serpent and with Greed (in the form of Logi, who can eat even more than Loki), these living within his realm of illusions. As a power, Hel is probably older and more independent than all that. Her realm Níflhel was there since before this universe came into being. When the poets assign Hel the status of "Loki's daughter," it is a way of saying that Death is the hidden result of Passion. As a female, Hel or Death is the secret, unseen result of the union between Passion and Aggression (Loki and Angrbóða). She is also the female counterpart to Sleipnir. Death is the unknown and hidden side of that which Sleipnir represents. The power to move between worlds. It is no coincidence that Snorri chose the name Helblindi to cover for Óðinn/Spirit in this presentation. He could have chosen several other Óðinn names, but he chose Helblindi for a purpose: To indicate that Hel corresponds with the name Helblindi, another way of showing the ambivalence of death and spirit. The spirit of life is the counterpart of death.

The most important thing we learn when we look for and recognize poetical formulas such as the trinity of qualities coupled with mirror qualities, is that such formulas are used all the time in the Norse myths. No matter what religious or magical function or status a god, goddess or other power being had in the religious cults in various regions at various times, the poets, who created fiction in order to reveal spiritual messages, applied these characters in order to make their point, and their purpose was to aid human beings on the path towards illumination, knowledge and immortality. By using the metaphorical, symbolic language of myth, they speak to the unconscious as well as to the conscious. This is also how we have to approach the myth of Týr and Fenrir.

THE CHAINS THAT BOUND FENRIR

"The Aesir raised the Greed Wolf among themselves, but only Týr had the courage to go him and feed him. When the Aesir saw how much the wolf grew every day...they made a terribly strong chain called Wind Shield Council [Læðing, Levþing or Leðing] and went to the wolf and asked him to try his strength on the chain. The wolf meant that he would easily manage this, and let the Aesir do as they pleased. And even in the first battle he broke the chain, and thus he was free from the Wind Shield Council.

Then the Aesir made another chain, this too very strong, and this was called Fetter [i.e. Divine Power (ON Drómi], and...the wolf....tore off the chain so the bits flew widely apart. Thus he freed himself from Divine Power...Now the Aesir feared that they would never bind the wolf. Then All-Father sent someone called Illuminated One [Skírnir], the messenger of Freyr, down into the realm of the Dark Elves, where he found some dwarfs, and they made a chain called Open One [Gleipnir]...

This chain was soft and light like a rope of silk, but still as powerful as you are now about to hear. When the chain was brought to the Aesir, they thanked the messenger well for his errand. And then they went to a water called Black Darkener [Amsvartnir a metaphor for the Underworld] and there to an island called Heather Covered [Lyngvi], and they lured the wolf there. Then they showed him the silk rope and asked him to tear this off too..."

Gylfaginning, Prose Edda, Snorri Sturluson

In order to truly appreciate the myth of the Fenris-wolf, we have to bear in mind, at all times, that he represents the quality of greed he is the Greed Wolf. As such, the wolf represents a quality within human beings, within gods, and within the world at large. When we read, in Snorri's account, that the wolf was raised and grew among the Aesir, it is a way of saying that the quality of greed was raised and grew among the powers of consciousness and intelligence and the powers that rule our world. It is destined to destroy the present order of our world, but the myths also show that there are ways of overcoming it. When the Aesir attempt to bind the wolf, it must be read as a parable of how the quality of greed was checked or how they tried to keep it in check. At first, they tried to use a "chain" that they perceived of as immensely strong. This chain is called, in different sources, Læðing, Levþing or Leðing. The meaning is actually obscure but it is a possibility that the first part of the word is læ ["harm"], while the second word is þing [council or assembly or parliament] so that the meaning is "Harm Council" or "Harm Parliament" a place where harm, in this case the harmful effect of the growing "greed-wolf" is discussed in plenum and dealt with. This would be a very simple way of describing how the wolf was bound with a divine solution, the sacred parliament.

It would actually be a way of describing how the þing a democratic institution is the solution to the problem posed by the wolf. If this is the meaning, we are seeing, perhaps, one of the oldest written arguments for democracy as the first way to stagger the forces of greed among men. The word may also be made from the word hlé windshield. This interpretation makes sense in the light of other myths. Wind is a symbol of the power of death. Wind-shield is a reference to immortality Hlésey being the island of immortality where Aegir and his nine daughters are said to reside and where the gods will come together with the light elves (immortal souls) to drink the mead of memory at the end of time. Only if they can own a "cauldron" big enough for all the mead of memory will they be able to dine with the immortals. The wind-shield is also referred to in the grove of Barri, where Freyr after the nine nights of initiation will be able to enter his union with the illuminating maiden in the "breezeless grove" a place of immortality.

The "council" in the name of the chain indicates a sharing of knowledge. The sharing of the knowledge of immortality is the "chain" that first binds Greed. If this is the meaning of the chain, the story is a parable telling how the quality of Greed terminated the sharing of this esoteric knowledge, a theme that so many other myths also reveal as a key issue. Earlier, we saw how Wisdom succumbed to greed for riches and power. In the next, we shall look at a myth that tells how Divine Knowledge was once flowing freely in the world for everyone to grasp. In this story, we hear that Greed destroys the sharing of this esoteric knowledge, a theme that corresponds with the story of how Divine Knowledge no longer was freely available in the world. So the Aesir attempt to bind the wolf with a fetter called Drómi. As far as I can find, the only translation to this name is "fetter". At first, this does not seem very profound at all, but only until we realize that "bonds" and "fetters" are in fact poetical metaphors for gods or cosmic powers, as Snorri wrote in Skáldskaparmál:

> "What names are there for the gods? They are also called bonds, as Eyiolf Dádaskald said:
>
> ...Eirik draws land under himself to the pleasure of the bonds... ...and fetters, as Einar Skálaglamm said..."

Thus the second attempt, when the sharing of the knowledge of immortality was broken by Greed, involves religion. As a second solution, the belief in gods and divine rules may be a powerful check against the quality of Greed, but religion proved (as we may all know now), no match against the increasingly raging cravings of Greed within people and societies. The third chain which finally managed to bind Greed was an apparently soft, hardly even visible chain called Open One. It is a subtle chain with a subtle meaning, no chain at all really, and it could only tie the wolf in a place of deep water darkness covered with "heather" the subconscious, the unknown. The Greed is, finally, checked by oblivion and ignorance, lest Greed finds a way of destroying the gods forever. The knowledge of immortality that Greed would destroy is forever hidden in the underworld, for its protection. It can only be sought by those who have the courage to overcome Greed and similar qualities. When young Helgi Hiǫrvarðsson in the heroic Edda poems goes into the Hatafiord "The Fjord of Hatred", fighting the giants called Hati "Hatred", Hróðmarr "Furious Water" (i.e. Aggression, anger), and is called upon to win the battle of the Frekasteinn "the Rock of Greed" it is a reference to the need to overcome the qualities of hatred, greed and fury within himself.

In his first life of initiations, Helgi Hiǫrvarðsson wins over hatred and aggression, but fails in the battle of Greed. He must repeat this battle in his next life as Helgi Hundingsbani, and only then can he reach Valhǫll, the land of immortality. The same theme is present in numerous initiation stories. In the myth of Sígurðr, fear and greed must be overcome before the hero can find and wake up his sleeping Valkyrie and receive the knowledge that will lead to immortality. In his story, Fear takes the shape of the serpent Fafnir, "Embracer", a version of the Middle World Serpent, who coils himself around the red gold of divine wisdom, snorting poison against intruders and wearing the Aegishjalmr "The Helmet of Fear".

Only when Sígurðr "kills" the serpent may he know his own fears (symbolized by putting on the helmet while carrying all the divine red gold of wisdom), and then he can destroy Greed in the shape of Reginn "The Ruler", brother to the serpent of fear. Reginn symbolizes Greed, with its raging lust for vengeance and its craving, which leads it to use its cunning in order to manipulate others for his own purpose. As soon as Sígurðr has killed the serpent that forms the border between his world and the divine knowledge, he understands the quality of Greed and "kills" it, slaying Reginn in the process.

TÝR AND THE FENRIS WOLF

"The wolf said: "If you bind me and I cannot get loose, you have tricked me...I do not want to try on this chain. But no one shall accuse me of cowardice, so let one of you place his hand in my mouth as a security measure to prove that this is not deceit."

The Aesir looked at one another...no one wanted to dare his hand. Finally, Týr offered up his right hand and placed it in the mouth of the wolf. But as the wolf began to struggle with the chain, the chain hardened, and the harder he struggled, the tighter the chain became. Then all the Aesir laughed all except Týr; he lost his right hand."

Gylfaginning, Prose Edda, Snorri Sturluson

The god Týr is a Norse version of a very old Germanic god of war and warriors, Tiwaz, also known as Ziu. His origins are ancient, like Þór's, perhaps going 5000 years back, and he has Indo-European counterparts in the gods Dyaus, Zeus and Jupiter. Etymologically, his name is associated with words for "god" [Old Indian deva, Old Irish día, Latin dei and Old Norse tívar (plural of Tyr)]. His function as a god of war and council overlaps with the younger god Óðinn, and there are several overlapping themes in their mythology: Like Óðinn, Týr will fight a wolf at Ragnarǫk, although this time the wolf is called Garmr. Garmr, like Fenrir, is also bound, and the two are through their descriptions obviously the same. Týr's functions and importance seem to have given way to Óðinn over time, and the two melt together.

In the Edda, Týr is almost not mentioned, except as a power to call on for victory in all kinds of matters, and a power that accompanied Þórr on his initiation journey as a young boy to the giant Hymir. As I mentioned above, the Norse poets applied the mythical character in order to create meaningful fiction. Thus we should look at what Týr might represent in the myth where he binds the Greed Wolf. As a god of war and warriors, Týr might represent two things. He might literally represent war and warriors, or he might represent a more subtle "warrior spirit" the will to fight, stand up for himself or others, and the readiness to sacrifice life and limbs in order to protect the community. A warrior society such as the Old Norse would hone and honor this warrior spirit, even if most people did not crave war or battle as a lifestyle, and rather prayed for peace and prosperity. We must understand Týr in the light of the society that nurtured him. First and foremost, he represents the sacrifice of the warrior who readily protects his kin when necessary.

Secondly, he represents victory in all matters, whether it be victory in battle or in other efforts, and was called upon when something was started and needed to be completed to the benefit of the caller. Thirdly, he represents the mind of the warrior, the strategic analysis that is needed to win any kind of battle, and the will to conquer and fight for what is wanted. Another interesting thing about Týr is his name. Although it is certainly etymologically linked to ancient words for gods, there is a second meaning in the Old Norse version of his name: Týr can also mean "beast" or "animal". The poets would be aware of this secondary meaning and use it to their advantage. The "Beast" is a perfect image of the passion that makes things happen. There is something beastly to the energy of intent, passion and will the instinct for survival, life force, vitality, the warrior's energy to move on, break through and fight for life.

The god of war represents the power of intent and the will to fight for its existence. Týr as a warrior god overlaps in function with Óðinn as a warrior god, and as the Beast he corresponds with the aspect of Frenzy in Óðinn's name, which I also refer to as Passion or Intent. In poetry, we must understand Týr as a character that was used by the poets to describe the Passion aspect of the spirit trinity. As such Týr the "Beast" mirrors Fenrir the "Wolf": They are the two sides of Passion. Týr is the positive aspect of Passion, that which is passionate and which channels its intent on protecting its community and making courageous sacrifices. Fenrir is the negative aspect of Passion, that which only craves power and properties the greedy outlet of the power of passion. The two mirror each other like two possible outcomes of the animal instinct for survival, the selfishness of greed and the sacrifice of the warrior.

The myth of Týr binding Fenrir is the story of how the positive side of the warrior spirit must control the negative side. However, the outcome of this struggle turned out to be ambivalent, for the Beast lost one arm to Greed a way of saying that the warrior spirit or the intent of men was partly consumed by Greed, or that the warrior spirit "lent a hand" to Greed. That the warrior spirit, the Passion, lost his "right hand" the Greed is in itself a metaphor, perhaps having to do with the fact that the right hand usually is the hand that acts outwards and takes the lead, or perhaps the expression of being someone's right hand meaning that the warrior spirit at least partially began to serve Greed rather than focus on its original true purpose of survival and protection.

OUT OF EDEN (PARADISE LOST)

> *"And the serpent said unto the woman, Ye shall not surely die: For God doth know that in the day ye eat thereof, then your eyes shall be opened, and ye shall be as gods, knowing good and evil.*
> *And when the woman saw that the tree was good for food, and that it was pleasant to the eyes, and a tree to be desired to make one wise, she took of the fruit thereof and did eat, and gave also unto her husband with her, and he did eat.*
> *And the eyes of them both were opened…"*

Genesis 3.5-7

According to Judaic, Christian and Muslim worldviews, prehistory has been a linear event from Creation onwards, described in their sacred texts, such as the Bible. The Biblical belief in the Golden Age excludes large civilizations, and was something only our two first ancestors, Adam and Eve, ever got to see. The loss of Paradise is a divine punishment for their disobedience against God, inflicted upon their descendants ever since. This is how the myth of Eden has usually been presented.

The two first people, a man and a woman, lived happily and innocently in Paradise, and only one thing was forbidden to them; to eat from the Tree of Knowledge. The Serpent, usually thought to be the Devil, then tempted the woman to eat of the fruit of Knowledge. When the woman ate from the tree, she could discern the difference between good and evil. She transmitted this knowledge to her man. God became jealous of their knowledge, and feared that next, they would eat from the Tree of Life and become immortal, like gods:

> *"And the Lord God said, Behold, the man is become as one of us, to know good and evil; and now, lest he put forth his hand, and take also of the tree of life, and eat, and live forever. Therefore the Lord God sent him forth from the garden of Eden…so he drove out the man, and he placed at the east of the garden of Eden Cherubims, and a flaming sword which turned every way, to keep the way of the tree of life."*

Thus he expelled them from Paradise, let the man know that he would have to work and suffer for his daily bread, while the woman would have to accept male domination and suffering in childbirth. The lost garden of Eden Paradise was barred from humankind by a flaming sword. Those who have professed this myth as actual truth have almost exclusively focused on the sex, which is not actually a theme or even present in the myth, but which nevertheless, according to countless religious leaders, has become the great clue by which to interpret this myth. Since no sex is actually mentioned in the myth, we must assume that the emphasis on the (non-existing) sexual part has to do with the fact that it is a woman who offers the fruit of the Tree of Knowledge to the man.

Although this fruit is expressly said to symbolize divine knowledge, it is automatically translated into a symbol of sex, the loss of sexual innocence. I cannot presume I understand exactly why religious leaders believe that this myth has to do with sex at all, but I suspect it has something to do with the fact that the fruit-offering comes from a woman, and that this in itself is enough to shudder and shout "sex!" within the patriarchal, gender-obsessed, sex-obsessed brotherhoods that have dominated and monopolized the myth of Eden. The myth itself clearly reveals the fruit of the tree to be a myth about divine knowledge. Knowledge that might enable human beings to learn about immortality, and thus to become like gods.

That a woman is the first to eat from the tree does not mean that this myth originally had anything to do with sex although a sexual union between the goddess and the initiate often is used in various mythologies to symbolize the consecration of the successful initiate. It might also be a story that reflects what people once knew, namely that the first wisdom keepers were women, who shared their knowledge with men. From archaeology, we see that the norm in the earliest civilizations were female priests. We also see that the symbol of the serpent was a very important part of early religious cults. The snake might not originally have been the Devil, but rather the symbol of the religion that came before the Judaic one, in which we know without doubt that the serpent was a symbol of wisdom itself the hidden, transformative wisdom of the underworld, a symbol wielded by priestesses of the ancient temples all over the Bronze Age world, from Sumer and Minoan Crete to Scandinavia.

Some historians and thinkers have suggested that the myth has to do with how a male-dominated monotheistic-to-be religion overthrew the ancient religions that were dominated by priestesses and a belief in goddesses or a great goddess. This is perfectly possible. We could also try to decipher the myth in a more psychological fashion, which does not exclude the historical approach just mentioned. As I see it, from a personal point of view, the myth of Eden is a parable of how humanity, closing in on knowledge that would lead to their awakening to their own divinity, somehow were stopped by a feeling of unworthiness and sinfulness. They started to look at themselves from the outside and feeling ashamed of their nakedness ashamed of their true, animal selves.

They began to feel a need to cover themselves up, to hide who they were. This was what kept humans from enjoying the fruit of knowledge, and what kept humans from reaching out for the tree of Life and become, truly, like gods. This belief in our own unworthiness, in our sinfulness, has kept us from our inner Paradises to this day. Then God comes, sees their shame, and throws them out of Paradise, allegedly for their disobedience. As a personal observation, I will say that I am convinced that the Biblical myth of Eden is an ancient parable about wisdom and what keeps us barred from wisdom and from our own divinity.

I also believe that most lay believers think of God as a loving, infinitely wise presence, and of their religion as a way of living morally and being "good". I am fully aware that everybody has a personal view of their god, and often a deep personal relationship with their god. However, the three main religions and all their branches, who build upon the myth of Eden, have a history of being used or abused by ruling elites. Although they claim that their sacred texts are the words of God himself history shows that these elites time and time again have been editing the sacred texts to their liking, and that they have been monopolizing and dogmatizing the religions of which they profess to be the sole valid interpreters. Whereas most lay people believe in a loving God, the God of the ruling elites is in fact as described by themselves or, as they claim, by God himself, a jealous and vindictive, often very blood-thirsty God who craves blood sacrifice and violent punishments for the slightest offence.

This depressing image of the divine is the cause of centuries of cruelty, torture, persecution, warfare and terrible and unfair punishments in the name of these three religions. Accordingly, the myth of Eden, I believe, was early enough used or abused by those who sat down to edit the Bible to their liking in order to keep people in their places. From the point of view of those who have been leading these religions in their own images, humanity deserved to be thrown out of Paradise, deserved to feel unworthy and sinful and ashamed, deserved to live in suffering, unequal relationships and hard work. This is how the religions that have monopolized this myth can provide, to the great joy of ruling classes everywhere, a legitimization for the suffering and inequality in the world today.

That God, revealing an "ungodly" pettiness, did not want to see humanity achieve divine knowledge and divine power and immortality has little to do with sex and probably a lot to do with his famed "jealousy", which is frequently referred to in the Bible. The promoted image of this God seems to reflect the personalities of the dogmatic elite priests themselves, who cast their God as they are themselves. Theirs is a jealous, angry and vindictive Lord who wants total submission from his subjects, their complete acknowledgment of his greatness and their own littleness. Theirs is the kind of God who wants his children to humble themselves and indulge in self-loathing, guilt and shame.

To turn the focus negatively on one of humanity's most basic natural traits, sexuality, has proved an excellent way to keep humanity in thrall to their own perceived sinfulness. There is just no way out of that state of sin, since we, being alive, are of the flesh, and the flesh is sinful. In our lowly, fleshly, sinfulness, there is just no way we can ever aspire to possess divine wisdom or achieve a state of illumination. We can only crawl before the Lord, hoping that he will forgive us for being such lowly creatures. The theme of gods jealous of the human capacity to become as omniscient and powerful as themselves exists in other mythologies as well. In the 16th century Mayan script known as Popol Vuh, we hear that the gods were anxious when the first human beings became wise:

*"The first human beings on Earth were called The Killing Laughter Wizard,
The Night Wizard, the Coarse, Black Wizard...They possessed intelligence and
had knowledge about all things in the world.
The moment they looked around, they discovered everything that surrounded
them, they had thoughts about the shape of heaven and then on the round
face of Earth...(Then the creator gods spoke)"They have been let to know
everything...What are we supposed to do with them? We shall let them see
only that which is close to them, only a little part of the Earth's surface! Are
they not simple creatures of nature, created by us? Do they have to be gods as
well?"*

Several ancient, Pagan paths of spirituality had a very different view on humanity
and its role in cosmos. The wisdom keepers of Old Norse Paganism, for one, seem
to have cherished the quest for knowledge as the most noble of all life paths, a path
staked out for us by the gods and goddesses, in whose footsteps we are invited
to walk. The myths are crammed with stories about how divine knowledge once
was freely available, but that the powers of fear, ignorance, aggression, greed and,
indeed, jealousy, made it necessary to hide the knowledge in the underworld. In
fact, the poems seem to suggest that this knowledge is our rightful human heritage
a heritage lost to us, but which can still be sought in the hidden realms.

When Óttarr in the Hyndlulióð poem goes into Hel with his goddess in order to
seek the knowledge that is guarded and hidden there, we are frequently told that
he does this in order to "claim his heritage". It is necessary to retrieve this heritage
in order to resurrect from Misty Hel and reach Valhǫll. The quest for knowledge
was not unproblematic, but rather than being sinful, it was merely challenging. The
path was crooked and could lead one astray, and the lore was careful to describe
and warn everybody of the pitfalls, as we see in the stories of Gunnarr and Sígurðr.
However, if one could maintain ones integrity, conquer hatred, fear and emotional
turmoil, the quest for knowledge was also a quest that would ultimately lead to
immortality and divinity.

This spiritual purpose in the sacred lore of our Pagan ancestors is the exact
opposite of that found in the dogmatic Monotheist religions, where such spiritual
aspirations are the ultimate source of sin. One might ask how people of other, more
profound spiritual traditions reacted when confronted with the very aggressive,
conquering, vindictive, angry and jealous priesthood of the medieval Christian
Church when it first came, ready to make sure that no one would believe that
they could ever find Eden or become like gods. The wisdom keepers of Old Norse
Paganism seem to have made several observations of their own, including a
warning of what happens when someone tries to monopolize divine knowledge.
The Edda lore about the Golden Age may be much older than Christianity, the
ancestral wisdom of people who actually did see a Golden Age and its destruction.
The lore of the lost Paradise could also have been created or re-created in response
to the new faith.

However it is, we are not seeing a Norse version of the Genesis, where humanity
is punished for the sin of disobedience. We are seeing a Norse myth of an era of
peace, wisdom and prosperity which was destroyed through the folly, the greed and
the petty mindedness of certain ruling elites. As usual in Norse poetry, this story
is told in countless ways. We will begin with the myth of Kvasir, since it is directly
related to the previous Chapter (3) about the sacred mead.

5.4: WHEN WISDOM WAS FREE THE MYTH OF KVASIR & HEIMDALLR

"It so happened that the Aesir had conflicts with that people which is called the Vanir. And then they held a peace-gathering and made a truce in this way: that both parties went up to a cauldron and spit their juice into it.

When they separated, the Aesir thought that this sign of truce ought not to be wasted, and they took and made a man out of it. His name is Kvasir, and he is so wise that whatever is asked of him, he knows the answer. He traveled widely around the world and taught knowledge to people.

Then he was a guest at two dwarfs, Fialar and Galar, and they tricked him into their private confidence and killed him. They let his blood run into two small vessels and a huge cauldron. The Cauldron was called Óðrerir, and the vessels were called Són and Bodn. They mixed honey into the blood, and from this they created a mead that transforms anyone who drinks it into a poet or a sage. The dwarfs said to the Aesir that Kvasir had drowned in his own knowledge, for there was no one wise enough to ask the knowledge out of him."

This is the story of Kvasir as told by Snorri Sturluson in the Prose Edda book Skáldskaparmál. It is obviously related to the mead-lore discussed in the previous Chapter. The blood of Kvasir, blended with honey, is in fact the origin of the precious mead served by the Mead-woman in the underworld. The name Kvasir is related to the Norwegian word kvase and the Russian kvas, referring to fermented juice of berries. In archaic cultures, the method for the production of fruit wine was to chew berries and spit the juice into a vessel, a work that was usually performed together in large groups.

In this way, we could say that Kvasir's name means "Brew Ingredient", an early indicator that he is deeply connected to the sacred mead even from the start. He is in fact the result of the blended essence of all the gods and goddesses from both the Aesir and Vanir experience, which is why he represents all divine knowledge put together in one being. He incarnates all divine knowledge and becomes the very precious mead that gives the initiates wisdom, knowledge, eloquence, magical powers and resurrection in death.

As such, Kvasir is Divine Wisdom, and once upon a time, Divine Wisdom flowed freely through the world, available to anyone who cared to ask. Two "dwarfs", representing lesser, limited beings, tried to monopolize this wisdom for themselves, legitimizing their act by claiming that no one else were wise enough to ask the right questions. It has been pointed out that the names of the two dwarfs seem to point towards a priesthood. Galar, at least, refers to the singing of spell-songs. Lotte von Motz has made an extensive analysis of how dwarfs and smiths tend to represent Pagan priests and priesthoods in the lore of Northern Europe.

In any case, the "dwarfs" of this myth certainly represent the kind of people who are convinced that only they can possess true knowledge, and that only they have the right to knowledge, and that others are too stupid to seek it or to even have access to it. Like the elite brotherhoods of certain dogmatic religions, they put themselves up as the only ones who could gain access to and keep divine wisdom. Obviously, being the sole keepers of Divine Wisdom, hiding Divine Wisdom away from the world at large, the dwarfs could hold great power in the world, being the only ones who knew anything in a largely ignorant world. This is a perfect description of dogmatic and exclusive priesthoods, seen from the point of view of people who believed that Divine Wisdom ought to be freely accessible to anyone who asks, as the gods had once decreed.

The Norse myth bears the exact opposite message of the Biblical one. That the great harm happens not when wisdom is sought and freely available, but when wisdom is hidden and monopolized. As such, we might be seeing in this story a subtle Pagan comment on the Church that had begun to leave its mark in Scandinavia towards the end of the Viking Age. However, it might also be dealing with a far older problem, and carry yet deeper meanings on more personal levels. The dwarfs had a deeper purpose with their monopolizing of wisdom, they wanted to gain immortality. This purpose is certainly a Pagan endeavor, being thought as sinful in the Christian tradition, and it is a purpose that is revealed symbolically, to be understood only by initiates or those who can figure out the riddle. I believe I have figured it out. To understand it, we must have a look at what happened next: After the dwarfs have killed Kvasir, they pour his blood into three cauldrons:

1. The biggest cauldron is called Óðrerir ["Poetry Stir"] the very cauldron from which Óðinn later drinks during his initiation among the giants.

2. Són: This means "Reconciliation" or "Atonement", a reference, perhaps, to the truce between the Aesir and the Vanir,

3. Boðn: a name that simply means "Vessel".

In his book Lady with a Mead Cup, Michael Enright suggests a connection to the many ritual drinking vessels with three interconnected cups (drinking from one, you drink from all three at the same time), found in countless Northern European graves from 500 B.C.E and onwards. This is about the same age as the first graves revealing the existence of actual "mead-women".

The dwarfs proceed in mysterious ways; they invite a giant couple to their home, only to kill the couple, no real explanation given, as Snorri continues to explain:

"Later, the dwarfs invited to them a giant called Gillingr, and his wife. Then they asked Gillingr to row out at sea with them…Gillingr could not swim, and drowned…They told the wife of Gillingr what had happened. It was hard news for her, and she wept loudly…then he… let a millstone down on her head. He was weary of her howling, he said."

The giant couple appears to be just an elderly couple of little consequence, and the story appears meaningless as long as we do not understand what they really represent metaphorically. Gillingr means "the Screamer" or the "Noisy One", and as such, he falls right into a line of giants with similar names indicating sounds, such as Ymir [the Sound] and Skrymir [the Loud Speaker] and Hymir [the Hymn]. These are giants of cosmic creation. Ymir is the giant on whose limbs the entire universe is built. Skrymir is identical to Utgarðsloki "Loki of the Outer World" or "Outer Space Loki" as I like to call him, a giant who seems to be ruling the great illusions of cosmos.

Hymir is a giant who lives by the borders between the universe, and who owns a cauldron that can contain all the mead of Aegir, which means all the oceans of the world. He is identifiable with Gymir [Hiding] and Aegir [Terrifying One], who rules the movement (sic winds and waves) of cosmos and is the father of the nine sorceresses who birthed the world. His wife, too, is described very much by the loud sounds she makes, and is associated with a millstone, which is a symbol of fate, as we shall see in the next section, and of death. The Well of Death in Hel is, significantly, called the "Howling Mill", in which the dead souls are ground and recycled.

The loud sounds associated with the giant couple, the ocean and the fate-stone are keys to unlock the meaning of the parable. The giant couple represent the two original cosmic beings. The giant who lives on an island, steering the "winds and waves" of the great cosmic ocean, and his wife, who receives the dead. They are sometimes, more famously, called Aegir and Rán, and seem to be the grandparents of this universe. They appear in numerous guises, but are recognized by their attributes. When the dwarfs "murder" these powerful (and immortal, endless) beings, it is a metaphor. They can obviously not murder these cosmic powers as such, but they can try to "murder" their impact on their lives.

This theme is repeated several times in the initiation myths, where the initiate has to overcome, sometimes kill or make sink dangerous giants and giantesses. By killing the couple, the dwarfs are trying to conquer death and become like gods. The dwarfs do not succeed, however. The giant couple reappears, this time in the guise of their "son" Suttungr [Heavy with Drink] and their granddaughter Gunnlǫð. Suttungr lets the dwarfs drown, and lets his daughter guard the precious mead, which must now be sought in the Underworld for ever after.

The myth of Kvasir serves many purposes. It indirectly describes a Golden Age when Divine Wisdom flowed freely through the world, accessible to all, as the gods had decreed it. Then it describes how this Divine Wisdom was hidden away, "killed" and monopolized by petty minds who wanted it all for themselves, and who disrespected their fellow creatures as being too ignorant to be worthy of access to Divine Wisdom. The lesson of their failure is that this act of monopolizing wisdom makes one fail utterly, becoming truly unworthy of Divine Wisdom.

Not only does this myth clearly describe the tragedy of dogmatic religions and sects upon the world and upon their adherents. It is also a warning to all those who on a personal level are prone to imagine that they have all the answers, that their way of looking at the world is the only one of value. Such an arrogant attitude is surely the downfall of wisdom and leads to self-destruction, yet it is the trademark of organized religions, sects and even various political ideologies from right to left which have it in them to compare the destruction of opponents with the crushing of eggs in order to make an omelet. It is also a possible pitfall for individuals or small groups who believe that they have access to ultimate truth. Thus the Norse myth, created so many centuries ago, is still highly relevant for people today.

The story describes a great pitfall on the long quest for wisdom; a pitfall that might open beneath the feet of those who are trying to achieve "immortality" or spiritual awakening, enlightenment, union with the divine, whatever the quest is thought to be. The quest for spiritual wisdom is not unproblematic. The dwarfs attempt to fight and conquer death itself, and fail miserably, mainly because in their attempt to monopolize Wisdom, they killed it. Ultimately, the new path is described: We cannot fight death, but we can befriend it. After the terrible consequences of the dwarfs' actions, Divine Wisdom is now hidden in the Underworld, guarded by the giantess of death herself.

The only way to access Divine Wisdom and reach immortality is through accepting death in the most intimate way; the initiate, like Óðinn, has to temporarily die and lay in the embrace of death, loving her like a husband, and only through this loving will he be restored to life, imbued with Divine Wisdom. The story of Kvasir is not only a myth of the Golden Age and how it was lost, but also a story that explains the origin of the sacred mead and the reason for the spiritual path of initiation that was instigated and adapted for a less golden era. Divine Wisdom no longer flows freely through the world, but is accessible for those who dare to go into Death's dark embrace and find the light there. It is the origin myth explaining why the Mead of Poetry, Memory and Immortality must be sought in the Underworld.

THE VANIR'S GIFTS TO THE AESIR

In the Skáldskaparmál, Snorri lets Kvasir be created of the very essence of all the Aesir and Vanir gods. In another source, the Ynglinga saga 4, Snorri reveals a different version of this myth:

> "Óðinn went with an army against the Vanir, but they stood well against him and defended their country; victory changed between them, they harried each other's lands and made great injuries. Then both parts grew tired of this, they asked each other for peace and exchanged hostages. The Vanir gave away their greatest men, Njǫrðr the rich and his son Freyr....and the Vanir gave the wisest man in their flock, he was called Kvasir."

In this version, Kvasir is not the joint essence of all Aesir and Vanir gods, but is one of the Vanir gods who arrives as a hostage together with Njǫrðr and his children Freyr and Freyia. Then we do not hear much more about Kvasir at all, except in the form of the precious mead that is his life blood the essence of Divine Wisdom. In this other version, Divine Wisdom emerged from the Vanir tribe and was shared freely with the Aesir. If we look to the Vanir gods, we find that three male gods and one female arrive with the Aesir after the truce. According to the same Ynglinga saga Chapter 4:

> "Njǫrð's daughter was Freyia, and she was a sacrificial priestess [blótgyðja]. She was the first to teach the Aesir how to perform seiðr, as the Vanir used to do. When Njǫrðr was among the Vanir, he was married to his own sister, for it was legal there, and their children were Freyr and Freyia. With the Aesir it was not legal to marry such close kin."

The clue about Freyia and her art of seiðr is significant here. Upon the arrival of the Vanir, the Aesir receive tremendous gifts! They receive Freyia, Njǫrðr, Freyr and Kvasir. The Vanir represent the great natural powers of the cosmos and of Earth. Freyia, the Vanadís Goddess of the Vanir carries with her that "most powerful of arts", the art of seiðr, which can transform fate itself, even the ultimate fate which is death. Njǫrðr is the lord of winds and waves, which is one of the features which suggest that he is a friendly version of Aegir. The winds and waves are metaphors for vibrational movement in the universe, the winds being associated with death, the waves with fate.

Freyr is the lord of growth and fertility as such he is the power that makes all things grow. Finally, we have the gift of Kvasir, who is the essence of Divine Wisdom, the embodiment of the precious mead. What did the Aesir give in return? Hardly anything at all, the myth goes, the Aesir gave hostages of little value to the Vanir in return, and thus tricked them in the end. This is where we need to ask ourselves what the Aesir and the Vanir tribes represent. As already mentioned, the Vanir seem to be embodiments of natural powers, and the four Vanir given to the Aesir are indeed the most important of all natural powers. The Aesir all seem to be related to mental and spiritual powers. Their names and function shows this: Their leader Óðinn has a name which indicates that he is The Spirit, The Poetry and The Frenzy. His brothers Víli and Vé mean Intent and Awe. When the three Aesir first walked this Earth, they gave gifts to humanity: Breath, Spirit, Thought, Intelligence, Life Force and Colors.

The Aesir's gifts to the Vanir are two, Hænir, who gave thought to humanity, the art of mind, or intelligence, and Mímir [Memory/ Murmuring] who represents universal memory (he is also the guardian of the Well of Memory at the root of the world tree). The myth relates that the Vanir were very impressed by Hænir's gorgeous appearance and made him a chief, the metaphor is that the natural powers and natural functions of, say, a body, made intelligent, conscious thought into their chief. Yet Hænir, although good looking, never spoke a word or made a decision without having to consult Mímir. The Vanir, natural forces, have little use for this quality, being unable to see the value of a Thinker who has to rely completely on Memory all the time. Not big on logical connections and rational thought, they send the gifts back in part. Feeling tricked, they chop the head off of Memory and sends that back, keeping the body only.

Óðinn, however, makes use of the head Memory ever after, as Snorri lets us know, and it is an important feature during his initiation, perhaps even during cosmic creation, as the Sígrdrífumál, st.14 reveals:

> *On the Mountain he [Óðinn] stood with the blades of the Flame, on the head he wore a helmet then Memory's head spoke in wisdom the first word*
> *And uttered the true runes*
>> *A biargi stoþ*
>> *meþ Brimis eggiar,*
>> *hafdi ser a hofði hialm;*
>> *þa melti Mims hafuþ*
>> *froþlict iþ fyrsta orð*
>> *oc sagdi sanna stafi.*

It would seem that the temporary journey of Thought and Memory into the mysterious world of the Vanir was beneficial indeed. This primeval journey may not have been the only one. Óðinn regularly sends his "ravens", Huginn and Muninn, whose names literally translate as "The Intent/Thought" and "The Memory", into the various worlds of cosmos in order to bring back tidings.

As is said in the Grímnismál, st. 20:

> *The Intent/Thought and The Memory fly every day across the great world I am worried about The Intent/Thought that he may not return though I worry more about The Memory*
>> *Hvginn oc Mvninn*
>> *flivga hverian dag*
>> *iormvngrvnd yfir;*
>> *ovmc ec of Hvgin,*
>> *at hann aptr ne comiþ,*
>> *þo siámc meirr vm Mvnin*

Indeed, it is Memory that is nearly lost among the Vanir: only his head returns. This is a metaphor that has something to do with the Aesir being "of the head", the mind, whereas the body the natural functions belongs among the Vanir. The body may die there, but in the realm of Spirit Óðinn, The Memory survives. With Óðinn, who has now learned the art of seiðr from Freyia, the head of The Memory is restored by magic, and may speak "the first word" and utter "true runes".

In the Sígrdrífumál, these are the runes of fate that are scattered with sacred mead and sent on their wide ways, to dwell in all worlds, but only after they have ran through Óðin's húgr his thought, soul or intent. It is hard to put the pieces of the puzzle together here, but there is certainly an intimate connection between the truce of Aesir and Vanir, the exchange of "hostages", and the initiation journey of Óðinn, where he hung on the world tree and sought the mead of wisdom in the embrace of Gunnlǫð.

KVASIR AND HEIMDALLR

The Vanir obviously represent cosmic and natural forces. At close scrutiny, there is no difference between them and the giants except for them being more benevolent. Like the giants, they belong to the primeval cosmic energies and the natural forces. In other sources, the third Vanir male god, Kvasir, is replaced by Heimdallr, who is said to be a wise Vanir, as in the Þrymskvíða 15:

> Then spoke Heimdallr The White Shine among Aesir
> He possessed great wisdom like all Vanir:
>> Þa qvaþ þat Heimdallr,
>> hvítastr ása,
>> — vissi hann vel fram
>> sem vanir aþrir —:

Is Kvasir identical to Heimdallr? Heimdallr is a Vanir god possessing great wisdom, and he is not mentioned in Snorri's tale of hostage exchange, but appears later as one of the three Vanir among the Aesir gods. Like the Vanir, he has a universal, cosmic, natural function; His name simply means Great World, and as such, he represents the universe, the world tree, the living, hearing, seeing world which hears all and sees all. Kvasir is identified as the life blood of the precious mead. In the previous Chapter 1 discussed how the ingredients of the precious mead were revealed to be the exact same as the ingredients that caused the young Heimdallr, the Great World, to grow:

> That drink was imbued (made to grow)
> With the Power of Earth
> With the Cool Cold Sea
> And the Blood of the Reconciliation/
> Atonement (Sacrifice)
>> ...þat var vm aukit
>> Iarþar magni,
>> svalcaldom se
>> oc sonar dreyra

These lines from the Guðrunarkvíða ǫnnur, 23, describing the contents of the precious mead, are identical to the lines of the poem Hyndlulióð 38, describing the growth of Great World:

> He was imbued (made to grow) by the Power of Earth, by the
> Cool Cold Sea and by the Blood of the Reconciliation/ Atonement
> (Sacrifice)
>> Sa var aukinn
>> Iardar megni,
>> sualkaulldum sæ
>> ok sonardreyra

It would seem that Heimdallr really is the "true face" behind Kvasir, Divine Wisdom incarnate, and that he is one of the four "hostages" that came from the Vanir tribe of natural powers to the Aesir tribe of mental powers. The mental powers had great use for the natural powers, whereas natural powers had no use at all for the mental ones. So how does all this relate to the Norse Golden Age?

I relate the myth of Kvasir with the Golden Age first and foremost because the Norse name for the Golden Age is Fróðafríðr, which means the Peace of Wisdom, which was ruled by "King Wisdom". One of its great attributes was the presence of a "gold ring lying on the heath", free for everyone to take, yet no one stole it. The gold ring symbolized divine wisdom. Thus the golden era is intimately associated with the presence of and dominance of wisdom in the world, and also with the presence of free-flowing, available Divine Wisdom, accessible to everyone who would wish to seek it. It was the time before the gold ring was stolen, before the dwarfs killed and monopolized the life blood of Divine Wisdom.

5.5: WHO REALLY KILLED BALDR? A MURDER MYSTERY

> *3. Forth rode Óðinn the Earth Path resounded as he reached the path to the*
> *High Hall of Hel*
> > *3. Framm ræið Óðinn,*
> > *folldvægr dvndi,*
> > *hann kom at háfv*
> > *Hæliar ranni.*

> *4. Then rode Óðinn to the east of death's door*
> *There he knew of a witch's grave He knew wisely to sing the spells of Choice-Death he made her rise, and reluctantly, she sang the words of the dead*
> > *4. Þa ræið Oðinn*
> > *fyrir austan dyrr,*
> > *þar ær hann vissi volv læiði.*
> > *Nam hann vittvgri*
> > *valgalldr kveða,*
> > *vnz nauðig ræis,*
> > *nas orð vm kvað*

> *Vegtamskvíða, st. 3-4, Poetic Edda*

The myth of Baldr's death has so often been interpreted as a "fertility myth" or a myth of the changing seasons that it is hard to introduce a new way of understanding it. Baldr is so easily discarded as the "young god", the "vegetation god" or the "Sun god" the latter otherwise completely unknown in Norse myths and religion, where the Sun goddess is a fact, and no Sun god ever shone on the sky.

Why? The "seasonal" interpretation of the Baldr myth is based on comparative mythology where Baldr is likened to ancient African, Middle Eastern and Mediterranean gods such as Attis, Dumuzi, Adonis, Osiris and so on, young gods who were the lovers and sons of the Great Goddess, in ritual dying annually interpreted by moderns to represent the death of vegetation and growth during winter. They were mourned, buried and reborn by the Goddess each year. When it comes to Norse Baldr, the place name material and other sources strongly suggest that Baldr was not a god that was worshiped at all.

He is a mythical character, just like Loki a character made up by poets in order to create good stories that reveal important messages. Whereas Attis, Dumuzi, Osiris and the other "dying gods" were real gods in their time, worshiped and mourned annually, celebrated at their return in spring, there is no sign whatsoever that Baldr was worshiped the same way or that he was ever worshiped. The Norse poets may have borrowed the theme of the dying god from other cultures, as the Norse people, like most ancients, always happily borrowed wherever they liked something.

They borrowed it with a purpose, to convey an important message to their audience, and to the initiates. They may very well have borrowed the deeper purpose of this basic myth too a purpose that transcends the "obvious" fertility myth. When the myth of Isis and Osiris became incorporated into Classical Mystery religions, Osiris no longer represented the dying and reviving vegetation, but the dying and reviving soul of human beings, reborn through his union with the great All-soul his sister-wife Isis. Isis was, significantly, called the Savior many centuries before the Christ was even conceived of, since she saved the souls of her devotees from Hades, resurrecting them from the shadow lands and offering them a place in bright Elysium, the divine realm.

Modern interpreters often seem obsessed with interpreting Pagan myths within the frame of "fertility cults", especially when a goddess takes precedence, yet the Classical interpretations show that people in olden times were not always that obsessed with fertility after all, they were in fact concerned with the fate of their souls in death and the purity of their souls in life. It is from the point of view of a spiritual mystery that we ought to read the Baldr myth. When I first began to interpret Norse myths based on translating the names of characters and places, the Baldr myth was one of the first to provide me with a revelation. The myth of Baldr is partly told in Snorri's Gylfaginning, where Baldr is first introduced:

"Another son of Óðinn is Baldr, and about him there is much good to relate. He is the best, and all praise him. He is so fair to look at and so bright that he illuminates shine… He is the wisest of the Aesir, and the one who speaks most eloquently, and he is also the most compromising. But that quality means that no judgment of his can possibly stand. He lives where it is called Breidablik [Broad Vision], it is in heaven. In that place, there can be nothing unclean, as it is said here:
It is called Breidablik where Baldr has his halls raised
In that country I know lies the least harmful runes"

Later, we hear of his death:

"This story begins with this, that Baldr the Good dreamt great dreams that foretold of a danger to his life. When he had told the Aesir about his dreams, they held a counsel, and they agreed to pray for Baldr's life to be saved from all dangers.
Frigg demanded of fire and water, iron and all kinds of minerals, the rocks, the Earth, the trees, the diseases, the animals, the birds, the poisons and the serpents, that they should not harm Baldr.
When this task was completed and declared, Baldr and the Aesir entertained themselves thus; that he should take a central place on their parliament fairs, and that they should shoot at him, others should axe or maim him, and others throw rocks at him. And whatever they did caused him no harm, and this game thought the Aesir to be great fun. But when Loki Son of Leaf Island (Laufeyjarson)saw this, it made him angry that nothing harmed Baldr. He took upon himself the shape of a woman and went to Frigg in the Moist Hall (Fensalar).

Frigg asked the woman what the Aesir were doing at parliament. The woman replied that they were all shooting at Baldr, and that it did not harm him. Then said Frigg: "Neither weapon nor tree will harm Baldr, I have made everything swear to that."

"Has absolutely everything sworn to never harm Baldr?" Asked the woman. Frigg replies: "There grows a small plant to the west of Valhǫll, he is called the Mistletoe. I thought him too young to demand oaths from." Then the woman went away.

Loki took the Mistletoe and tore him apart and went to the parliament. Strife (Hǫðr) stood outside of the circle of men, because he was blind.

Loki asked him: "Why are you not shooting at Baldr?"

"Because I am blind", Strife replied, "and besides, I have no weapons."

Then said Loki; "You should be able to do as they do, and show Baldr the proper respects like they are doing. I shall direct you about where he stands. Shoot at him with this twig!" Strife took the Mistletoe and shot at Baldr, as Loki directed him. The shot went right through Baldr, and he fell dead to the ground. And this is the greatest sorrow that has ever happened to both Aesir and to human beings."

THE COURAGE OF BROAD PERCEPTION THE WISDOM PARABLE OF BALDR

To sum up the myth very short: Baldr is the child of Óðinn and Frigg. He lives in a realm called Breidablik. He is married to a woman called Nanna Neprsdottir, and they are very much in love. He is beautiful, wise and much loved by everyone. He is so objectively fair ("compromising") that he cannot pass judgments. He represents all that is good and precious. Then he has dreams that are interpreted as omens by the other gods, omens of his early death. His mother, the goddess Frigg, moves about the world and asks all things to not harm Baldr.

The gods, ever fun-loving, plays at harming Baldr, since nothing can actually harm him. Then the tragedy occurs as Loki, moved by his jealousy, wrests out the knowledge he can and proceeds to actually harm Baldr, letting another, Hǫðr Blindi, perform the crime and thus receive the punishment. I translate the name Baldr as "Courage", based on the Old Norse adjective baldr, meaning "bold", or "daring". There are other possible translations as well. The name could be related to Indo-European bhel [white] (Lithuanian baltas), Old English bealdor [Lord], and Old Nordic baloram [power]. Now let us try what the story sounds like if you translate the names of the characters and the places.

Let us begin with the first three sentences of my summary above, now with translations, allowing us to come closer to what the Old Norse audience actually heard:

> *"Courage is the child of Spirit and Love. He lives in a realm called Broad Vision. He is married to a woman called Understanding, Daughter of the Ring, and they are very much in love."*

The moment names are translated, we begin to perceive the myths differently. As soon as the parable is deciphered, it becomes easy to see. It is such a simple way of relating the most basic, yet profound of all wisdoms. The myths are no longer just stories about some mythical people, but parables that convey a deeper message; that true courage is born of the union between spirit and love, and that this leads to broad vision broad understanding, broad perception. This is the best of all qualities: To take a non-judgmental attitude, to nurture one's capacity to grasp the wider picture rather than make judgments, and to nurture a deep love for learning and wholeness, with which this quality lives in union.

The ring represents wholeness. As long as Baldr lives among the gods, the quality he represents also lives among them. Thus the world is a good place, where the quality of this true courage is available to men and women, just like when Kvasir, the Brew Ingredient, moved freely through the world. The message is clear: Nothing can harm the person or the society who possesses such a quality within. This sacred quality was once present in the world, yet another metaphor for the Golden Age. Only one thing can harm and destroy this inner quality, and that is another inner quality, represented by Hǫðr Blindi, whose name literally translates as Strife the Blind or Blind Aggression. Blindness is a metaphor for ignorance, for a refusal to see the truth, the aggression blinding one's understanding. I shall continue to call the killer Ignorant Aggression.

This negative quality has always been there as a potential, watching the games of the gods, but was harmless, not given weapons or direction. It is always our choice whether we will lend weapons and guide the hands of our basest qualities. Only Loki eventually decides to make use of Ignorant Aggression. Loki, whose name rhymes with logi "flame" represents the fire of passion, not necessarily a negative thing. It is the source of vitality, life force itself, the heat that gave "vital power and beautiful colors" to the first people, which is here in the thrall of jealousy, hatred and anger.

These feelings rank among the feelings that must be conquered in the myths of initiation, as we saw when young Helgi went into the Fiord of Hatred to vanquish the "giant" called Hati [To Hate], before he could be worthy of wedding his Valkyrie bride. This message of nurturing the proper inner qualities whether on an individual or societal level is the true meaning of the life and death of Baldr. The first answer to the murder mystery is thus that Baldr represents a human quality that was once nurtured the quality of courage, objectivity, non-judgment, kindness and wisdom. This quality was "murdered" by another quality ignorance, jealousy and blind aggression. However, there are more murderers on the scene hidden powers pulling strings for a secret and strange purpose.

FRIGG'S SECRET

As mentioned above, the myth of Baldr and his death is yet another parable of the Golden Age, and about how and why it was lost. The complex variety of myths surrounding this one single theme belies the common preconceptions that myths are superstitious fairy tales. Instead, we are presented with numerous aspects of the answers to difficult questions. Why the world is in such a sorry state, what caused it, and what is needed to restore the healthy balance. In the myth of the millstone, we learn that people of great knowledge [King Wisdom] abused and underestimated natural powers (the giantesses) because of unchecked greed. The solution to this problem is to wake up ones wisdom and listen to the ancient tales and to begin respecting the natural powers once more. In the myth of Kvasir, we learn that people of great knowledge began to disrespect their fellow beings, monopolizing wisdom and hiding it away from the world, hoping to attain immortality for themselves without succeeding. The solution to this problem is to dare the darkness of the underworld, conquer one's fears and reach the realm of universal Memory.

In the myth of Baldr, we learn about how wisdom was killed because the qualities of jealous anger and ignorant aggression, blindness and strife, took precedence instead of the great appreciation that the gods of the mind (the Aesir) showed for qualities such as broadmindedness and a non-judgmental attitude. The story does not end there. Just as Óðinn sought the lost mead in the underworld, restoring the path of wisdom to the world, so a path of initiation is instigated, and it would seem planned.

Trying to decipher myths is a bit like detective work. One begins to see suspects everywhere, and to investigate every odd detail rather than ignoring it. For example: Frigg, who made such an effort of protecting her son Baldr, freely allows Loki to obtain exactly the information he needs in order to kill him. The story implies that Frigg was tricked, since Loki had changed shape into that of a woman. I have, at least, never see anyone question this apparent naïveté. In reality, the shape-changing only means that Loki needed a woman's body in order to reach Frigg's realm Fensalar the Moist Halls.

It is difficult to make out exactly what this means, but we could at least suggest that these "halls" belong to the women's sphere, to women's mysteries, and that Loki can only reach the mother goddess in her hall if he "is" a woman. This could be explained in various ways. If we understand that Loki is, as are most mythical characters, a quality rather than a person, he can possess either sex.

As a quality, he is passion, desire, life force itself. The sex-change can also be an example of seiðr, since we know that obtaining hidden knowledge and changing shape were important features of the mysterious art of seiðr. Several sources suggest that this art of sorcery and divination was considered a particularly feminine art, although males also practiced it risking their "manly" reputations. Male practitioners of seiðr could be called seiðberendr, which literally translates as "seiðr-vagina" or the more elegant "magical womb". The title indicates quite strongly that a magical change of sex from male to female may have been an important part of witchcraft practiced by men. Thus the sex-change is not just about tricking the goddess into revealing her knowledge, although Loki might think so. In fact, the Edda poem Lokasenna lets Loki think just that, only to learn, to his great chagrin, that he has been seen through all the time.

In the poem, Loki tries his utmost to offend all the gods and goddesses, getting so provoked that he finally reveals to Frigg that he is responsible for her son Baldr's death:

28. " Still you want, Frigg that I tell more about my harmful carvings and I tell you that I caused this that you will never see ride Baldr, to these halls."	28. "Enn vill þv, Frigg! at ec fleiri telia mina meinstafi: ec þvi red, er þv riþa serat siþan Baldr at salom.»

As Loki thinks he has triumphed over the mother goddess, Freyia turns to him and informs him of a known fact. That Frigg knows all fate, and thus knew exactly what was happening when Loki wrested out her knowledge:

29. "Deluded are you, Loki when you brag, reckoning up all your lowly, hateful carvings Of destiny, Frigg knows all in totality, I believe, though she herself never speaks of her knowledge	29. «Orr ertv, Loci! er þv ydra telr liota leiþstafi; orlag Frigg hygg ec at all viti, þott hon sialfgi segi.»

This all-knowing quality in Frigg is also repeated by Snorri. Thus she cannot, as Freyia points out, possibly have been tricked by Loki. She must have known what would happen! Despite the great sorrow it caused her, the mother goddess, whose name simply means "Love", allowed the death of Baldr, and was even instrumental in its happening. So, next to Loki and Hǫðr, our detective work leads us to a third suspect. Baldr's own mother, Frigg! The good-bad polarity suddenly becomes less clear. If the goddess of love, omniscience and fate herself paved the way to this death, maybe there is a deeper reason to it?

ÓÐIN'S SECRET

54. Óðinn said: "Much did I travel, much did I try much did I test out the Powers What did Óðinn whisper as he climbed the pyre himself, into the ears of his son?"	54. Óðinn qvaþ: «Fiolþ ec for, fiolþ ec freistaþac, fiolþ ec vm reynda regin: hvat melti Oðinn, aþr a bal stigi, sialfr i eyra syni?»
55. Powerful Head Veil said: "No man knows that what you in the beginning days spoke into the ears of your son; With a mouth wed to death did I speak my ancient carvings and of Ragnarǫk. Now I have with Óðinn contended for all my eloquent arts you turned out to be the wisest."	55. Vafþrvðnir qvaþ: «Ey manne þat veit, hvat þv i ardaga sagdir i eyra syni; feigom mvnni melta ec mina forna stafi oc vm ragnarac. Nv ec viþ Oðin deildac mina orþspeci, þv ert e visastr vera.»

Vafþruðnismál, The Song of the Tremendous Veil, Poetic Edda

Baldr is laid to rest on his remarkable ship Hringhorni the Ring-Horn. The ring is a reference to wholeness and completion, the horn a reference to the Mead of Memory. None of the gods have the strength to push that kind of ship onto its death-journey, so they have to call upon the most powerful of all beings, the wolf-riding giantess Hyrrokkin "the Fire Spinner". As she pushes the ship onto its death-journey, Baldr's wife Nanna dies with him on the pyre, representing the understanding that his courage loved so much.

Then we come to our fourth suspect in the story; Óðinn. Why is he also a suspect? Because he, too, seems to have a purpose with the death of Baldr. Just before the pyre is lit, Óðinn puts his ring Draupnir onto the pyre, and whispers something in the ears of his son. We do not learn what he whispers it is a secret. We do know that the ring Draupnir is the very golden ring that drips eight new rings every ninth night. This golden ring is continuously referred to in the lore, representing esoteric knowledge, divine wisdom, secret powers, wholeness and immortality.

We also know that this secret what Óðinn whispers in the ears of his son Baldr is the secret that saves Óðinn's life when he meets the giant Vafþrúðnir in a duel of eloquence later. The giant's name means Tremendous Head Veil and represents, as I see it, Illusion, the illusion of the world, which only Óðinn, through his endless questioning, may overcome. It is the answer to the question of what Óðinn whispered in Baldr's ears that saves Óðinn from succumbing to illusion for this is the one thing that illusion does not know. The secret which Baldr takes with him to the Underworld may be uncovered there a place where the recycling ring of divine knowledge is retrieved by those who manage to reach it. It is the key to conquering illusion and resurrect from Misty Hel.

THE PATH BEGINS, THE JOURNEY TO THE UNDERWORLD

The text that follows the death of Baldr in Snorri's work provides an important clue to understand the secret purposes of Frigg and Óðinn. After the death of Baldr, we learn that the Aesir are speechless, unable to utter any other sound than sobs of grief. Óðinn himself is broken by grief. None of the male Aesir are able to act in the shock, not until Frigg comes forth, as Snorri tells:

> *"When the Aesir had calmed down somewhat, Frigg took the word
> and asked which one of the Aesir would be willing to win all her
> good will and her love by riding the Hel-road in an attempt to find
> Baldr, offering to Hel a ransom so that she may release Baldr and let
> him return to Ásgarðr."*

In light of Chapter 3, where I explored the initiation myths of a journey into the underworld in order to wake up the bright maiden and receive her mead and her embrace, the stated purpose of winning the good will and love of the goddess by riding the Hel-Path is in fact the answer to understand what is happening: The path of initiation is instigated, the path that leads the initiate into Hel in order to restore the lost treasures of the human and divine heritage, symbolized by Baldr. It is also symbolized by the union between Baldr and Nanna Courage and Understanding by the dripping ring, and by the precious mead, and the maiden who serves it. This is our heritage as human beings, as the poems often suggest. When Óttarr (see Chapter 3.5) claims the knowledge of the She-Wolf in Hel, he is claiming, as Freyia repeatedly states, his heritage the heritage which will lead him to Valhǫll.

As we saw in 5.1, Baldr is ultimately connected with the mead that is hidden in the underworld, just like Kvasir. His is the essence of the mead; knowledge, wisdom and immortality. In the beginning of Snorri's story, he mentioned the omen dreams of Baldr that led the goddess to demand an oath from all things. In the Poetic Edda, there is a poem called the Vegtamskvíða eða Baldrs draumar "The Song of Way-Wont or the Death of Baldr". In this poem, we hear that Baldr dreams terrible dreams which lead Óðinn on a journey into Hel. Óðinn has made the journey before, we learn, and is "way-wont", thus his nickname in this story. Having been in Hel before, Óðinn has the knowledge needed to avoid the dangerous, deadly walls of Hel's High Hall, and rides to the east of it. The east indicated the sunrise, new life, a new possibility, and regeneration.

To the east of Hel's hall is the grave of a vǫlva an ancient witch. Óðinn sings "spells of Choice-Death" [valgaldr] before the ancient mound, making the dead woman rise from her grave. This is exactly what the young Svípdagr did before his mother Gróa's grave in order to learn the spells needed to reach the bright realm of Menglǫð, and like Óðin's dead woman, Gróa was also a vǫlva. In the poem, Óðinn asks questions as to the fate of Baldr. The dead woman reveals that the precious mead, the bright power drink, is brewed in Hel for Baldr! She also reveals who shall kill Baldr, and who shall avenge him. The "avenger" is called Váli, which means "The Choice" and refers to the word vál, which is used to describe the chosen dead of Valhǫll. As Óðinn learns this, he asks a most curious question: What the maidens are called, who are weeping and sobbing and "throwing their veils to the sky". Still curiously, the vǫlva refuses to answer the question, accusing Óðinn of trying to trick her, since he calls himself Way-Wont rather than Óðinn.

Óðinn replies that she is no wise woman, no vǫlva, but "the mother of three trolls" a metaphor for Loki or his lover Angrbóða ("Bids Rage"), who mothered the three trolls of death, greed and limitation (Hel, Fenrir and the Miðgarðr serpent). Thus ends the poem. All this seems confusing only until one puts two and two together; the poem refers to the path of initiation, where mead is offered by a maiden in the underworld. This is connected to the alternative afterlife in Valhǫll, and to Baldr's resurrection. The Choice will restore Baldr by "avenging" him, and The Choice will "avenge" Baldr by putting Ignorant Aggression to the pyre. The restoration of Baldr on a personal level depends on the ability to let Ignorant Aggression (or Blind Strife) burn out.

The reference to the weeping maidens is clearly a reference to the inner maiden, as we saw in the previous essay, the maiden who weeps, eagerly awaiting her lover to find her in the underworld, a maiden who seems to represent the inner soul, the personal fate goddess, wisdom and resurrection from death. This is hinted at only, given as a riddle to be solved. The dead woman refuses to reveal the identity of the maidens, like the old ogress of death and oblivion always resists the passing of the mead to the living. Hermóð's journey then begins. His name means "Army Courage", implying that he as one person has the courage equivalent of a whole army. This is a reference to the meaning of Baldr's name. It takes courage indeed, to go into the Underworld while still alive. The references to the mead that awaits Baldr, the dripping ring and the theme of resurrection from Hel are all powerful indicators that the path of initiation into the Pagan Mysteries have begun, and that this may be the ritual truth behind the Baldr-myth. His death the death of limitless perception and knowledge is the reason why it has to be sought in the Underworld forever after.

5.6 THE RAPE OF THE REJECTER

Óðinn said:
10.".....who will kill Aggression achieving due vengeance by bringing the bane of Courage to the funeral pyre?"
   Óðinn kvað:
   10.....hverr man hæipt Hæði
   hæfnt of vinna
   æða Balldrs bana
   a bal væga?»

The Witch said:
   11. «The Rejecter bears Choice in the Western halls
   The Spirit's son will fight from the first night of his life:
   He washes not his hands nor combs his hair until he carries to the funeral pyre the bane of Courage's spirit..."
      Volva kvað:
      11. «Rindr berr Vala
      i væstrsolvm,
      sa man Oðins sonr
      æinnættr væga:
      hond vm þvær
      næ hofvð kæmbir,
      aðr a bal vm berr
      Balldrs andskota;... »

Vegtamskvíða, st. 10-11, Poetic Edda

When Óðinn traveled to Hel in order to learn more about the death of Baldr in the Vegtamskvíða poem, he naturally asks who will avenge his son Baldr. From a Viking Age perspective, this was expected, a murder, even when carried out by mistake, must always be avenged. Although the gods may have known that young Hǫðr Blindi only wished to partake in the game that everybody else were playing, and although they may have known that Loki had manipulated his hand, it was Hǫðr's shot that killed Baldr, and the law of the time dictates that the is responsible, and that Baldr must be avenged. Someone related to Baldr must do the killing, and "bring Baldr's murderer to the funeral pyre". Since the other gods seem to be also related to Hǫðr, through relation or oaths of co-dependence, they must find someone from the outside, and Óðinn is given directions: He himself will father the avenger, a boy named Váli, to be mothered by a woman in "Western halls", name Rindr.

The name Váli translates as "The Choice", from vál "choice" the same word that is used to describe the chosen dead of Valhǫll and the choosers of the dead, the Valkyrie. The name of his mother Rindr derives from hrinda "to throw away, throw back, reject". The Prose and Poetic Eddas do not offer any explanations to why the mother of Choice is called "The Rejecter". In the Prose Edda, we hear only briefly of Rindr and Váli:

> "Then there is the one who is called Áli or Váli, son of Óðinn and Rindr. He is courageous in battle, and a particularly good bowman....Earth, mother of Þórr, and Rindr, mother of Váli, are counted among the Ásyniur [female Aesir]"

Snorri also reveals that Váli is among the Aesir who will survive Ragnarǫk, and recites the Vafþrúðnismál, st.51:

> « The Expander and the Choice shall build in divine shrines when the flames of Black Soot Acid are extinguished;"
>> «Viþarr oc Vali
>> byggia vé goða,
>> þa er slocnar Svrta logi;

Váli is also briefly mentioned in Vǫluspá 32, where we basically hear the same story as earlier, that Baldr's avenger in born swiftly and begins to fight from he is one night old. On their own, the Eddas give very little information, but the story can still be deciphered to a considerable degree if we keep the meaning of names in mind. If we insist on reading the story of Baldr, his death and the vengeance as a story about people (mythical and divine people, that is), the myth is little more than entertainment. But if we remember the fact that both Baldr and his murderer have names that indicate that they represent qualities the inner personal qualities of human beings the story becomes a beautiful and elegant parable about the plight of humanity. Baldr is the Courage born of the union between Spirit and Love a Courage that resides in Broad View a place of objectivity, ability to see widely, a meaning that is strengthened by the information given about Baldr's personality, that he is incapable of passing judgment because he sees all aspects of a situation and thus must always compromise.

The courage to remain in such a state is tremendous and leads to a union with completion, the wholeness of understanding, symbolized in his marriage. This beautiful quality is treasured by the gods, who rejoice in its ability to withstand all onslaughts it is invulnerable. The only thing that it is vulnerable to, it turns out, is another quality; jealousy motivating blind aggression. The myth continues, letting us know that the quality that Baldr represents may still be found through trials of initiation, but it also requires a sacrifice, it requires the birth of a Choice, a valiant, courageous Choice that does not hesitate to "bring Blind Aggression to the pyre". The Choice that destroys Blind Aggression will restore the Courage of Broad Perception. In itself, this parable is astonishingly relevant to people today as it was when it was created. There is more to the myth.

What about **Rindr**, the mother of Choice, who was found in Western halls, yet is counted among the Aesir goddesses? Why is she called The Rejecter? Snorri and the Poetic Edda speak nothing more of her, as if the poets were ashamed to mention what seems to have happened to her. In Denmark, a contemporary of Snorri called Saxo Grammaticus wrote a work in Latin called Gesta Danorum, "The History of the Danish People". He offers a clue. Saxo was a devout Christian who despised the Pagan religion with all his heart. Like Snorri, he explained the Aesir as a sort of ancestral tribe, and described them as extremely dishonorable, despicable and unsympathetic people. His story of Baldr is very different from that of Snorri and of the Edda, possibly relating a different continental version. In Saxo's story, "Baldrus" of the despicable Aesir tribe contends with "Hötherus" over the maiden Nanna, which ends with Hötherus stabbing Baldrus with a magical sword. Óðinn [Othinus] then proceeds on a mission to father his son's avenger, a strange story indeed.

In the Danish version, Óðinn consults seers on how to get revenge, and they advise him to travel to the Ruthenians, disguised as a human warrior called Roster. He becomes a great asset to the king of the Ruthenians and is made general. The king's daughter is called Rinda, and Óðinn knows that he has to impregnate her to get his avenger. But Rinda refuses him twice. She thinks he is too old, and she is not impressed by the gold he offers, since she has more than enough in her father's halls already. Óðinn then strikes Rinda with a thorn that causes her to go insane and ill. He turns into a medicine woman called Wecha, pretending to have the medicine needed to cure Rinda. But the medicine is so bitter that they will have to tie the girl up in her bed.

The people tie the princess to the bed and leave her alone with the medicine woman. Óðinn takes advantage of the situation he has orchestrated, and rapes the girl. From the rape was born a boy called Bous who would later avenge Baldrus. Óðinn was punished by the other gods and sent into exile for the crime of rape. We are used to hearing of Vikings who "raped and pillaged", but although this did happen, especially in raids abroad, there was no honor in raping women. In the poem Vǫluspá 35, rapists are counted among the murderers and oath-breakers, who will have to wade forever in the turbid streams of Hel after death and during Ragnarǫk. It is entirely possible that Snorri omitted the truth of Váli's conception, as did the poets of the Edda, because it was so shameful.

Contrary to Saxo, who cared nothing for the old gods, Snorri and the Icelanders who wrote down the Edda poems may have wished to tone down mythical events that could put the ancestral gods in a negative light. The massive silence about the fate of Rindr suggests that there really was a myth where the otherwise esteemed All-Father actually committed the lowly deed of raping the mother of his child. In fact, there are a few clues in the lore. In a skaldic poem by the skald Kormákr Ǫgmundarson called Sígurðarkvíða, verse 3 mentions that 'Óðinn seið til Rindar' which indicates that Óðinn used magic against Rindr. Another clue is found in the Edda poem Gróagalðr, where the old dead witch Gróa sings her spell-songs to guide her son on his journey to woo the maiden in the underworld.

In the first spell, Gróa declares that the spell was first sung by Rán to Rindr:

Mother said: 6. "I sing the first charm then I sing it well and completely, this was sung by Ráni to Rindr: That you shake off your shoulders that feels bad to you; Lead you yourself your own self!"	Móðir kvað: 6.«Þann gel ek þér fyrstan, þann kveða fjǫlnýtan, þann gól Rindi Rani, at þú of ǫxl skjótir því er þér atalt þykkir; sjálfr leið þú sjálfan þik.

Not only does this verse refer to an aspect of the myth which is otherwise lost when Rindr got advice from Rán the goddess of the ocean, that mistress of death by drowning. The importance is on the meaning of the name: "The Robbery" referring to the rape itself. It is also advice about letting go of bad feelings, of letting go of the past and not let it control you anymore. Good advice for any rape victim. In order to truly understand the myth of the rape, we have to delve even deeper. We understand that Óðinn was willing to go into exile as a punishment for a very dishonorable crime, his need to impregnate the unwilling Rindr, prophesied to be the mother of Váli being more important than his good name, reputation and status among the gods.

Rather than ignoring the story because it is unsavory, we should ask ourselves why he was willing to do that, and why the story was invented and told at all. We are moving into territory that is difficult and sensitive because we are still living in a time when women must fight to free themselves from shame and sin when it comes to sexual abuse. Blame is so often placed on the victim, and it is and has been a long struggle to overcome these kinds of attitudes. At first sight, the parable, once deciphered, could give the impression that it blames the victim. This is not so. This myth was created in a time when women's sexuality was quite acceptable and little shame attached to it, and certainly not sin. It was also created in a time when rape was unacceptable, yet could happen.

However, there is only one way to really understand the entire myth, and that is through translating the names and taking the translations seriously. I would like to emphasize the fact that this is not a story about real events committed by real people, but a parable. A parable will use a situation that is recognizable from real life such as a rape yet use that story to convey a deeper meaning. All the myths do this, but rarely do they use rape in parables. The rape, as all other mythical events, is a metaphor. To understand the metaphor, we need only understand that a rape is essentially the loss of freedom, the loss of free will, the loss of choice. It is the humiliation of being used, the fear of violence the feeling of being abused.

In a parable, a woman getting pregnant is a metaphor where she represents humanity creating something new how this happens illustrates how the new creation is brought about. The parable is revealed when we understand that Óðinn actually does mean "The Spirit". If we understand him as The Spirit as such, he represents The Spirit not only of the world, but also of the individual, and of society. He also represents poetry and passion. The point is that The Spirit is not a man, nor a nasty rapist, but simply that subtle thing which creates breath and inspiration in living things the spurrer of all experience and all knowledge. We understand the myth of Rindr only when we understand that her name indicates that she "rejects the Spirit".

Her name, from hrinda to reject, hurl away from herself speaks for itself. She rejects The Spirit because it is "too old" and because she is content with her material wealth. As such, The Rejecter represents a human society or an individual which rejects The Spirit. Significantly, she is the princess of a realm which experiences constant battles. In this society, the representative for humanity goes crazy. In this society, the representative for womanhood is "tied to the bed" and raped, robbed of her strength and her self-respect. The impression that this is a metaphor for human society is strengthened by the mention of "Western halls".

In Norse myths, only the west is not mentioned among the directions belonging to gods, death or giants leaving the human world. The sadness of the story is overwhelming. Not only do the spirit-rejecting human societies experience madness, meaningless battles and severe oppression.

The Spirit is exiled from the divine realms! However, after the Rejecter manages to shake the bad feelings from her shoulders and learns to lead her own way, she births The Choice the choice to destroy Blind Aggression forever. It is a valiant Choice that will restore the quality of Baldr the greatness of mind, the fairness of understanding and the courage of heart.

5.7 THE SONG OF THE SACRED GROVE-VǪLUNDARKVÍÐA

"...The building of megalithic monuments would concur, in all likelihood, with the rise of special crafts...reason for allying the group of craftsman-priests of our texts with the culture of the builders of the megaliths...The capture and suppression of a master of smith-craft...may symbolize the ascendance of a new social order. In this order, the highest praise would no longer go to mysterious, non-human forces, represented in earth by a craftsman-priest-magician, but to the deeds of strength and courage, accomplished by a human fighter and to the god who is modeled in his image....We find, indeed, evidence in the Europe of the second millennium BCE, of the rising of a warrior aristocracy which imposed its rule on the peasant villages of the Stone Age."

Lotte von Motz: "The Wise one on the Mountain: Form, function and the significance of the subterranean smith; a study in folklore" (1983)

Vǫlundarkvíða, or The Song of the Sacred Grove, as I translate it, is one of the most mysterious Edda poems. The poem is based on a very ancient and widespread legend. It is referred to in the Old English poem known as the Lament of Deor, and in a short story told within the Þiðrekssaga af Bern the Saga of Theodoric the Great, where it is called Velents þáttr smiðs, The Story of Velent the Smith. Velent is usually called Wayland in English, but in various versions he is known as Wieland, Veland, Velent and Vǫlundr. The names of the smith are all related to something sacred; vé is a Norse word referring to a sacred space whether it be a natural grove sanctuary, a temple or a shrine. Landr means "land" and lundr means "grove", so that the name of the smith could be translated as either Sacred Land or Sacred Grove. In the Edda version, it is the latter meaning that has survived. Groves were commonly used as natural temples in Pagan times.

A MEDIEVAL VERSION: VELENT THE SMITH

In the story of Velent the Smith, which is a late, medieval and very Christianized version, we learn that Velent was the son of the giant Vaði [Danger, Misfortune] in Sjaelland, Denmark. As a young man, he went to learn the blacksmith's art from Mímir [Memory], a Hunnish smith. We are reminded of how Óðinn sought the Mead of Memory from the giant Mímir who guards the Well of Memory at the root of the World Tree. Mímir is a giant in Norse mythology, representing universal memory and intelligence. That he shows up as a Hun is typical. The Huns were foreigners from the east who in literature and poetry could easily replace the giants, or be a poetical disguise for the giant race. While at Mimi's, Velent is an apprentice together with several others, among them Sígurðr, who in the Edda poems is apprenticed to the dwarf smith Reginn rather than to the giant smith Mímir, showing that the storytellers identified the two smiths. Sígurðr beats all the apprentices, and Velent, humiliated, is sent to learn the art of forgery with two dwarfs. To sum it up, Velent's father, who represents misfortune, danger and harm, dies in an avalanche, and Velent kills the two mischievous dwarfs who taught him, much like Suttungr killed the two dwarfs who kept the mead of memory.

Velent went to Denmark, where King Níðungr [Underneath-Descendant] ruled. Velent forged a sword called Mimungr [Memory Descendant] with which he kills a rival smith and enters the service of the king. The king promises his daughter and half the kingdom to the one who can bring him his victory-stone, but breaks his promise when Velent shows up with the stone Velent ends up banished after killing the knight who got the girl and the kingdom in his place. He is later caught and hamstrung, but takes his revenge, killing the king's two sons and raping his daughter. He later married the princess, who gave birth to a son called Viðga, whose name means "To Expand". The story of Velent is a late version displaying several interesting associations and details that are not present in the Edda poem, yet missing completely the depth and coherence of the older version.

THE SONG OF THE SACRED GROVE

1. The maidens flew from the south across the Dark Forest
All-Wise the young to fulfill her fate:
On the Shore of the Soul they sat down to rest the southern red goddesses spun
the precious linen.

> *1.Meyiar flvgo svnnan*
> *Myrcvið igognom,*
> *Alvitr vnga,*
> *orlog drygia;*
> *þer a Sevarstrond*
> *settvz at hvilaz,*
> *drosir svðronar*
> *dyrt lín spvnno.*

Vǫlundarkvíða st.1, Poetic Edda (The Song of the Sacred Grove)

In the Edda version, we get the story told in the usual metaphorical allegory, or spiritual parable that is so crucial to our understanding of the Edda lore. It begins with a prose introduction:

> *"Niðuðr [Undercurrent] was the king of Svithioð [Sweden]; He had two sons and a daughter, Bǫðvildr [Battle Will]. There were three brothers, sons of the Finn [Sami] king. One was called Slagfiðr [Battle Finder], the other Egill [Awe], the third was Vǫlundr[Sacred Grove]. They were skiing and hunting animals. They came to Ulfdal [Wolf Valley] and made their settlement there, and there was a lake called Ulfsiár [Wolf Sea]. One morning, the brothers found on the beach three women, who were spinning linen. They had with them their bird hides, and they were Valkyrie.*
>
> *There were the two daughters of King Laðvé [Sacred Storage] , Hlaðgvþr Svanhvit [Divine Storage Swan-white] and Hervor Alvitr [Army-spring All-wise], and the third was Avlrvn [Ale-Rune], the daughter of Kiar [The Pusher] from Valland [The Land of Choice]. The men brought the women to their homes. Awe had Ale-Rune, Battle-Finder had Swan-white, and Sacred Grove had All-wise. They built together seven winters, but then the women flew to seek battles, and they did not return. Then Awe went to look for Ale-Rune, and Battle Finder went to look for Swan-white, but Sacred Grove remained in Wolf Valley. He was the most skillful man ever known in ancient lore. King Undercurrent had him taken as a prisoner, as is here sung of..."*

From the very beginning of the story, the names of the characters provide the clues as to how we may decipher the true meaning of the poem. First of all, we have a king called Undercurrent, indicating hidden streams, underlying motifs, unconscious drives. He rules in "Sweden", a geographical assignment indicating that he rules the human world. Then there are the three sons of the Sami king. The Sami, like the Huns, belong to the "other" category of people who may represent the giants of the east, beings from the Realm Outside. The trinity formula is recognizable from countless myths. In part two, lecture 22, I have given an extensive analysis of the trinity formula and how it represents the three qualities of human consciousness. Spirit, mind and passion, as reflected in the three meanings of Óðin's name: Spirit, Poetry and Frenzy, and in the meanings of his two brothers.

Vé means Sacred Space, but it can also mean Awe, while Víli refers to the Will, the Intent. These three qualities were given to human beings in the Vǫluspá poem, where the first man and woman are given breath and spirit from Óðinn, intelligence and thought from "Hænir", and vitality and colors from "Hlóðurr" [The Heat]. In the Song of the Sacred Grove, the three brothers have names that easily identify them as representing the three divine qualities of human consciousness. Egill is a name that corresponds with Vé, meaning Awe and representing the mind, thought and poetry. Slagfiðr is a name that corresponds with Frenzy or Intent-Will and passion, meaning Battle Finder. Vǫlundr himself, whose name means Sacred Grove or Sacred Land, is the Spirit. His name has given the Norse word for labyrinth; Vǫlundarhús, the House of the Sacred Grove.

It is the place of prayer and sacrifice. That the three brothers come from the giant realm in the east, the great Outside, corresponds with the fact that Óðinn and his two brothers, the first Aesir, gods of human and cosmic consciousness, were born of giants. When the three brothers come to "Wolf Valley" and "Wolf Sea", it is a metaphor for how the three qualities entered the physical realm. Wolves represent the physical, passion, desire, lust, hunger and greed. Thus I will continue to refer to the valley and the sea as the Valley or Sea of Desire.

The entry of the three brothers in the "Valley of Desire" is the equivalent of the entry of the three brothers on Earth, as told in the Vǫluspá, st. 17, when the three Aesir come out of the host of dwarfs and enters Earth in order to offer their gifts of spirit-breath-inspiration, intelligence thought mind and vitality intent passion color to the first people. In the Vǫluspá, this event is immediately followed by the emergence of the three fates. Urðr, Verdandi and Skuld [Origin, Becoming and Debt] who represent past, present and future, and who are said to come from the "sea beneath the ash".

The ash is the world tree, and the sea beneath is the Well of Origin, from where Snorri explained that the Norns came. Snorri also let us know that there were swans in that same lake. It is the same lake that nourishes the world tree. In Snorri's account, not only the three original Norns came from the Well of Origin, but also the individual Norns, those that follow a human being throughout his or her life, spinning our fates. They have three origins, divine, elfin and dwarfish. In the Song of the Sacred Grove, the emergence of the fates is repeated, this time in the shape of three women with bird hides in fact swan hides spinning the precious linen, a metaphor for their shaping of fate. No attempt is made to disguise the identity of the women. They are southern, which is the direction of the Norns and the Aesir, they have swan feathers and can take a bird shape, they spin the linen of fate, and they are called Valkyrie.

Valkyrie are also Norns. Thus the Song of the Sacred Grove is a poetical rewriting of the creation story where the three qualities of divine and human consciousness enter the physical world of hunger and desire, and marry the three aspects of fate. The oldest of the Valkyrie is Ale-Rune, a name which refers to the oldest Norn, Origin, who guards the precious mead and who takes the ale or mead or water from the Well of Origin to nourish the world tree. Her origin in the Land of Choice is a hint towards her belonging in the land of the immortals. She marries the mind aspect of the trinity.

The other lady, Divine Storage Swan-white, seems to represent Skuld, the future aspect of fate, married to the Intent-Will, the Battle Finder. Finally, the Sacred Grove, the Spirit-Breath quality, is married to "Army-spring All-wise", the "happening now" aspect of fate. She is the one who must "fulfill her fate" in the poems, driving the southern ladies towards the Dark Forest, seeking battles. Not only is the creation myth repeated in the Song of the Sacred Grove, but so is The Golden Age myth. It is the sacred union between the three men and the three women the qualities of consciousness and the aspects of fate and their life together in the Valley of Desire.

The Sacred Grove laments the loss of this age in the poem, declaring that they had an abundance of "red gold" a metaphor for divine wisdom, when they all lived together:

13. Then said Undercurrent lord of those Beneath
"Where did you, Sacred Grove you wise elf! Find our gold in the Valley of Desire?"

13. Kallaþi nv Niþvðr
Niara drottinn:
«Hvar gaztv, Volvndr,
visi alfa!
vára aura
i Vlfdolom?»

14. The Sacred Grove said:
"The gold was not there on the path of Initiation, I think our land is far from the Rhine mountains;
I remember, that we had more riches in our ownership when we were all whole within our worlds.
Divine Storage and Army-Spring were born to Sacred Storage
Ale Rune was wise in magic the daughter of the Pusher."

14. Volvndr qvaþ:
«Gvll var þar eigi
a Grana leiðo,
fiarri hvgða ec vart land
fiollom Rínar;
man ec, at ver meiri
moti attom,
er ver heil hiv
heima vorom.
Hlaðgvðr oc Hervor
borin var Hlaðvé,
kvnn var Avlrvn
Kiars dottir.»

The path of **Grani** refers to initiation Sígurð's path of the divine red gold that his horse Grani **carried** when he went through the flames and woke up the sleeping Valkyrie within, learning about the runes. The gold and the "red rings" referred to throughout the poem are metaphors that have to do with initiation and divine knowledge.

The Sacred Grove is called a "wise elf", and also "the lord of elves", in this poem, a fact that may possibly relate him to Freyr, who was also the lord of elves. More importantly, the elves represent the souls of dead people, of which the Spirit certainly is lord. Sacred Grove, the "wise elf", clearly refers to the presence of the three maidens in marriage with the three brothers as crucial to the existence of the red gold.

Their marriage and living together for nine winters. The introduction says seven, but the **poem** clearly says nine, represent a happy and harmonious era. The impression of a sacred union is implied in the second stanza:

2. One of them took Awe to protect the beautiful maiden enclosed him in her bright embrace;
Another was Swan White, she wore the feathers of a swan (text vanished) and the third their sister embraced the white neck of the Sacred Grove.

2. Eín nam þeirra
Egil at veria
fagr mer fira
faþmi liosom;
onnor var Svanhvít,
svanfiaðrar dró,
enn in þriþia,
þeirra systir,
varþi hvítan
hals Volvndar.

In the first stanza, we learn that the maidens were discovered at Sefarstrǫnd the Shore of the Soul or, alternately, the Shore of Sleep. I have discussed the possible connection between the fate-goddess and the soul in previous essays, this poem only serves to strengthen this impression. It is the union with the inner soul that is at stake here. The bright embrace is recognizable in the countless stories of the maiden who awaits her hero in the underworld.

It is interesting to notice how it is unusually enough the women who are said to embrace the men, enclosing them in brightness and in death, as indicated by the "white neck" of the Spirit. The women are no longer there, the brothers have separated from each other, and Spirit has been taken captive by the warriors from "Beneath". What has happened? The Golden Age ended. We are not given exact reasons. We learn only that the maidens live happily with their husbands for a symbolical seven winters. The eight winter, they begin to yearn, and in the ninth winter, we hear that "need separated them".

4...need separated them; the maidens hastened through the Dark Forest, All Wise the Young would fulfill her fate.	4....nauþr vm scilþi; meyiar fýstoz a myrqvan viþ, Alvitr vnga orlog drygia.

No further reason is given for the end of the golden era in this poem. The maidens simply wanted to leave their husbands, in order to seek battles, and for Army-spring All Wise to "fulfill her fate". There was a need in it, a need to experience the separation. We can only speculate if the focus on "All-Wise the Young" indicates an unspoken meaning. The young fate goddess needs to fulfill her fate, a fate that is perhaps indicated by her name, omniscience. In order to achieve this, she needs to know all aspects of existence, even the battles and the conflicts.

In her study of the Fylgjur the follower guardian spirits of men and women, professor Else Mundal pointed out the fact that the loss of the fylgja in the sagas always means the loss of fortune and of life. The fylgja may actually leave her human being if she no longer likes him or her. I have argued that the Fylgjur, often just called Dísir, overlap in function and identity with the Norns that are connected to human beings. In the Song of the Sacred Grove, the women seem to grow impatient and no longer want to be with their men. We hear of no reason except need and fate, but the other Golden Age myths keep referring to the negative qualities of greed, hatred, jealousy, aggression and ignorance, and the destructive actions that follow these qualities.

In the Song of Much Knowing, we hear that the two dogs called Gífr and Geri Greed and Doer are the obstacles that keep a soul apart from the immortal maidens. As the three brothers return from their hunting, they find their women gone. Awe, representing the mind, goes to the east after Ale Rune the east being the direction of giants. Battle Finder, representing passion, goes to the south after Swan White the south being the direction of the Norns and the gods. The last direction is the north the direction of death. In the beginning of the story, when the brothers found the maidens at the Shore of the Soul, the Sacred Grove, representing spirit, had his "white neck" embraced by Army-spring All Wise. The white neck is a metaphor for death, and her embrace is the embrace of death.

Death in omniscience. But Sacred Grove does not go into the northern realm of death. He remains in the Valley of Desire all by himself, forging countless red golden rings while awaiting and hoping for the return of his beloved. This hears king Undercurrent, lord of the Beneath, and he sends his warriors to capture the smith "beneath the waning moon". A big point is made out of how the warriors of Beneath "walk the entire hall to its end" when they arrive at the Sacred Grove. They see all the seven hundred red rings "owned by the warrior", and take them all off their bast rope before putting them back on again.

Only one ring is left off, for the Sacred Grove to find. When the Sacred Grove returns from the bear-hunt, we hear that he travels "the very long path". He roasts the meat of a brown she-bear and watches while the fire begins to burn high with the "wind-dried wood". The wood is a metaphor for the flesh, the human being, the wind is a metaphor for death. The fire that begins to burn from this wood is the rekindling of life and passion. It is in this state of passion that the Spirit discovers the one red ring that has been left off the ropes, and believes that his wife has returned. He waits a long time for her, but falls asleep. When he wakes up, he is bound and fettered. King Undercurrent asks his prisoner where he has found "our gold in the Valley of Desire", and the Sacred Grove replies that it was not found on the "path of Grani", which means the path of initiation.

Grani was the horse that Sígurðr rode through the fire, carrying the divine red gold of the gods, before he found the Valkyrie within and woke her up. The Sacred Grove declares that there was "gold" when the three brothers lived whole in their worlds with their wives. Before the Spirit can continue to inform the king of underlying intentions of the truth of the red gold the divine knowledge, the king's unnamed wife appears, and, like the warriors of Beneath, she "walks the entire hall to its end". We can only understand the allegories if we keep in mind at all times that the characters and places of the poem represent human and divine cosmic qualities. The king, by his name, represents the underlying streams of human consciousness, the king of the subconscious (the Beneath ones). Women usually represent fate in one aspect or another, so that the Queen of Undercurrent, as she is called, represents the fate of Undercurrent.

The "hall" represents a body, an individual, or a society en enclosed space within which the qualities operate, whether on a cosmic, societal or individual level. The warriors of Beneath, and the fate of Undercurrent, have now taken over the entire "hall". It is the nature of the fate of Undercurrent to maintain the nature of Undercurrent. He must remain unconscious, driven by subconscious streams rather than a wakeful spirit. She will not have Spirit free and talking to her man about the bygone state of union and wholeness. Consequently, she advices the king to hamstring the elf and put him away.

The now injured and powerless [hamstrung] Spirit is placed on an islet called Sævarstaðir, which means the Place of the Soul or the Place of Sleep. King Undercurrent gives the red ring to his daughter Battle Will, and keeps the sword of Spirit himself. The Sacred Grove sits in his captivity, forging great treasures for the king, as he is forced to do. But like the giantesses who were forced to grind treasures for king Wisdom, the Spirit forges vengeance upon his captor. When the two young and unnamed sons of Undercurrent come to the Place of the Soul in order to see the red gold that is, come to seek the divine knowledge of the Sacred Grove he sees that they have evil intentions, and kills them both.

From their limbs and bones he forges jewelry and cups which he sends to the king, the queen and the princess of the Beneath ones. The princess, Battle Will, is a daughter. In the poetry, children always represent the result of their parent's union. Sons represent the obvious and seen result, whereas daughters represents the hidden result. Battle Will is the hidden result of the marriage between Undercurrent and the fate of Undercurrent, and as a woman, she represents an aspect of fate. In this new era, there are two women, a mother and a daughter, a queen and a princess of the Beneath ones. The princess represents the new growing fate of their subjects, as opposed to the old one. Battle Will cherishes the red ring of the Sacred Grove, but discovers that it is broken.

The ring represents wholeness, and the red gold indicated divine wisdom. Thus it is the wholeness of Divine Wisdom that is broken. Battle Will is the new fate, and unlike her mother, the old fate, who wanted to keep the Spirit locked away and powerless, Battle Will now seeks the Sacred Grove on the Place of the Sleeping Soul. When she returns the red ring to the Sacred Grove, his health is immediately restored. The Spirit is whole once more. He offers to the young woman his precious mead and rapes her. We do not get any details, but the story is the equivalent of what happened when Óðinn raped the Rejecter.

Battle Will gets pregnant, but we do not hear anything about her child, except that the Sacred Grove made her father swear to never harm "the woman of the Sacred Grove", although she would give birth to his child in Undercurrent's hall. In the story of Velent, we saw that the child of Battle Will was the boy Viðga "To Expand". The name is the equivalent of Óðin's son Víðarr, The Expander a god of inner silence who serves the precious mead to Loki in the halls of Aegir. He is among those gods who will survive the Ragnarǫk together with Baldr (who returns from Hel) and The Choice. The entire poem of Vǫlundr is a parable about the original wholeness of spirit, about what happens when the wholeness is broken, and what it takes to restore the wholeness. Sometimes, only the loss of freedom, the shock of abuse, can wake a person or a society up from subconscious slumber, in order to give birth to a new choice, in order to expand the soul.

5.8: LOST IN ILLUSION

Óðinn said:
1. "Advise me now, Frigg! As I intend to travel to visit the Powerful Head Veil
A great knowledge-hunger I have in me to contend about ancient runes with that
all-knowing devourer/giant."

> *Óðinn qvaþ:*
> *1. «Raþ þv mer nv, Frigg!*
> *allz mic fara tíðir*
> *at vitia Vafðrvdnis;*
> *forvitni micla*
> *qveþ ec mer a fornom stafom*
> *við þann inn alsvinna iotvn.»*

Vafþrúðnismál st. 1, Poetic Edda

When Frigg was Married to Víli and Vé

"Óðinn had two brothers, the first was called Vé [Awe/Sacred Space], and the second was called Víli [Will/Intent]. These brothers ruled the realm when he was gone. There was a time when Óðinn had traveled so far away and been so long away from home that the Aesir no longer believed that he would return. Then the brothers took the heritage after him and shared it between them; his wife Frigg became the wife of them both. But just after that happened, Óðinn returned home, and then he claimed his wife back."

Ynglinga Saga 3, Snorri Sturluson

Loki said:
26. «*"Be silent, Frigg! You are the Maiden (fate) of Life Struggle (Earth) and you have always been man-hungry; Awe and Intent, did you, wife of the Expanding/Wooden One, both receive in your embrace!"*

> *Loki kvað:*
> *26. «Þegi þv, Frigg!*
> *þv ert Fiorgyns mer*
> *oc hefir e vergiorn veriþ,*
> *er þa Vea oc Vilia*
> *leztv þer, Viþris qven!*
> *bada i badm vm tekit.»*

Lokasenna, Poetic Edda

There are several references in the Norse myths about the disappearance of Óðinn. The above indicates a myth of how Frigg was left alone with Óðin's two brothers, Víli and Vé, and had to marry them because her real husband, Óðinn, had disappeared. The only way to decipher the parable of the story is, as usual, to break down what each character represent. Óðinn is all the three aspects of the human/divine consciousness at once, as testified by his very name; The Spirit, The Poetry and The Frenzy. When he appears next to two other male gods, he usually represents The Spirit, while the other two will represent either the Poetry or the Frenzy.

In the case of Óðin's two brothers, Vé, whose name means Awe or Sacred Space, corresponds to Poetry, and thus to the creative, conscious, thinking mind (that which makes poetry happen), while Víli, whose name means Will or Intent, corresponds with the Frenzy and thus to the passion that moves us forward. In other stories, Víli is replaced by Loki, although he may also be replaced by Freyr or Týr, both gods of passion in its various aspects. Vé may be replaced by Bragi, the god of poetry, but also by Þórr, who is the protector of the known world, and whose servants have names that mean "Putting Together Ends" and "Digging Up" or "Maturing" (Þialfi and Rǫskva). In this story, no other gods take the place of Óðin's "brothers", who simply represent the thinking mind and the passionate survival instinct, the Mind and the Passion. Without the presence of Spirit, the Mind and the Passion can be very destructive and foolish, although we can only deduce what happened, since Snorri's story says nothing about it.

What he does say, however, is that they married Frigg.

We know that this goddess was called upon in childbirth as well, but to call her a "goddess of childbirth and motherhood" is too simplified. Frigg is a goddess of the hidden depths, living away in the mysterious Moist Halls where no men can enter perhaps a reference to the bogs and mosses where the goddess received her sacrifices or to the womb. She has the knowledge of all fate, but says nothing about this knowledge. She is a mother goddess who has power over all nature. As a deity, she is related to several other goddesses. Her knowledge about all fate relates her to the Norns. The fact that she keeps her knowledge hidden relates her to Hel and the giantesses of the underworld who also guard their knowledge in the dark and unknown realms. Her residence in moist depths relates her to the womb and particularly to the universal womb of origin to the lady of the cosmic ocean, Rán, who brought forth the nine waves that made our universe.

The fact that she is called Fiǫrgyn's maiden relates her to the Earth goddess: Fjǫrgyn is a name for the Earth goddess and means Life Struggle or Life Woman. The choice of that particular name of the Earth goddess indicates that Frigg is particularly related to survival. Frigg is also called Fjǫrgvínsdóttir The Daughter of Life's Friend. The fact that she has the power to demand oaths from all nature strengthens the impression of an earth-goddess. Her residence in the moist depths also relates her to the ancient mother goddess Nerthus who lived by a lake, as does the oldest Norn Urðr. The name Frigg is derived from the earlier Frija, the wife of Wodan, who was also the predecessor of the name Freyia, so that the two were once the same goddess.

The countless significant associations of one dís with other Dísir (female powers) is typical, indicating a very fluid overlapping between the various female powers that seem to border on identification. Ultimately, there seems to be a goddess of countless names and shapes who rules nature, life-fate and death, and who secretly possesses all the divine knowledge that gods and men are seeking through trials of initiation. When we want to understand Frigg's function in the poetical lore, however, we must also go to the meaning of her names. The root of the names Frigg and Freyia is related to sovereignty, wisdom, fertility and love. Frigg could be translated as Beloved or simply as Love, but she is also known as Saga "History", and as Hlín "Tranquility". With her three names, she corresponds with the three aspects of Óðinn [Love/Wisdom with Spirit] a union which produces the great Baldr, Poetry with History, and Frenzy with Tranquility. The union of these six complimentary aspects of human and divine existence is sacred and brings great fortune. But in the myth, two of these aspects are separated from each other. Spirit is lost to Love/Wisdom, and so she must be alone with Mind and Passion.

Since Frigg also represents history the history of humanity and the history of the individual we are faced with a history of humankind where Spirit has an empty seat, and Love is in the hands of Mind and Passion rather than Spirit. The tragedy of this separation can only be understood properly if we remember that the union between Spirit and Love was what created Baldr and all he represents: The objective, non-judgmental understanding that leads to true courage and fulfillment of wisdom. The death of Baldr is one way of saying that these qualities were lost to our world, our history, the separation of Spirit and Love is another way of saying exactly the same thing. Luckily, Óðinn returned and reclaimed his wife, but the myth is timeless, a description of a state of being or the state of a society, with a prophecy foretelling that if only Spirit returns to Love, divine wholeness will be achieved once more, both on the level of the individual and the level of society.

When Freyia became many

"A sixth is called Freyia. She is the most glorious besides Frigg. She was married to someone called Óðr. Their daughter is Treasure [Hnoss], she is so fair that after her, all things precious and beautiful are called Treasures. Óðr traveled far away, and Freyia wept for him. Her tears are pure red gold. Freyia has many names, and the reason for this is that she gave herself different names while she was with different people in order to search for Óðr. She is called Great Ocean [Mardǫllr], Fate [Hǫrn = "Flax" = Fate], Provider [Gefn] and Sow [Sýr]. Freyia owned the Jewel of Flames [Brisingamén]. She is also called the Goddess of the Vanir [Vanadís]"

(Gylfaginning, Prose Edda, Snorri Sturluson)

Snorri's account actually explains why the great goddess has many different names and shapes. Over the course of time, lots of tribes worshiped the goddess of all nature, fate, death, birth and initiation the protective goddess and often also the ancestral mother of their tribe, or the goddess that ruled their land, responsible for its prosperity and harvest. This is probably the origin of the Sacred Marriage, where the king showed his dedication to his tribe and their land by ritually marrying the goddess of the tribe or land.

Each tribe had a different name for her, and a different focus on what powers they most cherished. This ancient background must, in my opinion, be one of the most important reasons why the goddesses of Norse myths remnants of thousands of years of interaction between various tribes all share most attributes and functions. The myth-makers of Scandinavia were probably aware of this history to some degree, and made all the female powers the Dísir come together in one ruler. The name Freyia is in fact not a name, but a title, meaning "Lady Sovereign".

This strongly Pantheist streak, where other gods are real yet ultimately aspects of a singular deity, in Norse mythology may have ancient Indo-European origins. The Norse Dísir are etymologically and mythically related to the Old Indian dhisanas, who were goddesses of intelligence, fortune and fertility, "the wives of the gods", and who guarded the precious drink of immortality called Soma. The Soma was sometimes called Madhu, "honey", which is the same root word that makes up the precious miǫðr, "mead", of Old Norse lore.

It is easy to see that the Dísir and the dhisanas are very close, since the Dísir also guard the precious mead of immortality. From the Indian tradition, we know that the dhisanas all came together in the one Dhisana, otherwise also known as Aditi, the goddess of Infinity. The names of Freyia listed by Snorri identify the goddess as an ocean goddess, like Rán, her daughters and Frigg, as a fate goddess like Urðr and Frigg, and as a goddess of abundance and provisions, like the Earth goddess herself. The Jewel of Flames gives associations to the Sun goddess.

There are several other names that describe Freyia and identify her as something other than an Ásynia. In the Flateyjarbók, Freyia disguises herself and shows up as the huge fate-giantess called Magician [Gǫndul]. Most studies agree that Freyia is at least behind the figures of the giantess Menglǫð and the elfin goddess Iðunn.

The Grímnismál poem and the Hyndlulióð poem of the Poetic Edda clearly identify Freyia as a Valkyrie, whereas the former poem also suggests that she rules fate when it says that she "arranges the seating in the hall" of People Field [Folkvangr], which, by the way, is her field. In the Lokasenna, st.21, Óðinn speaks up for Freyia's alter ego, The Provider [Gefion, the long form of Freyia's listed name Gefn], and declares that she, like himself, knows all fate. That there was a great goddess in Scandinavia has been suggested by several professors and experts on the Norse religion, beginning, as far as I know, with Folke Ström in the 1950s. In later decades, the overwhelming evidence in the lore has re-convinced most experts on Norse mythology to accept the idea that the Lady Sovereign may really be an attempt to unite all the goddesses in one ultimate goddess, based on the fact that all the goddesses and other female powers seem to fluidly blend together as one.

This was strongly argued in the Swedish professor Britt-Mari N sström's hitherto undisputed work Freyia- Great Goddess of the North (2004). Although the above is an undisputed and well-argued thesis, much acclaimed, the knowledge of the Scandinavian, Pantheist Great Goddess keeps being ignored in most media. I have noticed a great deal of resistance especially from those who have made a modern religion out of whatever they know about Old Norse lore, the resistance seems to be based partly on an unwillingness to accept a female sovereign deity, partly on an unwillingness to understand Pantheism, since their religion is supposed to be Polytheist.

Religious beliefs and assertive attitudes often make it very difficult to think again and really explore what the ancestors of these religious beliefs actually believed. It is in fact impossible to really understand the female figures of Norse mythology and how the male figures relate to them without understanding the profound stream of Pantheism that runs through the religious lore or the Norse people like the very red thread needed to unlock the key to its secrets. As a goddess of fate, death and birth, she is also a goddess of initiation, and her loving embrace is the ultimate goal of the initiation the state of union where the soul is restored and renewed forever, which is what immortality is really about.

When Freyia is accused of having slept with all the gods and elves in the Hall of Aegir, we have to realize that all the gods and elves, souls which have reached the Hall of Aegir have reached a state of immortality. Aegir's hall is situated in Hlésey, the Wind Shield Island, and a place where the winds of death cannot reach. They have come to this state of existence only through the union with the Great Goddess, through her loving embrace, a union that could only be achieved after conquering the "giants" of fear, hatred and greed. The fact that she can take numerous shapes means that the ultimate unity of the one goddess can also separate into countless individuals. As such, each person has his or her individual fate spinning Dísir, Norns or Fylgjur, representing his or her own fate and soul. The goal of the initiation is to unite with one's own fate and soul, "waking her up", like Sígurðr woke his Valkyrie and achieved immortality, that is, the Valkyrie went after him into Hel after his death and saved him from the "rock bride" of darkness. The individual fate-soul-goddess may have her own characteristics and personality, but she is ultimately the same Gullna dís the same Golden Goddess, that is at the core of all the others. Snorri's account explains why the one goddess had numerous names and appearances.

His story may be partially based on the historical understanding he and the knowledge keepers that preceded him may have had that the same goddess was worshiped by various people under different names but there is also a spiritual message about the story. This can only be understood when we integrate our understanding of the goddess as the ultimate divine soul of everybody and everything. As such, the goddess corresponds with the god, Óðinn, who is the divine Spirit of everybody and everything. When Snorri says that Freyia was married to Óðr, the disguise for Óðinn is very thin indeed. Óðr is the very word that makes up the name Óðinn, which is derived from the word óðr and hinn.

Hinn is just a suffix, meaning "the", so that Óðinn is "The Spirit" or "The Poetry". In the short form Óðr, we are dealing with exactly the same concept that makes up the Óðinn character. It simply means Spirit, Poetry or Frenzy. In the Flateyjarbók, the writers make no secret out of it, Freyia is clearly said to be Óðin's wife. In earlier times, Óðinn was called Wodan and was married to Frija, which was the one goddess that turned into both Frigg and Freyia. Snorri, who had learned to see the two goddesses as separate beings, solved the problem of identification by letting Freyia's husband appear a little bit different.

The story of Freyia and Óðr resembles the story of Frigg and Óðinn related above. They are both stories of how the husband disappeared from the wife, and now that we know the identity of the husband and the wife is really the same in both stories, we understand that we are dealing with a different and complimentary version of the very same story. In the Freyia story, she is not married to his two brothers, but rather begins to walk the Earth looking for her lost husband. It is the loving fate-soul of the world and of the individual who seeks the lost Spirit, the lost Poetry, and the lost Frenzy of spiritual and sexual ecstasy.

On her long search, which is happening at all times, within all human beings, and within all societies, the fate-soul produces the very red gold that is so cherished by the gods; the "gold" of Divine Knowledge, the "gold" that will lead to wisdom, eloquence, healing, transformation and ultimately to immortality or eternal resurrection. The purpose of the separation is clear. It is the very yearning of the fate soul her tears that produces the knowledge.

Goddess flanked by two human figurines, what appears to be a male with a beast, boar, hound (?) to the right, and a woman involved with some plants, Gundestrup cauldron, Bronze Age Denmark

To say it in other words, the meaning of the myth is ultimately to show how suffering is transformed into divine wisdom how the yearning attitude, the passionate search for one's lost Spirit will produce the Divine Knowledge that is needed to accomplish the union between the all-knowing soul-fate and the learning spirit within. From the two stories, we learn that there are two options when the Spirit is lost, to remain in "marriage" with the mind and the passion, but without spirit, or to search passionately for spirit, producing the red gold of divine knowledge, our lost heritage.

WHERE DID ÓÐINN GO THEN?
(VAFÞRÚÐNISMÁL)

Frigg said:
2. "At home I would prefer (to keep) the Father of Rulers in the divine halls; for no giant I believe to be equally powerful as the Powerful Head Veil."

Frigg qvaþ:
2. «Heima letia ec munda Heriafa/ðr i ga/rðom goða; þviat engi iotvn ec hvgða iafnramman sem Vafðrvðni vera.»

Óðinn said:
3. "Much did I travel much did I try much did I test the powers; This I want to know, how the Powerful Head Vei keeps his hall."

Oþinn qvaþ:
3. «Fiolþ ec fór, fiolþ ec freistaða, fia/lþ ec reynda regin; hitt vil ec vita, hve Vafðrvþnis salakynni se.»

Frigg said:
4. "May you travel whole! May you return whole! May you keep a whole mind! May your knowledge be sufficient when you, Father of Ages, are to speak with the giant!"

Frigg qvaþ:
4. «Heill þv farir! heill þv aptr komir! heill þv a sinnom sér! oþi þer dvgi, hvars þv scalt, Aldafa/þr, orðom mela iotvn!»

Vafþrúðnismál, st. 2, 3, 4, Poetic Edda

None of the stories above reveal why Óðinn left or why he was lost, but we can look for cues in other myths. Saxo Grammaticus claimed that after the rape of the Rejecter, which I related earlier in this chapter, Óðinn was actually exiled from Ásgarðr as a punishment for the rape. To apply the approach of the parable, we realize that in his quest for creating the Choice that could destroy Ignorant Strife, and thus restore Baldr, Spirit had to force humans into cultivating that Choice. Humans, represented by the Rejecter, would not see the need to make that Choice. So Spirit, who is the power that inspires us to learn, evolve and expand at all costs, made the humans experience madness, loss of freedom and abuse. Only through suffering would the eyes of stubborn and ignorant humans be opened so that the Choice could be birthed.

During the stage of post-traumatic stress that inevitably follows an experience like that, the Spirit will be temporarily "exiled". Only through healing, through letting go of the past and begin one's own path of knowledge will the Choice be made to restore both Spirit and everything that Baldr represents. In the Hyndlulióð, we learned that the Rejecter was advised by Robbery to shake all the past troubles from her shoulders and begin leading her own way in life. When the Choice was finally birthed, it began acting and producing results at once. As to where the Spirit went in his exile, we get another clue in some Edda poems, such as the Vafþrúðnismál. In this poem, Óðinn goes to contend with the all-knowing giant Vafþrúðnir. The name of the giant is derived from the noun váf, which means a head veil, and þrúðnir, which is derived from the adjective þrúðr, meaning "powerful", "overwhelming" or "tremendous".

I translate the name as The Powerful Head Veil. This is a very elegant way of describing the veil of illusion that covers the minds (heads) of most people. To The Spirit, the giant of illusion is a formidable opponent. In the poem, Óðinn and The Powerful Head Veil engage in an exchange of knowledge about the nature of cosmos that provides us with a lot of useful information about Old Norse cosmology, but the ultimate message of the story is a parable. The Spirit will either have to outwit the Illusions of the mind, or succumb to them and die. The only key to outwit Illusion turns out to be the knowledge of what Spirit whispered in the ears of Baldr before he went to the underworld. When Óðinn asks that question, the giant of illusion can no longer answer, because what Óðinn whispered to Baldr is beyond illusion, it is the actual truth of what is, the Divine Knowledge that is hidden in the underworld. Since the discourse between Óðinn and the Tremendous Head Veil is about the entire cosmos and all its dimensions, we may assume that the giant of the head veil represents a cosmic illusion that the world is illusion, as discussed in a previous essay.

As such, we are hearing of the Spirit of the entire cosmos trying to use intelligence in order to break through the veil that threatens to devour it. When The Spirit, in the shape of the god Óðinn, is "exiled" and separated from The Soul in the shape of a goddess, the original union between the all-soul that knows all fate and the all-spirit that seeks all fate is broken. Perhaps it could be a way of describing the border between the conscious and the subconscious, the known and the unknown, physical reality and spiritual reality. It is the Spirit-Mind-Passion, the seeker of knowledge, that is lost in the realm of the "head veil", while the Soul-Fate, who stores and rebirths the knowledge, and awaits his return, like a distant wife and true love. The story of Óðinn and the Powerful Head Veil begins with a farewell between husband and wife, where Óðinn explains that his curiosity compels him to seek the giant of illusion in order to understand how "his hall is kept". It is the Spirit who must seek knowledge, and who must overcome Illusion through entering it and understanding it. Ultimately, the message of the stories of separation may be parables about life itself and its ultimate purpose, to enter the physical realm, understand its illusions, and to remember the true union with the cosmic soul, return to it and restore divine knowledge. It could also be a parable describing what is needed to restore wholeness within the individual while alive, or within the world at large.

5.9: THE SLEEPING GODDESS

"There is no coming to consciousness without pain. People will do anything, no matter how absurd, in order to avoid facing their own soul."

-Carl Gustav Jung

In the next Chapter, we will cover several stories where Óðinn seems to lurk clandestinely in the shadows, eagerly awaiting another warrior into his realm, but needing the goddess of resurrection and fate in her many shapes to make this possible. As we shall see in the next chapter, one of his important (and vile) methods is to have the necklace of the goddess stolen, so that she will be willing to create the conflict between human beings that is somehow necessary to reach his ends. In the Edda poems, his means is to make the goddess sleep, like Sígrdrífa reveals in the Sígrdrífumál:

2. Long did I sleep, long was my slumber, long is the woe of the peoples: *Óðinn caused this, that I could not own the power to break the carvings of slumber."*	*2. «Lengi ec svaf,* *lengi ec sofnoþ var,* *long ero lyða le;* *Oþinn þvi veldr,* *er ec eigi mattac* *bregða blvnnstafom.»*

After stanza 4, in a prose interlude, the Valkyrie reveals the reasons Óðinn had given for causing this "woe of the peoples":

"She said that there were *two kings, one was called* *Hjalmgunnarr [Helmet Warrior],* *he was old and a great warrior,* *and Óðinn wanted him to have* *victory, but:* *Another was Respect/Awed* *Warrior brother of Abundance* *and no one in the world would* *help him*	*...annarr het Agnarr* *Avþo broþir,* *er vetr engi* *vildi þiggia."*

Sígrdrífa wanted to help Agnarr [Respect Warrior], and chose him for victory instead of Óðin's favorite, Helmet Warrior [Hjalmgunnarr]. The helmet is a direct reference to the famous helmet in Sígurð's story, The Aegishjalmr ["the Helmet of Fear"]. The helmet would be a metaphor for the mind. This is the helmet that the serpent Fafnir wore when he kept human kind away from the divine red gold of Alert Spirit [Andvari], snorting poison. Thus the Helmet Warrior, unloved by the goddess, is a man whose mind is clouded by fear, despite his apparent fierceness.

On the spiritual quest, courage is a far more complex quality than the ability to fight fiercely, and profound fear may secretly rule the minds of the most brave-looking warrior. The goddess repeatedly states that she can only love a man who knows no fear, and the great test lies not in battle but in the courage to ride through the fire and the shields that cover the mead and the sleeping fate.

This is not the courage that the Helmet Warrior possesses, and so the goddess chose Agnarr despite Óðin's preference. Agnarr is the name of Frigg's favorite in the Grímnismál poem, while Óðinn favors Geirrǫðr [Red Spear], who turns out to be a cruel and stingy king. This king is unable to recognize his own god when he arrives in his halls, and binds him between two fires. Only when the king's son, called Agnarr after his uncle, offers a drink to the bound god on the ninth night, is Red Spear conquered and Agnarr a fusion between the favorites of the goddess and the god receives the sacred teachings of The Spirit. The conflict between the Valkyrie goddess and Óðinn is repeatedly alluded to in the Edda heroic poetry. In Sígrdrífumál, we hear that Óðinn caused the Valkyrie to sleep and "long is the woe of the peoples".

This is further elaborated in the poem called Helreið Brynhildar [Brynhild's Ride to Hel]. Wearing the name Brynhildr [Armor Battle], the Valkyrie previously known as Sígrdrífa, a reincarnation of Helgi's Valkyrie, rides to Hel in order to save the dead Sígurðr from the oblivion of the Underworld. Her name is a direct reference to the armor she wore when she was found by Sígurðr. Only when the hero releases her from the armor that has grown into her body may she wake from her slumber. The Goddess of Gold [Vár Gullz] is met in Hel by an ogress, a "Bride of the Rock Cave" [Bruðr or Steini], who challenges the goddess to defend her actions when she lived in the world as a woman. The ogress points out that the task of the Valkyrie goddess is to stay in Valland (Valhǫll), spinning and weaving (fate). Instead, she has entered the human realm, where she has "been a Viking", bloodied herself and caused war and misery among the people, and a perpetual battle between tribes.

That is when the goddess stands up to explain her cause:

5.«I, the wise one in the wagon,
must tell you, of much witlessness,
if you want to know:
How the lineage of Giuki treated
me:
They raped my love and broke
their oaths.

6. The king full of intent stole our
hides, we were eight sisters born
beneath the oak.
I was twelve winters old, if you
want to know, When the oaths tied
me to the young hero

7. In the Valleys of Tunes they
called me
"Battle beneath Helmet", where I
resided

5.«Ec mvn segia þer svinn or reiþo
vitla/ssi mioc, ef þic vita lystir,
hve gorðo mic Givca arfar
astala/sa oc eiþrofa.

6.Let hami vára hvgfvllr konvngr
átta systra vndir eic borit;
var ec vetra tolf, ef þic vita lystir
er ec vngom gram eiþa seldac.

7.Heto mic alliri Hlymdalom
Hildi vndir Hialmi hverr er kvnni.

In the first two lines of these stanzas, the goddess from Valland declares a distinction between herself and the Underworld ogress. The latter is "of much witlessness", like the death that the ogress represents a death in oblivion where all consciousness is vanquished. She herself is the wise one the death that leads to resurrection and knowledge, as during initiation. In the next two lines, she is referring to the betrayal of the Niflungar the Children of the Mist, also referred to as Burgunds and as the lineage of their legendary ancestor, king Giuki.

The betrayal was to give her in marriage to a prince who was in fact too timid to complete his initiation a prince that could not ride through the flames that surrounded her while she slept. In the next stanza, the Valkyrie begins to explain the background story, so as to reveal why this was such a terrible event. The king full of intent is Óðinn, who stole the hides and thus the powers of the "eight sisters", the Valkyrie of Hlésey, the land of immortality. She, the oldest of the sisters, was tied to the young hero the initiate who would be worthy of her love. In stanza 7, the goddess proceeds to tell about her career as a Valkyrie, beginning by identifying herself as the metaphorical "Battle beneath Helmet" in the "Valley of Sound".

The helmet may be a reference to the Helmet of Fear, and she is that battle which may overcome fear. The helmet would also be a symbol of the mind. The Valley of Tunes (from hlým a tune, a roar) may thus also be an image of the mind, or the world itself, since the world is made up of the many pieces of the original cosmic sound. Her career as a Valkyrie takes and end, however, when she chooses her own favorite Agnarr over Óðin's favorite, Helmet Warrior. Stanza 8 relates this, as it was earlier related in the Sígrdrífumál, and the Valkyrie continues to explain how Óðinn bound her in slumber. In stanza 9, she explains that the god locked her up inside the Grove of Trunks [Skatalundr].

The trunk is a metaphor for a man, and the particular word, skati (m.sg.), While being used as a metaphor for a chief or a ruler, literally refers to a tree without branches or roots. A tree is a metaphor for a human being, and the trunk is the masculine part, whereas the roots and branches are the feminine parts. In Chapter I.8, I referred to a stanza where Guðrún warns her husband Atli that a tree will topple and wither if the branches and roots are cut from it before she apparently submits to his total dominance, declaring that he shall now rule alone, without her.

The submission is only skin-deep, however, since Guðrún immediately begins to plot a terrible revenge, serving his own sons to him for dinner before killing him and giving all his men to the fire. When Óðinn deprives the goddess of her power, she becomes locked up within the masculine, a masculine that has been deprived of its roots and branches, its feminine counterpart with the terrible consequences that this leads to. I personally suspect that the "Grove of Trunks", also may refer to the brain or a part of the brain, since it is the "grove" atop the spinal cord trunk of our bodies. That there are two or more meanings is entirely within the range of Old Norse poetical methods. The poet could have used several words for trunk in order to describe the spinal cord, yet he chose the word skati, which then also gives the association to masculine power without a feminine counterpart. Within this grove, the sleeping goddess is hidden behind red and white shields. If this is a reference to some aspects of the body, we may be seeing the blood (red) and the bone (white).

Of course, we today know that the blood consists of red and white corpuscles, but it is less likely that the Norse did but that the inside of the body is mainly red and white would have been obvious. Around her hall of red and white shields within the grove of the trunk, Óðinn put up a blazing high fire, and her hall turns towards the south. This either means downwards in the body (from the top grove), or towards the land of the Norns and gods, which is situated in the south, the origin of life-giving heat. Only the one who held no fear would be able to break through the barriers, carrying on his horse the gold of the Embracer, the serpent who with poisonous fear separates us from the divine red gold of Alert Spirit.

The one was Sígurðr, and the Valkyrie was happy to receive him, although she had never wanted marriage before. In stanza 12, she explains how they slept together for eight nights, but without uniting, for Sígurðr was then wearing his foster-brother Gunnar's shape, and the marriage was deceitful. Brynhild's lament is repeated in another poem, Sígurðarkvíða hin skamma [The Short Poem of Sígurðr], where Óðinn is replaced by her brother Atli. The name Atli is derived from atla, which means "to intend", and Óðinn is also the king of intent.

Atli is also based on the historical Attila, but the poems clearly reveal that he plays the role of Óðinn in disguise, thirsting for the red gold. After the death of Sígurðr, the human-incarnated Valkyrie explains that the murder had been the plan of her brother Atli all along. She explains that she had been woken form her slumber by Sígurðr, who owned no fear and who was now shining with the red gold as he entered her secret chamber. There would be no mistaking him for Gunnarr, yet Atli forced her to marry the Burgund king lest he take from her all her land and all her power. The goddess submitted under threats and married the wrong man, although she, the "Valkyrie of the necklaces" [mén-skagul], could never love a man who owned fear.

Now she had been pressured beyond her limits, and chooses to die. She proceeds by calling herself the "lady of the necklaces" [morc ménia], sharing out her treasures to her people before killing herself with her own sword. When she asks her servants to join her in death, and they refuse, she declares that when they come to her later (when they die in their own time), they will have no "treasures of the Necklace-lady" [neit Menio god] to burn with their bones. Being an immortal entity, her death is only her death in the human realm. She is still able to save her beloved Sígurðr from Hel, with whom she will be forever. Yet as the Valkyrie goddess leaves the world of the living, a veritable Ragnarǫk begins for the people who betrayed her. As Brynhildr retreats from the world, she is, however, replaced by her younger sister, Oddrún [Edge Symbol].

Oddrún lives in Hlésey "The Wind-Shield Island" of Aegir and the realm of the immortals. Yet she leaves her immortal realm in order to save the woman Borgný [New Fortress] of the "Land of Tomorrow" [Mornaland], an indication that this is a future event. The woman gives birth to a boy and a girl after Oddrún sings powerful galðr to ease the birth. Afterwards, Oddrún repeats the story of her older sister, who once ruled "men and lands" while she worked on her "embroidery" (the workings of fate) until her "stronghold was seized". Her death caused the wrath of her brother Atli-Óðinn, who had not anticipated this outcome, and when the Children of the Mist tried to compensate for his sister's death by asking for Oddrún's hand in marriage, he refused.

Yet Oddrún had her own mind and her own heart, like her older sister had before, and gave the drink to Gunnarr anyway yet Atli-Óðinn kept them apart and had Gunnarr killed. Oddrún was not able to save him from the serpent pit of Hel, and returned to her land of immortality where she would stay, grieving for her lost love, until the maiden of the Land of Tomorrow invoked her yet again.

The male-female divine conflict is one that also appears in the Hávamál poem, where Óðinn relates his own experiences on the path of initiation. This poem is divided into three main sections, the first of which offers the first stage of practical wisdom, mainly about social interaction. From stanza 84 onwards, the second part begins, when Óðinn first talks about the relationships between men and women.

First, he declares the fickleness of women, how women's hearts are like wheels on fire, whose feelings are fleeting and impossible to trust completely an observation quite in tune with the Norse view on feminine energy as equal to that of streams and rivers, branches and roots going in all directions, seemingly at random. Thus a woman's love may be fierce in one instant, yet it will easily move on or be distracted by other options. Masculine energy is far more firm it is the masculine that is provides the power of holding together and maintaining a structure. Yet Óðinn, who in stanza 91 declares that he has either known both sexes, or been both sexes, may speak truly ["I may speak in truth, for I have known both sides" Bert ec nv meli, þviat ec beði veit].

Men are just as deceitful towards women, speaking most fairly when they think most falsely. The god proceeds, advising against judgmental behavior, since no one may know the mind or heart of another, and because love and desire can cloud the wisest of minds. This wisdom, he reveals, was gained when he himself first felt the throb of passion for a fair maiden. Curiously enough, he was "sitting in the reeds" [er ec i reyri sat] when this happened a statement which can only be partly deciphered if we keep in mind that this is a divine entity representing Spirit, Mind and Passion, and not a human male. The reeds would be a symbol for something, and I am inclined to think that this too has something to do with the human body, in which the qualities that make this god resides. The word reyr is usually translated as "reeds" in Edda translations, but it could also mean "tubes" or "pipes", long narrow passages. It is not entirely unlikely that they refer to blood veins or other similar physical passages in a body.

Also, the girl in question is not an ordinary human woman, but Billings mey "The Maiden of the Twin". I think we may assume that we are speaking of Óðin's own "twin" his counterpart. Like the fate-goddess within, the maiden is found sleeping, and, significantly, "sun-bright" [solhvita]. There is little doubt that this is a revelation disguised as an ordinary love story, about The Spirit's first encounter with his female counterpart the Fate-Soul that resides within. As he discovers the sun bright maiden, he is overcome by passion residing in the pipes of the body, this is the Passion aspect of the god and acting rashly. We do not know what his fault is until the end of this anecdote. When the maiden wakes, she asks him to return in the evening, since it would be shameful for them to be discovered together. Why it is a shame is not explained, unless it is the fact that they are siblings, like when the god of passion, Freyr, fell in love with his own sister, Freyia/Gerðr. Like with Óðinn and the Twin's Maiden, there is the theme of shame if other gods discover them, and the reluctance of the female, who rejects him to begin with.

We learn how Óðinn failed only when he returns that night. Instead of the maiden awaiting in her bed, he finds a bitch tied to the bed. The pun is a great humiliation, but reveals what the maiden perceived in him. That he did not truly want her love. What he really wanted was an obedient dog, "tied to the bed". That was what he got, a bitter truth thrown right in his face, causing him to leave the place in shame. In the case of Freyr and Freyia/Gerðr, Freyr learned that he would be able to have the maiden if he could manage to reach the "breezeless grove of the Pine Needle" a place of immortality within nine nights.

In Óðin's case, he immediately sets out to find the halls of Suttungr [Heavy With Drink], where he woos the giant's daughter Gunnlǫð. He is now in his mind aspect, where his eloquence and wit convinces the giant to allow the marriage. As he swears the sacred oath of the ring [baugeiðr], the lady who guards the precious mead offers him a drink from her golden chair. Later, after their three nights together, she helps him escape from the deadly grasp of the giant world, but is left weeping when he fails to take her with him. Óðinn, aware of his fault, calls himself Bólverkr "The Harm Causer" after this story, declaring that he would never have managed to survive the trial without the help of that good woman, who had embraced him. Looking at these stories, many would probably emphasize the "gender war" that is apparently a theme in Edda poetry.

My own first inclination was to think that this was a mythology describing the conflict between an older, matriarchal, goddess-oriented culture and a newer, patriarchal one, where male gods usurped the ancient power and position of the goddesses. There are many myths across the world that could possibly reflect such events. It is also thinkable that the myths reflect some kind of internal conflict within the Norse society where the path of the golden goddess increasingly posed problems for her male followers.

Not only sages walked the path of initiation, but also warriors and kings, whose political interests may sometimes be at odds with the spiritual values of their paths.

The warriors and kings would be represented by Óðinn, who may have found it difficult to adhere to the spiritual teachings of the initiation, symbolized by the goddess. The Edda myths clearly show that this conflict between the political and the spiritual was considered devastating by the myth-makers. However, I have come to realize that the Norse myths provide a system in their own right, like a language. A language is continuously influenced by other languages and cultural experiences and attitudes, yet at any point in history, the language also stands on its own, carrying its own self-explanatory meanings. As we have seen, the myths often seem to reflect legendary memories of actual history. Yet in all these cases, the poets turn the stories in order to reveal a deeper message.

This is also true in this case. The Aesir gods provided men and women equally with their essence of Spirit, Mind and Passion thus these "masculine" entities are present within each one of us, whether we are women or men. The masculinity is not a matter of actual, biological gender. They are "masculine" because these are qualities that hold the world together they give structure and form. Thus Óðin's threefold quest is the quest of all people and both genders, beginning with the Passion that must be tempered, made aware of its true intentions. Secondly, the Mind, that must be whetted in order to achieve knowledge. Thirdly, the Spirit, which must learn how to integrate the sacred power by creating its own spells from the ones it has learned.

This effort is beyond gender, it is relevant to all people who walk the path of knowledge and spiritual awakening. The maiden that the threefold Spirit seeks is his sister his feminine counterpart and also his lover, with whom he wants to unite. Just like the masculine trio resides within all people regardless of gender, so the hidden female resides within us all. In the Vǫluspá story of the creation of human beings, the driftwood that the Aesir find is said to be "without fate" [orlǫgslausa]. As soon as they are endowed with breath, spirit, thought, poetry, vitality and colors the gifts of the male Aesir they are also endowed with fate represented by the fate goddess in all her aspects.

Being feminine, fate is the hidden, unseen, yet moving element that makes our lives go forward. The feminine energy is the perpetual flow of energy that streams in all directions, nourishing life like the branches and the roots of a tree, the limitless awareness and omniscience that may be reached only through union between the male and female counterparts within for it is only when she is "embraced" and held by the masculine that her power may be channeled into our structured consciousness. The entire path of knowledge is to find the way to reach her, wake her, and hold her, symbolized by the god's or male hero's path towards the bright maiden.

Óðinn is obviously perfectly aware of his need to have the maiden in his embrace, yet the big question is HOW to do this. He tries all kinds of methods, he even tries to reach the red gold of wisdom without her constantly failing. It is my personal experience, and something I believe I might share with other people who work with therapy or who have followed a spiritual path for a long time, that Óðin's many crooked paths and vile attempts to control, trick and betray the goddess is a perfect metaphor for how the human consciousness will do almost anything to avoid uniting with our true inner self, our soul, and our fate.

What is fate, really, but the history of our lives? Few can truly embrace and love every aspect of their fate there will usually be a lot of resentment, hatred, rage and greed standing in our way exactly the kinds of qualities that our Norse heroes must conquer before reaching their Valkyrie. These are the trials of our Passion aspect, to overcome all the emotional obstacles that stand in the way of our knowing our true selves. To accept every aspect of our personal history our fate embracing it, loving it, and allowing it to unfold freely into the future, unhindered by our fear and greed is a challenge that will overwhelm anyone. We will be fearful for we instinctively know that our true soul-self may destroy the self-image we have spent years to build and maintain.

This is great trial of our Mind-aspect. Óðinn complains that his love for the maiden caused him to forget about his ambitions and his career, as well as his self-image as a man of high standing. He says this when he declares that his passion caused him to no longer care about his position as an earl (In earlier days, the earl was a kind of sage). In stanza 113-114 he warns a man that if he stays too long in the arms of the sorceress, she will make him forget politics and power issues. This may be where our greatest challenge lies. To leave all worldly ambitions, our self-image and the image other people have of us. That is a very hard challenge that requires total spiritual devotion. The final challenge is for the Spirit-aspect.

It is when Óðinn has overcome his fears and been wizened by experience. He looks back and remembers all the aspects of learning that he has encountered on the way, and then declares that it is time to speak from the Seat of the Sage [þularstólinn]. This is when he reveals the full story of his initiation, when he hung for nine nights in order to reach not only the maiden with her mead, but also the knowledge of runes and spells, and begins to give an account of the runes and the spells that he has learned. The first nine spells were spells he learned during his initiation, transmitted to him from his mother's father. As he begins to count up the nine spells he learned, he adds nine more that he has made himself an ability gained only through the true integration of knowledge. The three last spells form a climax, as the god of our learning spirits finally finds a way to reach the soul-fate-maiden, maintain the maiden, and finally share with her, his own sister, the most sacred and secret of spells.

LEFT AND RIGHT SIDE BRAIN FUNCTIONS

The idea that there are two sides to existence a feminine and a masculine counterpart may in my opinion be based on the human experience of having two different sides to our brains. The actual, biological division may not have been known to the myth-makers, but the experience of perceiving in two completely different manners may have been better known to them than to most moderns, since the ancients tended to seek the "other side" of perception through their rituals and magical practices. The human brain is divided into two completely different compartments which are only united through some nerve bridges, and through the "triune brain" situated in the lower middle part of the whole brain.

The right brain is wired through the nervous system so as to steer the functions of the opposite, left side of the body. The left brain is equally wired through the nervous system to control movement in the right side of the body. Apart from that, the two sides of our brains operate like to almost completely different personalities with their own unique way of processing information. The left side brain, connected to the right side of the body, is the part that likes to organize and categorize information from the environment, continuously referring back to prior experiences and attitudes. It is the part of our brain that "makes sense" out of our world and which enables us to identify ourselves as separate from everything else, creating a sense of "I am". Analytic thought and what passes for logic and reasoning (i.e. theories) happens in this part of the brain, as does our ability to speak coherently and understand language and numbers.

The right side of the brain, connected to the left side of the body, is the part that appreciates art, music and beauty, gets inspired to create such arts, provides us with intuition, insight and a holistic awareness an awareness that connects us to the larger universe and dissolves the sense of "I am". When the famous Dr. Jill Bolte Taylor, author of My Stroke of Insight (2012) experienced a stroke in the left side of her brain, her awareness moved over to the right side of the brain, leaving her in a happy state of interconnectedness with all life, free from all emotional baggage of the past yet unable to speak, understand letters and numbers, or even remember who she was. Obviously, both sides of the brain will be employed in all healthy human beings, and from the side of nature, the two sides should be equally employed and balanced throughout our lives.

Yet our society tends to condition us to exaggerate the use of our analytical left brain, shutting out a large part of our intuitive right brain. This does not mean that our right brain is not working at all times, it is, but we tend to ignore and suppress its impact, much of the processing of the right brain does not reach our conscious attention. To the culture we have been conditioned to live in, most parts of the right brain function represents the "unknown", the spiritual "other" side of existence. That the one side is masculine and the other is feminine is of course a cultural concept. Both genders employ both sides of the brain. There are general tendencies towards more flexibility in women's brains, however, where movement between various compartments of the brain happens swifter, often causing women to draw more associations between matters that often appear totally unrelated to men, hence many men's boast that they are more "rational", although the correct observation would be to say that men and women's rationality may work a bit differently on a general basis, and that men tend to be more compartmentalized, focusing on the contents of one "brain box" at a time, while women usually open all the boxes, attention bouncing from one to the other at great speed. Individual differences are, however, more important than gender, and even with a more flexible attention span, women may be as closed to the right brain reality as men are, limiting most of their "bouncing" to the compartments of the left brain, where personal memories and the emotions attached to them, are also stored, alongside categories, numbers and grammars.

The Old Norse myth-makers obviously perceived the fact of the two kinds of realities, the two kinds of minds, the two states of being that exist within us all. They associated the fluid, fleeting, intuitive, inspired, holistic reality with femininity, and the analytical, thinking and personal-emotional reality with masculinity.The latter may come as a surprise to some, since we are culturally conditioned to believe that women are more emotional than men. However, our understanding of our own emotions actually takes place in the left, "masculine" side of the brain where the "I am" person who may be emotionally hurt resides. When women appear more emotional than men, this is not due to the "feminine" right side of the brain but rather to the tendency of making more associations between different experiences and the feelings attached to these. When the Old Norse myth-makers associate the mind-poetry, the breath-spirit and the passion-intent with male deities whereas female deities are associated with a stream of revelations and a larger, unknown reality within the apparent, the soul, intuitive wisdom and hidden fate-knowledge, they are actually in tune with how our left and right brains function.

When the male deity must seek, wake and embrace the female deity in order to achieve divine knowledge, it is in tune with how the left, analytical brain must seek, wake and embrace the right, "unknown" intuitive side. The reality of this right, "feminine" brain can only be made manifest and "known" through the reality of the left, "masculine" brain. The initiate will move into the world of the unknown in order to get in touch with a larger reality, but his success is only true when he manages to remember, integrate and employ that which he has learned, into the known world of structure and shape. Both (or all) genders are capable of employing both sides of the brain and may be trained to employ both sides equally. The biological fact is that we have both the mind of the left side and the mind of the right side functioning within us, and that we will never reach our full potential and the totality of our selves unless we learn to employ both sides in a harmonious and balanced way.

6: Ragnarǫk And the new age

6.1: The build-up to ragnarǫk

Ragnarǫk could roughly be translated as "Apocalypse", since the word refers to the prophecy of a great social and natural upheaval towards the end of the known world. A more literal translation is "The Destinies of the Rulers". Ragna is genitive plural of Reginn ["Ruler"], whereas rǫk (n.pl) refers to "developments", "circumstances", "causes", "ends" or "destinies". The rulers in question are usually thought to be the gods.

The Apocalypse is sometimes referred to as Ragnarǫkr, where the word rǫkr (n.sg) refers to "twilight". All the stories of the previous Chapter (5) actually deal with the events that led to Ragnarǫk. The anger of the giantesses who draw the mill of fate when they experience abuse ultimately cause them to "grind" the apocalypse. The death of Kvasir and the death of Baldr, the loss of the goddess and the growth of the Greed-wolfall these are events that together explain the path towards destruction that was already perceived by people of the Middle Ages.

The loss of poetry's maiden

The build-up towards this time of violent upheavals is described in the Vǫluspá poem through a series of hints. In Chapter 2, we worked through the stanzas 1 to 24, from creation of the universe to the establishment of society and religion. The arrival of the vǫlva Gullveigr-Freyia and her art of seiðr, followed by the war and the truce between the Aesir and the Vanir formed the climax and a turning point in the history of the world. These events involved the introduction of ritual and mystical elements that lay at the core of Norse Paganism.

The initiation, the precious mead, the runes and the spell-songs. In Chapter 3, we looked more closely at these elements through a scrutiny of the precious mead and the goddess and/or priestess who served it during initiation. In Chapter 4, we saw how this goddess may have been considered the very fate-soul of the Aesir gods, who, just like human beings, are in constant danger of losing her to the powers of oblivion and destruction and often represented by the giants. This event is referred to in the Vǫluspá poem in stanza 25 and forms the first step towards the series of events that will lead to the Apocalypse:

25. Then all the powers went to the chairs of fate [parliament] the high holy gods to discuss this matter: Who had blended the air all with harm? Or to the giant kind given Poetry's Maiden?	25. Þá gengu regin ǫll á rǫkstóla, ginnheilug goð, ok um þat gættusk: hverr hefði lopt allt lævi blandit eða ætt jǫtuns Óðs mey gefna

"Poetry's Maiden" Óðs mey would refer to Freyia, who was the wife of Óðr (a disguise for Óðinn), although it could rather seem to refer to the theft of Iðunn, who was also the wife of the god of poetry (Bragi), and who is famous for having been given away to the giant world by Loki, as we saw in Chapter 4. We know of no myth where Freyia wearing that title is actually given over to the giants. She is threatened a few times, but never actually given over.

In the Þrymskvíða, Þórr tries to convince her to go as a bride to the giant world, but she refuses with so much anger that the whole Earth shakes, and Þórr has to go as a bride himself. Only if Iðunn is an aspect of Freyia does the sentence actually make sense. As such, we should probably regard Poetry's Maiden as a symbol for the fate-soul whether on the divine or the human level. The loss of and abuse of this goddess is the first event that leads to the destruction. In Chapter 5.9, we saw how this is not just a societal event, but also something that happens within the individual.

THE BOUNDARY BETWEEN THE WORLDS

Snorri links the Vǫluspá stanza about Poetry's Maiden to the story of how the horse Sleipnir was born: In his Gylfaginning, we hear that the Aesir hired an unnamed craftsman to build a wall around the divine realm in order to separate it from the giant realm and that the craftsman demanded Sun, Moon and Freyia for his reward. The Aesir went to the parliament chairs and discussed the matter, since they needed the wall built, yet would be unable to meet the terms. Listening to the advice of Loki, the gods decided to hire the craftsman anyway, since they thought they could trick him. He would have to finish the work in one winter only, and if it was not finished by the first day of summer, he would not have his reward.

The Aesir were certain that it would be impossible to make the wall in just one winter. However, the craftsman brought with him a stallion called Svadilfari [Harm Traveler], and this horse was so powerful that the wall was being built much faster than the Aesir had anticipated. By the night before the first day of summer, the wall was almost finished even to the opening of the gate. This was when the Aesir met once more at parliament in order to discuss what they ought to do, as described in the stanza above. They were anxious now, since they could not bear the thought of losing Freyia to the giant world, or lose the lights of the heavens by giving away Sun and Moon.

The Aesir asked each other who was to blame for the predicament they found themselves in, as in "who had blended the air with harm and given Freyia to the giant world". According to Snorri, they decided that Loki Laufeyjarson [Son of "Leaf Island", i.e. Earth] was to blame, since he had advised the Aesir to allow the craftsman to use his stallion. To save his skin, Loki vows that he will make the craftsman lose his reward. That evening, Loki, who is a notorious changer of both shape and sex, turned himself into a mare in heat, running past the working stallion. The stallion was immediately distracted from his work and began to run after the mare. The horse couple ran all night together, and the following morning, the stallion was so tired that he could not work as hard as before, and the craftsman was unable to finish his wall on time.

As the craftsman realized that he had been tricked, he became furious, and it became clear to everybody that he was a mountain giant. The Aesir called upon Þórr for their protection, since Þórr was away in the East, hunting trolls. Þórr arrived at once and hurled his lightening hammer Miǫllnir [Grinder] at the giant, whose head was crushed into tiny particles and sent into Misty Hel. Loki, on his side, remained a mare until he was ready to give birth to a foal: Sleipnir [Glider], an eight-legged steed who could carry his rider through all cosmic dimensions. I believe that Loki may represent humanity as such in many cases.

He is one of the Aesir, yet not of them his divinity is due to the blood-brotherhood with Óðinn, and the two often blur together in their ambivalence. Where Óðinn represents the Spirit, the Poetry and the Passion as a universal, divine power, Loki seems to represent the same on a more local level on the human level. Like a man, he is the servant of the gods, often functioning like a shaman. Like humanity, he can have two genders. Like humanity, he provides the physical vehicle for divine spiritual/non-physical consciousness when he births Sleipnir. Like humanity, he takes dire chances, and often has to mend what he has broken.

He lacks the wisdom of the other gods, yet is often more resourceful when it comes to make things happen. As an Aesir, he is a symbol of conscious intelligence, as a human, he is a symbol of all our challenges and pit-falls, as well as our resourcefulness and solution-mindedness. The gods want the boundary built, Loki makes it happen, and takes great risks in doing so, almost selling his own soul. Before the craftsman began building the wall of the Aesir, oaths were sworn, and to break an oath was a serious offense in the Old Norse world. Snorri tries to excuse the Aesir by saying that the craftsman had been a giant in disguise, only revealing his true identity when angry. Snorri also points out that Þórr was not present at parliament, so that he was exempt from the oaths that the other gods had sworn to the craftsman. Thus only Þórr can legally break them. But even the Vǫluspá poem emphasizes the serious matter of breaking oaths:

26. Þórr was then the only one striking seized by anger he seldom sits when he hears such things Oaths were broken then words and promises all the powerful words that had passed between them

26. Þórr einn þar vá þrunginn móði, hann sjaldan sitr er hann slíkt um fregn; á gengust eiðar, orð ok sœri, mál ǫll meginlig er á meðal fóru

Establishing universal borders, laws and rituals seems to be an ambivalent matter in Old Norse myths. In the story just told, the border that protects the divine world from that of the giants is built at a cost. The cost of having to break an oath, with the fateful consequences that such a crime will bring. Enmity with the giants a perpetual war. This theme is a recurring one. In order to bring the mead of poetry back to the living entities of divine, elfin and human realms, Óðinn broke a sacred ring-oath. When Óðinn waged war against the Vanir, the truce led to positive things.

The arrival of the Vanir gods in Ásgarðr, and with them the ritual of initiation, the secrets of seiðr, runes and spells yet these are the very things that also lead Óðinn the Spirit onto many a blind path. Enmity with the giants is a metaphor for the perpetual warfare with the powers of destruction that the Spirit must wage in order to achieve his goal a goal symbolized by the protected, separate, divine realm.

ÓÐIN'S EYE AND HEIMDALL'S HEARING

Things are getting out of hand, the maiden of the gods is in danger, and Óðinn seeks the ancient witch asking her to look into the past, the present and the future. In the Vǫluspá, this happens just after Þórr has chased away the master builder and caused the Aesir to indirectly break their oaths. The vǫlva, now alternating between talking about herself in the first and the third person, sees widely into all the worlds, looks back to the beginning and into the present time, until she arrives at the moment where Óðinn seeks her:

27. She knows that Great World's listening attention is disguised beneath the bright radiant sacred tree; she sees a torrent of water poured mixed with mud-sand from the Choice-Father's wager: *Do you understand now, or what?*	*27. Veit hon Heimdallar hljóð um fólgit undir heiðvǫnum helgum baðmi;* *á sér hon ausask aurgum forsi af veði Valfǫðrs.* *Vituð ér enn eða hvat?*

This stanza is impossible to understand without prior understanding of Norse cosmology. The mud-sand [aurr] mixed with water that is poured is a reference to the water mixed with mud, sand or gravel that the Norn Urðr uses to nourish the World Tree, the Universe every day. It is the water of the Well of Origin [Urðarbrunnr]. The "bright, radiant, sacred tree" is the World Tree.

Something is disguised in the mud of this water, namely "Choice-Father's Wager", as well as Heimdall's "listening attention" [hljóð], which seems to be identified with each other in this stanza. "Choice-Father's Wager" is the famous eye of Óðinn. According to Snorri, Óðinn gave away one of his eyes to the water beneath the World Tree's roots:

> "Beneath the root that turns towards the frost-thurses, there is the Well of Memory [Mímisbrunnr], and in it is hidden wisdom and intelligence. Memory [Mímir] is he called who owns the well. He is full of wisdom, for he drinks from the well through the horn called the Bellowing Horn [Gjallarhorn]. There came All-Father (Óðinn) once and asked for a drink from the well, but he was not allowed one before he wagered one of his eyes."

Thus one eye of the Spirit is hidden wagered in the Well of Memory, which in the Vǫluspá is obviously also identified with the Well of Origin. That the two wells are the same, essentially, is not problematic. There are three wells at the three roots of the World Tree, and they are all just three different aspects of the same essential phenomenon. The liquid source of our cosmos and the hidden depths of our souls. What might be more confusing at first sight is that Óðin's eye seems to be associated with Heimdall's ears (or listening attention).

According to Snorri, Heimdallr sees and hears everything that happens and moves in the entire universe. He can even hear the wool grow on the sheep and grass on earth. He also owns a horn called the Bellowing Horn [Gjallarhorn], an attribute which makes it possible to identify Heimdallr with the giant Mímir, the Memory of the world. Since the name "Heimdallr" actually means the Great World, we must assume that the god is a divine representation of cosmos, able to see and hear everything that takes place within itself. His hljóð, his "listening attention" is able to perceive every sound ever made by anything that moves and grows, and this listening is hidden in the life-giving mud of the Well of Origin or the Well of Memory and with Óðin's wager. The Vǫluspá elaborates further, as the god seeks the knowledge of the ancient witch:

28. *She alone sat outside when the aged one arrived the old-young of the Aesir (Óðinn) and she looked him in the eye:*
"Why do you ask me?
Why do you test me?
I know everything, Óðinn!
Where you hid your eye: in the famous
Well of Memory:
Memory drinks the mead every morning from the Choice-Father's wager."
Do you understand now, or what?

28. *Ein sat hon úti,*
þá er inn aldni kom
yggjungr ása
ok í augu leit.
"Hvers fregnið mik?
hví freistið mín?
alt veit ek, Óðinn!
hvar þú auga falt:
í inum mæra
Mímis brunni;
drekkr mjǫð Mímir
morgin hverjan
af veði Valfǫðrs.
Vituð ér enn eða hvat?

The mystery of the wager is better revealed if we think of Óðinn not as an individual, not as a god, but as the Spirit, operating on all levels and realities of cosmos, including the realities of each living individual. As the Spirit of the universe itself and all its creatures and entities, there is no significant difference between the Awareness of the Great World [Heimdallr] and the Spirit of the Great World [Óðinn], nor its Memory [Mímir]. On a cosmic level, the god Heimdallr, the god Óðinn and the giant Mímir are the same. The awareness of the universe, its listening, its seeing and its remembering.

When the seeing Óðinn sacrifices one eye to the remembering Mímir, it might be this universal awareness that sacrifices a part of its seeing for a part of its intelligence, and it is this sacrifice which makes our awareness less than whole and possibly why Óðinn sometimes hides behind the name Half or Half Lord [Halfdan]. The eye of the cosmic Spirit has been half hidden away as a wager to itself, just as when Óðinn sacrifices self to self in the Hávamál stanza 138, "given to Óðinn, given self to my self" [gefinn Oðni, sialfr sialfom mer] in order to discover and bring light to the runes of fate and share his knowledge with the world. Like with all the others pursuits for the sake of knowledge and enlightenment, it comes at a cost, the danger of oblivion. It is no secret that the awareness in human beings is vast, yet only a tiny portion, a few per cent only, reaches the conscious mind and even less stays put in our conscious memory.

Unless we employ methods of uncovering the totality of our awareness, the vast majority of our experience stays forever hidden in the depths of our personal Underworlds and our personal Outside Worlds what today is often referred to as the subconscious.

THE WAR OF THE FLAMING NECKLACE

The following stanza, 29, reveals how Óðinn, after hearing the witch mention the wager that is lost in the Well of Memory, pays the witch for her knowledge, and how she looked into all the worlds (described in Chapter 2.2). Stanza 30 heralds the arrival of the Valkyrie for the first time the fates of war:

She saw Valkyrie widely arriving
Ready to ride to the divine peoples
Debt held a shield, and Battle another
War, Fighting and Magician and Spear Battle;
Now are they counted, the women of the Ruler
Valkyrie ready to ride the Earth

> *Sá hon valkyrjur vítt um komnar*
> *gǫrvar at ríða til Goðþjóðar:*
> *Skuld hélt skildi, en Skǫgul ǫnnur,*
> *Gunnr, Hildr, Gǫndul*
> *ok Geirskǫgul;*
> *nú eru talðar nǫnnur Herjans,*
> *gǫrvar at ríða grund valkyrjur*

Of the six Valkyrie listed here, four have names that simply indicate war and violence. These are the "seven sisters" of the new and warlike era. To complete the number nine, there are two more Valkyrie, characters otherwise known as a Norn and a goddess. There is Skuld [Debt], the Norn of the future and Gǫndul [Magician], a name for Freyia, who is the ultimate Valkyrie and the goddess of fate. The use of the name Gǫndul for Freyia proposes a significant riddle that would have given associations to the myth of Gǫndul that we today only know from the medieval Flateyjarbók, in the short story known as Sǫrla þáttr [Sǫrli's Story].

Gǫndul is the name that Freyia wears after her lover Óðinn has forced her to create fate according to his decree. He has had Loki steal her precious necklace Brísingamen [Necklace of Flames], the attribute that before anything else identifies the goddess. As a condition for returning the Necklace of Flames to its rightful owner, Óðinn charges Freyia who is a goddess of fate with causing two sworn friends to become enemies forever, engaging in an eternal battle that will only end when a mysterious "third" arrives. Only then will Freyia retrieve her necklace.

In another short story, the Húsdrápa, the savior of the necklace is Heimdallr, who hunts down Loki and the necklace until they meet at Singasteinn. The original meaning of this place-name is very uncertain. Steinn means a rock or a stone, but the word singa is very uncertain. It may be derived from some other language than Old Norse, such as Gothic or Old English, or be the result of distortion or mis-spellings. It has been suggested that it may mean The Ancient Stone, based on Gothic sineigs, or the Magical Stone, from Old English sincstan, or the Sacred Stone, if the name is a mis-spelling for Old Norse Signasteinn.

It has been suggested that it could be a mis-spelling of Sǫngvasteinn The Stone of Songs. Since the meaning is so uncertain and the words or spellings may have been distorted, I would point out that the Old Norse words singirni/singjarn has to do with stinginess, selfishness and egotistic behavior, exactly the attitudes that lay behind Óðin's and Loki's motifs for stealing the sacred necklace of flames. In the story, Loki has transformed into a seal, and Heimdallr does the same thing, wins, and delivers the necklace back to the goddess. As pointed out many times already, Heimdallr, The Great World is a personification of the world itself as a sentient being. It is the very universe itself that fights the spirit that would steal the necklace from its rightful owner.

However, Heimdall's knightly deeds are not mentioned in the story of Gǫndul, who does what she has to do in order to retrieve her necklace. Changing fate according to Óðin's will and ambition. Wearing the name Gǫndul, the goddess appears before a princeling called Heðinn [The Fur-Clad One], son of Hiarrandi [Hinge from hiarri (m.sg) also a name of Óðinn], the king of Serkland. Serkland is a Norse reference to all Arab countries, where men wore serkr a loose shirt being it was only the undergarment for a Viking, which is why they emphasized the Arabs' use of it as a proper garment.

The Arab prince, Heðinn, harried Spain and Greece while his father ruled in Serkland, but one day, the young prince met an unusually large, yet beautiful woman who sat on a chair in a grove in the forest. The image of the goddess on her chair is one well-known from the archaeology of Iron Age Europe, as is the image of her offering a drink. The goddess introduces herself as Gǫndul and asks the young prince about his great deeds. After Heðinn has given a good account of his deeds, he asks if she knows about any warrior who can match him. She replies that king Hǫgni [The Thinker or The Fortunate] of Denmark, son of Halfdan [Half Lord] can match him. At spring equinox, Heðinn begins his journey to visit Denmark, and by spring equinox the following year, he arrives in Denmark and is well received.

King Thinker invites Prince Fur-Clad to compete in various games to find which of the two royal warriors are best, and find that they are equal and match each other in all warrior pursuits. They become such good friends that they swear foster-brotherhood a connection just as sacred and intimate as the connection between real brothers. They have become the best of friends. Heðinn meets Freyia again in the forest grove, and this time, she offers him a magical drink that makes him forget all his oaths to Hǫgni, and while this one is away, he murders his friend's queen and abducts his daughter Hildr [Battle]. As he escapes the furious Hǫgni, he meets Freyia-Gǫndul a third time, and she releases him from the effect of the magical drink before she weds Heðinn and his men to Óðinn, which means that she weds him to death. Although the Arab prince is longer deluded by the drink, the damage is already done.

After Hǫgni finds Heðinn, an eternal battle begins where all the warriors die but the Danish princess, Hildr, distressed by the conflict between two men that she loved equally her father and her lover walks the battlefield every night, singing a galðr [charm, spell-song] which wakes all the warriors up again to fight once more. Thus Freyia has fulfilled her promise to Óðinn, albeit reluctantly. The image of the eternal battle is also mentioned in Saxo Grammaticus' Gesta Danorum (I.31). The hero Hadingus is taken into the Underworld or the "land of the dead" by a sorceress (probably a vǫlva) who shows him many wonders there. Among them is an everlasting battle between two armies.

The witch tells him that: *"These are they who, having been slain by the sword, declare the manner of their death by a continual rehearsal, and enact the deeds of their past life in a living spectacle."* Another passage of the Flateyjarbók also relates a similar theme, where two companies, one black and one red, fight perpetually within a burial mound.

They are only released from their eternal struggle when a Christian hero conquers them and deals them the blow that may let them rest in peace within the mound (the source was written as late as 1387 and may have added Christian solutions to ancient legends). The story as it has been transmitted to us in this medieval source may have been inspired by an historical backdrop.

During the Viking Age, Christian Europe, with its unprotected villages and monasteries, was the main victim of Viking raiders, while relations between Pagan Scandinavia and the Moslem Arab countries were friendly and based on trade. Arab fashions and other merchandise were very popular in Scandinavia, and there was a great deal of friendly interaction (and slave trade), especially during the ninth century, when the Arab rulers of Spain among other things sent their ambassadors, such as Al-Ghazal, to Denmark. By the time that the Flateyjarbók was written, however, Scandinavia had joined Christian Europe with its enmity towards the Arab world an enmity that appears to have lasted over the centuries and even into our day. The story-tellers seem to have let this historical backdrop inspire the myth, where the Arab prince breaks the peace and friendship yet only because the gods have decreed it so and because Óðinn wants these warriors for himself.

The spiritual message of the story is, however, the one that counts. When we break down the parable to its essentials, we may see that the theme of the story is one that is repeated over and over in Old Norse myths. The theme of the two enemies who are like brothers. In the Hyndlulióð, which was transmitted to us in the same Flateyjarbók source, young Óttarr [Fear Warrior] must contend with Angantýr [Pleasure Beast] about the "gold of Valland" in order to claim his "heritage", the gold of Valland. He can only do so by asking the goddess Freyia for help.

The goddess takes the young man into the Underworld where she makes the Underworld witch Hyndla [She-Wolf] reveal the secret of Óttar's "lineage", a lineage that shows that he is related to all the entities and beings in the whole world, and that they all come together as one, a message that is repeated in the poem by listing up one mythical lineage after the other, repeatedly concluding: "they are all your kind, Óttarr of the narrow mind" [allt er þat ætt þin, Ottar heimski!]. After the witch has revealed that all the lineages in the world is his kind, and that they are all united in the one being that was born of nine sorceresses, Heimdallr, the Great World, the goddess offers the Mead of Memory so that he may remember the revelation when he returns to the world of the living.

In the beginning of the poem, the reason for the initiation is clearly stated it is so that they can "ride to Valhǫll, and the holy shrine" [rida vit skulum til Valhallar ok til vess heilags.] How does this story relate to the story of Heðinn and Hǫgni? If we look closely at the story, we see that the enmity is between two "brothers", as they are both seeking the same "heritage". If we assume that these myths and legends originated in the Viking Age, the audience back then would immediately associate such as setting to two competing sons of a king, both seeking kingship.

Viking Age laws did not automatically make the oldest son of a king into a king: All men who could claim that the king was their father even if born out of wedlock, could make a claim to the High Seat. They would have to show their worth through trials, where the one (or the ones) who succeeded could stand before the sacred þing [parliament] of the tribe and be elected as king. However, this "heritage" is obviously of an esoteric kind. It will lead to an alternative afterworld, Valhǫll, and it is a matter of overcoming the brother, who in the case of the Hyndlulióð seems to represent the baser needs, the beastly nature, the one that is bent on pleasure and desire. Angantýr means Pleasure Beast, and only spiritual knowledge gathered, through initiation, from the depths of the unconscious, remembered in the conscious state, may conquer this beast. Óttar's name, "Fear Warrior", seems to be a reference to the need to overcome fear, which is part of the beastly nature.

In the case of Heðinn and Hǫgni, there is a similar theme. Heðinn may be a bold and brave warrior, yet his name means Fur-Clad, which is another way of hinting towards his beastly nature. When I use the expression "beastly nature" I do not mean "bad" it is rather that part of us all which is connected to the animal world, ruled by instincts and often causing impulsive, passionate acts. The Fur-Clad lets his desire and beastly nature conquer him when he breaks his oath and steals his friend's daughter. The name Hǫgni on the other hand indicates the mind, that of the Thinker. The theme of Valhǫll is present in the myth, since the warriors are wed to Óðinn and must, like the einherjar ["one-harriers" or "sole rulers"], fight, die and be restored to fight another day on the same battlefield for an eternity.

The fight is actually about a girl but not any girl. In this story, the girl is a witch with the power to resurrect the dead, acting on the demands and with the power of the goddess Freyia, whose secret agenda is to retrieve her Flaming Necklace a symbol of wholeness and spiritual illumination. The theme is repeated over and over. In the heroic poetry, we have Helgi, who in both his lives has to conquer giant opponents who threaten to take his golden goddess, his Valkyrie. The giant opponents have names that indicate negative, base qualities such as hatred, rage and greed. Sígurðr has to overcome his dwarf mentor Reginn, who represents such qualities, in order to reach his sleeping Valkyrie and wake her, so that she may reveal to him the esoteric teachings. Like his brother Helgi, Sígurðr must also face the Hundingar "The Lineage of the Dog". Like the wolf, the dog in Norse poetry represents the beastly nature, animal instincts, survival instincts, desire, greed and rage.

THE TWO BROTHERS: MIND AND PASSION

In the story of Heðinn and Hǫgni, we saw the theme of two foster-brothers who turned enemies. We also saw that they seem to resemble the mind and the passion within a human being, as did Óttarr and Angantýr in the Hyndlulióð. The theme of the two brothers or friends is an important one in Norse myths. In the first life of Helgi, the young man is helped and aided by the sorcerer Atli, whose name is derived from atla, "to intend".

Thus Atli is The Intender the passion aspect whereas Helgi [The Sacred One] resembles Óðin's brother Vé, whose name indicates a sacred space [the Mind]. In the second life of Helgi, the Intender is replaced by Sinfiǫtli [Pale Fetters] a sorcerer with the ability to change shape into that of a wolf a symbol of the beastly nature yet beneficial when operating in service to the Mind.

The paleness is a symbol of death, the fetters a symbol of ruling forces showing how this beast aspect of our consciousness is a ruling power in our lives which eventually leads to death, unless employed in the service of the Mind. The two brothers also show up in the characters of Gunnarr and Họgni in the heroic poetry that follows Sígurð's story. After his initiation on the sacred mountain, Sígurðr arrives in the land of the Burgunds an historical tribe.

Yet the Burgunds are also called the Níflungar ["The Children of the Mist"]. The mist refers to Níflheimr [the Misty World] the world of the dead, showing that these are people who belong to the worlds ruled by Hel, that is, by death. As such, they represent all ordinary mortals. The Children of the Mist are ruled by a queen, Grímhildr [Masked War] and her three children, a daughter, Guðrún [Divine Symbol] and two sons. Gunnarr [Warrior] and Họgnir [Thinker]. Despite his fierce-sounding name, Gunnarr the Warrior is more efficient with his harp than with his blade.

He has a timid nature, controlled by fear and base urges, acting rashly out of passion rather than intelligence. His brother, Họgnir the Thinker, tries to counsel and reason with him, but it is Gunnarr who is the oldest brother, and thus the one who makes the decisions, to the woe of the Children of the Mist. The Children of the Mist receives the now initiated and enlightened Sígurðr with joy, the brothers swear foster-brotherhood, just like Heðinn and Họgni did, and offers him marriage with their sister Guðrún. The marriage immediately causes Sígurðr to become the king of the Burgunds, indicating a memory of a time when succession followed the matrilineal descent. It is Guðrún who is the heir to the High Seat, and her husband who becomes the lord protector and high king of the Burgunds.

Matrilineal descent being an age-old tradition, the brothers do not complain, and all five rulers (Grímhildr, Guðrún, Sígurðr, Gunnarr and Họgnir) rule together in perfect harmony, for a while. It would seem that a prince aspiring to marry a princess would have to go through the same initiation as that of the sage-king Sígurðr. When Gunnarr is to marry the sister of the Hunnish "King Atli" (Attila the Hun), he has to show his worthiness by seeking the Valkyrie on the sacred mountain. However, Gunnarr is too timid to go through the dangerous fires in order to wake the goddess within.

Sígurðr, wanting to help his foster-brother and save his friend from the shame of being a coward before his people, changes into Gunnar's shape and rides through the fires for him. Thus Sígurðr, in all his well-meaning goodness, betrays the oaths of the Sacred Marriage and offers the bright maiden to an unworthy man resembling how Loki offered Iðunn or "Óð's maiden" to the giant race. The first step towards Ragnarọk. The secret betrayal of a sacred union is discovered, and the powerful Hunnish princess, Brynhildr, threatens to leave her marriage unless her husband becomes high king and makes certain that his (and her) shame is hidden.

She declares that she will rather "sleep her life away" than be married to an unworthy man, a reference to her ultimate identity as a Valkyrie, who sleeps unless a man without fear can wake her, yet on this level the story can be read with a pseudo-historical (legend inspired by history) backdrop. The alliance with the Huns was a matter of life and death to the Burgunds, but to break an oath of blood-brotherhood was a sacrilege. When Họgnir the Thinker is unable to persuade Gunnarr not to meet his wife's demands, his thinking is employed in the matter of how to kill Sígurðr without becoming direct oath-breakers and brother-murderers.

At Hǫgnir's advice, the siblings make their hitherto unknown third brother, Gothormr [Gothic/Human Serpent], a halfwit, kill Sígurðr. The poems make it clear that their intention was to usurp the throne of their sister and her husband in order for Gunnarr to become king, introducing patrilineal descent for the first time, inspired by the Hunnish conquerors, as the "Fragment of a Poem about Sígurðr" [Brot af Sigurðarkviða] reveals:

8. Spoke then Brynhildr Budli's daughter: *"Well shall you enjoy the weapons and the land, Sígurðr would have ruled all this alone if he had owned life a little more.*	*8. Þa qvað þat Brynhildr Bvdla dottir:* *«Vel scolot niota vapna oc landa; einn mvndi Sigvrþr a/llo raþa, ef hann lengr litlo lifi heldi.*
9. It would not have been fitting that he should rule the inheritance of Giuki and the hosts of Goths..."	*9. Veria þat semt, at hann sva reþi Givca arfi oc Gota mengi*

We see how possible memories of historical events are employed to reveal a deeper message. Gunnarr and Hǫgnir obviously represent the brothers Mind and Passion who ruled alone after Óðinn had been sent in exile, and married his wife. The goddess would only be reclaimed by the god upon his return. This myth was discussed in the previous chapter. At this stage, we will see that the trio, Gunnar, Hǫgnir and Sígurðr, are molded in an original divine division of human and cosmic consciousness.

BALDR

The sage-king Sígurð's death, which we touched upon earlier in this chapter, resembles very much the death of Baldr. The theme of a secret divine agenda that has to do with Ragnarǫk and Valhǫll (Óðin's desire for the Red Gold of Alert Spirit) is very much present, as is the conflict between the Valkyrie goddess and the god Óðinn in all their disguises. In the previous chapter about Baldr, we saw that there seems to be a secret conspiracy going on, where conflict, blind aggression, ignorance and repeated suffering is caused by the gods in order to obtain some higher goal. The resurrection of divine wisdom. The arrival of the Valkyrie is certainly linked to the death of Baldr, since the stanzas that follow deal with this event, when the vǫlva switches back to the first person:

31. I saw for Baldr, the bloodied god Spirit's child, his fate concealed: *There stood on the hill, grown above the plain the mistletoe, slender and very fair.*	*31. Ek sá Baldri, blóðgum tívur, Óðins barni ǫrlǫg fólgin: stóð um vaxinn vǫllum hæri mjór ok mjǫk fagr mistilteinn.*

The two stanzas that follow deal with the death of Baldr as he was shot by Hǫðr, and how Váli, Óðin's son, began fighting to avenge Baldr from the moment he was born. In the previous chapter, I discussed how the meaning of the names indicates that we are speaking of human qualities here. Baldr represents the courage that derives from a broad mind, someone who perceives broadly, whereas his "killer" is the blind Aggression. The "avenger" is the Choice that was born after its "mother" realized the horror of living without Spirit.

THE THIRD

Earlier, we mentioned how Óðinn was bound between two fires by his ward, unable to recognize his own god when he entered his halls. The god that is bound between two fires is a metaphor that can be better understood by looking back to the Flateyjarbók story. The two war-leaders, Hǫgni and Heðinn, must fight their eternal battle but their conflict will be resolved when a mysterious "third" shows up in the future will the enemies find peace. We are reminded of Óðin's own name Þríði "Third" which the god wears when he appears as a trinity, where the two other aspects of himself are called Hár [High] and Jafnhár [Equally High].

In Snorri's Gylfaginning, these three aspects of the one god take turns answering the questions of Gangleri [Wandering Learning], another aspect of Óðinn. If one looks closely at Snorri's story, one might notice that it is always Þríði the Third who reveals the most esoteric and deepest of the mysteries. The Third of the trinity represents The Spirit in Óðin's name. The High One and the Equally High One would represent the two other aspects, representing the Passion and the Mind, just like Óðin's brothers Víli [Intent] and Vé [Awe/Sanctuary] represent these aspects of divine and human consciousness. As a trinity, they form a perfectly balanced wholeness, residing in Valhǫll and able to offer divine knowledge to the Wandering Learner.

The Third is seated between the "two fires" of the Mind and the Passion, which must also be balanced in order to succeed. The Passion and the Mind may burn the Third unless the Third is given nourishment, symbolized by the drink offered by the young Agnarr. The three gods that are ultimately one is a formula that is repeated continuously throughout the Edda poetry and other Norse myths and legends. In the story of Baldr, we find the same formula. Although Óðinn has many sons, there are only three that count in the Baldr story. Hǫðr Blindi [Strife the Blind], who, moved by jealousy (represented by Loki), kills his own brother Baldr, and Váli [The Choice], who in turn kills Hǫðr in order to avenge Baldr.

The two brothers represent Passion in its negative aspect. Blind (i.e. ignorant) Aggression, and the Mind, which makes the sound Choice of destroying this negative quality. Baldr is the Third, the quality of Spirit united with Love, who possesses the Broad Vision, able to see the grand picture, and thus acting with fairness, compassion and a broadness of mind. In the story of the Children of the Mist, the brothers Gunnarr and Hǫgni likewise represent the Passion of the "Warrior" and the Mind of the "Thinker". Sígurðr, the initiated sage king, was their Third, the one who arrived to rule both with them and above them. He is married to Gunnar's sister Guðrún, a sibling couple who seem created in the mold of Freyr and Freyia. As long as Sígurðr was their brother and their king, and they sat in his council, glory was theirs, or as his widow Guðrún laments in the "Greenlandic poem of Atli" [Atlamál hin Grænlenzku]

98. *We were three siblings [two brothers and a sister] we had never been conquered, we left our land to follow Sígurðr, we hastened our ships forward, each of us ruled one ship, we roamed where fate led us until we reached the east.*	98. *Þriv vorom systkin, þottvm ovegin, forvm af landi, fylgðom Sigvrþi; sceva ver létom, scipi hvert vart styrþi, a/rkoþom at auþno, vnz ver austr qvomom.*

The three men and the one woman is another formula as well the trinity of the conscious qualities united with the mysterious maiden. The formula is seen in the relationship between Frigg, Óðinn, Víli and Vé, where misery begins when Óðinn disappears or is exiled because his need to create the Choice to kill Ignorant Aggression turns him into a rapist, forcing the Choice upon a human woman after she rejects him. A female usually represents, ultimately, fate, and the princess of the "west" (the human realm) represents the fate of humanity.

While The Spirit is in exile, the greater divine fate, represented by Frigg, is married to Víli and Vé, the Passion and the Mind, who without Spirit can be quite destructive. The formula of the fate-goddess and the male trinity is also seen as in the arrival of the Vanir quartet, Freyia, Njǫrðr, Freyr and Heimdallr. We also see this formula in Snorri's Skáldskaparmál story of how Þórr travels to the giant world together with Loki, Þialfi and the maiden Rǫskva, whose name may mean either to "dig up" or "to mature". In this story, the female heroine, representing the growth of consciousness, is balanced with the ogress Eldi [Old Age], who defeats Þórr in combat. The appearance of a somber, older and terrible female counterpart to the fate-soul-maiden is part of the formula, repeated over and over in all the stories where the maiden is present.

The ogress is actually present in the Baldr story as the lady of the dead herself, Hel, who claims Baldr for herself where he was before married to the maiden Nanna. Nanna is, however, staying with her husband in Hel's realm, and we are reminded of the fact that Hel has two sides to her, one bright like a maiden, the other dark as death. In the Vanir quartet, the ogress is indirectly present as Freyr and Freyia's mother and Njǫrð's sister-wife, a lady who receives the drowned, a recipient of human sacrifice. In the Guðrún-Sígurðr-Gunnarr-Hǫgnir quartet, Guðrún is also balanced by another female in some instances it is the Valkyrie Brynhildr who plays a destructive and deadly role, in other instances it is her own mother Grímhildr, who rules behind the scenes.

Guðrún's relationship to the male trinity should be understood as another version of the same basic formula. In the next stanza, it seems clear that the quartet is of a higher nature than what it may appear at first:

99. We conquered a king there
first then we chose land there
rulers went into our service
through our battles, we brought
from outlawry, those we wished
to rescue, we gave fortune to
those who owned nothing

99. Konvng drapom fyrstan,
kvrom land þaþra,
hersar oss a hond gengo,
hrozlo þat vissi;
vagom or scógi
þannz vildom sycnan,
settom þann selan,
er ser ne attiþ.

The stanza shows an otherwise unknown myth of how the quartet conquered the world that was ruled by giants (the "east") and destroyed its king, before bringing justice and fortune to those who served them. If we look at the quartet as a unity of inner qualities. Spirit, Mind, Passion and Soul/Fate, where the latter is married to the first and sister to the other two, conquering the baser nature (the giants) and toppling the ruling "king" of that baser nature, we may better understand the meaning of this stanza. Everything is destroyed when Sígurðr dies and Guðrún, is given over to the Hunnish tribe, like Óð's maid was given to the giants.

The two brothers then rule alone, but not in happiness and not for long. The king of the Huns destroys them, and even though Gunnarr still manages to gain the love of the Valkyrie, it is too late, and she cannot save him from the pits of death a story that is retold in the poem Oddrúngrátr. A veritable Ragnarǫk follows, as both Huns and Burgunds meet their dramatic end. After having seen her people massacred, Guðrún, the sole survivor, makes sure that all the warriors and shield maidens of the High Hall of "Atli the Hun" perish in flames. Thus both sides of the conflict, both "brothers" perish as the ultimate result of their inability to appreciate and cherish their Third and his union with the maiden whose name here means Divine Rune, rune as in "symbol" or "fate". I think we may be fairly certain that the Third represents the highest or deepest aspect of divine, cosmic and human consciousness.

The Spirit, that offers breath, inspiration and the potential for enlightenment. The two brothers represent the two other aspects of consciousness, the thinking Mind which has to make choices, and the Passion, which has to resolve emotional turmoil. The two brothers may be the best of friends, yet they may also be in perpetual war with each other, not so difficult to understand, we are often drawn between our instinctual and emotional nature, and our mind, our ideas and theories. This battle will, according to the Norse lore, only be resolved when the Third appears, causing an end to the perpetual war. I personally suspect that the Third is also related to what has become known as the "third eye" or the "inner eye", possibly explaining the true meaning of the eye that Óðinn wagered on his quest for knowledge. In some Indian traditions, such as Kundalini Tantra and Kundalini Yoga, the "third eye" is chakra, an energy center called ajna, which means "command", and is considered as the eye of intuition and the psychic channel. It is invisible, yet situated in the middle of the cranium behind the middle of the eyebrows.

When this energy center is activated through meditation, it feels like an opening between the eyebrows and upwards, in the middle of the forehead. It is the eye that "sees" when we dream or have visions, and which allows us to have telepathic contact with others. The Ajna is the seat of a goddess called the Shakti Hakini, who has six faces and six arms, crowned by a downward pointing triangle within which is a lingum, a masculine symbol. A deity called Ardhanarishwara, which is a hermaphrodite form of the union between Shiva (the god) and Shakti (the goddess), resides within the lingum.

A Cambodian Shiva head showing a third eye.
Public Domain Image

Above the triangle is another, smaller triangle where the mantra Aum, the supreme sound is situated. Other Eastern traditions such as Tibetan Buddhism, other Tantra traditions, as well as the Chinese Taoist traditions such as Qigong have similar concepts. In the West, various modern schools have employed a similar concept, often inspired by the Eastern schools, especially since Theosophists of the 19th century introduced the concept on western terms, identifying the third eye with the pineal gland and/or in the pituitary body of the brain, which are situated exactly where the third eye chakra is said to reside.

In all the traditions, the awakening of the third eye is the path towards enlightenment. It is my personal opinion that anyone who has seriously practiced meditation on the third eye will be aware that this idea is not just a fancy and that its power is beyond question. When we hear that the perpetual war between the mind-poetry aspect and the passion-intent aspect of our being can only be resolved at the arrival of the Third, I suspect that we are seeing a concept quite similar to that of the Tantric and Yogic traditions of India, a basic concept that may once have been known in many world-wide traditions.

I have earlier mentioned that the hawk that is seated between the eyes of the eagle in the top of the world-tree (as well as the human-tree) may be related to Freyia, Freyr and Frigg. The reason for this is that the hawk can be poetically replaced by the falcon as a symbol, and this is the bird that these three own. There are three mythical instances where Loki borrows the falcon hide, once from Freyia, once from Freyr, and once from Frigg. When he does so, he is capable of moving into the unknown realms and find things that have been hidden away there. I believe we are seeing a description of the third eye, situated between the eyes, owned by these deities. Yet anyone may seek to borrow this power and cloth themselves in it. When Óðinn becomes the Third, it is consciousness that moves into the third eye, since Óðinn is, ultimately, consciousness.

It is in this state that Óðinn, representing the totality of the male side, is married (and is able to maintain his marriage) to the sister-wife on the female side, just as the awakening of the third eye resolves the separation between the left and the right sides of our brains. I believe that the myths of Óðin's exile, when the wife must contend with the lesser aspects (or else leave her home to search for him), is ultimately a metaphor for how the consciousness of the third eye is absent.

LOKI'S BONDAGE

35. She saw a captive lie beneath the Grove of Cauldrons
Loki's harmful likeness she recognized;
There sits Victory Woman, very unhappy
Unhappy with her husband.
Do you understand now, or what?

      35. Hapt sá hon liggja
      undir Hvera Lundi
      lægjarnlíki Loka áþekkjan;
      þar sitr Sigyn þeygi um sínum
      ver vel glýjuð.
      Vituð ér enn eða hvat?

Vǫluspá, st. 35, Poetic Edda

We have seen how Váli was the son of Óðinn, born to avenge his brother Baldr. Yet there is another Váli another "Choice". He is the son of Óðin's blood-brother and alter ego Loki. In the Vǫluspá, the stanzas go:

34. Then war-bonds were twisted from Choice, *The rather hardened ones, made from entrails.*	*34. Þá kná Vala vígbǫnd snúa,* *heldr váru harðgǫr hǫpt ór* *þǫrmum.*

These lines are explained further in the poem Lokasenna, where the editors of the manuscript added a prose ending. In the poem itself, Loki enters the Hall of Aegir where the gods and elves are seated, waiting for Þórr to arrive with the cauldron that may hold all the mead of Aegir the Ocean Lord. As mentioned before, this is a realm of immortality, where the light elves and the gods are aspiring to enjoy an eternal banquet providing the cauldron is found. Loki enters the sacred hall where peace is the law, and begins to provoke the gods and goddesses by offending them one by one. The goddesses are mainly accused of promiscuity and adultery, whereas the gods are accused of cowardice and unmanly behavior. The accusations sound conspicuously like those that would have been proposed by a Church hostile to the Pagan religion, and may very well be a way of dealing with such accusations. For it is Loki who stands out the fool, the one who cannot fathom the deeper meaning of each myth that he understands literally and thus fails to understand completely.

The gods and goddesses patiently stand up for each other and try to let Loki know that he has not understood their myths, but Loki, blinded by rage and hurt, continues his rant until he openly and mockingly admits that he is Baldr's true murderer. Then he admits to having killed Þiazi, Skaði's father, and for abusing the goddess Síf's gift of precious mead.

Þórr arrives with the priceless cauldron that may hold all the mead of Aegir, and chases Loki out of the hall. This is how the poem ends, but the editors of the Edda collection added a prose ending:

> "And after that Loki hid in the waterfall of Fránangr [Seething Rage], disguised as a salmon. There the Aesir caught him. He was bound with the guts of his son Nári [Dead One] But his son Narfi [Narrow One] changed into a wolf. Skaði [Injury] took a poisonous serpent and fastened it over Loki's face; poison dripped down from it. Sígyn [Victory Woman], Loki's wife, sat there and held a basin under the poison. But when the basin was full, she carried the poison out; and meanwhile the poison fell on Loki. Then he writhed so violently at this that all the earth shook from it; these are now called earthquakes."

In this version, Loki's son is not called Váli [Choice] but Nári [Dead One] and Narfi [Narrow One]. This apparent confusion is solved by Snorri, who in Gylfaginning identifies Nári with Narfi, and lets Váli be the second son:

> "Then they took the sons of Loki, Váli and Nári or Narfi; the Aesir made Váli into a wolf, and he tore apart his brother Narfi. Then they took his entrails and tied Loki over three edge stones, the one beneath his shoulder-blades, another beneath his pelvic bones, and a third beneath his knees, and these bonds were turned into iron."

The use of the name Váli should in my opinion be understood literally, it means Choice, and its actions are the results of Loki's choices. In the poetic language of metaphors, a father is but a cause, a son an effect, so the "son" in question is simply the result or the effect of Loki, his Choice. Loki's Choice is turned into a wolf, a symbol of desire and greed, and one that identifies the son with the wolf Fenrir [Greed], who is also said to be the son of Loki. The other son, Nári or Nárfi [Dead or Narrow one] is the one that is killed by its own brother, quite like Baldr was. Given the emphasis placed on entrails and particular body parts in the story, it is interesting to also note that the word nári or nárfi could in fact also refer to the narrow iliopsoas muscle which reaches from the insides of the thighs, through the front of the pelvis and up to the lower back.

Working with bodywork therapy myself, I find it interesting to note that this is a muscle that often develops a chronic tension due to emotional stress such as fear and rage. Chronic muscle tensions due to long-term emotional stress may very well feel like iron bonds, and the three areas mentioned by Snorri, the shoulders, the pelvic area and the knees, are exactly the areas that take on most tensions. When Loki bathes like a salmon in the falls of Seething Rage, it is a way of saying that he is moving upstream, like salmon are wont to do moving forward in the face of severe rage, probably the rage of the gods. It is his own Choice that causes him to be bound and according to the Vǫluspá, at least, our oldest source, it is by the "entrails" of his own Choice that he is bound, until the areas of his body where many muscle groups are connected turn into "iron" [emotional tension].

The story is an allegory of a very common human condition and what happens when we by ignorance live in anger, fear and resistance. Loki is the heat-giver, the one that offered the gift of vitality and color to human beings, to life itself. He represents the passion, the emotional spirit of life, for better and for worse. It is this quality within each one of us that is described in the stories about Loki stories of great achievements as well as stories of deep pain. There are three versions of Loki's bondage. Vǫluspá, the oldest, tells us that Loki was bound by the entrails of his son Váli, the Choice. Those who wrote down the Edda poems added to the Lokasenna poem that the entrails came from Nári while the other son, Nárfi, was turned into a wolf. Snorri offers a third version, where Nári and Nárfi is the same person, whereas Váli turns into a wolf who kills his brother.

Each one is told by the poet with a purpose, and none is actually "wrong", the differences are due to different poets trying different ways of describing the same essential message in poetical terms. From Snorri's Gylfaginning and various poetical expressions in Old Norse poems, we know that Loki had two sons as well, the wolf Fenrir and the Miðgarðr-serpent. The wolf represents the negative quality of greed, whereas the serpent represents the border between the known and the unknown worlds, it keeps the world of gods and men separated from the world of giants much like the wall that was made by the craftsman and his stallion who fathered Sleipnir on Loki, as we saw above.

Since Loki's surviving son is turned into a wolf in two of the versions, quite like Fenrir, we may assume that the other son, the one whose entrails are used to bind the father, is to be likened to the Middle-World serpent who with its body "binds" the world and forms a border against the Outer World of the giants, being ultimately the border between the known and the unknown realm. On the level of individual mentality, the serpent represents the limitations of the mind, the protection we all put up to shield our worldview, whatever that is, from input and influence that may challenge and change it. The Lokasenna poem clearly shows how Loki is unable to allow new information and new perspectives into his worldview. Blinded by jealousy and resentment, he ignores all the approaches offered by the gods and continues to rant on from the limited perspective of his self-destructive worldview where valor is nothing but feminine chastity and masculine aggression.

God handling two fighting male figures, Gundestrup cauldron, Bronze Age Denmark.

The gods and goddesses are trying to make him open his eyes and expand his mind, but he refuses to listen. The result is, finally, that he is bound by the entrails of his own Choice, or, alternately, by the entrails of his own limited perspective. According to Snorri's Gylfaginning, Loki had a daughter as well, Hel, the goddess of the underworld, and one whose face is half dark and rotted like a corpse, half pink and rosy-cheeked like a maiden's. In the story of Loki's bondage, the "daughter", a metaphor for a hidden result, in this case a very ambivalent one, is replaced by two goddesses who represent each half of the face of the Underworld's lady.

His ex-lover, Skaði [Injury], who lets him suffer the dripping poison of an underworld serpent hung above his face, and his present wife Sígyn [Victory Woman], who protects his face from the poison by holding a bowl beneath the dripping stream just above his face. However, the bowl is filled with poison and must be emptied, and it is when the bowl is emptied that the poison falls into Loki's face, causing a perpetual cycle of agony. The myth is an excellent and poetical way of explaining the very human condition of being "bound" by one's own choices and one's own limited perspectives, creating a hard and iron-like tension in the body and in the soul, resulting in the bitter truth regularly making its painful existence known no matter how much we try to avoid and suppress it.

6.2: RAGNARQK

We live in a time and age where we have learned to read our myths literally. Ever since the Church decided that the Bible should be read literally, and thus we have been conditioned to think of dooms day prophecies as literal descriptions of an apocalypse that is to take place in the near future, destroying our world. As such, we can choose to either believe it or not. We forget to scrutinize the myths more closely, forget to look for clues that will take us beyond the simple message of a futile future where everything must be destroyed and everybody must die on a societal and natural level. It is in fact scientifically true that our world will, one day in several million or even billions of years, collapse, and that humanity or civilization may collapse long before that happens. It is also true that countless civilizations have flourished, more or less similar to our own, only to be reduced to rubble, over the course of history.

Some such downfalls have evidently been connected to huge natural disasters, such as the decline of the Minoan empire, which happened in connection with volcanic eruptions, earthquakes and tsunamis and the terrible after-effects. To those who found themselves within the range of such events, it must have seemed like the end of the world. Apocalyptic visions may very well be based on legends, in their turn based on the actual memories of survivors. Indeed, Ragnarqk is in some places described in a way that is credible and highly reminiscent of a terrible natural disaster caused by volcanoes, earthquakes and tsunamis. But the idea of a universal societal and natural apocalypse is not the only way to understand Ragnarqk.

What we are seeing in the Vǫluspá is that all the events that lead to Ragnarqk are in fact of a spiritual, mental and emotional nature. The build-up towards Ragnarqk is in this poem completely the result of internal conflicts that often happen within the individual human being. The loss of the Goddess who represents our inner souls, the loss of Spirit' seeing eye, the loss of the Great World's listening attention, the loss of Baldr of the Broad Perspective, and the captivity each one of us may experience when we choose to be blinded by our own resentments and our own limited perspectives. These are the themes that lead to the internal "war" of our being a battle and an apocalypse that may take place within each and every one of us on an individual level.

Whereas most readers of the Edda have turned their attention to the final battles, the wars and the natural disasters that are described in the apocalyptic vision, the actual emphasis of the Edda poem is on the experience of death in Hel for those who walked in the footsteps of the negative aspect of Loki during life: Ruled by greed, jealousy, hatred, resentment, fear and rage.

THE RIVER OF ILLUSION

36. A river falls from the east through the poisonous valleys full of knives and swords she is called Sharp One
>   *36. Á fellr austan*
>   *um eitrdala*
>   *söxum ok sverðum,*
>   *Slíðr heitir sú*

Voluspá st. 36

After the Voluspá describes Loki's captivity in the Grove of Cauldrons, we are introduced to the river from the east. The east is the mythical direction of the giant world, which is often a metaphor for destructive forces (although, as we have seen, the giants may be ambiguous in nature, possessing great wisdom). Before we learn more about this river, we are told of three different halls. To the north the direction of the Underworld is a plain called Niðavǫllum, which may be understood as the plains where the moon is dark, or simply the plains below.

Here stands a glorious hall made out of gold divine knowledge which belongs to the "lineage of Sindri". The name Sindri refers to cinders or sparks of fire, or the action of releasing or spraying out such sparks (from the verb sindra). It is the name of the dwarf master smith who forged some of the most important divine attributes: The hammer Miǫllnir, for one. Another is the ship Skiðblaðnir, which is alternately described as Óðin's or Freyr's ship. Its name roughly means "assembled from thin pieces of wood", and we should bear in mind that wood is nothing but a metaphor for matter. The "ship" is large enough to carry all the gods and will always have fair winds when its sails are set yet it may also be folded up like a small piece of cloth that can be carried in a pocket.

A third creation of Sindri's is the golden boar Gullinborsti [Golden Bristles], which according to Snorri was given to Freyr, and which draws his chariot. However, according to the poem Hyndlulióð, Freyia received a boar called Hildisuin [Battle Swine] described as Gullinborsti [with golden bristles] from two other dwarfs, Dáinn and Nabbi [Dying One and Neighbor (to dying)]. She uses it to ride into the "darkest of darkness" [rauckr rauckra] to seek her sister of the rock caves, and its body contains the soul of her initiate and protégé Óttarr. According to Snorri, the boar can run faster than any horse, through air and water, and will be able to find its way in darkness due to its golden blisters. The final and most precious of all Sindri's gifts is, however, the ring Draupnir [Dripper], a golden ring that drips eight new ones like itself every nine nights.

It is the ring that Óðinn places on Baldr's funeral pyre before whispering his mysterious secret into the ears of his son a secret that enables the god to conquer the giant of illusion in the poem Váfþruðnismál (see previous chapter "Lost in Illusion"). It is also the ring that the hero Hermóðr received from Baldr in Hel to bring back to the world of the living. Obviously, Sindri's lineage are dwarfs, and dwarfs symbolize in some way or other the small compartments that enable limitless divine consciousness to enter the physical world of limited and separate shapes. His particular lineage may refer to the kind of dwarfs that create such divine gifts, most of which seem to belong to the realm of spirit travel and the transcending of realities. It also belongs to the northern realm of the dead from where resurrection and new life also begins.

The second hall that is described in the Vǫluspá is the "beer-hall" of the giant Brímir, whose name may either be derived from the noun brim (n.sg) which refers to the movement of the ocean or the phenomenon of waves crashing against the shore, or from brími [fire]. The latter would possibly be more in accordance with the realm in which this hall of brews is situated, called Ókólni. This means "Un-Cool", a typical Norse understatement referring to a place of terrible heat. The third hall that is described is an unnamed hall "standing far from the Sun", on the Beach of Corpses [Nástrǫnd]. Its doors face the north, the realm of death and it is woven by the spines of serpents, dripping with poison.

The three halls may resemble the three realms and the three wells, or it may be a reference to the creation story. Creation happened within the Ginnunga Gap [The Open Mouth of the Sacred Descendants] where the first movement began as streams from the cold northern realm of the dead met with streams from the hot southern realm of the brew-abundant cow. Both places are deadly and poisonous, yet it is their interaction that spurs life in the universe. The golden hall of Sindri's lineage is in my opinion another way of expressing this point of encounter between the hot brewing place of life's streams, and the cold, misty place of death.

The introduction of the river Sharp is, after a presentation of these three "halls", described in further detail as a place where the souls of unworthy people struggle in vain against the currents:

39. Here she saw wading in heavy currents oath-breakers greedy murderers and those who by force takes another's ears' secrets (= female confidantes) There sucks the Below/Shame/ Waning Biter from the dead bodies And wolves tear them. Do you understand now, or what?

39. Sá hon þar vaða þunga strauma menn meinsvara ok morðvarga ok þanns annars glepr eyrarúnu; þar saug Níðhǫggr nái framgengna, sleit vargr vera. Vituð ér enn eða hvat?

The description of this river seems related to other descriptions of similar rivers. In the poem Reginsmál, Loki encounters a dwarf called Andvari [Alert Spirit or The Surrenderer] in the "Fall of Andvari", and asks him, curiously enough, what kind of "reward" people will receive if they "wound each other with words". The dwarf replies:

4. *"A terrible reward is given to the sons of men: They must wade in No-Movement-Bellower; words of untruth and lies about others have terribly long branches."*	4. *«Ofrgiold fa gvmna synir þeir er Vadgelmi vaþa; osadra orða, hverr er a annan lygr, oflengi leida limar.»*

The name of the river, Vadgelmir, is derived from the word vad, which means a standstill, a lack of movement, a blockage in the flow of the stream. The "bellowing" in the word gelmir is consistent with other names for rivers, cauldrons and primeval creative forces based on sound (vibration). Its feminine counterpart is found in the name of the river that provides a border between the world of the living and the world of the dead. The river Giǫll, which according to Snorri is closest to the Hel-gates, deriving, like all rivers, from the Well of Hel known as Hvergelmir [Mill Bellower or Cauldron Bellower].

The stanzas above seem to indicate that the dead souls of people who in life have spread lies, murdered other people because of greed, broken sacred oaths or abducted women [the confidantes of others], or else broken trust between people, are destined to wade forever in heavy, poisonous, cutting currents and standstill. As I see it, this may mean a state of being, a situation that may occur in life as it may occur in the afterlife. In the poem Vafþrúðnismál, we hear of a river called Ifingr. The name means "Head-Veil", exactly like the váf in the name Vafþrúðnir [Powerful Head Veil].

It is the river that separates the world of giants from the world of men and gods:

16. *«Head Veil that river is called which separates the sons of giants the earth between the gods freely she flows as she will do forever and that river never freezes over*	16. *«Ifing heitir á, er deilir meþ iotna sonom grvnd oc meþ goðom; opin renna hon scal vm aldrdaga, verþrat íss a á.»*

Since the river seems to symbolize a state of being, I suspect that the river called a Head Veil, which divides the ground between the destructive powers of the giants and the constructive powers of the gods, is a matter of illusion. A veil of separation that descends upon the mind.

THE WOLF-MOTHER

Stanza 40 of the Vǫluspá introduces "The Old One" [in aldna], a female old one, who sits in Jarnviðr, The Iron Forest. The place may associate "The Old One" with the giantess Skaði, who in poetry is referred to as the "maiden from Iron Forest". Her name, meaning Injury, it is hardly surprising that she there nourishes Fenris kindir [The Lineage of Fenrir]. Fenrir being the wolf of Greed. It could also refer to Fenri's mother Angrbóða [Bids Anger]. This lineage of "wolves" will swallow the Moon and the Sun. As soon as the wolf-mother is introduced, we hear of many deaths. The gods' dwellings are reddened with blood, sunshine becomes black during the summer, and the weather is vicious. The poem appears to have taken us from the personal. The experience of death or negative states of being to a more universal destruction.

However, the following stanzas take us back to the three worlds of creation and death. We hear of three roosters crowing, One is called Fjalarr [fair red], crowing in "Gallows-Wood" [Gaglviðr]. Another is Gullinkambi [Golden Comb], crowing for the Aesir, and a third is sooty red, crowing in Hel's halls. The three crowing roosters seem to resemble the three halls mentioned earlier. Hel to the icy north, and Ásgarðr to the hot south. The third is the mysterious "Gallows' Wood", where a man called Egðér [Armed Servant] sits on a (burial) mound and plays his harp happily, being the "Guardian of Giantesses" [Gygjar Hirðir]. Since we are hearing of giantesses, we are likely in the east, and likely in the same place as the hall of Sindri, where gifts for the gods have been forged.

The guardian of the giantesses is encountered in some other Edda poems and may tell us more about this place. In the Skírnismál, the unnamed guardian of the giantess Gerðr sits on a mound and is called a "shepherd", although his function is to guard the halls of the maiden, challenging the intruder. The same guardian archetype is found in the Fjǫlsvinnsmál, where the giant Fjǫlsviðr [Much Knowing] is the servant and guardian [armed servant] of the maiden Menglǫð. Since these poems are both about initiation into the higher mysteries, where the goal is the reach the halls of the Maiden, the gallows in question may be a reference to the initiation by hanging which was introduced by Óðinn.

The gallows could also refer to trees, since Óðin's gallows was a tree, in fact, the World Tree itself. Perhaps we are being directed to a place with many such world trees? After all, the empty Mouth of the Sacred Descendants is a place of potential for the creation of new worlds. It is the middle ground between the hot and the cold realms. As soon as the three roosters have introduced us once more to the three worlds of creation, we hear about a wolf or a hound once more. A dog called Garmr barks before the Gnípahellir [The Overhanging Rocks], and when it breaks free from its chains, freki "greed" runs free.

We are likely seeing another version of Fenrir, the Greed wolf who is chained but is destined to break free in order to attack Óðinn during the battle of Ragnarǫk. The vǫlva concludes that "she knows much, I see more", as of to suggest a difference between herself and Freyia. She is the older sister or the older version, the dark face of Hel, and she is the one who may look farthest. The lines about the barking Garmr, released from his chains, are repeated several times throughout the rest of the poem. It also brings to mind the barking of the hound in Hel when Óðinn enters this realm in order to seek knowledge about the fate of his son Baldr in the poem Vegtamskvíða.

THE ATTACK OF THE GIANTS

The barking of the Greed-wolf introduces us to the societal Ragnarǫk. The famous lines of stanza 45 describe an age of war and betrayals:

45. Brothers will fight each other and be their kin's slayers children of sisters will betray their relations:
Hardness is in the world, prostitution abounds, axe age, sword age, shields are cleft asunder wind [death] age, wolf [greed] age, before all the world plunges no man will spare another

45.Brœðr munu berjask
ok at bǫnum verðask,
munu systrungar
sifjum spilla;
hart er í heimi,
hórdómr mikill,
skeggjöld, skálmöld,
skildir 'ru klofnir,
vindöld, vargöld,
áðr veröld steypisk;
man engi maðr
öðrum þyrma.

The age of war during Ragnarǫk is also described in the Grottasǫngr. In the previous chapter about the Loss of the Golden Age, we began with a study of this poem, where two giantesses, Fenia and Menia, are made to draw the Mill of Fate for King Wisdom. When they experience abuse because the king is blinded by greed, they begin to draw bad fortune for the king and his people. In stanza 18 and 19, they describe how hands shall grip the hard shafts of bloodstained weapons, and that a fire will begin to burn in the east, armies will march and settlements burn. All the while, the maidens call for Wisdom to wake up, to wake up and hear the ancient tales of the giantesses. The events of the human realm resound in the divine world.

In stanza 46, the "sons of Mím [Memory]" are "at play", and the "mead-wave" [mjǫtuðr] catches fire at the ancient Gjallarhorn [Bellowing Horn]. The god Heimdallr blows loudly through this horn in order to call the gods to attention. According to Snorri, this is a warning of the giants' attack. However, it could also be understood in a more complex manner. The Bellowing Horn belongs to both Mímir [The Remembering One] and Heimdallr [Great World]. The Remembering One drinks from this horn the intelligence of the universe or its memory of all experience of the world. When his alter ego Heimdallr blows through it, and it could be the release of all this knowledge. My interpretation is strengthened by the fact that in the next line, Óðinn then speaks with the head of Mímir, consulting its knowledge.

In the following stanza, Yggdrasill, the World Tree, begins to shudder and groan, and we hear that the giant is loose. This is generally thought to be Loki, released from his bondage in the Grove of Cauldrons. All beings are terrified on their path towards Hel before the kindred of Surtr swallows the path itself. Surtr means either "Sooty One", "Blackened by Fire" or "Acid"/"Sourness". According to Snorri, he is the ruler of Muspell, the southern world of heat and fire. Again, we hear that the dog-wolf Garmr barks loudly and runs free, that "she" knows much, yet "I" know more.

We hear that the land of giants roars, that the Aesir meet in parliament, and that the dwarfs stand howling before their rocky doors, and that they are the rulers of the "rocky walls". In stanza 50, a giant called Hrymr arrives from the east with a shield before him. His name may be related to the word hrymast "to become weak" from hrymdr "weakness". Then the great Middle World Serpent, here called Jǫrmungandr [Tremendous Magic] writhes in giant's rage a way of saying that the border between the worlds dissolves violently. The eagle shrieks in anticipation. Knowing that the eagle often is a symbol of the receiver of the dead, this anticipation is one of dying multitudes, and the next line describes how the eagle tears at the corpses of the dead.

Then the ship Naglfari [Nail Traveler] breaks loose. According to Snorri, this is a ship made out of the nails of the dead. Stanza 51 describes how a ship journeys from the east carrying all the people of Muspell, the realm of hot and poisonous gases. Loki steers this ship, bent on destroying the gods. I suspect that we are here seeing the greater Loki [Utgarðsloki, Loki of the Outer World], who rules the Outer World and creates ever-changing illusions for the gods, as described in Snorri's Skáldskaparmál.

But the eastern ship from the giant's land is crowded with the people of the southern realm of Muspell, and we hear that its lord, Surtr, now arrives from the south. The name Surtr bears association to scorching fire, soot and acid. Rocky cliffs crack open, releasing the giantesses within. As mentioned in the first chapter of this book, the giantesses within the rock or wood seem to represent the animating power within matter. When the cliffs crack open, this animating power is no longer contained, and impossible to control. The stanza ends with a sad revelation, all men will thread the path of Hel, will die, and the heavens will be torn asunder.

THE DEFENSE OF THE AESIR

53. Then comes Tranquility's [Frigg's], second sorrow when The Spirit [Óðinn] goes to fight the wolf [of Greed] and the Slayer of the Bellower [Freyr], the bright one, [goes to fight] Acid Then must fall Frigg's pleasure [Óðinn/Freyr].

53. Þá kemr Hlínar
harmr annarr fram,
er Óðinn ferr
við úlf vega,
en bani Belja
bjartr at Surti;
þar man Friggjar
falla angan

Stanza 53 (above) of the Vǫluspá describes in short the death of Óðinn and Freyr, and how Frigg grieves over them both. Her name Hlín [Tranquility] is applied in the first line, an aspect where the goddess is paired with the opposite quality represented by the meaning of "Frenzy" in Óðin's name, a frenzy he no doubt experiences when he goes to his final battle. Essentially, it is The Spirit who must engage in his final battle against Greed. The most dangerous quality of the conscious realm. Will the human/divine spirit ever conquer greed?

Even back in the Viking Age, it was clear to the myth-makers that the quality of greed will be the major enemy of all life, a fact which becomes increasingly clear in our day. This battle may on one level be seen as a battle between the immense powers of greed that rules our world to this day against the knowledge-seeking spirit of humanity. On another level, it is also a personal battle for the individual. This personal and societal battle is paired with another battle that which takes place between Freyr and Surtr, another curiously relevant battle in our days. After all, Freyr is the lord of fertility, natural growth, harvests, prosperity and plenty. He is the male earth-god, who protects cultivated nature and a just society. His enemy is the acidic power to scorch all this with poisonous gases and fire.

When Freyr is called the Slayer of the Bellower, it is a reference to a myth where Freyr, having given away his sword for the sake of his love for the maiden Gerðr, used an antler to kill the giant Beli [Bellower]. The most curious thing about this line is the fact that the two gods, Óðinn and Freyr, seem to be almost identified with each other. Frigg is said to mourn for them both as if they were one. Knowing that Frigg and Freyia derive from the same original goddess Frija, it could mean that she mourns her brother and her husband at once, and that there is a mysterious connection between the two. However, although the two gods fall, Óðinn is avenged by his son Víðarr the Silent.

The name could either mean "Expander" or "Wood Warrior" as in one who stands up for the "wood" our world, or our life. He is the son of Óðinn by the giantess Gríðr [Truce], whose name indicates a truce between the Aesir and the giants or the Vanir. It could be a reference to the truce between the Aesir and the Vanir, which led to the creation of the Mead of Poetry, as described in chapter 2 and 5, or to the truce between the Aesir and the giantess Skaði, as described in Chapter 4. In stanza 55, the result of this truce, Víðarr the Silent, finally slays the wolf of Greed. The silence, which is a major attribute of Víðarr, could refer to inner silence, the kind that shuts off the brain's chatter and opens the mind to new learning.

Then it is the time of Þórr. In stanza 56, we hear of his battle:

56. *Then comes the glorious son of Heat Woman [Earth] Óðin's son [Þórr] goes to fight the serpent: In wrath he strikes, The Protector of the Middle World [Þórr], All [humans] must now leave their homesteads: He walks the nine steps, the son of Life Struggle [Earth] from that serpent, death-wed he is yet no scorn will be spoken [of him now]*

56. *Þá kemr inn mæri mögr Hlóðynjar, gengr Óðins sonr við orm vega; drepr hann af móði Miðgarðs véurr; munu halir allir heimstöð ryðja; gengr fet níu Fjörgynjar burr neppr frá naðri níðs ókvíðnum.*

The son of Earth and the son of Spirit, Þórr represents the protector of the world of gods and human beings, the Middle World. The serpent represents the border between the known and the unknown, a border that dissolves when the serpent writhes. Þórr manages, finally, to kill the serpent, although it takes his life as well. However, he has walked the nine steps, death-wed, a reference to initiation. The last line shows that the god who struggled most with this particular challenge finally wins the battle and transcends ordinary perception.

In Chapter 11, "The Son of Earth", we will discuss the role of Þórr and his challenges on the path towards wisdom. His journey begins when he realizes that, for all his might and glory, he is unable to enter the realm of the gods unless they take him there. They will only take him there if they find him worthy, and in the poem Hárbardsljóð, they plainly find him unworthy. They will not take him across the river that forms the border to the divine world from that of the giants. He will have to walk the "left hand path" until he reaches the realm of human beings, where he will be found by his dying mother, the Earth, who will show him the way to the divine lands.

The border as a river was earlier in this Chapter recognized as a state of being or perception, where there is either standstill or currents too sharp and heavy to allow the ones who are captured there to be released. The serpent represents much the same thing as the river, a border. In Chapter 11, I will also discuss Þór's role as a representative of the Mind in the Spirit-Mind-Passion trio. As such, his battle is one of perception. When it is said that all humans must leave their homesteads, it might be that we are hearing that all humans must leave their ordinary state of perception, because the border between the worlds is opening up. That a home could be a metaphor for a state of perception is clear. In the poem Hyndlulióð, young Óttarr is repeatedly addressed as heimski, literally meaning "homebound", yet actually referring to ignorance and narrow-mindedness. Óttarr is "homebound" as long as his perception is narrow. His initiation will broaden his mind so as to perceive the true interrelatedness of all creation.

THE WARRIORS OF VALHǪLL

With his initiation, Óttarr aspired to become an Einheri [One-Harrier or Sole Ruler] a warrior of Valhǫll. Their role during Ragnarǫk is not mentioned in the Vǫluspá, but another poem. Grímnismál, confirms Snorri's description of how the Sole Rulers assist Óðinn in his battle against Greed:

23. Five hundred doors and forty more, I believe there is in Valhǫll Eight hundred Sole Rulers Go through the door at the same time. When they move to fight the Witness [Fenrir]	23. Fimm hvndrvþ dvra oc vm fiorom togom sva hygg ec á Valhallo vera; átta hvndrvþ eínheria ganga senn or einom dvrom, þa er þeir fara við Vitni at veg

There appears to be a significant riddle in the stanza above which may have to do with time, or with the timing of the Ragnarǫk. There are 540 doors in Valhǫll, and at Ragnarǫk, 800 warriors move out of these 540 doors at the same time. One could marvel at the size of the doors, or wonder if the numbers in themselves are significant. A similar numeric riddle is presented in the stanza that follows, where it is said that Þór's hall Bílskírnir [Passing Shine] possess five hundred daises and forty. The numbers 800 by 540 gives the number 432000. Remove the last two zeros, and we have the number 4320, which is the exact number of years it takes for the sun to move through two astrological signs.

This is related to a phenomenon known as the Precession of the Equinoxes. A full cycle of equinoxes takes 25920 years, where the astronomical constellations appear to slowly rotate around the earth. Every 2160 years, a new constellation rises behind the rising sun on the vernal equinox, beginning a new cycle. Many ancient cultures were obsessed with such astronomical-astrological cycles, celebrating the equinoxes, inventing methods and even huge monuments for calculating the. I have little knowledge about astro-mythology, and as far as I know there is scant evidence for this kind of knowledge in the Old Norse culture, but I do not doubt that the numbers are significant and chosen with care, and that they provide a riddle within the riddle.

NATURAL CATASTROPHES

The Vǫluspá description of natural disasters continues in its stanza 57, apparently describing volcanic activity and tremendous tsunamis phenomena not unknown to the ancients:

57. The Sun is blackened Earth sinks into the ocean disappearing from the heavens the bright stars steam rises up and from huge fires, a high flame plays against heaven itself.	57. Sól tér sortna, sígr fold í mar, hverfa af himni heiðar stjörnur; geisar eimi ok aldrnari, leikr hár hiti við himin sjálfan.

Freyr's battle against Surtr can probably be understood as a way of describing a scorching, flaming power that destroys all cultivated nature, followed by the stanza quoted above. This scenario of natural disasters is the one that has captured most of the attention of those who study Ragnarǫk. Yet it is only one stanza in the Vǫluspá, which immediately proceeds to the new beginnings. We have to look to another poem in order to find further descriptions. The Hyndlulióð, where Óttarr receives his initiation teachings. The last parts of the revelations he receives during his initiation include a description of the natural disasters of the end-times:

49. I see a fire burning and the earth aflame. When suffering, most will attempt to buy their lives; carry to Óttarr [Fear Warrior] the mead, to his hands, much blended with poisons and ill fortune.	49.Hyr se ek brenna enn haudr loga, verda flestir fiorlausn þola; ber þu Ottari bior at hendi eitri blandinn miok illu heilli.»

For more information about natural disasters, we have to look to Snorri, who in the Gylfaginning describes Ragnarǫk:

> *"First comes a terrible winter which is called Fimbulvetr [The Great Winter]. Then snow will drift from all directions. There will then be great frosts and keen winds. The Sun will not be beneficial for anyone. There will be three such winters together and no summer between. But before that there will come three other winters during which there will be great battles throughout the worlds (...)*
>
> *Then something will happen that will be thought a most significant event; the wolf will swallow the Sun, and people will think this a great disaster. Then the other wolf will catch the moon, and he also will cause much mischief. The stars will disappear from the sky. Then there will take place another event, the whole Earth and the mountains will shake so much that trees will become uprooted from the earth and the mountains will fall, and all fetters and bonds [i.e. gods, beliefs, the powers that bind the structure of the world] will snap and break. Then the Greed-wolf will get free. Then the ocean will surge up onto the lands because the Middle Earth Serpent will fly into a giant rage and make its way ashore..."*

INITIATION AND RAGNARǪK.

We have seen that a revelation about the apocalypse was offered during the initiation of Óttarr in the Edda poem Hyndlulióð. The connection between the disasters of Ragnarǫk and initiation is often emphasized. In the poem, the vǫlva Hyndla returns to the subject of the disaster when Freyia claims that her initiate will be saved by his initiation and the precious mead:

49. I see a fire burning and the earth aflame When suffering, most will attempt to buy their lives; carry to Óttarr [Fear Warrior] the mead, to his hands, much blended with poisons and ill fortune.	*49. Hyr se ek brenna enn haudr loga, verda flestir fiorlausn þola; ber þu Ottari bior at hendi eitri blandinn miok illu heilli.»*

This "ill fortune" that is blended with the mead may be a reference to earlier stanzas in the same poem, stanzas which form a build-up towards the disaster. In stanza 40, Hyndla explains that Loki had a wolf of Greed, by the giantess called Angrbóða [Bids Anger]. Thus the Passion unites with the power of rage and anger to create Greed. A reference is then made to Loki's birthing of Sleipnir by the stallion Svadilfari, whose name means Harm Traveler. Thus, the very steed that enables the gods to move between the worlds is a result of harmful powers used to build the wall that separates the gods from the giants, another reference to the boundary between the worlds.

In the next stanza, another curious piece of information is offered:

41. *Loki ate a heart from the linden's [woman's] fire he found, half-burned the intent-stone [heart] of a woman; The Airy One [Loki] was pregnant from the wicked woman from this all the earth's evils have stemmed.*	41. *Loki af hiarta lindi brendu, fann hann halfsuidinn hugstein konu; vard Loptr kuidugr af konu illri; þadan er a folldu flagd huert komit.*

The linden is a feminine tree and thus a metaphor for a woman, or a goddess. It would seem that Loki intruded upon a feminine sphere, eating the half-burnt heart of a woman, burnt on the woman's fire. The only woman's fire known to us is the fire that burnt the witch-goddess Gullveigr/Freyia. As I have shown earlier, this burning was her initiation, and the moment where she instigated the path of initiation by showing how death may be conquered.

Loki often represents the negative aspect of Passion, ruled by baser feelings, so this stanza may be a way of telling us that such negative aspects have abused the sacred path of initiation, and thus blended the precious mead of knowledge with ill fortune. Freyia then repeats that she will offer the precious mead to her initiate anyway, that her words of ill fortune will then bear no harm, and that all the gods will help him.

Obviously, the goddess firmly believes that the Mead of Knowledge is still the solution to the disasters of Ragnarǫk. Freyia is the only one who promises a solution to Ragnarǫk, as she has the last word of the Hyndlulióð argument:

50. *"Your decrees of ill fortune shall not rule effectively Though you, the bride of giants/ devourers, calls down disaster; For he shall drink the precious power drink and I order all the gods o help Óttarr!"*	50. *«Ordheill þin skal engu rada, þottu, brudr iotuns! baulfui heitir; hann skal drecka dyrar veigar, bid ek Ottari aull god duga.»*

It is not a coincidence, I think, that one possible interpretation of the name Óttarr is Hope Warrior, or that the revelation of this warrior is the unity of all lineages and all life. If the precious mead and the initiation is a solution to Ragnarǫk, I cannot help but see a connection here to the arrival of the Third to put an end to the perpetual battle between brothers, the awakening of the Third Eye to see beyond the conflict.

Bronze amulet of woman with drinking horn, Stockholm, Viking Age Sweden.

In fact, the arrival of a great personage is also prophesied by Hyndla, who cannot see further, on account of being a maiden given over to the giants:

44. Then comes another even mightier, of him, I cannot even speak his name; Few can now see any further than when the Spirit must fight the wolf [of Greed].	*44. Þa kemr annar enn matkari, þo þori ek eigi þann at nefna; fair sia nu fram vm leingra, enn Odinn man vlfui mœta.»*

Hyndla cannot see further, but Freyia can. The two sisters represent the two sides of fate, Hyndla is the maiden trapped in the underworld, surrounded by fire, wishing only to sleep, wishing only oblivion, seeing no further than the disaster. Like our own souls when they are trapped in oblivion. Freyia can see, just like when the vǫlva of the Vǫluspá repeats her mysterious message: "She sees much, but I see more."

6.3: THE RESURRECTION

59. She sees, coming up a second time, Earth from the Ocean eternally green waterfalls rushing the eagle soars above the one who in the mountains hunts the fish.	*59.Sér hon upp koma öðru sinni jörð ór œgi iðjagrœna; falla forsar, flýgr örn yfir, sá er á fjalli fiska veiðir.*

The resurrection of the Earth goddess in the Vǫluspá (above) is paired with the resurrection of the Sun goddess or actually the birth of a new Sun in the Váfþruðnismál:

47. "One daughter is born of Elf-Splendour [Sun] before she is taken by Greed; she shall ride when the rulers have died in the path that her mother staked out."	*47. «Eina dottvr berr Alfraðvll, aþr hana Fenrir fari; sv scal riða, þa er regin deyia, modvr brautir mer.»*

According to the same poem, new life will be stored as a potential within a mysterious place called the Holt of Treasure Memory [Hoddmímir] during the Great Winter:

45. *"Life and Inheritance-Tracker and they will hide in Treasure Memory's Holt; the morning dew they shall have for their food and from them generations will spring."*

45. *«Lif oc Leifþrasir, enn þa/ leynaz mvno i holti Hoddmimis; morginda/ggvar ðav ser at mat hafa, enn þaðan af aldir alaz.»*

THE NEW WORLD

In the Vǫluspá, the resurrection of the flooded Earth is followed by a scene where the Aesir, the powers of conscious intelligence, find themselves in a place outside of the ordinary. A way of saying that perception has been altered. They gather on the Iðavellir. I believe the place-name is derived from the word iðr (f.sg), which means a stream that separates from the main stream and returns to the water-source, exactly the same word that makes up the name of the goddess Iðunn, who offers eternal life through eternal resurrection. The first thing the gods do is to discuss the Middle-World Serpent the boundary of our perception, the border between the known and the unknown:

60. *The Aesir find themselves on the Plains of the Streams Returning to Source and about the Earth-girdler they discuss and there they remember the great events and the Great Sage's ancient runes.*

60. *Finnask æsir á Iðavelli ok um moldþinur mátkan dœma ok minnask þar á megindóma ok á Fimbultýs fornar rúnar.*

Remembering the ancient runes of the Great Sage causes them to find the golden checkers of the gods that went before them, scattered in the ground of the new Earth. They take possession of these "checkers" and find that they can make a world where the fields sow themselves and all ills of the past are healed. Baldr returns to the living, a symbol of how the Broad Perception that he represents is returned.

He is reconciled with his brother Hǫðr, who slayed him, and the brothers live happily together. Hænir, the god of thought and mind, chooses "the twigs of prophecy", the runes of fate and decrees that "both brothers' sons" shall live together in the Wide World of the Winds [Vindheimr Viða], a way of saying that the descendants of the two brothers, Mind and Passion, shall live together in the mortal world.

Then we see a hall called Gimlé [Shielded from Fire], where free from deceit (delusion and illusion) may dwell after their deaths which happened during the Ragnarǫk:

64. She sees a hall standing as fair as the Sun with golden roofs at Shielded from Fire; There shall deceit-free rulers build and for all eternity enjoy their happiness.

*64. Sal sér hon standa
sólu fegra
gulli þakðan
á Gimlé;
þar skulu dyggvar
dróttir byggja
ok um aldrdag
yndis njóta.*

THE NEW GODS

The Vǫluspá mentions the return of Baldr from Broad Perception and his brothers Hǫðr and Váli. As such, they form the new trinity where the Passion, the Mind and the Spirit now live together in peace. Hænir is also mentioned, another symbol of the Mind, who now is able to choose the proper runes of fate. In the Gylfaginning, Snorri adds to the new pantheon:

"The Earth will shoot up out of the sea and will then be green and fair. Crops will grow unsown. Víðarr and Váli will be alive, the sea and Surt's fire not having harmed them, and they will dwell on Iðavellir [Plains of Streams Returning to Source], where Ásgarðr had been previously. And then Þór's sons Móði [Furious One] and Magni [Strong One] will arrive, bringing Miǫllnir [the Thundergod's hammer]. After that, Baldr and Hǫðr will arrive from Hel. Then they will all sit down together and talk and discuss their mysteries and speak of the things that happened in former times, of the Miðgarðr serpent and the Fenris-wolf. Then they will find in the grass the golden playing pieces that belonged to the Aesir (...)

And in a place called Treasure Memory's Holt two people will lie hid during Surt's fire called Life and Heritage-Tracker, and their food will be the dews of morning. And from these people there will be descended such a great progeny that all the world will be inhabited (...) And this will also seem amazing to you, that the Sun will have birthed a daughter no less fair than she is, and she shall follow the paths of her mother (...)"

To sum it up, we have six surviving Aesir who now dwell in the realm that was once the realm of the gods [Ásgarðr], but which now has become the "Plains of Streams Returning to Source". Remembering that Ásgarðr was situated by the Well of Origin, we may imagine that the world of the gods has returned to its source. The Norns are not mentioned, but they are the original residents of this realm. Adding to the six male Aesir that are named is another male, Life-Tracker [Lífþrasir].

In Snorri's account, Life-Tracker appears to be a human male, but when looking at Snorri's source (the Vǫluspá), one may suspect that Life-Tracker and his female counterpart, Life [Líf], are beyond human, rather they constitute the power of life (the feminine) and the power to find life (the masculine). It would be very difficult for actual human beings to survive the fires and floods and quakes that are described, and it would be impossible to live on morning dew.

Particles of life surviving in small spaces, on the other hand. Three females are also mentioned. The Earth goddess, the daughter of the Sun goddess, and Life. Together, they form the original mold for all goddesses. With the three Norns, we have six females. Coupled with the seven males, we have the magical number thirteen, the number of Óðinn, who placed twelve gods to rule the world. The divination of the witch concludes, as the witch herself, that the corpses of all the rest of those who fell during the apocalypse will be carried away in the feathers of the serpent that once lay sleeping beneath the World Tree [Níðhǫggr, the Biter Below]. Sprouting these corpse-holding feathers and flies across the land. It is first described as dark, then as bright shining. As it flies away, the witch "sinks". There are two other places where a witch "sinks". In the poem of Brynhild's Hel-Ride and in the Vegtamskvíða. The witch "sinks" into the Underworld as the Valkyrie goddess and the god (respectively in each poem) conquer her power of darkness and oblivion and resurrect from the Underworld.

THE HALLS OF AEGIR

What of the gods that perished during Ragnarǫk? I believe we have to look for them at Hlésey [The Wind-Shielded Island] because this is the place of immortality in the cosmic ocean that is, ultimately, the Well of Origin. In Snorri's Skáldskaparmál, the gods invite the grandfather of our present universe, Aegir, to come and dine with them in Ásgarðr:

> *"There was being called Aegir or Hlér [Wind-Shield]. He lived on an island which is now called Wind-Shield Island. He was very skilled in magic. He set out to visit Ásgarðr, and when the Aesir became aware of his movements, he was given a great welcome, though many things were illusions.*
> *And in the evening when they were about to start drinking, Óðinn had swords brought into the hall and they were so bright that light shone from them, and no other light was used while they sat drinking. Then the Aesir instituted their banquet and twelve Aesir who were to be judges took their places in the thrones and their names are as follows: Þórr, Njǫrðr, Freyr, Týr, Heimdallr, Bragi, Víðarr, Váli, Ullr, Hænir, Forseti and Loki; similarly the Ásyniur; Frigg, Freyia, Gefion, Iðunn, Gerðr, Sígyn, Fulla, Nanna."*

The twelve gods and the eight goddesses entertain their guest by letting Bragi, the god of poetry, explain the rules of poetry and poetical metaphors to Aegir, also telling the mythical origin of the metaphors. When it is over, Aegir invites the Aesir to visit him in his hall, an invitation that ultimately means an invitation to immortality. However, the Aesir must bring a cauldron large enough to hold all the mead of Aegir if they are to enjoy a banquet in the hall of the immortals. They send Þórr and Týr, and when the cauldron is delivered by them, they and arrive in the hall of Aegir with the cauldron, awaiting the return of Þórr, who must still fight giants in the east.

Their waiting is described in the prose introduction to the Edda poem Lokasenna:

"Aegir, who with another name is called Gymir ["Hides Something" the father of Gerðr], had prepared an ale-banquet for the Aesir when he had received the great cauldron that it is now told about. To this banquet came Óðinn and Frigg, his wife. Þórr did not come, for he was in the eastern paths. Síf was there, Þór's wife, and Bragi and Iðunn, his wife. Týr was there, he had only one hand, the wolf of Greed tore off his hand when it was bound. Njǫrðr was there, and Skaði his wife, and there was Freyr and Freyia and Víðarr, son of Óðinn. Loki was there and Frey's servants, Byggvir [Corn-Man] and Beyla [Bean-Woman]. There was a multitude of Aesir and elves. Aegir had two servants, Clever Fingers and Maturity. Shining gold was used there instead of fire to brighten the hall, and the beer carried itself around the table. The place was strictly wed to sacred peace."

In the Skáldskaparmál, we learn that the gold which illuminates the hall of the immortals is equal to the rivers, the waves, and the daughters of Aegir, corresponding with the fact that one of Aegir's daughters, Gerðr, has shining arms that illuminate the world. The place is also the home of the Valkyrie, as confirmed by the Oddrúnargrátr. The nine daughters of Aegir are also the mothers of the present universe. This is a place of origins, from where gods and elves may observe the world and recollect its history, and where the destructive powers such as Loki must meet the day of reckoning. It is a place where all the mead of knowledge is finally shared by all participants. The elves of the hall are, as we shall see in the next chapter, the souls of the dead, the illuminated ones, who, like the gods, have all been embraced by the golden goddess. I suspect that they are the Sole Rulers who perished with Óðinn, sharing his self-sacrifice.

THE LAND OF TOMORROW

The story of the resurrection of the new world in the Vǫluspá is complimented by another story in the poem Oddrúnargrátr [The Lament of Edge Rune]. This poem begins with a very informative prose interlude:

"There was a king called Bright Wandering [Heiðrekr], and his daughter was called New Fortress [Borgný]. Source of Intent [Vilmundr] was the name of her lover. She could not give birth to her children until Edge Rune [Oddrún] sister of Intent [Atli], came; she had been the lover of Battle Warrior [Gunnarr], son of Giuki. About this tale, it is told..."

Oddrún was the younger sister of the Valkyrie who went before her in the heroic poetry. For each new hero, a new Valkyrie appears, and she is usually the reincarnation of her previous aspect. In this poem, we get to hear the story of Gunnar's death after Oddrún gave him the precious mead, and how his call for her help came too late. Oddrún heard his death-song from her place in Hlésey, the Wind Shielded island of her father Aegir, the place of immortality where gods and elves will meet at the end of the world. She rode with all her might to save her beloved from the pit of serpents in which his death was taking place, but just as she arrives, the mother of her brother Atli [Intent], the only being on Earth remained unmoved by the song of the warrior, changed herself into a serpent and bit his liver.

That was his death. Oddrún's recollection of previous events is balanced by the new events, where a maiden called New Fortress is pregnant on the fifth winter, yet is unable to give birth. She dwells in the Land of Tomorrow [Mornaland], but no one "above earth" is able to help her, as the first stanza reveals:

1. I heard it said in the ancient lore that a Maiden came to the Land of Tomorrow; No one had the power above the Earth the daughter of Bright Wandering to successfully help [her].	*1. Heyrþa ec segia i sa/gom fornom, hve Mer vm kom til Mornalanz; engi matti fyr Iorþ ofan Heiþrecs dottvr hialpir vinna.*

The Maiden who arrives in the Land of Tomorrow is Oddrún, who obviously does not live "above (on) Earth", since she is the only one who is able to help New Fortress. When she learns of the plight of the pregnant woman, she rides the "black steed" across "smooth paths" until she arrives at the "High Hall", being the first to speak the words "what happened?"

5. "Who has caused this pain of the wise woman? Why is New Fortress so suddenly ill?"	*5. «Hverr hefir vísir vamms vm leitað, hvi ero Borgnyiar braþar sóttir?»*

The immortal Valkyrie is told that the reason why the "wise woman" is in this terrible pain is because she has been trying to hide her pregnancy from her father after she had slept with The Source of Intent [Vilmundr]. Thus the birth of the girl and the boy that will be the children of the Land of Tomorrow has been stalled until their mother has become ill. After the Valkyrie goddess has spent a long time away from the world of the living, dwelling in her immortal realm, grieving for her beloved, she has finally returned to save the day. She sings rich and powerful spells for New Fortress, who then brings forth the babes that will be the ancestors of new lineages. It is the return of the goddess that is described, invoked by the wise woman of Tomorrow, mother of new life.

The pregnant woman is another formula of Old Norse myths. She represents the growing potential of new paths. In the poem Vǫlundarkvíða, the maiden Bǫðvildr [Battle Intent] is raped by the lord of elves, Vǫlundr, and becomes pregnant. The elf is her father's enemy, and the maiden finds herself in a terrible position, terrified of the wrath of her father, anxious about her "lover". The lord of elves puts her under his protection, calling her the Woman of the Sacred Grove, making her father promise that he will never harm her. There is also the story of Rind [the Rejecter], who was raped by Óðinn. She became "pregnant" with the Choice [Váli] that would put an end to Blind Aggression [Hǫðr Blindi] as soon as it was born. The poem Gróagaldr suggests that she was healed from the trauma of rape by the giantess Rán, who sang a spell-song for her that would help her to shake all pains from her shoulders and lead her own way.

Thus the Choice could be born, and Baldr could be restored to the world after Ragnarǫk because of this. The wise woman New Fortress is possibly a metaphor for Earth, the mother of all life, who was both the daughter and the lover of Óðinn, the Spirit. Her father, Bright Wandering, and her lover, Source of Intent, both have names that may be applied to The Spirit. As New Fortress, she is the resurrected Earth, pregnant with new potential for life. We also learn that she and the Valkyrie once walked the Mother Earth together as if they were the daughters of brothers, so that the "wise woman" may possibly represent humanity, or its wise women, bearing the new life of the Land of Tomorrow. She cannot birth this new life before she has invoked her ancient friend, the long lost goddess of fate, who takes her through the past and into the future with her spells and her recollection of the past. We learn that the Valkyrie and the mother of new human life had a falling out in the past, as the human woman judged the divine Valkyrie for immoral behavior, not understanding the secret reasons for this behavior. The Valkyrie yet comes to the woman's aid because she had once sworn an oath to do so, and is rewarded with the new mother's blessing and appraisal:

9. *"May all the holy spirits come to your aid, Frigg and Freyia and many gods, for you removed from my hands the terrible illness."*

9. *«Sva hialpi þer hollar vettir, Frigg oc Freyia oc fleiri goð, sem þv feldir mer fár af hondom!»*

7: DEATH AND RESURRECTION

7.1: ELVES, SOULS AND REINCARNATION

"There lives the people called Light Elves [liósalfar]; but the Dark Elves [dǫkkalfar] live beneath the ground. These two elfin kinds are very different to look at, and even more unlike within. The Light Elves are brighter than the sun to look at, whereas the Dark Elves are blacker than tar."

Snorri Sturluson, Gylfaginning, Prose Edda

The elves were objects of worship in the Pagan religion. During the annual alfablót, "The Sacrifice to the Elves", the elves were honored as the spirits of dead ancestors. These were thought to reside underground and within the burial mounds or within mountains. The festival took place around the same time as the Halloween and the Day of the Dead is celebrated in other places and is clearly related to these ancient festivals, a very ancient and widespread ritual in honor of the souls of the ancestors. Some elves were particularly honored. When King Olaf Guðrǫðsson of Vestfold, brother to Halfdan the Black (810-860 AD) died, his burial mound at Geirstað became associated with great fortune for those who went there to pray. It was thought that the soul of Olaf heard their prayers.

The dead king was referred to as the Geirstaðalfr, "The Elf of Geirstað". Thus we see that in Old Norse lore, the elves are strongly associated with souls, the souls of the dead. Snorri describes the Dark Elves as darker than tar and offers a very somber vision of them, yet the sources to our knowledge about the Sacrifice to the Elves and other references to elves as the souls of dead people give a more complex picture. The Dark Elves are not evil, they are simply the souls of the dead that reside in the underworld, perhaps ready to be reborn at some point. In the Flateyjarbók, it is written that a bodyguard of King Olaf The Holy (995-1030 AD), who forced the Conversion to Christianity upon Norway, asked if he was the reincarnation of the older Olaf, the Elf of Geirstað, asking the king, as they rode past the sacred burial mound:

> *"Tell me, lord, were you buried here?" The King answered: "Never did my soul have two bodies, and it will never have, neither now nor on the day of resurrection, and if I say anything else, then the true faith [Christianity] is not truly implanted in me." Then the courtier said: "People have said that when you came to this place before, you exclaimed: "Here we are and here we go". The King replied: "I never said that and never will." The King was deeply disturbed...It was easy to see that Olaf wished to uproot and destroy this heretical superstition."*

There are several indications that Old Norse people believed that a soul could be aptrborinn "reborn" or endrborinn "born again". Stories of rebirth are important in the heroic lore of the Poetic Edda, where the hero Helgi Hundingsbani is a reincarnation of the earlier hero Helgi Hjǫrvarðsson, and the hero Sígurðr very likely a reincarnation of Helgi Hundingsbani. Those who wrote down the poems, explained in a prose ending to the second poem of Helgi Hundingsbani that "in the olden days, people believed that they were reborn, but this is now called the tales of old wives".

The reference to "now" belongs to the 12th century AD, when the poems were written down, indicating that now that Christianity had been introduced, people no longer believed what their Pagan ancestors had believed in, reincarnation. If we compare the concepts of reincarnation with the known, for example in contemporary Hindu religion, we learn that the concept of reincarnation is closely related to the concept of karma. Where the soul harvests that which has been sowed in a previous life. This concept is actually also evident on the Poetic Edda where Helgi has to repeat the challenges of his previous life, among other things, overcoming the obstacles that were not overcome before. We also see that there are alternative afterlives, realms of the dead that are brighter and better than the fate that most souls go through.

The recycling of the soul in the Well of Hel, where the soul is ground like the seed in a mill, the self-obliterated and forgotten, before the essential life-spark runs back into the world through the rivers that spring from that well. The fact that there are options may explain the differences between the Dark Elves and the Light Elves. Without the Christian obsession over "good versus evil", we may see the different elves as some representations of different possible fates of the soul after death. The variety of the sources' descriptions of death and the afterlife indicate various possible fates or various traditions. I believe that the Dark Elves represent the souls of the dead that still reside in the world, albeit in the underworld, still able to communicate with the living.

They may have been kept in the world by their descendants, who prayed to them and sacrificed to them for their wisdom, their guidance and their protection. People would sit on burial mounds or on the sacred hills and mountains where the dead were thought to reside, meditating until communication with the dead could be obtained. Their darkness is the darkness of the unknown, that which is not seen by the living, of the hidden reality that is death. The Light Elves, on the other hand, may very well refer to the souls of the dead that have achieved immortality. Perhaps they have become shining bright and transparent through their bath in the Well of Origin, a feat achieved through spiritual training and initiation, leading to the transformation and the immortality of the soul.

The silent Light Elves dine with the gods and the immortals in the Hall of Aegir at Hlésey [The Wind-Shielded Island], where the history of the world is recounted and the nine Daughters of the Ocean provide the golden light of illumination for this mysterious banquet. Wind-shield is a metaphor for immortality. The Light Elves belong to the three upper heavens, where not even the gods may dwell; shining, bright heavens to the south. The first of these heavens is called Gimlé ["The Glittering"] brighter even than the Sun, where "deceit-free" lineages live for all eternity. The second is called Andlangr ["Long Breath"], and the third is called Viðbláinn ["The Wide Death"], where only Light Elves may dwell.

It is interesting to note that these three upper heavens of immortality, brightness and Light Elves are counted as the three last among the twelve cosmic dimensions in the Edda poem Grímnismál. The remaining nine worlds belong to various gods, and we should bear in mind that Snorri stated that Hel the personified Death "rules in nine worlds". In the Grímnismál, the ninth world is the place where Freyia rules the fate of people in life and in death. This is where the goddess receives the souls of the dead, deciding which path they will take from that point.

In the Edda poem Lokasenna, it is said that the goddess has held all the gods and Light Elves of the Hall of Aegir [the Hall of Immortality] in her bright embrace. The dark elf should not be confused with the draugr. This was the Viking Age version of a zombie, a kind of harmful wraith or "undead" that could only be vanquished by cutting off the head and then burning the body, burying the ashes far away from human habitation. Such folklore is described in Grettis saga and Eyrbyggja saga. According to Snorri in the Ynglinga saga, Óðinn is sometimes called Draugardrottin [the King of the Wraiths] because of his ability to wake the dead from their graves. The dark elf is more clearly a soul, not a dead body made to rise again.

7.2: INTO THE DARKNESS-THE UNDERWORLD JOURNEY

"One does not become enlightened by imagining figures of light, but by making the darkness conscious."

Carl Gustav Jung

Detail from the Kivik stone, Bronze Age burial art, Scania, Sweden.

The journey to the Underworld is a central theme in Old Norse mythology, and the aspect that most clearly shows the importance of shamanism as an influence in Norse religion. In various shamanic traditions, the shaman will enter a trance which allows the soul or awareness or "astral body" to move into the Underworld, where the souls of the dead are gathered.

Such a journey is often undertaken with the purpose of bringing something back. Most often a person's soul, but also hidden or forgotten knowledge. It is crucial to the fledgling shaman's journey of initiation, a phenomenon that appears to have been adapted by later Pagan religions such as the Classical Mystery schools, where a symbolic or experienced death is followed by resurrection into a higher state of being. Pagan Underworlds are sometimes confused with the Christian concept of an afterlife of eternal suffering and punishment. The modern English word for the Christian "Hell" is directly descended from the Norse name Hel, and I have noticed that some translations of the Edda, such as C. Larrington's, translate Hel to "Hell".

In Scandinavia, the conversion to Christianity transformed the Pagan Hel into Helviti, which means "Hel's Punishment". Yet both the English Hell and the Norse Helviti were adaptions from the Latin, Christian name Inferno that were applied after the conversion to Christianity, probably a rather effective way of identifying Pagan concepts with evil. This place of suffering, punishments, and demons is a Christian concept which has nothing to do with the original Pagan Hel. Hel was the name of the Underworld and also of its queen, a word which may be related to the verb helja "to hide", or to the noun helu- "frost" or "cold".

There is also an association to the noun hella, which refers to "stone", particularly to large, flat, smooth rocks that often provided overhanging cliff shelters and shallow caves. In Old Norse myths, the queen of the dead is often associated with rocks and caves. She may be a "bride of the rocks [brúðr ór steini]" or, according to Freyia in the Hyndlulióð, "the sister who dwells in the rock shelter [systir er i helli byr]", or a "provider of the mountain realm [berg-gefn]". The association with rocks, mountains and caves is a reference to burial mounds and to the idea that spirits live within rocks and caves. Even into modern times, Scandinavian folklore is ripe with legends about a people who live underground or within mountains, ruled by a queen.

In Norway, these people are called the "People of Huldra" [huldrefolket], and Huldra is their queen. Huldra is described as an alluring female forest spirit with a cow's tail, prone to lure attractive young males into her rocky realm with a kind of siren's song. She would also lure children whom she wanted to raise as her own. Another Norwegian folkloric version is the "thurses" [tussene], which is sometimes ruled by a king instead, called tussekongen [The King of Thurses], who was prone to lure young women into his underground mountain castle. The thurses also existed in Old Norse lore, known as þurs, associated with the giants and with the world of the dead, and with mortal danger.

The name Huldra is etymologically linked to the Old Norse Hel and its meanings. When people disappeared in the mountains or forests as people have often done it was thought that they had been claimed by the Huldra or her people. Huldra is also conceptually and etymologically linked to continental folklore such as that of Frau Holle and similar characters that appear to have originated in Pagan worship of a Germanic goddess associated with birth, death and marriage, spinning (fate) and livestock, as well as witchcraft. It is very probable that Norse Hel, too, was far more complex than the one-dimensional figure presented to us in Snorri's Edda, some aspects of which we shall touch upon next (VII.3: The Kiss of Death).

Some have seen the word Hel in connection to helgi "sacred" and indeed, the Underworld is sometimes thought of as the insides of a sacred mountain a helga fjall. One could also point out a similarity to the world heill which means "whole" and "healthy". In modern Norwegian, the word for "to heal" is hele, "healing" is helbredelse ["returning to wholeness"]. The word for "whole" is hel in some dialects, heil in others. None of these interpretations need exclude the others. Far back in time, the name Hel may have begun as one particular meaning of the above, yet the similarity to other meanings as well as cultural associations would not have escaped the ancient myth-makers or their audience. Old Norse poets often played on multiple meanings. The important thing is that all these possible meanings were indeed associated with the realm of Hel, who rules the nine worlds of mortality, and each meaning throws a further light upon her abode and may explain why gods and heroes sought her realm.

*Scene where a large goddess (ponytail) chooses warriors from an army to
go into her cauldron of Death.
Gundestrup cauldron, Bronze Age Denmark.*

THE DARK, RESOUNDING PATH

*10. «It is dark out there I say it is time to travel over the slippery mountains
across the lands of the thurses;...*

> 10. «Myrct er vti,
> mal qveþ ec ocr fara
> vrig fioll yfir,
> þvrsa þioþ yfir; ...

Skírnismál, st. 10, Poetic Edda

Snorri provided us with a detailed description of a typical Underworld journey
called a Helreið [Hel-Ride] or referred to as fara Helvegr to travel the Hel-Path.
After the death of Baldr, Frigg asks what hero will travel to Hel and ask the goddess
of the dead if she will release Baldr. Hermóðr [Courage of an Army] is he called
who takes upon him the challenge of the goddess. Hermóðr is allowed to use Óðin's
horse Sleipnir [The Glider], a steed that has the ability to move between realities.
Snorri describes the Helvegr [The Hel-Path] thus:

*"About Hermóðr it is said that he rode for nine nights through dark and deep valleys,
so that he could not see a thing before he reached the river Bellowing [Gjǫll] and
crossed the Bellowing Bridge [Gjallarbrú]; she is covered with bright shining gold.
Battle Courage [Móðguðr] is she called, the maiden who guards the bridge. She asked
him his name and his lineage, and told him that the previous day five armies of dead
men rode across the bridge, "but the bridge bellows no less beneath you alone. And you
do not have dead man's color. Why are you on the Hel-Path?"*
*He replies: "I am going to Hel to find Baldr. Have you seen him on the Hel-Path,
perhaps?"*
*She replies that Baldr has crossed the Bellowing Bridge, "and to the north and down
lies the Hel-Path."*

Thus Hermóðr rode on until he reached the Hel-Gate. Then he got off the horse, made sure his saddle was tight, got back up again and spurred the horse on. The horse made such a jump across the Hel-Gate that it did not come close to her. After that, Hermóðr rode up to the hall, got off the horse and went inside. There he saw Baldr, his brother, sitting in the High Seat. Hermóðr stayed overnight.

The expression "north and down" remains a metaphor for death to the present day in Norway, where it is often part of a curse. The Old Norse words were norðr ok niðr, which sounded poetical. It was the direction of Hel not a geographical direction but an allegory. In myths and poetry, the North always refers to Hel and to death, which was associated with darkness and cold. North is the cold direction from where the Sun does not shine. The "down" emphasizes the Underworld aspect. The journey to Hel described by Snorri is very similarly described in many Edda poems. The path is dark, slippery, moist and deep, and it resounds with a kind of bellowing noise when one who is not actually dead travels it. In the Skírnismál, the maiden Gerðr remarks on this resounding just as Móðguðr did:

14. " What is that sound of sounds that I am now hearing within our dwellings? The Earth trembles, and all the courts of the Hiding One are vibrating."	14. «Hvat er þat hlym hlymia, er ec heyri nv til ossom ra/nnom i? iorþ bifaz, enn allir fyr scialfa garðar Gymis.»

In the Vegtamskvíða, Óðinn traveled to Hel in order to inquire about Baldr's omen dreams before his death, and we get even more details about the Hel-Path, which is here, interestingly, called the Earth-Path:

2. Up stood Óðinn, the aged ancestor and he placed the saddle on Glider's back; he rode downwards from there unto Misty Hel, there he met the whelp the one who comes out of death.	2.Vpp ræis Óðinn, alldinn gautr, ok hann a Slæipni soðvl vm lagði; ræiþ hann niðr þaþan Niflhæliar til, mætti hann hvælpi þæim ær or hæliv kom
3. The hound was bloody on the chest and barked a long time at the Father of Charms Forth rode Óðinn, the Earth-Path resounded and he reached the High Hall of Hel.	3. Sa var bloðvgr vm briost framan ok galldrs foðvr gol vm længi. Framm ræið Óðinn, folldvægr dvndi, hann kom at háfv Hæliar ranni.
4. Then rode Óðinn to the east of the door...	4.Þa ræið Óðinn fyrir austan dyrr..

THE HEL HOUND

The Hel Hound: Three images showing the symbol of the dog, three of which with a woman associated with death: The first is a Bronze Age rock carving from Bohuslän, Sweden, where a giant woman has intercourse with a warrior, a dog behind her. The second is a sixth century AD image from a Gotland standing stone showing a Valkyrie with a drinking horn and a dog observing a battle. The third is a wolf-riding woman using serpents for reigns

In the story of Hermóðr, we do not hear of the Hel-hound, but it is prominent in the Vegtamskvíða, (quoted above) where it is called a "whelp" which is a humorous understatement of its terrifying proportions. The Hel-hound might be a dog or a wolf, a very ancient symbol of the Underworld. The unnamed, Norse Hel-Hound is probably related to the Greek Cerberus, who guarded the gates of the underworld by the river Styx. This fierce, three-headed dog was the offspring of a mother who was half serpent, half woman, and a fire-breathing giant. Cerberus' parents may show some ancient connection between the two traditions. Hel is not described as a serpent woman, but frequently depicted wielding serpents, and described as steering her wolfish steed with serpent reins.

Serpents are very prominent features of Hel's realm, and the serpent has been a symbol of the Earth goddess and the Underworld in many ancient traditions, not the least as a symbol of transformation (the shedding of skin) and wisdom. The serpent woman is a very ancient and widespread symbol of death. Like the Greek serpent woman, Hel is divided in two, she is half corpse, half young maiden. As to the serpent-woman's partner, a fire-breathing giant exists in Norse mythology as Surtr. In one poem (the Fjǫlsvinnsmál), this scorching giant is paired with the ogress Sínmara [Pale Mare], another name for Hel.

The Hel-hound is very old, being the companion of supernatural giant females in Bronze Age rock carvings across Scandinavia, and also the companion of Iron Age goddesses of death, fate and oracular divination, such as Nehalennia. From the early Viking Age, Valkyrie are sometimes depicted with a dog. One goddess associated with death, mountains and the Underworld is Skaði, who is said to enjoy the howling of wolves. In Norse mythology, the hound turns out to be a wolf the moment it appears together with a woman. Hyndla [She-Wolf], has a stable full of pitch-black wolves in her underworld cave, which like the Hel-Path itself is so dark that one is blinded.

Hyrrokkin [Fire Spinner], who pushed Baldr's funeral ship on its way to Hel, also rode a wolf. She used serpents for reins, and images of women riding wolves using serpents for reins are found as artistic motifs on standing stones dating from the Viking Age and before. In one of the Helgi-poems, an unnamed fylgja appears as an omen of death to young Helgi, riding a wolf. The Hel-hound of the Vegtamskvíða is described as bloody-chested. In the Vǫluspá, wolves are said to devour the corpses in Hel while serpents suck out their life-blood. There are other wolves too, such as Fenrir/Garmr who represent greed in ever-growing and more destructive proportions, wolves who will be the end of Sun and Moon and all the gods.

Like the Hel-hounds, they are recognized by their loud barking and the threat that they may break free. In poetry, wolves and dogs may represent the survival instinct in its many aspects, for better and for worse, such as Óðin's wolves Geri and Freki, who represent Action and Desire, but the canine connection to death and the underworld, particularly to the devouring aspect of death, the complete obliteration of the self, is very strong. In the Hel-Path descriptions, the hounds of Hel are mostly described as fierce guardians of the Hel-Gates. They appear frequently in the Mead-woman myths where they guard the dangerous gates of the Mead-woman, such as in the Skírnismál:

> The Shining One rode to the realm of the Hiding One in the Giant world. There were vicious dogs [hvndar ólmir] there, bound outside the fence that was protecting the Hall of Gerðr.

Skírnir is clearly experiencing the same world on his journey to woo Gerðr as Óðinn and Hermóðr experienced when they traveled to seek Hel about Baldr. Skírnir may be traveling through the dark paths of the giants, but he reaches a hall which, like the Hall of Hel, is guarded by vicious dogs. Like Óðinn when he sought Gunnlǫð, Skírnir is in danger of losing his life to a mysterious great giant. Like Hermóðr, he meets a guardian, this time a "shepherd", who, like the maiden who guarded the bridge, comments upon the fact that he is not dead. First, Skírnir asks him how to get past the fierce hounds:

11. "Tell me this, shepherd, as you
sit on the burial mound guarding
all the paths:
How may I come spirit to spirit
with the young maiden past
Gymir's grey ones
(= Wolves = Hounds)?"

11. «Segðv þat, hirþir!
er þv a haugi sitr
oc vardar alla vega:
hve ec at andspilli komvmc
ens vnga mans
fyr greyiom Gymis?»

How to get past the hounds seems to be the million dollar question of Old Norse myths. In the Skírnismál, the shepherd declares that it would be impossible to get past the dogs for one who was still alive, but the maiden, Gerðr, has the power to open the gates to anyone she likes, for as she notes the vibrations that emanates from the intruder, she is curious to meet him.

A similar theme is described in the poem Fjǫlsvinnsmál, where the hero is trying to find the right question, the question that will provide the answer as to how to gain entry into the halls of the Great Maiden. One of the first things he does is to ask about the hounds:

13...what are the dogs called that I hear bark louder than any barking I have ever heard?"	13...hvat þeir garmar heita, er gífrari hefik ǫnga fyrr í lǫndum litit?»
14. "One is called Greed the other is called Doer if you want to know it: they guard the immortal maidens and they will guard them for as long as the world exists."	14. «Gífr heitir einnarr, en Geri annarr, ef þu vilt þat vita; varðir ellifu er þeir varða, unz rjúfask regin.»

THE COLOR OF DEAD MEN

The journey into the Underworld is taken by all who are dead or dying, but for one who is still alive, it is a marvel. When Skírnir asks the shepherd guard how he can get past the hounds and meet the maiden Gerðr, the guardian replies with a question:

12. "Are you dying or dead (moved on) already...?"	12. «Hvart ertv feigr eþa ertv framgenginn...?"

As soon as the guardian understands that Skírnir is neither dead nor dying, he declares that the encounter with the maiden is impossible. The shepherd's comment is the equivalent of Móðgúð's comment: "You do not have the color of dead men". In the shepherd's case, this seems to disqualify Skírnir from entering Gerð's halls, but Skírnir does not give up. Eventually, the maiden herself allows the gates to open up, and comments, like Móðguðr, on the bellowing, resounding noise his presence in this realm creates. Like Móðguðr, Gerðr marvels about the fact that he is alive within the realm of the dead:

17. "Are you of the elves, or a son of the Aesir Or of the wise Vanir? Why do you come alone across the wild fire to seek our company?"	17. "Hvat er þat alfa ne asa sona ne víssa vana? hvi þv einn vm komt eikinn fvr yfir ór salkynni at sia?»

Skírnir replies that he is neither elf, Ás nor Vanir, but reveals not that which is implied by this. That he is a man, a human being, who ought never to enter the realm of death without being either dead or dying.

THE GATES AND WALLS OF HEL

When Óðinn rides to seek knowledge in Hel about the death of Baldr, he makes sure to ride "to the east of the door" of Hel. The east is the direction of the sunrise a new beginning, where an old dead witch rises from her grave. The mention of the door, and the fact that he does not touch it, is significant. When Hermóðr later rides the Hel-Path after Baldr, he also makes sure not to touch the Gates of Hel, jumping successfully over it. It would seem that this is very important if one wants to come back out alive. The theme of the wall or gate is repeated in the Mead-woman stories, although they vary in some detail. In the Sigrdrífumál, the hall is situated on top of a Sacred Mountain [Helga Fjǫll] called Hindarfjǫll, [The Mountain of Obstacles (from hindr, n.sg)].

The walls that surround the sleeping Maiden are high flames reaching up to heaven, and behind these, shields. Total fearlessness is necessary to pass these obstacles, and it is only because Sígurðr already carries the shining red gold of Alert Spirit that he is able to pass. Skírnir also has to go through a wild fire, as does Sígurðr and Gunnarr (Chapter 4.8). The fire is impossible to pass if one possesses fear, but fearlessness obviously brings down the obstacle of the fire. In some cases, we learn that the maiden within has declared that she will only accept the hero who has no fear, and who can show his fearlessness by passing the fire. In other cases, it is enough that the maiden wishes to open her gates for the visitor, often impressed by the resounding vibrations that emanates throughout her realm when the hero arrives.

We are reminded of a passage in Flateyjarbók where Freyia is said to own a beautiful hall that will only open its doors for those that she wishes to see. Freyia is indeed a recipient of the dead. In the Grímnismál, we learn that Freyia both chooses and receives the chosen dead, the einherjar, in her realm. In the Egils saga Skallagrimssonar, a woman, Þorgerður Egilsdottir, declares her intent to commit suicide by self-starvation with the following words: "I shall not eat until I sup with Freyia", obviously regarding life after death as a banquet in the hall of the goddess. In the Fjǫlsvinnsmál (ch.IV.10), fires are mentioned, but the wall, the gates and the hounds that we know from the stories of Óðin's, Hermóð's and Skírni's journeys are also described in detail. Like Skírnir, who has to cross wet and slippery paths, the young hero Wind-Cold [Death-Cold] has to pass urgar brautir slippery paths, as well as a great fire. He then floats about outside the high halls in Utgarðr [The Realm Outside] and watches a beautiful, glittering hall owned by the Great Maiden [Þióðmæra]. However, he has to face severe obstacles before he can reach it.

The all-knowing giant Fjǫlsviðr [Much Knowing] answers his questions about the obstacles surrounding the golden hall:

Death-Cold said:
9. "Tell me this, Much Knowing
as I am asking you and I want to
know it: what is this gate called
that is sown with the gods is there
a more terrible thing?"

Much Knowing said:
10. Bellowing Drumbeat she is
called and she was made by the
three sons of Sun-Blind;
The fetters are fastened around all
travelers who try to lift her from
her hinges."

Vindkaldr kvað:
9. «Segðu mér þat, Fjǫlsviðr!
er ek þik fregna mun
ok ek vilja vita:
hvat sú grind heitir,
er með goðum sáat
menn it meira forað?»

Fjǫlsviðr kvað:
10 .«Þrýmrgjǫll hon heitir,
en hana þrír gerðu
Sólblinda synir;
fjǫturr fastr verðr
við faranda hvern,
er hana hefr frá hliði.»

The description of the gate provided here may explain why the heroes take such care to not touch it. The dangerous gate is only matched by the walls surrounding the high hall of the Maiden:

11....what is the wall called that
is sown with the gods is there a
more terrible thing?"

Much Knowing said:
12."Guest/ghost-Strangler is he
called and he was made by me
from the limbs of Clay-Fire;
Thus have I forged him that he
will always stand forever through
the life of the ages."

11 ....hvat sá garðr heitir,
er með goðum sáat
menn it meira forað?» "

Fjǫlsviðr kvað:
12.«Gastropnir heitir,
en ek hann gǫrfan hefk
ór Leirbrimis limum;
svá hefik studdan,
at hann standa mun
æ meðan ǫld lifir.»

RITUALS, SACRIFICE AND WAKING THE DEAD

...With the golden necklace did the Goddess of Flames hoist him high in the air,
he who by Taur was to tame the cool horse [i.e. "die"]...
...með gollmeni
> *Loga dís*
> *at lopti hóf,*
> *hinn's við Taur*
> *temja skyldi*
> *svalan hest*

From Þjóðólfr ór Hvini's Ynglingatal st.10

The lines from the 9th century Norwegian skaldic poem above describes a king sacrifice by hanging performed by a queen who is identified with Freyia through the attributes of flames and a golden necklace and death. The cool horse is in itself a well-known Norse poetical metaphor for death. Most of the Edda poems describing the Underworld journey describe something that may have been experienced as an internal, personal vision. Some poems offer clues as to what rituals or practices may have been involved externally.

The Norwegian archaeologist Britt Solli has suggested that many hanging sacrifices may actually have been "mock hangings" where a light strangulation could lead to altered states of consciousness and ecstasy.

Óðin's description of fasting, thirsting, hanging and piercing has as much in common with severe ascetic, yogic and shamanic techniques of ecstasy in order to reach the border of death, as it has with actual sacrifice. Sagas such as the Gautreks saga show that the idea of a mock sacrifice during rituals was common enough, and there are some indications that kings were expected to let themselves by symbolically hanged. Such drastic efforts should not surprise anyone who has studied the history of ancient religions or shamanism, where initiation rituals could be a very dangerous affair with the purpose of bringing on a near-death experience, sometimes ending in actual death.

When Freyr in the Skírnismál sits in a seat that provides vision into all the worlds, and this seat belongs to Óðinn [The Spirit] I take it to mean a state of meditation. In the poem Helgakvíða Hiǫrvarðssonar, the shaman Atli moves into the Land of Sleep [Svávaland] by passing a river. The river would symbolize the river Gjǫll [Bellowing], which according to Snorri was closest to the Hel-gate and made up the border between life and death. Preparations were made before the crossing, including an ascent to the top of a Helga mountain, from where one can look into the Land of Sleep (death).

It is observed that the Land of Sleep is surrounded by high fires. Before ascending the mountain, however, visions are sought in a sacred grove and sacrifices and prayers are offered to the talking birds of the grove. This description of Atli's preparations and actions is in my opinion one that probably reveals how the rituals and preparations before an actual Underworld journey were in fact conducted during Pagan times. In the Hyndlulióð, the Underworld is described as the "darkness of darkness" itself [rauckr rauckra], and the ogress who rules there is said to live in the rock caves. Her wolves are pitch-black.

Óttarr enters this realm by the help of Freyia, who descends with him by transforming him into a dying boar. This happened during a sacrifice, at the moment when blood from the sacrifice [the boar] splattered the altar. This led to a vision of the alter becoming pure crystal, and the appearance of the goddess. The sacrificial animal is here used as a steed for the spirit of the man, riding the boar's spirit and shape as it dies. Such a concept may throw further light onto the meaning of sacrifice [blót] in Old Norse Paganism. The sacrifice may on one hand be a gift to the gods, as this boar was a gift to the goddess, but it may also hold magical properties. During the act of slaughter, the killer and the victim may become one, sharing the journey to the Underworld.

The power of the sacrificed to move between the worlds for some time after the sacrifice seems to have been a crucial concept, and there are some indications that Old Norse sorcery could involve necromancy. To sit beneath a hanged man was a common practice, where one could seek answers from the dead. Poets and other spiritual leaders were expected to practice this kind of morbid meditations. The hanged men were sacrificed to Óðinn, and thus they shared in Óðin's visions. Óðinn himself was said to be able to wake the dead and let them speak tidings from the other side. In the Vegtamskvíða, Óðinn sings válgalðr, charms of choice, to a dead witch in order to wake her up and hear her prophecies. He does this before her grave, and as the corpse rises, she complains:

5. [...]I was covered with snow and beaten by rain and moistened by dew; I was long dead.	5. [...]var ec snivin sniofi ok slœgin rœgni ok drifin da/ggv, da/ð var œk lœngi.

In the Gróagalðr, the young boy who must seek the Maiden who rules the World Outside wakes his mother, a dead witch, from her grave to obtain her counsel and magical charms. He invokes his dead mother at "the doors of death":

"Wake you up, Gróa! Wake you up, good woman! I wake you at the doors of death (...)	«Vaki þú, Gróa! vaki þú, góð kona! vek ek þik dauðra dura;(...)

Perhaps more than any other feature of Old Norse mythology, it is the many descriptions of the Underworld journey and the rituals to wake the dead that most clearly shows that these myths were not invented after the Conversion, as some people today still claim. The detailed descriptions of ritual and the emphasis played on the journey to an Underworld in order to seek knowledge and healing would, in my opinion, never have been invented by Christians.

These are thoroughly Pagan features, belonging to age-old traditions, in every detail and in every respect recognizable from ethnographic studies of shamanism across the world, and from historical studies of Classical, Pagan Mysteries. Even the major purpose of the Old Norse death journey is undoubtedly Pagan in character. The waking of an ancient, many-shaped goddess whose slumber is described as the woe of the world.

WHY THE DEATH JOURNEY?

"There were many an age before the Earth was created that Misty World [Niflheimr] was made, and in its midst was a source called the Bellowing Mill/Cauldron [Hvergelmir], and from it runs [all the rivers of the world]. Bellower [Gjǫll] is the river that lies close to the Hel-gate"

Gylfaginning, the Prose Edda

Snorri described Hel as a somber place where those who have died from old age or sickness have their residence. This is far from the picture drawn up by the older source, the Edda poems. Baldr and Sígurðr are both heroes connected to courage and wisdom, one divine, another semi-divine.

Sígurðr even dies in battle, avenging himself. Yet they end up in Hel. Sígurðr is saved by his Valkyrie, who comes after him in order to save him. Hel, also known as Níflhel [Misty Hel] or Níflheimr [Misty World] is the place where the souls of the dead are drawn into the Bellowing Mill or Cauldron, to be ground and dissolved. It is the place where symbolical animals devour the corpses. Serpents, symbolizing transformation (the shedding of skin), suck out the life-blood the vitality and color that was given by the gods of heat. Wolves, symbolizing that which devours, tear apart the physical body. The ogress of darkness receives the dead and bids slumber and oblivion to the waking world of the living. The eagle called Corpse Devourer lives up to its name. Yet it is from this same bellowing cauldron or mill that all the rivers of the world spring, mothers of life. It is from the corpse-devouring eagle that all the winds unseen movements of the world originate.

The earthly Misty World is preceded by the cosmic Misty World. In Norse myths, this icy, frost-covered realm is a place where potential for the revival of slumbering life resides. It is from Misty World that the Aesir emerge, brought to life by the hot tongue of the great cow. It is from Misty World that the first giant, Ymir, takes its nourishment. The world of the dead is a place where not only death and oblivion takes place, but also resurrection. In many ways, the Underworld could be compared to the hidden realm of the subconscious that all human beings carry within. If we are to know ourselves and dig out our hidden potential and powers, we must move into that realm and discover it, know it, become, like Óðinn, "Way-Wont" [Vegtamr].

There might; however, be more to the Underworld journey than modern psychology could ever attempt to explain without entering the realm of the mysterious. It is an aspect belonging to forgotten traditions where the quest for immortality through knowledge about death and resurrection was central. To enter the world of the dead while still alive may have been thought to enable the practitioner to know his or her way out when the moment of actual death arrives. Why else should Freyia introduce the path of initiation by displaying her ability to conquer death? Through the path of initiation a practitioner could, like Óðinn, become a Helblindi or one who blinds death, or is blind to death and is an immortal.

7.3: THE KISS OF DEATH

Loki said:
"Be quiet, Freyia!
I know you thoroughly, you are not in lack of shame:
of the Aesir and elves that are seated in this hall [of
immortals], each one has been your lover."
   Loki qvað:
   «Þegi þv, Freyia!
   þic cann ec fvllgerva,
   era þer vamma vant:
   asa oc alfa,
   er her inni ero,
   hverr hefir þinn hór veriþ.»

Lokasenna, st. 30, Poetic Edda

Golden plate with couple kissing, Roman Iron Age, Rogaland, Norway.

   Both from the Edda- the Skaldic and the saga- literature there are examples of death presented as an sexual encounter between the dead/dying and a female power associated with death, such as Hel, Rán or Freyia. The death-experience could be described in poetry as the act of climbing into Ran's bed, or as being embraced by the death-woman. In the poem Ynglingatál, composed by the skald Þióðolfr ór Hvini during the late ninth century the combination of sex and death is repeated over and over. In that poem, the poet describes the death of various Ynglinga kings, and their deaths are described as a sexual encounter between the king and Hel, the queen of the dead:

7...And the ruler of the people of Yng	*7...ok allvald*
	Yngva þjóðar
Loki's maiden [= Hel] has taken as a lover [= he had died].	*Loka mær*
	of leikinn hefr.

   In another written version of the same poem, the stanza translates: "I do not deny that the Goddess of Glitnir [Hel] is taking lustful pleasure in the corpse of Dyggvi", the king [Kveðkat dul, nema Dyggva hrǫr, Glitnis Gnǫ at gamni hefr]. That Hel is known as "the Goddess of Glitnir" [Glitnis Gná] in such an ancient source speaks volumes about how she was conceived during the Viking Age. We will be discussing Glitnir further in the next section for now it is sufficient to say that Glitnir means "Glittering", a bright shining place where the gods will dwell after Ragnarǫk. The name used for "goddess" is Gná, a goddess associated with divine messages sent rapidly through the air. Snorri claimed that Gná was Frigg's messenger, and that she has also been called the goddess of completion. It is this kind of energy that is taking such "lustful pleasure" in the corpse of the king. In stanza 32 we read that Hel has invited the king to "parliament".

It was an established and well-known metaphor in Old Norse poetry to describe love-making through the metaphor of a female inviting a male to parliament:

32. And to parliament [= love-making] for the third time Hveðrung's [= Loki's] maiden [= Hel] invited him away from the world [of the living], thus Halfdan [the king] [...] in the Judgment of the Norns [= death] could have pleasure...	*32. Ok til þings þriðja jöfri Hveðrungs mær ór heimi bauð, þás Halfdanr [...] Norna Dóms of notit hafði;*

This Viking Age presentation of Hel as an seductive lover is in sharp contrast to medieval Snorri's dark description, which must have be strongly influenced by Christian concepts. In an article on the subject by the Norwegian professor Gro Steinsland, several examples of Skaldic poetry where Hel is described as an attractive maiden have been pointed out. In Þorbjǫrn Brúnason's ransom song from the early 11th century, we find that epli Heljar "Hel's apples" is a kenning for death. The kenning alludes to Iðunn's apples, and as Steinsland reminds us, apples were ancient symbols of lovemaking. In the Edda poem Baldr's draumar [Vegtamskvíða], Hel is presented as a hall decorated and well-furnished for a party awaiting the arrival of Baldr to the realm of death. This gives the image of a rich húsfrú [lady of the house] hall who takes good care of her realm, and has not a trace of Snorri's tale of hunger and misery.

Towards the end of the 900's, the Icelandic poet Tindr Hallkelsson, described Hel [death] with the kenning "the bendable branches of Gerð's shoulders", that is, as Gerð's [Hel's] arms. Moreover, in the same stanza, Hel is preparing a bed for the earl who was fighting on the battle-field. In Norse poetry, the hint to a woman's arms is always a hint to the lover's embrace and has erotic overtones. With these examples from poetry, Steinsland pointed out that we have probably moved a step closer to genuine, Pagan, Viking Age concepts of Hel as an erotically attractive entity, which makes it easier to grasp the image of death as a loving union between the dying and the mistress of the death-realm. This seems to be connected to death on the battle-field or at sea. It is possible that the Valkyrie who takes the dead to Valhǫll were part of the same motif, as the heroes of the Edda are married to their Valkyrja. In the Helgakvíða Hundingsbani II, Helgi's death is followed by the entry of his Valkyrie into the grave and a reference to "high goddesses" being with the dead:

46...now has the bride arrived into the burial mound, the high goddesses are with us dead ones.	*46....nv ero brvþir byrgþar i ha/gi, lofda disir hiá oss liþnom.*

Image from a burial urn lid, Bronze Age Denmark

Another example of Steinsland's is a stanza from the Viking Age skald Hofgarda-Refr Gestsson, where the idea of courageous death in battle is described as an act of vigorous love making in the "golden bed" of the "maiden": "The generous Freyr-god [warrior] climbed the Golden Bed of the Maiden/ the warrior showed great virility [Gjǫfrir As-Freyr gekk i Golli stokna Sæing Meyiar/ Hǫars drífu askr viðrinn þroska]".

Death on the sea can also be described as a sexual union between the dying and the nine daughters of Ran. In Flateyjarbók we hear that a crew that struggle to survive in a tempest are being tried seduced by the daughters of Ran: *"Ran's daughters tried the men, inviting them to their fiery embrace [reyndu Ranar dætr dreiningina ok budu þeim sin fadmlog]."* In Fridtjiof saga hin frækni, chapter 6, death is described as climbing the bed of Rán: *"Now I shall soon climb the bed of Rán"* as in *"I am going to die soon"*. The expression of Skaldic poetry *"to climb Ran's bed"* is equivalent of losing life at sea. In Sonatorrek 10, the poet Egill Skallagrimsson describes his grief after the death of his son Bodvar. His life has been radically changed.

Man wearing the emblem of the Sun goddess has intercourse with larger than life female accompanied by dog (symbol of the underworld), Bronze Age rock carving.

He described his son's death journey as "walking the path of lust [a munvega]". Since the 1990s, the Norwegian professor Gro Steinsland has published several studies on the myths of Sacred Marriage in Old Norse sources, and is one of the few scholars who has emphasized the connection between death and sex as a theme that goes beyond mere poetical imagery.

The Old Norse poets associated the death of males with a sexual encounter not just because it gave a thrilling, poetical swing, but because it was a concept deeply embedded within the Old Norse culture and religiosity. Steinsland believes the connection between death and sexuality originated in the cult of Sacred Marriage, where the king ritually married the goddess of the land or the ancestral mother of his people (often the same thing). The marriage is mythically conducted during a symbolic death or whilst in the Underworld.

I believe that there could be more influences on this concept than the ritual of Sacred Marriage alone. I think that a very important backdrop to the combination sex and death in poetry may simply be the fact that the realms of death are dominated by female rulers. After all, the sexual theme only happens when a man dies. The woman who imagined she would sup with Freyia after her death clearly envisioned a banquet, but no sexual encounter or marriage is ever mentioned in connection to women's' deaths.

Óðinn may have achieved power in one of the afterlife spheres, Valhǫll, but even there, the actual choosers of the slain are the Valkyrie, and the power of resurrection derives from the mead that runs from the teats of the she-goat Heiðrún, who is subtly identified as Freyia in the Hyndlulióð. It is Freyia who ultimately chooses the slain and receives them in her hall, letting half of the chosen go to Óðinn. The heroic poetry clearly shows that Óðin's influence in the choice of dead souls and their afterlife fate completely depends on his ability to control the Valkyrie goddess.

In the Norse world, Death is personified, and is always a female. At sea, it is not Aegir but his wife Rán who receives the drowned in her net. Her daughters, the waves, assist their mother by luring sailors to their death. The ladies of the ocean represent death by drowning. In the mountains, the "Lady of the Rocks" is another female, Skaði, who represents death by injury, which often happens in the mountains. Hel is Death in general, and appears to have been associated with illness and old age by the time of Snorri in the 13th century.

Image from Kivik burial chamber, Scania, Sweden, ca. 1300 BC (Bronze Age), showing a couple involved in sacred marriage during a ritual.

As Steinsland pointed out, actual Viking Age poetry, which is far older than Snorri's account, appears to consider Hel an attractive female whose seductive power lures all kinds of males to all kinds of deaths. In the poem Sólarlióð, the dying man is called on by the "Maidens of Hel" [Helju Meyiar].

The dying men are often described as helpless play-things in the arms of the lustful death-woman, although the courageous man of the honorable death would be described as vigorous and virile, one who showed ability to satisfy her by being manly and taking control.

Females dominate the afterlife realm, corresponding with the tendency in Old Norse lore to associate feminine powers with the secret and hidden realms, and with fate. For the ultimate fate for all mortals is death. In the poem Sólarlióð, death involves a nine-night trial in the Seat of the Norns [nórnarstólinn], where the Norns would decree their judgment on the dead person. The "judgment of the Norns" [Nornar dómr] is also mentioned in the poem Fafnismál, said to be something that will be received before one has "crossed the river" (of death). As to the personal Norns of the individual, there is ample evidence that a person's Fylgjur would arrive at a person's death, bidding the dying person "home" that is, to their home.

Most Fylgjur appear to have been the souls of dead female ancestors, who had as one of their afterlife tasks to help those who died to cross over. Sexual unions between shamans and spirits of the opposite sex abound in various shamanic traditions, and the Mysteries and other mystical and devotional religious traditions have emphasized a romantic relationship between the initiate and the deity, where the union between a soul and the divine is metaphorically described as a sexual encounter. In all these traditions, the union would happen during the initiation whilst in the Underworld.

Such concepts may have found their way into the general perception of death as a place where the female ruler or rulers of that realm embraced the male newcomers, perhaps promoted by Viking Age poets who often described death as a sexual encounter. The fact that female powers receive the dead is in my opinion the most important reason why Norse poets promoted sexual metaphors for death, but there may certainly be more to it. Sacred Marriage is one influence, as Steinsland argued. I think that the myths of the mead-woman is another, which is not necessarily always about Sacred Marriage but about the mysteries of initiation and resurrection, where the love of the mead-woman is essential for the successful return to life as a new, reborn initiate worthy of a sacred office.

7.4: AFTERLIVES

> 22. *She is called The Gate of Choice*
> *standing on the plain*
> *holy she is, before the holy doors*
> *ancient is that gate*
> *and few know*
> *how she is closed and locked.*
>> 22. *Valgrind heitir,*
>> *er stendr velli á*
>> *heilog fyr helgom dvrom;*
>> *forn er sv grind,*
>> *enn þat fáir vito,*
>> *hve hon er i lás vm lokin.*

> *Grímnismál, st. 22, Poetic Edda*

After the Conversion to Christianity, people were presented with two afterlife options, Heaven and Hell. Snorri's presentation of the Norse Pagan afterlife could easily be mistaken for a similar two-dimensional option, Valhǫll or Hel. From that perspective, the Christian version appears more fair, and I remember quite distinctly being taught in school that common Norsemen and women embraced the new religion because it gave them a hope for a blissful afterlife where the old religion only offered hope to those who died in battle. But the Pagan concepts of what happens after death were far more complex than that. We have already seen that Hel was a far more complex figure than Snorri's account allowed for, just as her afterlife realm is a far more complex place.

The belief in reincarnation may explain the image of the well into which the life-force of the dead continuously drips, while "rivers" of new life emerge from that same well. Such beliefs appear to have existed simultaneously with other beliefs in various afterlife realms. It is almost impossible to pinpoint one particular concept of the Pagan afterlife, as there appear to have existed many.

Apparently, whole clans may have lived on within certain mountains or mounds sacred to that clan, providing a link to the ancestors. Female ancestors may have lived on as Fylgjur, guardian spirits for their descendants. Male ancestors may have lived on as elves whose wisdom could be sought at the mounds where they had been buried. Even such ancestral spirits could eventually decide to be reborn as humans, often as their own descendants or name-sakes. The clue to understand Pagan concepts of the hereafter is to realize that the Pagan religion was not dogmatic, and that no texts were written down to ascertain one belief above the other, so we must assume that several different concepts may have existed side by side, and that they may easily have overlapped with one another. It is certainly possible that death was considered a complex affair of several stages or even several different options.

THE TWELVE HEAVENS (GRÍMNISMÁL)

"They say there is another heaven south of and above this heaven of ours, and that heaven is called Long Breath [Andlangr]; and that there is a third heaven still further above that one, and that place is called Wide Death [Viðbláinn]... only light-elves ... inhabit these places for the time being."

Snorri Sturluson, Skáldskaparmál, Prose Edda

In the Edda poem Grímnismál, Óðinn counts up twelve different "heavens", all spheres ruled by different gods. They could be called different worlds, different dimensions, different realms yet some of them are certainly also afterlife realms. It is impossible to know if these are all afterlife realms, but we should bear in mind that concepts of the soul's fate after death appear to have been fluid and varied. Some of these realms are definitely afterlife realms, and it is possible that they all are. However, each realm may be more than just afterlife realms they may represent various dimensions of being or states of perception.

It may appear that one realm leads to the next, or that the realms belong together as four trinities. Within each trinity, one realm corresponds to Mind, another to Passion/Intent, and a third to Spirit. Each trinity appears to represent a "higher" or "deeper" stage than the one before. The first heaven is Þrúðheimr [Power World], where Þórr rules "near the Aesir and the elves". It is obviously situated in the sky. In Chapter 2.8, I discussed Þór's realm as related to the electromagnetic field around Earth. In Chapter 10, I shall discuss the thundergod's role as a representative for the human mind. A bit later on in the same poem, we hear that Þór's hall has "five hundred roofs and forty" and that it is the greatest of all halls. The second heaven is Ydalir [Valleys of the Yew], also known as Alfheimr [Elf-World]. It is ruled by Freyr or his older aspect, Ullr. The reference to elves is in itself a powerful indicator that we are speaking of an afterlife realm.

The yew is a male tree and thus a metaphor for man. Freyr is also a representative for human passion. The third heaven is called Valaskialf [The Seat of the Choice], a silver-roofed hall made by a mysterious god simply called hin Ás ["the god"]. It is probably a reference to Óðinn, the foremost among the Aesir. As such, the three first heavens correspond with the three aspects of Óðinn, the Mind, the Passion and the Spirit where the Choice is made. The Choice is a reference to Váli, the Choice that put an end to Blind Strife. The fourth heaven is called Sǫkkvabekkr [Sunken River], where Óðinn and Saga drink happily from golden cups every day. Óðinn here corresponds with the Mind/Poetry, since he is paired with an aspect of his goddess wife called Saga [The Story (or the History)].

The happy fulfillment of drinking together from golden cups is a reference to the precious mead and the union between the male and the female aspect, to knowledge and completion. The Sunken River may be a reference to Frigg's realm Fensalar [Moist Halls] and/or to a realm of hidden knowledge. Since Frigg knows "all fate" and here goes by the name Story, it may represent a place where the entirety of fate and thus history, whether personal or universal, is known and embraced. The realm corresponds with the Mind aspect of the trinity. The fifth heaven is Gladsheimr [World of Happiness], where gold bright Valhǫll is situated, from where Óðinn as Hroptr [The Shattered One] chooses his chosen warriors each day. It is also in his aspect as The Shattered One that Óðinn received knowledge of the runes, as the Sígrdrífumál declares: "Through the Shattered One's Intent [húgr] they [the runes] ran".

The word for Intent is húgr, which refers to intent, thought, heart and passion. It is a place of passionate ecstasy, corresponding with Passion and Intent. The sixth world is Þrymheimr [The World of the Drum], associated with the giants Þrýmr and Þiazi. It is the realm where both Iðunn and Þór's hammer were hidden and retrieved, and is now ruled by Skaði, the bride of the gods. It corresponds with the Spirit aspect, a place of hidden, unknown treasures. The seventh heaven is Breidablik [Broad View], Baldr's abode. It is said to be the place with the fewest evil plots a place of broadmindedness. It corresponds with the Mind in a state of perfection. The eight is Himinbiorg [Heaven Fortress], where Heimdallr rules "the sanctuaries" [veom], the Great World's abode, where good mead is drunk in a comfortable hall. It corresponds with the Passion/Intent.

The ninth heaven is Freyia's heaven, where the Lady Sovereign rules "the seating of People Field [Folkvangr]" and chooses the chosen, as well as receives them. It corresponds with the Spirit, the realm of the chosen dead. The tenth heaven is Glitnir [The Glittering]. In the previous section, we saw that Hel was called the Goddess of Glitnir, which associates the place with an afterlife realm. It is both golden and silvery, and is a place where the god of justice, Forseti [Front Seat], puts an end to all quarrels. It is followed by the eleventh realm called Noatún [The Ships' Harbor], where the god Njǫrðr receives the "ships" of life. We have earlier identified this god with Aegir, the ruler of winds and waves, father to the rivers that bring forth the world and husband to Rán, who receives the drowned in her net. His place is actually Hlésey the Wind Shield Island a place of immortality, where the Valkyrie live, or the giantesses who gave birth to the present universe. The twelfth world is called Viðars land Viði "the Wide Land of Víðarr".

The name could mean "Wood Warrior", yet I am tempted to translate the name Víðarr as "The Expander" (from viða to expand, make wide). Víðarr the Silent is Óðins son by the giantess Gríðr [Truce]. This giantess acts as the mentor of Þórr in one of Snorri's stories, where Truce offers her sacred wand, her belt and her iron gloves to the thunder god, who has forsaken his own thunderbolt-gear. The gear of the giantess provides the same kind of power to hurl thunder and lightning. Her name may hint towards Skaði, who made a truce with the Aesir, or to the truce between the Vanir and the Aesir which led to the path of knowledge. In any case, the mysterious, silent god Víðarr appears to represent the silent expansion of the soul, being the only male deity who offers the precious mead alongside the goddess in the hall of Aegir. His realm is described as overgrown and unknown, but is the place where the "son will avenge the father". This is a reference to how Víðarr is the one god who will conquer the Wolf of Greed and bring about the new world after Ragnarǫk.

SNORRI'S TEN HEAVENS

Snorri has a different description of the various heavens or "worlds" [heimir]. In one place, he asserts that Hel rules in nine worlds. This could correspond with how Freyia is said to receive the chosen in the ninth world up until this stage, death rules in all the realms. This could mean that the three upper heavens the fourth and last trinity represent the immortal stages. However, his own account appears to count ten heavens where the tenth and highest heaven is a place of immortal light elves. I think it ought to remind us of the place where the Great Maiden sits beneath the Tree of Memory upon the Mountain of Medicine, dreaming while awaiting the return of her beloved surrounded by nine maidens. We have seen how the nine maidens may represent worlds previous worlds thus the Great Maiden would be the tenth world where immortality is attained.

In his Gylfaginning, Snorri describe the following heavens, the first is Hvergelmir [Mill/Cauldron Bellower], which belongs to Hel and Níflheimr. This is the place where all the moisture (life-force) from the consumed leaves of the world tree return, and from which all the rivers of life originate. It is obviously the first world of death. Hel [Death] is said to rule eight more worlds. The second is Mímisbrunnr [The Well of Memory] which belongs to the frost thurses and the giant of universal memory, Mímir, and where the eye of Óðinn and Heimdall's hearing is hidden. The third is Urðarbrunnr [The Well of Origin], from where the Norns continuously emerge to follow each individual through their lives. It is a place of rejuvenation and restoration possibly a way of describing reincarnation.

The fourth heaven is Alfheimr [The World of Elves], where the Light Elves dwell a blessed and sun-bright realm different from that of the Dark Elves, who live underground. A fifth heaven is Breidablik, Baldrs realm of broad perception, which Snorri identifies with Glitnir, the Glittering abode of Justice. The sixth heaven, according to Snorri, is Himinbiorg, which is not only Heimdall's abode but also the place where Bifrǫst [Shivering Voice] connects the world of the gods with the other worlds. It is often thought of as a rainbow bridge. The seventh heaven is Valaskialf [The Seat of the Choice] which Snorri believes was made by Óðinn and identifies with Hlíðskiǫlf [The Seat of Openings], the seat from which the seated one may look into all the worlds.

The eight heaven mentioned by Snorri is Gimlé [Glimmering] which in the Vǫluspá is identified as the place where deceit-free lineages shall dwell for all eternity after Ragnarǫk. In the Gylfaginning, Snorri lets Gangleri ask how this place will be spared the fires of Surtr. The High One mysteriously replies that there is a place south to and above Gimlé [the ninth] called Andlangr [Long Breath], and above that one a tenth, even higher heaven called Viðbláinn [Wide Death], where only Light Elves dwell. Somehow, the survival of the Glimmering abode of the righteous depends on these two higher realms. Unlike the Grímnismál, Snorri's account does not actually give a number to each of the worlds, so that his account of ten heavens and the chronological order in which they are presented may be coincidental, which would explain why the numbering differs from the Grímnismál source. Snorri's identification of some worlds, such as Glitnir with Breidablik, appears to be based on a different source.

7.5: Salvation-The old norse elysium

Freyia spoke:
1. "Wake, maiden among maidens, wake, my friend,
She-Wolf, sister! Who lives in the rock cave;
Now is the darkness of darkness itself
We ought to ride to Valhǫll and to the holy sanctuary."
     Freyia qvaþ:
     1. «Vaki mær meyia,
     vaki min vina,
     Hyndla systir!
     er i helli byr;
     nu er rauckr rauckra,
     rida vit skulum
     til Valhǫllr
     ok til vess heilags"

Hyndlulióð, st. 1, Poetic Edda

Concepts of salvation and alternative, blissful afterlives abound in ancient, Pagan religions, preceding the Christian concept of salvation by many centuries. Classical sources speak of ancient Greek concepts that appear to have similarities to Old Norse concepts, as we shall see. According to the Greek story-teller Homer, who lived sometime during the ninth century B.C.E, the blissful afterlife realm was called the Elysian fields or Elysium, and had a particular geographical location here in Earth, described as a place where heroes and other mortals belonged.

Later sources describe the place as an afterlife for the blessed, the righteous, those chosen by the gods, where they could live a blessed and happy life indulging in their favorite pastimes. The poet Hesiod (seventh century B.C.E) described Elysium as the "Isles of the Blessed" and as the "Fortunate Isles", whereas Pindar (522-443 B.C.E) spoke of a single island. Elysium is sometimes described as an island, or as various isles, but also as a plain or as fields. All describe the place as one of bliss, beauty, peace, pleasure and of music, art and inspiration. Many describe it as a place where good people are rewarded after death.

The Roman poet Virgil (70B.C.E.-19 B.C.E) claimed that there were two paths where souls go after death:

"Here comes the place where cleaves our way in two: Thy road, the right, towards Pluto's dwelling goes, and leads us to Elysium. But the left Speeds sinful souls to doom, and is their path to Tartarus the accursed." (Aeneid).

In the same work (the Aeneid), Virgil describes Elysium in further detail:

"In no fixed place the happy souls reside. In groves we live, and lie on mossy beds. By crystal streams that murmur through the meads...all the shining fields below. They wind the hill, and through the blissful meadows go."

The Classical concepts of Elysium were intimately connected to the Classical Mysteries. The Greek word mysteria simply means "to initiate" and the Mysteries were schools of initiation, sometimes called "cults" (Mystery cults) or "religions" (Mystery Religions). The oldest, known European Mystery School was situated in Eleusis near the city-state of Athens. The city-state itself supported the Temple economically. The Temple of Eleusis originated in a very ancient, cult like center of goddess worship primarily devoted to Demeter, the mother goddess, and her daughter Persephone, the corn maiden.

Archaeological finds show that the iconography of the goddesses and their symbolic attributes (the sow, the mare, the serpent, the cow, the hallucinogenic mushroom and the poppy, among other things) reach back thousands of years into prehistoric times around the area of Eleusis. Yet, the Temple and the Mysteries were said to have been introduced by emigrants from Crete, survivors of the catastrophe that destroyed the Minoan empire during the 15th century AD. Like the labyrinthine temple of Knossos in Crete had once been a thriving center of pilgrimage for Bronze Age Europe, Eleusis became a similar center of religious pilgrimage for the next two thousand years, until it was destroyed by Christian invaders (Goths, actually) in 392 AD.

Between the 15th century B.C.E and the 4th century AD, approximately two thousand people from all over the Classical world were initiated every year during the annual nine-day festival of Demeter at Eleusis. Both genders and all classes, even slaves, were admitted and could participate in the Mysteries, which also had three stages, one higher and more secret than the other. Most people were content with the first stage, where most of the procedures were quite public, except for the personal revelations that were supposed to happen during the climax of the initiation ritual. An ancient myth of how Demeter searched for her daughter, who had been abducted by Hades, the Lord of the Underworld, provided the great myth of the Mystery, where the initiate would walk in the footsteps of Demeter for nine days and nights, fasting and submitting to various trials.

It was said that the myth was a disguise for deep spiritual truths that could only be revealed to the initiate and which would not be truly understood by those who had not experienced the initiation. The true meaning of the myth would be revealed step by step to the initiate during the re-enactment. After the initiation, the reborn initiate would perceive the world, life, fate and death, in a different manner, having become purified and reached a higher state of awareness and knowledge. The initiate would now be able to know a different fate in death, a fate that would lead his or her soul to Elysium rather than to dark Hades. As such, the Mysteries provided a Pagan kind of salvation.

According to Goblet D'Alviella [The Mysteries of Eleusis, the Secret Rites and Rituals of the Classical Greek Mystery Tradition, 1981], the theology of the Mysteries went through different stages. He based the theory of the stages on the written evidence. The degree to which it is possible to prove that a concept existed at a particular time. I would say that the only thing the written evidence proves is that we have the first written evidence for a concept at certain times, it is entirely possible that the concepts themselves existed a long time before they were written down, or that concepts were written down in texts now lost to us.

The earliest evidence we have for a concept of resurrection and rebirth during initiation is dated to the 9th century B.C.E, where the highest purpose of the initiation at Eleusis was a kind of salvation where the initiate could look forward to a blessed and bright existence after death. During the 6th century B.C.E, we have the earliest evidence that the cult of Dionysus, earlier a cult open to women only, was integrated into the Eleusinian Mysteries. At the same time, we find evidence of the so-called "Orphic Doctrine" as an important part of the Mystery revelations.

The Orphic Doctrine was a Pantheist doctrine teaching that all gods and goddesses are but aspects of the great Supreme Being, called the Universal Life, the Universal Being, the Supreme Spirit or the All-Soul. The individual souls of people are temporary, separate parts of the original All-Soul. At Eleusis, the goddesses Demeter and Persephone, as well as the god Dionysus, are all mythological expressions of the All-Soul, the Ultimate Being. This Pantheist revelation was at the heart and core of the secret teachings that would be integrated into the soul and knowledge of the initiate during the initiation. It was no less than a school of salvation, where salvation involved the union of the individual soul with the Universal All-Soul.

APULEIUS' INITIATION AND THE OLD NORSE MYSTERIES

The Greek-Roman civilization represented two thousand years of Mysteries. Not only the Mysteries of Eleusis. Various schools and cults flourished all over the Hellenistic and Roman empires. One school that became immensely popular, almost to the point of becoming more popular than the Eleusinian, was the Mysteries of Isis. Isis began as an Egyptian goddess known as Aset. In the Hellenistic and Roman empires, she became known as Isis, and her adherents identified her as the ultimate face of the great Universal All-Soul.

All Mystery initiates recognized all deities as aspects of the Supreme Being and were inspired by other Mystery schools, so that it is difficult to see any actual differences between the theology of Isis and the theology of Demeter. Sometime around 180 B.C.E, an Algerian-Roman poet and priest of Isis known as Apuleius wrote a novel called The Golden Ass or Metamorphoses, where the Mystery initiation is described in as much detail as the Mysteries could allow. Some things would not be revealed to the uninitiated, but Apuleius let slip that what could not be said directly would be said in symbol and metaphor, through mythical and poetical language.

When I read Apuleius' work for the first time, I was struck by the immense similarity in structure and content between the Mysteries of Isis and the initiations described in the Poetic Edda. To sum up the journey of our Edda heroes and gods, much of which was described in Chapter 3. The initiation always began with a Vision Quest, where the hero would seek a vision of the bright golden maiden of the Underworld through some kind of ritual or meditative activity. The Vision follows, where the hero would usually see or hear of the golden lady.

She, or those who talk of her, would point out the path that he must follow. Then follows a Descent, where the hero moves into the Underworld. He is there faced with various trials, which I have called the Trial Theme. The Consecration involves the embrace of the goddess and the imparting of her wisdom, often symbolized by the precious mead. Then there is a Resurrection, where the initiate returns to the world, often with a new name or new profession such as king or sage. Often, he lives life with the Guidance of the golden goddess, until he dies when he experiences Salvation through the love of the goddess. The exact same structure is described in Apuleius' initiation journey.

The hero, Lucius, seeks a vision by ritually immersing himself seven times in the ocean during the night of a full moon. The ritual cleansing is accompanied by intense prayer. The Quest is followed by a Vision, where the goddess reveals herself before him through the night sky and the full moon. He learns that she is the primary mover of the universe and the true identity behind all goddesses, and the mother of all gods.

Just like in the Norse myths, the goddess then points out the direction that young Lucius must take next seeking the Mysteries of Isis. Only then will Lucius [Light] be able to restore his human shape, much like Helgi must seek the path of initiation in order to earn his true name, Helgi [The Sacred One]. Lucius seeks the Mysteries, and after initial preparations and guidance from an ancient priest of Isis called Mithras, he is allowed to take the initiation, which is described as a voluntary death and a descent into the Underworld:

> *"I approached the borders of death, I put my foot on the doorsteps of Persephone, I traveled through all the elements and returned, I saw the sun by midnight, shining in a white light, I came close to the gods of the higher and lower regions, and worshiped them in their closeness...*
> *Both the keys to the gates of the Underworld, as well as the guarantee of Salvation were in the hands of the Goddess; The Initiation itself was like a voluntary death and a gracious salvation."*

The philosopher Plutarch described the experience of dying and compared the experience of the soul at death with the experiences of the initiates during a Mystery initiation. The soul wanders around in tiring circles, on scary roads through absolute darkness that lead nowhere, and then, just before the final end to all cruelties the soul experiences panic, perspiration and trembling. Then a wonderful light approaches the soul, it is met by clean spheres and fields that welcomes the soul with sacred words and sacred sights, and there the initiate will, now in its most perfect form, free of bondage, wander about, crowned with laurel, celebrating great festivals with others of sacred, pure souls. After such an experience, Plutarch concludes, the initiate will look at the uninitiated with new eyes and see all their impurity. The revelations of the Underworld are described in symbol and metaphors, and one central theme is highly recognizable from Norse initiation myths.

The concept of the light within the darkness, the "sun by midnight", and the appearance of the gracious, savior goddess just as the darkness of death descends upon the soul. In Apuleius' account, the Savior Goddess declares that she will forever provide guidance in life for her initiate, and that she will save and deliver his soul after death, exactly in the manner of the Valkyrie of the heroic Eddas:

> *"You shall live blessed in this world, you shall live in honor through my guidance and my protection, and when, after your given life-span, you descend into the Underworld, you shall see me there, shining."*

Isis as Creator and Savior made her the hardest competition to Christianity towards the end of the Pagan era. By then she was the most popular deity of all, offering her worshipers salvation, healing miracles and a deep religious experience of unity with the divine. When Bishop Cyril argued his successful doctrine of Virgin Mary at Ephesus, 431 AD, he was struggling hard against the faith in Isis and the popular Gnostic belief that Mary and Isis shared the same basic characteristics and that they were ultimately the same. As R.E. Witts describes it in his work Isis in the Graeco-Roman World (1971): "A bitter struggle had to be fought before the Greek-Roman world at last accepted Jesus instead of Isis."

THE NORSE "ISIS" AND THE GOLDEN HALL

Norse myths and folklore reveals a complexity of thought about the afterlife, but the Edda poems appear to insist on one particular concept where death is represented by a female, and where that female ultimately has to do with fate. Fate is not just the fate of life, but also the fate after death. As we have seen, the "death-woman" in various guises was a widespread and well-known concept from other sources as well.

In Chapter 3, we explored the "maiden with the mead", and we have been touching upon her realm on several instances. Summing up, we can safely say that the bright, golden hall of the mead-woman is situated in the dark depths of the Underworld, the realm of the dead. Like Isis and any other Mystery deity can boast of a single identity behind countless aspects, the mead-serving maiden of the Eddas may change name, status and appearance, yet remains, ultimately, the same. A powerful entity that provides light within darkness, life within death, and resurrection to the initiate who is accepted into her hall after overcoming the trials of the dark realm.

As we have seen, the basic structure of initiation and salvation is identical to those that are revealed in Classical Mystery initiations. In the Norse sources, the darkness and the oblivion of death is often represented by a wizened and omniscient old ogress who may reveal her infinite knowledge to the residents of and visitors to Hel, yet will work against any attempt to return to life with the memory of that knowledge, whether it be in this life or in the next incarnation. The ogress is represented in myth and in art as a wolf-riding ogress using serpents for reins and the myths show that she is the most powerful of all entities more powerful, even, than the strongest of gods. After all, she is that power which not even gods can bend, the ultimate fate, which is death. The ogress of oblivion is only countered by the "Great Maiden", the bright, life-giving, rejuvenating face of Hel, and her gift of mead is the gift of memory of the whole self even as the body dies.

The importance of this bright golden maiden in Old Norse myths has been obsessively ignored for centuries on end, yet once she has been pointed out it should be obvious that the maiden with the mead and her realm are central to our understanding of Norse myths, and probably to our understanding of Old Norse Paganism, and particularly to Old Norse concepts of death and salvation. I believe that the Ogress and the Maiden represent to different kinds of fates after death, a death that leads to total oblivion of the self, and the fate that leads to resurrection.

Whether it is a resurrection into a better life where the previous lives are remembered and thus may be learned from, or into a better afterlife, resurrection into a realm where the soul may live in a blissful state in proximity to the divine realities. In Chapter 3, I have given several examples of the golden abode of the mead woman. There is no need to repeat all the descriptions or point out once more all the details which show that they are basically the same. There is no doubt that the Maiden with the Mead may hide behind a wide variety of female entities yet is, ultimately, always the same. It is tempting to suggest that the Pantheism of the Classical Mysteries, which we know date back to at least the fifth century B.C.E in Europe, if not much earlier, found its way into Scandinavia at some point in history.

The Pantheist unity of the Norse goddesses could easily be a far older concept. Such Pantheist concepts of the goddesses find correspondence in what little we know of Pagan goddess celebrations. During the annual dísablót [Sacrifice to the Goddesses], all the female powers were worshiped together as a collective. Yet the temple that was raised in honor of this celebration was called Dísarsalinn "The Hall of the Goddess" emphasizing the one dís, the one, unifying goddess. The Old Norse word for female powers, Dísir, is etymologically linked to the Old Indian word dhisana. The dhisanas were goddesses of abundance, intelligence and fertility, linked to Aditi, the goddess of infinity.

The dhisanas are described as the wives of the gods and as the guardians of the holy soma the nectar of immortality. Most importantly is the idea that the plural dhisanas are really just aspects of the one great Dhisana. The conceptual and etymological link between the Scandinavian Dísir and the Indian dhisanas may be five thousand years old. Snorri explained that one goddess could be disguised in poetry by using the name of any other goddess.

Thus any goddess or female entity would serve the function of All-Soul yet the Mysteries all seem to have favored one particular goddess as the face of the Great All. If there were Mysteries in Scandinavia, who, then, would be the ultimate Norse Viking Age candidate for the great Universal Being? Who would ultimately have represented the All-Soul that hides behind the other giantesses, Valkyrie, Norns and goddesses of the Edda lore?

When Óttarr of the Hyndlulióð sacrificed to the plural goddesses, the one goddess appeared before him. Freyia, whose name, it should be pointed out, is not a name at all but a title, "The Lady Sovereign". To understand what the Golden Hall is, we need only remember this most basic feature of Old Norse poetry. That one thing may be described in endless variation, that one place or one character will be disguised behind other places and other characters, recognizable through attributes and function.

Rather than repeating all the descriptions of the High Hall of the Golden Goddess, I shall simply suggest, based on the previous accounts, that the Golden Hall within the darkness can be identified as the hall of the great dís Freyia, where she receives the Vál the Chosen dead. Snorri describes Freyia's hall in Gylfaginning, and quotes from the Edda poem Grímnismál, where we learn that Freyia rules the "seating of the hall" in "People Field", choosing and receiving the einherjar the chosen dead before half the chosen are sent to Óðinn:

> "Freyia is the greatest among the Ásyniur. She owns that court in heaven that is called People Field [Folkvangr]. And whenever she rides to a battlefield, she owns half of the Chosen, and Óðinn owns the other half, as it is said here [quotes from Grímnismál st. 14]: (...) Her hall, Room-For-Seats [Sessrumnir], is large and beautiful..."

In the Flateyjarbók, we also hear about Freyia's hall:

> "She owned a hall that was so beautiful and so powerful that people said that if the door was locked and closed, nobody could enter unless she wanted it so."

Freyia's hall sounds conspicuously like that of Gerðr or Menglǫð, which will only open if the lady within wishes it so. The only ones who may enter the Golden Hall are those who have conquered their fears, their hatred, their greed, and displayed their courage and wisdom during the Underworld journey. The Golden Hall is the place where the initiate is united with the goddess and where he may receive the precious, ancient Mead of Memory, the Mead of Poetry, or the Mead of Knowledge.

As we have shown, the Golden Hall is associated with the three wells of the three roots of the World Tree: The Well of Memory, the Well of Origin, and the Well of Hel. The embrace of the goddess and the drinking of the mead ultimately lead to the resurrection of the initiate, the initiate returns from death carrying the knowledge that was previously hidden in the Underworld. Upon return to life, the initiate will be a sage, a poet, a king, a witch or a sorcerer. In actual death, the Lady of Valland would save her chosen from oblivion in Hel. As the Hyndlulióð strongly suggests, one important result of the initiation journey and the precious mead would be to become an Einheri a Sole Ruler a resident of Valhǫll.

LIFE IN VALHǪLL

In the Gylfaginning, Snorri offers a description of Valhǫll:

> "Gangleri [Wandering Learning] asked: "You say that all who have fallen in battle from the origin of the worlds, now have arrived at Óðinn in Valhǫll. What does he have to give them for food? I think there must be a great deal of people there."

The High One said: "It is true, what you are saying, there is a great deal of people there, and larger it grows, and still it seems too small when the wolf comes, but never is there so many people in Valhǫll that they do not get enough food out of the boar called Sæhrimnir [Water Burner]; he is cooked every day, and is whole again come evening. The question you put forth, I believe that few people are wise enough to truly answer. Andhrimnir [Breath/Spirit Burner] is the name of the cook, and Eldhrimnir [Fire Burner] is the name of the cauldron.

Thus it is spoken of this [Grímnismál, st. 18]:

23. Five hundred doors and forty more, I believe there is in Valhǫll eight hundred Sole Rulers go through each door at the same time when they go to fight the Witness [Fenrir]	*23. Fimm hvndrvþ dvra oc vm fiorom togom, sva hygg ec á Valhallo vera; átta hvndrvþ eínheria ganga senn or einom dvrom, þa er þeir fara við Vítni at vega*

Yes, few will ever know what truly nourishes the Einheri the vál the Chosen resident of Valhǫll. The stereotypical notion of this place as a paradise for primitive brutes with a taste for eating, drinking, sexy serving maids and ongoing fights is hard to overcome. This stereotype is stubbornly repeated in everything from popular media to serious research papers. It is an appealing and humorous image that is brought to mind, one that serves to emphasize an image of the barbarian, primitive brute of a Viking. Today, it is my experience that Scandinavian intellectuals and teachers will put on an embarrassed grin before repeating the image, chuckling condescendingly.

Neo-Pagans embrace the stereotype with cheerful toasts, and Christians present it as an example of why their own religion is spiritually superior. Apparently, the chosen dead drink large quantities of alcohol that stream from the teats of a she-goat called Heiðrún, served by sexy bar-maids (the Valkyrie), and gorge themselves on the meat of a boar that resurrects itself every day, only to be cooked once more come morning. The eternal banquet takes place after a happy day of fighting, as Snorri later describes: "...what entertainments have the Sole Rulers when they are not drinking?" The High One said: "Every day when they have dressed themselves, they take their army-gear and walk out into the courtyard and fight and kill each other, this is their entertainment.

When it is time for dinner, they ride home to Valhǫll and sit down at the table, as it is said here [Vafþrúðnismál, st. 41]:

41. "All Sole Rulers in Óðin's courtyard clash in battle every day they choose the Chosen and ride from the strife then sit together in peace."	*41. «Allir einherjar Oðins tvnom i ha/ggvaz hverian dag; val þeir kiosa oc riþa vígi fra, sitia meirr vm sáttir saman.»*

As Snorri may have been the first to point out, there are messages that have been cunningly disguised in symbols throughout both his own Prose Edda and in the Edda poetry. The happy-go-lucky image of an afterlife for burly warriors may be based on popular notions that actually existed during the Viking Age. Such imagery may very well have served the purpose of spurring on men who were expected to face death in battle and show little fear while doing so. Another image that may have served such a function is the imagery of joyful sexual encounters with death-women.

To ease the horrors of an actual battle situation by emphasizing a joyful afterlife of (consequence-free) battles, booze and babes would have been the main purpose of the war band's skald. However, as the cryptic remarks of Edda poetry suggest, the funny, yet superficial image of Valhǫll is an allegory, a metaphorical disguise for deeper spiritual truths. As the Edda poetry suggest, the path to Valhǫll was not as simple as the act of dying in battle. Helgi had to conquer the giants Hatred and Rage Ocean before he could conquer the ogress of death and see her replaced with the glorious Valkyrie bride who would save his soul in death. He had to return to life once more when he failed the battle of the Rock of Greed, and go through the same initiation challenges before he could finally achieve residence in Valhǫll. His younger brother, Sígurðr, had to go through similar, severe trials of initiation, and his escape from dark Hel depended on the rescue of his Valkyrie bride.

Óttarr had to seek the knowledge of the Underworld and remember it before he could actually claim his "heritage" the "gold" of Valland. The Edda poetry clearly suggests that the path to Valhǫll in death depended on a path of initiation during life. Some, like Svípdagr of the Fjǫlsvinnsmál, would find bliss in the embrace of the Great Maiden others, like Óttarr of the Hyndlulióð, would be taken by the goddess Freyia to the hall of Óðinn. These two possible situations of afterlife bliss are mentioned in the Grímnismál stanza 14, where we learn that Freyia owns half of the chosen, and Óðinn the other. The importance of the initiation is a powerful clue to read all the details about Valhǫll as spiritual parables. First of all, we have the eternal battle. By all accounts, the Sole Rulers of Valhǫll engage in a daily battle. Every day, they fight all day and kill each other.

Then they are restored to life and return to the hall where they feast and drink with their enemies. It is of course easy to see in this image a rather rough opinion of a "paradise" seen from the view of Viking warriors, thinking of battle as fun and glory, despising death. A healing of enmities seems to take place during the banquet. However, it is also possible to see the situation as a metaphor for reincarnation where life on Earth is seen as an eternal, repetitive battle. The battle, after all, happens in "Óðin's court", which could easily be a metaphor for the world and for Earth. One name for Earth is Fjǫrgyn, which could translate as Life Battle. Saxo Grammaticus, who wrote his chronicles in the early 13th century AD, tells the tale of the hero Hadding, whom Óðinn has guided to the Underworld. There, they see two armies fighting.

Óðinn tells Hadding that: "...these are they, who having been slain by the sword, declare the manner of their death by a continual rehearsal, and enact the deeds of their past life in a living spectacle." Hadding has been shown the true after-life fate of the warrior. In the Flateyjarbók, there is the story of the maiden Hildr [Battle] which is also retold in other chronicles and which I discussed in the previous chapter. Hildr is the name of a Valkyrie representing the Fate of battle. Hildr was distressed because her father and her lover were fighting each other. Every night, she walked among the slain warriors and raised them back to life with her spell-songs. Thus, the battle never ended. Hildr, torn by two sides, expresses a wish for settlement and will not let the warriors die properly as long as they are fighting each other but for each resurrection the battle is played out anew.

A better metaphor for a concept of karma in reincarnation can hardly be found. Hildr is another representation of Freyia, who earlier in the story caused the battle to begin because Óðinn forced her to do so if she wanted her Necklace of Flames back. She, as the goddess of fate, was thus tricked into making two kings fight each other for all eternity until a third would appear that would cease all battle. When this happens, the goddess who may represent the Universal Soul will have her symbol of completion back. I have suggested that the two kings fighting each other are symbols of the Passion, and the Thought aspect of the soul, whereas the Third is the Spirit, who has been driven into exile. Until the Spirit returns with the necklace of completion and reunites with his true wife, the goddess, the battle will continue throughout the ages. This is a situation that exists within the individual as well as in the world at large.

A battle can be a metaphor for life itself, just as the Earth goddess is called "Life Battle". Óðinn says that he sends his Intent and his Memory [Húginn and Múninn] every day into the "battlefield" of Earth into life itself. When someone dies in "battle", the Chosen ones are received into the splendid halls of the goddess Freyia. She will keep half of the Chosen to herself in those beautiful halls, but the other half are set to Óðinn and his Valhǫll. Those who are admitted into the golden hall of the goddess may find peace. The Fjǫlsvinnsmál poem strongly suggests that the soul will be reincarnated no more once it has returned to its true union and remembered its true self. In Valhǫll, on the other hand, the souls reenact the battles of their lives. They are called the einherjar [The Sole Rulers]. The title could signify that they rule only one, themselves. Before the doors of Valhǫll, there is a tree called Glasir, whose leaves are of gold. It is of course the divine gold of wisdom that shines on that tree. The meaning of the name Glasir has to do with shine, crystal or glass symbols of brightness and illumination.

As Snorri says it:

"Glasir stands with golden leaves, before the halls of the victorious gods"

In Valhǫll, the Sole Rulers are given the precious mead of wisdom, poetry and immortality, served by the Valkyrie and milked from the she-goat Heiðrún Bright Rune/Symbol. The She-goat is Freyia, the All-Soul, who brews the mead within herself after taking her nourishment from the "leaves" of the World Tree, the lives of the departed. The meaning of the mead was thoroughly explored in Chapter 3, and its ingredients had much to do with the ingredients of universal creation. Like the Great World itself, the mead was brewed and made to grow by the power of Earth, the cold cool Sea, and the blood of the Reconciliation. The Sole Rulers are also given a very special meal, as is said in the Grímnismál, st. 18: "Andhrimnir cooks Sæhrimnir in Eldhrimnir".

Let us take a look at the stanzas again, this time with a translation of the names of the cook, the boar and the cauldron: "Spirit/Breath Burner cooks Water/Sea Burner in Fire Burner". The word hrímnir may mean either "burner" or "freezer". The most common interpretation is "burner". Obviously, the word points towards an alchemical process of changing substance into something else, either by freezing it or by burning it. Spirit/Breath, Sea/Water and Fire are also symbolical but of what? Let me suggest that the symbolical meanings of the cook, the boar and the cauldron have something to do with creation as well. In the beginning, back before creation, there were three realms.

The icy Mist World [Níflheimr], the fiery Muspell, and the empty, "breezeless" Mouth of the Sacred Descendants [Ginnunga Gap]. Creation happened as streams from the two realms of hot and cold met within the Mouth. The heat melted the cold and vibration issued, growing into the great, primeval Sound [Ymir]. The sea, the water element, comes from the Misty World of the dead, the source of all rivers. The resurrecting "boar" represents the transformation of the water element within the "cauldron" which represents the transformation of the fire element. Fire comes from the hot regions of fire and acid. During creation, these two opposites met within the empty Mouth the origin of breath, and grew there.

In the secret "meal" of the Sole Ruler, the transformation of the Breath, which in Old Norse equals Spirit, is the "cook" that causes the resurrection. There is no way that this process of resurrection can be explained in simple terms. Suffice it to say that the mysterious "meal" of the Sole Rulers of Valhǫll involves an alchemical process of transformation that repeats the resurrection of the early Universe within the individual after death. In my opinion, Valhǫll represents, primarily, a place of transformation and resurrection.

The image of Óðinn seated in the hall of the Chosen is one of the perfect Spirit, who rules his actions, his desires, his intent and his memory. The Grímnismál poem as well as Snorri emphasized how Óðinn sits in Valhǫll between his two wolves or his two ravens. The wolves are called Geri and Freki. The name Geri is derived from the verb gera, "to do". The name Freki has to do with "desire" or "gluttony". The wolves of Óðinn represent the Spirit's Action [the Doer], and the Spirit's Desire. The two ravens represent "The Intent" [Húginn] and The Memory [Múninn].

The Spirit feeds his "wolves", yet drinks only wine himself, the precious mead. One important detail that may allow us to understand the deeper function of the transformation that takes place in Valhǫll is the purpose of the Sole Rulers. To ride out with Óðinn on the day of the final battle, which to the individual would be the day of death. The great battle stands between Spirit and the wolf of Greed. The Spirit may be consumed, yet will be "avenged" by the son, Víðarr, the silent expansion of consciousness that eventually conquers Greed.

THE CRYSTAL FIELDS

Þórr spoke:
21."Tell me now, All-Wise!
About everything in life:
I expect, dwarf, that
you know: what is that
Tranquility called that shall
lie within every world?"

All-Wise spoke:
22"Tranquillity it is called
among humans
Quenching among gods
Wind-less among Vanir
Death-Air with the giants
Day-Ceasing among elves
Day-Peace among dwarfs."

Allvìsmàl, st. 21-22, Poetic Edda

Þórr qvaþ:
21.«Segðv mer þat, Alvíss!
oll of rauc fira
voromc, dvergr! at vitir:
hve þat logn heitir,
er liggia scal,
heimi hveriom i?»

22«Logn heitir eþ monnom,
enn Logi meþ goðom,
kalla Vindslot vanir,
Ofhlý jotnar,
alfar Dagseva,
kalla dvergar Dags Vero.»

Old Norse equivalents of the Elysian fields actually abound. There is the golden hall of the goddess, and there is Valhǫll, both places where resurrection take place. They may be identified with or perhaps be points of entry into the shining fields of immortality that appear in other terms such as the Glasisvellir, meaning the Shining Fields. These fields are also encountered in the Helgi poems, then called the Rǫdullsvellir, which means the same.

There are also other concepts in Norse mythology such as the Ódainsakr, literally the "Field of the Immortals", as well as the Iðavǫllr, a field where the "streams return to source", in fact the place where the gods once met in order to create the cosmic order, and where the children of the gods will meet again after the end of this world. Ásgarðr, the World of the Aesir, is another divine afterlife, where the center is the Well of Origin, from which a soul will come out transparently bright and shining. Another description is Gimlé, which means "Fire-Shielded", and Glitnir, "Glittering", as Snorri described them:

> "One place is called Wide Perception [Breidablik], and no fairer place is there. Also there is one called Glittering [Glitnir], and its walls and columns and pillars are of red gold (...) There is also a place called Seat of the Choice [Valaskialf]. That place is Óðin's (...) and is there in this hall that the Seat of Openings [Hlíðskiǫlf] is, the throne of that name. And when All-Father sits on that throne he can see out over all the world. At the southernmost end of heaven is the hall which is fairest of all and brighter than the Sun, and it is called Shimmering [Gimlé]. It shall stand when both heaven and Earth have passed away, and in that place shall live good and righteous people for ever and ever."

When the present world-story is finished, the gods and the illuminated Light elves will gather at the Wind-Shielded Island of Immortality, the Hlésey, where they will gather and drink the precious mead of memory, and memorize the history of the world, the sacred story.

8: THE WAY OF THE WAND-WITCH

8.1: RESTORING THE WISE WOMAN

"Granny turned slowly in her seat to look at the audience. They were staring at the performance, their faces rapt. The words washed over them in the breathless air. This was real. This was more real even than reality. This was history. It might not be true, but that had nothing to do with it.

Granny had never had much time for words. They were so insubstantial. Now she wished that she had found the time. Words were indeed insubstantial. They were as soft as water, but they were also as powerful as water and now they were rushing over the audience, eroding the levees of veracity, and carrying away the past.

That's us down there [on stage], she thought. Everyone knows who we really are, but the things down there are what they'll remember three gibbering old baggages in pointy hats. All we've ever done, all we've ever been, won't exist anymore (…) Whoever wrote this Theater knew about the uses of magic. Even I believe what's happening, and I know there's no truth in it."

Terry Pratchett: Wyrd Sisters

After centuries of witch-hunts and methodical, indeed systematic tarnishing of the reputation of wise and crafty women we might find it hard to even recognize the tremendous importance of the wise woman, the witch of the Pagan European tradition. Even to this day, the archetypal wise woman tends to be presented as an hysterical, ridiculous old woman pestering her surroundings with superstitions, warts and a high-pitched, screeching voice, or as an evil stepmother whose beauty is the result of illusory magic. The precious mead of knowledge that she once brewed became a slimy, stinking mass consisting of dead frogs and fetuses. Her wand of authority became a broomstick on which she rode to orgies with the Devil.

The fact is that the Pagan world of ancient Europe revered a dignified group of highly educated women well versed in herb lore, medicine, and magic, who were regarded as keepers of ancient wisdom and guardians of sacred initiations. In Scandinavia, these were the vǫlur the wand-carrying priestesses who traveled the world, offering their services which could range from anything to oracular divination to healing, witchcraft and spiritual guidance. These women were highly respected wherever they went, and were above or beyond the normal hierarchy of society. I have described the vǫlur and their art of seiðr on several occasions in this book, so this chapter will only add a little to what has already been said. To fully cover the role and character of the vǫlva would take a whole book. The most famous vǫlva of the Icelandic sagas is probably Litilvǫlva [The Little Witch], the last of a group of nine witches that came with the Icelandic settlers to Greenland during the 10th century.

Her name was Þorbjǫrg, and she is described as the leader of a ritual of seiðr performed by the women on a farm in the Eirik Saga Rauða. Several other sagas describe vǫlur and their rituals, but the story of The Little Witch is particularly interesting because it indicates that people would bring with them as coven or a veritable priesthood when they emigrated to new places. A similar scenario appears to have taken place according to Gothic legends of how the Goths emigrated from southern Scandinavia (possibly from Gotland in south Sweden) to the Baltic area, possibly sometime during the first century B.C.E. Apparently, these proto-Goths brought with them a group of women that the scribe Jordanes in his Getica (551 AD) called haliurunnae.

The Getica was written in Latin, so the term haliurunnae is a Latinized form of some old Gothic or Norse title. I would suggest that the Latinized word is derived from an original helju-rúnar. Helju- would be the genitive singular form of the name Hel, a goddess later known as the queen of the Underworld. Rúnar is the plural form of the word rún, which means "letter", "symbol" or "secret". The title would refer to women who knew the secrets of the goddess Hel, the secrets of death, the Underworld and the initiation. It could well have been a title worn by those we otherwise known as the vǫlur. The haliurunnae are only mentioned in Getica because they were expelled from the tribe after having been accused of performing "necromancy" and "black magic" by their king, Filimer.

Five hundred years later, the Goths believed that the conquering Huns were the descendants of these women, come to avenge their fore-mothers. The expulsion of the priestesses had obviously left its mark, and I believe the event should be regarded as a change of religion. After the Goths let go of their wise women in favor of the King's monopoly of power, their religion changed, and they were the first German tribe to embrace Christianity. Most other German tribes, however, maintained and cherished their wise women. Votive altars from Iron Age Europe show thousands of oracular priestess-goddesses and groups of so-called matronae [mothers], goddesses who had their real life counterparts in institutions of priestesses who played an important role as counselors to the tribes.

The institution of the priestesses was common both from the Celtic and the Germanic areas. Vǫlur abound in the Poetic Edda. There is the incredibly ancient vǫlva of the Vǫluspá who remembers a time before the present world existed. She is followed by the vǫlva Gullveigr-Heiðr, who introduces initiation and who is identified as Freyia. Freyia is the prototype of a vǫlva, the priestess and spiritual mentor of the gods. Óðinn seeks an unnamed vǫlva in the poem Vegtamskvíða, where the old woman is buried to the east of the Hel-gate and must be made to rise from the dead. Another dead vǫlva is invoked in the Gróagalðr, and then there is Hyndla of the Hyndlulióð. In Snorri's Edda, the vǫlva Gróa heals the wounds of Þórr after a battle, and another wand-carrying vǫlva, Gríðr, acts as the Thunder god's mentor. It is the only place where we hear that the function of her sacred wand is described.

Detail from the Oseberg tapestry (Norway 834 AD) showing two females performing ritual movements and three swastikas (ancient symbols of the Sun goddess). The Oseberg ship burial was the grave of two women who may have been witches or priestesses.

It possesses the same power of creating lightening as the hammer Miǫllnir. In the heroic poetry, the Burgund princess Guðrún learns how to weave fate while staying in the realm of the Norns, and her mother Grímhildr has obviously learned the art before her, since she is able to read into her own weave what her daughter is shaping.

Guðrún later displays her ability to put her hand into boiling water without any harm coming to her, and to make a hall full of warriors fall asleep. Archaeology shows that vǫlur indeed existed and were buried with their sacred gear, particularly the wand. The great ship burial of Oseberg, Norway, appears to have been the grave of two high-standing vǫlur, buried in 834 AD.

It was the most splendid grave ever known from the Viking Age, surpassing even that of Sutton Hoo. In this Chapter follows two transcripts from two YouTube videos, one dealing with the vǫlur in general, and the other dealing with evidence of initiation rituals where witches may have been the mentors of young men, as indicated by several sagas.

8.2: THE VǪLVA'S PATH

We are seeing that the Edda myths are composed as parables using metaphors, where what appears to be a straightforward story may hide many deeper levels of meaning. The other side of the coin is that what appears as very imaginative fairy tales may also cover up very straightforward tales. We are now speaking of rather down-to-Earth and literal descriptions of Pagan rituals hiding within the structure of the parables that are the myths. We will now begin to reveal the underlying structures of the myths and give a little taste of how almost all the myths of the entire Poetic Edda collection may be read as accounts of such ritual. I am talking about one level of these myths now, as said before, the myths may be read on several levels.

One level may be read like a manual on how initiation rituals were conducted, offering a variety and at the same time, telling their story and how they originated. One of my first revelations during my initial studied of the Poetic Edda was that the poems read together actually take the form of a monograph, and may be read as a book. I do not believe the Edda was in any way a random collection of poems. I believe that the poems, whatever their origin, were placed in a sensible sequencedesigned to reveal the story of the great ritual of initiation that was at the heart of a genuine Old Norse Pagan mystery cult. The first poem of the Poetic Edda is the Vǫluspá, the Prophecy of the Witch.

It tells the story of our present universe from the beginning to the end, mentioning, of course, only very important events in cosmic history, things that affected the destiny of the entire the Cosmos. It is an introduction to all the other poems, and also a summary. Everything that is mentioned in the Vǫluspá is repeated throughout the subsequent poems. Now, among these great cosmic events is the story of the burning of a witch called Gullveigr. Her name is derived from gull, gold or golden, and veigr, which means a strong beverage, a drink, and it may also just mean power. Gold is a metaphor for divine light and knowledge, so the name of the witch indicates what she represents, the power of divine knowledge, or else identifying her as the precious mead, indeed a golden drink of cosmic memory and knowledge, which is so important in the myths.

Now, the Vǫluspá tells how the witch is burned and stabbed in the Hǫll Hárs the Hall of the High One meaning the Hall of Óðinn. Now, before we go on accusing Óðinn of being a patriarchal witch-burning old scoundrel, we need to stop and look at what he and the witch represent, metaphorically. Óðinn has a name that identifies him as Spirit, as Poetry, as Frenzy. He is the giver of breath to women and men. He is spirit, he is breath, he is inspiration, he is poetry, he is passion, and he, in short, is life. We are all Óðinn, he is present in all of us, and he is our breath and our spirit, and everything Óðinn does in the myths is being spirit, and what he does in the myths is learning, perpetually.

He is that in us which makes us continually seek knowledge and new learning. He is that which scrutinizes everything. He is that which wants, and wants more than anything else, to know, and from his quest for knowledge, the universe spins into a grand saga, thus the meaning of poetry in his name. His hall is the hall of spirit, which I would say, giving an educated guess, is the world or on a micro cosmic level, the "hall" of each individual. What happens here is something that happens in us as individuals, and in the world at large.

21. *She remembers the first war in the world*
When Gold Drink was hoist on the spears and in the High One's hall they burned her
Three times they burned the Three Times Born often, not seldom [did they burn her] yet she still lives!

21.*Þat man hon fólkvíg fyrst í heimi,*
er Gullveigr geirum studdu
ok í hǫll Hárs hana brendu;
þrysvar brendu þrysvar borna,
opt, ósjaldan,
þó hon enn lifir

22. *She was called Bright One/ Illuminated One, when she came to the settlements [of people]*
The well-divining witch she could cast spells, she did seiðr wherever she could she did seiðr with a playful intent
She was always loved by wicked women.

22.*Heiði hana hétu,*
hvars til húsa kom,
vǫlu velspá,
vitti hon ganda,
seið hon hvars hon kunni,
seið hon hugleikin,
æ var hon angan illrar brúðar.

Now what happens? Well, in the "Hall of Spirit", Divine Knowledge [Gullveigr] is being burned and stabbed. The witch has been identified as Freyia in this book so many times that, in short, she is Freyia, the Goddess, in her aspect as cosmic witch and pure knowledge, and if he is the spirit that seeks knowledge, she is the soul that contains knowledge. There are so many reasons to say this and one of these reasons is what Óðinn and the goddess as Frigg, his wife, represent. It is said that while Óðinn seeks knowledge, Frigg knows all. A perfect match, you might say, however, it is then said that Frigg does not speak.

So her poor husband has to find out everything on his own (there wouldn't be any fun otherwise now would there?). So, what is going on in this Hall of the Spirit? A witch is being burned, and stabbed, and then she resurrects. She resurrects not only once, but three times, indeed, countless times. She is, in short, immortal. She is the soul, and all this happens in the presence of that which wants to understand. Óðinn [The Breath] who is not immortal. That, I think, is the highest level of this myth. On a more literal level, let us just imagine Óðinn and the Aesir as a group of gods, who watched a witch being burned in their hall, and then watched how she conquer death as the first being in the universe to do so. Now as the gods eventually let the Goddess leave the hall, realizing that nothing will kill the immortal one, they observe how she walks out into the world, now bearing a new name and a new role.

She has become Heiðr, the Bright One, or we may say the Enlightened One, perhaps. She proceeds by traveling the world, teaching all the unconventional women, the wicked ladies, how to conquer death and rule fate, how, in short, to perform the art of seiðr, which is fate magic, the most powerful magic there is. She teaches witchcraft to the women, and serves the communities like a witch. This is a story of initiation. It follows the basic structure of a Pagan, a shamanic initiation ritual known to the entire world. A structure that involves symbolic death, a symbolic resurrection, and then a restoration to society with a new role, a new name, and a new profession.

This is probably a description of how the initiation of a witch was perceived. I don't mean to say that the poor novice witches were literally burned. The burning must be metaphorical, but that the witch experienced a sort of spiritual trial by fire in the halls of the gods before she was considered ready to serve the community. The myth tells the story of how the first witch did this. The first witch was the goddess herself, and she taught it to the women, to those women who were "wicked" enough to choose witchcraft rather than being a wife. The fact that this story is given two whole stanzas in a rather short poem that describes all the important cosmic events also shows that the theme was important to the whole Cosmos, or at least to the Cosmos of the religious community that created the myth.

Indeed, witches, the vǫlur, were important women in Old Norse society, and they had been for a long time. Roman sources dating back two thousand years or so, tell us how all these Germanic tribes let themselves be guided by communities of women, who were well-versed in spells and magic. This influence of witches did not restrict itself to the home and hearth. The so-called Vandals, a Germanic tribe that went into Africa and seem to have had something to do with the ancestry of the Berber people, or so I have heard, did not make a military move until they had listened to the declarations of the so-called "mothers" [matronae] of the tribe, according to the Romans, a group of old women.

The Bructeri, another German tribe, let the oracle Veleda, which means the Seeress, rule their military moves in all respects, and so on. Some German tribes parted with their witches early on, namely the Goths. The Goths ancestral story is like this, in short [from Jordanes' Getica]: About 100 B.C.E, the Goths left their homeland in Sweden and sailed across the sea and into the Baltic countries. They brought with them a community of women known as the haliurunnae. That is, I think, a Latin version of the Norse word heliurún, which means the secrets of Hel. Now Hel is the underworld or also a name of the goddess in her death-aspect. Rún means a secret. So these women knew the secrets of the goddess, or the secrets of death, or both probably.

They had influence in Gothic society, so much influence indeed that the king, Filimer, became a little annoyed with them. Now it is not the first time that a priesthood clashed with a royal authority, but this was probably the first time in Germanic/Norse history that the royal authority won (these being exiles, it was probably easier to dispel old customs). The witches were accused of performing dark and evil magic, and were expelled. Apparently, this female priesthood was last seen moving eastwards into the Siberian steppes. The Goths experienced a great change in their religion, in which they started to worship ancestors [ansis] and the king himself, he was worshiped too. Maybe that was what the witches were trying to avoid and maybe that is why Filimer accused them of evil magic.

In any case, without their priestesses the Goths became king worshipers and started to bully everyone else around them, conquering here and there. However, it is not as if the expulsion of the representatives of an entire ancestral religion went unnoticed by the lay Goth. The event had a great impact on the minds of the Goths. Five hundred years later, a people arrived in Europe, who were even greater bullies than the Goths, the Huns. As the Mongolian Huns swept across Europe and made all the Germanic peoples their vassals, the Goths were convinced that this was the revenge of haliurunnae, the witches, who must have been mating with Siberian demons to produce such a fierce tribe and we are talking five hundred years later!

The expulsion of these witches was an event that was remembered. Now the Goths were about the only tribe that refused the counsel of their witches, everybody else kept witches, and when Vikings moved from Iceland to Greenland during the 10th century AD, they brought a group of nine witches with them. The Saga of Eirík the Red contains a tale regarding the last surviving witch among this group of nine witches, the Litilvǫlva. That means "the little witch", and referred to her being the youngest of the original group. At the time the little witch appears she has become an old woman and is the last of the group.

A ritual of seiðr is being described, where the witch receives the greatest honor as she comes to the farm, and how she makes all the women on the farm, regardless of class and status, come together and hold hands to make a circle around her. They sing the song called Varðlokur, which means Calling the Spirits, and then the witch performs her divination and calls down fertility on a land that had been plagued by drought. Numerous graves have been found containing the remains of Germanic witches or priestesses. They are all very splendid, showing that these women were highly honored, and they invariably contain three kinds of items: a sacred wand, a collection of magical herbs and amulets within a pouch, and the necessary items for serving mead. Yes, mead.

Most of these ladies were buried with a spoon for serving mead in their hands, which goes to show, according to archaeologists, that the serving of mead was extremely important to the witch-priestess profession! (Main source: Michael Enright's Lady with a Mead Cup). Now I think this brings to mind the maiden with the mead of the Poetic Edda, and also the reference to a golden drink in the name of the first witch that I talked about earlier. In my next video, I shall continue this subject as I will be talking about the male initiation ritual, and how witches participated in these.

Now just summing up, the very first witch was the Goddess herself, come to show the secret of immortality and to teach the art of ruling fate to so-called wicked women. This myth may be read on various levels. To move on with the "historical" (mythical-historical) level, the god Óðinn watches this event and then covets the knowledge of seiðr, which he rightly perceives is the most powerful of arts. The other gods apparently said: "Oh no, Óðinn, that's women's business! He says: so what! If women know the secrets that give the greatest power, why shun their wisdom? I want some!" To get it, he instigated the first war that was ever known in the whole world, just to make the Vanir come into his world with their art of seiðr.

8.3: WITCHES AND WARRIORS

In Norse myths and legends, supernatural women goddesses, giantesses and Valkyrie often appear to teach young men during their initiation. Snorri,in his Heimskringla, Ynglingatál, stated that it was Freyia who taught the art of seiðr to the Aesir. An Edda poem also relates how the goddess Freyia initiates young Óttarr by taking him down into the Underworld, in which a giantess, Hyndla, the she-wolf, teaches him about universal interconnectedness through a séance of seiðr [divination]. In the Edda poem Gróagalðr, a young man called Svípdagr invokes his dead mother, Gróa [Growth] at her burial mound, so that she may guide him and teach him spell-songs. The name Gróa is otherwise known to be that of a vǫlva, a witch-priestess, who heals the god Þórr by singing spell-songs over his wounds.

In the Prose Edda we learn about how Þórr, who has vowed to go unprotected and unarmed into the world of the giants, seeks the aid of a giantess called Gríðr ["Truce"], who after teaching him about the true nature and the weak points of his opponent, lends him her magical wand, her power-belt and her gloves so that he may defeat his opponent. In the heroic poems of the Edda, Valkyrie brides are responsible for transmitting knowledge, purpose and esoteric teachings to the young men, to guide them in life and to magically protect them in battle. Now, to another source which is not the Eddas. The fornaldarsǫgur ["The Sagas of Old Times"] written down during the 13th and 14th centuries AD, but claiming to tell the legends of very old times. A lot of these sagas repeatedly present the theme of a witch or giantess who teaches a young man.

The stories seem to resemble initiation stories told in a fairy-tale-like manner. In Kjalnesinga Saga, the hero Búi [Inhabitant] walks through a cold and uninhabited wilderness before he finally knocks on a door leading into a mountain. He is on a quest for a special and magical game-board. He meets The Mountain King's daughter Friðr [Peace], who can tell him that many have come to the mountain before him "without having shown themselves worthy", and it has resulted in their death.

Búi and Friðr enjoy a long erotic adventure together within the mountain during winter. When spring comes, the maiden assists Búi in his quest for the magical game-board, and it is stated that he could not have done it without her help. The mountain, especially the inside of the mountain, the cold, the winter and the wilderness, are all typical Norse metaphors for death and the underworld, as is the theme of making love to a giantess in the underworld. The game-board itself is symbolic of fate, and the story faintly echoes the initiation story of the god Óðin's adventure with a giant's daughter inside the mountain of Suttungr.

In the saga of Þorsteinn Geirnefjufostra, the hero Þorsteinn has to win over the giant Sǫkkolfr [Dark Wolf = Dark Death] before he can win the love of the giantess Geirnefja. Her name means Spear-Beak, which refers to a deadly vulture. Þorsteinn is named after her in a manner that shows her role in his upbringing, or, indeed, his apprenticeship. He is called Þorsteinn Geirnefjufostra ["Fostered by Geirnefja"]. In the same saga, another version of their relationship is presented in which Geirnefja brings the wounded warrior, Þorsteinn, to her hall. She heals his wounds and teaches him to hunt with bow and arrow. He loves her until she dies. In the saga of Illugi Gríðarfostra [Illugi, Fostered by Gríðr], the hero Illugi encounters problems at sea as his ship is wrecked against dangerous cliffs. Illugi is picked up from the shore by the giantess maiden Hildr [Battle], daughter of the eagle-clawed giantess hag called Gríðr [Truce].

Hildr, the daughter, treats Illugi harshly and violently, but Illugi shows no fear. His courage causes a spell to be lifted from the two women, and they are transformed into beautiful and helpful ladies. They reveal to him that the unfriendly introduction was a test that few could pass. Illugi is called Gríðarfostra after his apprenticeship to the mother giantess within a cave. The theme of a hostile giantess turned good and helpful is present in several other sagas. In the saga of Illugi Tagldarbani [The Bane of Tǫgld], a hostile giantess called Tǫgld [Chewing One = Death] sends mist and a storm in order to wreck Illugi's ship.

Illugi has to fight the giantess Hrímgerðr [Frosty Enclosure = Death by freezing water], and as he wins the battle, it turns out that this was a test, and by showing his fearlessness and conquering death, he also wins the eternal allegiance, guidance and protection of the giantess that he has conquered. In the same saga, Illugi frees a princess from captivity among the giants. Another saga relates how the hero Gunnar wins over the giantess Fala [To Bid For (your life)] in battle, and thus wins her allegiance, help and protection in further battles against trolls. The hero Sǫrli conquers the giantess Mána and she swears her eternal allegiance and help. She gives clothes to the hero, magical clothes that may not be penetrated by weapons, and she gives him a sword that cuts through steel and stone.

The theme of the healing and protecting giantess is also prominent. In the saga of Halfdan Brǫnufostra [Halfdan, Fostered by Brána] the hero Halfdan encounters the giantess Brána [The Norse word brá means eyelash or eyelid] in a giant's cave, which is a metaphor for death and the underworld. Brána remains a helping and guiding power in the life of Halfdan. She offers magical gifts, herbs, a protective and warning ring, and a ship. She chooses his bride, saves him from fire, saves his sister from being raped, and turns up in his dreams in order to remind him of an old oath he must honor.

In the saga, Halfdan also frees a princess, who is a captive of the giants, another
repetitive theme. The saga of Þorsteinn Vikingssonar Skellinefjas relates how the
hero, Þorsteinn, almost drowns, but is saved by a giantess called Skellinefja. Her
name means Shouting Beak/Nose, which may refer to the high pitched nasal
sound used for performing spell-songs known as galðr, hinting to the giantess'
role as a witch, a volva. The fact that Þorsteinn is called Skellinefjas refers to her
having ownership over him. In the saga, she heals his wounds. Þorsteinn has to
accept marriage with the horrible-looking giantess, but the moment he accepts, the
giantess is transformed back into the beautiful princess she really is.

The same theme, ogress turned princess, appears in Grímr Loðinkinna's saga,
where the hero, Grímr, lies on the battlefield, close to death after having conquered
twelve men, when he is saved by the giantess Geirríð [Spear-Ride = Death], who
heals his wounds. Grímr has to promise marriage to Geirríð, who immediately
turns into the beautiful princess with whom he was originally engaged. In the saga
of Qrvar [Arrow's Odd], the hero Odd traverses a rocky mountain-landscape before
he arrives at a violent river fall. He finds no way to cross over to "the other side."
The wilderness is a known metaphor for the Underworld, and close to Hel there is a
Bellowing and terrible river that forms the border between the living and the dead.
Suddenly, a huge eagle, another known metaphor for death, lifts him up and flies
up into the mountains with him, placing him in her nest.

Odd has to conquer the hungry eagle-chicks, and through cunning he manages
to kill the eagle [= conquer death]. He calls on the aid of a giant, who can take
him across the river of death, where he is taken to the giant's daughter, Hildigunnr
[Battle Warrioress], and Odd remains there through the winter as her lover. She
allows him to leave as spring comes, but lets him know that he would never have
got out of the world of the giants if it had not been for her help. Like in the first case
I mentioned, this clearly echoes the initiation story of Óðinn and Gunnlöð. In the
saga of Egill and Ásmundr, the heroes set sail until they arrive at the shore of the
world of the giants, where they go inland. They travel through deserted wilderness
and almost starve to death. After several months they see a herd of goats and try
to catch one to eat. Just as they are hunting, they are disturbed by a huge female
monster who asks, in a high-pitched bell-like voice, who they are and why they are
trying to steal the goats of the Queen.

The two heroes try to placate the monster, calling her beautiful, and she takes
them home to her mother. The mother of the monster is the mighty Queen Eagle-
Beak, who rules over Iotunheimr [The World of the Devourers = Giants]. The
heroes are well received at the house of the two giantesses, and at the dinner table
they share each other's life-stories. Queen Eagle-Beak reveals the existence of two
beautiful princesses, who are being held captive in the World of the Giants, and
who are to be married off to the Queen's two giant uncles. The Queen and her
daughter aid the heroes in their effort to trick the giants and save the princesses,
who finally become their wives. The Queen of the giants heals the heroes' wounds,
even to the point of restoring Egill's severed hand.

Real life warriors' priestesses, or warrior's guardian spirits?

Several more sagas relate the stories of heroes who free princesses from captivity among the giants [see also Egill Einhendas saga and Jǫkull Búasonar þottr]. Almost all of these sagas relate how the heroes have to overcome cold, frost, ice, solitude in the wilderness and shipwreck, before they are either saved by, or have to fight giantesses, who later promise their eternal help and allegiance [also see Ármans saga unga, Ásmunðr Atlasonar saga, Ketils saga]. The giantesses are very often associated with eagles, which are metaphors for death. The trials of the heroes in many respects resemble the typical trials of the shaman initiate, although it would appear that these are warriors' initiations. The sagas in which these strange fairy-tales occur are very late renderings of the 13th and 14th centuries, some written even as late as the 15th century. Thus it is problematic to use them as sources of actual Pagan religion, even though the writers claimed that they were faithfully rendering the oldest ancestral lore.

However, the elements of Pagan initiation rituals in these stories are so obvious that they clearly represent some oral memory of the real thing. The dangers, the trials, the encounter with death, the staying "on the other side" [often literally described as such], and the mysterious female who saves the hero's life, teaches him, helps him and in many cases become his wife or mistress. The home of this giantess is in almost all the cases situated within a mountain or hill, a stone or rock dimension. This is important in the light of the fact that caves and stone-formations and mounds had a religious function in Norse Paganism, as burial-places and the home of "elves," or souls, vettir [spirits] and other underworld inhabitants to whom one could sacrifice and pray. The dark, tomb-like home of the giantess often reveals a hidden palace filled with brightness and beautiful, magical treasures. This basic formula is repeated throughout the Norse myths, testifying to its widespread importance and probable antiquity.

According to the rules of Norse poetry, any name or character in a story may and will be a metaphorical disguise for an actual character, which is known to the listener/reader through their attributes and the various meanings of their many names. In the case of these stories, the giantesses seem to represent either human women and/or the actual mythical forces of death. The one possibility does not necessarily exclude the other, a real, human priestess-witch could very well be representing a mythological character in a ritual setting. One candidate is the sea giantess Rán [Robbery a name referring to her tendency to rob people of their lives]. She and her daughters cause shipwrecks and drowning, but are also identifiable as "the lights of the gods," according to Snorri [Skaldskaparmál]. The numerous shipwrecks and near-drowning scenes hint to these goddesses of the ocean and the waves. Another, obviously, is Hel, the giantess of death, who is famous for having two sides to her character, one of fertile maiden and one of rotting corpse, hence the very ambiguous nature of the giantesses in the stories. A third possible actual character is Skaði [Fatal Injury], who symbolically "hunts with bow and arrow" in the rocky mountain, enjoying the howling of wolves, another metaphor for death.

She too has a two-sidedness to her: As a wife of the god of winds and waves, Njǫrðr, she spurs her foster-son Freyr to undertake initiation [Skírnismál], and her love-relation to the gods staggers her natural wish to devour them all (being a personification of Death) and allows them to keep the bright Iðunn and her apples of immortality. Of course, the three giantesses of death are probably just various aspects of the same original character the Lady of the Underworld. In the stories, the giantess also takes on the role of a sort of guardian spirit. If the legends reflect real life initiation experiences or rituals for young warriors, as I think they do, the giantess may have been represented by a witch who possibly performed a role as a personal priestess to her "foster-son", offering guidance and spells of protection throughout his life.

There is enough evidence that women performed this role dating back to Iron Age German societies at the very least. At the same time, the giantess may very well have been identifiable as a typical Fylgja ["follower"], a female guardian spirit, who was thought to "follow" a human individual throughout their life, and is probably the same figure described by Snorri as a personal Norn, a fate-goddess, who appears at birth and who follows the individual through life, spinning their fate. Both Snorri and the Prose Edda assert that bad lives are caused by bad fate-goddesses not bad because they are evil, but because they are in a state of coma ["the daughters of Hibernation [Dvalinn]"].

The theme of young men's apprenticeship with giantesses, who might easily represent real life priestesses, is so overwhelmingly present in the lore of the Vikings that one has to wonder if this is not actually reflecting real-life initiation stories in which vǫlur, witches, may have played a part as teachers. I am convinced that they do, even more so as the much older source of the Poetic Edda seems to be telling the same stories of initiation as its main plot. The almost countless stories of heroes trying to save captive princesses [often, indeed, sleeping in their captivity] or transform horrible-looking ogresses into the beautiful and helpful maidens "they really are", seems to me to be reflecting an initiation ritual in which the waking up of one's sleeping fate, so as to acquire a powerful, divine fate, is the real goal. I dedicate this Chapter to the research of Lotte von Motz, who pointed out the initiation pattern in these sagas and who was the first to compare them (Lotte von Motz, "The Beauty and the Hag").

9: THE PRIESTESS AND THE KING

9.1: THE SACRED MARRIAGE INSTITUTION

"The people of Sumer gather in the palace in that house which rules the land
The King builds a throne for the Queen of the palace he sits beside her on the
throne.

The King walks with a lifted head towards the sacred vagina
Dumuzi walks with a lifted head towards Inanna's sacred vagina
He lies down beside her on the bed
Gently he caresses her, whispers the words of love;
"Oh my sacred jewel, oh my marvelous Inanna!"

Oh my Lady, Queen of Heaven and Earth!
Queen of Heaven and Earth!
May he live long in thy embrace!"

Sumerian hymn to Inanna and the Sacred Marriage

Kinsley, David; The Goddess's mirror: Visions of the Divine from East and
West (1989)

One of the oldest human civilization known and recognized was established
between the rivers Euphrates and Tigris in present day Iraq. The area was known
as Sumer from the earliest of days, and was later called Mesopotamia. From
the beginning, the culture consisted of several city-states and many different
deities. The cultural organization and religious concepts of Sumer appear to have
held tremendous impact on the Middle East and Europe from an early stage,
particularly during the Bronze Ages. Their religion was polytheist, but the creator
deity was almost always a goddess. The order of the universe happened through
sexual unions between gods and goddesses.

The great goddess Ishtar was widely worshiped throughout a period of three
thousand years despite great changes and migrations. She stood in the center of
the most popular and widely spread cults, and was revered as the Great Goddess
by many Sumerians. She was primarily a goddess of war and fertility and credited
with establishing culture as such, the mother and creatrix of human beings. She
was increasingly worshiped as the source of all ethical qualities, involved in the
personal lives of her worshipers. Her name is etymologically identical with the
west-Semitic goddess Astarte and Athart. Around 2300 B.C.E, the priestess and
poet Enheduanna (who was the world's first known and named poet with a written
legacy) identified Ishtar with another popular Semitic goddess, Inanna, the Queen
of Heaven.

Ishtar/Inanna was the main character of an important ritual known as the Sacred Marriage, a ritual that dominated the official and royal cult throughout the entire Mesopotamian period (around 4500 B.C.E- 1750 B.C.E), that is, over a period of more than three thousand years. According to mythology, the first Sacred Marriage happened between the king Dumuzi and an avatar of Inanna, or between the king Tammuz and the goddess Ishtar. Since then, the wedding was repeated thousands of times, essential in all royal inaugurations. It may even have been a part of the annual celebration of the new year.

The ritual took the form of a wedding between the kings and a priestess who incarnated the goddess Inanna/Ishtar, a priestess who was trained for this particular role. All the surviving literature show that it was the goddess who was the dominant partner in the marriage. She appoints the ruler and enjoys him sexually in very detailed vocabulary. The sexual joy of the union leads to fertile vegetation, the stability of the government and to the king's ability to rule the country. The goddess will lead the king to victory in battle and help him maintain the social order. The marriage was celebrated publicly as a great and joyful event. The kings called themselves the "grooms of the Goddess" or the "caretaker of the Goddess". They ruled in her sacred name and with her blessings. The goddess was called the Carrier of the King, the Source of the King, his Power and his Prestige.

The goddess was clearly seen as the source of the king's power, and it is through her love and her sexual satisfaction that his success as a king may be guaranteed. The texts that treat the Sacred Marriage describe the goddess as an active sexual partner, whose sexuality is unambiguously blessed and fortunate. Her sexual pleasure blesses the king and the entire society. Her sexuality is celebrated as non-monogamous and is not connected to human reproduction, the central theme of the erotically laden ritual was her power over the fertility of the land, victory in war and the fate of society. Connected to the ritual of the Sacred Marriage was the annual death of the god of vegetation, who is also the king in his mythical aspect. The goddess will grieve and descend into the Underworld in order to restore her lover to life. It has been speculated that the king was sacrificed and replaced during the ritual that accompanied the myth, but there is no evidence that this was actually the case.

The ritual of the Sacred Marriage was so important and well-established over so many millennia that it continued into later eras. Including the Babylonian and the Hebrew eras that followed after 1750 B.C.E and into several centuries AD. The ritual or its basic concepts had by then long spread across the ancient world [Main sources: Judith Ochshorn (1983) and Mircea Eliade]. The Norwegian archaeologist Camilla Helene Fari ranks among the scholars who have argued that there is considerable evidence for a cult of Sacred Marriage in Bronze Age Scandinavia, and that these evidently also were related to the Sumerian form. Sexual scenes abound in Bronze Age Scandinavian rock-art, and are made in such a fashion and in such places that there is no doubt that the sexual scenes were connected to ritual and religion. Numerous such scenes are depicted within burials or on burial lids, and the scenes often depict public rituals surrounding the sexual scene.

Bronze Age Scandinavia was not an isolated place but powerfully connected to the rest of Europe. In fact, the whole of Europe was culturally connected, not only from Scandinavia in the North to the Mediterranean in the South, but also to the Middle East. There is little doubt that the Sumerian ritual of the Sacred Marriage became a powerful hit in cultures as distant as the Scandinavian as a means of legitimizing the rule of a king by symbolically marrying him to the goddess of the land or tribe that he was to rule. We can only guess that many of the underlying concept found in Sumerian texts may have influenced the Scandinavian version.

As the Icelandic writer Svava Jacobsdottir has pointed out, Sacred Marriage myths abound Irish legends, and are connected to the offering of precious mead. The goddesses of the legends appear as magical women whose names are either associated with the red golden drink that they serve, or with sovereignty. Only through winning her love may a young man become king. The Norwegian professor Gro Steinsland has shown that Old Norse myths display similar myths of Sacred Marriage, and suggests that the many golden icons of a kissing couple from the Scandinavian Iron Age are in fact amulets depicting the Sacred Marriage. In this chapter, I have rendered transcripts from two YouTube videos where I explore the Sacred Marriage of Norse myths.

9.2: Precious mead and sacred marriage

I have already touched upon the Hávamál initiation myth, where Óðinn explains that he hung on the world tree and descended into the realm of the fate goddesses in which he picked up the runes of fate, understood them and shared them with the beings of the world (see Chapter 10). I discussed how the description of his trial could reflect real rituals of initiation that actually took place in the Pagan world of the Vikings and their Iron Age predecessors. These people are known to us as Germanic people. This was a name assigned to them by the Romans two thousand years ago. From the outside, the so-called Germans looked similar. From the inside they were, quite obsessively, tribal.

The tribes shared a common root language and could understand each other, they seem to have all originated in Bronze Age Scandinavia, from which, during the early Iron Ages, many a tribe migrated, and thus shared certain cultural and mythological basic structures. However, it is important when you look at the past to realize that history is a matter of editing down masses of contradictory and confusingly diverse information into a coherent whole. To say that all the Germanic people, all over Northern Europe for a thousand years, thought this and did that is a bit too simple. The truth is that despite a common Bronze Age root; even that root would turn out to be amazingly diverse if you started to look at it closely.

The truth is that people in the past were as different and diverse in outlook and experience as we are today, sometimes even more so because there was no TV or Internet or newspapers and many tribes would not see much of the outside world for many generations, there would be trading and traveling, but not for the majority of people. When it came to war and peace, class structures and gender roles, matriarchy and patriarchy, and which gods were the most popular, things changed, and it changed all the time, from tribe to tribe, from century to century.

Apart from language, there are only a few things that seem to have been shared by most of the tribes, and one of these was the presence of a powerful group of women, who seem to have been something between priestesses and witches. Their power and influence was quite strong throughout the tribes, independent of the changing roles of women in general or the degree of warlike behavior in the tribe. If their tribe was warlike, the priestesses participated in war strategy and many are the sources, showing how Germanic chiefs listened intently to their advice, as these priestesses were considered to be allied with the goddesses of fate and thus the outcome of anything, even war. However, whether the tribe was comparably peaceful or very warlike, the priestesses of the tribe were considered to be the source of wisdom, and I think perhaps, generally, they were. As I talked about in Video 11 [see Chapter 8], some Germanic tribes, such as the Goths, denounced their priestesses quite early.

They were also among the first tribes to become Christians and to sack the great Goddess Mystery temple of Eleusis and to actually even sack Rome, destroy civilization and start the Dark Ages. Priestesses partook in male initiation rituals and one of their most important functions. There seems to have been the ritual serving of a magical brew, usually referred to as mead. Archaeology testifies that all over Northern Europe from about 700 B.C.E and until the end of the Viking Age during the 10th century AD, great ladies were buried with full ritual paraphernalia, in graves that show their importance and power in life, as well as their profession, leaders of rituals and users of magic and not the least as servers of the precious mead. The ladies serving mead are part of a very important recurring theme in the Norse myths, that of a supernatural lady in the underworld, who serves the precious mead after the hero has undergone dangerous trials of initiation.

There is also a sacred marriage involved. As we have seen, the lady of the myths is, through metaphorical and mythical attributes, identified as the goddess Freyia, who indeed is supposed to meet the chosen dead in her ninth realm of Cosmos. It seems probable that the ladies who participated in such rituals in real life were also supposed to represent the goddess, temporarily present in a living woman during the ritual. You may wonder why I am talking about this when I was going to continue the talk about the hanging of Óðinn. We know that the god hung and then descended to the roots of the world tree in which he grasped the runes of destiny. This was not the only thing that happened there.

In the following Hávamál stanza 140, Óðinn explains how he was taught nine fimbulljóð, which means nine powerful songs by his maternal uncle. I shall talk about what that may have meant in a ritual context later, for now I shall move on to how these nine spell-songs led Óðinn to a place where he, according to this stanza: "received a drink of the precious mead, poured from Poetry Blend [Óðrerir]". Nothing more is said about this event in these particular stanzas, but that is a typical Old Norse poetic way of making a metaphorical riddle, referring to something the listener is expected to already know and be able to deduce for themselves. Luckily the precious mead and the poetry blend is mentioned and described in more detail earlier in the same poem, which is why the theme is not elaborated more, if you paid attention to what was being said earlier, you would realize that here comes another piece of the puzzle that adds to our knowledge of the whole sacred story.

Now those of you, who already know a little about Norse mythology, have probably heard the story of how Óðinn stole the mead of poetry from the giants. If you have, you have probably been presented with the version told by Snorri in the Prose Edda. I am going to stick to an older version, the version of the Hávamál poem of the Poetic Edda, because that version is older and more authentic, and it does not try to hide what it was all about. I am convinced that Snorri was trying to disguise the initiation theme so he could get away with talking about the Pagan lore in the first place. He told us how Óðinn tricked a giant maiden into sleeping with him so that he could drink all her mead and run off. He describes the girl as loose-lived and dim-witted, but the Hávamál tells another story.

In the Hávamál, we are told that Óðinn went to the land of the age-old giant called Suttungr, which means Heavy with Drink. This is, I believe, one of the many names of the world giant who lives in the Cosmic Ocean beneath the World Tree together with his wife Rán and their nine daughters. In his halls, Óðinn, helped by the nine spell-songs taught to him on the way, displays his eloquence and in this way, mysteriously saves his life. It is made very clear that he would have died if he could not talk himself out of it.

The world he has come to is a realm of death, an underworld, as shown by its attributes of being dark, rocky and deadly, situated, in fact, within a mound a burial mound. It is not so difficult perhaps to imagine that a people, who let the initiates hang for nine days and almost die, would not hesitate to place them in a mock burial mound afterwards, in which they were to achieve their consecration, the marriage with the lady of the dead. You see, when Óðinn has managed to use his intelligence and eloquence to survive in this underworld, he swears a sacred ring-oath, which is the same as being married. Then the giantess called Gunnlǫð, whose name means Invitation to Battle, is revealed to him, sitting on a golden chair, offering him the precious mead that she guards. They get married, and later she helps him turn into a drill, snake or an eagle so that he can escape death and return to earth.

What is being described in this story is as close as a myth can get to describing real life ritual. There is evidence that people did go through mock sacrifice to Óðinn, in which they were mock hanged and mock stabbed, in which they fasted for nine days and definitely faced death, but with a certain chance of returning to life. In Gautreks saga, we hear of how King Vikarr was to hang in a supple rope made out of calf-entrails. He was not meant to die, because it was supposed to be a mock sacrifice. Thus he was hanged from a lithe branch, and was to be "stabbed" with twigs.

As much as this sounds relatively safe, the saga reveals that things could well go wrong; in the story, Óðinn interferes and turns the lithe branch into a spear that really does pierce the king, and the supple rope turns into hard rope, and the king is claimed by death. That kings went through such mock sacrifices is clear, as testified by the old Nordic title wiðu-hundaR known from runic inscriptions, meaning "Tree/Gallows King". Gautreks saga suggests that such mock king sacrifices were usually expected to be quite safe, but only quite. We have the examples of kings, but what about men who were in fact, like the god himself, also great sorcerers? Another title known from runic inscriptions is wiðugastiR, often the title of the rune master himself, and interestingly, it means "Tree/Gallows Guest".

We may think it impossible for a man to hang in a tree for nine days and nights without eating or drinking, while bleeding and being close to suffocating. But there are in fact people who exercise ordeals quite as "impossible" within traditions of asceticism and yoga. The Norwegian archaeologist Brit Solli (2002) has suggested that the hanging ritual may be better understood in light of the phenomenon known as "erotic asphyxiation", or else as "breath control play" where intentional restriction of oxygen to the brain gives sexual arousal. Whereas this may seem incomprehensible from the outside, the experience may in fact induce something more than sexual arousal, it may create a sensation of ecstasy and what science refers to as hallucinations.

When the carotid arteries on either side of the neck are compressed during strangulation, the sudden loss of oxygen and the accumulation of carbon dioxide will cause light headedness and pleasure, which can be heightened by sexual stimulation. It is a fact that the myth of Óðin's hanging includes a myth of sexual intercourse when the mead is served and the knowledge is grasped, described in the Sígrdrífumál as a very ecstatic experience where the runes flowed like liquid mead through the soul of the Shattered god. Hanging is not the only way to the mead of knowledge. There is textual and archaeological evidence that people would indeed meditate on top of or even walk ritually into burial mounds in order to converse with spirit beings of the underworld.

There is even archaeological and textual evidence that priestesses existed whose job it was to preside over a sacred mead drinking ritual and that they were even buried with the serving spoon in their hands, ready to offer the mead to the brave warrior, who dared to seek her underworld abode. Historians and archaeologists alike all agree that some sort of sacred marriage in connection with initiation rituals seem to have taken place during both the Scandinavian Bronze Age and in the Iron Age tribes known to us as Germanic, as well as during the Viking Age. I think that it all adds up.

The story of Óðinn hanging reflects, describes and attempts to explain the origin of a very important ritual of initiation undergone by men, who sought to rule their own fate, to wake up the sleeping fate goddess within and symbolically marry her, to gain access to esoteric knowledge and abilities, and to become something apart from the ordinary, whether it was to become a sorcerer, a priest, a bard or a king. The story of the hanging also tells the tale of how the path of initiation for men was instigated, it was first staked out by Óðinn, who learned it from the ancient witch, and because of this deed, it is stated in the poem, because he did this, because he died, learned and resurrected, and became a god and an immortal: Resurrected, he «came among the bonds", or as st.109 of the Hávamál expresses it; "ef hann veri meþ bandom cominn eþa hefdi hanom Svttvngr of sóit"["(they asked if Óðinn) had come among the bonds, or if Suttungr had slain him"].

"Bonds" is a well-known heiti for the gods, the ruling powers, and we learn thus that the outcome of the trial would either be death, or immortal divinity. Since he succeeded, and he became a god, a god with the right to receive the annual apple of restoration from the Goddess, an apple that ensures his divine immortality, which is not so accurately immortality, but rather the ability to transform death over and over as his youth is restored every year. I have earlier discussed how Freyia, in the shape of a witch, showed Óðinn how to conquer fate, the ultimate fate being death, and that this led him to seek that knowledge.

In that myth, the goddess is called "Golden Brew (or Drink)", which refers to the precious mead. Throughout the myths, the mead is referred to and described as precious, ancient, filled with universal memory, power, poetry, creative power, knowledge and the power to transform. It is guarded by the goddess in all her countless shapes, Hel guards it, but keeps it under lock, giantesses offer it when heroes have had the courage to reach their underworld halls, Freyia guards it, and offers it to those who are allowed into her halls after death, in fact it seems to actually be the essence of the goddess herself. The Valkyrie offer it to the chosen of Valhǫll and they draw the mead from the teats of the goat Heiðrún, which means Bright Secrets, and this she-goat, identified as Freyia herself in a poem [Hyndlulióð], produces the mead by nourishing herself from the World Tree. This World Tree, again, is nourished by the Well of Origin, the Urðarbrunnr, by the oldest fate goddess called Urðr, meaning Origin.

In the Raven Spell-song of Óðinn [Hráfnagalðr Óðins eða Forspjallsljóð] we learn that the keeper of the mead of poetry is in fact the fate goddess Origin, so that ultimately, we may say that the mead is essentially the waters of origin, the waters of fate, death, resurrection and memory. As Snorri describes those waters in his Prose Edda, those who come into that sacred water will emerge transformed, shining and transparent like the membrane of the inside of an eggshell.There is a great difference between the Hávamál version of the story and the story told by Snorri. Snorri explained how Óðinn sneaked into the hall of the giants and secretly had sex with the girl and tricked her into giving him the mead. This older version, however, shows Óðinn as a man who asks a father for a girl's hand in marriage. His eloquence, and remember now, eloquence was a most valued virtue during the Viking Age, his eloquence wins him the bride, who is not at all shown as a silly girl, but as a lady seated on a golden throne, who freely offers her mead to him after he has proven himself worthy.

There is plenty of archaeological evidence that the offering of mead by a woman was indeed an important part of Germanic rituals, and there were women, who seem to have been priestesses or witches, who specialized in such mead-offering rituals. There is also evidence that rituals of sacred marriage as part of initiation rituals were very common in Northern Europe from the Bronze Age and onwards. So, what is described here, the hanging, the teachings, and the subsequent offering of mead by a woman, as well as the sacred marriage in the underworld, all have parallels in real life rituals that actually happened in Pagan Scandinavia.

However, let's go back to the mythical aspects. Now this mead has a story. In the Poetic Edda it is often referred to as the minnisdrykk, the Mead of Memory, or as hin m ra miǫðr, the Precious Mead, or as the forns miǫðr [the Ancient Mead or more literally the mead of the past], and it is offered by a female figure, who is always associated with gold, and the mead-provider always dwells in the underworld, which is what the world of the giants is. Her halls are always well guarded and surrounded by dangerous fences, indeed, the hall of Freyia may only be entered by those she invites. The mead gives infinite wisdom, power and transformation. The mead is, basically, the drink of immortality, and it is always guarded by the goddess in one of her countless shapes. According to Snorri, the mead began as the essence of all the gods and goddesses together.

Through the art of seiðr, Óðinn and Freyia created a being from this mead who wandered the world, just like its creators did, and who was accessible to everyone who asked for wisdom. However, the wisdom was monopolized by two dwarfs, who wanted it all for themselves, and then the personification of Wisdom was killed. This was basically how the mead of poetry, inspiration, wisdom, knowledge and transformation ended up being hidden beneath shields in the underworld, guarded by the goddess. It is accessible only to those who, like Óðinn, dare to undertake the initiation trial of death and who manages to make his way into the realm of the goddess, the realm of the soul, the light within the darkness of the darkest pits of Hel. This is his initiation. Óðinn drinks the precious mead, and is married, technically, to the lady of the dead, who dwells in the underworld, but he has other plans. He wants to bring the mead back with him to the living world and he wants to share it with others. He wants to place the mead in what he refers to as the ancient shrine of earth.

So, helped by the goddess, he escapes, first by becoming a serpent of death, the underworld is crammed with serpents, symbols of transformation, and then he becomes an eagle of death, like Hræsvelgr, the Corpse Swallower, and he flies. According to Snorri, he is followed by Suttungr in Eagle's disguise, and the wind blows as the eagle flaps his wings. Suttungr, the "Mead-Heavy", is no other than the eagle of death. Óðinn makes a narrow escape and the last stanzas of the story explain how he now has become a god, living among gods. That means he had to work for his divine status. Another big point is made out of how he betrayed the Goddess. He laments how she loved him and helped him and saved his life, without her he would never have made it.

However, he betrays her, he betrays the ring-oath of sacred marriage to the goddess, and leaves her behind in the Underworld, weeping. What does this mean? Well, I have been uncertain about what exactly that means myself. Óðinn seems to be the villain here, who leaves his wife, and she cries. There is a second parallel story to this one told by Snorri. Freyia was once married to Óðr, which is of course the same as Óðinn, since Óðinn is just the word óðr put together with the suffix [h]inn to indicate "the", "The Spirit". So the Spirit and the Soul were married, they even had two daughters, and then he left, vanished mysteriously, and we are not told why in this version of the story. As Óðinn left, Freyia started to travel the world in search of him, teaching as she went, and leaving behind her tears of pure red gold, which is a metaphor for divine enlightenment and wisdom.

Moreover, there is a third parallel story told by Saxo Grammaticus, a Danish medieval storyteller. After the death of Baldr, who symbolizes wisdom, Óðinn sets about to ensure that someone will be born, who can avenge Baldr. Metaphorically that means someone who can destroy the blind and ignorant aggression that killed wisdom in the first place, but to do that, Óðinn ends up committing a crime. He is the Spirit, and after the loss of wisdom in the world, people no longer want Spirit they want material riches. This is illustrated in how Óðinn tries to make love to a woman whose name is Rindr, which means to reject [from the verb rinda], that is, she rejects spirit when he arrives. Óðinn, knowing that the woman will give birth to the choice that will restore Baldr, causes the spirit-rejecting woman to go mad, has the people tie her to the bed, and then he rapes her.

This can mean a lot of things, it may refer to Óðinn as the representative of a patriarchal (and oppressive) system, but then, remembering that he is Spirit, she may represent women and the fate of women when they no longer assume spiritual authority, or the woman may even represent human beings and their fate when they reject the spiritual. The latter is what I think, firstly because females in Norse poetry almost always represent an aspect of fate, and a human woman would represent the fate of humanity. Secondly because the goal here is to force the spirit-rejecter to give birth to a Choice the choice to destroy Ignorance and blind aggression forever.

When the spirit is rejected, he causes a great trauma, and through trauma, human beings may learn, even though it may take a lot of pain before we finally decide to seek the spirit in ourselves. When the other gods hear about his crime, Óðinn is expelled from the divine realms and has to travel the world as an exile. This is Spirit we are talking about, and it is a grave matter when Spirit is expelled from the divine order of things. Suddenly, the divine union between god and goddess, between spirit and soul, between wisdom and love, between poetry and history, is disrupted, and it affects us all.

To get to the point of my interpretation, the story of how Óðinn betrayed the goddess is the story of how the spirit of humankind has separated itself from its sacred union with the all-soul. After that event, the god and the goddess are scattered across the universe, both appearing in countless shapes. We are them, and history happens, because they are constantly on the move, constantly changing shape, constantly learning, constantly teaching. Freedom from this endless world story happens to each and every one of us, who decide to make a choice of reuniting with the wholeness of soul and spirit.

He was taught these songs from the "famous son of Bolþorn, Besla's father". Now, Besla is Óðin's giantess mother, so the son of her father is Óðin's maternal uncle. The maternal uncle is a very important teacher figure in Germanic initiation myths. He appears again and again, and is probably derived from the fact that once upon a time. Some Germanic tribes were matrilineal rather than patriarchal, and there are many indication that the brother of the mother had a duty to teach and raise his sister's sons. This is described in Tacitus' Germania, among other sources, where this Roman writer, Tacitus, who wrote this around the year 98 AD, explained that maternal uncles were more important role models and educators to men than their own fathers.

In the mythical and legendary sources, these maternal uncles also had a priestly or shamanic function in society, which may reflect a certain hereditary tradition when it comes to learning spiritual practices. In the Vǫlsunga Saga, a maternal uncle teaches his nephew, who is also his son, to change shape into animals, and to heal wounds and illnesses. In the initiation myth of Sígurðr in the Poetic Edda, the maternal uncle performs divination in the style of seiðr, which I have been calling witchcraft. In this initiation story, the maternal uncle teaches powerful songs. All these stories show the shamanic maternal uncle in the process of helping his nephew to begin his journey of initiation. Óðinn is taught nine powerful songs, which is of course a significant number of songs, as we discussed in the previous video, the number nine reflects the worlds in which death is the rule.

Powerful songs may be another name for the art of galðr, spell-songs. The word galðr is derived from the verb gala, which means to sing in a high-pitched tune. It was a way of casting spells and was a well-known practice in Norse society. Other names for spell-songs are varðlokur, "Calls for the Spirits", or seiðlæti, the "Sound of the Craft [seiðr]". To sing a spell-song could be a way of casting spells, but it could also have a healing effect. In the poem Oddrúngrátr, spell-songs are used by a Valkyrie to help a woman through childbirth. Snorri relates how the wounded god Þórr was healed by the spell-songs of a witch giantess called Gróa. This giantess later appears in an Edda poem called the Gróagalðr, the Spell-Songs of Gróa, where the spell-songs are meant to help a boy through his initiation. No less. So do the spell-songs of the maternal uncle help Óðinn? Yes indeed, because the next line tells us how he finally received the precious cup of mead, poured to him from the cauldron called Óðrerir, the Poetry Blend. And then, apparently, Óðinn just returns and has become a wise man.

9.3: ÓÐINN AND THE GODDESS

We do not know exactly how old the god Óðinn is. The first evidence of his cult date back almost two thousand years, but I will take us still further back in time, to the Bronze Age. I am not an archaeologist, so what I am saying now is based on the book called "The Chariot of the Sun and other Rites and Symbols of the Northern Bronze Age", published in 1969 by Peter Gelling and Hilda Ellis Davidson. In their book, Gelling and Davidson analyzed rock paintings made by Bronze Age people in Scandinavia dating between 1800 and 500 B.C.E, which is roughly the era of the Bronze Age in Scandinavia. Gelling and Davidson concluded that there was substantial evidence that despite the existence of other deities or powers, there were four major deities which completely dominated the religious scene.

At the center was the worship of the sun. Countless images show the sun disc in some mythical situation and countless others show people worshiping the sun disc in all kinds of ways. The sun was worshiped by warriors parading with their sun-disk shields and weapons, the sun was carried as an emblem above the priests heads, fastened with sticks to people's hands, the sun was worshiped by acrobats and dancers, most of whom were female, and often performing aboard a ship, sacred to the sun. Gelling and Davidson do not make a conclusion about the sun's gender, but suggest that it may have been female or at least androgynous, because it is often showed as being penetrated or adored by a man with a very large and erected phallus that may not in any way be misunderstood.

The conclusion is that the sun disc often engaged in sexual activities with male gods or worshipers. Personally, I think it is obvious that the sun was a goddess, since from the very beginning absolutely all the Nordic and Germanic languages name the sun as a female, and because in later times, Sol of Scandinavia and Sunna of Germany were clearly goddesses. Snorri counted Sol, the sun, among the Ásyniur, the goddesses. In the Poetic Edda, it is said that the sun gives birth to a daughter, who will follow in her mother's path. The sun goddess is also important in creation, when she comes from the south and gathers all the horses of heaven [which I guess are the planets] with "her right hand", whatever that means and then begins to shine on the rocky surface of the earth goddess, who then brings forth life.

Another reason for claiming that the Bronze Age sun was a goddess is the fact that all its attributes, chariot, ship and spirals, are all attributes of Northern goddesses, who are always described as bright, golden-white, golden-red, shining, bringing forth rays of light and rays of lightning, not to mention Freyia, who weeps tears of gold and who owns the Brisinga-men, which means the Jewel of the Flames, which I take to be a heiti for the sun. So we have a Bronze Age scenario in Scandinavia where a sun goddess was at the center of public festivities, worshiped by men doing warrior dances and women doing acrobatics, and priests walking in procession with the lady's disc and spiral emblems. Next to this goddess, three male gods very obviously male, no doubt about it, basically ancient Scandinavians were even less demure than modern ones; well, three very male and let us say very virile gods take up the flanks around the golden lady, interacting with her, having sex with her, and carrying her emblem on their bodies, on their shields or above their heads like priests.

That these gods were divine or supernatural priests is very likely. Not only do they appear like worshipers and as lovers of the sun goddess, so that they could be taken for priests, but they are also larger than life and have their own emblems or attributes, so that they must be recognized as gods in their own right at the same time, even as they act like worshipers and priests. In this light I think it is significant that Snorri actually called the Aesir god for priests. The gods, according to Snorri [Ynglinga saga], were hófgóðir and blótgoðir, which means temple priests and sacrificial priests, and both in Edda and skaldic poetry we encounter Aesir gods in the act of performing a sacrifice and ritual incantations in honor of powers even greater than themselves. The three male gods are recognized by their attributes or emblems, which sometimes take their place.

A virile giant-sized man wielding an ax, or just the image of an ax as his emblem, representing him, is called the Ax-god by Gelling and Davidson. Then there is the Sword-god, who is an equally virile man wielding a sword, or just the sword emblem on its own, and finally, there is the Spear-god, represented by the spear as an emblem, or by a huge man wielding a spear. Gelling and Davidson pointed out that the three Bronze Age gods are symbolized by attributes that clearly belong to later Norse gods of the Viking age. The Ax-god would be an early predecessor of Þórr the Thunder god, the one god whom we know existed in Europe and Asia at least five thousand years back.

Knowing this, it is very reasonable to assume that the ancient Thunder god is identical with the ax-wielding god of the Bronze Age rock carvings. The Sword god could be an early predecessor of Freyr, an assumption which is powerfully strengthened by the fact that the sword god is often associated with pigs or boars, as well as horses, which were later animals sacred to Freyr. Then there is the Spear-god, we know that the god Óðin's favorite weapon was the spear, and that his spear symbolizes his choices. When he points or hurls his spear at someone, it is to choose them for his own. So is this proof that the gods Þórr, Freyr and Óðinn were already worshiped almost four thousand years ago in Scandinavia? No, it is not proof, but as Gelling and Davidson suggest, it is quite remarkable that the three major male deities of the Bronze Age pantheon share the primary attributes of the three major male deities of the Viking Age, namely ax-hammer, sword, and spear.

This is hardly coincidental, and could at least be evidence that the three Viking Age gods, as well as the goddess Freyia, inherited some central symbols associated with a much older religion, dating back almost four thousand years. Is there any other evidence that the Viking Age religion is based on a Bronze Age prototype? Not really, as far as I know, but we could turn to Snorri's tales in the Edda and in the Heimskringla. From a modern point of view, Snorri was not a great historian. In fact, when I studied Norse literature, one of my co-students asked if there could be any real foundation for Snorri's historical approach to the origin of the Norse gods.

Our tutors immediately warned us to never go there if we wanted an academic career. To claim that there is any historical basis to Snorri's tale whatsoever, would be academic suicide. Some of us tried to ask why, exactly, pointing out that Tor Heyerdahl had tried to excavate evidence about this, but had to stop his diggings due to lack of funding. The answer was that Tor Heyerdahl was a mock scientist and should never be referred to by serious scholars. So, I later figured out what exactly was the reason why Snorri's tale are not believed by modern scholars, it is said that his tale bears evidence of a European medieval tradition of claiming classical ancestry in order to glorify ones past, with no real basis in history whatsoever.

I shall nevertheless dare to go where no serious scholar is allowed to thread. I do not believe that Snorri's tale is actual history, but I believe that there may indeed be shreds of truth in it, shreds of ancient memories. We know that myths and legends can be communicated orally over thousands of years, and that they sometimes refer to historical events, so why not, really? Snorri claimed that Óðinn was a prince of Troy, a Bronze Age city in Anatolia, present day Turkey. He was married to a clairvoyant woman called Frigid, and they were descendants of Þórr the Thunder god and his clairvoyant wife, Sibylla, hence Viking Age Síf. If there is any trace of real history in this tale, I would suggest that what could be the reality behind the legend is that there were a people dwelling in the southeast, possibly, Anatolia, possibly even Troy, as Snorri suggests.

A people who worshiped the ancient Thunder god and his wife, and saw themselves as their descendants. The Óðinn of this legend may be covering for a distant memory of a certain leader, general or king who claimed to be the descendant of the Thunder god. Even more likely, Óðinn in this legend is a singular archetypal representation of many such leaders, who all were seen as incarnating a divine king while holding the royal office. I actually think that this is quite likely, and I will explain why later. In Snorri's tale, Óðinn leads his people on a quest towards the lands of the North, conquering some people, marrying into other people, spreading their language and their religion, which was strongly based on good, old fashioned, Pagan sorcery and shamanism.

Only when they came to the land of the wise Vanir did they meet real resistance, but managed to make a truce with them, and soon, the two divine tribes blended in friendship and marriage, instigating an era of peace and prosperity and wisdom available to everyone. This was also when their religions blended the goddess of the Vanir and her three male companions became members of the Aesir tribe. The Aesir, according to Snorri, were so called because they came from Asia. Now, could there be any truth in this story?

Again, I shall blaspheme against the ruling paradigm and say that yes, there is likely to be a shred of truth in this. Let us ask the first question, is it likely that a people led by some kind of Óðinn-like figure or worshiping a divine prototype of Óðinn, descendant of the Thunder god, incarnated in their kings, who did move from the southeast to the northwest and came to dominate the cultures of Northern Europe? Certainly. We have to go back a bit before the Scandinavian Bronze Age, into the late Neolithic, that is, we have to go back four thousand years from now, to find plenty of evidence that a new culture did indeed spread over time, beginning in the southeast and moving slowly to the northwest, during the millennium preceding the Scandinavian Bronze Age.

It is quite likely that they may have eventually brought the Bronze Age with them, since the Bronze Age began a lot earlier in the southeast than in the northwest. The new, invading culture was completely different from the old one. The old culture of Scandinavia during the late Neolithic was a megalithic, clan-based culture. It was communal and egalitarian, as we see that no individual was significantly elevated above others. This is shown both in graves where everybody, no matter what gender or age or status in the tribe, were buried as equals in big communal clan graves, and in their dwellings, which show that everybody in the clan lived together in the same big house. They were peaceful, as there is no evidence of war, and they were matrilineal, which we know because of modern DNA. The women of the burials are all related, whereas the men came from the outside.

This means that the women remained within their clans their whole lives, together with their mothers, sisters, aunts, grandmothers and cousins. The men, on the other hand, had to move into the clan of the wife and thus had to live and deal with the in-laws for the rest of their lives. We do not know much about the gender relations, as said the graves and buildings bear evidence of basic equality, but in such a society it is likely to assume that the women were the backbone of the clan, those who did not change or move away, and could expect the support of their families in everyday life, and thus most probably had a very strong position. I think that the cult of the ancestral mothers that was still strong in the Viking Age may very well be a remnant of this ancient megalithic culture.

The new, invading culture was completely different from the older culture insofar it was a hierarchical, caste-based, warlike and patriarchal culture. During the Bronze Age, these two cultures blended and compromised, and I think that the truce between the Aesir and the Vanir of Norse myths may likely reflect this historical event. This merging may also explain the institution of the Sacred Marriage, where a king had to marry the ancestral mother of the tribe in order to legitimize his rule.

What we have to dismiss completely; however, is the idea that this invasion happened during the lifetime of one king called Wodan or Óðinn. Archaeology shows that the spread of their warrior culture happened slowly, over many generations. What is possible, however, is that they did worship a Wodan-Óðinn-figure, and that their kings were seen as living incarnations of this god, married to a clairvoyant goddess, as Snorri explained that all the kings of Troy from Thonar to Wodan were married to clairvoyant women. The earliest known hard evidence for a Wodan-cult does indeed picture the god as a king married to a fate-knowing goddess.

We will come back to that later. Second question is, if a particular culture that worshiped a king god and a clairvoyant goddess, did indeed move up to dominate northern cultures before the onset of the Bronze Age, could they have come from Troy or thereabouts? This is pure speculation, but it is certainly possible. Troy was already a big town by 3000 B.C.E, so the place already has existed by the time of the south to north migration of the new culture. The migration could, technically, have begun there, and there is no doubt whatsoever that there were strong cultural connections between the Bronze Age Trojans, their Greek counterparts, and the Scandinavian culture during the Bronze Age. No doubt whatsoever, and there must be a reason for why Bronze Age cultures all over Europe had so much in common. Migration from Anatolia to Scandinavia just before the Bronze Age began is a very probable reason.

The third question is what about the Vanir tribe, who met the Aesir with such resistance? If the legend of the war and truce between the Vanir and the Aesir gods has any basis in history, we have to consider when this could have happened, and where. Tor Heyerdahl believed that it took place somewhere in Eastern Europe, basing it on certain place names there that resemble place names mentioned by Snorri. Then, why is the event only remembered in Scandinavia? We don't know, but let us ask who, exactly, did the newcomers from Asia encounter when they came up here? They would have encountered at least two different types of Neolithic cultures existing in Scandinavia at the time. The hunter-gatherers, who became the ancestors of the Sami people, and the megalithic farmers. Denmark and southern Sweden are scattered with remnants of megalith constructions. I have already said something about that culture.

They were communal, clan-based, there was a basic equality between the members within the clans, and they followed a matrilineal law of descent where men moved into their wives families and ancestral mothers were the focus of ancestral worship. In the Norse sources, the Vanir are described as exceedingly wise, a lot wiser than the Aesir, they are the know-alls whose magic was powerful enough to withstand the Aesir attack where no one else had succeeded. They were seen as great magicians. Indeed, it was the goddess of the Vanir, who taught Óðinn how to master the art of seiðr.

In my personal opinion, without claiming any scientific proof, I would say that the Vanir of the legend could represent the megalith builders of the Scandinavian Stone Age, inheritors of a grand tradition of an astronomical and architectural science that we today still find completely mystifying. How did they build the megaliths? If we find them mystifying, knowing all the things we know, imagine what they must have appeared like to a tribe of barbarians! To their contemporaries, to the barbarian invaders, who for all their warrior aristocratic bravado, these guardians of the megaliths must have appeared to be exceedingly well versed in mysteries and magic. If the legends are to be believed, the newcomers were certainly impressed and sought to be initiated into the mysteries of the native Scandinavians. I think it is actually quite remarkable that in the Norse world-view, there were three great tribes of power-beings: The Aesir, the Vanir, and the Jotnir.

They could all represent a legendary version of the three cultures that actually coexisted during the late Scandinavian Stone age. One, the invading warrior culture from the southeast, two, the megalith farmers, and three, the hunter-gatherers. By the time of the Bronze Age in Scandinavia, the megalith farmers had indeed merged with the invading culture, whereas the hunter gatherers maintained their separate identity and became the Sami people. This could be reflected in the legend of how the Aesir and the Vanir people merged, whereas the iotnir remained a separate tribe associated with the wilderness and great magical powers. We also know that the new invading culture brought with them the ancient, Indo-European Thunder god. They may also have brought with them the cult of a sacred king, who impersonated one of their most important gods, Wodan or Óðinn, or at least his predecessor, who was seen as a descendant of the Thunder god. Later, we know that Óðinn became the all-father and the father of the Thunder god, but in earlier times, the descent was reversed.

This reversal may have happened quite late, because in the year 80 AD, Tacitus claimed that the German tribes believed that the Thunder god was their ancestor, their all-father. Anyway, this culture of the Thunder god and the divine king-god merged with the megalith farmer culture, who may have worshiped a goddess, the Vanadís, which literally means the goddess of the Vanir, and according to the legend, she had three male companions. Her father Njǫrðr, her brother Freyr, and her mysterious protector and hero, Heimdallr, the god of the universe, who returned the fiery jewel to the goddess. Óðinn and the Thunder god may have merged with two of these three companions, leaving only two original Vanir gods in the ancient formula of one goddess and three gods.

The original Vanir gods in the formula were Freyia and Freyr, who are, significantly, siblings, from the original Vanir tribe. By the time of the Bronze Age, the great goddess of the Vanir was probably worshiped, in the shape of the sun goddess, surrounded by her brother the Sword god, and the two newcomers with their axes and spears, Þórr and Óðinn, who in many ways blend easily with respectively Njǫrðr and Heimdallr. If there is any historical truth in the legend, as I have now suggested, although it would be difficult to prove for certain, it is quite interesting to note that Snorri described the prototypical Óðinn as a prototypical king god married to a clairvoyant priestess-goddess.

This brings us into the Iron Age and the first known temples dedicated to Wodan, the Iron Age predecessor of Óðinn. This part is based on the work by the historian Michael Enright in his book "Lady with a mead-cup Ritual, Prophecy and Lordship in the European War band from La Téne to the Viking Age". In this book, Enright points out that the earliest representations of Wodan is as a sacred king god married to a clairvoyant goddess called Rosmerta.

Shrines to this divine couple were erected almost two thousand years ago in Western Europe. Rosmerta means the Great Provider, which brings to mind one Norse goddess, Gefion, whose name means The Provider. A short form of the name is Gefn, which Snorri says is one of Freyia's names. We know that Frigg and Freyia were once the same goddess, and that both were married to Óðinn. Are there any other indications that the Iron Age Rosmerta, the Great Provider, could be associated with Freyia or other Norse goddesses? Indeed.

Rosmerta, like Freyia, is depicted in the shrines as a clairvoyant oracle goddess, who owns a necklace, carries a cult like staff or wand, and whose central function is the serving of sacred mead. She is the prototypical divine witch-priestess of Norse and Celtic religions. So where did Rosmerta come from? Bearing the name Rosmerta, this goddess came from the Celtic region and was earlier married to the Celtic god Lugh. In regions where there was a lot of Roman influence, Lugh's place as Rosmerta's consort is taken by the Roman god Mercury, and in the German regions, Mercury's and Lugh's place by Rosmerta's side is taken by Wodan. Dear old Óðinn. This means that the earliest hard evidence for a Wodan cult two thousand years ago emphasizes his role as a king in sacred marriage to a divine priestess. How old is this sacred marriage? There is plenty of evidence for a sacred marriage cult in Scandinavia already during the Bronze Age.

Marriage scenes, or let us say ritual sex scenes, that is, a sexual act is depicted, surrounded by religious symbols and images of people performing ritual movements around the couple. These images abound in Bronze Age art, but where do they abound? They are found close to sacred places and groves, but most of them are actually found within graves. This is why these sex scenes are not interpreted as Bronze Age pornography despite all their explicitness. They are clearly depictions of a sacred act, the Hieros Gamos, or sacred marriage between two deities or between a human and his goddess. We do not know if the Bronze Age sacred marriage was associated with kingship, but it is very likely. Moving forward to the Iron Age, especially towards the 3rd, 4th, 5th and 6th centuries AD in Northern Europe, there is new evidence for a bloom in the ancient ritual of sacred marriage in connection to kingship inauguration. One Norwegian professor of Norse mythology, Gro Steinsland, has shown how the memory of the sacred marriage and kingship cult is strongly present in Norse myths.

Comparing these to similar Celtic myths and to other religions where the sacred marriage was an institution already five thousand years ago, such as in ancient Sumer, a picture emerges. When kingship was introduced in Europe during the late stone age and early bronze age, a new institution was established almost everywhere. The Sacred Marriage, where a king, in order to be accepted by his people, had to be accepted by the goddess of the land, and marry her. The goddess represented both the land and the people living in the land, she was their ancestral mother, their provider. The king was responsible for keeping the goddess happy. If she was satisfied in her marriage, she would provide abundance and make her children happy.

If she was unsatisfied with her husband, she would withdraw the bounty of the land and send famine, war and pestilence onto her children. The lady, basically, had to be pleased. Thus the people had to choose a king carefully, one who could please her and inspire her to create abundance and prosperity, peace and happiness. In ancient Sumer, a great deal of emphasis was placed on the king's ability to please the goddess sexually. He had to offer her many gifts, prostrate before her, sing her praises, raise a throne to her, seduce her with caresses and loving words, and when she had consented to wed him, she would bed him. Many of the oldest religious hymns ever written down in our world are detailed and very explicit descriptions of how the Sumerian goddess finds pleasure in her husband during Sacred Marriage.

The funniest thing for us is that all this happened on stage with thousands of onlookers, the goddess being represented by a priestess. The sexual pleasure of the goddess was emphasized in the hymns as something great, beautiful and sacred, because when the goddess thrived in this way, she would automatically bring forth bounty. As she was enjoying herself, the flowers would bloom, the fields would grow, and good fortune and prosperity would come to the people. If the crops failed, if there was pestilence, if the king failed to protect the peace by holding back enemies, it would be said that he was a bad husband for the goddess, and there are several indications that he would be sacrificed, just as many sagas, particularly the Ynglinga saga, frequently describe how Norse kings were sacrificed in times of famine and other disasters, or else claimed by the goddess of death in some form or other. Is this ancient Mesopotamian tradition in any way relevant to the Northern ritual of sacred marriage and kingship?

There are indeed many parallels, but we do not know as many details, because unlike the Sumerians, the Scandinavians had not yet discovered writing. Apparently, the institution of Sacred Marriage had dwindled by the late Viking Age, if not even earlier, and the only texts we have are much earlier than that. However, there are quite a few indications, such as the sacrifice of a king which certainly happened when there was famine in the land. Then the body parts of the sacrificed king would be brought around the land with the hope that the land would provide once more. There is also a very significant story about a king, who ritually rode in a circle around the Dísarsalinn, which means the Temple of the Goddess.

During the great dísaþing, the Parliament of the Goddesses, which was the name of the annual assembly at Uppsala in Sweden during the Viking Age, the king had to show his worth by circling the temple of the goddess, and if his horse stumbled or he fell off, he was no longer favored by the goddess and no longer fit to rule. I and many others believe that the Scandinavian sacred marriage in connection to kingship is powerfully related to the much older Mesopotamian ritual, and it is thought that the idea spread from there and into Europe during the Bronze Age, which would explain why the rituals are so similar everywhere.

The only thing that makes the Northern traditions stand out as different from the Sumerian, as far as I know, is the emphasis on a drinking ritual in connection to the sacred marriage. The drinking ritual is probably particular to an Indo-European tradition, known to the Celts and the Norse and German cultures, with clear connections to Soma, the sacred drink of the Indian Vedas, and to Haoma, the sacred drink of the Iranian Avesta texts. These ancient Indo-European traditions blended with the originally Mesopotamian ritual of Sacred Marriage as the ritual became established all over Europe during the Bronze Age. My theory is that the ritual of Sacred Marriage is a result of the emergence of a warrior aristocracy, who wanted the people to be ruled and protected by a strong military leader the king. In order to legitimize kingship the power of one man over many people, the king had to prove that he was worthy of leading the people by being accepted and loved by the goddess on whom the people depended for their fortune and prosperity.

As long as the king managed to keep his people happy, it was seen as the blessings of the goddess, and as proof that the king incarnated the husband-brother of the goddess. In the beginning, the kings of Sumer were quite humble in their role, they were titled as the overseers and caretakers of the goddess, like men who ruled under her guidance, a bit like caretakers of the land on behalf of the goddess.

As long as he pleased the goddess, she would provide. The king was elected by the people in Sumer, as he later was in Northern Europe. Yes, the kings were elected by the parliaments even towards the end of the Viking Age. Both the Sumerian and the Norse king knew that if he failed to please his people, protect them, secure the peace and inspire fertility in the goddess of the land, he would be sacrificed and another would replace him. In both cultures, power relations changed over time and the kings became more secure in their positions, but the age-old ritual of Sacred Marriage continued as a powerful symbol of why the king was allowed to rule.

10: THE WISE MAN'S PATH

Once a student of the Edda myths knows how to look for the ritual elements and ritual structures, it becomes obvious that rituals of initiation are central to the lore and that they are even literally described, in great detail. The question is not really if there is an underlying theme of initiation rituals, but what kind of initiation ritual we are talking of. On the dusty shelves of Oslo University library, I have found many studies and papers discussing this, suggesting everything from shamanic rituals to rituals of manhood or initiation into the status of the Einheri.

The Swedish professor, Britt Mari N sström, has suggested a similarity to the initiations of the Classical Mystery cults, a similarity that in my opinion cannot be overlooked. Sadly, the general attitude seems to be that there has to be only one kind of initiation that may explain the myths, at the exclusion of any other. In Norway, the last decades of research on Old Norse initiation mythology has focused almost exclusively on the Sacred Marriage since Gro Steinsland put forth her powerful analysis of various Norse myths as the myths of the Sacred Marriage in connection to royal inauguration. As much as I am inspired by and hold Steinsland's research in great esteem, I must interfere. There is no way, in my opinion, that these rituals, described in such detail, were only relevant to young kings-to-be. The male gods and young men who play the roles of initiates learn of runes, healing, spell-songs, magic, eloquence, poetry, warrior hood and leadership: arts that would have been relevant for warriors, chieftains, healers, poets, priests and shaman-like offices alike.

When Bishop Biarni Kolbeinsson of the Orkney Islands in the year 1200 declared that he had never learned the art of poetry by the water-source, never sung galðr and never sat beneath a hanged man, his statement must have been a pious Christian response to the general and popular expectation of what a spiritual leader would have done in order to come into that position. What Bjarni never did as a Christian bishop was what Pagan spiritual leaders would have done before him a popular expectation that to all appearances was still strong in the year 1200. The actions that he never did are very much the actions described in various accounts of initiation in the Edda lore and strongly suggest that the initiations were not restricted to princes. In the myths of Óðin's initiation, for example, it is not kingship that appears to be the main theme.

Rather, Óðinn stands out as the Fimbulþul [The Great Reciting Sage] a kind of sage or skald, who could recite sacred lore, which Óðinn then proceeds to do during the last part of the Hávamál. Another goal of his is apparently to conquer death and "to come among the binding powers", i.e. the gods that is, to become divine and immortal. In other places, Óðinn is described as a seiðmaðr [male seiðr-practitioner, the masculine counterpart to the vǫlva] and as a viðki [a wise man or wizard]. He is also the prototypical skald or poet. I would suggest that the initiation structure that is described is of a general kind. What is described could be anything, the initiation of a king-to-be, a shaman-like professional such as a þul [reciting sage] or a seiðmaðr, a skald [bard], a góði [priest] or an Einheri, possibly the initiate of a Mystery school devoted to the secrets of immortality. Whatever their purpose, their initiation into a new identity went through the Underworld, their resurrection through the embrace of the Golden Goddess the ultimate fate of the soul.

10.1: HANGING THE SORCERER

*138. I know that I hung on the
wind-swept tree for nine whole
nights stabbed with spears and
given to Óðinn given self to own
self on that tree few know whence
its roots have run.*

*138. Veit ec at ec hecc vindga meiði
a netr allar nío, geiri vndaþr
oc gefinn Oðni,
sialfr sialfom mer,
a þeim meiþi, er mangi veit,
hvers hann af rótom renn.*

*139. Bread was not given me nor
drinking horn
I looked downwards
I picked up the runes
Screaming, I took them then I fell
back there.*

*139. Við hleifi mic seldo
ne við hornigi,
nysta ec niþr,
nam ec vp rvnar,
opandi nam,
fell ec aptr þaðan.*

*140. Nine powerfuil spell-songs
I learned from the famous son
of Harm-Thorn, Bestla's father
[Bestla is Óðin's mother] and I was
given a drink from the precious
mead poured out from Poetry
Blend.*

*140. Fimbvllióð nío
nam ec af enom fregia syni Balþorn
Bestlo faðvr;
oc ec dryc of gat
ens dyra miaðar
ausinn Oðreri.*

*141. Then I learned how to become
wise and to be wise to grow and to
find my well-being
Words from words found more
words for me deeds from deeds
found more deeds for me.*

*141. Þa nam ec frovaz
oc froþr vera
oc vaxa oc vel hafaz;
orð mer af orði orz leitaði,
verc mer af verki vercs leitaþi.*

These are the words of Óðinn, the All-father, greatest among gods, the giver
of breath, spirit and inspiration to all of us. In these stanzas, he is telling us how
he was initiated by hanging, being stabbed, and refused drink and food for nine
whole nights. If you saw my video number seven, that which is disguised in runes,
I talked about how Snorri in his prose Edda did not mention certain important
mythological events, because he was trying to make a version of the myths that
would be acceptable to the Christian Church. The hanging of Óðinn, the self-
sacrifice of the All-father, is one of those events not mentioned by Snorri.

One reason is that the hanging of Óðinn referred to a practice that was simply
too Pagan for the medieval church, another reason might be that the event actually
offered a certain Pagan competition to the Christian faith, namely the self-sacrifice
of a god that led to a kind of resurrection from the dead. Many scholars have
suggested that the hanging of Óðinn is actually a Pagan adaption of the Christian
crucifixion story, that it was never a part of the Norse Pagan faith at all, but simply
a late attempt of the Viking age Pagan, or of a mystic Christian, to show a certain
mysterious connection, even identification, between Óðinn and Jesus.

However, as other scholars have pointed out, references to hanging are very old and found in Iron Age runic inscriptions, and the hanging on the world tree might as well be a very typical and exceedingly ancient shamanic practice known from Siberia among other places. We also know that hanging was a very important religious practice during the Viking age and before that among Germanic tribes. We are talking about human sacrifice, and there is overwhelming evidence that human sacrifice by hanging was common practice among Germanic tribes long before Christianity was even conceived, and that the hanging happened to honor Óðinn and Freyia or their predecessors/counterparts on the continent.

While talking about human sacrifice, I think I should point out here that I am not talking about my personal values, I am just talking about how things actually were. There is no reason to beat around the bush. These people offered other people to the gods, as gifts. To be sacrificed was a great honor, often granted to captured enemy warriors, and why was it an honor? A free man was meant to be a warrior who defended his people, and for a man to be captive after having lost a battle was a great shame, to be a male captive meant being a hostage that could be used against his own people, which was the opposite of his life purpose, or it meant to be a slave, disarmed and dishonored forever. To be sacrificed, however, allowed you a chance to show courage and to die honorably and to be welcomed among the gods after death.

Which is why Germanic tribes were so surprised when their Roman captives cried and begged for mercy when they were about to be offered the honor of being sacrificed after battles won by the Germans. Cultural misunderstandings may have a gruesome outcome sometimes. There are some rather heart-wrenching descriptions of this in the writings of Roman generals, who were appalled at the sight of priestesses cutting the throats of prisoners and filling great cauldrons with blood from which they could divine the will of the gods, and stabbing men hanging from trees. If we are to look at the many Iron Age bodies found in mosses across Northern Europe, the most common way of sacrificing a human being in those days was through a threefold slaughter. The victim would be strangled in honor of Óðinn, stabbed, to honor Þórr, and finally drowned in the moss, given to the Goddess in her moist halls, where she would receive them and assign them to their places in the afterlife.

The markings of a sacrifice were possibly a way to signalize to which gods people hoped that she would send them. The written sources make it pretty clear that Hel or Freyia or the Norns had the power to decide where the souls would go, as the soul would sit for nine days in the "Judgment of the Norns" [Norna Dómr]. We have mentioned how Óðinn observed the hanging and burning of the witch-goddess in his High Hall, and how he observed how she conquered death. Then he observed how she started to walk the Earth, to practice witchcraft and to teach the women, and the god wanted to learn what she had shown, namely immortality and the power to conquer fate, and he was willing to go to extremes to get what he wanted. He actually challenged the people of the goddess, the Vanir, among whom Freyia was called the Vanadís, the Goddess of the Vanir, with a war that he almost lost, but through his cleverness, he managed to make a truce that ensured that the Goddess came to live with him in Ásgarðr.

What happened then, between the god and the goddess, is shrouded in mystery. Apparently, they got married, but then, they were separated, and after their separation, both of them moved around in the world in the shape of witches. According to Snorri, the Goddess taught the art of witchcraft to Óðinn [Heimskringla 4: "Njǫrð's daughter was Freyia, and she was a sacrificial priestess, she was the first to teach the Aesir how to do seiðr, such as the Vanir knew"]. Óðinn was the first male among the Aesir to receive her teachings, and he taught all the other gods, even though they were reluctant to practice it, because it was deemed unmanly. This had for a long time been the sphere of women. Óðinn, wanting knowledge more than anything else, did not care. So what happened in this time this encounter between the goddess and the god, in which she taught, he was taught, they were married, and then separated?

What happened? First of all, let us remember what we know about the high god and the great goddess. She is the ruler and origin of all souls and fates. She knows everything, but keeps her knowledge hidden in the underworld. He is the god who seeks knowledge, he is the very image of the spirit of conscious intelligence, in fact, he is the spirit, he is life, he is breath, he is inspiration, he is passion, through his quest for knowledge, the history of the universe is unfolding. His quest and his initiation affects us all, it is part of our spirit. I think that what happens when he lures the goddess and her people, her knowledge, from the realms of dark unordered space, into his ordered divine realm, is that he receives his initiation. The Goddess has a solar origin, she is the owner of the Brísingamén [Flames' Jewel], from her arms rays of light shine and illuminate the world, she is golden, she is bright, she is fiery.

So her trial is by fire. Óðinn, on the other hand, is spirit. His very name means the spirit. And, he is the giver of breath. So his trial is going to be by strangulation. He lets himself be sacrificed to Óðinn, to the spirit, in the same manner that people were later offered to the god. However, in this case, the sacrifice is part of an initiation ritual. The victim does not die and move on to the next world. He conquers death, he resurrects, bringing with him from that place he went, new knowledge that allows him a new status in life. He learns to become a wise man. Before I go further, let us stop and ask if hanging could have been used as part of initiation rituals in Germanic cultures.

The answer is probably yes. The Icelandic sagas have some examples of what was called a mock sacrifice, in which people were hanged from a noose that was not supposed to actually kill them, just give them a bit of a hard time and a slight lack of breath. They would not be actually stabbed, but a pretend stabbing would happen, more like poking, perhaps a surface slicing. Apparently, victims or mock victims at the temple of Uppsala during the Viking Age would be hanging for nine nights, exactly like Óðinn hung for nine nights. The lack of food and drink would add to the hardships. Imagine hanging from a tree without food and drink for nine whole nights maybe you would start to get visions as well? This kind of practice would certainly give you something like a near death experience or an altered state of consciousness. It is a practice that is certainly similar to the hardships that shamans and ascetics have been facing for thousands of years. Did Óðinn have a near death experience? I have been talking a lot about metaphors, and we will look at the metaphors for death in the first stanza. First of all, Óðinn says that he hangs on the vindga meiði [wind-swept tree].

Snorri taught us that the wind that runs across the worlds originates in the flapping of the wings of the great giant eagle called Hræsvelgr. This name literally translates as Corpse Swallower. This giant, swallowing corpses, producing wind, that is, destroying the movement that is life and at the same time creating the movement of air, life, this giant lives in the North, which is another metaphor for Hel, the world of the dead. Anything that is "wind-swept" is deadly. Just as anything that is wind-shielded or breeze-less is about immortality. Second, he hangs for nine nights. That is no coincidence.

As I have said before, nine is the number of the goddesses. According to Snorri, Hel, the goddess of death, wields power in nine worlds. There are twelve worlds to which we all relate, so there are three worlds of immortality, and they belong to the light elves, who are the immortal souls, not even the gods have reached there yet. Rán, a second goddess of death, has nine daughters, who are identified as worlds, who continually bring dead souls to their mother. Freyia, another goddess of death, lives, according to the Poetic Edda (Grímnismál), in the ninth of the twelve worlds. The ninth realm is where she receives the chosen dead and decides their after-life fate.

The wind and the number nine are metaphors that indicate that Óðinn is having a death-experience when he hangs, and what happens when he almost dies? He looks down. The roots of the world tree are referred to, and at the roots are situated by the Well of Origin, the Cosmic Ocean owned by the goddess of Fate. As it is said in the poem Vǫluspá (St. 20) the goddesses of fate carved the runes of destiny into the wood of the world tree. What Óðinn does next, is to pick up these runes, screaming. He grasps the runes of fate. According to another poem, the Sigrdrifumál, Óðinn carved off the runes, let them flow through his soul in the shape of precious mead, understood them completely, and then sent them out into all the worlds, so that gods, elves, giants and human beings may enjoy them. This was his sacrifice on our behalf.

10.2: THE RITUAL BEHIND THE MYTH
A CHRISTIAN INFLUENCE OR A PAGAN TRADITION?

I have been talking about initiation rituals and how both the myth of the burning of the Goddess in Vǫluspá and the hanging of the god in Hávamál probably reflect real life rituals. We know that mock hangings took place during the Viking age and that these may very well have been parts of a ritual of initiation that follows the path staked out by Óðinn as is described in detail in the Hávamál poem. The hanging, fasting and stabbing leads to Óðinn traveling down to the roots of the World Tree in which he finds the runes of fate and receives the precious drink of poetry, knowledge and transformation. As well as, the embrace of the lady of the dead. Before he returns to life with new knowledge and a new status, that of a "binding force" as a god, and of a wise sage to whom people come to ask for guidance. The gods were known by metaphors such as "fetters" and "bonds", and there are still several aspects of Óðin's initiation story that should be discussed, but I am still concerned with the ritual aspect of the myth.

There is an on-going debate among scholars as to whether the myths of the Poetic Edda may be understood as real sources to pre-Christian religion, or whether the myths should be understood only as sources to the minds of the people who wrote them down during the already Christianized 12th and 13th centuries. One thing seems pretty clear to everybody. In Scandinavia, Pagan elements and folklore survived strongly in Scandinavia up until the witch trials of the 15th and 16th centuries when most of these elements were finally and brutally destroyed. Perhaps I shall talk about that another time. The question is, how good were people's memories really?

Are these Pagan elements just faint echoes that may have been disfigured by the new Christian mentalities, or are they part of a truly Pagan heritage that had survived? More importantly to us, are the poems of the Edda true renderings of Pagan poetry and Pagan myths, or are they inventions of the 12th century Christian poets, who just let themselves be inspired by whatever had survived of the poetic language of the past? I firmly believe that the Poetic Edda is a true Pagan heritage. I believe this because I am convinced that the myths describe credible Pagan rituals, such as that of Óðin's hanging. Supporters of the Christian Medieval line have claimed that the hanging is just a version of the Crucifixion story and has no roots in Pagan thinking at all. However, as I have been pointing out lately, Óðin's hanging is a good description of what archaeology has proved happened to victims of sacrifice for more than a thousand years, beginning in the Iron Age and even before the birth of Christ.

Wooden figurine from Norway, Viking Age, showing the god with one eye.

Many written sources about the Viking Age at least describe such hangings, both real and mock hangings that happened in honor of Óðinn and of Freyia. His receiving mead from a woman in the underworld has its ancient archaeological counterparts, as do the Sacred Marriage in the Underworld theme, these three, the hanging, the ritual serving of mead and the Underworld marriage are all mythical elements that are dating back at least two thousand years and are often even older. Now the whole structure of the myth reflects a typical, well known and almost universal pattern of initiation ritual in Pagan societies.

➤   One, the hanging is a typical archaic technique of ecstasy as described by Mircea Eliade in his famous book on shamanism. A technique of ecstasy is designed to cause the subject to alter their consciousness, so that they may travel out of their bodies and into other worlds. These kinds of techniques are known from shamanic, ascetic and other Pagan traditions. We may also call it a vision quest, since the goal is to open up ones vision. Óðinn, indeed, has a vision, as he "peers down" and discovers the runes. I personally can see NO Christian element whatsoever in this vision quest story.

➤➤ Two: The next step of the ritual pattern is the vision itself. Óðinn sees the runes, secrets that had been hidden since the birth of the universe, secrets held by the ladies of the well of origin. We KNOW that the runes and the fates and the World Tree belong to an age-old Pagan tradition, that is, there is NO Christian medieval element to this vision.

➤➤ Three: The third step of the pattern is the descent, when Óðinn travels into the underworld. Again, is this a Pagan or a Christian medieval element? Pagan, of course.

➤➤ Four: The fourth step of the pattern is the trials. Óðinn has to prove his worth and courage, and through his training, having received the powerful, magical spell-songs from his maternal uncle. He manages to convince the guardian of the underworld realm to let him live and marry his daughter. Is this a Christian or a Pagan element? Pagan.

➤➤ Five: The fifth step of the path of initiation is the consecration. This is where Óðinn is rewarded for his trials, receives the knowledge of the runes and the love of the goddess. Symbolized as the serving of a mead that lets the knowledge of the runes enter his very soul, and in the marriage with the lady of death. Here, I can see similarities to proven and long-standing, five thousand year old rituals of sacred marriage from Sumer and with the five thousand year old texts that speak of soma, the drink of immortality, in the Vedas, but I can see no Christian, medieval element whatsoever.

➤➤ Six: The sixth step is the return and the result. Óðinn has become, as he says, a sage, a magician, and a god. Again, a Pagan and very ancient element. So my point here is, from beginning to end, and in every detail and with any purpose, the story of Óðin's hanging is completely Pagan in origin and there is no way that it could have been invented within a Christian framework.

This in itself is one of the many pieces of evidence that the Poetic Edda is a genuine source to Pagan lore. The pattern I just described is typical of Pagan initiation rituals, and it includes detailed descriptions of real life ritual practices that are proven to have existed during the Pagan eras. Furthermore, the story of Óðinn is not the only one in the Poetic Edda. There are in fact so many that I have to pick out a few and stick to only the two first steps of the initiation here. The vision quest with its technique of ecstasy, and the subsequent vision. The vision always leads to the other steps, the descent, the trial, the consecration and the return, but I shall now focus on the two first steps.

The poetic Edda provides us with several different kinds of ritual descriptions. Obviously, not everybody had to hang. Sometimes, it would be enough to sacrifice something else, or someone else, perhaps. In the Hyndlulióð, The Song of the She-Wolf, the human being called Óttarr makes a sacrifice to the Ásyniur, the goddesses. According to the poem, Óttarr had always been devoted to the Ásyniur, but this sacrifice is special, because he has decided that he wants to claim his heritage, which is the "gold of Valland". Valland is another name for Valhǫll, the afterlife of the chosen ones, gold is a metaphor for wisdom and divine light. So what Óttarr is praying for is the wisdom of the afterlife, and we are told that this will lead to Valhǫll, a chosen death. As Óttarr makes the sacrifice and blood covers the altar, the rock of the altar turns into crystal and the goddess Freyia appears, turns Óttarr into a boar and rides him down to Hel.

The sacrifice is the technique of ecstasy by which Óttarr receives his vision, this time of the transformation of his sacrifice, the appearance of the Great Goddess, and his own identification with the sacrifice as he becomes the sacrificial animal and moves into the underworld. The structure of the whole myth is exactly like that of Óðinn on a structural and thematic level. Sacrifice followed by a vision followed by a descent into the underworld, followed by trials and teachings below, followed by the goddess offering him the so-called drink of memory and calling him her husband. The goal is to reach Valhǫll, an alternative afterlife.

This one element, the alternative afterlife, has led some to believe that there is a salvation theme in the story and that there must thus be a Christian element in the story. However, who says that Pagans did not think about salvation? The Mystery cults that were everywhere in the Pagan Hellenistic and Roman empires were all concerned with the salvation of the soul after death, salvation that could only come if in life you had gone through the initiation into the mysteries of the Goddess. Again, I must say, I can see nothing Christian about this myth at all. It is Pagan through and through, even with its Pagan (and older, I should say) version of salvation. We have the several heroic poems that follow the same structure of initiation, all offering new alternatives and details as to how one seeks the necessary vision. The stories of King Hiǫrvarðr and of Sígurðr both describe how heroes seek visions in sacred groves and suchlike.

In the Poem of Helgi Hiǫrvarðsson, we first learn that earl Atli, on behalf of his king, enters the so-called Svávaland, "Land of [going to] Sleep", in which he stays for a while, trying to convince the king, Svafnir, which means "the Sleep-Maker" to give his daughter as a wife to the king. When this fails, the earl Atli returns to the land of the waking and goes into a grove in which he dozes off and then, miraculously he understands the speech of birds, and a little bird speaks to him. The bird makes demands for a sacrifice, Atli makes a sacrifice, and then the bird gives him a vision of the beautiful maiden of the Underworld, and explains that she is guarded by a giant in eagle's disguise.

This eagle is familiar, it is the eagle Hræsvelgr [Corpse Swallower], death itself that keeps the bright, golden, shining maiden in darkness. The bird explains that the eagle needs to be killed before he can take the maiden. During the third part of the story, the king and the earl ascend a sacred mountain together, from which they can both look into the "Land of Sleep". There, they see the eagle and realize that the eagle of death is guarding a maiden for both of them, one for the king and one for the earl. Finally, the two of them go to sleep, again, by the river that is a border to the Land of Sleep, and while the king sleeps, the earl enters the Land of Sleep, kills the giant eagle of death and returns with both the bright golden maidens. What at first sight appears like a fairy tale may be broken down into the elements of the structure of initiation as I talked about earlier, and each element actually describes what would happen during an actual ritual.

Image on 7th century Gotland memorial stone

One: When one bothers to translate the names of the places, it makes sense that Atli and the king always fall asleep before they travel to Svávaland, which is in fact the land of going to sleep. This element is about dreams. Everything in the story happens in the realm of dreams, which was obviously deeply connected to reality, again, a Pagan element. The goal of the dreaming, the maiden, is a magical maiden. This bride lives in dreams.

Atli's title of earl, iarl, is not a coincidence. The title is derived from an old Nordic title erilaR, which actually refers to a magician, a sage, a priest or shaman. This is why the "earl" does all the dreaming and traveling into the dream realms. He is a shaman type. Although the bride is intended for the king, the king's shaman does most of the work and the king is only required to spend a night at the borders of the dream realm with his shaman. Another part of the ritual here is seeking the advice of birds within a sacred grove. This is not an element of fantasy and fairy tale; it is a detailed description of an age-old religious tradition.

Two thousand years ago, Roman sources explained that the Germanic tribes all worshiped their gods within sacred groves, in which they would also talk to birds and other animals. The action, meditating within a sacred grove, followed by the building of an altar and the sacrifice of cattle within the same grove, all with the purpose of having visions of the supernatural maiden of the land of dreams. To me it seems obvious that these are all descriptions of Pagan practices. All these activities lead to a journey into the otherworld in which the bright maidens are rescued from the guardianship of the eagle of death and brought back to the waking world as brides of those who have undertaken the journey.

10:3 THE VISION QUEST

We are still talking about techniques of ecstasy or vision quests described in the Poetic Edda, showing that the poems of the Edda were indeed created within a completely Pagan context. I ended the last chapter with a description of how king Hiǫrvarðr and his earl, that is, his royal shaman, used dreams, meditations and sacrifice in order to move into the realm of dreams and bring the bright maiden of dreams out from the darkness of death to the world of the living and the waking. Now Hiǫrvarðr had a son by his maiden, and he was a special one. No name would set with him, he kept to himself and spoke little.

One day this prince sat down on a mound, a burial mound, and this Old Norse Pagan practice was called utiseta, "to sit outside", when someone would seek communion with spirits and suchlike by sitting beneath a hanged man, on a burial mound, or at a crossroads. We may safely call this practice a vision quest, a Pagan technique of ecstasy that required meditation in powerful places. This meditation performed by the prince is followed by a vision. Nine Valkyrie suddenly appear before the young man. As most of you know, the Valkyrie is a goddess of the dead, who resides in Valhǫll. From her functions and names we learn that she is a sort of fate goddess, and it has been established that the Valkyrie are aspects of or else closely related to Freyia, who like them "chooses the vál". The structure is clear the vision quest is as usual followed by a vision of the supernatural "maiden". In this vision, the young man sees nine maidens riding together in a group. They are golden and bright, and rays of light flash from them as they move. The leader of the group of nine Valkyrie is called Svava, which means "the Sleeper". She addresses the young prince by giving him his true name, Helgi, the sacred one.

Helgi Hiǫrvarðsson asks her counsel and her hand in marriage, she advises him and sets him trials that he has to overcome. Before he can marry the Valkyrie, he has to, among many other things, move into a place called the Fjord of Hatred [Hatafiorðr], and destroy the giants called Hatred [Hati] and Unrest Ocean [Hróðmarr], and overcome the advances of the giantess called Frosty Enclosure [Hrímgerðr], who lives in the waves and is one of Ran's nine daughters. She tries to sink his boat and is only kept from doing this through the incantations of the sorcerer Sinfiǫtli, and finally the Valkyrie come to their aid. Hrímgerðr reveals that only the protection of the Valkyrie prevents her from drowning the men. Her attack means that the hero has to overcome death, or the fear of death. The Valkyrie represents the opposite fate in death as that of Hrímgerð's frosty "enclosure". After he has succeeded, he marries the Valkyrie, but she continues to live with her group of nine Valkyrie and to ride the air and sea.

When she and her sisters move through the sky, flashes and rays of lightning and sunlight surrounds them, and they are continually referred to as golden and bright. As soon as he has passed the trials, they are married, but she is no ordinary housewife. She continues to live within her own band of nine women, riding the air and sea, and illuminating the world with her rays of light. However, she also comes to him as a wife, protects and guides him in battles and in life as a whole. When he finally dies, she follows him into the grave and swears that she will find him again in his next life, and be his Valkyrie once more. So Helgi is indeed reborn, this time as Helgi Hundingsbani, son of Sígmundr, who is a sorcerer king. To make a long story really short, the story of Helgi is described in the two poems of Helgi Hundingsbani and they have slightly different versions.

I am just going to give a brief resume. Helgi is born and grows up as a prince and a warrior and acts unwisely until one day he dozes off the dreaming theme again. After having performed a very odd ritual of drinking the blood of a bear, alternately after having fought a battle and faced death. He falls asleep by the so-called Arasteinn, which means the Rock of the Eagle. The eagle, as we know, is a symbol of death. As he falls asleep, the Valkyrie appears to him and announces herself, revealing that they were married in his previous life and that he ought to get his act together unless he wants to lose her love.

She rebukes him for having destroyed the Fróðafríðr, the Piece of Wisdom, and for needlessly shedding blood. Hardly what we would normally expect from a Viking Age poem or from a Valkyrie's words, but then we do have a lot of stereotypical ideas about what Viking Age people thought about things. We tend to discredit them as mindless bloodthirsty barbarians and fail to recognize that there may have been more diversity in opinion among our ancestors and deeper spiritual aspects to some of their lore. Now, Helgi does get his act together as he learns that his previous death happened as he lost the battle of the rock of Greed, and indeed in this life he manages to win it. He overcomes Greed. As before, the Valkyrie comes to his aid in life and in death.

Death occurs as the god Óðinn decides that he wants to have Helgi as a warrior in Valhǫll and lends his spear to an enemy who kills Helgi. This is to say that he has an honorable death. The Valkyrie bride goes to him in the burial mound and describes herself as the hungry raven of Óðinn, who wants to drink her lover's blood. Which is a suitable and expected line of thought for a Valkyrie, a goddess of death, and shows what she is capable of. However, she will not devour this one. She remembers her love for him and declares that they shall drink the precious mead within the grave, before they move on to Valhǫll.

Helgi's younger brother, Sígurðr, is the next one to go through a ritual of initiation. Sígurðr is born after the death of Helgi and one may wonder if there is another reincarnation of Helgi, but it is not said directly. This story is so long that I shall not go into it in much detail. The important thing is that Sígurðr decides that he wants to learn about magic and wisdom and is taught by a dwarf smith. This is not coincidental, just as the "earl" of King Hiǫrvarðr was not coincidental. The scholar Lotte Motz has shown that in Germanic folklore dwarfs always represent a sort of priest character. The same is true of blacksmiths, who were regarded as the keepers of sacred knowledge.

So the young prince Sígurðr is in fact seeking the teachings of a type of priest or sage. During his learning period, Sígurðr learns about sacred legends and other things. He seeks his own maternal uncle, just like Óðinn did and is told about his fate, and more importantly about a beautiful, golden maiden, who sleeps on a sacred mountain, awaiting his arrival. It is stated that the golden maiden, the Valkyrie and sister of Óðinn, has slept ever since Helgi died. This spurs Sígurðr on, and he wants to seek the maiden, but he has a duty, namely to avenge his father, so before his initiation, he goes to war. On the way, he meets Óðinn, the spirit, standing quietly and balanced on a rock in the middle of a stormy ocean, and he asks his advice. After Sígurðr has won the battle and killed all his enemies, he is being praised by his teacher, but Sígurðr takes no pride in the killings, declaring that many a courageous man never killed another.

Now, Sígurðr finally carries on with his initiation. His teacher is an evil man and does not teach Sígurðr about the maiden at all, but Sígurðr has already heard about the maiden from his maternal uncle, so he has his own plans. After having killed a serpent and drunk its blood, Sígurðr has learned all the secrets of the serpent of death, and now he can understand the speech of birds, and they tell him about the Valkyrie that sleeps on the sacred mountain. Sígurðr, now shining with divine gold, rides up to the mountain, breaks into the walls of fire that surrounds the maiden, cuts her loose from the armor and wakes her up. She offers him the mead of memory and teaches him about runes.

When Sígurðr later dies, the Valkyrie rides after him into Hel and saves him from the all-devouring ogress of death, bringing him back to her home-country, Valland. Two other Edda poems, the Gróagalðr and the Fjǫlsvinnsmál tell about the young hero called Svípdagr, who wants to find the maiden called Meng-lǫð, which translates as Invitation to Blend. The usual translation is based on separating the name into men-glǫð, which would mean Jewel Happy, but my translation follows the suggestion of Svava Jacobsdottir [see bibliography]. In order to find his way, he goes to the grave of his mother, who had been a witch.

This witch is called Gróa, which is the name of a giantess witch, who once healed Þórr after a battle by singing spell-songs. Now the lady is dead, but the young boy sits on her burial mound and invokes her spirit with prayers. The dead woman's spirit rises from the grave and sings nine powerful spell-songs to her child sounds familiar, doesn't it? The sitting on a burial mound is the ancient technique of ecstasy known to the Vikings as utiseta, "to sit outside", and is also what young Helgi did when he had his vision of nine Valkyrie.

The nine spell-songs echo the nine spell-songs given to Óðinn before his descent. After having sung the spell-songs, the dead witch gives her son advice as to how to proceed if he wants to have luck with the maiden. To make a long story short, young Svípdagr gets to the impenetrable halls of the maiden where he, just like Óinn and the earl Atli, has to show his eloquence to a giant guardian. It is revealed that the bride waiting for him behind dangerous and deadly gates is seated at the Mountain of Medicine [Lyfjaberg] below the Tree of Memory [Mímameiðr] together with her nine handmaidens, another repeated theme, sleeping as she awaits her true husband. In this poem, the Fjǫlsvinnsmál, the maiden is said to be the ruler of all the halls and fields, and she is referred to as the Þióðmæra, the Great Maiden, surrounded by her group of nine ladies.

As Svípdagr looks into the hall he suddenly remembers that he has been married to the maiden all the time, but that he had forgotten his true union with the Maiden, because he had died so many times, and as he remembers, the impenetrable walls open wide and the lady of the halls and fields wakes up and greets him as her true husband. As I have said time and again, all the details and the very structure of these stories are deeply Pagan in origin and reflect typical aspects of Pagan rituals. They all follow the same structure. The hero seeks a vision through some Pagan ritual that serves as a technique of ecstasy.

He has a vision, and that vision usually includes the bright golden maiden hidden in the underworld, a vision that leads to the hero moving into that world and facing dangerous trials before he finally enters the halls of the great maiden, and receives her drink and her embrace. The goal, when it is stated, is usually to reach Valhǫll, the alternative after life. The maiden that is sought by the hero is always described in the same way and has exactly the same function and lives in the same kind of place. She is sometimes a giantess and sometimes a goddess and sometimes a Valkyrie. Some of the poems make it clear that the Valkyrie reincarnates, or that she falls asleep on sacred mountains and returns with a new name every time she wakes. As I have said before, the maiden with the mead is an aspect of the Great Goddess and to every human being she is fate.

The goal of the initiation is to wake up and unite oneself with one's personal fate goddess, an aspect of the great goddess yet an individual fate. What I want to stress here is that all these stories follow the same structure, the same pattern of initiation, and all show that they have the same goal. The Poetic Edda is crammed with these stories, they actually completely dominate the whole collection of Pagan poems. This is the reason why I believe that the Poetic Edda is in fact a testimony to actual Pagan, pre-Christian lore, remembered by certain people, who managed to maintain the poems quite unaltered until they were written down during the 12th century. Furthermore, I suspect that the deeply Pagan character of this collection of ancient poems, and especially the fact that they all deal with a kind of salvation, is the real reason why the manuscript was hidden away from the 13th century and did not resurface until the 17th century AD.

11: The trials of Þórr-The son of Earth-

11.1: Þórr in Hárbarðsljóð

This chapter is dedicated to Þórr, god of thunder, lightning and protection. In my second video in this series, I talked about how the Þórr mythology may reflect some ancient knowledge about electricity and the electromagnetic sphere around Earth (see Chapter 2.8). I am going to talk about a different aspect of Þórrlore. According to Snorri, Þórr was foremost among the gods after Óðinn, and was the son of Óðinn with the Earth goddess. Several Edda poems refer to Þórr as the son of Óðinn, as well as the son of Earth, so this was probably how people looked upon it during the Viking Age. However, a different and probably earlier version of this exists; in which Þórr is the ancestor and the original god of the Aesir, and Óðinn a human descendant. It is impossible to say which version is correct, because both versions would be correct to those who believe in either, but that Þórr is the older god is historically true.

He is a European version of the Indian god Indra, who was worshiped in India at least five thousand years ago. The Thunder god was the most prominent deity of the first Indo-European invaders in Northern Europe, and two thousand years ago a Roman writer told us that the German tribes all believed that they were descended from the Earth goddess and her son, Þórr. He was the first born of mother Earth and thus the big brother of all human beings, and ancestor at least to the Aesir gods, including Óðinn. His popularity during the Viking Age was immense at the temple of Uppsala in Sweden he took the central space and was flanked by Óðinn and Freyr. In Iceland too, he was the most popular, something which is reflected in the Prose Edda written by Snorri about 1225 AD, more than two hundred years after conversion to Christianity.

No Pagan god receives more attention in the Prose Edda than Þórr does, which does not actually tell us anything else than that his lore was the part of the Norse lore that was most easily remembered by the general public, probably due to the high action level. Þórr lore is very entertaining and easily remembered. His mythology was the ancient equivalent of modern action movies, the James Bond, Indiana Jones or Bruce Willis type of movies. At least on the surface. I am going to take a peek under the surface and look towards the hidden structures of initiation and messages of a spiritual quest that can be drawn from the lore of Þórr, and I will focus mainly on the Poetic Edda as a source, because this is the oldest source we have.

The Poetic Edda does not give Þórr the same overwhelming, dominating space as Snorri does out of 34 Edda poems, only three are dedicated to the Thunder god, although he is of course mentioned in a couple of other poems. So, I will put these three together and look at the story they tell as a whole. I will be using Snorri's Edda only in the manner it was meant to be used, to explain the metaphors of the Edda poems. It is my conviction that the Poetic Edda represents not the totality of the Norse Pagan world, but rather represents a particular tradition with a particular message. In this tradition, Þórr is not taken as seriously as he probably was by the common man and worshiper. He is actually ridiculed a lot. Why?

Because if you look beyond the awe-inspiring concept of Þórr, the mighty Thunder god and our protector and ancestor, if you look past the possible connection between Þórr and ancient science, and to the metaphorical spiritual message level, Þórr represents something metaphorically. He represents us, the human species, especially the males. His mother, the Earth, was considered the ancestral mother of all humans, and Þórr is her first-born son. He is the archetypal man in the Indo-European tradition. His character is in every respect the ideal Indo-European or Viking Age peasant warrior. Brute strength and courage is the ideal. Intelligence, on the other hand, is not particularly emphasized. Now, imagine you are a poet, a highly educated person, a sensitive, thinking person, initiated into great spiritual mysteries, living in a world dominated by, well, "Thors".

I think I can relate to how frustrating that sometimes would be, but that was what a Viking Age poet had to relate to on an everyday basis. Now, how to make use of this? How to employ the Þórr character in a poetic tradition that requires parables and allegories to convey spiritual truths? To the Norse poet, Þórr is fantastic material, how to make this simple-minded and rather uneducated warrior into a learning initiate? Let us take the first Þórr poem of the Edda, Hárbarðsljóð [The Song of Long Beard]. This poem is a perfect example of Edda Þórr-bashing. The mighty god is completely ridiculed as a simple-minded brute. Many scholars have thought that this poem must be reflecting the arguments between those who primarily worshiped Óðinn and those who primarily worshiped Þórr. Óðinn stands out as the god of smart noblemen, while Þórr is the god of ignorant peasants.

I do not believe it is that simple, and I am uncertain about whether anyone living in Pagan times would dare to offend each other's gods that much. Remember that they believed in all of them. Even the poet would probably pray to Þórr for protection. I think we should look more closely at this poem and reconsider its metaphorical nature. The poem begins with a dilemma, Þórr wants to get into Ásgarðr, the land of the gods, and stands by a river, needing the "ferryman" to take him across into the lands of Óðinn. The ferryman is Óðinn, but Þórr does not recognize this, and stupidly enough believes the old god when he says that he is called Long Beard. This is a little hint to the reader, you need to understand that one character may turn up with new names and new shapes in all the stories, but it is easy to be fooled if you are blind, like Þórr is in this poem.

Another thing we have to ask ourselves is why Þórr is not just crossing the rainbow bridge like all the other gods do when they move between worlds. The answer lies with Snorri, who says that Þórr cannot use the rainbow bridge like all the other gods, because he is too "heavy". He has to cross the river like a mortal. Let us just stop there at the bridge. The rainbow bridge is the bridge between the different dimensions of the Cosmos. It has names, one of the names is Bifrǫst, which means "Shivering Voice", or "Vibrating Voice". Another name of the rainbow bridge is Bíflind, which means "Gentle Vibration" [from bífa to shiver [vibrate] and lind, gentle]. Obviously, Þórr doesn't have a soft vibration. Now, before we continue, remember that poetically, Þórr represents human beings, especially male human beings, and just like us mortals, he has to cross the river of death to get to the other side. Þórr tries to make the ferryman do his job and take him into the spirit/divine realm, but to his surprise, the ferryman refuses. Þórr's immediate reaction is typical of him, stupid and simple, he rages, becomes furious and demanding.

Bronze figurine of Thor from Akureyri, Iceland, 1000 AD

He threatens, and he boasts about his grand, heroic deeds, only to experience, probably for the first time in his life, that his listener is not in the least impressed. The ferryman seems to just point out the stupidities in Þórr's actions. Þórr starts to ask the ferryman what he did then, since he is not impressed by Þórr's heroic deeds, and the ferryman, Óðinn in disguise, replies [stanza 16]:

«I was with Much Alert/Wise Spring for five winters on that island [of immortality] which is called Ever Green we fought men there and fell many Chosen Tried many things and met some maidens."	*«Var ec meþ Fiolvari fimm vetr alla i ey þeirre, er Algron heitir; vega ver þar knattom oc val fella, margs at freista, mans at kosta.»*

The mention of women immediately catches Þórr's attention. He asks how the "girls" behaved, and Óðinn replies [stanza 18]:

«The women would have been life-sparks, had they only been docile with us The women would have been wise, had they only been benevolent towards us; They spun threads out of the sand They dug the ground out of the valleys, I was the one who prevailed and ruled them, I rested with the seven sisters had all their love and pleasure. What did you do then, Þorr?	*«Sparkar atto ver konor, ef oss at spa/kom yrði; horscar atto ver konor, ef oss hollar veri; þer or sandi síma vndo oc or dali divþom grvnd vm grofo; varþ ec þeim einn a/llom efri at raþom, hvilda ec hia þeim systrom siav oc hafða ec geþ þeirra allt oc gaman. Hvaþ vanntv þa meþan, Þorr?»*

This needs some clarification. The girls, the seven sisters, are not ordinary women. The reference to spinning threads indicates that they are Nornir, fate goddesses, and the fact that they are digging valleys also indicates that they are giantesses, because giantesses were the original shapers of Earth, as it is said in another Edda poem, the Grottasǫngr. Óðinn encountered these primeval female forces, the fates, and despite their wild nature and lack of docility, he managed to seduce them into loving him.

It is a metaphor. Þórr doesn't really understand this and feebly continues boasting about his manly deeds, getting more and more frustrated by the fact that the ferryman, Death, remains completely unimpressed. Again, let us stop for a moment to consider what this means. Óðinn is the spirit and he is the spirit of that realm which Þórr is seeking to enter, the realm of the gods. The message here is that even if Þórr gains mundane popularity through his strength and abilities as a warrior, this will take him nowhere spiritually. No matter how much he flexes his muscles and displays his manliness, spirit doesn't care. Spirit cares about other things, and after having endured a little more of Þórr's self-important rambling on about his own greatness, the ferryman turns the focus back towards supernatural women.

Óðinn says (stanza 30):
«I was to the east [= the giant world] and made love/wooed someone, I made love to the Linen White woman in secret I met her and I made the Golden Fair happy she allowed me pleasure.

«Ec var austr
oc við einhveria domþac,
lec ec við ena línhvito
oc la/nþing háþac,
gladdac ena gvllbiorto,
gamni mer vnði.»

So, according to the interpretations I have been presented with by others than myself, this is supposedly about a bragging contest between the two gods, where Þórr brags about his warrior abilities and Óðinn brags about his seduction abilities, but that interpretation is to disregard the allegorical nature of the myth. We have to ask, who is the Linen White woman? Well, first of all, she lives in the east (like Menglǫð in the Fjǫlsvinnsmál). In Norse Cosmology, the east is the direction of the giants, just as south is the direction of the gods and the north is the direction of Hel.

This means that the Linen White woman is a giantess, or a maiden living among giants. Having read through this book, you may find this familiar. Not only is she a giantess, but she is also associated with linen, which connects her to the Nornir and the Valkyrie as well as to fate again. She is described as bright and golden, which is the formula used to describe the consecrating maiden in all the initiation stories throughout the Edda.

To confirm this interpretation, we need only look at the next stanzas in the poem, where Þórr gets confused and asks if the "girls" were nice, and the ferryman, Óðinn, replies angrily:

32: "I was in need of YOUR assistance, Þórr! if I was to keep the Linen White maiden!"

32: «Liþs þins var ec þa þvrfi, Þorr!
at ec helda þeirri enni linhvito mey.»

And Þórr replies:
33: "I would have helped you with that, if I had only been there!"

33: «Ec mvnda þer þa þat veita, ef ec viðr of komomc.»

Is this not an odd exchange? It gets even odder, because

Óðinn asks:
36: "What DID you do then, Þórr?"

36: «Hvat vanntv [þá] meþan, Þorr?»

Yes, what did Þórr do when he was supposed to help Óðinn marry the Linen White woman? Well, Þórr replies:

37: «"Berserk brides did I battle at the Wind-Shielded Island, they were worse than anything! They made all people wild!"

37: «Brvþir berserkia barþac i Hléseyio, þer hofðo verst vnnit, velta þioþ alla.»

Óðinn says:
38: "It was a shameful act, Þórr, when you beat up women."

38: «Kleki vantv þa, Þorr! er þv a konom barþir.»

And Þórr exclaims: "But..!
39: «She-Wargs they were, they were not women; They broke my ship that I had built with such care They threatened me with iron bars And they chased Þialfi away!"

39: «Vargynior þat varo, enn varla konor; sceldo scip mitt, er ec scorþat hafdac; ogðo mer iarnlvrki, enn elto Þialfa.»

In truth, the ladies of the Wind-Shielded Island are not actual women. Their island is the Island of Immortality, where gods and elves will meet to drink the precious mead and recapitulate the history of the world. The women of that island are the daughters of Aegir, the mothers of the universe, the golden lights of the gods, the Valkyrie followers of the fates of men. One Edda poem, Oddrúnargrátr, clearly identifies the same island of immortality as the home of the nine original Valkyrie, identifying it thus with Valland and Valhǫll, and it is the place where they spin fates.

As I have said before, the division between giantesses, Nornir and Valkyrie is not as clear-cut as is commonly believed. Also, this ocean is situated below the World Tree, which is the same ocean from which the Nornir emerge. This is just one of countless so-called "confusions" in the Edda, which is to my mind not confusion at all, but proves the fact that all the female forces are connected and may identify with each other.

The point here is that the women that Þórr tries to fight are primeval forces connected to fate, and they are not being nice to him. They are she-wolves, representing the destructive face of fate. Wolves in the metaphors of the Old Norse poets always indicate either greed and destruction, or mortality and death. Yet to the ignorant, these "women" are nothing but a threat to the known world and the limited mind. While Þórr, in this poem, as in many others, represents the mentality of a human, especially a human male, in this poem Óðinn represents as in many others, the spirit in this case. Þórr's spirit, the divine spirit part of the man Þórr.

We know the importance of waking up the bright fate sleeping within during initiation. The spirit of any human has already known the bright fate goddess, but could not keep her, because the Þórr-human was not "there". The mentality, the mind, wasn't present. Instead of being in the place of spirit, our average human representative, especially our average male representative, was out battering women. As Þórr says, in his defense, these women were not really women (battering women was considered thoroughly dishonorable and shameful for a man), as already explained above. When Þórr tries to get to the land of immortality just like he is trying now without much luck, when he gets there, he is tested by giantesses/Nornir /Valkyrie, who have existed before this universe was born. They are the unknown. They are the real power in this universe, but Þórr recognizes no power besides his own manly heroism.

The wolf-skin that the fates wear when meeting Þórr indicate that Þórr, like all human beings, is struggling with the fate of mortality and greed, and when they attack his ship, the ship that he has made so carefully, and chasing away his servant Þialfi we must ask what Þialfi means. His name means "holding together". These mind-blowing ladies disturb the holding together of Þórr's mind. They challenge his "ship" that he has made so much effort to build his paradigm of understanding. They knock it over, and he, representing the average man, is too stupid to react with anything but rage and getting nowhere in the spirit world. In the end of this poem, Óðinn says to Þórr that his wife Síf has a lover, and that his mother, the Earth, is dying. Þórr takes all this as an insult and is getting angrier and angrier, while Óðinn remains calm and repeats that this is the case. Now we have to ask ourselves what Síf represents. Her name simply means "female relative", which might bring the Fylgjur to mind.

The followers that guide the individual and spin of our fates. Some may be the souls of dead female relatives, others more closely linked to the individual's actual soul. On this level of meaning, where Þórr represents the human being, the "wife" or "female relative" always represents his fate. What is being said here is that the fate who spins Þórr's destiny is not faithful to him that is, his course of life is destructive and traitorous, and his mother Earth whom he was born to guard, is dying. He has lost his true purpose. He was supposed to use his strength to protect the Earth and human kind, but has been wasting time fighting his fate and boasting about his manly deeds, and now she is dying. Before Þórr angrily stomps away, still not really understanding the message, he has the sudden insight to ask the Ferryman what he can do in order to get into the land of the gods after all. The Ferryman tells him that he will find the way into Óðin's land, into the world of the gods, if he only keeps to "the left path", because then he will be found by his mother, the Earth, and she will tell him the way to the lands of Óðinn.

This is actually reminiscent of a passage in the Rig Veda (10.18), where it says: *"Crawl you, to your mother the Earth, for she will save you from the void."*

We are leaving Þórr here in a state of anger and on a destructive path, but there is hope. When he asked for the way, he has finally asked the right question, and received valuable counsel. Will he follow that counsel? In the following chapter, I will tell the rest of the story.

11.2: Þórr in Þrymskvíða and Hymiskvíða

In the last chapter, I discussed how the great god Þórr was humiliated and ridiculed in the Edda poem Hárbarðsljóð, the Song of Long Beard. I would draw an example from a very good Chinese Kung Fu movie. It is called Fearless and stars Jet Li. The story is about a young man, played by Jet Li, who has trained Kung Fu all his life and is now almost unbeatable. He takes down one champion after the other and is very proud of himself. Yes, he is a great fighter, but there is no wisdom in him. The driving force behind his learning Kung Fu in the first place, is a fear of humiliation and loss, and a need to show them all. He gets into brawls, he drinks, he thinks that winning fame by winning fights is the meaning of life and what gives him worth, and his students are bullies, with his blessing.

One day he ends up killing an opponent for a perceived offense, giving into rage without having investigated the circumstances that led to the fight. It turns out that Jet Li's character was wrong about his opponent and that he has now killed a very honorable man, widowed a decent woman and made an innocent child fatherless. Also, there are repercussions, and his own mother and daughter are killed. Jet Li's character almost tries to avenge them before he understands that he himself is to blame. He realizes that he has been incredibly boastful, blind, stupid, ruthless and cruel, and that despite him winning a fight, he has lost his beloved ones, his honor and face. Everything in his life falls apart and he leaves his home and almost dies in the wilderness.

However, he is picked up by a humble farmer's family, and lives with an old peasant grandmother and her blind daughter for several years, learning to appreciate the earth, humility and simplicity. Through gentleness, he finds his true spiritual strength, which ultimately leads him to become a greater warrior than before. When he finally returns, he has truly become a great master, who acts with true courage and true fearlessness, for he no longer fears losing and he has no need to show off for his own sake. He has learned to not abuse the power of his supreme fighting skills.This is a theme that repeats itself in many stories, especially warrior stories.

You have the Karate Kid movies, for example, where the theme is always a young foolish boy who wishes to learn to fight to get back at his enemies, yet he encounters a wise teacher who, often through humiliation, teaches him to be humble, perceptive, meek, soft, respectful and invincible. A similar idea is found in Taoism, where it is said that a master of Tao, if he is a man, needs to become "like a woman". Not to become a transvestite (not of modern LGBTQ+ concepts), but to assume the qualities that are traditionally associated with women. Perceptive, humbleness, meekness, gentleness weakness, only with those qualities may Tao enter the body and mind, and wisdom is born from within. In many shamanic traditions, a very important part of the initiation is to break down the initiates' pride, boastfulness and self-importance.

You get nowhere spiritually through beating your chest. If anyone has read the books of Carlos Castañeda for example, you may have noticed how much poor Carlos, a student of native Mexican sorcery, is teased endlessly by his teacher, and how hard it is for him to let go off his self-importance. However, the teacher says to him that self-importance and self-pity are the greatest obstacles to wisdom and transformation on the path of the spiritual warrior, and this is especially valid for men, who are taught and raised to be self-important.

I personally, have had many teachers, and one of them was a Siberian (Tuvan) shaman, a man, who told me that it is often easier for women to learn and to change, because we tend to be more flexible because we listen and are perceptive and humble and often assume the position of someone who learns. The only thing women generally have to work with, he said, is self-confidence. Given that, there is no limit to the speed and efficiency with which a woman can transform into wisdom and light. Men, on the other hand, he said, struggle, often for a lifetime, with the obstacles of self-importance, self-pity and boasting. They want to teach before they have learned. They want to beat their chests. They have heavy energies, like Þórr, if you recall my last video. This shaman told me that the most important and difficult part of learning for men especially, is the breakdown of the ego.

As far as I have been able to observe the world, I think this is rather true, although I do find that women in modern Western societies often struggle with the same issues of self-importance because we are no longer raised to be so much humbler than men, at least not to the same degree as before or in other cultures. I think that generally, women and men who are on the path of spiritual transformation, all struggle with the same things, and that the major difference between women and men is that women struggle with lack of self-worth, while men also struggle with a lack of self-worth, but this real and innermost insecurity is often hidden in men behind thicker layers of pride, boasting and learned self-importance. This difference may make it easier for most women to accept that their big problem is low self-esteem, so that they can face this obstacle and deal with it, whereas letting go of pride is far more difficult.

As I think I have made clear, this is not a modern phenomenon. You find traditions stressing these same obstacles all over the world and in many indigenous cultures, and Kung Fu movies. Sometimes, often, a prideful man needs to learn humility in order to learn true greatness. Sometimes, the higher and more blinding the pride, the greater is the humiliation applied in order to break down the obstacle of self-importance. The moment an ego is broken down, it is easier to access new wisdom. Many shamanic and other spiritual traditions have developed strong guidelines for how to expose a young man to humiliation in order to teach him humility. This appears to have also been true of the Norse tradition, in which initiates, young men were often met and attacked and taunted by monstrous women. We saw earlier how the mockery and assaults of female monsters are very common themes in the Saga initiation stories, and the key to success is always to endure the mockery with grace. I think that in macho cultures like the Old Norse being taunted and teased by females, who were culturally expected to respect men as higher ranking warriors, was a monstrous experience for young men. The grace and fearless acceptance with which the young men met this humiliation determined the outcome and success of their initiation.

They succeed when they handle that treatment and the initial fear with grace, often calling the monster beautiful, and then seeing how she turns into a helpful creature. In at least one of the stories, the she-monster actually reveals that this was a test, a test that few could pass and then she turns into a beautiful bride. So, getting back to Þórr, you may now understand where I am going. In the precious chapter, the son of Earth encountered a teacher who showed him that no matter how heroic and strong and invincible a warrior he was, he could not get into the divine realms by boasting of that. He is humiliated and ridiculed, and told that his course of action is wrong. We are told how he struggled with the "she-wolves", who attacked his paradigm of beliefs, and how he reacted with rage rather than learning. The fact that the women wore wolf-cloth signifies death, the death of his ego, which, if he had accepted it, would have led him to discover the beautiful brides that they really are.

Sadly, Þórr's encounter with the she-wolves is a test that Þórr witlessly fails, because he is so eager to defend the mental system he had worked so hard to build. A similar myth is told by Snorri, actually. In that story, Þórr goes to Utgarðr, the Outer World, and tries to act the big man, only to be shown time and time again how small and insignificant he is among the real powers of the universe. It is a long story, so I won't retell it here, but it is available in the Prose Edda. Now, in the end of the last video I told you how Þórr, in the Hárbarðsljóð poem, finally had the wits to ask how he would be able to reach the divine lands, and he was told that he had to follow the path to that land until he was found by his mother, the Earth, and that she would help him to find the way. Off he stomped, not quite believing this. However, something obviously gave. It took some time though. In the next poem about Þórr, we learn how he wakes up one morning and realizes that he has lost his hammer. The beginning line of the Þrýmskviða goes as follows:

> *Angry was Friend--Þórr when he awoke and missed his hammer". Reiðr var*
> *þa VingÞórr, er hann vacnaþi oc sins hamars um sacnaði*

Þórr immediately seeks the great shaman of the gods, Loki. We tend to think of Loki as a bad guy, but the truth is that he is just rather complicated, like any human being. Loki, more than willing to serve Þórr, immediately goes to Freyia, the great goddess of shamans, and asks if she will kindly lend him her falcon hide, and a point is made of how happy the goddess is that he asks, and how gladly she accepts his petition:

4. Freyia said:	*4. Freyia qvaþ:*
"I would have given it to you even	*«Þo mvnda ec gefa þer,*
if it had been made out of gold	*þott or gvlli veri,*
even if it were made out of silver."	*oc þo selia at veri or silfri.»*

Loki flies off in her falcon body until he comes to the world of the giants to be exact, the world of Þrýmr, whose name means "drum". There are some shamanic aspects here as you see, drumming, shape-changing, going into other worlds to seek hidden answers. The giant Þrýmr says that he has got the hammer and that he will return it if the Aesir bring him the goddess Freyia as a wife. Loki returns with the message, and Þórr, thoughtlessly, runs to Freyia and tells her to get ready for marriage with the giant. Upon which the goddess displays her independence and power and makes the whole earth shake with her rage. In short, she blankly refuses.

13. Angry was Freyia and snorted;
so that the entire hall of the gods
trembled from beneath and her
powerful Jewel of Flames burst:
"You must think I was desperate
for a man if I went with you to the
giant world!"

13. Reið varð þa Freyia oc fnasaþi,
allr ása salr vndir bifðiz,
staucc þat iþ micla men Brisinga:
«Mic veiztv verþa vergiarnasta,
ef ec ek meþ þer i iotvnheima!»

Note that Freyia's anger in the Norse first line of the stanza is described exactly like Þórr's anger is described, making an intentional rhyme with the poem's opening line Reiðr var þa Vingeþórr er hann vacnaþi. This is not without importance, the loss of the goddess to the giant world is compared with the loss of the hammer, and may, ultimately, be the same thing. A point has been made in Freyia's two reactions to two different requests. Freyia represents soul, light and wisdom, immortality even. The soul, light and the wisdom is happy when someone wishes to seek knowledge, like Loki did when he asked for the falcon hide. She gets angry, however, when someone wishes to "marry her off" to the forces of destruction and greed. It's a metaphor.

Then, all the gods gather in parliament. It is of vital importance that Þórr retrieves his hammer, because this is necessary in order to defend Earth and the gods from the destructive forces of the Outer World. The wise god Heimdallr, who represents the Universe, suggests that Þórr dress up like a bride himself in order to trick the giant Þrýmr into giving him his hammer. Þórr protests, claiming that the Aesir will laugh at him and call him unmanly if he dresses up like a woman. However, Loki then intervenes and tells him that he must do what is needed and not think about his male pride before the welfare of the gods.

Þórr has to accept. Loki, who has never had a problem with cross-dressing, helps Þórr to dress up like a maiden. The two of them go to the world of the drum in the shapes of a bride and her handmaiden, and at the wedding, the giant places Þórr's hammer in the bride's lap in order to seal the marriage. A rather symbolic act. In fact, the groom placing a Þórr's hammer in the bride's lap symbolizes penetration. To Þórr, who is known as "the manly god", even the symbolic act of being penetrated by another male is a moment of utter emasculation and thus humiliation. However, it is in this moment of humiliation, when the hammer is placed in his lap as if he was a bride that Þórr throws his head back and laughs. Laughs because he realizes that it is now that he will retrieve his true power.

He seizes his hammer, kills the giant and the giant's sister, who had asked him for his red rings. This sister symbolizes old age and death, and the red rings symbolize life, so this means that Þórr manages to conquer death. So, I see this in connection with the first story. Þórr failed the first test of initiation, because he started to fight the she-wolf witches, who attacked his masculine ego paradigm and self-image. Then, a new and even more humiliating test is presented to him, in which he himself has to assume the role of a woman. In this context we should say a couple of things about Old Norse Pagan attitudes towards gender roles. At first sight, Old Norse society was obviously patriarchal and strictly gender divided.

Women were highly respected for wisdom and medicine skills and actually ruled the economy, but men ruled supreme the spheres of politics and war, and there were strict codes of masculine honor. Homosexuality was acceptable behavior (within certain limits), as there are quite a number of examples from old Norse texts were men, who had been lovers before, argued in public, for all to hear about it. About who had played the active, masculine, penetrating part. What can we learn from that? We learn that Norse warriors who had sex with other men were open about it and felt no shame, but that they would feel embarrassed if people thought that they had been "the femme" of the relationship.

They were not persecuted for it, they were not attacked, there was no punishment. Obviously homosexuality was one of those things that happened and that people knew about, but if the man in question was a warrior, one of those fierce Vikings, his manliness could be doubted, and if there was a rumor that he had been the passive, receptive part of the act, this could be a source of amusement and it could be used to tease and taunt and cause grave dishonor. As to homosexual/lesbian marriages, the only thing we know is that it was outlawed in the first Christian law-texts. Which strongly suggests that same-sex marriage or co-living was not unlawful and certainly happened before the conversion. What about cross-dressing?

There is plenty of evidence from archaeology that some sort of transgender behavior happened and was recognized, acknowledged behavior with a place of its very own within the otherwise rather gender-divided Norse Pagan society. They even had a title reserved for male to female transsexuals, and that was seiðberendr, which means "a womb by seiðr" or, in other words "a magical vagina." This title was applied to male shamans or some of them. Transgender behavior and lifestyles happened, and it seems to have happened within the context of shamanism, ritual and religion. An example of this is the infamous Ragnvaldr "Spreading Legs" Rettilbeini, son of King Haraldr Hárfagri, who went openly and proudly by his rather suggestive nickname yet wielded great political power and held his father's trust until a certain point where Haraldr became suspicious about the sorcery practiced by Ragnvaldr and his Sami mother. Ragnvaldr was a powerful seið-man.

Norse, Viking Age society was a society with clear-cut gender roles, but without Church doctrines and sexual morals. When children emerged, who clearly did not fit into the expected gender roles, they were not considered freaks. They were considered magical, and sent off to learn magic. Some boys returned from their initiations with so-called magical wombs, and there was a space for them in Norse society. Only later on, when Christian descendants wrote down the lore of their Norse Pagan ancestors did they feel a certain embarrassment about these facts and wrote that there were aspects about ancestral customs that were sexually perverted. Archaeology, however, shows that these special people were acknowledged and buried respectfully as they had lived, as transgender people [as recently argued by the Norwegian archaeologist Brit Solli]. This tolerance towards transgender and homosexual behavior did not mean that the average warrior male would feel comfortable with being personally associated with it. As said, ridicule could fall upon a warrior who was accused of being the feminine part in a homosexual relationship, or if he was in any other way feminine.

I think that Þórr's trial of cross-dressing, was to him, the manly god, a tremendously difficult trial, and that it was not intended to make him more feminine but to break down his masculine pride and boastful ego. I also believe such humiliation was part of the initiation traditions, and that the Thunder god's trial is an example of what is amply documented from the Norse material, namely that cross-dressing and transgender often took place in ritual contexts, even for those who usually fitted into the norm of male-female polarity.

The second poem of Helgi Hundingsbani describes how the high-born prince Helgi lives for a time in secret among his enemies, being disguised as a female servant. Those who comment on him believe that he is a manly woman, who would be better off as a female warrior. The poem later relates how the sorcerer Sinfiǫtli is castrated and openly argues with his ex-lover Guðmundr about which of them was the masculine part of their relationship. One of Óðin's names is Ialk, which means "The Gelding" or "Castrate". In the Lokasenna, Óðinn is said to have lived as a vǫlva and done sexually "dishonorable things best not mentioned". Why? I think that in a society where gender differences are the norm, transgender is potentially a very powerful transformative experience. The more unthinkable it is to act like the opposite gender, the more effect such an act will have on the mind.

When a society makes gender into such a big issue as it was in the Norse world, the application of the role of the other gender could be a deeply transformative experience. Everything you thought you knew about yourself would disappear. Anyone who ever tried to be the opposite of what they thought they were knows what a great mind-opening power there is in this, and this is possibly a reason why the technique was applied in many ancient traditions. Obviously, this is another and more complete story telling the same tale.

At initiation, there is a very important paradox; the need to let go of pride and self-importance, of the male ego, even, if one is to retrieve ones true, lost potential, one's true power. In another story told by Snorri, Þórr is challenged by the giants to come and visit them without all his weapons and gear. As we know, Þórr has a power-belt, two iron gloves, and a hammer that represents lightning, perhaps even electricity, and that is also symbolic of power and manliness.

He often fights giantesses, who hurl rocks towards Middle earth, and a giantess representing death and old age is his sworn enemy, one he always tries to conquer. However, in this story he must show his true courage by walking unprotected into the giant world without his iron gloves, without his hammer, and without his power-belt. Suddenly, it occurs to him to seek the aid of his old enemies. He seeks the cave of a giantess called Gríðr. Her name means Truce, which tells a lot, and she is the mother of Óðin's son Víðarr, Víðarr the Silent. Víðarr means to expand. It gives me, at least, an association to the expansion of the mind and the spirit when inner silence is achieved.

In fact, I think that this is what Víðarr the Silent represents. He is one of those gods that only appears in poetry, a pure metaphor for silent expansion of spirit. Gríðr, by being his metaphorical mother, is the one who helps to "give birth" to this state of consciousness. Þórr spends some time with the giantess in the cave, where she teaches him how to conquer his enemy. The enemy is the giant Red-Spear and his daughters, who literally urinate the waters of death in which Þórr later almost drowns. Red-spear, of course, is another metaphor for death.

I analyze this story as such:

> ❧ The giantess represents a female teacher, a wise woman or witch, and also represents the earth, because the earth is a giantess, and as we know, Þórr was told to let Earth show him the way to the spirit lands. So this is what happens, mother Earth finds her son and teaches him. That the manly god allows an old woman to teach him is the Truce hidden in her name, he learns from what he previously fought. When Þórr has finished his apprenticeship with the giantess, she lends him her power wand indicating that she is a witch indeed, and also her very own power belt and her iron gloves. In this way, Þórr is again armed, only this time with the weapons of the old lady, and needless to say he wins the battle eventually. ❧

So we have a common thread between the various Þórr myths here. In the last chapter, Þórr was told to seek out his mother Earth for guidance. In another story, a giantess in a cave. Who could very well represent the earth offers him guidance, and he conquers death. In two stories now, Þórr has had to give up his attributes his hammer and his manhood in order to succeed. In one, he had to become humble like a maiden bride, in another he had to go unprotected, and apply the weapons of an old woman. It is all about letting down the guard of self-importance and discover one's true courage behind the mask. In a third story, Þórr becomes a young boy in order to complete his task. In all the stories, the great manly god has to humbly accept the lower ranking roles of woman, apprentice to a woman, and a young boy before he can discover his true power.

This story is the Hymiskvíða, the Song of Hymn, a giant of frost. That story begins with another giant, Aegir. Aegir is the father of the nine giantesses, who gave birth to the universe and who manifest as light or waves, and he is husband to Rán, who receives the dead in her net. He lives on the island called Hlésey, the Wind Shielded Island. We have been talking about that place a few times now, and basically, this is the island of immortality associated with the Cosmic ocean below the World Tree, an ocean that provides the water to the three Cosmic wells, the well of memory, the well of fate, and the well of death and renewal. All of them, basically, are the same well. Aegir, who then lords over the immortal realms, invites the gods to a party there.

Now remember one thing, the gods, the Norse gods, the Aesir, were not immortal. They were completely dependent on the goddess Iðunn, the aspect of the great goddess that offers the apples of eternal resurrection. Every year, they have to eat these apples, and will grow old and die unless she offers these fruits to them. Thus the gods live long through the help of the Lady, but they are not immortal. So, being invited to the island of immortality is a big thing for them, but in order to get there and party, they have to bring a cauldron that is big enough to hold all the mead of Aegir.

The task falls on Þórr, who accompanied by the god of war, Týr, travels to the Outer World of the giants. In the Outer World realm, a giant called Hymir, "hymn", a frost giant, owns a cauldron that is of the appropriate size. When Þórr and Týr arrive in his halls, they are lucky to find that the giant is out for the day. However, someone else is there Þórr's maternal grandmother, and she is a scary one. The poem tells:

The son found that Grandmother
was fierce to behold nine hundred
heads the old one had but another
(Mother) came forward all bright
and golden bright browed she
offered the power drink to her
son."

Ma/gr fann a/mmo
mioc leiþa ser,
hafði ha/fda hvndrvð nío;
enn a/nnvr gecc
algvllin fram
brvnhvít bera
biorveig syni:"

We know that Þórr's mother is the earth, so the golden friendly woman is actually his mother Earth, the very person he was told to seek out for help and guidance. We know Earth's mother is Nǫtt, which means Night, a terrifying giantess with, as is said, nine hundred heads. The theme is one of endless repetition in Norse lore, we have by now seen countless stories in which the hero of the initiation stories is met with a horrible ogress and a beautiful woman, sometimes the two are just aspects of the same person. It is the life-death contradiction. In any case, as the gods do not let themselves become too terrified of the ogress, the beautiful and benevolent maiden aspect appears and offers strong beer a symbol of the initiation.

She also offers counsel, and because of her advice and warnings, Þórr manages to conquer the giant Hymir. In the same story, Þórr also goes on a fishing trip and almost catches the Middle world Serpent, famous story, full of meaning. Sadly I cannot go into every detail about the Þórr mythology here, it's too much, so let us stay with this particular common thread of essentials. With the help of his mother Earth, Þórr manages to outwit Hymir, puts the "cauldron" over his head so that it covers his entire body, a metaphor, and runs off. As a result of his success, he is able to reach the Island of Immortality and let the gods drink the mead of memory, wisdom and resurrection.

He also manages to retrieve his wife. We remember how Óðinn mocked Þórr because his wife Síf was being unfaithful. Actually, it turned out that the lady had only tried to help Loki, offering him the mead of the gods with the hope that he should calm down and take to his senses, but the god of jealousy and intrigue abuses the gift, that; however, is a different story. The most important thing is that Þórr, at the island of immortality, takes his wife back and thus his own fate back. Through trials harsher to him than any giant opponent. Trials that require him to let go of his pride, his boastfulness, his masculinity, his protection, his very identity. Trials that require him to seek guidance from women, even, through all this "humiliation", he finally retrieves all his powers and reaches the island of immortality.

*Illustration from medieval
Prose Edda manuscript.*

11.3: ÞÓRR AND THE MIND-A PERSONAL REVELATION-

As I have made clear, the Norse, Pagan lore of the great, very popular and ancient god Þórr, actually gives the impression that this god is ridiculed and humiliated. Is he really? My analysis offers a reason for why this is the case because in the myths Þórr represents mankind and man's quest for wisdom, and honestly relates all the pitfalls and blind spots that may be encountered along the way. Maybe Þórr is not ridiculed at all. Maybe he is instead honored for having paved the way for others, and for letting all the aspects of his experience be a map for others to follow, even when and almost especially when it involves the less flattering tales.

To openly relate and in retrospect laugh, at one's own stupidities in the past, yet stupidities that were overcome. Is not a sign of weakness, as dear old Þórr, I am sure, would be the first to point out. It is a sign of real greatness. I don't want to knock Christians, Muslims or Jews for that matter. I am fully aware that any one individual's personal relationship to their god is varied and that any religion may have room for real spiritual insights, perhaps even to evolve the soul. I also happen to think that Norse mythology is not the only mythology where it would be fruitful to apply a metaphorical and allegorical understanding, I think that the Bible, for example, could also be read in this way, and there have been some attempts to do that.

However, these monotheist religions have, in my opinion, been sort of hijacked by powerful political institutions, such as the Church, and as such, they have developed doctrines that tend to offer an image of god that is not necessarily the only way to perceive divinity. Although these religious institutions claim that theirs is the only way. In these institutional faiths, god has become someone up there, far away from here, above, outside of creation, better than us, higher than us, a million times more sacred than us and we, his creatures, are lowly, bad, sinful, shameful, and our only hope is that god will have mercy on us despite all our lowliness. For this purpose, we are supposed to kneel and bow and beg and pray and display our utter submission and declare our uselessness and our guilt and so on. This has to an overwhelming degree been the effect of the totalitarian institutionalized religion, no matter what the real and originally spiritual message was really about. Obviously, in this setting, there is no room for making fun of god.

That is blasphemy, that is sacrilege, and if those institutions get their way, making fun of god will be severely punished. Since this has been the way of people for quite some time now, it can be difficult to understand a previous tradition, a Pagan tradition, in which the gods are the objects of funny stories and engage in all kinds of activities, even sex, and even sexual transgression. It is easy, when you think that god has to be an angry, humorless, strict old man with supremacy and jealousy issues and sexual conduct hang-ups to think that the old Norse religion was no religion at all since, obviously, their gods were more fun. This is actually the subject of one poem of the Poetic Edda, which is known as Lokasenna, meaning Loki's Mocking.

In this poem, all the gods and goddesses have gathered together with the immortal light elves in the hall of Aegir. The nine daughters of Aegir function as their light and the gods try to entertain the old giant while they wait for Þórr to arrive with the cauldron of Hymir, which we talked about in the last video. While they are waiting, Loki, the blood brother of Óðinn and the constant companion of Þórr, arrives late and drunk, and he kills the two servants of the gods, called Fímafengr and Eldi. Those names mean Cleverness and Maturity. That is obviously a metaphor, because after having "killed" these aspects of intelligence and wisdom within himself, Loki approaches the gathering of the gods and angrily starts to accuse them of all kinds of lowly behavior.

Basically, the goddesses are accused of having immoral and casual sex outside of marriage, whereas the gods are accused of unmanly behavior and cowardice. This poem, where the gods are criticized, has been taken as yet another example of how spiritually empty the Pagan religion was. However, what most people have not really paid attention to when analyzing this poem is that the gods do not attempt to deny the accusations, but they do stand forth, one after the other, and try to explain to Loki that he has not understood the real meaning behind these stories. The result of his failure to understand the deeper meaning of the divine actions is devastating for Loki, because when Þórr returns with a cauldron of wisdom that covers the totality of his being, Loki is expelled and ends up suffering terribly from the poison that he has created. So, what kind of religion was Norse Paganism?

When Christianity was introduced, people at first made the distinction between the new religion, which they called Kristinndómr [the Rule of Christ] and the old Pagan religion, which they called Heiðindómr, the Rule of Heiðr. The word Heiðindómr is derived from the word Heiðr, which means brightness or heath, and which by the way was a common name for witches. It was the name Freyia bore when she walked the earth at the dawn of time and taught seiðr to the people as it is told in the Vǫluspá poem. I think that is interesting although the term Heiðindómr is usually understood as referring to the fact that this religion was usually practiced outside, in groves, on mountains, and on heaths. Later, when most people had adapted to the new faith, the old faith was remembered as forn siðr, the "old custom". I think that there was a great degree of flexibility in this religion. They were pragmatic people. They had an acute awareness of the universe as something highly mysterious, something even the gods had not fully grasped. The great god of wisdom, Óðinn, does not stand out as a know it all. He stands out as a seeker of wisdom, one who never stops learning. Curiosity and an openness of mind was the essence of wisdom.

In the myths, Þórr is learning, and Freyr is learning. This religion was not based on set doctrines. It was based on mystical experience and a consciousness about how knowledge always develops. I am going to tell you two stories about mystical experiences I have had in relation to Þórr. Let me first emphasize the fact that I have an academic background and an academic approach to the mythology. I always consider the evidence and check my conclusions again and again, and change them if necessary. However, there have been times when I have felt that dreams and visions have actually helped me to deeper understanding, or have pointed out the way for me. I cannot say whether that is just my subconscious working on material I didn't manage to figure out in an ordinary state of mind, or if the powers really give me messages, or whatever, that really depends on what you are inclined to believe and it doesn't really matter to me as long as it works. So I will just tell you the story.

THE THUNDER GOD'S MAZE

I was in my early twenties, and I was living in England, and had just begun to seriously study the Edda. I had a very good Japanese friend, and she suggested that we take a short holiday in York together, and I agreed and tagged along. I didn't know anything about York at the time. I didn't even know that York was an ancient Viking town, or that it was famous for its ghost sightings. There is possibly no place on Earth were ghost sightings are more common than York. People who never believed in or thought they would not see ghosts, have reported seeing ghosts in York. I didn't know this, but the moment I came within the ancient city walls, I felt like, wow, it is like this place has no real time, as if time blurred together.

I don't think everybody feels that in York, but I did. I kept looking over my shoulder, because I felt that I kept seeing these historical scenes and images. It was like time just became, relative. It was very odd and it made me very alert and nervous. We had arrived quite late, so the only thing we did that evening was to eat and have a half-pint of Guinness in a local pub, because the next day we were going to do some sketching, visit museums and other things. So when I went to bed at the B&B, I still had no idea about the Viking past or about the apparent ghost presence in York.

I fell asleep almost immediately, and then I dream. I dream of flying through York looking for something that was hidden. It was a starlit night, but the moon was dark. I flew and searched all over the place, circling the city walls, and then, finally, I found and realized what I was looking for. It was an ancient temple dedicated to the Old Norse god Þórr. The temple was hidden below the ground, but as I recognized it, the temple surfaced, revealing itself to having been built in stone in the shape of a maze, and in my head I heard a woman's voice say: *"This is Vé Þórs [Þór's Sanctuary], and you will be initiated. Do you consent?"* I said, *"eh, ok!"* Then I felt this pull towards the labyrinth. So I entered the labyrinth, flying just above ground level. As I kept moving through the maze my body was gradually disintegrating, beginning with my feet, then my legs, and then most parts of my torso. Finally I had only my head, shoulders and arms left, and I knew that these too would disintegrate if I continued into the maze.

The more I disintegrated, the brighter everything was becoming, and by the time I realized that I was disappearing, there was daylight in my dream, and I could see a huge green oak tree standing majestically in the center of the labyrinth. The oak is a female tree in Old Norse, yet it is associated with the Thunder god. As I felt myself disappearing, I tried desperately to hang onto something, and I grasped the air with no arms to grasp with, really, and I caught my heart. My center, and I heard, in my dream, a woman's voice saying: *"Þórr is protection"*. I woke up, I thought, with a beating heart and her words still ringing in my ears, but my trials were not over, and I was catching my breath and trying to feel whether I still had a body. Then I felt something standing beside the bed, just behind my back. I felt my hairs rise and a cold shiver ran down my spine.

It was a black shadow that I had seen earlier in the day, one of those things that had made me feel nervous. I lay still for a while, hoping that it would go away if I ignored it and pretended that it wasn't there, but it didn't. Its oppressive energy was right there behind me, intent on me, focused on me, and it didn't feel reassuring. I knew I would have to face it. So, I turned around slowly and felt myself freeze with terror as I saw it. The ghost was a huge dark figure clad in a black mantle, looking perhaps like a medieval monk or rather, because of the sword it was holding, like some ancient warrior. He held his sword with both hands pointing it towards the ground, and he just stared at me. I could not see his face, shadowed by his hood, but I could feel his icy stare piercing right through me, and then I felt angry. When I now tell that I talked to him, even screamed at him, I didn't do so physically. My body was frozen, motionless, staring at the ghost.

Perhaps I was sleeping and it was a nightmare, but it felt very real and I remember it very clearly, but some part of me that was like myself in a dream rose up from my body and screamed anyway. What I was screaming surprised me, because I had never thought of myself as a witch, but there I was, and I was screaming; *"How dare you?" I screamed, "I am a witch! I am a witch! I do not fear you!"* Some part of my mind reacted to what I was saying with puzzlement. I am a witch? Well, that was what I was screaming, very assertively, out loud with my dreaming body. "I am a witch! Get the hell out of here! You do not belong in this room!" The ghost just stood there, staring at me as if daring me to prove my point, that I was a witch and that I was more powerful than him. He seemed to be mocking me, laughing at me. I could see his hands clutching his sword more tightly. My thoughts raced through my brain until I remembered those words: "Þórr is protection".

Then I just called him, I invoked the god. I heard myself screaming, at the top of my dreaming lungs, summoning Þórr for my protection. Then I felt a strange surge explode in my body and then I felt and saw this dark reddish thundering figure with eyes like glowing embers emerge from out of my belly, tall, huge, powerful and majestic. He was wielding a weapon, and as he emerged I could see the ghost actually take a step back. Then Þórr suddenly became like a black and red wall of impenetrable energy around the bed, surrounding me like a fortress against the black shadow ghost, and you know how sometimes the mind works very quickly, especially in dreams, and you can have a series of revelations and insights and feelings in very short time? Well, I had these insights.

One, this thundering, impenetrable, protective, massive, static, energy was the essence of Þórr as a Cosmic power. Two, it was also the essence of masculinity, of masculine energy. Three, this Þórr energy, this masculine energy, was, by protecting me, serving its true purpose. At that realization, I felt a pang of grief, because as a woman on this planet, and this is valid for women all around the globe it has for much too long been a matter of life and death, that we are cautious around men. Men may potentially be dangerous, harmful to us. Men may violate us, abduct us, use us, objectify us, imprison us, sell us, buy us, trick us, condemn us, and this awareness has been engraved into our hearts as an age-old truth, a matter of survival. Even the men that were closest to us could not automatically be relied on.

The concept of relying on men for support and protection, so that we may relax and concentrate on developing and teaching our wisdom to the children and nurture them with our love, that concept became empty a long time ago. It became a bad deal for us. Those who were supposed to support us, turned against us, and the wall of protection became a prison. I realized how much I missed real men, real brothers. It was as if our brothers had been lost in some sort of violence and supremacy psychosis, and I realized why the Goddess weeps. All over the world, the goddess weeps and in Norse myths the goddess Freyia weeps her golden tears, because of the loss of poetry, the loss of spirit, and the loss of the sacred union and of true partnership.

Well, as these thoughts and emotions ran through me, I also made another observation. That this energy, this essence of masculinity, had emerged from within me, and that was almost incredible, because I had always been told that I was very feminine, and I just didn't think that I possessed that kind of energy in me. I looked at it, and knew that even though it came from me or through me, it was still the opposite of me, and that led me to the ultimate question, what am I? What is my power? If this is the god, what is the goddess? Then she came, but not in any way I had ever experienced or imagined before. She came, like the Þórr-force, from within me, as a very real force of energy shooting through my body like lightning. I didn't know what Kundalini Shakti was then, but in retrospect, I am sure that I had my first encounter with that particular serpentine energy, because it emerged from my womb and then moved up my spine in the shape of a double helix until it reached my head, which it simply blew open.

My head was open and a stream of blue electric energy seemed to be shooting out of me like a fountain. It was the first time I experienced the goddess as something more than mild and blissful love, and I knew that this was the true power of the goddess, that this was what she really was. As this immense power was contained within the protective walls of Þórr, it started to circuit. I could feel my body suddenly give a jolt as the blue serpentine lightning spiraled itself down through my body and out through my feet. As soon as it had moved through me, it encountered the walls of Þórr, turned, and moved back into my feet. She kept spiraling her way up and down through my body and out through my head, and back, until I felt utterly and completely charged with electrical power that filled all of my veins. Then I felt myself rising again, hovering above the wall and telling the ghost that he should be gone, because I was a witch, and this was my power, and I would wield it against him, and finally, the ghost vanished.

Then I felt the wall of protection that had been Þórr descend back in to my belly, and then I felt the Lady gradually retire into my womb, although I felt her electrical energy sizzle through me all night, and for several days afterwards, I felt charged and wide open. The day after I was not surprised to learn that York was an old Viking town and a ghost town, but very disappointed that there was no known temple of Þórr, because I was certain that it must be there and I wanted to go and give my thanks.

As far as we know, it's not physically there. I am sort of still expecting some kind of discovery. Instead, I spent a whole day walking around the entire city wall, as a sort of homage. Now this experience helped me in my research on Þórr-lore. A lot of my personal experience seemed to be highly compatible with the mythology and as I wrote about in Chapter 2, Þórr-lore seems to reflect some ancient understanding of electricity conduction, the electromagnetic field around Earth, of polar opposites coming together to create tremendous power, and I started to realize all these things after this experience. I found that I could scientifically argue most of the aspects of my understanding of Þórr.

Sadly, we know so little about Þór's wife Síf, that I have to admit that my interpretation of her as being the lightning and the electrical power is based on some evidence, and on reasonable deduction, but still, the evidence is uncertain. It is not an incredible thesis, but it is impossible to prove with scientific certainty. On a personal level, however, I am certain. That certainty is based on my personal mystical revelation, and I am also certain that my kind of experience was of the type that the ancients would induce on a regular basis. That also led me to think that things in mythology are not always what they appear to be at first sight. The second story, many years later, I had begun my first attempt to write a book on Norse mythology, and I struggled a bit with Þórr.

I had the electrical conduction theory going, but there was so much more to the lore of Þórr, and then one night, after a day of having read through all the Þórr lore of the Eddas, I dream. In this dream, I was suddenly before the great, Pagan temple of Uppsala in Sweden and it was the Viking Age. I knew that there would be a Þórr statue within the temple, so I went inside. There I was met by an old woman, who looked very much like a witch, with her staff and all, and I asked if I could see Þórr, since I had something to ask him. She sort of stepped aside and made a gesture and there I suddenly saw this huge middle-aged warrior standing there, his hair and beard was red and his eyes were like ember lights.

I stared at him, and he stared back, and suddenly I felt a thought emerging from his forehead, and enter my forehead, like an electrical jolt. The thought that he sent me consisted of three sentences: *"Thought is electricity. Mind is the conductor. I am the conductor"*. I woke up, and it was like everything suddenly fell into place. I had to grab my laptop and start writing, and I kept writing until the morning. When I later in the day looked at my notes, everything I had written as if in trance during the night, made sense, and it opened up an entirely new realm of my understanding of the myths. It began with the certain knowledge that on one important, metaphorical level, Þórr represents the human mind, the conductor and filter of thought. I wish to sum up and conclude the story of Þór's initiation.

We have seen how his journey started when he wanted to enter the land of the gods and realized that for all his manly deeds, he could not enter. He was told to seek the guidance of his mother the Earth, and that if he did not succeed in his quest, she would die. As we know, Þór's major purpose is to protect the Earth, the mother, and Miðgarðr, the world. At first, he failed. As he tried to enter the Island of Immortality, he refused to let go of his preconceptions and his pride, and started to batter the women who tried to teach him. Then he was presented with a bigger trial still, the loss of his hammer and the adaption of a feminine role, to which is his polar opposite.

As he became the opposite of himself, he was able to grasp the power, and now he was on his way. The next step was to dare to lay aside all his weapons and walk unprotected into the unknown. Wise enough to seek the guidance of the mother giantess, he is given her ancient weapons and manages to overcome the second trial. The third step was to become like a young child again, entering the unknown. First he is faced with the terrifying aspect of the feminine power, the giant ogress grandmother with the nine hundred heads, but as he stands his ground and does not let fear take him, the gentle, guiding, teaching aspect of the feminine steps forth and offers him strength and advice. Then he manages to trick the frost-giant, who freezes everything, makes an effort to catch the world serpent and gets to look it in the eye.

Miðgarðr, the Middle World, is the Earth, or the human world, that Þórr protects against the onslaughts of Utgarðr, the Outer World. However, to every macro Cosmos, there is a micro Cosmos, and on the micro level, the Middle World is human consciousness, the known. If we think of Þórr as the metaphor for mind, the human mind, then the "world" he protects is the consciousness, human awareness, what we know. We know that the conscious mind is like a filter that puts all the impressions and thoughts and feelings that we experience into a certain order. That order is something we have learned, it is often strongly cultural and becomes a framework of preconceptions by which we understand the world. To protect that order, everything that does not fit into the framework is expelled or ignored, and if something really tries strongly to get inside, but which does not fit into our preconceptions, we will often react with anger, like Þórr reacted when giantesses reminded him of his mortality, before he understood that he could learn from that. So if we take this approach, we may reconsider the Middle World Serpent.

That serpent, which has more than one name, in one poem he is called Fafnir, the Embracer, and he embraces the known world, forms a border against the unknown. He is the limitation of the human mind. A limitation against which Þórr has to fight. It is when Þórr lifts the veil that is the serpent of limitation, of illusion, perhaps, that he sees it in the eye and sees his world start to tremble, it is when the known and the unknown meets, that Þórr can finally gain new knowledge. This is the point where he gathers the courage to steal the cauldron of knowledge and lets it cover the totality of his being, so that he may arrive victorious at the banquet of the immortals.

12: THE ONE AND THE MANY

-MYSTERIES AND PANTHEISM IN OLD NORSE MYTHS-

It is time to speak from the Seat of the Sage:
Out by the Well of Origin
I saw and was quiet
I saw and I contemplated
I listened to the speech of people

About runes I heard speak and counsel was given by the High One's Hall in the High One's Hall

I heard them speak like this....

Hávamál, st. 111, Poetic Edda

12.1: AN OLD NORSE MYSTERY SCHOOL?

"And as the rites are called Mysteries,
So in very truth we have learned from them the beginnings of life,
And have gained the power not only to live happily,
But also to die with a better hope."

Cicero, Laws.

In Chapter 7.4, I discussed the initiation of Classical Mystery schools in connection to the initiation structure in Old Norse myths, as well as the concepts of a salvation and an alternative afterlife. During the 2nd century B.C.E, an African-Roman initiate of Isis, Apuleius, wrote his novel Metamorphoses, in which he tells the tale of his path towards enlightenment as an initiate of the Great Goddess. Like the myths of the Mysteries, his novel is written as a metaphor, and he describes how his main character Lucius was, before initiation, walking the world as a beast, a donkey, suffering the lack of free will as he is enslaved to mean, ignorant and perverted people.

Then one night he cannot take it anymore, he wants to be restored to his true human shape. The process of restoring his humanity is described as a sequence of events that is following the same carrying structure that we have observed in the Edda poems, as summed up in Chapter 7.

➻ His Vision Quest begins as Lucius desperate about his condition as an enslaved beast runs down to the shore and "baptizes" himself in the water seven times, while praying fervently to the Goddess.

➻ The Vision appears as the Goddess reveals herself to him as being the true face behind all other goddesses and the supreme ruler and mother of all gods, and she gives him advice as to what he should do.

➤ His first Trial is to dare to approach a procession of priests, initiates and worshipers of the Goddess while still in his shape as a mere donkey. As he walks up to the priests, his human shape is restored and he is acknowledged as an initiate of the Goddess.

➤ The initiation itself is so secret that no details are revealed, except for the fact that Lucius walks through the "gates of Persephone", which is the world of the dead and that the Goddess mercifully saves him. She declares that from now on she will guide and protect him, and that he shall have a blessed life as her beloved. At the moment of death, when the great darkness surrounds him, she shall wait for him there like a light in the dark.

➤ This is his Consecration and his promise of salvation.

The Isis-Mysteries in Rome were greatly influenced by the Greek Mysteries of Eleusis, which were thought to have been established by the goddess Demeter. We do not know the exact details of the initiations, but the Eleusinian Mysteries included a nine day ceremony where the initiates would fast and relive the suffering of the Goddess, when she was searching for her daughter this could be seen as the Vision Quest. The identification with the Goddess and her original, archetypal ordeals of initiation. The initiation itself was described as an encounter with death and a salvation at the hands of the Goddess. The drinking of Kykeon and the entering of a marriage bed was also part of the ritual.

Initiates reported that they had seen light in the darkness, the sun by midnight and that their perception was changed forever after the initiations. Thousands of people of all classes and genders would attend the annual initiation ceremonies together, which were sponsored by the Athenian government, and people would come on a pilgrimage from all over the Ancient world in order to attend. Yet we also know that there were two "higher mysteries" for those specially inclined.

The Old Norse Mysteries, if there were any, must have resembled the Ancient Mysteries and been deeply influenced by them. I assume they existed, because I can find no better explanation as to why the Old Norse myths are carried by almost identical structures and descriptions as the Ancient initiates dared to reveal in writing. The carrying ritual structure of the myths, the Savior Goddess, who appears as a light in the darkness, the magical number nine, the precious drink and the Sacred Marriage, as well as the idea of a Supreme Being with whom the individual souls must strive to be reunited with are all common themes both in the Old Norse poems and in the writings of those ancients, who attended the Mysteries. The Greek-Roman world was a complex world in which religion was multifaceted and polytheistic. This is the same as in the Old Norse world.

In both Pagan worlds, people carried out numerous different rites and ceremonies, some people or even some areas would attend to particular deities with their own particular cults. There were great public cults, local cults, military cults. Cults of the home. People could attend to many different cults or concentrate on some in particular. There were numerous kinds of religious officials, some more specialized than others. There were also oracles, wise women, healers, witches and sorcerers operating on their own or in guilds, perhaps connected to particular cults. So far, the Pagan Old Norse and the Pagan Greek-Roman worlds shared exactly the same basic traits.

Then there were the Mystery schools, whose attendees used ancient myths as metaphors to explain the secret of their Mysteries, the quest of the soul for immortality and union with the divine. These cults were based around particular temples (such as Eleusis), and anyone could attend ceremonies there or come to the pray at the shrines and receive help from the priests and priestesses. In that way, the Mystery temples served as common public religious centers for the benefit of local worshipers, but they were also the centers for the great Mysteries to which people who were so inclined would travel far and wide in order to save their souls.

We know that this was the case in the Hellenistic and the Roman empires, and that some cults date back into prehistory, but was it the case in the Old Norse world? We cannot know that for sure, but we could ask ourselves whether the Old Norse peoples only worshiped in groves and little shrines, or whether there was any great public temple that ever served as a grand religious center during Pagan times and which could have been the center of such Mysteries. Indeed there was at least one: The Temple of Uppsala, as we shall see in section 12.2. Before we take a closer look at this possible center of Pagan initiations and Mysteries, we shall go a little further back in time, when Isis was said to have been worshiped in Germany.

ISIS IN GERMANY OR A NORTHERN MYSTERY RELIGION?

"Some of the Suebi also sacrifice to Isis. I cannot determine the origin and meaning of this foreign cult, but her emblem, made in the form of a light war-vessel, proves that her worship came in from abroad."

Tacitus, Germania, 9.

Sometime before the year 98 AD, the Roman historian Cornelius Tacitus wrote a little summary about what the Romans at the time knew of their German neighbors. Despite the occasional bloodshed and warfare between Rome and Germany, a lot of the interaction between the two peoples was actually peaceful, involving trading and visiting, even intermarriages. From this interaction, information about the German tribes and their religions and customs seeped into the Roman Empire. One of the many interesting things that Tacitus claimed was this: "the Suebi make sacrifice to Isis." Who were the Suebi? They were a large alliance between various tribes that considered themselves related to each other.

Langobardi, Chatti, Tencteri, Semnones, a whole cluster of tribes that dominated what today is known as central Germany, just outside the borders of the Empire. Two thousand years ago, according to contemporary sources, Isis was worshiped in Central Germany. Isis, an African goddess with roots in Ethiopia and Egypt. Now, that is a bit odd. Odd, yes, but impossible? Not really. The goddess Isis had already been worshiped in Ethiopia and Egypt for thousands of years. When Alexander the Great annexed Egypt into his Hellenistic Empire, which was later to be taken over by the Romans, the extremely ancient religion of this African goddess seeped into the Mediterranean world.

By the time Tacitus wrote between 80 and 98 AD, the religion of Isis was among the most popular cults in the whole Empire, reaching all its corners and this Empire was huge. It was a cult that spoke of the salvation of the soul. For the last couple of thousands of years we have seen how religions that began as local cults have spread out all over the world. So it is definitely not impossible that the religion of Isis could reach as far as Germany, but the strange things about this idea are these. One: Germany was outside of the Empire. The Germans seemed to be very devoted to ancestral, tribal cults. There is no archaeological evidence for actual Isis worship in Germany.

Like all Romans, Tacitus believed that people all over the world worshiped the same gods, but by different names, so he thought it was perfectly valid to translate the names of barbarian gods into the Roman or Greek gods that he believed were really being worshiped here, based on the particulars of the cult and the attributes of the gods. Following this rule, Tacitus claimed that the Germans worshiped and sacrificed to Mercury, which in reality was Wodan/Óðinn, and to Mars, which in reality was Týr/Tiwaz, and to Jupiter, which in reality was Þórr.

So what we are looking at is probably Tacitus' way of saying that the Germans had a religion that was very similar to the religion of Isis, and that they worshiped a goddess very much like Isis. Seeing as he chose Roman names for the barbarian gods, we must ask ourselves why he did not choose a Roman goddess to describe this German goddess. Why did he not use Juno, or Venus, or Vesta, or Proserpina or Gaia? Why? Why the foreign goddess Isis? Why was she the most similar goddess to the one worshiped by the central Germans?

Historians generally agree that the reason he believed they worshiped Isis was because there is archaeological evidence that a German goddess was worshiped widely in central Germany at the time, and one of her important attributes was a ship, just like with Isis. I think that is a bit too simple. I think we need to consider what Isis was in the Roman world. At the time Tacitus was writing, a Pantheist philosophy had for a long time been extremely common throughout the Empire. Pantheism means that people, who worship many gods and goddesses, actually think that these gods and goddesses are aspects of a unifying whole, a supreme being, a very common notion in contemporary India, just as it was common in the Classical world.

Most Pantheists claim to know exactly which one deity really covers all the others, and at the time of Tacitus, it was widely believed that Isis was the one true goddess behind all other gods and goddesses, the one Supreme Being in which all the others come together as one. She was the Great Goddess, first among heavenly beings, the mother of the universe, whom even the gods revere and "must bow to". Another relevant attribute of the Pantheist Isis-religion is that it was one of the great classical Mystery religions and had initiation rituals at its core. Other important Mystery religions were that of the ancient Greek goddess Demeter and that of the exceedingly ancient Anatolian goddess Cybele.

They all had great Goddess Pantheism and mystery initiation as core attributes. In all of them, initiation rituals took place. Anybody could worship the Great Goddess in her temple, but some people would have a special passion, a vocation, and would become initiated into the secrets of immortality that the Goddess presided over. Anyone, man or woman, slave or free, if only they knew the language and did not have a criminal record, could apply for permission to become initiated. Among those who underwent initiation were famous Roman orators, philosophers and emperors. The initiation involved several steps. First, the initiate had to purify them self and pray for visions. When the Goddess appeared in their visions, she would give them permission to proceed with the ceremonies.

The initiations were secret and could only be revealed through poetical metaphors. The metaphors show that one experienced a sort of voluntary death, a journey through the underworld, and that the Great Goddess would appear as a light within the utter darkness of Death and save the sold through resurrection. People who came out of the Mystery halls claimed that they had been reborn and no longer feared death, and that they had been given deep insights into the nature of existence and the meaning of life and death. All this happened through the grace of the Great Goddess, and the union with her as the origin of all souls was sometimes described through metaphors as a marriage.

This is comparative mythology from the classical world showing a basic structure of initiation which is more or less identical to that which I claim exists in the Poetic Edda. The Viking Age poets described the vision quest that caused a vision of the goddess, the subsequent journey into the underworld, where the initiate experiences death and then resurrection through marriage to the goddess, who appears as a golden light within the utter darkness of Hel. Usually, a drink is served to consecrate the hero and offer him wisdom. We do not know if that was part of the Mystery initiation of Isis, but it was certainly a part of the Mystery initiation of Demeter, where the drink was called Kykeon.

Two thousand years ago, the Suebi tribes of Central Germany had a religion centered around a goddess, and I think that this religion and the goddess herself may have been basically similar to that of Isis, meaning that we are not talking about Isis herself, but about a mystery cult which included a goddess whose attributes basically covered all the attributes of all other gods and goddesses. The next question is, was there a Native German goddess that could fit this description? Historians usually think that the goddess described as Isis was in reality Nehalennia, who was widely worshiped in Germany at the time. She may be identical to the goddess Nerthus, the mother of gods, who was also worshiped by the Suebi tribes as a goddess that united all the tribes in peaceful co-existence, and whom most linguists believe is the female version of the Norse god Njǫrðr, who was said to have a sister, with whom he begot Freyr and Freyia.

Let us have a look at Nehalennia and see if she could possibly be perceived as a Great Goddess. I cannot prove this, but I can point to the many attributes of Nehalennia that resembles a whole ensemble of later Viking Age goddesses. One, the ship. From the Stone Age and Bronze Age, the ship was an important symbol of the afterlife journey, and from European mythologies we know that the journey "to the other side" is often happening by ship, and that there is a ferryman, or indeed, a ferry woman. Nehalennia is shown as a woman steering a ship. Another goddess associated with the ship during the Bronze Age is the Sun. Yes, some of you might think that just because the Greeks and the Romans believed that the sun was masculine, everybody else did too. Actually, around the whole northern part of the globe, a feminine sun is the rule, not the exception. In the Germanic languages, the sun is a feminine noun and in Norse mythology there is no doubt whatsoever that the Sun is a lady.

The Sun was the center of worship in Scandinavia during the Bronze Age, no surprise there, and the three major male gods, who were phallic figures carrying either a spear, a sword or a battle ax, all seem to center around the sun disc. Spear, sword and battle-ax are attributes later associated with Óðinn, Freyr and Þórr. To cut it short, the sun goddess was the object of reverence and ritual, even from the other gods, who sought to unite with her, just like Óðinn, Freyr and Þórr all go through initiation rituals in which they receive knowledge from a bright, golden lady, whose "arms" illuminate the ocean and the lands.

The Sun is also known as Alf-Rǫðull, the "Elf-Shine". That leads us to the second attribute of German Iron Age goddess Nehalennia, the basket of fruits, apples actually. The Norse goddess associated with fruits is Iðunn, whose name has been discussed earlier, and basically indicates the Returning to the Source of all Streams. She keeps the apples of immortality and resurrection, which the gods need to stay immortal. There is only one myth about Iðunn, and that explains how dependent the gods are on her, as when she is abducted, they grow old and would have died if the goddess had not been restored. The fact that she is sort of identical with the apples may be indicated in the poem known as Óðin's Raven Spell Song, where she is called the Seed of Yggdrasill, the World Tree.

She is also called the oldest and the youngest child of the inner ruler, and it is said that she is of elf-kin, notice the resemblance to Elf Shine the sun goddess. The third attribute of Nehalennia is the dog that accompanies her. In Norse mythology, the dogs and the wolves are the residents of Hel and accompany the Lady of the Underworld. This makes sense when we look at the three possible meanings of the name Nehalennia. One meaning is, well, "to kill". That reminds us of the Norse goddess Skaði, whose name means harm or injury, and who was widely worshiped in Scandinavia. The other meaning is "to hide", which reminds us of Hel, the goddess of death, whose name means exactly the same to hide. The third possible meaning is "goddess of seafaring".

Now that reminds us of Rán, the goddess of the ocean, but it could also remind us of one of Freyia's names, which is Mardǫllr and means "the great ocean". As seafaring was what happened when traveling from life to death, we must also assume that it could be a metaphor for the death journey. I would like to also point out that Nehalennia was part of a trinity, just like the three Nornir. All these things go to show that this Iron Age goddess, who seemed so similar to the Great Goddess Isis of the Mystery initiations, could actually have been worshiped as a Great Goddess in Germany, since her attributes cover all the major female superpowers of Viking Age Scandinavia. I have already talked about how they all came together in one being, Freyia, the Lady. When Tacitus talked about Isis, he may very well simply have been telling us that the Germans worshiped the Great Goddess and that her religion was a sort of Mystery religion, with initiation and Pantheism at its heart and core.

12.2: The temple of uppsala

Old Norse myths show several interesting similarities to Classical Mystery schools, especially to those dedicated to the oldest of goddesses, Demeter from Eleusis, Greece, and Isis from North Africa. References to castration of initiates in Old Norse myths, particularly the character Sinfiǫtli in the Helgi Hundingsbani poems, and the name Ialk [Castrate] for Óðinn, may even bring to mind the Mysteries of Cybele/Kubaba, a goddess also known as Magna Mater [Great Mother] by the Romans, who adopted her religion as their own. The latter goddess was depicted flanked by two felines or drawn in a chariot by two great cats in an iconography which had persisted since the early Neolithic ages.

It is interesting indeed that in the Gylfaginning, Snorri claimed that Freyia was drawn in a chariot by two large cats during Baldr's funeral. The Old Norse myths show a basic structure and a focus on themes that are strikingly similar to those of ancient Mystery schools, particularly to the initiation structure of the Mysteries of Isis that was revealed by Apuleius during the 2nd century B.C.E. In my opinion, it is highly probable that Scandinavia had a Mystery school of its own. It may have been very old indeed. There are indications that the Mystery schools were already flourishing during the Bronze Ages in the Mediterranean areas and we know with certainty that Scandinavia had an old and strong connection to this part of the world during that era.

However, an Old Norse Mystery school may also have been one adopted from a Classical school, and then adapted to Old Norse cultural and mythological context. This kind of flexibility would have been typical of the Mystery schools which professed that the Great Goddess showed herself with different names and different shapes among different people and in different languages, yet was ultimately always the same. Interestingly, Snorri claimed [in Gylfaginning] that Freyia was a goddess who took upon herself a new name and a new shape wherever she came among different people. Like the goddesses of the Mystery schools, she was searching for a lost beloved, an allegory for the All-soul's search for its own wholeness, shattered into billions of individual souls. The importance of the initiation lore and the resurrection theme in Old Norse myths is so crucial and central that in my opinion, it must have originated in a school of thought that was well established and powerful.

Powerful enough to shape the mythology of an entire culture. If one such school existed, it would have had at least one powerful center a publicly or nationally sponsored temple complex and center of pilgrimage like that of Eleusis in Greece. Indeed there was one place that in my opinion could possibly have nurtured such a center: **The Temple of Uppsala in Sweden**. Old Uppsala is situated a few kilometers north of the modern city of Uppsala in Sweden. It is famous for having been a large Pagan cult like center and for its three great burial mounds that are aligned and oriented towards where the sun sets on 3rd November and 8th February. The Pagan New Year happened after the first new moon after 21st October, so that the first full moon would happen around 4th November. Three lunar months later, on 8th February, the sun would again set in the direction to which the mounds were oriented. Three lunar months later, on 29th April, the sun would rise in the exact opposite direction. All the dates were connected to important Pagan festivals.

During the full moon that occurred between 28th January and 26th February, an important ritual would take place for nine days and nights, devoted to the Dísir, the goddesses. There was a temple of the Dís, the Goddess that served as a focal point for this ritual. It was a grand, public event and the kings and the chiefs were expected to partake in the ritual. We know very little of the ritual itself except that it included a sacrifice and that the king was expected to consecrate the site by riding around the Temple of the Goddess [Dísarsalinn]. A dísting is held in Sweden at Old Uppsala to this day, an annual market named after the Pagan Dísaþing, the Assembly (Parliament) of the Goddesses. While the only aspect of this event to survive into our day is the market that was certainly also held during Pagan days, this market once took place with a great political and religious backdrop. Here, the Viking Age aristocracy would meet to hold a national parliament dedicated to the goddesses, just like the gods of the myths held parliament at the Well of Origin, the abode of the fate-goddesses.

The Temple of Uppsala by 17th century artist, Rudbeck's Atlantica

The Assembly of the Swedes was held in conjunction with the Dísablót, the Sacrifice to the Goddesses, and there were celebrations and a grand public fair or market associated with it the latter tradition surviving unto this day. Snorri describes the custom in his Heimskringla from 1225 AD:

> *"In Sweden, it was the old custom, as long as heathenism prevailed, that the chief sacrifice took place in Goe month at Uppsala. Then sacrifice was offered for peace and victory to the king; and thither came people from all parts of Sweden. All the Assemblies of the Swedes, also, were held there, and markets, and meetings for buying, which continued for a week; and after Christianity was introduced into Sweden, the Assemblies and fairs were held there as before. After Christianity had taken root in Sweden, and the kings would no longer dwell in Uppsala, the market-time was moved to Candlemas, and it has since continued so, and it lasts only three days."*

As to the three burial mounds, we do not know exactly how old they are or what purpose they served, but their alignment and orientation towards important ritual dates are the same as the orientation of other Swedish passage graves, and the tradition of this alignment of mounds dates back to at least 3300 B.C.E. There was a well-developed and prosperous society around the Uppsala Mounds during the early Iron Ages, at least, since time immemorial, the kings had their estate here and the Swedes gathered here to worship. There is a long-lived myth about the three mounds containing the remains of Pagan gods, and the East mound was said to be Óðin's mound, while the West Mound was Þór's, and the middle mound belonged to Freyr. In 1874, the East and the West mound were excavated, apparently only revealing that those buried there had been influential and prominent people, but otherwise little is known about them. Snorri wrote that Freyr had built the Temple of Uppsala as his abode. Freyr was the most important deity in Sweden, and said to be the ancestor of the royal lines there:

> *"Freyr built a great temple at Upsal, made it his chief seat, and gave it all his taxes, his lands, and goods. Then began the Upsal domains, which have remained ever since. But after Freyr was buried under a cairn at Uppsala, many chiefs raised cairns, as commonly as stones, to the memory of their relatives."*

Snorri's older contemporary, the Danish scholar Saxo Grammaticus, confirms the notion that Freyr was said to have established the center at Uppsala:

> *"Also Freyr, the regent of the gods, took his abode not far from Uppsala, where he exchanged for a ghastly and infamous sin-offering the old custom of prayer by sacrifice, which had been used by so many ages and generations. For he paid to the gods abominable offerings, by beginning to slaughter human victims."*

Saxo was, as one may notice, less than favorably inclined towards the Pagan gods. He continues to tell the story of the hero Starkaðr, who came to Uppsala and was appalled:

> *"...because when stationed at Uppsala, at the time of the sacrifices, he was disgusted by the effeminate gestures and the clapping of the mimes on the stage, and by the unmanly clatter of bells."*

As disgusted as Saxo was, we may read something valuable from his information that there was a mime-stage at Uppsala. The mime stage means that it is possible that myths were played re-enacted as in what could have been Mystery Plays. The actors or the participants appear to have been playing music, dancing or moving in a way that to an outsider of the New School of continental, Christianized machismo were "effeminate" and "unmanly". In the previous chapter, we mentioned how transgender behavior may have been a part of the initiation rituals. Initiates like Þórr, Helgi and Óðinn, at least, would don the garments of women and pretend to be serving maids, witches or even brides in order to reach their spiritual goals. This was a powerful transgression of gender roles that was designed to perhaps humiliate, perhaps to challenge the self-importance of the initiate, or else in order to access some power that had to do with femininity and the womb.

THE GOLDEN HALL OF THE MAIDEN

Adam of Bremen, a German chronicler of the 11th century, wrote an account of the temple at Uppsala, based on other accounts by witnesses that were there when Uppsala was still a Pagan center:

> "At this point I shall say a few words about the religious beliefs of the Swedes. That nation has a magnificent temple, which is called Uppsala...In this temple, built entirely of gold; the people worship the statues of three gods.
> A general festival for all the provinces of Sweden is customarily held at Uppsala every nine years. Participation in this festival is required of everyone....those who have already adopted Christianity buy themselves off from these ceremonies. The sacrifice is as follows: of every kind of male creature, nine victims are offered...
> Their bodies, moreover, are hanged in a grove which is adjacent to the temple. This grove is so sacred to the people that the separate trees in it are believed to be holy because of the death...of the sacrificial victims. There even dogs and horses hang beside human beings...The incantations, however, which are usually sung in the performance of a libation of this kind are numerous and disgraceful, and it is better not to speak of them.
> Near that temple is a very large tree with widespread branches which are always green, both in winter and summer. What kind of tree it is nobody knows. There is also a spring there where the Pagans are accustomed to perform sacrifices and to immerse a human being alive. As long as his body is not found, the request of the people will be fulfilled. A golden chain encircles the temple and hangs over the gables of the building.
> Those who approach see its gleam from afar because the shrine, which is located on a plain, is encircled by mountains so situated as to give the effect of a theatre. For nine days feasts and sacrifices of the kind are celebrated. Every day they sacrifice one human being in addition to other animals, so that in nine days there are 72 victims which are sacrificed. This sacrifice takes place about the time of the vernal equinox."

We do not know if these accounts are exactly true, since they are all written by Christian outsiders, who had never actually observed the temple or the rituals themselves. However, through these filters several elements from the mythology emerge. Firstly, the temple site is connected to the worship of the many Dísir and the one Dís.

The Dísir is a word that covers all the numerous female powers, whether they are giantesses, goddesses, Valkyries or Norns. In the myths, we have seen that the role of the consecrating Maiden with the Mead, who takes the initiates into her sacred embrace, may be played by a giantess, a goddess, a Valkyrie or a Norn. They all come together in the one great Dís, Freyia, "The Lady Sovereign". Moreover, the temple is said to be all golden, surrounded by a golden chain that glimmers and shines and might be seen from afar. This is exactly how the Hall of the Maiden is described in the myths. It is also standing on a plain surrounded by mountains. In the myths we have seen how the heroes ascend mountains in order to see into the great land. We learn about the Resplendent Fields, the Crystal Fields and so forth.

People travel far and wide to get to the temple, just as the initiates have to travel long distances to get to the Golden Hall. The rituals last for nine days and nights, just as the initiation lasts for the same duration of time. There is a grove dedicated to a sacred tree and a lake which can only resemble the World Tree or the Tree of Memory and the Well of Origin. Both the Hávamál and the Fjǫlsvinnsmál emphasize the presence of a sacred tree in the latter poem, the Tree of Memory is growing out of the halls of the Maiden. According to Adam of Bremen, the lake was used for a drowning sacrifice, which was the kind of sacrifice that has been connected with goddess worship since at least the Iron Age.

Tacitus, writing in 1st century AD, described how people were sacrificed to the Great Mother of the Gods, Nerthus, by drowning in a lake. However, what is described as a drowning sacrifice in severely hostile sources, may easily have been cleansing rituals where the initiates re-enacted a myth of being transformed in the Well of Origin, sacred water from which anyone, according to Snorri, would re-emerge transparent and shining, resurrected. Another sacrifice that is described is the hanging sacrifice where nine human males were sacrificed alongside male animals. We have touched upon sacrifice as a way for the one sacrificing to unite with the dying victim in order to move into the Underworld while still alive. We have also touched upon hanging as a ritual a mock hanging, designed to copy the initiation of Óðinn as he hung nine nights on the World Tree.

In her study of seiðr, the Norwegian archaeologist, Brit Solli, argued that the hanging of the men at Uppsala may have been rituals of initiation where the men hung within the grove in an attempt to follow in the footsteps of the great god of seiðr. I heartily agree. I would add that in the Oseberg ship burial, where I argued (Chapter 9) that the two priestesses presided over various important public ceremonies, such as the royal inauguration and Sacred Marriage, a tapestry was found showing nine men hanging in a grove full of serpents, presided over by three females.

The similarity between the motif of this Norwegian tapestry, dating back to 834 AD, and to the later medieval descriptions of the nine men hanging in the Uppsala grove is hardly coincidental. We may remember that the Oseberg priestesses seem to have played a role in a ritual of Sacred Marriage. As we have seen, a symbolical sexual union was very much a part of the mythical initiation structure, even those that had nothing to do with kingship. The embrace of the goddess was the ultimate consecration, the symbolic or actual death that leads to a spiritual rebirth. After centuries of suffering the theologies of misogynists with severe sexual hang-ups, it may seem strange to us moderns when sexuality is so obviously associated with spiritual resurrection and enlightenment.

The closest thing we can find in contemporary religions may be in Tantra, where a sexual union is indeed the ultimate metaphor for spiritual wholeness, and even practiced physically in a ritual context. A sacred grove of serpentine trees with nine men hanging, Three females preside over the hanging ritual, beneath the feet of the middle woman there is a fly agaric. The scene from this tapestry found in the Oseberg ship burial may be a depiction of initiation trials rather than sacrifice. The females are shown carrying different symbolic attributes. The first carries a sword, giving associations to the warrior and to the Valkyrie. The second carries a weave, giving association to the Norns and to fate. The third carries three serpents, giving associations to Hel and specifically to the transformation (the shedding of skin) that happens in the Well of Hel.

The three may represent the threefold goddess, Valkyrie, Norn and giantess and they may also represent the three possible fates of the initiate, the warrior/ prince, the poet/seer and the sorcerer/sage. Three gods were indeed associated with the temple of Uppsala. The three burial mounds at the site were said to belong to Óðinn, Freyr and Þórr in folklore. Adam of Bremen also later identifies the idols of the three gods as belonging to Óðinn, Freyr and Þórr, and that Freyr was, indeed, situated in the middle wearing a huge erect phallus. In the myths, I have often identified a trinity of gods representing Spirit, Passion/Will/Intent and Mind/Poetry. I have also shown how Óðinn is the ultimate representation of Spirit, whereas Freyr in such a trinity would take the place of Passion, and that Þórr is the mind. These three qualities of human consciousness must come together in their union with the Linen White maiden, the goddess in whose embrace the soul is reborn. The formula of a great goddess and three gods is one that is repeated throughout the mythology and is recognizable even from Bronze Age rock carvings.

A caste and class matter?

Some may remember the three-fold Indo-European class hypothesis of Dumezil, but this old die-hard theory does not actually apply to Norse society or to the trinity of the Norse gods. In Dumezil's theory of the three functions, Óðinn represents the king and the priestly caste, Þórr represents the warrior caste, and Freyr the peasant class. However, Norse sources clearly show that Óðinn is more associated with war than Þórr is, and that the Thunder-god is primarily concerned with fertility and marriage as well as protection. In the Hárbarðsljóð, the Thunder-god is clearly related to the "crowd of thralls" and the peasant class, an association that is confirmed by the fact that Þórr was obviously a god of the common people, worshiped by the common man.

Yet he was also a warrior, as the myths clearly show. Freyr was certainly strongly related to fertility and sexuality, yet he was as much a king as Óðinn, and also a warrior, and the Skírnismál poem clearly suggests that this prototypical king god also went through a spiritual initiation. The functions of the three gods relating to three distinct classes simply do not fit the bill. Looking at Viking Age society, we also see that the "threefold function" theory falters. Scandinavia during the Viking Age was rather flexible when it came to social function. Every free man, who could hold a blade, was expected to be able to wield it. Every free man could and would be a warrior, regardless of social status and occupation. Every man or woman who wished to pursue a spiritual career could do so if the intent was strong enough and the opportunity presented itself.

Anyone with a talent for poetry could pursue the art of poetry. Everybody was essentially a farmer. Economically dependent on the fertility of the land that their clan tended. In fact, this was more of a clan society than a class society, and although there were clans that would have been more aristocratic and higher than others, due to greater riches and long traditions of power, no clan was exclusively concerned with a particular profession. A clan needed to be able to tend to all matters of survival and well-being, to be, as it were, self-sufficient. That meant that they were all farmers, and they were all warriors, and each would nurture the skills of the clan-member, who showed a talent for a particular craft. No matter how small and insignificant the clan, each head of any household was a priest and a priestess in their own right, within their own household.

The important trinity formula of Old Norse Paganism must have had a different meaning that had little to do with caste. From my own analysis of the three aspects of awareness, Spirit, Mind and Passion, I deduce that the basic idea behind the trinity formula originates in a philosophy about human and divine awareness or consciousness, rather than in a class structure. As far as I am concerned, the medieval descriptions of the great Pagan Temple of Uppsala are perfect descriptions of the mythical concepts and themes that have to do with the initiation where the hero or god walks through the Underworld in order to reach the Golden Hall of the Maiden. Initiations that may very well have been played out and re-enacted in great public rituals, similar to those of Eleusis and to those of the temples of Isis.

12.3: THE GREAT GODDESS AND THE UNIVERSAL SOUL

I approached the borders of death, I put my foot on the doorsteps of Persephone , I traveled through all the elements and returned, I saw the sun by midnight, shining in a white light, I came close to the gods of the higher and lower regions, and worshiped them in their closeness…

Both the keys to the gates of the Underworld, as well as the guarantee of Salvation were in the hands of the Goddess; The Initiation itself was like a voluntary death and a gracious salvation…[The Goddess said to Lucius:] "You shall live blessed in this world, you shall live in honor through my guidance and my protection, and when, after your given life-span, you descend into the Underworld, you shall see me there, shining."

The Speech of Great Goddess Isis to her initiate, Metamorphosis. XI.6

The possible existence of a Mystery school of initiation in Pagan Scandinavia should also point attention to the possibility of Pantheist ideas within the otherwise polytheistic world of the Viking Age Pagan. Pantheism is a concept that may be understood in different ways, so to clarify what I mean by the term. It is basically the idea that one unifying deity or universal soul lays at the core of all deities, a one within the many, or a many within the one. The concept also includes divine immanence, the idea that the divine unity is immanent in "creation", "nature" or "the universe", not outside of and apart from it. In many Pantheist traditions, the divine is the soul of existence itself, as a whole, and thus we are all aspects of the ultimate divine soul.

We do not know how old the oldest European version of Pantheism is. According to the late archaeologist Marija Gimbutas, there is considerable evidence in symbology and iconography for a Pantheist goddess tradition stretching back to the European Neolithic, if not even before that. This hypothesis has met with a lot of resistance of a more or less scholarly nature. Less controversial scholars must at least agree that Pantheism was evidently in existence by the 6th century B.C.E in connection to Mystery Schools such as that of Eleusis in Greece through the so-called "Orphic Doctrine". Pantheism is strongly associated with but not necessarily the same as the concept of a "Great God" or "Great Goddess".

A so-called "Great" deity is a deity within a polytheist tradition, who wields power, often ultimate power, in all important matters of the world. The "Great" deity is recognized by its universal function, it is not a specialized deity, but concerned with creation, life, fate, death, war, politics and so-forth, every major issue in a given culture is somehow affected by the "Great" deity. The "Great" deity exists together with other deities that are more specialized, or even share the "Greatness" with a few others in the same culture. It stands out, because it is a deity that is worshiped by everybody regardless of class or gender. In Old Norse Paganism, Freyia was certainly one such "Great" deity, wielding her influence in a wide range of areas, both fate, death, war, births and politics.

She was worshiped by all classes and both genders for a wide variety of reasons, whether it was the peasant midwife, who called upon her aid during a difficult birth, or the king who invoked her during his inauguration. She took many shapes and forms, and appears to be the true identity behind many, if not even all of the female powers. All this is sufficient to assign Freyia ["The Lady Sovereign"], to her rightful place in the High Seat among the gods, alongside her brother or her husband. To assign her the role of "Goddess of Love" is in my opinion ridiculous when we look at how she actually appears in the Norse sources, since it gives the wrongful impression that love was her specialty and her main purpose.

It was, simply, not the case, but old stereotypes die hard. Like many Scandinavian scholars of the last sixty years or so, I personally regard Freyia as the Old Norse version of a Great Goddess. This personal opinion is based on sound reasoning and overwhelming evidence in the literary sources, much of which has been presented in Chapters 2, 3, 4 and 7 of this book. The evidence strongly suggests that the border between the various female mythical characters of various mythical tribes are extremely fluid and overlapping to the extent of being no real border at all the one may easily replace another and many may be one.

Scholars such as Britt Mari N sström and Folke Ström have used other angles to argue the same case: That there is a Great Goddess in Norse myths, a Lady Sovereign, who hides behind the countless masks or aspects represented by the many, like avatars or hypostasis. The evidence is overwhelming, yet in our day, there is a powerful tendency to aggressively reject the concept and ignore the importance of a Great Goddess in any ancient culture, no matter how overwhelming the archaeological, even the written evidence is. For the most part, the evidence is simply ignored. In some cases, however, there are counter-arguments, if they may actually be so called. Cutting out the counter-arguments I have heard or read down to the core, it seems obvious to me that the intense refusal to even consider the idea of a Great Goddess derives from nothing better than a profound fear, an irrational, yet stubborn fear at the very idea of feminine power, even if it is just mythical at any time in history.

If there is any comfort to those who feel the throng of fear at the idea of a Great Goddess, let me say that the Great Goddess does not exclude the Great God, and that the Great Goddess also exists within patriarchal societies. Many traditions nurture a concept of both a Great Goddess and a Great God, such as the Tantric concept of Shiva-Shakti. Even in contemporary, patriarchal India, the female deities tend to represent the dynamic and creative divine power, while the males tend to represent the passive and observing divine power. There are many temples in India dedicated to a goddess, who stands on her own, yet the temples that are dedicated to male gods always add the god's wife.

The reason for this is that without his Shakti, his "Power", the male god cannot act in the world, and thus prayers become futile. The god needs his goddess to practically answer prayers, to be able to act in the physical world. Old Norse Paganism shows evidence for both a Great Goddess and a Great God, the latter position may once have belonged to Freyia's brother and lover Freyr, whose name is also a title; The Lord Sovereign. The myths as they have been transmitted to us show that Óðinn most probably grew into the role of Great God at some point. But the existence of a Great Goddess and a Great God may not necessarily mean Pantheism, it could rather mean that these were considered the Lord and the Lady of the divine pantheon. Actual Pantheism would consider all the goddesses and gods to be faces of the Ultimate Divine, only that some faces are more specialized while others are more universal, covering more of the divine wholeness than others. Ultimately, the Pantheist would realize that the soul is in itself an aspect of the Universal Soul, and thus the separation between the mortal and the divine is extinguished.

Understanding the profundity of Pantheism requires a great deal of contemplation, meditation, perhaps indeed an initiation where the unity within the variety is grasped through experience. I believe that Pantheism lies at the heart and core of Old Norse myths, yet Pantheism may easily have been an underlying message that could only truly be grasped by the initiated. Only the few would be able to integrate the experience of universal, divine immanence and unity. Most people would be polytheist, yet honoring certain goddesses and gods as divine royalty. The Great Goddess and the Great God, or one of these. However, true Pantheism makes no distinction between the mythical faces of the Divine All and certainly not between the feminine and masculine faces of the Supreme Being. In the subsequent chapters, we shall explore the masculine faces of the Universal Soul in Old Norse myths, of which evidence also abounds. Since the evidence for Great Goddess Pantheism in Norse myths has been presented throughout this book, particularly in Chapters 2, 3, 4 and 7, I will only add two edited transcripts here from some of my videos that address this subject. In the next sections, I will explore how Pantheism is also evident in the myths of Heimdallr, Óðinn and the mysterious giant at the end of the world.

"THE GREAT GODDESS"

On account of that fair maid neither of them cared for games or joyous days
No other thing could they in memory bear than that bright form

The Song of the Sun, st. 12, Poetic Edda

Whenever anyone is introduced to Norse myths, they learn that Freyia was the goddess of beauty and "love", and we all know what kind of love they are referring to. Now, WHY is Freyia the goddess of beauty and, you know, love? I asked myself the same question once. I had already been reading the prose and the poetic Edda at least fifty times I am sure, and years of studies had passed before it occurred to me to ask that question, because it was something I had been taking for granted. When I finally asked myself that question, I realized that the only place I had ever read that Freyia was the goddess of love and beauty was in modern literature.

I had, in the original sources, never once read a passage where it said that Freyia was the goddess of love and beauty. So I set out on a little research, scrutinizing everything that was being said about Freyia, and about all her alter egos, and not once did I find any reason to say that she was the goddess of beauty and love. I tried to find descriptions of the goddess, such as what did she look like? If she was the goddess of beauty she should be described as beautiful, right? The only descriptions I could find described the goddess Freyia as bright, shining, golden, cunning, wise, crafty, scary and large. One man who claimed he had met the goddess emphasized how wise and how big she was. He was very impressed by her size, she had been as tall as two men.

Then I tried to find anything that could support the idea that she was the goddess of love. I found that Snorri wrote she was the most formidable and powerful of the goddesses, that she had a beautiful hall that was impenetrable unless she herself wanted you to enter. She frequently traveled the world alone in the search of her lost husband called Óðr, which means poetry, and she wore endless disguises, new names and shapes wherever she went. She loved to visit people and teach them her art, and that would be the art of witchcraft, actually. She chose who should die on the battlefield and received the dead warriors and offered half of them to Óðinn. She was the master of seiðr, the art of operative divination, an art that was very similar to shamanism, and she taught that art to Óðinn and the Aesir [this is told in Snorri Sturluson work Heimskringla] and, Snorri added, as an afterthought, she especially loved poetry.

That little sentence has, apparently, completely drowned all the other things that are said about this lady and has been taken as proof that she was the goddess of love. I looked to the Poetic Edda and found that the myths describing Freyia doing something, describes her as enabling people to change shape and travel into the underworld in order to seek knowledge. She had complete power over her own person. When Þórr lost his hammer, he stupidly asked her to save his pride by getting married to a giant, so that he would be given his hammer in return. Freyia got so angry that the whole earth shook and the end result was that Þórr had to dress up as a bride himself. Her many alter egos indeed do have love stories about them, but the loving encounter always seems to take place in the darkest core of Hel, the Underworld, in which Freyia's impenetrable halls are to be found.

The embrace of the goddess is equivalent of death and perhaps, it seems, resurrection. There are a couple of stanzas in the whole Edda where **Freyia is accused of having had several lovers, but is that enough to say that she is the goddess of love?** What about her brother then, Freyr? He is the one who was represented all over Scandinavia by having huge big standing stones erected in his honor and with a very unambiguous shape to them.

You won't find most of them if you travel in Scandinavia nowadays, because after Christianity was introduced lots of people didn't know a good thing when they saw it, so lots of these nicely shaped stones were destroyed, but they were literally all over the place, supposedly they inspired the fertility of the land. The rituals in his honor? I will say no more. Freyr is the one god with a poem dedicated to him in the Edda which describes him being intensely, passionately in love [Skírnismál]. The sculptures found representing that god had a huge phallus.

So, why isn't Freyr known as the god of love? Local women sat on the stone in order to increase fertility up to the present time. What about Þórr? Lots of things may be said about Þór's hammer, and one of these things is that it was used to seal a marriage contract. The contract was sealed when a replica of Þór's hammer was placed in the bride's lap, a symbolic penetration. The hammer itself had the power to restore life. Now why isn't Þórr called the god of love, marriage and fertility? Or what about Óðinn? He traveled far and wide and wherever he went he seemed to have made someone pregnant. He had sons all over the place! All with different mothers. Countless stories of seduction, so why isn't Óðinn the god of love?

I will tell you why neither Freyr, Þórr or Óðinn are called gods of love by modern scholars, even though they are at least as sexually active as Freyia they are not called that because of a very stupid tradition called patriarchy/ sexism/ misogyny/ male supremacy. A tradition that dictates that no matter how sexual a male is, there is always so much more to the man. He has so many more layers, oh so high spiritually, so that his sexual aspect is something that only adds to his personality on some low and unimportant level. However, the tradition dictates, if a female is sexual in any way that is all there is to her, and then everything else about her becomes rather unimportant. It is the same kind of tradition that dictates that if a woman has many lovers she has loose morals and has a bad reputation, whereas if a man has many lovers he is a tough guy, who ought to get a business card.

However astoundingly stupid, it is still a line of thought that has been immensely popular for quite some time now here on earth. And it is the reason why everything that is really important about Freyia has drowned behind a stereotypical image of her as the goddess of love, safely dismissed into what is for some reason assigned the "women's arena". Now of course modern scholars do tend to point out that she is also associated with death and witchcraft, but the image has still struck. So I will go into those couple of lines in the Edda that are taken as proof for her role as love-goddess. In two poems, she is accused of being promiscuous. One, in the Hyndlulióð, the Song of the She-Wolf, where she is compared to the goat Heiðrún, who runs with the bucks, wild with passion for her husband, Óðr. Well, Heiðrún is the goat that produces the sacred mead that gives immortality and regeneration to the one-harriers of Valhǫll, and her name means Bright Secrets, so that this "accusation" is actually a description of Freyia's function as a giver of sacred knowledge in the afterlife. The second poem is the Lokasenna, in which Loki plays the role of an ignorant person, who takes the myths of the gods and goddesses too literally.

In this poem he accuses all the gods of being unmanly and dishonorable, and all the goddesses for being promiscuous. All the things he says are true, but the whole poem is about how he does not understand the real meaning of the myths, and it ends very badly for Loki. In this poem, he accuses Freyia of having had all the elves and all the gods in the Hall of Aegir as lovers, and that is true.

The only defense given against these accusations in the poem is when Njǫrðr, Freyia's father, remarks: "So what? What difference does it make if a woman has many lovers? What's the big deal?"[Or to be precise: Þat er válitit, þótt ser varþer vers fái hóss eþa hvars, "It makes little difference whether a woman plays with a husband or a lover." (Lokasenna St. 33)]. Now, that's Pagans for you. They were sensible enough to realize that a woman's sex life was her own damn business and didn't have that much influence on her worth and value or honor. To understand something important. The Hall of Aegir is the Cosmic ocean from which the universe was born, elves are metaphor for souls, and those present in that hall are the elves and gods that have managed to achieve immortality, that means they have all undergone an initiation over which Freyia presided, they have faced death, the embrace of the goddess, and obtained the right to receive her apples of regeneration.

When I was about to start writing my master thesis on Old Norse religion many years ago, I was trying to figure out what exactly to focus on. Then I had a revelation of sorts. Now I had just been through a couple of Old Norse language exams, so maybe that is why I had the revelation I had. I was walking around thinking about this subject, what am I going to write about exactly, when suddenly I had a vision of the goddess standing right in front of me, offering me a horn of mead, a bit like this, and she said, in Old Norse: "Verþu heill, systir, ok taka minnisdrikkin fullom mæra miaðar", which means: "Be whole sister, and take the drink of memory filled with precious mead". Then I was sort of left standing there, gaping, and thinking: How could I have missed her? I hurried home and started to flick through the pages of my favorite translations of the Poetic Edda, and there she was, over and over, featuring in almost all the myths: the maiden offering the precious mead.

The mead of memory, the mead of poetry, the mead that was precious, made from the substance of the World Tree, the mead that would renew your life, the mead given only to those who went into death without fear and had the courage to challenge her impenetrable walls, asking her leave to enter. The maiden with the mead was always there with a different name and a different shape, but she was always the same bright shining maiden hidden deep within the darkest pits of Hel. To reach her, gods and heroes sought visions, let themselves be sacrificed or went through horrendous trials, moved into the underworld and faced their deepest fears and only reached her when they remembered themselves and who they really were. I was lucky I didn't really have to argue that there was a Great Goddess behind all the goddesses in the Edda, because someone else had already proven that. Britt Mari N sström, a Swedish authority on Old Norse Paganism, made an acclaimed study on this subject published under the title "Freyia Great Goddess of the North", where she proves how the other goddesses all seem to replace Freyia's wide functions, being but hypostases of the "Lady".

Other renowned scholars, who have argued this point, are Folke Ström and Anne Holtsmark. The hypothesis of goddess hypostasis in Old Norse religion has not been disproved or even challenged due to the overwhelming source evidence, although it is often ignored due to an academic tradition of ignoring the importance of such finds. All the female forces, all the female powers that are in the whole Norse pantheon, no matter whether they are Nornir or Valkyrie or giantesses of goddesses, all of them are known as a collective, the Dísir, who received homage as a group, and unifying all the Dísir was the Great Dís, who is Freyia, and whose name simply means the Lady, just as monotheists today call their god simply by the title Lord. The word Dísir is derived from an Old Indian word, the dhisanas of the Vedas. The dhisanas were also aspects of the one great Dhisana, who unified them all. They were the guardians of the sacred soma, a honey mead drink that supposedly gave immortality and inspiration exactly the same way the Dísir of the Poetic Edda guarded the precious mead of the poetry.

THE UNIVERSAL SOUL

The Valley Spirit never dies
It is named the Mysterious Female
And the Doorway of the Mysterious Female
Is the base from which Heaven and Earth sprang
It is there within us all the while;
Draw upon it as you will
It never runs dry.

Tao te ching VI, Waley 1958.

Norse Pagans as was the case with many Pagan cultures believed in a universe that was ruled by multiple forces, powers that be, and that they did not divide these powers into good or evil, but rather related to all of them in a pragmatic manner. All the powers in the universe were divided into various tribes, and perhaps surprisingly, these Cosmic tribes were usually also only of one gender. That is, you had female tribes and male tribes. I am going to talk about all of them, but since I am continuing the Goddess theme here, I will focus on the female tribes first. Among the female tribes, the female superpowers are counted.

1. The so called giantesses, the Gýgjur. They are the oldest creatures in the whole Cosmos, considered the mothers of everyone else including the universe we live in. Throughout the Edda, the giantesses are described as creative primeval powers, they gave birth to the universe, and they shaped the earth, dug out the valleys, built the mountains, that kind of stuff. In our dimension they physically manifest as waves and rivers and light. Nine giantess sisters together gave birth to the present universe. These giantesses are also identified as the nine previous worlds. These nine mothers were the daughters of Rán, the oldest among giantesses, who manifests in our dimension as the ocean.

2. This ocean is also known as the Cosmic Ocean from which the World Tree was born. Giantesses are also perceived as sorceresses, indeed, a giantess is always portrayed as the prototypical witch. In the sagas, the idea of a witch and a giantess is always mixed up. Mind you, people didn't think that witches were evil in those days. They were wise women and honored as such.

3. Nornir, English, "Norns". They are closely related to the giantesses, probably identical, but as Nornir they specialize in fate, so we may just call them fates. They are all descended from the oldest Norn called Urðr, which means Origin. She owns the Cosmic Ocean that goes by the name of Urðarbrunnr, which means "the Well of Origin". Snorri relates how all the other Nornir, that is, all the other fates, ascended from the Well of Origin. This Well is described by Snorri as sacred water that has the power to transform and renew everything. It is the Well that nurtures the World Tree, and Urðr, Origin, the oldest among fates, waters the tree every day. The Nornir carve the runes of destiny into the World Tree and decide the laws and the destiny of the universe, of men and of gods alike. No one is more powerful than these ladies. The gods actually hold their parliament next to the Well of Origin, which is said to be placed in the heart of the divine realms. Countless Nornir ascend out of the Well of Origin every day. They do that because they are called to every birth that ever happens, each person, each individual, is assigned a personal fate goddess at birth, and she will follow them through life, shaping our fates as we go.

4. Fylgjur (f.pl.)So-called 'followers'. They were female guardian spirits that followed human beings throughout their lives. They are probably identical to the individual Nornir that Snorri described as following people through their lives. (F.sg: Fylgja)

5.Hamingjura Hamingja means a shape-walker and is the aspect of the human soul that may walk around without its body attached. We all have one. That is, if you have an out of body experience or the power to let your soul move in the shape of an animal, it is the Hamingja, who is performing this. There is a little confusion about what a Fylgja is and what a Hamingja is, since they seem to overlap in function. Basically, the follower and the individual fate goddess and the out of body shape-walker are all expressions of the human soul. The soul, you will notice, is essentially female, the Norse word for soul, sál, is indeed a feminine noun. Do you find that odd? We often think of the spiritual as a masculine sphere, but that is cultural. The Scandinavian religion was not entirely Indo-European, it was strongly influenced by another and older spiritual tradition, brought into Scandinavia during the end of the last Ice Age by the ancestors of the Sami, a Finno-Ugric people, who were the first to inhabit the Scandinavian Peninsula. They believed that all souls were generated by the great Sun maiden, Beaivi Nieida, and that all souls were female until half of them were changed within the mother's womb by the decree of the "Bow Woman". This idea was typical of Finno-Ugric peoples from Scandinavia to Eastern Siberia. The idea of the Sun as the mother of all souls was probably also a part of the Norse religion. During the Bronze Age, the Sun was the most central deity, Sól [Sun] was a feminine noun, and perceived as a goddess in Old Norse. She was called the Alfrǫðull, the Shine or the Wheel of Elves, and elves are in Norse poetry metaphors for human souls.

6. All right, I have mentioned all the female superpowers now, except the Valkyrie and the goddesses.

7. Valkyrie are just like the fates (described in the same way, spinning fates, wearing bird hides), they are the kind of fate that belongs to warriors. In the Poetic Edda, there are many stories about heroes, who manage to wake up their own personal Valkyrie through rituals of initiation, and she will follow him in battle to protect him and guide him throughout his lifetimes, and finally take him to Valhǫll or save him from oblivion in Hel. It is necessary to wake up your fate, because it is said, both by Snorri and in the Poetic Edda that most fates are sleepwalking.

8. Finally, goddesses. Actually, there is no single word for god or goddess in the Old Norse language. They had maktar, the powers, and among the powers were the Aesir, who were powers that seem to represent human mental and emotional capacities such as thought, intent, poetry, ecstasy, spirit, rage, passion, wisdom and so forth.

Their wives are called the Ásyniur, and Aesir and Ásyniur are usually translated as gods and goddesses. Essentially, the goddesses are giantesses of fate, who are married to the gods. They actually seem to become Ásyniur, goddesses, through their marriages. If you realize that the female superpowers always, without exception, represent creative power, soul, and fate, you will also realize that the goddesses represent the creative power.

Soul and fate of the gods they are married to, like the Indian notion of a god's Shakti, the ultimate name of the creative goddess, but also identical to the male god's power to act in the world, a power which in my opinion is equal to fate. Fate being all the things that happen in a lifetime. Above, I talked about the Great Goddess and how all the female superpowers in the Norse Pagan universe, no matter how they were otherwise classified, were worshiped together as a collective, the Dísir, and they were unified by the great singular dís, the Lady, Freyia. Now to clarify this further, the concept of a Great Goddess is a Pantheist concept. Pantheism is perhaps something in between monotheism, the belief in and worship of only one god, and polytheism, the belief in and worship of many gods.

The Pantheist thought is that all the gods and goddesses are real on one level, but ultimately aspects or expressions, avatars or hypostasis of one, unifying Supreme Being. This Supreme Being is usually identified as one particular deity, who was supposed to be the true face behind all the others. This did not mean that the other gods were not worshiped or perceived as real, they were, but there was a knowing that you were really just worshiping a particular expression of a greater whole. Pantheism is a much stronger element in Pagan and polytheist religions than is commonly known, it seems. We know for sure that Pantheism is very strong in the Hindu religion. Most Indians today perceive all gods and goddesses as being, on one level, real individual deities, but on an ultimate level they are but different expressions of the great one and that Great One is usually identified as a particular god or goddess among the pantheon.

There are three main candidates for the Supreme Being in contemporary India, Shiva, Vishnu, or Mahadevi, the "Great Goddess". As far as I have understood Hindu religion, only the Mahadevi, the Great Goddess, is perceived as quite independent of a partner, since there is a very old perception in India that the male gods need their Shakti, their feminine dynamic power, to act in the world at all. A male god will therefore always be accompanied by a female god so that his will actually be acted out in the world.

Action, you see, and power, force, is feminine, so even if a male god is perceived as superior, he is completely dependent on Shakti. The patriarchal tradition dictates that Shakti needs to be controlled by the passive, male aspect. On the other hand, there is also a strong and ancient matriarchal tradition that has survived in certain layers of Indian culture, and there are those who believe that Mahadevi, the Great Goddess, is the Supreme Being, that Shakti, the Power, is superior and (devotional movements to the Great Goddess are called Devi Bhakti ["goddess devotion"]). We also know that in classical times, there were many very important so-called mystery cults, a religious element that was very strong in the classical age and may have also been strong in ancient Egypt, Bronze Age Crete, Anatolia, and so forth.

The Mystery cults had a strong Pantheist concept and the oldest, biggest and most popular Mystery Cults believed that the Great Goddess was the Supreme Being. During the Roman Empire, the three main candidates for the position of Supreme Being were African Isis, European Demeter and Asian Cybele, there is a lot of discussion about how far back you can date the concept of the Pantheist Great Goddess behind these goddesses. Some, like me, believe that the concept stretches far back into the Ice Age and blossomed during the early Neolithic and just continued into the Bronze and Iron Ages as Mystery Cults, it is notable that the three main candidates for Supreme Being, Isis, Demeter and Cybele are extremely ancient goddesses evidently dating back into prehistory. Others believe that the idea of the Great Goddess just popped up during the Hellenistic age and was a rather new and local event that the same people who believed this would rather not talk about at all.

Summing up, the concept of the Great Goddess is a Pantheist concept, Pantheism meaning that there is supposedly one unifying whole, a Supreme Being behind all other divine individuals. This concept is often related to the concept of the All-Soul, a universal soul that is sort of the ultimate, supreme and unifying reality behind all other individual souls. That means that you and I seem to be different people, different individuals, and on some level of reality, we definitely are! However, on some other level of reality, a deeper, more cosmic level, we are all exactly the same. That is what the Mystery of Pantheism is all about. Not only are the gods and goddesses ultimately just expressions of the Great One, we, as human beings, are also expressions of the Great One, the source of all souls.

The great theme of the ancient Mystery cults was to unite your individual soul with the All-Soul, and this divine union was often described in metaphor such as marriage, a marriage between the individual human soul and the great divine All-Soul. So, how does all this pertain to Norse Paganism? As I have already mentioned, there is quite enough evidence that there was a Pantheist concept of the Great Goddess encompassing all female expressions of the divine. As I have also mentioned, the female superpowers all seem to be closely related to the soul. I am not only talking about the human soul. I am talking about the soul of the universe, the soul of every living entity in the Cosmos. The Great Goddess is the soul, the fate, the creation of the World Tree, and just as all entities in the universe are microcosmic replicas of the world tree, we all possess a microcosmic replica of the goddess within.

12.4: HEIMDALLR THE GREAT WORLD

Let us begin by completely clarifying what Pantheism actually means. It is such a complicated concept that it takes some time and contemplation to understand, actually, and I notice that several people who have asked questions regarding that concept in some way or another feel a bit confused, and some Pagans are perhaps also anxious that the concept kind of takes away the reality of their gods. It does not, actually. I will begin by quoting what Wikipedia has to say about the concept of Pantheism at the time of preparing this chapter:

> *"Pantheism is the view that the Universe [Nature] and God are identical. "The word ["Pantheism"] derives from the Ancient Greek: πᾶν [pan] meaning "all" and θεός [theos] meaning "God". As such, Pantheism denotes the idea that "God" is best seen as a way of relating to the Universe. Although there are divergences within Pantheism, the central ideas found in almost all versions are the Cosmos as an all-encompassing unity and the sacredness of Nature..."*

To sum it up, Pantheism is the belief in a living, conscious, divine Universe of which every living being is a part. To explain it on an even deeper level. All that exists on any level of reality is an individual manifestation of the great whole, a part of the great experience of the living Universe, endless in diversity, yet always the same. The concept usually involves the idea of a Source from which all creation springs and to which all creation returns. All creation is a part of that one, unified, original Source, often seen as a sort of All-Soul, or Universal Soul, yet within the living Universe, creation takes endlessly different shapes. I will explain this even further regarding the individual gods, but let us first take another peek at what Wikipedia has to say, this time of the history and spread of Pantheism:

> *"... Many earlier writers, schools of philosophy, and religious movements expressed Pantheistic ideas. They include some of the Pre-Socratic [philosophers living before Socrates], such as Heraclitus and Anaximander. The Stoics were Pantheists, beginning with Zeno of Citium and culminating in the emperor-philosopher Marcus Aurelius. During the pre-Christian Roman Empire, Stoicism was one of the three dominant schools of philosophy, along with Epicureanism and Neo-Platonism ....*
>
> *The early Taoism of Lao Tzu...is also pantheistic. It is generally asserted that Hindu religious texts are the oldest known literature that contains Pantheistic ideas. In Hindu theology, Brahman is the unchanging, infinite, immanent, and transcendent reality which is the Divine Ground of all things in this Universe, and is also the sum total of all that ever is, was, or ever shall be. This idea of Pantheism is traceable from some of the more ancient Vedas and Upanishads to [later Hindu] philosophy.*
>
> *All of the ... Upanishads, in one way or another, seem to indicate the unity of the world with the Brahman. It further says: "This whole universe is Brahman, from Brahman to a clod of earth."*

Good. What Wikipedia completely fails to mention is the role of Pantheism within ancient European Pagan, polytheist religions. It mentions philosophers and philosophical schools that were Pantheist without mentioning the role of Mystery religions in shaping such philosophical thought. I have talked about Mystery religions before, so I shall only sum it up very briefly, Mystery religions flourished in the Hellenic and the later Roman Empire.

THE SEED OF YGGDRASILL

They were often Pantheist, having chosen a particular deity to represent the divine Universal soul, and they were all based on secret initiations where great secrets were revealed Most Mystery Schools focused on a Great Goddess or a Great God, yet were not necessarily Pantheist. However, Pantheism was a very strong influence on several Mystery Schools such as that of Isis and that of Demeter in Eleusis. The Mystery initiates of these schools were devote Pantheists, who believed that all gods and goddesses were diverse expressions of the same Supreme Being, the source and unifying core of all creation. Those who had been initiated reported of some sort of divine vision of being united with the Source.

The profound teachings of the Mystery religions and their enormous influence on ancient society and philosophy were violently suppressed by the Church and are still largely ignored by mainstream education and media. We have, for example, Marcus Aurelius, the spiritual emperor. Aurelius was a Mystery initiate, and described the Mystery initiations as "one of three ways to be certain about the existence of the gods". The two other ways are through dreams and miraculous healing. Marcus Aurelius was by no means the only ancient philosopher, who embraced the Mysteries and was inspired by them in his thought. One of the more famous ones was Socrates, who praised the Mysteries and described his own initiation and vision at the Mystery Temple of Demeter in Eleusis with the following, sublime and secretive words, only to be fully understood by other initiates (From Plato's Phaedrus, 250):

> "There was a time when the rest of the happy band they saw beauty shining in brightness we philosophers following in the train of Zeus, others in company with other gods;
> And then we saw the beatific vision
> And were initiated into a Mystery which may be called most blessed, celebrated by us in our state of innocence, before we had any experience of evils to come, when we were admitted to the sight of apparitions innocent and simple, calm and happy, which we saw shining in pure light."

Another ancient orator, not exactly a philosopher, but a very famous scholar and politician, the Roman orator we know as Cicero, praised the Mysteries of the Great Goddess Demeter in Eleusis with the following words (Cicero, Laws II, xiv, 36):

> "For among the many excellent and indeed divine institutions which your Athens has brought forth and contributed to human life, none, in my opinion, is better than the Mysteries.
> For by their means we have been brought out of our barbarous and savage mode of life and educated and refined to a state of civilization;
> And as the rites [of the Mysteries] are called "initiations,"
> So in very truth we have learned from them the beginnings of life,
> And have gained the power not only to live happily,
> But also to die with a better hope."

The last statement that death was no longer to be feared after one had beheld the secret Mysteries of initiation is confirmed by many other sources, such as the words of the inscription above the entrance to the Temple of the Great Goddess Demeter:

> *"Beautiful indeed is the Mystery given us by the blessed gods:*
> *Death is for mortals no longer an evil, but a blessing."*

The philosopher Plutarch, another Mystery initiate, described the experience of dying and compared the experience of the soul at death with the experiences of the initiates during a Mystery initiation:

> *"The soul wanders around in tiring circles, on scary roads through absolute darkness that lead nowhere; and then, just before the final end to all cruelties the soul experiences panic, perspiration and trembling. Then a wonderful light approaches the soul, it is met by clean spheres and fields that welcomes the soul with sacred words and sacred sights, and there the initiate will, now in its most perfect form, free of bondage, wander about, crowned with laurel, celebrating great festivals with others of sacred, pure souls."*
>
> *After such an experience, Plutarch concludes, "the initiate will look at the uninitiated with new eyes and see all their impurity."*
>
> *Plutarch was also among the many Greek philosophers who regarded the origin of the Mysteries as coming from Egypt. Plutarch said he had seen a Mystery temple in Egypt honoring the goddess Neith as the Supreme Being. The inscription above her temple had said, according to Plutarch (this temple is lost to us):*
>
> *"I am everything there is, everything that ever was, and everything that will ever be. No mortal has ever seen beyond my veil."*

No wonder this goddess was known as "the goddess of existence". Her statement and her function is a perfect depiction of the concept of Pantheism: She is everything. That the Mysteries may have originated in Egypt is possible, since one of the most important Mystery religions of the Roman Empire was an imported cult. That of Isis and Osiris, where Isis was called the Savior Goddess and her brother and husband Osiris, shattered into many pieces, represented the fate of individual souls, that may be unified through the love of the Savior Goddess, who represented the unified All-Soul.

A 2nd century novel called Metamorphosis by the Greek-Egyptian writer Apuleius, where through the media of fiction he describes his own initiation into the Mysteries of Isis, begins with a revelation where Isis shows herself as the true face behind all other deities and the primary mover of all creation. Egypt had, throughout its long history, many traditions of Pantheism and several concepts of the divine "One and the Many". However, the longest lasting and the most important center of Mystery initiations of Europe was that of the goddess Demeter in Eleusis, sponsored by the Athenian city-state, and the one which most of the old Greek philosophers were involved with. The story of the mother goddess's search for her daughter in the Underworld was understood by the initiates as an allegory, a parable for the quest of the initiate towards union with the All-Soul.

Demeter herself was celebrated as the Supreme Being, such as shown in this
Orphic poem [D'Alviella, 1981, p. 81]:

> "Oh, All-Nature, Queen, Mother of all things, untiring Mother, exalted,
> creating, She who tames all, Unmentionable, shining, the first born who
> quenches everything, who brings the Light....
> Born of yourself, present everywhere and all-knowing...
> You Blessed One, who makes things grow and rot Father and Mother of all
> things, Universal Worker, you who walk forth in an endless maelstrom,
> conserving, you who uphold yourself through repeated metamorphosis...
> I pray to you give me peace."

Thousands of people were initiated at Eleusis every year for over two thousand
years, and it was a center of pilgrimage for the whole Mediterranean world.
According to the ancient historian Diodorus Siculus, the Mysteries of Demeter were
said to have originated at the temple of the Great Goddess in Knossos in Minoan
Crete [Book V, Diodorus Siculus : 1st century B.C.E], which was contemporary with
Egypt as an independent superpower.

So it would seem that the tendency towards Pantheist Mysteries may have
been widespread even during the Bronze Age. We know that Mysteries are also
mentioned in the Middle East, such as in the Assyrian history of Creation dating
back to 800 B.C.E at least. There it speaks of the Mysteries of Nisaba, otherwise
only known to us as the goddess of learning, the inventor of writing and the
patroness of scribes:

> "In the places where mankind was created, there was Nisaba established. Let
> the wise teach the Mystery to the wise."

I do not think we know whether Nisaba, goddess of learning, was identified as a
Pantheist representation of the All-Soul by her initiates, but we do know that such
ideas probably existed within the various Middle-Eastern cultures of the Bronze
Age, and that the priestess and poet Enheduanna of Ur identified the goddesses
Ishtar and Inanna as the same deity, ruling the motions of the universe and being
the greatest among the gods, indeed "to whom all gods must bow", exactly as Isis
was describing herself in Apuleius' novel. So here we are talking about an ancient
and widespread religious tendency towards Pantheism in connection with initiation
Mysteries that far precedes the Greek philosopher and which indeed nourished
their philosophies. The tendency was also present in ancient India five thousand
years ago and still flourishes in certain Indian traditions to this day.

Pantheism is at the heart of many Indian spiritual schools based on the Vedas,
and also very important in several Bhakti and Tantra traditions, such as those
dedicated to Mahadeva Shiva or Mahadeva Vishnu, or Mahadevi Shakti, the Great
Goddess [Mahadeva means "Great God" and Mahadevi "Great Goddess", terms
applied by Indian Pantheists to this day]. As with the ancient Mystery religions, the
Pantheist traditions of India emphasize initiation and various yogic or meditative
exercises in order to reconnect with the original, spiritual source of all being. So,
how does Pantheism actually work when it comes to the huge number of gods
and goddesses, and other super-powers within a polytheist society? Do Pantheists
disregard the individual gods and goddesses as not real? No, they do not, as far as
I know they rather incorporate all the individual deities as different faces of the
unifying whole.

All gods and goddesses are respected as such, and any deity may be served as a particular aspect of the one source behind all the masks. A Pantheist does not believe in a creator god removed from and outside of his creation, yet a Pantheist is not an atheist, who does not believe in divinity in anything. A Pantheist rather believes in the divinity within everything that lives. It is called divine immanence. There will always be different lines of thought about the gods within different traditions, but it is my strongest impression that the definition I am going to state next is what Pantheists of most of the Mystery religions and of the Old Norse tradition believed in. To a Pantheist, to say that the individual gods are unreal just because they share the same unifying core is as absurd as saying that we as living individual beings are unreal because we, also, share the same unifying, divine core.

The gods and goddesses and powers are real, and they are immanent in everything and everyone, united by a common source of origin: The living Universe. We are real, and so are the gods, according to the Pantheist traditions, but on the ultimate level we are all the same. Creation is infinite diversity, countless individual expressions of the divine living Universe. The great Mystery, as far as I have been able to deduce, based on my studies and on my personal contemplations, is to know the divine, unifying core within ourselves and grow into our divinity through a spiritual union with the All-Soul.

This was what the Pantheist Mysteries of Salvation were all about. Now that thought is very complex and it takes huge effort and long spiritual, mental and physical training to understand it truly. It takes a great deal of contemplation and meditation, for example, which was why only those initiated could truly appreciate it. To the initiated, all mythology was an allegory, a parable letting us know the many traps and pitfalls, as well as promises on the path towards union with the Whole. And that is when we come to the subject of Old Norse mythology as it appears in the best source we have available, the Elder Edda.

OLD NORSE PANTHEISM

Was there a Pantheist tradition, or various Pantheist traditions, in Old Norse Paganism? Was Pantheism influential and widespread? Was it connected to initiation Mysteries? And if Pantheism existed, what deities were usually assigned the position of Supreme Being? Let us begin with the concept of the living, conscious, divine universe. Did such a concept exist in Old Norse mythology? Certainly. We have the god Heimdallr of the Old Norse myths. I translate Heimdall's name as "Great World", from the words heimr = "world" and dallr = "great", "dazzling", "awesome" [The adjective dallr is also used in one of Freyia's many names in the female form: Mardǫllr"Great Ocean" or "Great Mare"]. Just by his name we get a strong hint, for Heimdallr by his very name seems to be identified as the great, dazzling, awesome, divine universe itself. Snorri said the following about Heimdallr:

> *"He is called the White Áss, and he is great and holy. Nine women bore him, all sisters. He is also called Hallinskíði ["The Sheath of the Hall"] and Gullintanni ["Golden Tooth"] as his teeth are made of gold. His horse is called Gulltopr ["Golden Top"]. He lives at Himinbjǫrgr ["The Mountain of Heaven"] near the bridge Bifrǫst ["Shivering Voice", the bridge between the worlds]; he is the watchman of the gods and sits at the end of heaven guarding the bridge against the mountain giants.*

He needs less sleep than a bird and can see things 100 miles off whether it is
day or night. He can hear the grass growing on the earth and the wool on the
sheep and everything else which is louder than that. He owns the horn called
the Gjallarhorn ["The Bellower Horn"] which can be heard throughout all the
worlds. Heimdall's sword is called Hǫfuð ["Head"]."

About him it has been said [Grímnismál 13]:

The Mountain of Heaven it is called	*Himinbiorg ero en atto,*
where the Great World is said to rule	*enn þar Heimdall*
the sanctuaries	*qveþa valda veom;*
The Guardian of the gods drinks in the	*þar vorþr goða*
beautiful halls	*dreccr i vero ranni*
Happily the precious mead.	*glaþr inn góða mioþ.*

He himself said in the Heimdalargalðr [The Spell-Song of the Great World]:

"Of nine mothers am I child	*Níu em ek mæðra mögr*
Of nine sisters am I son"	*Níu em ek systra sonr*

Let us have a closer look at the various names and attributes of Heimdallr as
listed by Snorri, beginning with his own name. As said, the name, which in its most
simple and direct translation just means the Great World, already points him out as
a strong candidate for the living Universe of Pantheist traditions.

ALL-SEEING AND ALL-HEARING

An important aspect of the Pantheist understanding of the Supreme Being, or the
All-Soul, is that it lives and experiences within the universe and within every living
being. It means that the Pantheist divine unity hears all and sees all, which is one of
the important attributes of Heimdallr mentioned by Snorri.

UNIVERSAL SOUND

Heimdallr also creates sound that can be heard in "all the worlds". In Norse
mythology, there are many worlds within the one universe, many layers of
existence. Heimdallr, the Great World, reaches them all with his sound. He is
also closely connected to the bridge between the worlds, which has a name that
indicates sound as well, The Shivering Voice. In Chapter 2, I strongly suggested
that the world giant Ymir [from ýmr = "sound" [m.sg]] represented the one, single,
primeval sound of the universe, which was later separated into numerous parts,
that is, tunes, which together make up the universe.

That is in itself a basic Pantheist idea. The importance of sound as a carrier of
the physical universe is probably very important, and also recognizable in many
other mythologies. In Vedic Pantheism, the universe came into existence by the
speech of Brahman, and the speech was called Vac, the goddess of speech [her
name, however, means "cow"]. In the Vedas we see an early version of a theme that
repeats itself in later Indian traditions, the male side of the Supreme Being is the
silent observer at the core of all movement, the female side of the Supreme Being is
the dynamic energy of sound that creates endless variation.

Later Indian traditions would deal with such concepts, for example in the image of Shiva, the meditating god, who dreams the universe, and Shakti, the dynamic energy of the goddess, who creates the dream through motion. Can we speak of a similar concept in Old Norse creation myths? Certainly, only the order seems to have been reversed. The Old Norse society was somewhat less patriarchal than the Old Indian, and the first being that appears is the female side, which gives birth, nourishes and activates the living Universe into being. Like both Vac and Shakti, this female side of the Supreme Being seems to represent the dynamic, creative energy of the Universe, and like Vac, she is pictured as a great cosmic cow, Auðhumbla ["Abundant Brew Ingredient"].

She is the first being to appear on the cosmic scene at the beginning. Her active intake of nourishment from Níflheimr ["Mist World" the world of the dead which existed before creation of the present universe] makes her able to nourish the great primeval Sound [Ymir], which was born by a female element, the great Wave [Alda [f.sg] = "Big Wave"]. Like a wave, too, does Auðhumbla's tongue ravish the frozen ice of death and so reveal the first conscious being from which conscious, creative, universal intelligence emerges in the shape of Óðinn ["Spirit", "Poetry", "Frenzy"], Víli ["Intent"] and Vé ["Awe", "Sanctuary"].

Unlike Indian traditions, the male element of universal divinity in Norse myths is not just the passive observer-dreamer, but rather the part that not only embodies the physical universe, but which also experiences actively while immanent in the universe, born, nourished and activated by the subtle and hidden female element. This is more akin to the ideas of ancient Mystery Religions that concentrated on the Great Goddess and her dying and reincarnating consort or brother.

BORN OF THE WAVES

So, how does all this relate to Heimdallr, the Great World? The sound-element relates them, as do the mothers of Heimdallr. They are nine in number, which is an important number discussed many times in this book. The important thing here is that these nine mothers may easily be identified as the nine daughters of Aegir, which are often referred to as waves or streams. Waves and streams, deriving from the world of the dead and from the world of heat and Auðhumbla's teats, were important in the creation and nourishment of Ymir, the primeval world giant and the embodiment of Cosmic sound.

The masculine element, sound, carries the universe and brings it into shape, when it is nourished and moved by the female element, streams and waves. Whereas Heimdallr is called the Great World, Ymir is identified as the body of which the Universe was built. Those of you who have read Snorri's Edda or the easier versions available, may be a bit surprised at my readiness to identify a god with a giant, when here I identify Ymir, the world giant, with Heimdallr, The Great World, because of Snorri's judgment on the giants. Snorri and most of the authors, who render easier versions of his stories judge the giants as an evil, demonic species.

This is a Christian influence of dividing the world into good versus evil, which does not exist in the older and more Pagan myths found in the Elder Edda. There, the giants are the origins of the gods and possessors of great wisdom and knowledge, and the borders between the two species are far from distinct. Like Mímir, Heimdallr is said to be exceedingly wise, and like Mímir, he originated among a different species than the Aesir, as it is said in the Þrýmskviða, Heimdallr is one of the "wise Vanir" alongside Njǫrðr, Freyr and Freyia.

THE REMEMBERING UNIVERSE

Heimdallr can also be recognized in another giant figure. Mímir, whose name means "Remembrance", representing universal memory. Just as Heimdallr drinks the precious mead and is the owner of the Bellower Horn that can be heard in every dimension of the Universe, so Mímir is the owner of the very same horn, which he uses to drink the mead from the Well of Memory in which all the experience of the Universe is collected. Being the owners of the same great Gjallarhorn helps to identify the two. Thus the Great World not only sees and hears everything, but also remembers everything, and like Heimdallr, Mímir is a wise giant that is also a god, one of the Aesir. The character called Ymir, the Sound, has his counterpart in Mímir, the Rememberer.

Also in Skrymir, "The Great Speaker", which further emphasizes the importance of sound as basic to existence. The Great Speaker Skrymir is identified with Utgarðsloki by Snorri, which means Loki of the Outer World, who rules the Outer World and who creates great illusions for gods and men. This attribute of creating illusions. Illusions of limitation and separation, in turn, identifies Loki of the Outer World with the giant Vafþrúðnir, whose name means "The Powerful Head Veil", whose so-called "halls" Óðinn, the Spirit, has to explore at the peril of his life. Snorri also identifies the world giant Aegir [The Terrifying] with Hymir, whose name may mean "Hymn" and further emphasizes the importance of sound.

In the Hymiskvíða, Hymir is the frost giant, who owns the one cauldron that may contain all the mead of the world giant Aegir, who fathered the mothers of the universe. Another identification is made with Gymir, whose name means "the One Who Hides [something]". What Gymir hides is revealed in the poem Skírnismál: His daughter Gerðr is what he hides, and she is the source of light, the illuminator of all existence, just like the daughters of Aegir are called the lights of the gods. She is the hidden Mystery within the living Universe.

THE SHEATH OF THE HALL AND THE SWORD THAT IS THE HEAD

In order to understand the metaphors offered by Snorri when he described Heimdallr, we have to make an effort to understand the symbolic significance of various terms. One of Heimdall's other names is Hallinskíði, the Sheath of the Hall. A "hall" will usually symbolize a sphere in the Universe, so here it could easily symbolize the very Universe itself. A sheath is something that contains something else a sword, usually.

Thus Heimdallr is that sphere which contains a "sword". The "sword" of Heimdallr is bluntly called the "head", which is the seat of consciousness. That this is symbolized by a sword brings to mind the sword's capacity for cutting through things, and should be understood metaphorically. The mind or the consciousness's ability to act and reason.

Thus the sphere that is Heimdallr is what contains consciousness. Knowing that Heimdallr is the Great World, this signifies a concept of the living universe containing all the consciousness there is in living beings, a concept strengthened by the image of the Rememberer, who drinks from the well at the root of the World Tree that contains all the memories of everything that ever lived, and of the universe itself.

THE GUARDIAN OF HEAVEN

Heaven is the typical ancient term for the greater, mysterious universe from which creation sprang, and Heimdallr is certainly connected with "Heaven", as is shown by him being the guardian of Heaven, the guardian of the "bridge" between the various Cosmic dimensions, and of his home called The Mountain of Heaven, and of him living at the "End of Heaven", like a Source being.

GOLD AND BRIGHTNESS

Heimdallr is also associated with gold and brightness. When he is called the White God, this does not refer to his skin-color as some would seem to think. At the time of preparing this speech I had long observed how some people had boycotted the feature movie "Þórr", because the actor playing Heimdallr is a black man. The movie may be mythically inaccurate in every sense, having more in common with various 20th century Super-being action movies than with Norse myths, but the Heimdallr character as a black man is not the problem. In fact, I thought he was the most credible and dignified divine character of them all. Seeing as Heimdallr is the Universe, his skin color is irrelevant, the concern of it is beside the point and takes attention away from the true meaning of the myth.

There is no racism in Old Norse mythology. Or as Hyndla says "They [every lineage in the world] are all your kind, Ottar of the narrow mind". Whiteness is the common Norse term for indicating brightness. The Great World is bright. If you look at Heaven in the day, you will see that it is very much a bright place. If you look at Heaven in the night, you see numerous dots of brightness called the stars, and they would appear as white. The Milky Way, our very galaxy, is also recognized by its white brightness. Another metaphor for divine brightness is the gold, with which Heimdallr is associated. No wonder, as his mothers are the very incarnations of the subtle "gold" in Old Norse mythology, and seems to represent divine wisdom and illumination.

Heimdallr in the poetic edda -A mystery revelation of the unifying world-

Now, let us move onto how Heimdallr appears in the Elder, Poetic Edda. The one and only poem that really explains Heimdallr is found in the revelation of the Hyndlulióð [The Song of the She-Wolf]. I am not the first to point this out, in fact the first time I thought about this was when I read the analysis offered by Gro Steinsland, the most highly regarded professor on Old Norse mythology at the University of Oslo, where she heads the department of Nordic Medieval studies. She has written a book that I am not sure is available in other languages than Norwegian, but if you can find it in your language it is well worth the read [Steinsland, Gro: Det Hellige Bryllup og Norrøn Kongeideologi En analyse av Hierogami-myten i Skírnismál, Ynglingatál, Háleygjatál og Hyndlulióð (1991)].

In it, she tries to analyze the Song of the She-Wolf as part of an initiation ritual for kings. I have also analyzed this myth as an initiation story, only I think it was not just for kings, but that is not the subject here. The point is this, in the poem, a young man called Óttarr worships the goddesses, and Freyia appears before him, turns him into the shape of a sacrificial boar and rides him into Hel, where they meet with an old giantess called Hyndla ["The She-Wolf" or just "The Bitch"], who lives in the rock caves, an image of the goddess of the dead. Through an act of oracular, divinatory seiðr, this somber lady reveals that every being in the universe is in fact connected and related and finally united in one great being.

The climax is reached after a long study of every mythical and human lineage in the world, stating at every point that "they [every lineage in the world] are all your kind, Óttarr of the narrow mind". The great Mystery is for Óttarr heimski to expand his mind and his feeling of kinship with all the cosmic species and human lineages as they are all one. Óttarr is repeatedly called heimski ["Narrow Minded"], "Ignorant" [someone who has never been away from home], because he has not yet understood the real truth about kinship in the universe. Steinsland identifies the unifying being as Heimdallr, for many good reasons, mainly because, like Heimdallr, this being is born by nine mothers.

I completely agree, as would any scholar who reads her analysis and who has studied the myths, that the concept of a universal being that unifies everyone and everything that has ever existed, is the major theme of the poem, and that the being is recognizable as Heimdallr. Steinsland sees this mainly from the perspective of kingship ideology where the king is sort of to be identified with the universal being, uniting all his people as one. I am also sure that this concept was an important part of the Norse kingship ideology, but I think that the meaning goes further and that we may be speaking of Óttarr as an initiate into the great Mysteries of Pantheism where the goal is to connect and unite with the universal being within the individual.

THE WORLD TREE

If Heimdallr and his countless namesakes in the giant world represent the living Universe, then what about the World Tree Yggdrasill? This is problematic only if one insists on thinking about the World Tree as a physical tree and not as a being. The Old Norse people would not have the same problem. As Snorri makes very clear in his Edda, male trees in poetry always symbolize men, whereas female trees always symbolize women. This is why the first man and woman are named after trees. The first man, Askr [Ash] is indeed called by the very same sort of tree as the World Tree, so that the World Tree may very well be known as "the first man", and that would be Ymir, the first male being. What about Yggdrasill meaning the "Horse of Yggr"? Actually, the word drasill [m.sg] means a steed, which is usually a horse, but basically is something that carries something else.

What does this steed carry? If you think of the Universe as a steed, and seeing that it is a container of consciousness in another metaphor, then we better understand why the Universe is the steed that carried Yggr. Yggr meaning either the "old one" or "the terrifying one". This is usually thought to indicate Óðinn, who before any other god seems to embody consciousness itself. Thus the universe is that which carries consciousness.

We could also be talking about another, older creature than Óðinn, namely the giant Aegir, whose name also means "The Terrifying One" and who is certainly the oldest of all male beings, he is the father of the mothers of the present universe, perhaps, in fact the Óðinn of a previous world. Seeing as he steers the waves that moves and gives birth to the universe, and the winds that draw everything back to the source in death, he could very well be the original image of both the universe and of consciousness.

This leads us to a new discussion, whether the great god Óðinn could qualify as the Supreme Being within a Pantheist tradition in Pagan Scandinavia. In the next video, we shall see that he does. For now, we will just have a quick summary. Heimdallr has been identified as the living universe of Old Norse mythology, the one being that unites all "lineages" of giants, gods and humans alike. His mythology fits perfectly into the Pantheist concepts of a living, conscious universe, a unifying, divine core in all existence, and the fact that his unifying power is revealed as the visionary climax of an initiation in the underworld also makes him fit perfectly into the pattern of a Pantheist Mystery religion.

12.5: THE WIND-EAGLE OF YGGDRASILL

I have sometimes pointed out that I believe that the Poetic Edda is a testimony to a spiritual tradition which ultimately transcends the borders of culture. Norse mythology is by all means obviously strongly flavored by Viking Age culture, which is why I sometimes talk about Old Norse culture and history, as a means to understand the background to their mythology. The imagery, symbols and metaphors applied by Norse poets when retelling the myths are without a doubt rooted in the often harsh realities of Old Norse culture. Yet, the imagery, the symbols and the metaphors applied also reveal deeper spiritual messages, which appear to be more universal than cultural.

Some of these messages are very subtle indeed and may have been recognizable, perhaps, only to those who were initiated into the mysteries of seiðr, galðr, poetry, runes and precious mead. I could well argue that what I just said is the case, based on proper academic research. I am not the only one who has discovered that hidden meanings in the myths are a fact, a fact that even corresponds perfectly with the rules of Old Norse poetry-making. There is really no doubt that the Norse poets tried to convey deeper meanings through metaphors, but what are those deeper meanings? Some would try to take the approach of Carl Gustav Jung, who believed in mythical archetypes and a sort of common archetypal mind shared by all humans.

I would take it a lot further than to the world of archetypes though. I have sometimes pointed out similarities to Old Indian traditions and to Classical Mystery cults, religious or spiritual paths that were concerned with spiritual transformation and illumination through union with the divine. Today I am going to make comparisons to a tradition of knowledge which at first sight seems very different. As I discovered for myself what I am now convinced is the nature of these hidden meanings in Norse myths, I came to personally believe that these deeper messages, the messages that are hidden behind the culture-specific imagery, belong to an age-old and almost pan-human tradition of spiritual transformation. I want to point out here that to say something like that is often thought of as controversial.

Furthermore, the lines between the two cultures that I am going to draw next are sometimes based on my personal convictions and all of them may not be scientifically proven. One of the reasons I point this caution out is that I am going to refer to a source that is very controversial seen from an academic point of view, so please be aware that the connections I am going to make between that source and Norse myths are strictly a matter of personal opinion.

So, this is my slightly controversial standpoint, there are some universal messages in the Edda, deep insights that transcend the borders of culture, insights found in countless cultures that to all appearances have nothing to do with each other. I believe that these deeper insights belong not to any particular culture or tradition, but that they belong to humankind, perhaps reaching back into a lost prehistory, or perhaps even testifying to some ultimate truths that have been perceived by different peoples at different time.

From this point of view, the Poetic Edda is one culture's testimony to a very ancient lore of knowledge, almost forgotten in the Western world after centuries of suppression. Sometimes, the universal messages cannot be easily traced back to any known historical cultural connections. I am going to take a swift ride to a culture that apparently has never had any connection with Viking Age culture whatsoever, namely pre conquest Mexico, in order to point out just one such amazing, conceptual parallel. I am going to quote a passage from a book called The Fire from Within by Carlos Castañeda. For those of you who have not heard about Castañeda, he was a social anthropologist, who from the 1960s onwards, became apprenticed to a Yaqui Indian sorcerer called Don Juan in Mexico. The sorcerer Don Juan instructed Castañeda on a number of issues that have to do with human perception of the great mystery that is the world.

The books are very recommendable I think, thought-provoking and mind-altering. They should also be read with great sobriety, because I have met some very self-important guys, who have become totally delusional after reading these books. However, for those who are more grounded and have a bit of self-insight to start with, these books can hold only great interest. They are also highly controversial from an academic point of view. Castañeda has been criticized for not really revealing the real identity of his source, Don Juan, that is, and for not attaching the teachings of Don Juan to any known contemporary culture.

He has even been accused of having made the whole thing up. After having lived in Mexico for several years myself and experienced a thing or two in my life as a whole, I am personally convinced that his books are based on actual experience and that the teachings of Don Juan represent an ancient, pan-human art of seeing, exactly as Don Juan himself claimed. Don Juan often spoke of the heritage of knowledge provided by the so-called "old seers". The "old seers" were sorcerers living in Mexico at some point before the European conquest. Don Juan never specified who they were or what culture they belonged to, although he named them Toltecs. It is believed that the Toltecs were a pre-Aztec culture and very war-like, but Don Juan claimed that the name was used not to describe a culture, but to describe the "old seers" and their art of seeing.

I am going to quote what Castañeda had to say about what some of these "old seers" witnessed about the greater the Cosmos, the part of the Cosmos that is inaccessible to ordinary human perception, but which could be glimpsed by trained seers, who were accustomed to altering their perception. When the terms "to see" and "seeing" are used in this context, Castañeda is referring to an art of perceiving the invisible which has nothing to do with "looking" at things.

It has rather to do with seeing realities that are hidden behind the apparent one:

> *"Don Juan said that the old seers, risking untold dangers, actually saw the
> indescribable force which is the source of all sentient beings. They called
> it the Eagle, because in the few glimpses they could sustain, they saw it as
> something that resembled a black-and-white eagle of infinite size. They saw
> that it is the Eagle who bestows awareness. The Eagle creates sentient beings
> so that they will live and enrich the awareness it gives them with life.*
> *They also saw that it is the Eagle who devours that same, enriched awareness
> after making sentient beings relinquish it at the moment of death.*
> *"For the old seers," Don Juan went on, "to say that the reason for existence is
> to enhance awareness is not a matter of faith or deduction. They saw it.*
> *They saw that the awareness of sentient beings flies away at the moment of
> death and floats like a luminous cotton puff right into the Eagle's beak to be
> consumed. For the old seers, that was the evidence that sentient beings live
> only to enrich the awareness that is the Eagle's food."*
> *...The Eagle is as real for the seers as gravity and time is for you, and just as
> abstract and incomprehensible..."*
> *Don Juan went on to explain that the Eagle transmits so-called "emanations",
> emanations of awareness, and he explained the emanations thus:*
> *"...the Eagle's emanations are an immutable thing-in-itself, which engulfs
> everything that exists, the knowable and the unknowable. There is no way to
> describe in words what the Eagle's emanations are...they must be witnessed
> by the seer. They are a presence, almost a mass of sorts, a pressure that
> creates a dazzling sensation. One can catch only a glimpse of them, as one can
> catch only a glimpse of the Eagle itself. It goes without saying that the Eagle is
> the source of the emanations."*

To sum it up in my own words, the seers of old Mexico, according to the sorcerer
Juan, as rendered by Castañeda, perceived a central, cosmic source of awareness.
Awareness runs through the universe at large in the form of "emanations" coming
out of this central source. As sentient beings, we all relate to these emanations, our
awareness is shaped by them, and we are shaped by our awareness by how and
what we perceive. The gigantic source of the mysterious, cosmic emanations was
called "the eagle", not because it actually was an eagle, but because it appeared
to resemble an eagle, and just as this "eagle" bestows awareness through its
emanations, so it also feeds on our awareness once we die. I am not going to
discuss the truth value of this claim about the Cosmic "eagle".

What I am going to say is that I believe that a very similar concept had an
important, even central place in Old Norse mythology, We are speaking of the great
giant in eagle disguise that frequently shows up in Old Norse sources. It appears
in the Prose Edda, it appears in the Poetic Edda, it appears in a 9th century skaldic
poem known as Haustlǫng, and it appears in numerous fornaldarsǫgur, that is, the
sagas of olden times, which carry a lot of mythical and folklore material. This is the
Eagle of Norse myths. The oldest Norse description we have of the Eagle is actually
found in the skaldic poem Haustlǫng, which was created by the poet Þióðolfr of
Hvínir, who was a skald at the court of the Norwegian King Haraldr Hárfagri.

The poem dates back to about the year 900 AD and is rendered and explained by Snorri in the Prose Edda. It relates the story of how the goddess Iðunn was abducted by the giant eagle called Þjazi. For now, we shall only have a look at the giant eagle Þjazi. The first question, as always in my research, is what does the name Þjazi mean? It is derived from the Old Norse verb þiaza, which means to enslave, bind, capture. So I translate the name Þjazi to mean "The Slave Binder". This in itself is an interesting name when compared to how Don Juan proceeds to describe the cosmic force known as the Eagle in his Mexican tradition. For he emphasizes how we are all literally slave-bound to this force our awareness stems from it, and returns to it in death.

Both Þióðolfr, and later Snorri, describe the Slave-Binder as being of enormous size, exactly as the Mexican Eagle is said to be of infinite size. There are many other names for this eagle in Thióðolf's poem: As always in Norse poetry, one character appears with countless names that describes its function. One of the other names for Þjazi is Valkastar. Val means "choice", but also refers to death, the dead, and more specifically to the chosen dead. Kasta means to throw, so that the name could be translated as the Death Thrower, linking the Norse Eagle to death. It could also possibly mean the Choice Thrower, which is equally interesting, as we shall see.

Other names that associate Þjazi with death describe him as "the ghost of the giant world", he is said to be very "hungry", is "the vulture of the flock" and the "seagull of entrails". Snorri explains that all masculine birds, such as the seagull, can be used in poetry and myth to replace the concept of the "eagle". That would include the raven, the rooster, and the vulture as birds describing the cosmic eagle. So we have a slave-binding force in the poem strongly associated with death. Þjazi is also described as flapping his wings, so that he creates whistling winds, and he is said to be seated in an age-old tree. Now these aspects of Þjazi links him with another eagle figure described by Snorri in the Gylfaginning, Prose Edda, where we hear that there is a giant in eagle disguise, who sits by the end of heaven, in the top of the World Tree, and from his flapping wings come "the wind across all people". His name is Hræsvelgr, a name that literally translates as "Corpse Swallower."

This giant in eagle disguise is also described in the Edda poem Vafþrúðnismál, where Óðinn is engaging the giant Vafþrúðnir whose name means the Powerful Head-Veil to a contest of wisdom. The god asks, and this is from stanza 36 and 37 in the said poem:

36. *"Tell me the ninth, as they say you are wise and if you, Vafþrúðnir, know: From where comes the wind that moves across the waves even if men never see him."*

36. *«Segðv þat iþ níunda, allz þic svinnan qveþa, oc þv, Vafþrvðnir, vitir: hvadan vindr vm komr, sva at ferr vág yfir? e menn hann sialfan vm siá.»*

Vafþrúðnir, "the Powerful Veil", replied:

37. *"His name is Corpse Swallower, sitting by the end of Heaven a giant in eagle's disguise; from his wings it is said that the wind comes across all human beings."*

37. *«Hresvelgr heitir, er sitr a himins enda, iotvnn i arnar ham; af hans vengiom qveþa vind koma alla menn yfir.»*

Whereas the Edda reveals that this eagle sits at the end of the world, Snorri said that he sits in the top of the World Tree and to the North. In Norse cosmology, Hel, the realm of death, is situated to the North. Just as the eagle swallows the dead, so Hel is the place to which all the dead return, although it is also the place from which everything began. In the Norse creation, misty Hel is a place that existed before time itself, and from which both the world giant and the first Aesir emerged from. The name Corpse Swallower is pretty unambiguous, revealing that this giant in eagle disguise devours the dead.

The imagery is in my opinion completely consistent with the Mexican idea of the gigantic Eagle-like figure which devours the awareness of the dead. That the Corpse Swallower is identical to the Slave Binder is clear through their descriptions, as well as the fact that they are both associated with an age-old tree, in which top they are seated. The tree is the World Tree, a metaphor for the universe itself. Like the Mexican Eagle, they sit at the very beginning and end of the universe. The Mexican Eagle emanates awareness which is compared to an unseen presence, like a pressure, which rules us, but nevertheless is invisible to our ordinary human perception. The fact that this awareness takes the form of "emanations" indicates a kind of streaming movement, originating in the cosmic source, creating the world and the awareness of living beings.

In the Old Norse myths, these emanations are called "winds". Winds which move through or across so-called "waves", that is, I believe, the same as vibrations. Is it possible to compare the Mexican Cosmic "emanations" with the Norse Cosmic "winds"? Well, both the "emanations" and the "winds" stem from a gigantic Cosmic force which is described as looking like an eagle, but not quite being an eagle, and which devours the dead. Another similarity is the fact that both the "emanations" and the "winds" are associated with awareness. Yes, winds and mind or awareness are very much connected in Norse poetry, as Snorri said: "Consciousness is called the wind of the giantesses". I rest my case. Well, not entirely. I am going to continue. Don Juan made it clear to Castañeda that the eagle was a metaphor, a way of describing the indescribable.

The Norse myths also reveal that the eagle shape is a disguise, a hide, for a giant. The image of the eagle appears in other places in the Edda lore. As a giant eagle, it turns up in the poem of Helgi Hiǫrvarðsson, where it guards two maidens in a land of fire and sleep, yes, the land is actually called Svávaland, which means the Land of Falling Asleep. The maidens can only be brought out of the sleeping realm if the eagle is "killed". There are associations to fire and flames in the realm of the eagle, a theme we shall return to. Another giant in eagle disguise is Suttungr, whose name means "Heavy with Drink" from sut drink, and tungr, "heavy".

He is the father of the maiden, who guards the precious drink of poetry and the one who allowed Óðinn to have both the maiden and the drink, although not without a price. There is also fire involved, but again, we shall return to that later. To get hung up on the eagle image will not take us all the way. The eagle is but a metaphor for something different, something mysterious and big that can only be described through metaphor. We shall look at other possible ways of describing this cosmic force. I cannot stress enough how important it is to realize that the Old Norse poets would use numerous ways of describing the same essential thing, through applying metaphors. The descriptive variations are countless, but the essential themes are actually quite few, and concentrated.

In order to identify the essential theme here, we have to look past the imagery, such as the image of the eagle, and into the essential meaning. As I see it, the essential meaning is that there is a Cosmic source to all awareness which is also the same as the source of death, a point of origin to which all awareness returns, as if drawn back by unseen movements. These movements are like winds emanating from the original source, permeating existence with awareness, and drawing awareness back into itself. Where, in Norse mythology, can we find symbolic, metaphorical imagery which seems to be describing this essential theme?

The Eagle is so clearly an image of the realm of death that another description of this realm is the most obvious place to begin, and Hel, Misty Hel, is the most obvious description of the realm of death that we find in the Edda. Within Misty Hel there is a well, or let us say a water-source. This is the well into which the dead are thrown in order to be consumed by serpents. The Well of Hel is called the Hvergelmir, which could translate as "The Bellower Mill" or the "Bellower Cauldron". The word hverr may mean either mill, where substance is ground into tiny particles, or a cauldron, where things are being cooked up. The word gelmir, which I have translated as Bellower, could, according to some old dictionaries, actually mean a young eagle.

Then we would be speaking of a Well in Hel called "The Eagle Mill" or the "Eagle Cauldron". However, it may just as likely mean Bellower. The Bellower theme is typical of the underworld. They have the Gjallarbrú, for example, which means the Bellowing Bridge, which is the bridge between the world of the living and the world of the dead. The river that this Bellowing Bridge is crossing, that is, the river that forms the border between life and death, is simply called Gioll, which means "Bellower". I have already explained how the name of the world giant Ymir is derived from the Old Norse word ýmr, which means "sound". When Ymir is slain, and his body used to shape the universe, this is a metaphor for how the original, unifying sound was separated into many different tunes, giving us the message that the universe is created by an orchestra of tunes, of sounds, which are also, in the myth, associated with waves and streams.

I take it that sound vibrations were perceived as essential to the creation of the Cosmos, and that the idea is that these sound vibrations originated as one, great sound-source. So, here we have Ymir, the original sound, becoming the material for the creation of the universe through the separation into countless tunes, but Ymir is not alone. He was nurtured by the Cosmic "cow" Auðhumbla, ["Abundant Brew Ingredient"] in fact by the rivers of "milk" that ran from her teats.

Enter the rivers and the streams. As a parallel, we see the Well of Hel, which is obviously related to sounds, and from which, it is said, "all rivers stem". In the Edda poem Grímnismál, we learn that all rivers in the world are derived from The Bellower Cauldron of Hel, the Eagle's Mill. What are these cosmic "rivers", really, if not another way of saying emanations, a streaming movement? Moreover, the so-called "rivers" get their so-called "water" from a very interesting source. Apparently, a stag stands at the roof of Valhǫll and eats from the World Tree, that is, we are speaking of a force which devours the universe itself. From this nourishment, water drips down into the Well of Hel and becomes the "rivers" that run through the world.

Again, we are speaking of a cosmic source of origin which continually emanates all movement of the universe, and which continually feeds on the experience of the universe itself. Into the Well of Hel, the dead go, just as in one image they are devoured by the Eagle, they are devoured in Hel's Well by serpents and wolves. The rivers of the world, the movement of the world, flow out from a place where the living relinquishes their awareness in death. This description of Hel is essentially exactly the same as the image of the Eagle.

Moving on, we might as well have a look at the other wells associated with the roots of the World Tree, the World Tree being of course an image of the universe. Replacing the Well of Hel and its running rivers, we may look at the Well of Memory, that is, the Mímisbrunnr. The name translates as the Well of Mímir, known as a giant friend of Óðinn, but whose name should be taken seriously: His name means the Rememberer, the Memory. According to Snorri, this well contains all the "tidings" of the world. That is, it contains the descriptions, the memories of the world and the beings that live in it. Mímir, the Memory, drinks from this well every day, so that he may be compared to Suttungr, whose name means Heavy with Drink. Now, the drinking of cosmic memories seems to me to be yet another image of a cosmic source that devours the awareness of the universe after lived lives. It is obviously a place where the memory of universal awareness is stored. But does it also transmit something akin to the wind-like, wave-like or river-like emanations of the Eagle?

Indeed, if you look closely at the myth, you will realize that the giant Mímir, that is, the Memory, drinks from the Well of Memory, much like the Eagle feeds on awareness, and he drinks through a horn called Gjallarhorn, The Bellowing Horn. This drinking horn not only associates the Well of Memory with the Well of Hel, through the Bellower gjallar-gjǫll theme, but also with the god Heimdallr, whose name means the Great World, and who, rather than drinking from the horn, blows out through the Bellower Horn whenever there is a meeting between dimensions. And what is he blowing out? Sound, obviously, sound imbued with the memories of the world. As I have said before, Heimdallr, who hears all and sees all, is identical to Mímir, who remembers all, and they are linked through their shared property, The Bellowing Horn. What went into the Well of Memory comes out in the shape of sound, a kind of vibration essential to creation. We are seeing the same theme of the cosmic source again, and again, and again.

Then to the third well, the one situated in the heart of Ásgarðr, the realm of the gods. This is the Urðarbrunnr, The Well of Origin. The Well is owned by the Norn Urðr, whose name means Origin, or Beginning, or Before. I like to use the translation Origin. She is the oldest of the Nornir [the fates] the most powerful beings in the Cosmos, since they create all cosmic laws and all destinies, and they created the runes that Óðinn discovered and made known. Runes are ultimately about fate and Cosmic laws. Anyway, the Well of Origin is the water from which the universe, symbolized by the world tree, is nourished. The old lady herself goes out every day to water the tree from her well. The water of the well replenishes, rejuvenates and heals the world tree.

It also has the quality, says Snorri, that if a person bathes in that water, he or she will be transformed, emerging like a transparent, bright, ethereal being. This water is also from where all the Nornir emerge, all the fates. What are they? They are the fates of the individual beings. At the birth of a human being, a fate will descend, or ascend, from the Well of Origin, in order to shape the fate of the newly born. She will follow her human throughout their life, continually spinning away, shaping the life unto death. Then, we must assume, she will return to the source of Origin in order to be renewed before a new birth. What does the Norn have to do with awareness, memories and the river-like, wind-like emanations of the source? Everything! What is fate, but the story of a life? The fate of a person is the story of that person, the fate of a society is the story of the society.

The Norn, the fate-goddess of each person, tells your story and holds your story in her hands. It will remind us of Óðin's wife Frigg, a goddess, who knows all fate and who also goes by another name Saga, which means "The Story". I have earlier claimed that the wives of the Aesir represent their personal fates, and Frigg is Óðin's fate, his story. So once again we find an interesting parallel to the Eagle's emanations. The emanations carry awareness out into the universe from the cosmic source, that is their purpose. The emanations also carry the echoes, the memories of experience back to the source. In the same way, the Nornir emerge from and later return to the Well of Origin carrying the stories, the experiences of lived lives, that part of our lives which requires awareness, perception. So may the Nornir somehow truly be identical to the emanations, to the rivers, to the winds, to the waves of the universe? Let us look a bit closer at these ladies who follow each of us through life, according to Norse beliefs. First of all, the concept of the spinning or weaving Nornir is significant.

In Pagan times, women would use the rhythmic and repetitive movements of spinning and weaving to enter trance and have visions about fate, which is probably why the Nornir are described as spinning and weaving the threads of fate, but let us stop and consider these threads of fate. Each thread, obviously, is a story [a life story]. In a weave, the story interacts with other stories. At birth, the Nornir would apparently arrive and start casting the stories [the threads of fate] around to begin the weave of life. In Castañeda's descriptions, the emanations of the Eagle are often described as fibers or filaments moving through the universe. I wonder if the fibers of the weave may be yet another image describing the emanations of awareness. The fate-goddesses of the individual men or women resemble, in the way they are described and named, a part of the human soul. That is what I think, anyway. Sometimes she is called a spádís, which means a Prophetic Goddess that is when she appears to her person with advice and guidance or warnings.

Sometimes she is called a Fylgja, a "follower", and operates like a sort of guardian spirit to her human. Or she may be called a dís, which just means a goddess, or a Hamingja, which probably means a "shape-walker", and which seems to refer to the part of the soul which can move outside of the body. Then she may turn out to be a Valkyrie, or simply be called a Norn. She is not only responsible for spinning the life, but also to choose a death and to carry the dead back into Hel, or to Valhǫll. It was thought that a person could have one, three, nine, or two or three by nine Nornir in their following.

The many would usually be just silent attachments to one leading Norn. The personal fate or fates could be of different kinds. What kind of fate-goddess you had would show through the fortune or lack of fortune in your life. Most people have sleeping fates, the daughters of Dvalinn, which means Hibernation. If your fate-goddess was sleeping, your life would be randomly spun and easily unfortunate. Other people had divine fates, like the heroes of the Edda, who woke up their fates during a trial of initiation, to find that they were powerful Valkyrie, who would lead her person to honor and glory.

Other people had elfin fates, akin to the light-elves, who were immortal and lived in the upper heavens. Through my studies over a long time I have come to believe that the often recurrent Norse theme of waking up a giantess, goddess or Valkyrie, who resides in a hidden, but glorious realm in the underworld, has to do with a path that is all about waking personal fate. When the fate is "woken" and released from her slumber in the "underworld", she becomes an important part of the hero's life, his life becomes rich in wisdom and power, and he is able to gain control over his destiny. I will just move on to draw the connection between the fates that emerge from the Well of Origin, and the "emanations," or rivers, waves or winds, that emerge from the cosmic source in so many different mythical versions.

What is the connection between the fate-goddesses and the emanations of awareness? We have mentioned the parallel between the Norn and the emanation, when it comes to creating and carrying the life stories from a source and returning it to the same source. Like the emanations, the Nornir emerge from the cosmic source. Like the emanations, they are closely linked to both awareness and death. We have also mentioned the possibility of the thread and the weave as images of fate as actually also being an image of the emanations of life. Are there any other aspects that link the Nornir with the rivers, waves and streams of universal awareness and experience, the stories woven through existence? There is a stanza in the Poetic Edda where the Hamingjur, another name for the follower Nornir, are compared with great rivers flooding the world, or as it is told in Vafþrúðnismál St. 48 and 49:

Óðinn said:
48."Much did I travel much
did I try much did I test the
powers: who are the maidens
streaming as one across the ocean
exceedingly wise as they travel?"

Powerful Head-Veil said:
49."Three great rivers fall across
the world which belongs to the
Kin-Tracker's maidens
They are all shape-walkers when
they are in the world although
they were born among giants."

Óðinn kvað:
48.«Fiolþ ec for,
fiolþ ec freistaþac,
fiolþ ec vm reynda regin:
Hveriar 'ro þer meyiar,
er liþa mar yfir,
frodgediaþar fara?»

Vafþrúðnir kvað:
49.«Þriar þioðár
falla þorp yfir
meyia Ma/gþrasiss;
hamingior einar
þer er i heimi ero,
þo þer meþ iotnom alaz.»

The fact that the Nornir are here described as streaming across the ocean and that they are like great rivers streaming through the world [the home of Kin-trackers maidens is a metaphor for the world] makes us once again think about the emanations flowing through the universe. It is also said that they are born among giants, a claim that is confirmed many times in the sources, the fates began as giantesses. So let us take a little detour into the realm of the giants. In the realm of giants we find yet another image of the same cosmic source of awareness. We find that there is a sort of ocean a cosmic ocean, I believe, in which the giantess Rán receives the dead, who have drowned at sea. Now this could be, as most people think, a sort of ocean goddess, but she is clearly also a death goddess. In poetry she is described the same way as Hel is, an attractive, beautiful woman, who invites people in to party and love-making. Her embrace is, however, death.

Yes, if what I just said surprised you, it is probably because you have been reading Snorri's version of Hel as a very grim-looking poor outcast girl. However, his description is a late one and does not correspond with earlier description from sources of Norse poetry. As said, Hel is a real beauty according to some poems, and so is Rán, although they are also terrifying and menacing. However, returning to Rán, the queen of the ocean, an alluring woman who awaits the drowned with her net. The fact that the ocean in itself is a poetic image of the realm of death is itself not so strange, during the Viking Age, death at sea or death by drowning was extremely common, and so the ocean becomes the earthly version of the Cosmic Ocean in which there is an ancient entity, who attracts and claims the dead.

It is the same image all over again, and Rán's net, with which she catches the dead, is yet another image of the weave of life, made out of countless different threads of fate. Now this Rán has a husband called Aegir, whom I have earlier identified with the other world giants such as Suttungr, Heimdallr, Ymir and so on. Aegir lives on an island called Hlésey, which means the Wind Shielded Island. Knowing that wind equals death and the emanations of awareness, we realize that Aegir lives in a place that is shielded from these forces. So I call it the Island of Immortality, but it might just as well be identical to the grove, the well, the source from which everything stems. The couple has nine daughters, and interestingly enough, these daughters are identified as waves.

They are also called rivers, and they are called the lights of the gods. Their father is said to be steering the winds and the waves. In one Edda poem, the Oddrúngrátr, we learn that the daughters, who emerge from the island called Hlésey are in fact Valkyrie, that is, they are fate goddesses. In several other places, we learn that nine sorceresses gave birth to this world at the end of heaven, which is the exact same location as the great Eagle. Thus we learn something interesting. The mothers of the world are giantesses and fate goddesses, who emerged from the realm of death as daughters of the primeval couple. The male in that couple stands in the ship harbor of his shielded island or grove of immortality, steering the winds and the waves his daughters. The female of the couple waits with her net as the daughters bring back the dead, and receives the results, the remnants of the dead, taking them into her net and, we suspect, devours them. However, just as she receives the dead, she also gives birth to the daughters that create fate, that create life stories. So, once more we have the same essential description of a cosmic source of awareness a source of fate and life stories, which also receives the memories of the dead.

People get easily hung up in geographical borders and individual characters when they try to understand myths. Look beyond all that and into the essence of what is being conveyed here and you realize that there is no difference between the three wells at the three roots of the World Tree. There is no difference between these wells and the image of the eagle, or the image of Aegir and Ran. It is the same story told over and over again using new imagery every time, following the rule of Old Norse poetry.

You have the Well of Origin and Fate, from which the fates come, you have the Well of Hel and Death, from which the rivers come, you have the Well of Memory from which intelligence and sound vibrations come, you have the Mead of Poetry, from where knowledge comes, you have the Cosmic ocean death realm, from which the mothers of the world emerge in the shape of rivers, waves and light, you have the story of Ymir, the great Cosmic Sound, whose body was divided into countless tunes, and you have the Eagle, from which the winds of consciousness emanate. All these different descriptions do not describe different geographical areas, they are all using different images describing the same awesome phenomenon, the Cosmic source, which is essentially exactly the same as that described by Castañeda in his book The Fire from Within: The Eagle and its emanations of awareness. So what is the point of knowing all this?

Why were Norse poets so obsessed with describing this cosmic source over and over again in various ways? I will look to Castañeda again in order offer a very possible clue. Now I am going to use my own words in order to summarize and simplify the explanations given, because Castañeda uses a lot of terms that are only understandable to those who have seriously studied his work. To explain it in simpler terms, a human being is, according to Don Juan, ultimately an energy being. We normally only perceive the physical reality of our bodies, but beyond that physical reality there is a greater reality where we are pure energy. This energy is made up of the threads or fibers or filaments of the cosmic emanations. The human energy body is like a cocoon made up of such fibers. However, the ordinary human being will not make any use whatsoever of most of these fibers. When a seer looks at the energy cocoon of a human being, the seer will observe that most of the cocoon is dimmed, and only a small part lit up.

That tiny light is our conscious awareness, but it only illuminates a very small part of oneself. We have a kind of glow of awareness that is normally restricted to only move within a very small part of the entire energy body. This is the reason why we hold on to a particular perception of the world and ourselves, but it is only a very tiny portion of what we really are. The seer is a person who learns to expand the glow of awareness to cover the entire energy body, so that we illuminate every part of ourselves and become whole beings.

When the glow of awareness has expanded to the entire energy body, we light up like a fire, and this is what is called the Fire from Within. It is to become aware of the entirety of ourselves, and when the seer has succeeded in lighting the fire from within, the seer becomes free of the devouring beak of the Eagle. At death, the seer will be able to maintain their awareness, so as not to become consumed into that great cosmic pool of memories. To maintain awareness is to maintain one's life on an energy level. It is a way to achieve individual freedom and immortality. To achieve this result is the reason why the old seers wanted to learn about the Eagle and its emanations in the first place.

THE MURDERED EAGLE

Now, to Norse mythology, there are countless stories of such feats, but I will concentrate mainly on the eagle stories. As far as I remember, there are three stories of how the eagle is "killed", and they all involve the rescue or the guidance of a bright maiden.

➻ Firstly, there is the story I mentioned earlier about how the hero succeeded in rescuing two maidens from the giant in eagle disguise, while in the Land of Falling Asleep. Significantly, there is a fire involved.

➻ Secondly, you have the story of how Loki rescued the goddess Iðunn from the giant in eagle disguise in the Land of the Drum. The eagle pursued Loki and the goddess, but lost when the gods set a great fire in their realm.

➻ In a third story, Óðinn rescues the Mead of Poetry given to him by the maiden Gunnlǫð, who also aids him in his escape from her father. Her father pursues Óðinn in his eagle disguise, but Óðinn escapes while also wearing an eagle disguise. He takes upon himself the same disguise as the great giant of the source. You can ponder the meaning of that yourself. The result is that Óðinn is able to come among the binding powers, that is, among the immortal gods.

So, what is being rescued in these stories? Basically it is mead, a maiden, or both. The mead of poetry is the mead that contains all knowledge, all memory it is indeed often called the Mead of Memory and the poetry that creates the stories of the lives. I supposed we could call that awareness, and when it comes to the goddess Iðunn, we know that she is the power that rejuvenates the gods every day, just like Urðr is what rejuvenates the World Tree. Significantly, the name Iðunn means the woman who returns to the water-source. She is described as the Seed of the World Tree and as the one Lover of all the Gods, the oldest and the youngest child of the Inner Ruler. She is clearly connected to life and life force.

She is also called dís forvitin, the Knowledge Hungry Goddess, and it is her hunger for knowledge that will make us able to draw the connection between the goddess and awareness, an awareness that is so essential to maintaining life. In the Edda, there are many stories and references to the golden lady that may be found in the world of the dead, and that by uniting with her and by drinking her mead, one will not only be able to access hidden knowledge, but also be able to escape death. The golden lady is strongly associated with fate and knowledge, especially the fate of death, and if she is ultimately a metaphor for the emanations of awareness that stream from the Cosmic source of life and death, then the idea that she has to be woken in order to reveal the hidden knowledge of personal power and immortality that is always being described in the Edda as our human heritage, then this concept is exactly the same found in the idea of lighting the fire of awareness until it covers the entirety of our being. In my opinion, what is being described is a path towards knowledge and immortality akin to that described by Castañeda, where the whole point is to reach the totality of oneself and to claim one's own fate. The Norse version of the Fire from Within is perhaps best described in the Vǫluspá story of the witch called Gullveigr, Golden Drink, another name for Freya. In that story, the divine witch displays her immortality by bursting into flames three times, emerging unscathed, and thus instigating the path of freedom from being consumed in death.

12.6: Óðinn, the universal spirit

It is time to discuss one of the most complex mythological characters in the Edda, the great god Óðinn, and how he may fit into the concept of Pantheism. Lots of Pantheists have paid reverence to all the gods in their religion, but focused particularly on one deity that in their minds serves best to represent the more or less unfathomable universal being. This does not mean that they disregarded other gods. It only means that the particular deity that they chose had a universal and all-encompassing character that served to provide an image of the great All. So, people seem to have, perhaps, always felt a need to worship something higher than themselves.

However, the ultimate conclusion of Pantheism is that if all entities in the Cosmos are but cells of the same universal body, then we are just as divine as the gods, sharing the same essence as them, although they might appear wiser, more ancient, and more powerful. Some Pantheist traditions have completely embraced this knowledge. When the concept of the immanent divinity of everything in the universe is truly grasped, the person who grasps it will usually leave all worship of gods completely, and rather focus on integrating their own inner divinity, symbolically uniting their individual soul with the great universal all-soul. This person will either regard the gods as figments of their imagination, symbols for Cosmic energies, or as real beings that possess great power and should be respected, and perhaps prayed to for help and guidance, yet are ultimately no more or less divine than him or herself.

When it comes down to the essentials, you could just worship a tree or some other entity as a symbol of the universal being, or you could start to revere your own body-soul as a microcosmic image of the Macrocosm. If we take another, more secular approach, we may begin to better grasp the concept of the one and the many. If we look towards the science of cosmology and physics, we quickly realize that the most common understanding is that the entire universe was born from an original source. Since I am not a physicist, I will use very simple terms here, so don't be too hard on me if you think it could have been explained better or in more scientific terms. I will just say the most basic understanding I have, that ultimately, we are all but energy at the core.

Despite all our individual differences, despite the difference between various species of life, despite the apparent difference between us and, say, our planet, our moon and our sun star, we and them are all made up of tiny particles that are, ultimately, completely identical. The only thing that make us all different are the way these particles create different configurations as they hook up with each other. The configurations are different and change over time, they come into being and then dissolve in death, yet the energetic essence and the particles are eternal and all the same, like the one cell which at conception begins separating into many cells. All the countless different ways of building entities in nature and the universe at large stem from a common origin. The Big Bang theory is now the prevailing cosmological model of the early development of the universe. The major premise of the Big Bang theory is that the universe once consisted of only one or two substances and existed in an extremely hot and dense state that expanded rapidly, creating a so-called "Big Bang".

This rapid expansion caused the young universe to cool and resulted in its present continuously expanding state. The theory was first proposed by a scientist called Georges Lemaitre, and although the theory has become known as the Big Bang theory, he called his theory the "hypothesis of the primeval atom". The early universe was a place of homogeneity, from which it expanded into numerous configurations of atoms. It is easy to see that this scientific understanding is somewhat similar to the religious concepts of Pantheism. Indeed, today, there is a line of thought called naturalistic Pantheism, or scientific Pantheism, which describes the opinion of those who believe in no other eternal being, but the universe itself. My point of saying this is to make it easier to grasp what the concept Pantheism actually means. Now there will still be someone who will rage and say: "The Old Norse people were not Pantheist, mainly because they think that as far as history is concerned, everybody in a historical culture must have believed exactly the same."

Also, this is what they have decided to believe a long time ago, and somehow the very idea is frightening, because it rocks their beliefs. So how should I answer that? I will say this, we actually do not know what most people believed during Pagan times in Northern Europe. The written evidence we are left with is actually rather scant, and describes only what some people cared to write down a few centuries after conversion to Christianity. Many scholars actually doubt the value of these writings as source material to Pagan beliefs, precisely because they were written down so late, and although Paganism took a long time to die out, the understanding of Pagan lore may have changed a lot during the centuries following conversion. According to the world-view and subjective experience of the archaeologists, archaeological evidence could be interpreted in numerous ways.

Then there is the place name material, which is important because it lets us know which gods were worshiped where and when. All over Scandinavia there are ancient place names that indicate the worship of particular deities in that area. To make an example, there is an area in my hometown, Oslo, which is still called Torshov. I have sometimes asked people, who live in that area if they know what the name Torshov means, but to most modern people, it is just a syllable that describes a certain area of the town. However, the name means "The Temple of Þórr" and indicates that this was a place where the god Þórr was worshiped. The place-name material gives us insight, into which gods were actually most important in practical life, insights that are often at odds with the importance of the gods in the mythology.

By comparing the place name material with the myths, we see that the god Óðinn, for example, was far less important in Scandinavia as a whole than the myths would lead us to believe. This does not mean that he was not important in some areas, or to some clans, or to some particular people, who had reason to be devoted to this god, such as to poets, who regarded him as the archetypal divine skald, the ultimate source of poetry itself. Due to my research on the ritual structure of the myths, I think I have proved that the poems of the Poetic Edda were actually created by Pagan poets and can thus be used as sources to Pagan beliefs. To be more exact, they can be used as sources to some Pagan beliefs.

What was remembered and written down was the lore of Old Norse poets, the skalds, and this is when we have to ask ourselves whether the skalds were actually representative for the entire Norse Pagan religion. They were probably not. We know that to be a skald, a bard, was actually a sacred office at some point in history. Óðinn, for example, does not refer to himself as a skald, but as the great þul, þul being the title of a skald, who recites sacred lore. The skald and the þul received initiation into the mysteries of the heathen lore. What kind of initiation?

Well, in the beginning of the 13th century, the bishop Bjarni Kolbeinsson of the Orkney Islands declared himself to be a good Christian by stating the following sentences: "I never learned the art of poetry by the water-source. I never sang spell-songs and never sat beneath hanged men." His denial of these Pagan practices was necessary, because people still believed that a religious leader such as this bishop must have gone through such events. His denial of having done so is a valuable source to what Pagan poets actually did when they learned the intricate art of poetry.

Like Óðinn, they went to the water-source, the Well of Origin, the Well of Memory, and the Well of Death, in order to complete their initiation. Like Óðinn, they sang spell-songs, and like Óðinn, they sought wisdom from the dead by sitting beneath hanged men. Men hanged in sacrifice to the god Óðinn. These were the people, who created the poems we now know as the Edda poems, and the importance of Óðinn in the myths we know reflect the world-view of the skalds. These people are our sources to Pagan myths. I think it should be almost needless to say that not everybody received this kind of initiation. It was the initiation of the special people, the poets, the witches and the wizards, and as we now know, the initiation of kings. These were the people, who learned the deeper wisdom and more profound meanings of the myths, so that they could learn to sing the hidden wisdom into riddles that people could solve on various levels according to the depth or shallowness of their personal understanding.

And the poets composed these poetic riddles consciously, letting them reveal at least three different layers of understanding at all times. So, what we are left with is written material which reveals the insights of people, who were initiated into Pagan mysteries. Then they composed the mythical poems. I have noticed that many people actually think that the myths are not stories made up by people. They think, somehow, that these myths came into being by themselves and quite literally tell the real stories of real entities. When I suggest otherwise, some people feel provoked, because they believe in the gods and the other powers. Some also want to impose modern concepts of aliens onto the myths, completely missing out the spiritual messages and the fact that all the mythical beings are metaphorical characters, applied by human poets in order to convey a message.

If we want to truly understand the profound spirituality of our ancestors, we have to realize that Old Norse poetry is fiction, composed by human poets, who may have believed in the old powers, yet whose sacred art of poetry it was to apply the supernatural beings of their culture as fictional characters in order to convey a spiritual and philosophical messages that are far more profound than the belief in particular deities. When Pagan poets chose Heimdallr or the Great Goddess to represent the universe, or chose to let them both represent the male and female aspects of the universe, they did not do so because they had monotheistic ideas of exactly this or that deity being the ultimate source of being.

They chose these characters because these were the gods whose functions were most universal and least specialized. This use of particular deities to represent the universal being does not necessarily reflect their importance in any cult or region or time period. Rather, it reflects the flexibility of their characters. Take Þórr, for example. Why is Þórr never employed as a universal source-being in poetry? We know from the texts, from the numerous hammer symbols and from the names of men and women, who were named after him, and from the place name material that he was a very important deity in Scandinavia during Pagan times. The reason why he is never used is because he is too specialized and too set in his character. Only flexible and shape-changing characters, who seem to meddle in all kinds of worlds and affairs, could poetically serve to represent the entire universal body.

Goddess Pantheism is actually more researched and easier to prove and detect than the Pantheist male figures in Old Norse mythology. The reason for this is probably that it is so easy to prove that the female entities are all flexible and overlapping in function, so that they could all easily represent the countless faces of a universal being. The most flexible and omnipresent of them all is Freyia, whose name is only a title which indicates sovereignty, and who is said to take countless shapes and names. So, when I talk about Goddess Pantheism, does that exclude God Pantheism? Of course not.

The whole point of Pantheism is that there is a unifying core to all gods and goddesses, indeed to all existence, so that the focus on a particular deity is only skin-deep. However, the Norse myths clearly show a focus on the balance and complimentary qualities of the two genders. We should always bear in mind that the poets who made up the myths applied metaphors to everything, and that even gender is a metaphor. The metaphor of gender reflects the Old Norse society's view on male and female qualities being different, but equally important, making up a whole.

It also reflects the Old Norse gender roles, where the males represented their clan to the outside world, while the women ruled the inner spheres. In the same way, gender in Old Norse poetry will only be understood if you realize that a female character always represents that which is hidden and guarded, that which is at the inner core, that which awaits and is sought. The male character will represent that which is seen, that which guards and protects, that which challenges the intruder, and that which seeks. A perfect image of this is found in the match between Óðinn and Frigg. Frigg is a being who knows all fate, yet reveals nothing of her knowledge. It is no coincidence that she is matched in marriage with Óðinn, who is the being who seeks to know all fate.

As such, they constitute two sides of the same coin the seeker and the sought, the learner of knowledge and the inherent, yet silent knowledge. The one is nothing without the other, and as it is stated in the Raven Charm of Óðinn, "the honor of the high seat belongs to both". In the poem Grímnismál, we learn that Óðinn and Frigg, with her name Saga, which means The Story, and corresponds to the Poetry meaning of his name, sit together within the sunken river of existence and drink the mead of knowledge together. If we take the fact seriously that male and female forces are matched and balance each other in Norse myths, then the concept of a Universal being should also reveal a similar gender balance, where the male face of the greater all represents the masculine qualities, and the female face of the greater all represents the feminine qualities that together make up the whole.

I have already mentioned one male character which serves to describe the unified the Cosmos, Heimdallr. Heimdallr, who is basically the world itself, hearing all and seeing all, is a perfect candidate to represent the universal being, since he shows up in many giant bodies and in the World Tree itself. Óðinn, as we shall see, is equally representative, especially when it comes to a particular type of universal energy; the quest for expanding one's knowledge, a virtue that lies at the core of life itself. As I have already argued in several videos, there is strong evidence of Pantheist concepts in the Edda lore. In my opinion, this proves that the concept of Pantheism existed in Old Norse religion. However, we have no way of knowing to what extent people who were not initiated had any understanding of this concept.

It is completely possible that the average Norse man and woman had very little understanding or even knowledge about Pantheist concepts, and that this was an understanding held only by the few, the cultural, religious, spiritual and political leaders. It is equally possible that the average Norse man and woman actually did have some understanding of Pantheism. We just do not know anything about the degree to which this concept was known and understood in general. The only things we can know, through interpretation of the metaphors and allegories, is that such concepts existed and were promoted by the skalds, and that it was at the core of the tradition followed by skalds, poets who received their initiation in mystical ways, and who left their lore to us. I will tell you about my own personal vision of Óðinn as a universal being towards the end of this section.

For now, I will only say that I had a sort of transcendental experience once, which made a lot of puzzles fall into place. Sometimes, intuition will help us to find new ways to look at something one has tried to figure out for a long time, and I had long suspected a deeper meaning to the myths of the Eddas. After my experience, I sat down with the Edda poems again, and began to scrutinize the lore of Óðinn in order to see if my intuitive visions were merely personal insights of my own, or if there was any correspondence with the actual myths that we know.

I found that my dream-like visions had directed me towards an approach that completely revolutionized my understanding of the myths. Óðinn has been an important figure in many of my talks already, and I will not go too deeply into matters that have already been touched upon before. I have discussed the myth where Óðinn hangs on the World Tree in order to grasp the runes and learn powerful songs, so that he may become a wise man. I also showed how this myth is actually connected to the myth of Óðinn seeking the Mead of Poetry in Gunnlǫð's hall, and that the two myths together make up one singular story. I have also discussed this god in relation to the theme of Sacred Marriage in Scandinavian prehistory.

As in, is all history that predates the art of writing in that particular culture. Despite the runes, the Vikings were a largely illiterate people and as such their history is prehistoric. This theme has been well known to scholars of Old Norse religion for several decades already, is still being researched and promoted in academic circles, and is actually crucial in the lore of and the history of the god Óðinn. However, it would seem that this knowledge has not yet found its way into mainstream education and media. I am actually a bit surprised about how many people, who have obviously been interested in Norse mythology, are surprised about this kind of information!

I have also discussed initiation rituals and showed how the path staked out by Óðinn when he sought the runes, the spell-songs and the precious mead, was actually followed by other gods and human beings. As such, he was the instigator of a spiritual path of initiation for males, the first to stake it out. I say it was a path for males, because all those who are described following the path of Óðinn are male, and the culmination of their path lies in marriage to the goddess. However, I also showed that Óðinn learned a significant part of his art from a female, and that females acted as teachers on this path of male initiates. As such, there was also a female path that we simply know less about. Furthermore, I have offered an in-depth study of the trinity theme in Old Norse Myths, showing how Óðinn and his two brothers make a sort of prototypical pattern that resurfaces in all the male trinities in the Edda, and that the three represent the three main aspects of human existence, Spirit, Mind and Passion.

I am going to continue a little where I left off. First, we have the name Óðinn. The name is derived from the Old Norse word Óðr, which translates as "Poetry", "Spirit", or "Frenzy". The, 'inn' ending, is a suffix which means the same as the English word "the". Thus we realize that the name Óðinn indicates that he not only is poetry, spirit and frenzy, but that he is The Spirit, The Poetry, and The Frenzy, as such. Obviously, we all have these qualities within us. The Spirit is that which gives us breath and inspiration, which is exactly what Óðinn is said to have given to men and women alike. The Poetry is the equivalent of the mind, that within us which creates the stories that are our lives, and the Frenzy is our passion, our desire, that which drives us forward and make us seek, rebelling against everything that limits the fullness of our being. All these three meanings are relevant and coexisting, and symbolized in the trinity that I talked about before.

I will not begin to explain the trinity issue again, so I highly recommend the reader to look back to previous chapters for a better understanding of what this means. If you have read carefully all I have written about both Óðinn and Þórr, will you understand what I mean when I say that the trinity formula of the myths indicate that the Old Norse poets, who left us their lore, not necessarily the lore of everyone, but certainly the lore if the initiated believed that other gods such as Þórr and Freyr, actually represented one of these three aspects of Óðinn. Þórr the poetry, the thinking mind, and Freyr the passion, the desire to experience. This in itself is a powerful indicator of a Pantheist concept behind the messages of Old Norse myths. So, again, since many seem to misunderstand this concept, yes, these gods were indeed worshiped as separate entities in Scandinavia. I am not saying that they were not worshiped in their own right.

What I am saying is that the poets applied these gods as characters in order to reveal deeper spiritual knowledge where the gods represent Cosmic, natural and human virtues at large, both outside of and within ourselves, and that they had a Pantheist understanding at the core of their mysteries. Mysteries that may not have been understood by those who were not initiated. Let us talk about Óðin's ravens, Huginn and Muninn. They are also a part of the trinity concept, actually. In the center stands the Spirit, the Inspiration and the Breath-Giver, Óðinn himself. On either side of him sit the two ravens. I remember reading someone claiming that the ravens of Óðinn were a sort of patriarchal adaption of the earlier goddess of ravens in Western European myths. That is certainly possible, but to stop at that is to not understand the meaning of the ravens within Old Norse mythology.

You see, no matter how much Norse myths may have changed and adapted and borrowed from other mythologies, the way they are presented to us reveals that they are a complete and whole system of beliefs in their own right, and the ravens as part of the trinity concept actually have a meaning of their own. The, *'inn' endings*, in the names of the ravens mean the same as theinn ending in the name Óðinn. That leaves us with the words húgr and múnr. The word húgr can be translated as desire, love, thought, soul or intent. The best translation is in my opinion "intent", since the húgr is basically something that intends and wants something in the Norse language.

A strong willed person would be praised for having a strong húgr. A cold-hearted person would be scorned for having a hard húgr. The reason it could be translated as desire, love and thought is because these virtues are all about intending and wanting. Thus the raven called Huginn is actually "The Intent". It corresponds with the frenzy and passion in the name Óðinn. The raven Muninn is derived from the word múnr, which means Memory. So the raven Muninn is The Memory. This corresponds to the mind, and thus to poetry. What we are seeing in the trinity of Óðinn and his ravens, is that we are not only about spirit, intent and memory, but also The Spirit, The Intent and The Memory, as such. I think we can all agree that we all have spirit, intent and memory within ourselves. They are virtues that exist at large, present within all humans and, some will agree, within all living beings. What about Óðin's wolves?

He is said to be accompanied by two wolves called Geri and Freki. Again, we have the trinity formula to deal with. Let us look at what these names mean. Geri could easily be derived from the Old Norse verb gera, which means "to do", or "to act". As such, the wolf Geri represents action. He is the doer. We all have the doer within us, do we not? Freki actually means the same as Fenrir, namely greed or gluttony. Obviously, this is the wolf that corresponds with the frenzied passion of the Spirit. That leaves the Action wolf to correspond with poetry and mind, that which creates the stories of lives, while the greed or the passionate desire drives us forward. After having looked at these Óðinic attributes, let us now move on to an Edda poem called the Grímnismál, which means the Speech of Grímnir, the Masked One or the Hooded One.

This is one of Óðins many names. In this poem, we learn that Óðinn visits the halls of his ward Geirrǫðr, whose name means Red Spear, in order to find out whether he really is as inhospitable and stingy as his wife Frigg claims. Inhospitality and stinginess were considered very bad form in Pagan times, and Óðinn is very disappointed to hear that his own ward could have sunk so low. Skipping a few details, as Óðinn arrives with Red Spear, his worry is confirmed and instead of being recognized and welcomed, he is chained between two fires that gradually burn their way towards him. If you realize that Óðinn represents The Spirit, you will understand the deeper meaning of this metaphor. Red Spear can no longer recognize the Spirit of knowledge and "chains" it, allowing it be consumed.

The result is that he ends up dying on his own sword. However, just as The Spirit awaits the fire, Red Spear's young son Agnarr, who is named after Frigg's ward Agnarr, and whose name means Honorable Warrior, offers a drinking cup to Spirit. To reward the young man, Óðinn begins to reveal secret knowledge about the twelve spheres of existence, and finally reveals who, or rather what, he is. If you have a translated copy of the Poetic Edda lying around, I recommend that you look up the Grímnismál now. It will probably be called either the Lay of Grímnir or the Speech of Grímnir. Find stanza 46 and read from there.

What you will probably find is that Óðinn starts to list all his names. Are the names translated? Probably not. As they are, and if you are not familiar with Old Norse, you will only read a long list of exotic-sounding names that are really nothing but meaningless words to you. Then consider the fact that the names actually mean something and that these meanings were known to both the poet, who composed the poem, and to his audience. Then consider the possibility that the meanings of these names are in fact essential to Óðin's revelation. I am going to offer my translation of the names in these stanzas, where Óðinn reveals his true names to the Honorable Warrior. The stanzas translated here are 46 to 50, and then stanza 54 of the Grímnismál in the Poetic Edda.

46. I called myself Masked/Hooded
I called myself Wandering Learning
The Ruler, the Helmet-Carrier [= Carrier of the Mind] Beloved and Third
Swelling One and Wave
Death-Blinder and High

47. Truth and Perishable and Truth-Guesser
Joy of the Moment and Pushing Forth Towards Sight, Fire-Eyed
Harm-Doer, The One Who Is Many Hooded and Masked
Bright Knowledge and Much Knowing

48. Broad Hat, Broad Beard
Victory Father and Pushed
All Father, Choice Father
Close/Approaching Weight and God of Burdens; Never did I have just one name as I moved among people

49. I was called The Masked One in the halls of Spear Source
Castrate in the house of Divine Water-source
Cauldron I was called when I pulled the sledge
Faith I was at parliament
Expander at the battleground
Ashes and Oven
Just-as-High and Vibrating Path
Magician and Long-Beard among the gods

46. Hetomc Grimr,
hetomc Gangleri,
Herian oc Hialmberi,
Þeccr oc Þriði,
Þvðr oc Vþr,
Helblindi oc Hár.

47. Saþr oc Svipall
oc Sanngetall,
Herteitr oc Hnicarr,
Bileygr, Baleygr,
Ba/lvercr, Fiolnir,
Grimr oc Grimnir,
Glapsviþr oc Fialsviþr,

48. Siþha/ttr, Siþsceggr,
Sigfa/ðr, Hnicvþr,
Alfa/þr, Valfa/þr,
Atríðr oc Farmatyr;
eino nafni hetomc aldregi,
siz ec meþ folcom fór.

49. Grimne mic héto
at Geirraðar,
enn Ialc at Asmundar,
enn þa Kialar
er ec kialca dró,
Þrór þingom at,
Viðvrr at vigom,
Osci oc Ómi,
Iafnhár oc Biflindi,
Ga/ndlir oc Harbarðr meþ goðom
[...]

50. The Burner and the Burned
I was called at Sunken Memory
I tricked the ancient giant when the son of
Mead-Witness the mighty warrior died in
battle with me
[...]

50. Sviþvrr oc Sviþrir
er ec het at Sa/ccmimis,
oc dvlþa ec þann inn aldna
iotvn,
þa er ec Miþviþnis varc
ins mora bvrar
ordinn einbani.

54. The Spirit, the name is now
The Old One I was before and Thin Mist
before that
Awakening and Shivering
Veiled Wave and Shattered God
Human Ancestor and Castrate among
gods
Opener and Closer and all, I believe, stem
from me only.

54. Oþinn ec nv heiti,
Yggr ec áþan het,
hetvmc Þvndr fyrir þat:
Vacr oc Scilfingr,
Váfvþr oc Hroptatýr,
Ga/tr oc Ialcr meþ goðom,
Ofnir oc Svafnir,
er ec hygg at orðnir se
allir af einom mer.

I don't know if I could find any better example of a true Pantheist revelation in Pagan lore than this poem. He even states that all [allir everybody/everything] stems from him. There are so many names that I cannot go through each of them in this talk, but if you listen, they actually speak for themselves. In the Prose Edda, Snorri describes Óðinn in a similar manner. In the Prose Edda Chapter called the Gylfaginning, which means the Visions of the Sorcerer, the sorcerer king Gylfi takes the name Gangleri, which means Wandering Learning, and visits the hall of the Aesir. As I already quoted, Gangleri, Wandering Learning, is actually one of the names that Óðinn reveals as his own.

So the sorcerer king is actually a disguise for Óðinn himself, and the most puzzling thing is that it is thus Óðinn himself who seeks the Aesir and is met by yet other aspects of himself in order to learn! In the story, Wandering Learning is met by a trinity called Hár, Jafnhár and Þriði, which means The High One, Just as High and Third. All these names are known and listed names of Óðinn, despite the fact that they all speak of him in the third person. Wandering Learning, too, is Óðinn, asking the other aspects of himself about the nature of himself.

They are all really speaking about themselves, yet using the third person. This can only be truly understood if we perceive the myths as a parable about the nature of the universal Spirit, a moving learner, who seeks knowledge about itself, who continuously asks questions and answers them from another point of view, yet which is also itself, a universal Spirit appearing in countless guises, who all relate to each other as if they were separate entities, yet are all the same ultimate being.

I quote:

"Wandering Learning began his questioning thus: "Who is the highest and most ancient of Aesir?"
The High One said: "He is called All-Father in our language, but in Old Ásgarðr he had twelve names. One is All-Father, the second Ruler, the third Pusher, the fourth Pushed, the fifth One Who Is Many, the sixth Ashes, the seventh Oven, the eight Shivering Path, the ninth Burner, the tenth Burned, the eleventh Expander, the twelfth Castrate."
Then Wandering Learning asked: "Where is this god, what power has he, and what great works has he performed?"

*And the High One said: "He lives through all ages and rules his entire
kingdom and governs all things great and small. [...]"
Then spoke Wandering Learning: "What was he doing before heaven and
earth were made?
The High One replied: Then he was among the Frost giants."*

The stanzas quoted from the Grímnismál, as well as the Prose Edda passage
above quoted from Snorri, not only state that Óðinn seeks knowledge from himself
in different guises, and that he has many names and shapes. The meanings of these
names show him as a universal character. He is the Burner and the Burned, he is
the Opener and the Closer, he is the pusher, and the pushed, he is the ashes, and
the oven. He is both parts of an interaction, the giver and the receiver.

That which causes and that which is caused. He is all-encompassing. We also
learn something of his origin. He is Poetry, Spirit and Frenzy now, as Óðinn, but
before that, he was the Old One, and before that, he was Thin Mist. What of this
"Thin Mist"? What of the Awakening, and the Shivering? What is the Divine Water-
source, where he was castrated, and why is he the Cauldron when he pulls the
sledge? What is the sledge, even? To understand the meaning of these names, we
have to look into the myths of creation.

THIN MIST THE PRIMEVAL BEING

The Thin Mist of his name, Þundr, refers to the thin mist that exists in the world
of the dead, the Níflheimr, which means Misty World. When he says that he was
Thin Mist in the beginning, before he became Óðinn, and also revealing that he was
among the frost giants, he is referring to the time of origin, before actual creation,
when Níflheimr, the icy world of the dead, was the only Cosmic sphere that existed,
next to the fiery heat of Muspellheimr. We know that the myths relate how the
present universe was preceded by nine previous worlds, its mothers.

Thus the presence of the realm of the dead at the beginning of the universe
strongly suggests that these previous worlds had left their remnants in the ice
of the Misty World. We know that the first conscious being of the present the
Cosmos actually came from the world of fiery heat in the shape of the giant "cow"
Auðhumbla, and that she began to nourish herself from the ice and mists of
Níflheimr, the Misty World. As she nourished herself from the icy remnants of dead
worlds, like the eternal goddess of the dead, who receives and consumes the souls
of the dead, she also created life at the same time.

As she fed on the mists of dead worlds, she also fed the world giant, the Cosmic
Sound, so that it expanded with her streams of milk, and as she slowly worked
her way into the core of the icy realm of death, she uncovered another frost giant
called Búr, and as she continued to feed on the ice, her warm tongue caused him to
defrost back to life. The name Búr means the Storage Room or the Cage, which is
also significant, he was something that contained something. What he contained,
obviously, was the potential for conscious intelligence. We must assume that
this giant belonged to the previous world, and that he had only been hibernating
within the death realm, waiting for a new cycle, carrying with him the seed of new
life. From the frost giant Storage Room comes a son, and his name is Bórr, which
indicates a drill, as if his main function was to drill himself out of the cage.

His wife was called Bestla, and her name indicates a rhythmic beat. United in a metaphorical marriage, the beat and the drilling power succeed in escaping the ancient Cage and, as the Storage Room opens up, three entities appear that are also just one; Óðinn, Víli and Vé, the three aspects of conscious existence that were to move through the universe and give it shape. This brings us to one of Óðin's names, Þundr, which refers to Thin Mist. Thin Mist was exactly the essence of the frozen world that contained the remnants of previous worlds.

This was what Óðinn was in the very beginning, when he was among Frost Giants. He is the result of the quickening of life that came out of the death of a previous world. My guess is that Thin Mist refers to the thin mists of the Underworld, the mist of the souls that were frozen before life could start afresh. It refers both to his being the original creature of the world, the first self-conscious entity that was created from the icy mists of a previous world and it refers to him being intimately connected with the souls that are recycled through this realm time and time again.

Awakened and shivering

This also explains the possible essential meaning of his name Awakened. The importance of vibrations in creating the early universe may account for why Óðinn was also called the Shivering. As the Aesir awake into consciousness after eons of hibernation, they observe the state of the early universe as it is described in the Vǫluspá. The Sun knows not where she has her halls (that is, I think, the planets), Earth is a barren rock, the Moon knows not of his powers, and the stars know no constellations. When the three gods of conscious energies "lift up the lands", or, as Snorri described it, "killed" the primeval Sound and parted it into numerous tunes, then the stars found their places in heaven, the Sun goddess threw her right hand around the "horses of heaven" and began to shine her elfin rays upon the Earth Goddess so that she bloomed with life, and the Moon god, we must assume, learned of his power.

The three primeval, original Aesir, representing the three aspects of conscious, learning energy, could now begin to play with their golden checkers, only to soon learn that fate rules everything and demands responsibility. Another of Óðin's names is the Shivering Path. That brings me back again to the parting of one original Sound into numerous tunes, or sound vibrations. Vibrations which could easily be called shivering paths. When I had my vision of riding the steed Óðinn through the universe, I certainly perceived countless such vibrating paths in the universe. I have experienced that kind of sensation so many times, and also read several accounts from others, that I am certain that this is something that many human beings before me have also perceived countless times.

What of the Divine Water-source? This is a reference to the Well of Origin, The Well of Memory and the Well of Bellower, the original source of all movement. That he was a castrate when he was there is a very interesting detail which I think I have to make an analysis of another time, because it will take too long. However, the fact that he was a Cauldron when he "pulled the sledge" would refer to the Cauldron that can contain all the so-called "water" of the Divine Water-source, the sledge being a symbol of a physical shape pulled through life, and which he pulls, containing the divine water of life.

In a poem of the Elder Edda called Reginsmál [the Song of the Ruler], Óðinn appears standing on a rock in the midst of a stormy ocean.

When the hero sees the god, he asks who he is, and the god answers:

18. " I was the Pusher when I pleased the Intent *...* *Now you may call this man of the mountain* *The One who Receives or The One Who is Many and I want to travel with you."*	*18. «Hnicar heto mic,* *þa er Hvgin gladdac,* *...* *nv mattv calla* *karl af bergi* *Feng eþa Fiolni,* *far vil ec þiggia.»*

As soon as the hero lets the god of Spirit come aboard his "ship", which is a metaphor for life itself, as it floats through existence, the storms are stilled and wise counsel given. It is not hard to see that Óðinn represents the spirit of knowledge and wisdom in such a story. The name which indicates that he is the one, who receives, probably refers to his receiving the dead. We usually tend to think about him as the receiver of the dead in Valhǫll, where he sort of cooperates with Freyia and the Valkyrie in the reception of the chosen dead. On a greater scale, we may have to think further, and wonder why Óðinn also wears an eagle hide on certain occasions. If you saw my previous video, you will know that the eagle represents both the recipient of the awareness of the dead, and the creator of Cosmic movement.

THE MANY AND MUCH KNOWING

Another good name is Fiǫlnir, which is derived from fiǫl, which means "many". The form of the name, however, as in Fiǫlnir, is singular, indicating one. The name must be translated as the One Many, referring to him being one and many at the same time. There is also the name Fjǫlsviðr "Much Knowing" which identifies Óðinn as the true character behind the guardian and servant of the Great Maiden, who questions and answers the young initiate of the poem Fjǫlsvinnsmál. When we look back at the stanzas I referred to earlier, we should by now begin to accept that only Pantheism could be behind such a revelation.

Óðinn is the Thin Mist at the beginning of time, the Shivering Paths of creation. As the spirit that seeks knowledge in all kinds of situations, in all kinds of worlds, he becomes both the actor and the acted. He is the Burner, but he is also the Burned. He is the Pusher, but he is also the Pushed. He makes it perfectly clear that he is a different kind of being in different kinds of worlds, and that he performs all the acts of the story that is life. I will just end this talk with one more stanza from an Edda poem, stanza 142 of the Hávamál the Speech of the High One. This is where Óðinn reveals his different aspects in different Cosmic spheres of existence:

142. Spirit with the Aesir *Dying one (Mortal) for the Elves* *Hibernation for the dwarfs* *Divine Tree for the giants* *I myself carved some (fate runes)*	*142. Oþinn meþ asom* *enn fyr alfom Dainn,* *Dvalinn oc dvergom fyr,* *Asvidr iotnom fyr,* *ec reist sialfr svmar*

In order to truly understand these lines, we have to understand what the Aesir, the elves, the dwarfs and the giants actually represent. The Aesir are the energies of conscious intelligence at large in the universe and within the individuals. To our conscious intelligence, he is, simply, the eternally seeking spirit. The elves are mysterious, and I have not made a public analysis of them yet, but for now I will just state that they probably represent the souls of people, either the souls that haunt the burial mounds as hidden, dark elves, or the souls of the three upper heavens of immortality, where they are light beings, higher even than the gods, associated with the splendor of the sun as well as with the so-called Ydalir, the Valleys of the Yew.

When we understand the elves as souls of dead people, we may more easily understand how Óðinn, as The Spirit among elves is Dáinn, the Dying One. The dwarfs have been accounted for in one my videos earlier called Of Dwarfs and Men, where I analyzed them as the images of men, limiting the limitless, and images through which the gods move into our world. As such, the Spirit often becomes dormant when it enters a limited physical shape, like the sleeping Nornir, who are the daughters of Dvalinn, Hibernation, and who, because they are hibernating, only spin random and unfortunate lives for those who have not yet woken their fates. As for the giants, they are mainly huge Cosmic entities of Utgarðr, the Outer World, which may very well refer to Outer Space. From their perspective, Óðinn is the Divine Tree, the World Tree itself, which is also called Yggdrasill, the Steed of Óðinn.

The World Tree is the Cosmos itself, through which the Spirit moves on his endless search for ever expanding knowledge. As I have shown here, there is plenty of evidence that Óðinn, as well as Heimdallr and the Great Goddess, are poetical characters that serve to reveal a Pantheist core in Old Norse myths. Lots of people will find it confusing that either of these different characters could, in different ways, represent a unifying and universal core. In order to understand this it is essential that you leave the old stereotypical preconceptions of separation between the mythical entities, that you leave all your worries about which god was more or less important, and begin to read the myths as they were made, as metaphors.

The poets who created the myths as we know them were taught to reveal deep spiritual meanings through metaphors, or as Snorri put it, they were taught to understand that which was subtly sung and hidden in words. What is revealed in the Edda is a spiritual path where the illusions of the gods are destroyed to reveal an even greater reality behind them. The Edda poems may not be representative of the lost common folk beliefs in Pagan times, but they certainly represent an ancient lore of spiritual and metaphysical mysteries, and outright philosophy, that in certain aspects is even sometimes close to what we today know as science.

Óðinn and Me, a Personal Revelation

I have reached the end of this book, and now is the time to tell a good story. Whether you believe this story is real or not is entirely up to you. It felt very real to me, and it helped me to look at the myths differently at a time when I felt stuck. This is my own story of Óðinn the Choice Father.

Around the age of fourteen, I began to see a man in my dreams and often in the states just before sleeping or waking. I called him the Shadow Man or the Wolf Man, and the only thing I remember is how he looked and what he made me feel. His appearance was very clear to me. He was extremely tall and very athletic, with strong, broad shoulders. He had a rather long and narrow face with very marked cheekbones. His nose was quite long and a little hooked. His hair was dark and flowed freely down to his hips. He wore a leather tunic and trousers, above the tunic was a silvery chain mail, and around his shoulders was a wolf skin fur. He looked like a barbarian warrior from very ancient times. He also had a scar where his left eye should be. Later, I always drew him with a scar over his right eye, but in my vision it was his left that was missing.

The scar went down to his left cheekbone and formed a little cross there. His remaining eye was dark with a sort of golden hue, shining and highly intelligent. I am quite sure that we spoke, but I have no recollection of the words. I think that most men will perceive Óðinn as a sort of father figure, a leader figure perhaps, or a teacher. I think that is perfectly understandable. However, I am not a man, and the Shadow Man was certainly not a father figure for me. Or a leader figure. A teacher, yes, but the strongest feeling I had when I saw him was of being held, in a fashion.

He made me feel comfortable, like I was not alone. He made me feel safe. He was scary looking, but that was certainly not intended to scare me, and before you start to get ideas, there was nothing untoward! Even though I will admit that he was very attractive. He remained in the shadows, at a certain distance, which was why I called him the Shadow Man. Then for a while, he disappeared from my dream-states. He returned one early morning when I was fifteen, after I had a series of dreams where I met several mythological characters. Even Jesus was there!

Anyway, when I thought that I had woken up, the Wolf Man was sitting in the shadows again, watching me with a sly smile on his face, and I asked, for the first time (as I recollect it), "Who are you?"

He replied; "I am the Watchman". (Or the Guardian? I am only translating the name from Norwegian (vokteren) and it could mean either).

So I went; "Oh...so, are you going to watch over me? Protect me?"

He grinned, with that sly smile of his, and said; "Well,"

In Norwegian he said the words "på en måte", which in English would translate as "sort of". So, I was a bit confused. When he said that he was the Watchman, it resonated with me, because he made me feel safe, but when he said that he was only going to "sort of" protect me, I began to wonder what kind of guardian he could be.

So, I asked again; "Who are you then, really?"

He said the oddest thing. He said; "I am you."

I was like, yeah, right. I mean, he was the furthest thing from me that I could think of! So I picked up the most obvious difference and exclaimed: "But...you are a man!"

He just grinned even more broadly and said; "Sort of".

I figured, OK, he is a man, but only sort of a man. Not really a man. His shape was a figment of my imagination, yet a being, a being without physical existence despite the very strong visual impression I had of him, and a man who claimed to actually be me, and to be a kind of guardian. It was very odd, and I became very curious.

At the time I started to drift back to sleep, quite exhausted, and the only thing I recollect is the feeling that he took my hand and started to walk with me into my dream, and that we talked a lot. Or mainly, I did the talking. He had a great ear for listening, and something about his presence made me raise and answer my own question, which always led to a new question and a new answer, forever. He taught me that there was never one singular answer to end all questions, only countless questions and countless answers. He taught me that the path of learning was endless, and that whenever we insist on remaining inside a world-view box, our wisdom becomes stale and our minds small.
I wrote a lot of these discussions down when I woke up after such dreams, because it was only the first of many.

He actually used to come just as I was falling asleep, and took me into a weird, philosophical dream state. I also had the sensation of being outside the world, in a dark blue place where we could see stars above and beneath us, and where we looked into floating water pools which he called "realities". After a period of time, the Watchman disappeared, and it was only several years later, when I had already studied the Edda poems for several years, that he returned before my inner eye. Only then did I start to suspect that he was a kind of Óðinn figure. When I first began to draw cartoons about Norse myths, I realized that I was drawing Óðinn almost exactly as I had envisioned the Shadow Man.

Then one night, as he appeared again in a state of meditation, I asked him; "Who are you, really?"

Like so many years before, he replied, "I am the Watchman".

Having remembered our previous discourse, so I didn't bother to try and make him specify. Instead, I asked; "Yes, but who are you really?"

Again, he replied, "I am you." So I decided to try to ask a different kind of question in order to make him reveal more.

I asked; "Have you been called by other names before?"

Then his face started to dissolve into the shadows, but his voice became very clear in my head.

He said; "Wuotanaz" and I knew that this was an ancient name of Óðinn.

At the time I had also started to suspect that Óðinn, as a mythical character, represented something more and deeper than just the divine yet human-like patriarch that most are accustomed to think that he is.

Realizing that I had finally made him identify himself, I asked the next question; "What are you, behind the names?"

That was obviously the right question, because the answer turned into the ride of my life. He actually turned into a horse, a black horse with burning coal eyes. He was exactly like a horse I had used to dream of and imagine when I was a child. I had called that horse the Fireball, on account of his fiery eyes, and I could ride that horse through the universe. He could jump from planet to planet, from star to star. I loved that horse! Now, I mounted the horse of my childhood imagination and then the speed of my visions accelerated.

It felt like we were moving at immense speed through countless energetic tunnels, and on the way I saw and understood what he was. I could not really express in words, what that revelation felt like. To remember it, even, is hard. The best way to explain what I saw was that he certainly was not a man in the sense of a human male. He was actually not really gendered at all, so that the best way to describe him would actually be to use the neutral form, "it", and it was like a particular kind of Cosmic energy. We humans will easily perceive this energy as masculine, because of its push-forward, penetrating and conquering nature, but in reality he was just a kind of non-gendered energy that could assume any form according to the eye of the beholder.

I perceived that he was the energy of ever expanding, seeking, conquering consciousness, an energy that wants to learn, to seek, an energy that is always expanding, learning more, seeking more knowledge, a desire to experience every possible and seemingly impossible quirks of conscious existence. This energy was simultaneously perceived by me as one unified and very real Cosmic entity, and at the same time as an impersonal energy that exists within all life. And that was why he said that he was me. He was in all things that ever lived and learned through the experience of existence. He was, truly, the Watchman, the great, Cosmic Observer. I also learned that if I was connected to this energy, if I assimilated this energy within myself, it would in fact watch over me and protect me, but that if I was not able to integrate it within myself, it could just as easily lead me into peril, just to learn from it.

He made no judgment upon any kind of experience or point of view. He was in all kinds of experiences and every point of view, in order to learn. He was in the dramas, in the comedies and in the tragedies, in the romances, the thrillers, and the horror stories. He was the poetry of every story that is a life. He was in every world, watching every experience, ever learning more. His lost eye lies in the Well of Memory, where all universal intelligence is collected. He is half there, half here. As he revealed himself to me, he also revealed the female aspect of himself, the eye that lies in the Well of Memory and receives all the knowledge, the part of the universe that is not frenzied for learning, as himself, but calm, cool and silent, the recipient of all the learning.

That part was the feminine aspect of the universe, although both energies were equally present within everyone and everything, and in all the stories. What I perceived as male and female aspects of universal divinity represented the seeker of knowledge and the recipient of knowledge, two sides of the same coin. There was no real separation between them, and no real conflict, just two complimentary virtues that make up the whole of universal consciousness. Now, just because a person has a vision that seems full of deep spiritual insights, does not mean that one has become enlightened overnight.

As I was to learn, such visions usually serve only to help and offer guidance on the incredibly long journey towards actually integrating the insights of the vision in your life as a whole being. To see visions is easy, but to integrate them into your life at every level is a time-consuming path that actually requires a lifetime of dedication and unwavering intent. There is no instant solution, but the experience became a powerful tool for me both in my personal life, like a reminder of what I ought to focus on whenever I wandered into crooked paths, and also as a tool that helped me look at the Old Norse myths with new eyes, even after several years of study.

EPILOGUE

Since I began sharing my research and thoughts in Old Norse myths on YouTube, many people have asked me about my personal relationship to the Old Norse powers, whether I believe in them and in what fashion I might believe in them. I think it is evident that I regard the mythical characters of the poems as literary characters that fulfill a function within a spiritual tradition. I can also reveal that as a private person, I gradually discovered Pantheism through my studies of Old Norse myths. To begin with, it was just another aspect of the myths that I could research, but the more I realized that Pantheism plays such an important role, the more the idea itself resounded in my own soul. In the Chapter about Þórr the Thunder-god, I offered a few stories about how the god appeared to me in dreams. In the last chapter on Óðinn as a Pantheist character, I shared some of my long relationship to that god.

In fact, lots of mythical characters have appeared in my dreams over the years, probably a natural result of my personal focus. Not just Norse characters, but all kinds of characters, some more famous than others, have had their turn in my subconscious, always with a benefit to my personal development and the development of my research and understanding of mythology. I am absolutely convinced that this kind of mystical and dream-state experience lies at the heart of ancient mythology. Whether the characters themselves have a real existence on their own, outside of our imaginations, is not for me to say. I accept the fact that I cannot know for sure what is real and what is not, only be certain that the human imagination is both powerful and without limits. There are two more Norse deities that have been very close to me, both emotionally and spiritually, Freyia and Hel. As for Hel, she appeared to me in powerful and somber dreams for years, especially during the time that I first began to discover Norse mythology.

I had a rather morbid mind in those days, and was so deeply fascinated by the realm of Hel that I easily slipped into it night after night, contemplating the lady who lived there. One night, I dream of sitting in a boat that was being rowed by a tall, skinny lady dressed in a ragged old fur cloak. She was taking me through forgotten underground rivers. I could see the houses of ancient civilizations in the misty darkness of the shores. For a moment, I let my hand sweep through the cold water. Then the lady turned towards me, and her face was the naked skull of a mare. The lady told me to seek, and I knew that she meant that I needed to seek the forgotten messages within the myths. In another dream, Hel came towards me and placed her skeletal hands on either side of my face, cracking my skull in two. I could still feel the mark of her fingers on my head when I woke up, and remembered that her fingernails had been long and green.

The dream marked a serious change in my life. Even from when I first heard about her as a child, Freyia had always appeared in my imagination in a very vivid fashion, very bright, golden, lively and funny. As an adult and a student of mythology, I had an awesome experience when I first began to compose my analysis of this goddess. I was living in Mexico at the time, in a little forest. For nine days on end exactly at the moment that I sat down to write about Freyia, a falcon landed just outside of my window, settling in the branch of a great dead tree that was there.

The falcon would shriek, and then settle in silence for hours while I wrote. When the heat drove me to finish the work for the day, the falcon disappeared. It did not escape me that the falcon is Freyia's bird. In 2010, just before deciding to share my knowledge about Norse myths on YouTube, I had an anxiety attack. I was afraid, somehow, of persecution! To share what I knew about Pagan lore, to expose myself, seemed to stir some ancient and hidden fears within. At night, I dream about people, grumpy old men of authority in particular, humorless, dry, angry old males with tiny minds and enormous egos, who would want to scare me away from sharing my insights.

It terrified me! I personally believe that centuries of oppression and witch-hunts has etched itself into the memories of us, who possess a taste for Paganism and also into the souls of women in general. In my dream, Freyia suddenly appeared, surrounded by intense brightness. She appeared exactly as one might envision, in a flying chariot drawn through the heavens by large tomcats, and she was laughing heartily. The dream became colorful and beautiful, and a bit cartoonish. The goddess laughed and pointed towards the row of grumpy old men. As I looked at them, they all seemed to turn into bowling pins with painted faces. The goddess Freyia then caught my attention by showing me a huge bowling ball. She winked at me and then threw the ball with perfection and all the grumpy old men-pins fell in all directions with a great rumble. I woke up laughing my head off. The goddess had given me a gift, to learn how to laugh at the self-important little fools and refuse to take them seriously.

For centuries, they have oppressed the goddess, oppressed women, and oppressed knowledge in all forms. It is time to throw the ball right at them and laugh while so doing. The very next day, I recorded my first video. Months later, I had the strangest sensation of actually having merged with the goddess in a dream. I was floating through the air, and beneath me was a winter ocean, filled with icebergs. The ice of the ocean was melting slowly as I moved across it. I was approaching a shore, and as I came closer, I could see an entire army of warriors standing on that shore, frozen. They had been frozen for a thousand years or more, I saw. The warriors, both male and female, though mostly male, appeared to belong to countless different ages, some were so ancient that I could hardly recognize what culture and time they belonged to.

They were frozen and covered with hoar frost, frozen in a state of terror and agitation. At first, I shuddered with fear, because they were in fact a fearsome lot. Then I overcame the fear and felt a deep compassion, indeed a powerful sense of love. Somehow, I felt that the frozen warriors were looking to me for a purpose and for freedom. This disturbed me who was I to take on such responsibility? And then I realized that I was not me, but I was looking through the eyes of the waking goddess. As she came closer, she began to blow gently on them, and the warriors began to defrost. It felt like they were melting, softening, and healing.

As I woke up, I felt that my work is part of a greater purpose, and that there is a great need to defrost the souls of all those who have become frozen in fear. There is little doubt in my mind that the entities of the myths have a certain reality of their own, but their exact nature is unknown to me. I prefer to keep an open mind rather than letting my mind be closed by beliefs. It is a fact that a great number of my insights appear to have emerged like gifts from the gods, as if they arrived in my dreams to let me know the answer to what I had been wondering about.

Even so, I could spend years on end trying to prove the basic content of my intuitive or visionary experience in a rational and scientific fashion. I am glad I did, although as it has turned out, my initial insights through dreams and visions have always proved themselves correct in the end. To the powers, whatever they be and to the myth-makers, whoever they were, I can only raise my drinking horn in awe and praise. As the poet said:

Now have been sung the words of the High One in the hall of the High One
To the prosperity of the Human lineage
To the downfall of the Devourers' lineage

Hail the one who sang it!
Hail the one who knows it!

Enjoy it, the ones who learned!
Hail to those who heard!

Hávamál, 164, Poetic Edda.

BIBLIOGRAPHY

Primary Sources Nordic Sources (Ancient Texts in Original Language):

Bugge, Sophus, red. (1867 / 1965): SÆMUNDAR EDDA HINS FRÓDA. Norrøn FornkvædiIslandsk Samling av Folkelige Oldtidsdigte om Nordens Guder og Heroer. Universitetsforlaget, Oslo

Bugge, Sophus (1867): Sæmundar Edda. Available online: http://etext.old.no/

Eskeland, Severin (1924): Eiriks saga rauða/Soga om Eirik Raude: gamalnorsk grunntekst og nynorsk umsetjing Gamalnorske bokverk; 2, Oslo, Samlaget

Halldórsson, Johannes (1959): Kjalnesinga saga. Jökuls thattr Búassonar. Viglundar saga. Króka-refs saga. Thórdar saga hredu. Finnboga saga. Gunnars saga keldugnúpsfifls, Íslenzk fornrit; 14, Reykjavik; Hid islenzka Fornritafélag

Jack, George (ed.) (1994): Beowulf, A Student Edition. Oxford University Press

Jónsson, Finnur, ed. (1907): EDDA Snorra Sturlusonar Reykjavik

Jónsson, Finnur, ed.(1912): Den Norsk-Islandske Skjaldedigtning (800-1200) udgiven af Kommisjonen for det Arnamagnæisk legat B: rettet tekst, 1. bind Gyldendalske Boghandel Nordisk Forlag København og Kristiania

Ólafsson, Gudmundur (1695): Illuga saga Gridarfostra (Svensk & norrønt) Sagan af Illuga Grydar Fostra, eller Illuga Grydar Fostres historie/ fordom på gammal gøthiska skrifwen, och nu på swenska uttålkad af Gudmund Olafsson Upsala
Dictionaries and linguistic literature

Den Arnamagnæanske Kommision (1989): Ordbog over det norrøne prosasprog/ A Dictionary of Old Norse ProseVol. I XI København

Fritzner, Johan (1886): Ordbog over det gamle norske sprog, Det norske forlags forening

Fritzner, Johan (1972): Ordbog over det gamle norske sprog, rettelser og tillegg. Universitetsforlaget
Heggestad/Hødnebø/Simensen (1975): Norrøn Ordbok Det norske samlaget

Hólmarsson, Sverrir /Sanders, Christopher / Tucker, John (1989): Íslensk-ensk orðabók, ráðgjöf: Svavar Sigmundsson. Orðabækur Iðunnar, Reykjavik

Iversen, Ragnvald (1972-1994): Norrøn grammatikk. Tanoannson, Sven (1986): Isl ndsk-Svensk Ordbog. Göteborg

Lind, E.H (1920-1921): Norsk-Isl ndska Person-Binamn, Uppsala

Rygh, Karl (1871): Norske og islandske tilnavne frå oldtiden og middelalderen. Trondhjem

Simek, Rudolf (1996): Dictionary of Northern Mythology Translated by Angela Hall, D.S. Brewer, Cambridge

PRIMARY NORDIC SOURCES IN TRANSLATION

Byock, Jesse L. (1998): The Saga of king Hrolf Kraki. Penguin Classics, England

Byock, Jesse L. (1999): The Saga of the Volsungs, the Norse epic of Sigurd the Dragon Slayer Penguin Classics, England

Donaldson, E. Talbot (1966): Beowulf: A New Prose Translation. New York

Faulkes, Anthony (1987): Snorri Sturluson: EDDA Snorri Sturluson. University of Birmingham Everyman, London

Fisher, Peter (Translation)/Ellis Davidson, Hilda(Ed.) (1996): Saxo Grammaticus: The history of the Danes, Books I-IX

Gyldendal Norsk Forlag (1944) Snorri Sturlusson: Snorres Kongesagaer (Heimskringla, Ynglinga Saga), Oslo

Hreinson, Viðar (Ed.) (1997): The Complete Sagas of the Icelanders, Vol.I-V. Leifur Eiríkson Publishing, Reykjavik

Eggen, Erik (1978):Snorre Sturluson: Den yngre Edda Det Norske Samlaget, Oslo

Hatto, A.T. (1969):The Nibelungenlied Penguin Books, London, New York, Victoria

Hollander, Lee M. (1986): The Poetic Edda. University of Texas Press, Austin

Holm-Olsen, Ludvig (1985): Eddadikt Cappelen, Trondheim

Jack, George (ed.) (1994): Beowulf, A Student Edition Oxford University Press

Larrington, Carolyne (1996): The Poetic Edda Oxford University Press, Oxford, New York

Lie, Hallvard (1970): Egils saga Skallagrimsonar [Norsk] Aschehoug, Oslo

Magnusson, Magnus/ Palsson, Hermann (1960): Njals saga. Harmondsworth

Magnusson, Magnus/ Palsson, Hermann (1972): Laxdaela Saga. Harmondsworth

Mortensson-Egnund, Ivar (1993): Edda-Kvede Det Norske Samlaget, Oslo

Nedrelid, Gudlaug (1989): Egils saga einhenda og Ásmundar (Norsk) Soga om Egil Einhendte og Åsmund Berserksbane; Tåtten om Norne-Gjest/ omsatt av Gudlaug Horgen Norrøne bokverk; 49, Oslo, Det Norske Samlaget

Pálsson, Hermann / Edwards, Paul (1985): Seven Viking Romances Penguin Books

Pálsson, Hermann/ Edwards, Paul (1972): The Book of Settlements, Manitoba

Rindal, Magnus (1974): Soga om Volsungane Det Norske Samlaget, Oslo

Tucker, John (red) (1989): Sagas of the Icelanders New York

OTHER PRIMARY SOURCES (ANCIENT TEXTS) IN TRANSLATION:

Berntzen, Arve Omtvedt (2009): Orfeus: Og tekster fra den orfiske tradisjon, utvalg og innledende essay av Arve Omtvedt Berntzen

Braarvig, Jens / Kittelsen, Erling (2004): Enheduanna: Til Inanna: Prinsesse Enheduannas dikt til gudinnen Inanna fra 2200-tallet før Kristus, gjendiktet dra sumerisk av Jens Braarvig og Erling Kittelsen. Aschehoug

Cohen, Signe / Reinvang, Rasmus (ed./Transl.)(2003): Vediske skrifter. Utvalg og innledende essay av Signe Cohen. Verdens Hellige Skrifter, Bokklubben, Oslo.

De Shing Meador, Betty / Maier, John (2010): Enheduanna: Princess, Priestess, Poet: The Sumerian Temple Hymns of Enheduanna (Classics and the Ancietn World)

Dewing, H.B. (red.) 1924: Procopius, London

Doniger O' Flaherty, Wendy (1981): The Rig Veda, an Anthology Penguin London

Foster, E.S. (red., overs.) (1925): Livy London
Green, Peter (2006): Diodorus Siculus, books 11-12.37.1 : Greek history 480-431 B.C., the alternative version / Diodorus, Siculus ; translated, with introduction and commentary, by Peter Green. Austin, University of Texas Press

Griffiths J. Gwyn (Translator and Editor) (1975) Apuleius, Lucius Madaurensis: Metamorphoses Book 11: The Isis-book Études preliminaries aux religions orientales dans l'Empire romain; 39, Leiden, Brill

Edwards, H.J (red) (1980): Caesar. The Gallic War. Cambridge

Foulke,William Dudley (Translator) (1974): Paul the Deacon: History of the Lombards. Philadelphia

Griffith, Tom (ed) (1996): Herodotus: Histories, Wordsworth Classics of World Literature

Hamilton, Walter (1951): Plato: The Symposium. Penguin

Kenney, E.J. (ed) (1999): Apuleius: The Golden Ass. Penguin Classics

Kramer, Samuel Noah / Diane Wolkstein (1983): Inanna : Queen of Heaven and Earth : her stories and hymns from Sumer; art compiled by Elizabeth Williams-Forte, New York, Harper & Row

MacKenna, Stephen (1991): Plotinus: The Enneads, Penguin

Mattingly, H. (1970): Tacitus: The Agricola and the Germania

Narasimhan, Chakravarti V. (ed.) (1965): The Mahabharata. Colombia University Press, New York

Nordin, Andreas (1997): Jordanes: Getica: om goternas ursprung och bedrifter Stockholm, Atlantis

Pritchard, James B. (Ed) (1958): The Ancient Near East: An Anthology of Texts and Pictures. Princeton University Press

Rackham, h. (Red) (1952): Pliny: Natural History. London

Rieu, E. V. (): Homer: The Odyssey. Penguin

Sandars, N. K. (1960): The Epic of Gilgamesh, Penguin, London

Tacitus, Cornelius (A.D. 98): Germania. Available in English translation online at http://www.ourcivilisation.com/smartboard/shop/tacitusc/germany/chap1.htm

Thorpe, Lewis (overs.) (1979): Gregory of Tours. The History of the Franks Harmondsworth

Tarrant, Harold / Tredennick, Hugh (1993). Plato: The Last Days of Socrates Eythyphro, Apology, Crito, Phaedo

Gantz, Jeffrey (1984): Early Irish Myths and Sagas

Godley, A.D. (red,overs.) (1950): Herodotus Cambridge

Van Voorst, Robert E. (2007): Anthology of World Scriptures: Eastern Religions

Wordsworth Editions Limited (1995): The Iliad

ANALYSIS ON OLD NORSE LITERATURE AND MYTHOLOGY:

Acker, Paul/ Larrington,Carolyne (red.) (2002): The Poetic Edda: essays on Old Norse mythology Routledge Medieval Casebooks, New York

Ahlb ck, Tore (ed.) (1990):Old Norse and Finnish Religions and Cultic Place-NamesAlmqvist & Wiksell International, Stockholm

Bartha, Antal (1992): Myth and Reality in the Ancient Culture of the Northern Peoples (in Hoppál, Pentik inen,1992)

Bessason, Haraldur / Glendinning, Robert J. (red.)(1983): Edda: a collection of essays- University of Manitoba Icelandic studies; 4 Winnipeg: University of Manitoba Press

Clover, Carol J. /Lindow, John (red.)(1985): Old Norse-Icelandic literature: a critical guideIslandica; 45, Cornell University Press

Clunies-Ross, Margaret (1987). Skáldskaparmál. Snorri Sturlusson's Ars Poetica and Medieval Theories of Language Odense University Press

Clunies-Ross, Margaret (1994): Prolongued Echoes, Old Norse Myths in Medieval Northern Society, Volume I: The Myths. Odense University Press

Cohen, Jeffrey Jerome: Of Giants, Sex, Monsters and Middle Ages

Cohen, Jeffrey Jerome: Monster Theory

Cohen, Jeffrey Jerome/Gail Wess (red.): Thinking the Limits of the Body

Damico, Helen (1984): Beowulfs Wealtheow and the Valkyrie Tradition Madison

Davidson, Hilda Ellis (1964):Gods and Myths of Northern Europe Penguin, London, New York, Toronto
Davidson, Hilda Ellis (1998):Roles of the Northern Goddess Routledge, London and New York

Davidson, Hilda Ellis (Hilda Roderick Ellis) (1968): The Road to Hel A Study of the Conceptions of the Dead in Old Norse Literature

Dick, Ernst S (1966): The Bridesman in the Indo-European Tradition: Ritual and myth in Marriage Ceremonies

Dillmann, Francois-Xavier (1982): Katla and her Distaff: An Episode of Tri-functional Magic in the Eyrbyggja saga (i Polomé, red. (1982)

Dronke, Ursula (1980): The role of Sexual Themes in Njals saga London

Dronke, Ursula (1997):The Poetic Edda, volume II: Mythological Poems
Clarendon Press, Oxford

Dumézil, Georges (1973): The Destiny of a King. Chicago

Dumézil, Georges (1973): Gods of the Ancient Northmen, Berkely

Fleck, Jere (1970): Konr-Otarr-Geirrodr: A Knowledge Criterion for Succession
to the Germanic Sacred Kingship

Fleck, Jere (1971): Odins Self-Sacrifice: A New Interpretation

Fleck, Jere (1971): The Knowledge Criterion in the Grimnismál: The Case
Against "Shamanism"

Gade, Kari Ellen (1988): The Naked and the Dead in Old Norse Society

Grimstad, Kaaren (1983): The Revenge of Volundr (in Bessason / Glendinning,
eds., 1983)

Gurevich, Aaron J. (1973): Edda and Law: Commentary upon Hyndluljóð

Halvorsen, Eyvind (et al) (1992): Eyvindarbók: Festskrift til Eyvind Fjeld
Halvorsen 4.mai Universitetet i Oslo

Harris, Joseph (1983): Eddic Poetry as Oral Poetry: the Evidence of Parallel
Passages is the Helgi Poems for Questions of Composition and Performance (in
Bessason H./Glendinning R.J. Editors, 1983)

Haugen, Einar (1983):The Edda as Ritual: Odin and His Masks (in: Bessason /
Glendinning, eds., 1983)

Hedeager, Lotte (1999): Skygger av en annen virkelighet. Oldnordiske myter
Oversatt av Kåre A. Lie Pax Forlag, A/S, Oslo

Heide, Eldar (1997): Fjölsvinnsmål. Ei oversett nøkkelkjelde til nordisk
mytologi Magister-avhandling i norrøn filologi. Universitetet i Oslo

Holm-Olsen, Ludvig (1995): Norges Litteraturhistorie bind I: Fra runene til det
Norske Selskab Middelalderens Litteratur i Norge J.W. Cappelens Forlag A.S,
Oslo

Hødnebø, Finn/ Fjeld, Halvorsen (et al) (1992): Eyvindarbók: Festskrift til
Eyvind Fjeld Halvorsen Universitetet i Oslo

Jakobsdóttir, Svava (2002): Gunnlod and the Precious Mead (Hávamál)(i
Acker/Larrington,reds.)

Jochens, Jenny M. (1987): The Female Inciter in the Kings Sagas

Kragerud, Alv (1989): Helgediktningen og Reinkarnasjon Scripta Islandica Isl ndska s llskapets årsbok 40/1989 Almqvist & Wiksell International, Stockholm, Sweden

Kvilhaug, Maria Christine (2004): The Maiden with the Mead, A Goddess of Initiation in Norse Mythology?. Thesis. University of Oslo, History of Religion Available online at: http://www.duo.uio.no/sok/work.html?WORKID = 18497&lang = en

Kvilhaug, Maria Christine (2009): The Maiden with the Mead, a Goddess of Initiation Rituals in Old Norse Mythology?. VDM Verlag Dr. Müller, Deutschland

Mac Cana, Proinsias (1958): Aspects of the Theme of King and Goddess in Irish Literature

Magennis, Hugh (1985): The Cup as Symbol and Metaphor in Old English Literature Speculum 60

Motz, Lotte von (1983): The Wise One on the Mountain: form, function and significance of the Subterranean Smith: a study in folklore Göppingen, Kummerle Verlag

Motz, Lotte von (1993):The Beauty and the Hag. Female figures of Germanic Faith and Myth Filologica Germanica 15 Fassbaender, Wien

Motz, Lotte von (1997): The Faces of the Goddess New York: Oxford University Press

Mundal, Else (1974): Fylgjemotiva i norrøn litteratur. Universitetsforlaget, Oslo

Mundal, Else (1990):The Position of the Individual Gods and Goddesses in Various Types of Sources with Special Reference to the Female Divinities (in Ahlb ck, 1990)

Mundal, Else (1992): Heidrun den mjødmjølkande geita på Valhalls tak (in Hødnebø, Fjeld Halvorsen, 1992)

Mundal, Else (1994):Mytar og diktning (in Schjødt, 1994)

N sström, Britt-Mari (1998): Frøya Den store gudinnen i Norden Oversatt av Kåre A. Lie Pax Forlag, A/S, Oslo

Schjødt, Jens Peter(red.) (1994): Myte og ritual i det førkristne Norden, et symposium. Odense Universitetsforlag, Odense

Røthe, Gunnhild (1994): Osebergfunnet, en religionshistorisk tolkning, Hovedoppgave i Religionshistorie våren 1994. Institutt for kultur og samfunnsfag, Universitetet i Oslo

Steinsland, Gro (1986): Giants as recipients of cult in the Viking Age (i Steinsland, ed, 1986)

Steinsland, Gro (ed.) (1986): Words and Objects Towards a Dialogue Between Archaeology and History of Religion Norwegian University Press, Oslo

Steinsland, Gro (1991): Det Hellige Bryllup og Norrøn Kongeideologi En Analyse av Hierogami-Myten i Skírnismál, Ynglingatal, Háleygjatal og Hyndluljód Solum Forlag, Larvik

Steinsland, Gro (1992):Døden som erotisk lystreise (i Hødnebø, Fjeld Halvorsen, 1992)

Steinsland, Gro (1997): Eros og død i norrøne myter Universitetsforlaget, Oslo

Steinsland, Gro (1998):Hedendom mot kristendom i norrøne myter(i Hjelde/ Ruud (ed.) (1998)

Steinsland, Gro/Meulengracht Sørensen, Preben (1999):Voluspå Pax forlag A/S, Oslo

Van Hamel, A.G. (1932): Odinn Hanging on the Tree

Ström, Folke (1983): Hieros-gamos-motivet i Hallfredr Ottarrssons Hákonardrápa och den norska jarlav rdigheten

Wagenvoort, Hendrick (1971): Nehalennia and the Souls of the Dead Mnemosyne 24

Williams, David: Deformed Discourse

GENERALLY ON MYTHOLOGY

Campbell, Joseph (1973): The Masks of God: Primitive Mythology. London: Souvenir Press

Eliade, Mircea (1965): Rites and Symbols of Initiation: the mysteries of birth and rebirth. Harper torchbooks Harper Colophon Books, New York: Harper & Row

Eliade, Mircea (ed.et al.) (1987): The Encyclopedia of Religion New York: Macmillan

Eriksen, ThomasH. (ed.) (1996): Sosialantropologiske grunntekster Ad notam Gyldendal, Oslo

Graves, Robert (1960): Greek Gods and Heroes. New York: Doubleday

Hjelde, Sigurd/Ruud, Inger Marie (red) (1998): Enhet i mangfold? 100 år med religionshistorie i Norge. Tano Aschehoug

Larrington, Carolyne (ed.) (1992): The Feminist Companion to Mythology Pandora Press, HarperCollins, London

Turner, Victor W (1996): Betwixt and Between, the liminal period in rites de passage (in Eriksen, ed., 1996)

Van Gennep, Arnold (1999): Overgangsriter = Rites de Passage Oversatt av Erik Ringen, Pax Labyrint, Oslo

ANCIENT NORTHERN EUROPEAN PAGANISM: RITUAL AND RELIGION

Bauchhenss, Gerhard/ Neumann, Günther (1987) (red.): Matronen und verwandte GottheitenKöln

Carver, Martin (red) (1993): In Search of Cult: Archaeological Investigations in Honour of Philip Rahtz. Bury St. Edmunds

Christensen, Arne Emil/ Ingstad, Anne Stine/ Myhre, Bjørn (1992): Osebergdronningens grav, vår arkeologiske nasjonalskatt i nytt lys. Schibstedt, Oslo

Colpe, Carsten (1987): Muttergottinnen und keltisch-germanischen Matronen: Ein historisch-psycologisches Problem (i Bauchenss og Neumann, ed, 1987)

Enright, Michael J. (1985): Iona, Tara and Soissons: The Origins of the Royal Anointing Ritual, Berlin

Enright, Michael J. (1990): The Goddess Who Weaves: some iconographic Aspects of Bracteates of the Fürstenberg Type
Enright, Michael J. (1996): Lady with a Mead Cup, Ritual, Prophecy and Lordship in the European Warband from La Tène to the Viking Age Four Courts Press, Dublin

Fari, Camilla Helene (2003): Hieros-gamos : en sammenligning mellom symbolets uttrykk i den nordiske bronsealderens helleristningstradisjon og myteverdenen i det østlige middelhavsområdet / Hovedoppgave i nordisk arkeologi, Universitetet i Oslo

Fari, Camilla Helene / Prescott, Christopher / Melheim, Anne Lene (2006): Myter og religion i bronsealderen : studier med utgangspunkt i helleristninger, graver og depoter i Sør-Norge og Bohusl n / Christopher Prescott (red.)

Flint, Valerie I. J. (1991): The Rise of Magic in Early Medieval Europe. Princeton

Flood, Jan Peder (1999): Volver, Seidmenn og Sjamaner: en komparativ analyse av norrøn seid- Hovedoppgave i religionshistorie, Universitetet i Oslo

Gelling, Peter / Davidson, Hilda Ellis (1969): The Chariot of the Sun and Other Rites and Symbols of the Northern Bronze age Frederick A. Praeger, Publishers, New York, Washington

Grieg, Sigurd (1926): Osebergdronningens grav Tidskrift om vårt land, 2.årg. nr.21 Oslo, Fabritius

Helm, Karl (1946): Wodan. Ausbreitung und Wanderung seines Kultes Giessen

Hoppál Mihaly/ Pentik inen, Juha (eds.)(1992): NORTHERN RELIGIONS AND SHAMANISM, ETHNOLOGICA URALICA 3. Budapest Akadémiai Kiadó, Helsinki. Finnish Literature Society

Kraft, Johrn (1985): The Goddess in the Labyrinth, Åbo Akademi Religionsvetenskaplige skrifter nr.11

Krausse, Dirk (1993): Trinkhorn und Kline. Zur griechischen Vermittlung orientalischer Trinksitten and die frühen Kelten Germania 71

Ljono, A. (1952): Hva Oseberghaugen gjemte-Vestfold Historielags småskrifter

Larson, Gerald James/ Littleton, Scott/ Puhvel, Jan (1974): Myth in Indo-European Antiquity Berkeley

Mitchell, Stephen (2011): Witchraft and Magic in the Nordic Middle Ages University of Pensylvania Press

Naumann, Hans (1938): Der König und die Seherin

N sström, Britt-Mari (2001): BLOTTro og offer i det førkristne Norden Oversatt av Kåre A. Lie Pax Forlag A/S, Oslo

Piggott, Stuart (1991): the Druids London

Polomé, Edgar C (1987): Muttergottheiten im alten Westeuropa (i Bauchhenss/ Neumann red)

Reese, Richard (red)(1977): Burial in the Roman World London

Rüger, Cristoph B. (1983): A Husband for the Mother Goddesses, Some Observations on the Matronae Aufaniae

Sayers, William (1989): Warrior Initiation and Some Short Celtic Spears in the Irish and Learned Latin Tradition

Solli, Brit (2002): SEID Myter, sjamanisme og kjønn i vikingenes tid Pax Forlag A/S, Oslo

Stafford, Pauline (1983): Queens, Concubines and Dowagers: The Kings Wife in the Early Middle Ages London

Steblin, Kamenskij, M.I. (1982): Valkyries and Heroes

Steinsland, Gro (2000): Den Hellige Kongenom religion og herskermakt fra vikingtid til middelalder Pax Forlag A/S, Oslo

Steinsland, Gro (2005): Norrøn Religion- Myter, riter, samfunn Pax Forlag, Valdres

Stein, Frauke (1967): Adelsgr ber des achtens Jahrhunderts in Deutschland Berlin

Ström, Folke (1954): Diser, Nornor, valkyrjor. Fruktbarhetskult och sakralt kungadöme i Norden Almqvist & Wiksell, Stockholm

Ström, Folke (1985): Nordisk Hedendom Tro och Sed I förkristen tid Akademiförlaget, Göteborg

Strömb ck, Dag (2000): SEJD och andra studier i nordisk sj lsuppfatning Kungl. Gustav Adolfs Akademien för svensk folkkultur, Gidlunds förlag, Uppsala

Turville-Petre (1975): Myth and religion of the North: the religion of ancient Scandinavia

Greenwood Press, Westport

CULTURAL HISTORY AND ARCHAEOLOGY OF NORTHERN EUROPE

Brøndsted, Johannes (1962): Danmarks historie bind I. De ældste tider Politikens forlag

Craik, Elisabeth (red) (1984): Marriage and Property, Aberdeen

Crawford, Barbara E (1984): Marriage and the Status of Women in Norse Society (i Craik, red. 1984)

Dickinson, Tania (1993): An Anglo-Saxon "Cunning Woman" from Bidford-on Avon (i Carver, red, 1993

Evans, D. Ellis (1981): Celts and Germans

Fell, Christine E (1984): Women in Anglo-Saxon England Bloomington

Ford, Patrick K. (1988): Celtic Women: The Opposing Sex Viator 19: 417-33

Grohne, Ernst (1932): Die Koppel-, Ring-, und Tüllengef se: Ein Betrag Zur Typologie und Zweckgeschichte keramischer Formen Bremen

Heather, Peter (1996) The Goths. Blackwell Publishers

Hedeager, Lotte (1984). A Quantitative Analysis of Roman of Roman Imports in Europe North of the Limes (0-400 AD) and the Question of Roman-Germanic Exchange (I New Directions in Scandinavian Archaeology, red. Kristiansen/Paludan-Muller)

Herlilhy, David (1990). Opera muliebria: Women and Work in Medieval Europe. New York

Hoffmann, Marta (1964): The Warp-Weighted Loom. Studies in the History and Technology of an Ancient Instrument Oslo

Howarth, Patrick (1994): Attila, King of the Huns. The Man and the Myth. Constable

Jahnkuhn, Herbert (1966): Archaeologische Bemerkungen zur Glaubwurdigkeit des Tacitus in der Germania Göttingen

Jesch, Judith (1991): Women in the Viking Ages, Woodbridge, Suffolk: Boydell Press

Jochens, Jenny M. (1986): The Medieval Icelandic Heroine: Fact or Fiction? Viator 17

Kristiansen, Kristian/Paludan ouller, Carsten (reds) (1984): New Directions in Scandinavian Archaeology. Odense
Kliman, Bernice (1977): Women in Early English Literature, Beowulf to the Ancrene Wisse

Konecny, Silvia (1976): Die Frauen des karolingisches Königshauses: Die politische Bedeutung der Jahrhundert Wien

Lamm, Jan Peder / Nylén (1987): Bildstenar. Katalog över samtliga på Gotland k nde bildstenar samt bibliografi över bildstenlitteratur. Gidlunds, Stockholm

Mac Cana, Proinsias (1980): Women in Irish Mythology The Crane Bag 4

Mohen, Jan Pierre (1991): The Princely Tombs of Burgundy (i The Celts, New York)

Paulsen, Peter (1967): Alamannische Adelsgr ber vom Niederstotzingen Stuttgart

Spurkland, Terje (2001) I begynnelsen var Futark, Norske runer og runeinnskrifter. Cappelen Akademisk Forlag/ Landslaget for norskundervisning

Thompson, E.A (1965): The Early German,s Oxford University Press

Thompsons, E.A (1999): The Huns, Blackwell Publishing

Todd, Malcolm (1987): The Northern Barbarians London

Todd, Malcolm (1977): Germanic Burials in the Roman Iron Age (i Reese, red.)

Vogelsang, Thilo (1954): Die Frau als Herrscherin: Studien "consors regni" Formel im Mittelalter Göttingen

Wells, Peter S. (1980): Culture Contact and Culture Change: Early Iron Age Central Europe and the Mediterranean World Cambridge

Qviller, Bjørn (1996): Rusens Historie Det Norske Samlaget

Qviller, Bjørn (2004): Bottles and Battles. The Rise and Fall of the Dionysian Mode of Cultural Procuction. A Study in Political Anthropology and Institutions in Greece and Western Europe. Hermes Publishing, Oslo

COMPARATIVE MYTHOLOGY: CLASSICAL/PREHISTORIC PAGANISM, PHILOSOPHY, PANTHEISM AND MYSTERIES

Barstow, Anne L. (1983):The Prehistoric Goddess (in Olson (ed.) 1983)

Bernabé, Alberto / Jiménez San Cristobal, Ana Isabel (2008): Instructions for the netherworld: The Orphic gold tablets. Leiden, Brill

Berntzen, Arve Omtvedt (2009): The culture of Orpheus: Traces of countercultural values in the Orpheus myth and the early Orphic tradition Oslo, Department of Culture Studies and Oriental Languages, Faculty of Humanities, University of Oslo

Blundell, Sue / Williamson, Margaret (red.) (1998): The Sacred and the Feminine in Ancient Greece Routledge: London and New York

Bowden, Hugh (2010): Mystery cults of the ancient world. Princeton University Press

Casson, Lionell (2002): Libraries in the Ancient World Yale University Press

Burkert, Walter (1987): Ancient Mystery Cults Harvard University Press, London

Castleden, Rodney (1997): Knossos, Temple of the GoddessEfstathiadis Group S.A. Athens

Castleden, Rodney (1994): Minoans. Life in Bronze Age Crete. Routledge, New York

Dahlström, Anna (1997): I gudinnans tecken? Analys och kritikk av Marija Gimbutas forskning kring en forntida gudinnakult, C-uppsats i Arkeologi, Arkeologiska Institutionen, Lunds Universitet

D'Alviella, Goblet (1981):The Mysteries of Eleusis the secret rites and rituals of the Classical Greek Mystery tradition The Aquarian Press

Deakin, Michael A. B. (2007): Hypatia of Alexandria. Mathematician and Martyr. Prometheus Books, New York

Dillon, John / Lloyd P. Gerson (2004): Neoplatonic Philosophy, Introductory Readings. Hackett Publishing Company, Cambridge, Indianapolis

Edmonds, Radcliffe G. (ed.) (2011): The "Orphic" gold tablets and Greek religion: further along the path. Cambridge University Press

Eisler, Riane (1995): The Chalice & the Blade. Harper, San Francisco

Evasdaughter, Susan (1996): Crete Reclaimed, A feminist exploration of Bronze Age Crete. Heart of Albion Press

Freke, Timothy / Gandy, Peter (2001): Jesus and the Goddess. The Secret Teachings of the Original Christians Thorsons, London

Freke, Timothy / Gandy, Peter (1999): The Jesus Mysteries. Thorsons, London

Gimbutas, Marija (1989): The Language of the Goddess. HarperSanFrancisco

Gimbutas (1991): The Civilization of the Goddess. The World of Old Europe, Harper. San Francisco

Graf, Fritz / Johnston, Sarah Iles (2007): Ritual texts for the afterlife: Orpheus and the Bacchic gold tablets. London, Routledge

Guthrie, W.K.C (1935): Orpheus and Greek religion: a study of the orphic movement. London, Methuen

Herrero de Jáuregui, Miguel (2010): Orphism and Christianity in late antiquity (translators: Jennifer Ottman and Daniel Rodrígruez). Sozomena, vol.7, Berlin, De Gruyter

Hornung, Erik (1996): Conceptions of God in Ancient Egypt, the One and the Many. Translated from the German by John Baines, Cornell University Press

Levine, Michael P. (1994): Pantheism a non-theistic concept of deity. London, Routledge

Macleod, Roy (Ed.) (2004) The Library of Alexandria. Centre of Learning in the Ancient World Tauris, New York, London

Marinatos, Nannó (2000): The Goddess and the Warrior, the naked goddess in early Greek religion Routledge, London and New York

Matthews, John (1991): Taliesin. Shamanism and the Bardic Mysteries if Britain and Ireland. Aquarian. Harper Collins

Pakkanen, Petra (1995): Interpreting early Hellenistic religion: a study based on the cult of Isis and the mystery cult of Demeter Avhandling (doktorgrad). Faculty of Arts at the University of Helsinki

Reid, Howard / Pollard, Justin (2007): The Rise and Fall of Alexandria. Birthplace of the Modern World. Penguin, New York

Rodenborg, Erik (1991): Marija Gimbutas teori om "Gamla Europa"s samh lle, kultur och religion Uppsats i fordjupningskurs i arkeologi.

Stockholms Universitet. A summary in English is available online at: http://potnia.theladyofthelabyrinth.com/the-critique-and-defense-of-marija-gimbutas%c2%b4-old-europe-thesis/

Sharma, Arvind (ed.) (1987): Women in World Religions. State University of New York

Skretting, Atle (1980): Innvielsene i antikkens Isis-mysterier. Hovedoppgave i religionhistorie, Universitetet i Oslo

Stone, Merlin (1976): When God was a Woman. A Harvest Book, Harcourt

Södergård, Peter J. (2003): The hermetic piety of the mind : a semiotic and cognitive study of the discourse of Hermes Trismegistos. Stockholm, Almquist & Wiksell: Coniectanea Biblica, New Testament series, no. 41/ Avhandling (doktorgrad) Uppsala Universitet

Torjussen, Stian Sundell (2008): Metamorphoses of myth: a study of the "Orphic" gold tablets and the Derveni Papyrus. University of Tromsø, Faculty of Humanities, Department of Culture and Literature

Trump, David H. (2004): Malta, Prehistory and Temples. Midsea Books LTD

Wagenwoort, Hendrick (1971): The journey of the Souls of the Dead to the Isles of the Blessed Mnemosyne 24

Witts, Reginald Eldred (1971): Isis in the Graeco-Roman World, Aspects of Greek and Roman Life. London, Thames and Hudson

COMPARATIVE RELIGION: SHAMANISM AND ETHNOGRAPHY

Bogoras (1904-1909): The Chuckchee. The Jesup North Pacific Expedition, edited by Franz Boaz Memoirs of the American Museum of Natural History

B ckman, Louise (1975): Sájva. Förest llningar om hj lp och skyddsv sen i heliga fj ll bland samerna Almqvist & Wiksell, Stockholm

Demant Jacobsen, Merete (1999): SHAMANISM, Traditional and Contemporary Approaches to the Mastery of Spirits and Healing. Berghnan Books, New York, Oxford

Diószegi, Vilmos (1968): Tracing Shamans in Siberia. The story of an ethnographical research expedition Oosterhout cap. Anthropological publications

Eliade, Mircea (2004): Shamanism, Archaic Techniques of Ecstasy. Princeton University Press, Princeton and Oxford

Grim, John A. (1983): The Shaman. Patterns of Siberian and Ojibway Healing University of Oklahoma Press

Hultkrantz, Åke (1953): Conceptions of the Soul among North American Indians A study in religious ethnology Ethnographical Museum of Sweden, Stockholm

Hultkrantz, Åke/B ckman, Louise (ed.) (1978): Studies in Lapp Shamanism. Acta Universitatis Stockholmiensis Stockholm studies in comparative religion. Almqvist & Wiksell International, Stockholm

Hultkrantz, Åke (1992): Shamanic Healing and Ritual Drama Health and Medicine in Native North American Religious Traditions Crossroad, New York, 1992

Hultkrantz, Åke (1992) (b): Aspects of Saami (Lapp) Shamanism (i Hoppál, P entikainen, 1992)

Narby, Jeremy/ Huxley, Francis (eds) (2001): Shamans through Time, 500 Years on the Path to Knowledge Penguin Putnam, New York

Pollan, Brita (2002): Noaidier, historier om samiske sjamaner De Norske Bokklubbene, Oslo

Comparative Mythology: Ancient Middle Eastern Religions and The Sacred Marriage

Kramer, Samuel Noah (1969): The Sacred Marriage Rite, Aspects of Faith, Myth and Ritual in Ancient Sumer. Indiana University Press, Bloomington, London

Kramer, Samuel Noah (1972): Sumerian Mythology: A Study of Spiritual and Literary Achievements in the third millennium B.C. Philadelphia: University of Pennsylvania Press

Crawford, Harriet (2004): Sumer and the Sumerians, Cambridge University Press

Hammer, Anita (1999): Inanna in Hieros Gamos, A Processual representation Skriftserie fra Institutt for Kunst og Medievitenskap 3 Trondheim

Lapinkivi, Pirjo (2004): The Sumerian Sacred Marriage: In the light of comparative evidence, Helsinki, Neo-Assyrian Text Corpus Project

Nissinen, Martti / Risto Uro (ed.) (2008): Sacred marriages : the divine-human sexual metaphor from Sumer to early Christianity. Winona, Ind. Eisenbrauns

Ochshorn, Judith (1983): Ishtar and her cult (in Olsons, Carl (ed.))

Olsons, Carl (ed.) (1983): The Book of the goddess, past and present: an introduction to her religion. New York: Crossroad

INDIAN RELIGIONS AND SPIRITUAL PATHS

Barthakuria, Apurba Chandra (2009): The Tantric religion of India: an insight into Assam's Tantra literature Kolkata: Punthi Pustak

Bhattacharya, Bikash Kumar (2003): Tārā in Hinduism : study with textual and iconographical documentation. Delhi, Eastern Book Linkers

Biernacki, Lorilai (2007): Renowned goddess of desire: Women, sex and speech in Tantra. New York, Oxford University Press

Brockington, J.L.(1996): The Sacred Thread. Edinburgh University Press

Coburn, Thomas B. (2002): The structural interplay of Tantra, Vedanta, and Bhakti: nondualist commentary on the goddess (in Harper/Brown ed.)

Flood, Gavin (1996): An Introduction to Hinduism. Cambridge University Press

Geoffrey, Samuel (2008): The Origins of Yoga and Tantra: Indic religions to the thirteenth century Cambridge University Press, UK New York

Harper, Katherine Anne/ Brown, Robert L. (ed.). (2002): The Roots of Tantra Albany, N.Y. State University of New York Press

Hawley, John Stratton (2005): Three Bhakti voices: Mirabai, Surdas and Kabir in their time and ours New Dehli: Oxford University Press

Kinsley, David (1989): The Goddesses' Mirror, Visions of the divine from East and West. State University of New York Press

Kinsley, David (1975): The Sword and the Flute. Kali & Krsna, Dark Visions of the Terrible and the Sublime in Hindu Mythology. University of California Press, Berkely, Los Angeles, London

Kumar, Samrat Schmiem (2010): Bhakti, The yoga of love: Trans-rational approached to peace studies. Wien: Lit Verlag

Mirdad, Michael (2011): An introduction to Tantra and Sacred Sexuality. Bellingham, Wash, Grail Press

Müller-Ebeling, Claudia/R tsch, Christian / Surendra Bahadur Shahi ; in collaboration with Mohan Rai and the shamans, Indra Doj Gurung..[et al.]; [Translated by Annabel Lee] (2002): Shamanism and Tantra in the Himalayas. London, Thames and Hudson

Nagar, Shanti Lal (1989): The Universal Mother. Delhi, Atma Ram & Son

O'Flaherty Doniger, Wendy (1975): Hindu Myths. Penguin Books

Pauwels, Heidi Rika Maria (1996): Kṛṣṇa's round dance reconsidered: Harirām Vyās's Hindi Rās-pañcādhyānī. London Studies on South Asia/ Centre of South Asian Studies / School of Oriental and African Studies, no. 12, University of London, Richmond, Surrey

Pechilis, Karen (1999): The embodiment of Bhakti. New York: Oxford University Press

Pintchman, Tracy (1994): The rise of the Goddess in the Hindu tradition. Albany, State University of New York Press

Pintchman, Tracy (ed.)(2001): Seeking Mahādevi: constructing the identities of the Hindu Great Goddess Albany, State University of New York Press

Robertson, S. (2006): Bhakti Tradition of Vaisnava Alvars and theology of religions. Kolkata: Punthi

Smith, Gilly (1996): Tantra and the Tao: The secrets of sexual ecstasy. London. Robinson Publishing

ABOUT THE AUTHOR

Maria Kvilhaug was born in Oslo, Norway, in 1975. She studied History of Religions and Old Norse Philology at the university of Oslo. She has written several non-fiction and fiction books concerning Old Norse pre-Christian culture and religion.

NON-FICTION:
The Maiden with the Mead (2004/2009)
The Seed of Yggdrasill (2013/2018/2020)
The Poetic Edda, Six Cosmology Poem (2017)
The Trickster and the Thunder god, Thor and Loki in Old Norse Myths (2018)

FICTION:
(Blade Honer novel series about the life of the Oseberg priestesses):
The Hammer of Greatness
My Enemy's Head
The Hel-Rune's Claim
A Twisted Mirror

http://www.bladehoner.wordpress.com
http://www.youtube.com/user/ladyofthelabyrinth

The Three Little Sisters

The Three Little Sisters is an indie publisher that puts authors first. We specalize in the strange and unusual. From titles about pagan and heathen spirituality to traditional fiction we bring books to life.

the3littlesisters.com

Made in United States
Troutdale, OR
12/20/2023

16234600R00332